Brief Table of Contents

Focus on . . . the Cover

How do you feel when you look at this cover? We hope the image on the book conveys a feeling of relaxation and overall peace of mind—both achieved by developing a solid financial plan. From cover to cover, this text's goal is to actively help you gain the financial literacy and personal finance skills you need to make sound financial decisions for life. Use this book as a tool to help you gain peace of mind about your financial future!

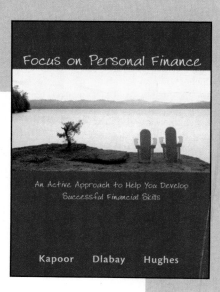

Focus on Personal Finance

An Active Approach to Help You Develop Successful Financial Skills

Kapoor   Dlabay   Hughes

The McGraw-Hill/Irwin Series in Finance, Insurance, and Real Estate

Stephen A. Ross
Franco Modigliani Professor of Finance and Economics
Sloan School of Management
Massachusetts Institute of Technology
Consulting Editor

FINANCIAL MANAGEMENT

Adair
Excel Applications for Corporate Finance
First Edition

Benninga and Sarig
Corporate Finance: A Valuation Approach

Block and Hirt
Foundations of Financial Management
Eleventh Edition

Brealey, Myers, and Allen
Principles of Corporate Finance
Eighth Edition

Brealey, Myers, and Marcus
Fundamentals of Corporate Finance
Fourth Edition

Brooks
FinGame Online 4.0

Bruner
Case Studies in Finance: Managing for Corporate Value Creation
Fourth Edition

Chew
The New Corporate Finance: Where Theory Meets Practice
Third Edition

Chew and Gillan
Corporate Governance at the Crossroads: A Book of Readings
First Edition

DeMello
Cases in Finance
Second Edition

Grinblatt and Titman
Financial Markets and Corporate Strategy
Second Edition

Helfert
Techniques of Financial Analysis: A Guide to Value Creation
Eleventh Edition

Higgins
Analysis for Financial Management
Seventh Edition

Kester, Ruback, and Tufano
Case Problems in Finance
Twelfth Edition

Ross, Westerfield and Jaffee
Corporate Finance
Seventh Edition

Ross, Westerfield and Jaffee
Essentials of Corporate Finance
Fourth Edition

Ross, Westerfield and Jordan
Fundamentals of Corporate Finance
Seventh Edition

Smith
The Modern Theory of Corporate Finance
Second Edition

White
Financial Analysis with an Electronic Calculator
Fifth Edition

INVESTMENTS

Bodie, Kane and Marcus
Essentials of Investments
Fifth Edition

Bodie, Kane and Marcus
Investments
Sixth Edition

Cohen, Zinbarg and Zeikel
Investment Analysis and Portfolio Management
Fifth Edition

Corrado and Jordan
Fundamentals of Investments: Valuation and Management
Third Edition

Farrell
Portfolio Management: Theory and Applications
Second Edition

Hirt and Block
Fundamentals of Investment Management
Eighth Edition

FINANCIAL INSTITUTIONS AND MARKETS

Cornett and Saunders
Fundamentals of Financial Institutions Management

Rose and Hudgins
Bank Management and Financial Services
Sixth Edition

Rose and Marquis
Money and Capital Markets: Financial Institutions and Instruments in a Global Marketplace
Ninth Edition

Santomero and Babbel
Financial Markets, Instruments, and Institutions
Second Edition

Saunders and Cornett
Financial Institutions Management: A Risk Management Approach
Fifth Edition

Saunders and Cornett
Financial Markets and Institutions: A Modern Perspective
Second Edition

INTERNATIONAL FINANCE

Beim and Calomiris
Emerging Financial Markets

Eun and Resnick
International Financial Management
Third Edition

Kuemmerle
Case Studies in International Entrepreneurship: Managing and Financing Ventures in the Global Economy
First Edition

Levich
International Financial Markets: Prices and Policies
Second Edition

REAL ESTATE

Brueggeman and Fisher
Real Estate Finance and Investments
Twelfth Edition

Corgel, Ling and Smith
Real Estate Perspectives: An Introduction to Real Estate
Fourth Edition

Ling and Archer
Real Estate Principles: A Value Approach
First Edition

FINANCIAL PLANNING AND INSURANCE

Allen, Melone, Rosenbloom and Mahoney
Pension Planning: Pension, Profit-Sharing, and Other Deferred Compensation Plans
Ninth Edition

Crawford
Life and Health Insurance Law
Eighth Edition (LOMA)

Harrington and Niehaus
Risk Management and Insurance
Second Edition

Hirsch
Casualty Claim Practice
Sixth Edition

Kapoor, Dlabay, and Hughes
Focus on Personal Finance: An Active Approach to Help You Develop Successful Financial Skills
First Edition

Kapoor, Dlabay and Hughes
Personal Finance
Seventh Edition

Williams, Smith and Young
Risk Management and Insurance
Eighth Edition

Focus on Personal Finance

An Active Approach to Help You Develop Successful Financial Skills

To my father, Ram Kapoor, and the memory of my mother, Sheila; my wife, Theresa, and my children, Karen, Kathryn, and Dave

To my mother, Mary Dlabay, and the memory of my father, Les; to my wife, Linda, and my children, Carissa and Kyle

To my mother, Barbara Y. Hughes; and my wife, Peggy

Focus on Personal Finance

An Active Approach to Help You Develop Successful Financial Skills

Jack R. Kapoor

COLLEGE OF DUPAGE

Les R. Dlabay

LAKE FOREST COLLEGE

Robert J. Hughes

DALLAS COUNTY
COMMUNITY COLLEGES

**McGraw-Hill
Irwin**

Boston   Burr Ridge, IL   Dubuque, IA   Madison, WI   New York   San Francisco   St. Louis
Bangkok   Bogotá   Caracas   Kuala Lumpur   Lisbon   London   Madrid   Mexico City
Milan   Montreal   New Delhi   Santiago   Seoul   Singapore   Sydney   Taipei   Toronto

McGraw-Hill
Irwin

FOCUS ON PERSONAL FINANCE:

AN ACTIVE APPROACH TO HELP YOU DEVELOP SUCCESSFUL FINANCIAL SKILLS
Published by McGraw-Hill/Irwin, a business unit of The McGraw-Hill Companies, Inc., 1221 Avenue of the Americas, New York, NY, 10020. Copyright © 2006 by The McGraw-Hill Companies, Inc. All rights reserved. No part of this publication may be reproduced or distributed in any form or by any means, or stored in a database or retrieval system, without the prior written consent of The McGraw-Hill Companies, Inc., including, but not limited to, in any network or other electronic storage or transmission, or broadcast for distance learning.

Some ancillaries, including electronic and print components, may not be available to customers outside the United States.

This book is printed on acid-free paper.

2 3 4 5 6 7 8 9 0 VNH/VNH 0 9 8 7 6 5

ISBN 0-07-299239-5

Publisher: *Stephen M. Patterson*
Senior sponsoring editor: *Michele Janicek*
Developmental editor: *Jennifer V. Rizzi*
Executive marketing manager: *Rhonda Seelinger*
Senior media producer: *Anthony Sherman*
Media project manager: *Ellyn Zydron*
Lead project manager: *Mary Conzachi*
Senior production supervisor: *Sesha Bolisetty*
Lead designer: *Matthew Baldwin*
Lead supplement producer: *Cathy L. Tepper*
Senior digital content specialist: *Brian Nacik*
Cover and interior design: *Kiera Cunningham*
Typeface: *10/12 Times Roman*
Compositor: *Cenveo Indianapolis*
Printer: *Von Hoffmann Corporation*

Library of Congress Cataloging-in-Publication Data

Kapoor, Jack R., 1937–
    Focus on personal finance : an active approach to help you develop successful financial
skills / Jack R. Kapoor, Les R. Diabay, Robert J. Hughes.
      p. cm.
    Includes index.
    ISBN 0-07-299239-5 (alk. paper)
    I. Finance, Personal. 2. Investments. I. Diabay, Les R. II. Hughes, Robert James, 1946–
III. Title.
HG179.K368 2006
332.024'01—dc22
                                             2004057913

www.mhhe.com

Jack R. Kapoor, *College of DuPage*

Jack Kapoor is a professor of business and economics in the Business and Technology Division of the College of DuPage, Glen Ellyn, Illinois, where he has taught business and economics since 1969. He received his BA and MS from San Francisco State College and his EdD from Northern Illinois University. He previously taught at Illinois Institute of Technology's Stuart School of Management, San Francisco State University's School of World Business, and other colleges. Professor Kapoor was awarded the Business and Technology Division's Outstanding Professor Award for 1999–2000. He served as an assistant national bank examiner for the U.S. Treasury Department and has been an international trade consultant to Bolting Manufacturing Co., Ltd., Bombay, India.

Dr. Kapoor is known internationally as a co-author of several textbooks, including *Business: A Practical Approach* (Rand McNally), *Business* (Houghton Mifflin), *Business and Personal Finance* (Glencoe), and *Personal Finance* (McGraw-Hill). He served as a content consultant for the popular national television series *The Business File: An Introduction to Business* and developed two full-length audio courses in Business and Personal Finance. He has been quoted in many national newspapers and magazines, including *USA Today, U.S. News & World Report,* the *Chicago Sun-Times, Crain's Small Business,* the *Chicago Tribune,* and other publications.

Dr. Kapoor has traveled around the world and has studied business practices in capitalist, socialist, and communist countries.

Les R. Dlabay, *Lake Forest College*

Sharing resources with the less fortunate is an ongoing financial goal of Les Dlabay, professor of business at Lake Forest College, Lake Forest, Illinois. Through child sponsorship programs, world hunger organizations, and community service activities, he believes the extensive wealth in our society should be used to help others. In addition to writing several textbooks, Dr. Dlabay teaches various international business courses. His "hobbies" include collecting cereal packages from over 100 countries and paper currency from 200 countries, which are used to teach about economic, cultural, and political aspects of foreign business environments. Professor Dlabay also uses many field research activities with his students, conducting interviews, surveys, and observations of business activities.

Robert J. Hughes, *Dallas County Community Colleges*

Financial literacy! Only two words, but Bob Hughes, professor of business at Dallas County Community Colleges, believes that these two words can literally change people's lives. Whether you want to be rich or just manage the money you have, the ability to analyze financial decisions and gather financial information are skills that can always be improved. In addition to writing several textbooks, Dr. Hughes has taught personal finance, introduction to business, business math, small business management, small business finance, and accounting since 1972. He also served as a content consultant for two popular national television series, *It's Strictly Business* and *Dollars & Sense: Personal Finance for the 21st Century,* and is the lead author for a business math project utilizing computer-assisted instruction funded by the ALEKS Corporation. He received his BBA from Southern Nazarene University and his MBA and EdD from the University of North Texas. His hobbies include writing, investing, collecting French antiques, art, and travel.

Owning a huge house and a luxury car?
Retiring at age 45 and traveling the world?
Having a sense of freedom from financial worries?

Though the first two suggestions are very appealing, most of you would welcome the third—being able to go out to dinner, occasionally splurging at a sale at your favorite store, just paying bills and credit cards in full—and avoiding arguments that many people experience because they never seem to have enough money. Enjoying *peace of mind* with regard to your financial situation is a very attainable goal, and you took the first step by enrolling in a personal finance course and purchasing this book.

Focus on Personal Finance is all about you—this text will not only get you thinking about your current situation and your financial goals, but it will encourage you to put these in writing to use as a guide and revise over the course of your life. The more you involve yourself in the Getting Personal self-assessments, the in-chapter exercises, and, most important, Your Personal Financial Plan worksheets, the more you will discover about your current habits and how to improve them for greater financial freedom. The fact is that there is no better time to start than now.

No matter your age, gender, family status, economic status, or stage of life, being financially literate—having the ability to make informed choices about spending, saving, borrowing, and investing—is critical. This book won't give you the hottest stock tips, tell you where you can get the best deal on a car, or offer secrets for instant wealth, but you will learn basic concepts that will increase your comfort in financial situations. These concepts include advantages and disadvantages of different investments, tips you need to know before purchasing a car, suggestions for financing a home, and how to calculate how much money you will need to retire comfortably. Not every topic will apply to your life right now, but this book will be a valuable reference when you do need to apply for credit or a loan, purchase insurance, or plan your estate.

Be sure to check the cover foldout for ways to use the many learning resources available and to get the most out of this text, CD, and Web site at www.mhhe.com/kdh. We hope that your active involvement with this text and the resulting financial plan brings you closer to peace of mind and the many financial goals you select for yourself!

Jack Kapoor
kapoorj@cdnet.cod.edu

Les Dlabay
ldlabay@lfc.edu

Bob Hughes
rjh8410@dcccd.edu

GET INSIDE THE BOOK

Getting Personal

Fill it in and get personal! Each chapter starts with a personal assessment questionnaire focusing on your current personal financial habits for the topics that will be covered in that chapter. Each assessment contains four to six questions that ask you to fill in, circle, or rate your answer.

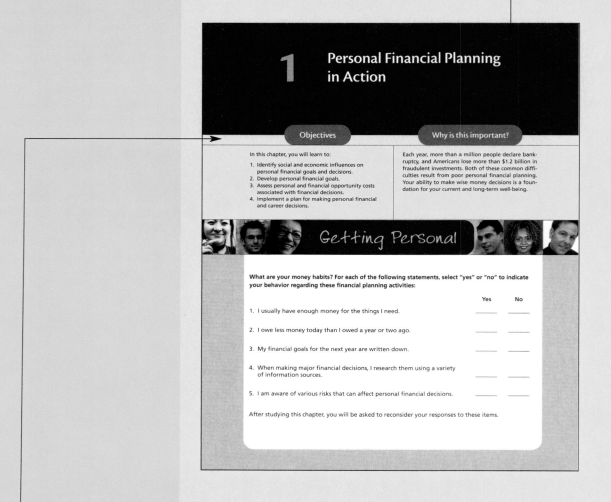

1 **Personal Financial Planning in Action**

Objectives	Why is this important?
In this chapter, you will learn to: 1. Identify social and economic influences on personal financial goals and decisions. 2. Develop personal financial goals. 3. Assess personal and financial opportunity costs associated with financial decisions. 4. Implement a plan for making personal financial and career decisions.	Each year, more than a million people declare bankruptcy, and Americans lose more than $1.2 billion in fraudulent investments. Both of these common difficulties result from poor personal financial planning. Your ability to make wise money decisions is a foundation for your current and long-term well-being.

Getting Personal

What are your money habits? For each of the following statements, select "yes" or "no" to indicate your behavior regarding these financial planning activities:

	Yes	No
1. I usually have enough money for the things I need.	_____	_____
2. I owe less money today than I owed a year or two ago.	_____	_____
3. My financial goals for the next year are written down.	_____	_____
4. When making major financial decisions, I research them using a variety of information sources.	_____	_____
5. I am aware of various risks that can affect personal financial decisions.	_____	_____

After studying this chapter, you will be asked to reconsider your responses to these items.

Objectives and Why Is This Important?

As each chapter begins, a list of the chapter objectives and why they are important is boxed off for easy reference. The objectives are also used to organize the end-of-chapter summary.

Key Web Sites and Your Personal Financial Plan Sheets

Lists of *key Web sites* and all of the *Your Personal Financial Plan* worksheets for each chapter in easy-reference boxes are presented at the start of each chapter.

Objective References

Citations in the margins next to the relevant text refer to corresponding chapter objectives, listed at the beginning of each chapter.

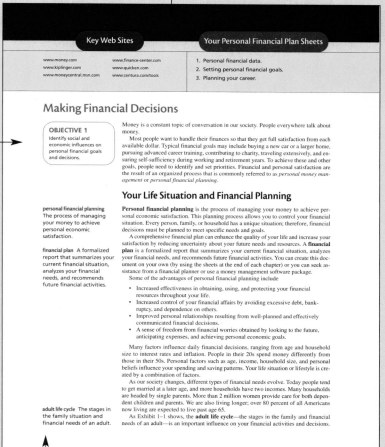

Key Web Sites

www.money.com   www.finance-center.com
www.kiplinger.com   www.quicken.com
www.moneycentral.msn.com   www.centura.com/tools

Your Personal Financial Plan Sheets

1. Personal financial data.
2. Setting personal financial goals.
3. Planning your career.

Making Financial Decisions

OBJECTIVE 1
Identify social and economic influences on personal financial goals and decisions.

Money is a constant topic of conversation in our society. People everywhere talk about money.

Most people want to handle their finances so that they get full satisfaction from each available dollar. Typical financial goals may include buying a new car or a larger home, pursuing advanced career training, contributing to charity, traveling extensively, and ensuring self-sufficiency during working and retirement years. To achieve these and other goals, people need to identify and set priorities. Financial and personal satisfaction are the result of an organized process that is commonly referred to as *personal money management* or *personal financial planning*.

Your Life Situation and Financial Planning

personal financial planning The process of managing your money to achieve personal economic satisfaction.

financial plan A formalized report that summarizes your current financial situation, analyzes your financial needs, and recommends future financial activities.

Personal financial planning is the process of managing your money to achieve personal economic satisfaction. This planning process allows you to control your financial situation. Every person, family, or household has a unique situation; therefore, financial decisions must be planned to meet specific needs and goals.

A comprehensive financial plan can enhance the quality of your life and increase your satisfaction by reducing uncertainty about your future needs and resources. A **financial plan** is a formalized report that summarizes your current financial situation, analyzes your financial needs, and recommends future financial activities. You can create this document on your own (by using the sheets at the end of each chapter) or you can seek assistance from a financial planner or use a money management software package.

Some of the advantages of personal financial planning include

- Increased effectiveness in obtaining, using, and protecting your financial resources throughout your life.
- Increased control of your financial affairs by avoiding excessive debt, bankruptcy, and dependence on others.
- Improved personal relationships resulting from well-planned and effectively communicated financial decisions.
- A sense of freedom from financial worries obtained by looking to the future, anticipating expenses, and achieving personal economic goals.

Many factors influence daily financial decisions, ranging from age and household size to interest rates and inflation. People in their 20s spend money differently from those in their 50s. Personal factors such as age, income, household size, and personal beliefs influence your spending and saving patterns. Your life situation or lifestyle is created by a combination of factors.

As our society changes, different types of financial needs evolve. Today people tend to get married at a later age, and more households have two incomes. Many households are headed by single parents. More than 2 million women provide care for both dependent children and parents. We are also living longer; over 80 percent of all Americans now living are expected to live past age 65.

adult life cycle The stages in the family situation and financial needs of an adult.

As Exhibit 1–1 shows, the **adult life cycle**—the stages in the family and financial needs of an adult—is an important influence on your financial activities and decisions.

Key Terms

Key terms appear in bold type within the text and are defined in the margins. A list of key terms and page references is located at the end of each chapter.

Did You Know?

Did you know each chapter contains several *Did You Know?* yellow "sticky-notes" containing fun facts, information, and financial planning assistance you can use in creating your personal financial plan?

From the Pages of . . . Kiplinger's Personal Finance

This one-page chapter feature presents an actual article from the well-known *Kiplinger's Personal Finance Magazine* related to a chapter topic. Each article presents a personal finance issue for you to debate and solve, using the questions at the bottom of the page. This is an excellent tool to develop critical thinking and writing skills!

Also, because money matters, subscribe to *Kiplinger's* at special student rates! With the purchase of a new book, you can subscribe to a year of *Kiplinger's Personal Finance Magazine* for a reduced student rate of $12.00. Please see the subscription card inside the back cover envelope of this book for more details.

Tackle AMBITIOUS goals

WHEN Casey and Pete Andrysiak were single, they lived large and invested like high rollers. Casey still talks about a $10,000 loss she took on IBM options years ago. Now married and parents of seven-month-old Mackenzie, they want to salt away $40,000 a year—and may just be able to. Pete, 36, is a major with the Army Corps of Engineers at Fort Leavenworth, Kan., where they live. Casey, 34, is a high-tech product-development executive and works two well-paid jobs from home.

So what are the problems? Setting priorities and making sense of too many investing choices, says Casey. The couple have already saved $170,000. But right now the money is scattered among 14 investments: mutual funds, retirement plans and a 529 college-savings account, with balances ranging from $52,000 down to $1,200. Casey and Pete would like to accumulate $5 million by the time they retire between the ages of 55 and 60. If they truly can invest $40,000 a year, they'll need to earn a doable 7.5% per year over 22 years to reach their goal. They'll also have Pete's military benefits.

Suggestions: To stay disciplined, Casey and Pete need a "policy statement," says Jeffrey Rattiner, president of JR Financial Group, in Englewood, Colo. That means putting goals in writing, estimating the timing and amount of income and expenses, and agreeing to stick to a savings plan. Casey and Pete want Mackenzie's tuition fund to grow to $150,000 in 16 years. But assuming a $200-a-month investment in the 529 plan and an annual return of 7.5%, they'd accumulate only $80,000 in that time. (Casey's father is also saving for Mackenzie; that may make up for the shortfall.)

The other key issue: where to invest the $40,000 each year. With their long time horizon and the safety net of Pete's pension, the couple should place at least 70% of their investments in stocks or stock funds. They should put 20% in bonds, 5% in real estate securities and 5% in cash. Seven or eight good funds should suffice for now, though they can add some long-term growth stocks if they wish. Casey and Pete already have 15% of their long-term investments in **Dodge & Cox Stock.** We'd fill out the portfolio with 15% in **FMI Focus,** 10% each in **Legg Mason Opportunity, ABN Amro/Montag & Caldwell Growth N** and **Aegis Value,** 5% in **Third Avenue Real Estate Value,** and the rest in either the **Artisan** or **Oakmark International** funds, or split between the two. A low-cost bond fund, such as **Vanguard Total Bond Market Index,** and cash complete the picture.

Source: Reprinted by permission from the April issue of *Kiplinger's Personal Finance.* Copyright © 2004 The Kiplinger Washington Editors, Inc.

1. What actions did Casey and Pete take that reflect wise financial planning?

2. Describe actions you might take based on the experiences of Casey and Pete.

3. What information is available at www.kiplinger.com that might be of value when making personal financial decisions?

From the pages of . . . Kiplinger's Personal Finance

Concept Checks

Concept Checks at the end of each major section provide fill-in-the-blank questions to help you assess your knowledge of the main ideas covered in that section. You'll know whether you have mastered the concepts and are ready to move on, or if you should stop and revisit certain topics.

✔ **CONCEPTCHECK 1–4**

1 What actions might a person take to identify alternatives when making a financial decision?
_____
_____

2 Why are career planning activities considered to be personal financial decisions?
_____
_____

3 For the following situations, identify the type of risk being described.
_____ Not getting proper rest and exercise.
_____ Not being able to obtain cash from a certificate of deposit before the maturity date.
_____ Taking out a variable rate loan when rates are expected to rise.
_____ Training for a career field with low potential demand in the future.

4 For the following main sources of personal finance information, list a specific Web site, organization, or person who you might contact in the future.

Type of information	Specific source	Contact information
Web site		
Financial Institution		
Media source		
Financial Specialist		

Your Personal Financial Plan Sheet References

The integrated use of the Your Personal Financial Plan sheets is highlighted with an icon in the margin. This visual, near the text material needed to complete each worksheet, helps you better integrate this study resource into your learning process and continue to track your personal financial habits.

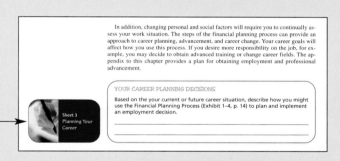

In addition, changing personal and social factors will require you to continually assess your work situation. The steps of the financial planning process can provide an approach to career planning, advancement, and career change. Your career goals will affect how you use this process. If you desire more responsibility on the job, for example, you may decide to obtain advanced training or change career fields. The appendix to this chapter provides a plan for obtaining employment and professional advancement.

Sheet 3 Planning Your Career

YOUR CAREER PLANNING DECISIONS

Based on the your current or future career situation, describe how you might use the Financial Planning Process (Exhibit 1–4, p. 14) to plan and implement an employment decision.
_____
_____

Apply Yourself!

Boxed activities, listed by chapter objectives, ask you to perform activities that apply concepts learned to your life situations.

Financial Planning in Our Economy

economics The study of how wealth is created and distributed.

Daily economic activities have a strong influence on financial planning. **Economics** is the study of how wealth is created and distributed. The economic environment includes various institutions, principally business, labor, and government, that work together to satisfy our needs and wants.

While various government agencies regulate financial activities, the Federal Reserve System, our nation's central bank, has significant responsibility in our economy. *The Fed*, as it is called, is concerned with maintaining an adequate money supply. It achieves this by influencing borrowing, interest rates, and the buying or selling of government securities. The Fed attempts to make adequate funds available for consumer spending and business expansion while keeping interest rates and consumer prices at an appropriate level.

Apply *Yourself!*

Objective 1
Using Web research and discussion with others, create an inflation rate that reflects the change in price for items frequently bought by you and your family.

GLOBAL INFLUENCES The global marketplace can have a significant influence on financial activities. Our economy is affected by both foreign investors and competition from foreign companies. American businesses compete against foreign companies for the spending dollars of American consumers. When the level of exports of U.S.-made goods is lower than the level of imported goods, more U.S. dollars leave the country than the dollar value of foreign currency coming into the United States. This reduces the funds available for domestic spending and investment. Also, if foreign companies decide not to invest in the United States, the domestic money supply is reduced. This reduced money supply can cause higher interest rates.

Exhibit [1-2]   Components of Personal Financial Planning

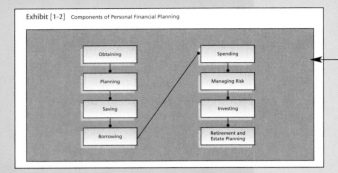

Exhibits and Tables

Throughout the text, exhibits and tables help to visually illustrate important personal finance concepts and processes.

Personal Finance in Practice

These boxes offer information that can assist you when faced with special situations and unique financial planning decisions. They challenge you to apply the concepts you have learned to your life and record personal responses.

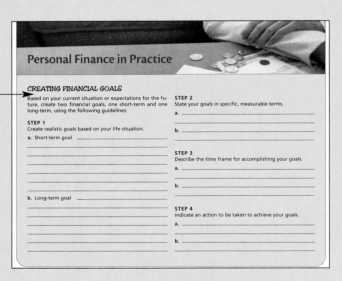

Personal Finance in Practice

CREATING FINANCIAL GOALS

Based on your current situation or expectations for the future, create two financial goals, one short-term and one long-term, using the following guidelines:

STEP 1
Create realistic goals based on your life situation.

a. Short-term goal _____

b. Long-term goal _____

STEP 2
State your goals in specific, measurable terms.

a. _____

b. _____

STEP 3
Describe the time frame for accomplishing your goals.

a. _____

b. _____

STEP 4
Indicate an action to be taken to achieve your goals.

a. _____

b. _____

Figure It Out!

ANNUAL CONTRIBUTIONS TO ACHIEVE A FINANCIAL GOAL

Achieving specific financial goals often requires regular deposits to a savings or investment account. By using time value of money calculations, you can determine the amount you should save or invest to achieve a specific goal for the future.

EXAMPLE 1
Jonie Emerson has two children who will start college in 10 years. She plans to set aside $1,500 a year for her children's college educations during that period and estimates she will earn an annual interest rate of 5 percent on her savings. What amount can Jonie expect to have available for her children's college educations when they start college?

CALCULATION:

$1,500 × Future value of a series of deposits,
5%, 10 years

$1,500 × 12.578 (Exhibit 1–3B) = $18,867

EXAMPLE 2
Don Calder wants to accumulate $50,000 over the next 10 years as a reserve fund for his parents' retirement living expenses and health care. If he earns an average of 8 percent on his investments, what amount must he invest each year to achieve this goal?

CALCULATION:

$50,000 ÷ Future value of a series of deposits,
8%, 10 years

$50,000 ÷ 14.487 (Exhibit 1–3B) = $3,452.80

Don needs to invest approximately $3,450 a year for 10 years at 8 percent to achieve the desired financial goal.

Figure It Out!

This boxed feature presents a variety of important mathematical applications relevant to personal finance situations and concepts.

Annotated Web Links

Web sites that are relevant to a section or concept in the text are presented in the margins.

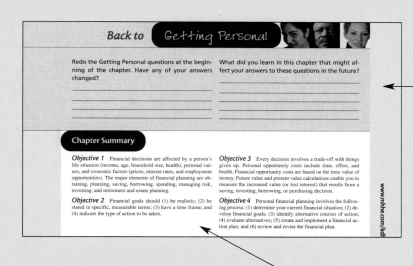

Financial Planning Activities

To achieve a successful financial situation, you must coordinate various components through an organized plan and wise decision making. Exhibit 1–2 presents an overview of the eight major personal financial planning areas.

OBTAINING   You obtain financial resources from employment, investments, or ownership of a business. Obtaining financial resources is the foundation of financial planning, since these resources are used for all financial activities.

PLANNING   Planned spending through budgeting is the key to achieving goals and future financial security. Efforts to anticipate expenses and certain financial decisions can help reduce taxes.

SAVING   Long-term financial security starts with a regular savings plan for emergencies, unexpected bills, replacement of major items, and the purchase of special goods and services, such as a college education, a boat, or a vacation home. Once you have established a basic savings plan, you may use additional money for investments that offer greater financial growth.

BORROWING   Maintaining control over your credit-buying habits will contribute to your financial goals. The overuse and misuse of credit may cause a situation in which a person's debts far exceed the resources available to pay those debts. **Bankruptcy** is a set of federal laws allowing you to either restructure your debts or remove certain debts. The people who declare bankruptcy each year may have avoided this trauma with wise spending and borrowing decisions. Chapter 5 discusses bankruptcy in detail.

Key Web Sites for Obtaining
www.rileyguide.com
www.monster.com

Key Web Sites for Planning
www.quicken.com
www.irs.gov

Key Web Sites for Savings
www.bankrate.com
www.fdic.gov

Key Web Sites for Borrowing
www.finance-center.com
www.debtadvice.com

bankruptcy A set of federal laws allowing you to either restructure your debts or remove certain debts.

Back to Getting Personal

Redo the Getting Personal questions at the beginning of the chapter. Have any of your answers changed?

What did you learn in this chapter that might affect your answers to these questions in the future?

Chapter Summary

Objective 1   Financial decisions are affected by a person's life situation (income, age, household size, health), personal values, and economic factors (prices, interest rates, and employment opportunities). The major elements of financial planning are obtaining, planning, saving, borrowing, spending, managing risk, investing, and retirement and estate planning.

Objective 2   Financial goals should (1) be realistic; (2) be stated in specific, measurable terms; (3) have a time frame; and (4) indicate the type of action to be taken.

Objective 3   Every decision involves a trade-off with things given up. Personal opportunity costs include time, effort, and health. Financial opportunity costs are based on the time value of money. Future value and present value calculations enable you to measure the increased value (or lost interest) that results from a saving, investing, borrowing, or purchasing decision.

Objective 4   Personal financial planning involves the following process: (1) determine your current financial situation; (2) develop financial goals; (3) identify alternative courses of action; (4) evaluate alternatives; (5) create and implement a financial action plan; and (6) review and revise the financial plan.

www.mhhe.com/kdh

Back to Getting Personal

Now, what would you do differently? At the end of each chapter, you are asked to revisit your initial responses to the chapter opening self-assessment, *Getting Personal.* Having read the chapter, you are now challenged to rethink your personal financial habits and record what you'd do differently and why.

Chapter Summary

Organized by chapter objective, this concise summary of each chapter is a great study and self-assessment tool, located conveniently at the end of chapters.

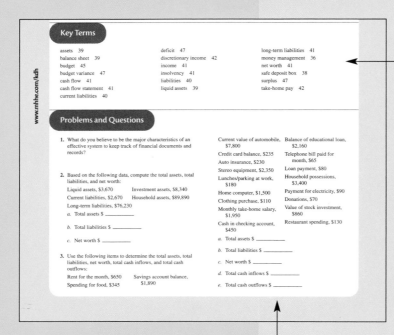

Key Terms

assets 39	deficit 47	long-term liabilities 41
balance sheet 39	discretionary income 42	money management 36
budget 45	income 41	net worth 41
budget variance 47	insolvency 41	safe deposit box 38
cash flow 41	liabilities 40	surplus 47
cash flow statement 41	liquid assets 39	take-home pay 42
current liabilities 40		

Problems and Questions

1. What do you believe to be the major characteristics of an effective system to keep track of financial documents and records?

2. Based on the following data, compute the total assets, total liabilities, and net worth:

   Liquid assets, $3,670 Investment assets, $8,340
   Current liabilities, $2,670 Household assets, $89,890
   Long-term liabilities, $76,230

   a. Total assets $ _____

   b. Total liabilities $ _____

   c. Net worth $ _____

3. Use the following items to determine the total assets, total liabilities, net worth, total cash inflows, and total cash outflows:

   Rent for the month, $650 Savings account balance, $1,890
   Spending for food, $345

Current value of automobile, $7,800
Credit card balance, $235
Auto insurance, $230
Stereo equipment, $2,350
Lunches/parking at work, $180
Home computer, $1,500
Clothing purchase, $110
Monthly take-home salary, $1,950
Cash in checking account, $450

Balance of educational loan, $2,160
Telephone bill paid for month, $65
Loan payment, $80
Household possessions, $3,400
Payment for electricity, $90
Donations, $70
Value of stock investment, $860
Restaurant spending, $130

   a. Total assets $ _____

   b. Total liabilities $ _____

   c. Net worth $ _____

   d. Total cash inflows $ _____

   e. Total cash outflows $ _____

Key Terms List

A handy list of all the boldface key terms from each chapter, along with page citations for easy reference while studying.

Problems and Questions

A variety of problems and questions that allow you to put your quantitative and qualitative analysis of personal financial decisions for each chapter to work in the spaces provided!

Internet Connection

COMPARING ONLINE MONEY MANAGEMENT ADVICE

Conduct an Internet search to locate two Web sites that provide information on budgeting and other money management activities. Compare the advice provided for the following categories:

Money management topic areas	Web site	Web site
1. What budget guidelines are provided for suggested spending amounts for food, housing, transportation, and other living expenses?		
2. How can a person avoid financial problems and money management difficulties?		
3. What suggestions are provided for saving and investing to achieve financial goals?		

What similarities and differences exist in the advice given by these Web sites? Which sites do you believe provide the most useful and reliable information?

55

Internet Connection

This end-of-chapter Web exercise asks you to apply concepts just learned to real-life situations and institutions by surfing the Web. Directions are given to help guide the way, and spaces are provided to record your findings for reference or for a class project.

Case in Point

A SINGLE FATHER'S TAX SITUATION

Ever since his wife's death, Eric Stanford has faced difficult personal and financial circumstances. His job provides him with a fairly good income but keeps him away from his daughters, ages 8 and 10, nearly 20 days a month. This requires him to use in-home child care services that consume a major portion of his income. Since the Stanfords live in a small apartment, this arrangement has been very inconvenient.

Due to the costs of caring for his children, Eric has only a minimal amount withheld from his salary for federal income taxes. Thus more money is available during the year, but for the last few years he has had to make a payment in April—another financial burden.

Although Eric has created an investment fund for his daughters' college education and for his retirement, he has not sought to select investments that offer tax benefits. Overall, he needs to look at several aspects of his tax planning activities to find strategies that will best serve his current and future financial needs.

Eric has assembled the following information for the current tax year:

Earnings from wages, $42,590

Interest earned on savings, $125

IRA deduction, $2,000

Checking account interest, $65

Three exemptions at $2,750 each

Current standard deduction for filing status, $6,350

Amount withheld for federal income tax, $3,178

Tax credit for child care, $400

Filing status: head of household

Questions

1. What are Eric's major financial concerns in his current situation?

2. In what ways might Eric improve his tax planning efforts?

3. Calculate the following
   a. What is Eric's taxable income? (Refer to Exhibit 3–1, page 64.)

   b. What is his total tax liability? (Use Exhibit 3–5, page 74.) What is his average tax rate?

   c. Based on his withholding, will Eric receive a refund or owe additional tax? What is the amount?

www.mhhe.com/kdh

Case in Point

You are given a hypothetical personal finance dilemma and data to work through to practice concepts just learned from a chapter. A series of questions reinforces your successful mastery and application of these chapter topics!

Your Personal Financial Plan Sheets

Listed at the beginning of each chapter and with in-text icons, at the end of each chapter are several worksheets—each asking you to work through the application and record your own personal financial plan answers. These sheets apply concepts learned to your personal situation and serve as a roadmap to your personal financial future. Fill them out, rip them out, submit them for homework, and keep them filed in a safe spot for future reference!

Also, key Web sites are given to help you devise your personal financial plan, and the "What's Next for Your Personal Financial Plan?" section at the end of each sheet challenges you to use your responses to plan the next level, as well as foreshadowing upcoming concepts.

Name: _____   Date: _____

Current Income Tax Estimate

Financial Planning Activities: Based on last year's tax return, estimates for the current year, and current tax regulations and rates, estimate your current tax liability.

Suggested Web sites: www.irs.gov   www.taxlogic.com

8

Gross income (wages, salary, investment income, and other ordinary income)		$
Less Adjustments to income (see current tax regulations)		– $
Equals Adjusted gross income		= $
Less Standard deduction **or**	Itemized deduction	
	medical expenses (exceeding 7.5% of AGI)	$
	state/local income, property taxes	$
	mortgage, home equity loan	$
	interest	$
	contributions	$
	casualty and theft losses	$
	moving expenses, job-related and miscellaneous expenses (exceeding 2% of AGI)	$
Amount – $	Total	– $
Less Personal exemptions		– $
Equals Taxable income		= $
Estimated tax (based on current tax tables or tax schedules)		$
Less Tax credits		– $
Plus Other taxes		+ $
Equals Total tax liability		= $
Less Estimated withholding and payments		– $
Equals Tax due (or refund)		= $

What's Next for Your Personal Financial Plan?

• Develop a system for filing and storing various tax records related to income, deductible expenses, and current tax forms.

• Using the IRS and other Web sites, identify recent changes in tax laws that may affect your financial planning decisions.

Your Personal Financial Plan

USE THE STUDENT CD

0072992468

Available with each new text for Windows use, the CD includes:

Your Personal Financial Plan Software

This Windows-based, computerized version of the Your Personal Financial Plan sheets (located at the end of each chapter) and other financial tools for handling personal finance calculations allows you to work through the sheets with the computer and print or save your personal financial plan for future reference. The software also provides a convenient way to update your personal financial plan as your life situation changes.

Self-Study Tutor

Need more practice? Created by Dr. Anne Gleason, University of Central Oklahoma, 50–75 multiple-choice and true-false questions per chapter test your knowledge. All of the questions are different from the end-of-chapter text problems and offer an additional way to master personal finance concepts and help prepare for quizzes and exams.

Web Links

Live links to the book Web Site, Personal Finance Online, and Business Around the World help you stay just a click away from additional study resources.

STUDY ONLINE AT www.mhhe.com/kdh

Here are some of the additional **FREE** online study tools you get with *Focus on Personal Finance.*

Online Self-Study Quizzes

Test yourself! Use these 10-question-per-chapter self-grading quizzes to help you master personal finance concepts from the text and prepare for class quizzes and exams.

Crossword Puzzles

Puzzled by personal finance? Each chapter's puzzle, created by Patricia Halliday, Santa Monica College, provides clues to fill in the puzzle with relevant personal finance topics and words. A fun way to study for class!

Flashcards

Learn in a flash! Virtual flashcards present key term definitions on one side and the key terms on the other side. You can choose which side you'd like to test yourself on, and flip the card when you are ready.

Personal Finance Online

Accessible through the book Web site, Personal Finance Online is an exclusive Web tool from McGraw-Hill/Irwin. This value-added site provides even more personal finance practice exercises and activities using the Internet. More than 50 exercises for 11 different key personal finance topics draw on recent articles, company reports, government data, and other Web-based resources!

Focus on ... Teaching

INSTRUCTOR SUPPLEMENTS

The *Instructor Resource CD* (0072992433) provides you, the instructor, with one resource for all of your *Focus on Personal Finance* supplementary material. It includes:

Instructor's Manual

Created by the authors, the *Instructor's Manual* includes a "Course Planning Guide" with instructional strategies, course projects, supplementary resource lists and sample syllabi. The "Chapter Teaching Materials" section of the Instructor's Manual provides a chapter overview, the chapter objectives with summaries, introductory activities, and detailed lecture outlines with teaching suggestions.

This section also includes concluding activities, ready-to-duplicate quizzes, supplementary lecture materials and activities, and answers to concept checks, end-of-chapter questions and problems and cases. A print version of the Instructor's Manual (0072992476) is also available through your McGraw-Hill/Irwin representative.

Test Bank

The *Test Bank,* also created by the authors, consists of close to 2,000 multiple-choice, true-false, and essay questions. These test items are organized by the objectives for each chapter. This resource also includes answers, text page references, and an indication of difficulty level. A print version of the Test Bank (0072992484) is available through your McGraw-Hill/Irwin representative.

Computerized Test Bank

Utilizing McGraw-Hill's *EZ Test* testing software for Windows to quickly create customized exams, this user-friendly program allows instructors to sort questions by format, edit existing questions or add new ones, and scramble questions for multiple versions of the same test.

PowerPoint Presentation

Created by Samira Hussein with contributions from Stephen Chambers, both of Johnson County Community College, it offers more than 350 visual presentations that may be edited and manipulated to fit a particular course format.

Instructor Resources and Optimal Text Packages to Help Enhance Your Course

VIDEOS

Our ten 30-minute videos, almost one per chapter, help to visually illustrate important personal finance concepts in potential real-life situations. Developed by Coastline Community College, these half-hour segments can be used with multiple chapters at any time during the course. For a list of videos and their descriptions, please see the Instructor's Manual.

ONLINE SUPPORT AT www.mhhe.com/kdh

Along with having access to all of the same material your students can view on the book's Online Learning Center (OLC), you also have *password-protected* access to the Instructor's Manual, PowerPoint files, and answer keys to the Crossword Puzzles.

OLCs can be delivered in multiple ways—through the textbook Web site (www.mhhe.com/kdh), through PageOut (see packages below), or within a course management system like Blackboard, WebCT, TopClass, and eCollege. Ask your campus representative for more details.

KIPLINGER'S PERSONAL FINANCE

With each new book is a special offer from McGraw-Hill/Irwin and Kiplinger's for you and your students to subscribe to a full year of *Kiplinger's Personal Finance* (12 issues) magazine for the special rate of $12.00—a huge 71% off of the newstand cost. With savings like this, and the Kiplinger's feature within the book, it's easy to integrate this resource into your personal finance course! Please see the subscription card inside the back cover envelope for more details.

Which Package Will You Choose?

Here are some available options to enhance your teaching and your students' learning experience. Please ask your campus representative for more details.

BusinessWeek

Your students can subscribe to 15 weeks of *BusinessWeek* for a specially priced rate of $8.25 in addition to the price of the text. Students will receive a passcode card shrink-wrapped with their new text. The card directs students to a Web site where they enter the code and then gain access to *BusinessWeek's* registration page to set up their print and online subscription.

The Wall Street Journal

Your students can subscribe to **The Wall Street Journal** for 15 weeks at a specially priced rate of $20.00 in addition to the price of the text. Students will receive a "How to Use the WSJ" handbook plus a passcode card shrink-wrapped with their new text. The card directs students to a Web site where they enter the code and then gain access to the **WSJ** registration page to set up their print and online subscription, and also set up their subscription to Dow Jones Interactive online for the same 15-week period.

PageOut at www.pageout.net

Free to adopters, this Web page generation software is designed to help you create your own course Web site, without all of the hassle. In just a few minutes, even the most novice computer user can have a functioning course Web site.

Simply type your material into the template provided and PageOut instantly converts it to HTML—a universal Web language. Next, choose your favorite of three easy-to-navigate designs and your class Web homepage is created, complete with online syllabus, lecture notes, and bookmarks. You can even include a separate instructor page and an assignment page.

PageOut offers enhanced point-and-click features, including a Syllabus Page that applies a real-world link to original text material, an automatic grade book, and a discussion board where you and your students can exchange questions and post announcements. Ask your campus representative for a demonstration.

We express our deepest appreciation for the efforts of the colleagues who provided extensive comments that helped to shape and create this text and contributed to the quality of the book you are using.

Chris A. Austin, *Normandale Community College*

Gail H. Austin, *Rose State College*

Tom Bilyeu, *Southwestern Illinois College*

Ross Blankenship, *State Fair Community College*

William F. Blosel, *California University of Pennsylvania*

Jennifer Brewer, *Butler County Community College*

Peg Camp, *University of Nebraska–Kearney*

Stephen Chambers, *Johnson County Community College*

Julie Douthit, *Abilene Christian University*

Bill Dowling, *Savannah State University*

Dorsey Dyer, *Davidson County Community College*

John D. Farlin, *Ohio Dominican University*

Garry Fleming, *Roanoke College*

Paula G. Freston, *Merced College*

Robert Friederichs, *Alexandria Tech College*

Caroline S. Fulmer, *University of Alabama*

Dr. Michael R. Gordinier, *Washington University*

Shari Gowers, *Dixie State College*

Michael P. Griffin, *University of Massachusetts–Dartmouth*

Ward Hooker, *Orangeburg–Calhoun Tech College*

Ishappa S. Hullur, *Morehead State University*

Samira Hussein, *Johnson County Community College*

Dorothy W. Jones, *Northwestern State University*

Jeanette Klosterman, *Hutchinson Community College*

Joseph T. Marchese, *Monroe Community College*

Kenneth L. Mark, *Kansas City Kansas Community College*

Paul S. Marshall, *Widener University*

Allan O'Bryan, *Rochester Community College*

Carl Parker, *Fort Hays State University*

David M. Payne, *Ohio University*

Padmaja Pillutla, *Western Illinois University*

Brenda Rice, *Ozarks Technical Community College*

John Roberts, *Florida Metropolitan University*

Joan Ryan, *Clackamas Community College*

Steven R. Scheff, *Florida Gulf Coast University*

James T. Schiermeyer, *Texas Tech University*

Joseph Simon, *Casper College*

Lea Timpler, *College of the Canyons*

Dick Verrone, *University of North Carolina–Wilmington*

Kent Weilage, *McCook Community College*

Sally Wells, *Columbia College*

Micheline West, *New Hampshire Tech*

Bob Willis, *Rogers State University*

Glen Wood, *Broome Community College*

Many talented professionals at McGraw-Hill/Irwin have contributed to the development of *Focus on Personal Finance*. We are especially grateful to Michele Janicek, Rhonda Seelinger, Jennifer Rizzi, Mary Conzachi, Sesha Bolisetty, Matt Baldwin, and Cathy Tepper.

We'd also like to thank the following people for their assistance in creating supplements: Samira Hussein, Johnson County Community College, for creating the Power-Point presentation; Stephen Chambers, Johnson County Community College, for contributing to the PowerPoint presentation; Anne Gleason, University of Central Oklahoma, for her creation of the self-study and online quiz questions; and Patricia Halliday, Santa Monica College, for her creation of the crossword puzzles.

In addition, Jack Kapoor expresses special appreciation to Theresa and Dave Kapoor, Kathryn Thumme, and Karen Tucker for their typing, proofreading, and research assistance. Finally, we thank our wives and families for their patience, understanding, encouragement, and love throughout this project.

Appendix

Index

Focus on Personal Finance

An Active Approach to Help You Develop Successful Financial Skills

1 Personal Financial Planning in Action

Objectives

In this chapter, you will learn to:

1. Identify social and economic influences on personal financial goals and decisions.
2. Develop personal financial goals.
3. Assess personal and financial opportunity costs associated with financial decisions.
4. Implement a plan for making personal financial and career decisions.

Why is this important?

Each year, more than a million people declare bankruptcy, and Americans lose more than $1.2 billion in fraudulent investments. Both of these common difficulties result from poor personal financial planning. Your ability to make wise money decisions is a foundation for your current and long-term well-being.

 Getting Personal

What are your money habits? For each of the following statements, select "yes" or "no" to indicate your behavior regarding these financial planning activities:

	Yes	No
1. I usually have enough money for the things I need.	_____	_____
2. I owe less money today than I owed a year or two ago.	_____	_____
3. My financial goals for the next year are written down.	_____	_____
4. When making major financial decisions, I research them using a variety of information sources.	_____	_____
5. I am aware of various risks that can affect personal financial decisions.	_____	_____

After studying this chapter, you will be asked to reconsider your responses to these items.

Making Financial Decisions

OBJECTIVE 1
Identify social and economic influences on personal financial goals and decisions.

Money is a constant topic of conversation in our society. People everywhere talk about money.

Most people want to handle their finances so that they get full satisfaction from each available dollar. Typical financial goals may include buying a new car or a larger home, pursuing advanced career training, contributing to charity, traveling extensively, and ensuring self-sufficiency during working and retirement years. To achieve these and other goals, people need to identify and set priorities. Financial and personal satisfaction are the result of an organized process that is commonly referred to as *personal money management* or *personal financial planning.*

Your Life Situation and Financial Planning

personal financial planning The process of managing your money to achieve personal economic satisfaction.

financial plan A formalized report that summarizes your current financial situation, analyzes your financial needs, and recommends future financial activities.

Personal financial planning is the process of managing your money to achieve personal economic satisfaction. This planning process allows you to control your financial situation. Every person, family, or household has a unique situation; therefore, financial decisions must be planned to meet specific needs and goals.

A comprehensive financial plan can enhance the quality of your life and increase your satisfaction by reducing uncertainty about your future needs and resources. A **financial plan** is a formalized report that summarizes your current financial situation, analyzes your financial needs, and recommends future financial activities. You can create this document on your own (by using the sheets at the end of each chapter) or you can seek assistance from a financial planner or use a money management software package.

Some of the advantages of personal financial planning include

- Increased effectiveness in obtaining, using, and protecting your financial resources throughout your life.
- Increased control of your financial affairs by avoiding excessive debt, bankruptcy, and dependence on others.
- Improved personal relationships resulting from well-planned and effectively communicated financial decisions.
- A sense of freedom from financial worries obtained by looking to the future, anticipating expenses, and achieving personal economic goals.

Many factors influence daily financial decisions, ranging from age and household size to interest rates and inflation. People in their 20s spend money differently from those in their 50s. Personal factors such as age, income, household size, and personal beliefs influence your spending and saving patterns. Your life situation or lifestyle is created by a combination of factors.

As our society changes, different types of financial needs evolve. Today people tend to get married at a later age, and more households have two incomes. Many households are headed by single parents. More than 2 million women provide care for both dependent children and parents. We are also living longer; over 80 percent of all Americans now living are expected to live past age 65.

adult life cycle The stages in the family situation and financial needs of an adult.

As Exhibit 1–1 shows, the **adult life cycle**—the stages in the family and financial needs of an adult—is an important influence on your financial activities and decisions.

Exhibit [1-1]   Financial Planning Influences, Goals, and Activities

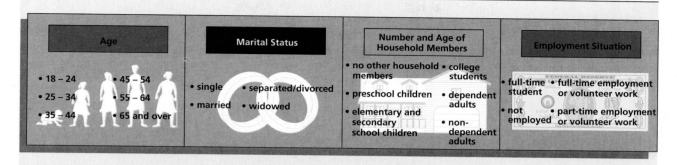

Age	Marital Status	Number and Age of Household Members	Employment Situation

• 18 – 24 • 45 – 54
• 25 – 34 • 55 – 64
• 35 – 44 • 65 and over
	• single • separated/divorced
	• married • widowed
		• no other household • college
		  members students
		• preschool children • dependent
		              adults
		• elementary and
		  secondary • non-
		  school children dependent
		              adults
			• full-time • full-time employment
			  student or volunteer work
			• not • part-time employment
			  employed or volunteer work

COMMON FINANCIAL GOALS AND ACTIVITIES

- Obtain appropriate career training.
- Create an effective financial recordkeeping system.
- Develop a regular savings and investment program.

- Accumulate an appropriate emergency fund.
- Purchase appropriate types and amounts of insurance coverage.
- Create and implement a flexible budget.

- Evaluate and select appropriate investments.
- Establish and implement a plan for retirement goals.
- Make a will and develop an estate plan.

Life Situation	Specialized Financial Activities
Young, single (18–35)	• Establish financial independence. • Obtain disability insurance to replace income during prolonged illness. • Consider home purchase for tax benefit.
Young couple with children under 18	• Carefully manage the increased need for the use of credit. • Obtain an appropriate amount of life insurance for the care of dependents. • Use a will to name guardian for children.
Single parent with children under 18	• Obtain adequate amounts of health, life, and disability insurance. • Contribute to savings and investment fund for college. • Name a guardian for children and make other estate plans.
Young dual-income couple, no children	• Coordinate insurance coverage and other benefits. • Develop savings and investment program for changes in life situation (larger house, children). • Consider tax-deferred contributions to retirement fund.
Older couple (+50), no dependent children at home	• Consolidate financial assets and review estate plans. • Obtain health insurance for postretirement period. • Plan retirement housing, living expenses, recreational activities, and part-time work.
Mixed-generation household (elderly individuals and children under 18)	• Obtain long-term health care insurance and life/disability income for care of younger dependents. • Use dependent care service if needed. • Provide arrangements for handling finances of elderly if they become ill. • Consider splitting of investment cost, with elderly getting income while alive and principal going to surviving relatives.
Older (+50), single	• Arrange for long-term health care coverage. • Review will and estate plan. • Plan retirement living facilities, living expenses, and activities.

Your life situation is also affected by events such as graduation, dependent children leaving home, changes in health, engagement and marriage, divorce, birth or adoption of a child, retirement, a career change or a move to new area, or the death of a spouse, family member, or other dependent.

In addition to being defined by your family situation, you are defined by your **values**—the ideas and principles that you consider correct, desirable, and important. Values have a direct influence on such decisions as spending now versus saving for the future or continuing school versus getting a job.

values Ideas and principles that a person considers correct, desirable, and important.

Financial Planning in Our Economy

economics The study of how wealth is created and distributed.

Daily economic activities have a strong influence on financial planning. **Economics** is the study of how wealth is created and distributed. The economic environment includes various institutions, principally business, labor, and government, that work together to satisfy our needs and wants.

While various government agencies regulate financial activities, the Federal Reserve System, our nation's central bank, has significant responsibility in our economy. *The Fed*, as it is called, is concerned with maintaining an adequate money supply. It achieves this by influencing borrowing, interest rates, and the buying or selling of government securities. The Fed attempts to make adequate funds available for consumer spending and business expansion while keeping interest rates and consumer prices at an appropriate level.

Apply *Yourself!*

Objective 1

Using Web research and discussion with others, create an inflation rate that reflects the change in price for items frequently bought by you and your family.

GLOBAL INFLUENCES   The global marketplace can have a significant influence on financial activities. Our economy is affected by both foreign investors and competition from foreign companies. American businesses compete against foreign companies for the spending dollars of American consumers. When the level of exports of U.S.-made goods is lower than the level of imported goods, more U.S. dollars leave the country than the dollar value of foreign currency coming into the United States. This reduces the funds available for domestic spending and investment. Also, if foreign companies decide not to invest in the United States, the domestic money supply is reduced. This reduced money supply can cause higher interest rates.

inflation A rise in the general level of prices.

INFLATION   Most people are concerned with the buying power of their money. **Inflation** is a rise in the general level of prices. In times of inflation, the buying power of the dollar decreases. For example, if prices increased 5 percent during the last year, items that cost $100 then would now cost $105. This means it now takes more money to buy the same amount of goods and services.

Inflation is most harmful to people living on fixed incomes. Due to inflation, retired people and others whose incomes do not change are able to afford fewer goods and services. Inflation can also adversely affect lenders of money. Unless an adequate interest rate is charged, amounts repaid by borrowers in times of inflation have less buying power than the money they borrowed.

Inflation rates vary. During the late 1950s and early 1960s, the annual inflation rate was in the 1 to 3 percent range. During the late 1970s and early 1980s, the cost of living increased 10 to 12 percent annually. At a 12 percent annual inflation rate, prices double (and the value of the dollar is cut in half) in about six years. To find out how fast prices (or your savings) will double, use the *rule of 72:* Just divide 72 by the annual inflation (or interest) rate. An annual inflation rate of 8 percent, for example, means prices will double in nine years ($72 \div 8 = 9$).

More recently, the reported annual price increase for goods and services as measured by the consumer price index has been in the 2 to 4 percent range. The *consumer price index (CPI)*, computed and published by the Bureau of Labor Statistics (www.bls. gov), is a measure of the average change in the prices urban consumers pay for a fixed "basket" of goods and services.

Inflation rates can be deceptive since the index is based on items calculated in a predetermined manner. Many people face *hidden* inflation since the cost of necessities (food, gas, health care), on which they spend the greatest proportion of their money, may rise at a higher rate than nonessential items, which could be dropping in price. This results in a reported inflation rate much lower than the actual cost-of-living increase being experienced by consumers.

INTEREST RATES   In simple terms, interest rates represent the cost of money. Like everything else, money has a price. The forces of supply and demand influence interest rates. When consumer saving and investing increase the supply of money, interest rates tend to decrease. However, as borrowing by consumers, businesses, and government increases, interest rates are likely to rise.

Interest rates can have a major affect on financial planning. The earnings you receive as a saver or an investor reflect current interest rates as well as a *risk premium* based on such factors as the length of time your funds will be used by others, expected inflation, and the extent of uncertainty about getting your money back. Risk is also a factor in the interest rate you pay as a borrower. People with poor credit ratings pay a higher interest rate than people with good credit ratings. Interest rates influence many financial decisions. Current interest rate data may be obtained at www.federalreserve.gov.

Financial Planning Activities

To achieve a successful financial situation, you must coordinate various components through an organized plan and wise decision making. Exhibit 1–2 presents an overview of the eight major personal financial planning areas.

OBTAINING   You obtain financial resources from employment, investments, or ownership of a business. Obtaining financial resources is the foundation of financial planning, since these resources are used for all financial activities.

PLANNING   Planned spending through budgeting is the key to achieving goals and future financial security. Efforts to anticipate expenses and certain financial decisions can help reduce taxes.

SAVING   Long-term financial security starts with a regular savings plan for emergencies, unexpected bills, replacement of major items, and the purchase of special goods and services, such as a college education, a boat, or a vacation home. Once you have established a basic savings plan, you may use additional money for investments that offer greater financial growth.

BORROWING   Maintaining control over your credit-buying habits will contribute to your financial goals. The overuse and misuse of credit may cause a situation in which a person's debts far exceed the resources available to pay those debts. **Bankruptcy** is a set of federal laws allowing you to either restructure your debts or remove certain debts. The people who declare bankruptcy each year may have avoided this trauma with wise spending and borrowing decisions. Chapter 5 discusses bankruptcy in detail.

> **DID YOU KNOW?**
>
> Not all consumer prices change by the same amount. In 1972, a 1-pound box of sugar cost 18 cents. In 1997, that same box of sugar cost $1.15, a 538 percent increase. During the same time period, a 5-pound bag of flour rose from 49 cents to $1.61, a 228 percent increase.

Key Web Sites for Obtaining
www.rileyguide.com
www.monster.com

Key Web Sites for Planning
www.quicken.com
www.irs.gov

Key Web Sites for Savings
www.bankrate.com
www.fdic.gov

Key Web Sites for Borrowing
www.finance-center.com
www.debtadvice.com

bankruptcy A set of federal laws allowing you to either restructure your debts or remove certain debts.

Exhibit [1-2]   Components of Personal Financial Planning

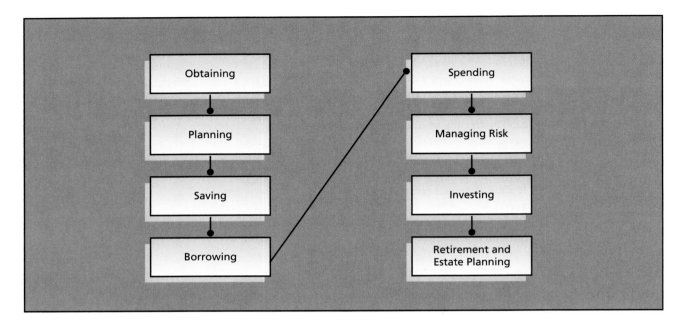

Key Web Sites for Spending
www.consumer.gov
www.autoweb.com

SPENDING   Financial planning is designed not to prevent your enjoyment of life but to help you obtain the things you want. Too often, however, people make purchases without considering the financial consequences. Some people shop compulsively, creating financial difficulties. You should detail your living expenses and your other financial obligations in a spending plan. Spending less than you earn is the only way to achieve long-term financial security.

Key Web Sites for Managing Risk
www.insure.com
www.insweb.com

MANAGING RISK   Adequate insurance coverage is another component of personal financial planning. Certain types of insurance are commonly overlooked in financial plans. For example, the number of people who suffer disabling injuries or diseases at age 50 is greater than the number who die at that age, so people may need disability insurance more than they need life insurance. Yet surveys reveal that most people have adequate life insurance but few have needed disability insurance.

Key Web Sites for Investing
www.fool.com
www.cbsmarketwatch.com

INVESTING   Although many types of investments are available, people invest for two primary reasons. Those interested in *current income* select investments that pay regular dividends or interest. In contrast, investors who desire *long-term growth* choose stocks, mutual funds, real estate, and other investments with potential for increased value in the future. You can achieve investment diversification by including a variety of assets in your *portfolio*—for example, stocks, bond mutual funds, real estate, and collectibles such as rare coins.

Key Web Sites for Retirement and Estate Planning
www.ssa.gov
www.aarp.org/financial/

RETIREMENT AND ESTATE PLANNING   Most people desire financial security upon completion of full-time employment. But retirement planning also involves thinking about your housing situation, your recreational activities, and possible part-time or volunteer work.

Transfers of money or property to others should be timed, if possible, to minimize the tax burden and maximize the benefits for those receiving the financial resources. Knowledge of property transfer methods can help you select the best course of action for funding current and future living costs, educational expenses, and retirement needs of dependents.

✔ CONCEPTCHECK 1–1

1 What personal and economic factors commonly affect personal financial decisions?

_____

_____

2 For each of the following situations, indicate if the person would tend to "suffer" or tend to "benefit" from inflation. (Circle your answer)

A person with money in a savings account.	suffer	benefit
A person who is borrowing money.	suffer	benefit
A person who is lending money.	suffer	benefit
A person receiving a fixed income amount.	suffer	benefit

3 Listed here are the eight main components of personal financial planning. Describe an action for one or more areas, that you might need to take in the next few months or years.

1. Obtaining	
2. Planning	
3. Saving	
4. Borrowing	

5. Spending	
6. Managing risk	
7. Investing	
8. Retirement estate planning	

Developing and Achieving Financial Goals

Sheet 1
Personal
Financial Data

Why do so many Americans—living in one of the richest countries in the world—have money problems? The answer can be found in two main factors. The first is poor planning and weak money management habits in areas such as spending and the use of credit. The other factor is extensive advertising, selling efforts, and product availability. Achieving personal financial satisfaction starts with clear financial goals.

Types of Financial Goals

What would you like to do tomorrow? Believe it or not, that question involves goal setting. _Short-term goals_ are goals to be achieved within the next year or so, such as saving for a vacation or paying off small debts. _Intermediate goals_ have a time frame of two to five years. _Long-term goals_ involve financial plans that are more than five years off, such as ensuring adequate retirement income, saving money for children's college educations, or purchasing a vacation home.

Long-term goals should be planned in coordination with short-term and intermediate goals. Setting and achieving short-term goals is commonly the basis for moving toward success of long-term goals. For example, saving for a down payment to buy a house is a short-term goal that can be a foundation for a long-term goal: owning your own home.

A goal of obtaining increased career training is different from a goal of saving money to pay a semiannual auto insurance premium. _Consumable-product goals_ usually occur on a

OBJECTIVE 2
Develop personal financial goals.

Apply _Yourself!_

Objective 2

Ask friends, relatives, and others about their short-term and one long-term financial goals. What are some of the common goals for various personal situations?

Personal Finance in Practice

CREATING FINANCIAL GOALS

Based on your current situation or expectations for the future, create two financial goals, one short-term and one long-term, using the following guidelines:

STEP 1
Create realistic goals based on your life situation.

a. Short-term goal _____

_____

_____

_____

_____

b. Long-term goal _____

_____

_____

_____

_____

_____

STEP 2
State your goals in specific, measurable terms.

a. _____

_____

b. _____

_____

STEP 3
Describe the time frame for accomplishing your goals.

a. _____

_____

b. _____

_____

STEP 4
Indicate an action to be taken to achieve your goals.

a. _____

_____

b. _____

_____

periodic basis and involve items that are used up relatively quickly, such as food, clothing, and entertainment. *Durable-product goals* usually involve infrequently purchased, expensive items such as appliances, cars, and sporting equipment; these consist of tangible items. In contrast, many people overlook *intangible-purchase goals*. These goals may relate to personal relationships, health, education, and leisure.

Goal-Setting Guidelines

An old saying goes, "If you don't know where you're going, you might end up somewhere else and not even know it." Goal setting is central to financial decision making. Your financial goals are the basis for planning, implementing, and measuring the progress of your spending, saving, and investing activities. Exhibit 1–1 on page 3 offers typical goals and financial activities for various life situations.

Effective financial goals should be:

- *Realistic,* based on your income and life situation. For example, if you are a full-time student, expecting to buy a new car each year is probably not realistic.
- *Stated in specific, measurable terms,* since having exact goals will help you create a plan to achieve them. For example, the goal of "accumulating $5,000 in an

investment fund within three years" is a clearer guide to planning than the goal of "putting money into an investment fund."
- *Based on a time frame,* such as a goal to be achieved in three years. A time frame helps you measure your progress toward your financial goals.
- *Action oriented,* because your financial goals are the basis for the various financial activities you will undertake. For example, "reducing credit card debt" will likely mean a decreased use of credit.

Sheet 2
Setting
Personal
Financial
Goals

✔ CONCEPTCHECK 1–2

1 What are some examples of long-term goals?

_____

_____

2 What are the main characteristics of useful financial goals?

_____

_____

3 Match the following common goals to the life situation of the people listed.

a. Pay off student loans	_____ A young couple without children.
b. Start a college savings fund	_____ An older person living alone.
c. Increase retirement contributions	_____ A person who just completed college.
d. Finance long-term care	_____ A single mother with a preschool daughter.

Opportunity Costs and the Time Value of Money

Have you noticed that you always give up something when you make choices? In every financial decision, you sacrifice something to obtain something else that you consider more desirable. For example, you might forgo current buying to invest funds for future purchases or long-term financial security. Or you might gain the use of an expensive item now by making credit payments from future earnings.

Opportunity cost is what you give up by making a choice. This cost, commonly referred to as the *trade-off* of a decision, cannot always be measured in dollars. Opportunity costs should be viewed in terms of both personal and financial resources.

Personal Opportunity Costs

An important personal opportunity cost involves time that when used for one activity cannot be used for other activities. Time used for studying, working, or shopping will not be available for other uses. Other personal opportunity costs relate to health. Poor eating habits, lack of sleep, or avoiding exercise can result in illness, time away from school or work, increased health care costs, and reduced financial security. Like financial resources, your personal resources (time, energy, health, abilities, knowledge) require management.

OBJECTIVE 3
Assess personal and financial opportunity costs associated with financial decisions.

opportunity cost What a person gives up by making a choice.

Financial Opportunity Costs

You are constantly making choices among various financial decisions. In making those choices, you must consider the **time value of money**, the increases in an amount of money as a result of interest earned. Saving or investing a dollar instead of spending it today results in a future amount greater than a dollar. Every time you spend, save, invest, or borrow money, you should consider the time value of that money as an opportunity cost. Spending money from your savings account means lost interest earnings; however, what you buy with that money may have a higher priority than those earnings.

time value of money Increase in an amount of money as a result of interest earned.

INTEREST CALCULATIONS   Three amounts are used to calculate the time value of money for savings in the form of interest earned:

- The amount of the savings (commonly called the *principal*).
- The annual interest rate.
- The length of time the money is on deposit.

These three items are multiplied to obtain the amount of interest. Simple interest is calculated as follows:

For example, $500 on deposit at 6 percent for six months would earn $15 ($500 × 0.06 × $^6/_{12}$, or ½ year).

You can calculate the increased value of your money from interest earned in two ways: You can calculate the total amount that will be available later (future value), or you can determine the current value of an amount desired in the future (present value).

future value The amount to which current savings will increase based on a certain interest rate and a certain time period; also referred to as *compounding*.

FUTURE VALUE OF A SINGLE AMOUNT   Deposited money earns interest that will increase over time. **Future value** is the amount to which current savings will increase based on a certain interest rate and a certain time period. For example, $100 deposited in a 6 percent account for one year will grow to $106. This amount is computed as follows:

$$\text{Future value} = \underset{\substack{\uparrow \\ \text{Original amount} \\ \text{in savings}}}{\$100} + (\underset{\substack{\uparrow \\ \text{Amount of} \\ \text{interest earned}}}{\$100 \times 0.06 \times 1 \text{ year}}) = \$106$$

The same process could be continued for a second, third, and fourth year, but the computations would be time-consuming. Future value tables simplify the process (see Exhibit 1–3). To use a future value table, multiply the amount deposited by the factor for the desired interest rate and time period. For example, $650 at 8 percent for 10 years would have a future value of $1,403.35 ($650 × 2.159). The future value of an amount will always be greater than the original amount. As Exhibit 1–3A shows, all the future value factors are larger than 1. Future value computations may be referred to as *compounding*, since interest is earned on previously earned interest. Compounding allows the future value of a deposit to grow faster than it would if interest were paid only on the original deposit.

Exhibit [1-3]

Time Value of Money Tables (condensed)

A. Future Value of $1 (single amount)

Year	5%	6%	7%	8%	9%
			PERCENT		
5	1.276	1.338	1.403	1.469	1.539
6	1.340	1.419	1.501	1.587	1.677
7	1.407	1.504	1.606	1.714	1.828
8	1.477	1.594	1.718	1.851	1.993
9	1.551	1.689	1.838	1.999	2.172
10	1.629	1.791	1.967	2.159	2.367

B. Future Value of a Series of Annual Deposits (annuity)

Year	5%	6%	7%	8%	9%
			PERCENT		
5	5.526	5.637	5.751	5.867	5.985
6	6.802	6.975	7.153	7.336	7.523
7	8.142	8.394	8.654	8.923	9.200
8	9.549	9.897	10.260	10.637	11.028
9	11.027	11.491	11.978	12.488	13.021
10	12.578	13.181	13.816	14.487	15.193

C. Present Value of $1 (single amount)

Year	5%	6%	7%	8%	9%
			PERCENT		
5	0.784	0.747	0.713	0.681	0.650
6	0.746	0.705	0.666	0.630	0.596
7	0.711	0.665	0.623	0.583	0.547
8	0.677	0.627	0.582	0.540	0.502
9	0.645	0.592	0.544	0.500	0.460
10	0.614	0.558	0.508	0.463	0.422

D. Present Value of a Series of Annual Deposits (annuity)

Year	5%	6%	7%	8%	9%
			PERCENT		
5	4.329	4.212	4.100	3.993	3.890
6	5.076	4.917	4.767	4.623	4.486
7	5.786	5.582	5.389	5.206	5.033
8	6.463	6.210	5.971	5.747	5.535
9	7.108	6.802	6.515	6.247	5.995
10	7.722	7.360	7.024	6.710	6.418

Note: See Appendix A at the end of the book for more complete future value and present value tables.

Figure It Out!

ANNUAL CONTRIBUTIONS TO ACHIEVE A FINANCIAL GOAL

Achieving specific financial goals often requires regular deposits to a savings or investment account. By using time value of money calculations, you can determine the amount you should save or invest to achieve a specific goal for the future.

EXAMPLE 1

Jonie Emerson has two children who will start college in 10 years. She plans to set aside $1,500 a year for her children's college educations during that period and estimates she will earn an annual interest rate of 5 percent on her savings. What amount can Jonie expect to have available for her children's college educations when they start college?

CALCULATION:

$1,500 × Future value of a series of deposits, 5%, 10 years

$1,500 × 12.578 (Exhibit 1–3B) = $18,867

EXAMPLE 2

Don Calder wants to accumulate $50,000 over the next 10 years as a reserve fund for his parents' retirement living expenses and health care. If he earns an average of 8 percent on his investments, what amount must he invest each year to achieve this goal?

CALCULATION:

$50,000 ÷ Future value of a series of deposits, 8%, 10 years

$50,000 ÷ 14.487 (Exhibit 1–3B) = $3,452.80

Don needs to invest approximately $3,450 a year for 10 years at 8 percent to achieve the desired financial goal.

The sooner you make deposits, the greater the future value will be. Depositing $1,000 in a 5 percent account at age 40 will give you $3,387 at age 65. However, making the $1,000 deposit at age 25 would result in an account balance of $7,040 at age 65.

FUTURE VALUE OF A SERIES OF DEPOSITS Many savers and investors make regular deposits. An *annuity* is a series of equal deposits or payments. To determine the future value of equal yearly savings deposits, use Exhibit 1–3B. For this table to be used, the deposits must earn a constant interest rate. If you deposit $50 a year at 7 percent for six years, starting at the end of the first year, you will have $357.65 at the end of that time ($50 × 7.153). The Figure It Out box on this page presents examples of using future value to achieve financial goals.

PRESENT VALUE OF A SINGLE AMOUNT Another aspect of the time value of money involves determining the current value of an amount desired in the future. **Present value** is the current value for a future amount based on a certain interest rate and a certain time period. Present value computations, also called *discounting,* allow you to determine how much to deposit now to obtain a desired total in the future. Present value tables (Exhibit 1–3C) can be used to make the computations. If you want $1,000 five years from now and you earn 5 percent on your savings, you need to deposit $784 ($1,000 × 0.784). The present value of the amount you want in the future will always be less than the future value. Note that all of the factors in Exhibit 1–3C are less than 1 and interest earned will increase the present value amount to the desired future amount.

present value The current value for a future amount based on a certain interest rate and a certain time period; also referred to as *discounting.*

PRESENT VALUE OF A SERIES OF DEPOSITS You may also use present value computations to determine how much you need to deposit so that you can take a certain amount out of the account for a desired number of years. For example, if you want to take $400 out of an investment account each year for nine years and your money is earning an annual rate of 8 percent, you can see from Exhibit 1–3D that you would need to make a current deposit of $2,498.80 ($400 × 6.247).

The formulas for calculating future and present values, as well as tables covering additional interest rates and time periods, are presented in Appendix A. Computer programs and financial calculators may also be used for calculating time value of money.

✔ CONCEPTCHECK 1–3

1 What are some examples of personal opportunity costs?

_____

_____

2 What does time value of money measure?

_____

_____

3 Use the time value of money tables in Exhibit 1–3 to calculate the following:

 a. The future value of $100 at 7 percent in 10 years.

_____

 b. The future value of $100 a year for six years earning 6 percent.

_____

 c. The present value of $500 received in eight years with an interest rate of 8 percent.

_____

A Plan for Personal Financial Planning

We all make hundreds of decisions each day. Most of these decisions are quite simple and have few consequences. However, some are complex and have long-term effects on our personal and financial situations. While everyone makes decisions, few people consider how to make better decisions. As Exhibit 1–4 shows, the financial planning process can be viewed as a six-step procedure.

OBJECTIVE 4
Implement a plan for making personal financial and career decisions.

Step 1: Determine Your Current Financial Situation

In this first step, determine your current financial situation regarding income, savings, living expenses, and debts. Preparing a list of current asset and debt balances and amounts spent for various items gives you a foundation for financial planning activities. The personal financial statements discussed in Chapter 2 will provide the information needed in this phase of financial decision making.

Exhibit [1-4]   The Financial Planning Process

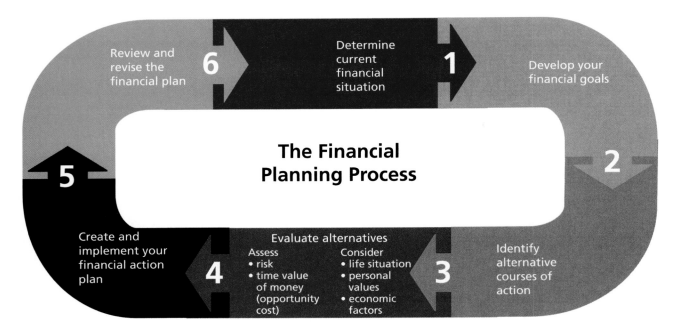

Carla Elliot plans to complete her college degree in the next two years. She works two part-time jobs in an effort to pay her educational expenses. Currently, Carla has $700 in a savings account and existing debt that includes a $640 balance on her credit card and $2,300 in student loans. What additional information should Carla have available when planning her personal finances?

_____

_____

Step 2: Develop Your Financial Goals

You should periodically analyze your financial values and goals. The purpose of this analysis is to differentiate your needs from your wants. Specific financial goals are vital to financial planning. Others can suggest financial goals for you; however, *you* must decide which goals to pursue. Your financial goals can range from spending all of your current income to developing an extensive savings and investment program for your future financial security.

The main financial goals of Carla Elliot for the next two years are to complete her college degree and to maintain or reduce the amounts owed. What other goals might be appropriate for Carla?

_____

(Continued)

Step 3: Identify Alternative Courses of Action

Developing alternatives is crucial when making decisions. Although many factors will influence the available alternatives, possible courses of action usually fall into these categories:

- *Continue the same course of action.* For example, you may determine that the amount you have saved each month is still appropriate.
- *Expand the current situation.* You may choose to save a larger amount each month.
- *Change the current situation.* You may decide to use a money market account instead of a regular savings account.
- *Take a new course of action.* You may decide to use your monthly saving budget to pay off credit card debts.

Not all of these categories will apply to every decision; however, they do represent possible courses of action. For example, if you want to stop working full time to go to school, you must generate several alternatives under the category "Take a new course of action." Creativity in decision making is vital to effective choices. Considering all of the possible alternatives will help you make more effective and satisfying decisions. For instance, most people believe they must own a car to get to work or school. However, they should consider other alternatives such as public transportation, carpooling, renting a car, shared ownership of a car, or a company car.

Remember, when you decide not to take action, you elect to "do nothing," which can be a dangerous alternative.

DID YOU KNOW?

In 2004, Congress created the Financial Literacy and Education Improvement Act to promote financial education and long-term financial security in the United States. This program will be administered by representatives from several federal government agencies. Additional information is available at www.treasury.gov/financialeducation.

Apply *Yourself!*

Objective 4

Prepare a list of questions that might be asked of a financial planning professional by *(a)* a young person just starting out on his or her own, *(b)* a young couple planning for their children's education and for their own retirement, and *(c)* a person nearing retirement.

STEP 3 EXAMPLE

To achieve her goals, Carla Elliot has several options available. She could reduce her spending, seek a higher-paying part-time job, or use her savings to pay off some of her debt. What additional alternatives might she consider?

EXAMPLE FROM YOUR LIFE

Step 4: Evaluate Your Alternatives

You need to evaluate possible courses of action, taking into consideration your life situation, personal values, and current economic conditions. How will the ages of dependents affect your saving goals? How do you like to spend leisure time? How will changes in interest rates affect your financial situation?

CONSEQUENCES OF CHOICES Every decision closes off alternatives. For example, a decision to invest in stock may mean you cannot take a vacation. A decision to go to school full-time may mean you cannot work full-time. *Opportunity cost* is what you give up by making a choice. These *trade-offs* cannot always be measured in dollars. However, the resources you give up (money or time) have a value that is lost.

EVALUATING RISK Uncertainty is also a part of every decision. Selecting a college major and choosing a career field involve risk. What if you don't like working in this field or cannot obtain employment in it? Other decisions involve a very low degree of risk, such as putting money in an insured savings account or purchasing items that cost only a few dollars. Your chances of losing something of great value are low in these situations.

In many financial decisions, identifying and evaluating risk are difficult. Common risks to consider include:

- Inflation risk, due to rising prices that cause lost buying power.
- Interest rate risk, resulting from changes in the cost of money, which can affect your costs (when you borrow) and benefits (when you save or invest).
- Income risk may result from a loss of a job or encountering illness.
- Personal risk involves tangible and intangible factors that create a less than desirable situation, such as health or safety concerns.
- Liquidity risk, when savings and investments that have potential for higher earnings are difficult to convert to cash or to sell without significant loss in value.

The best way to consider risk is to gather information based on your experience and the experiences of others and to use financial planning information sources.

DID YOU KNOW?

The main sources from which people get their money advice are financial professionals, friends and family, printed materials from work, newspapers and magazines, the Internet, and television and radio.

FINANCIAL PLANNING INFORMATION SOURCES

Relevant information is required at each stage of the decision-making process. In addition to this book, common sources available to help you with your financial decisions include (1) the Internet; (2) financial institutions, such as banks, credit unions, and investment companies; (3) media sources, such as newspapers, magazines, television, and radio; and (4) financial specialists, such as financial planners, insurance agents, investment advisers, credit counselors, lawyers, and tax preparers.

STEP 4 EXAMPLE

As Carla Elliot evaluates her alternative courses of action, she should consider both her short-term and long-term situations. What risks and trade-offs should Carla consider?

_____

EXAMPLE FROM YOUR LIFE

_____

Step 5: Create and Implement Your Financial Action Plan

This step of the financial planning process involves developing an action plan that identifies ways to achieve your goals. For example, you can increase your savings by reducing your spending or by increasing your income through extra time on the job. If you are concerned about year-end tax payments, you may increase the amount withheld from each paycheck, file quarterly tax payments, or shelter current income in a tax-deferred retirement program.

To implement your financial action plan, you may need assistance from others. For example, you may use the services of an insurance agent to purchase property insurance or the services of an investment broker to purchase stocks, bonds, or mutual funds. Exhibit 1–5 offers a framework for developing and implementing a financial plan, along with examples for several life situations.

Exhibit [1-5]   Financial Planning in Action

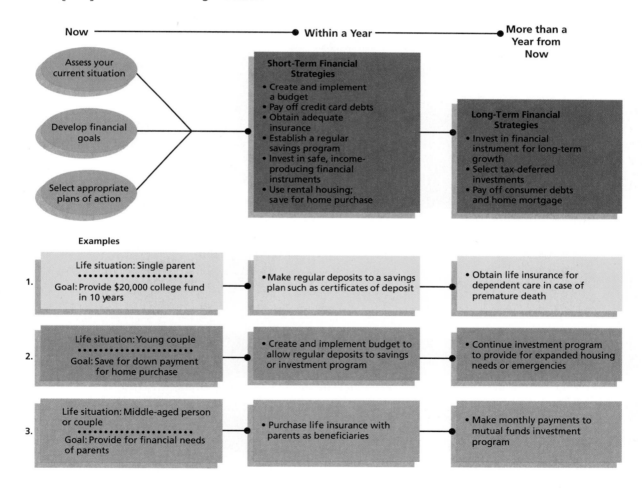

Tackle **AMBITIOUS** goals

WHEN Casey and Pete Andrysiak were single, they lived large and invested like high rollers. Casey still talks about a $10,000 loss she took on IBM options years ago. Now married and parents of seven-month-old Mackenzie, they want to salt away $40,000 a year—and may just be able to. Pete, 36, is a major with the Army

Corps of Engineers at Fort Leavenworth, Kan., where they live. Casey, 34, is a high-tech product-development executive and works two well-paid jobs from home.

So what are the problems? Setting priorities and making sense of too many investing choices, says Casey. The couple have already saved $170,000. But right now the money is scattered among 14 investments: mutual funds, retirement plans and a 529 college-savings account, with balances ranging from $32,000 down to $1,200. Casey and Pete would like to accumulate $3 million by the time they retire between the ages of 55 and 60. If they truly can invest $40,000 a year, they'll need to earn a doable 7.5% per year over 22 years to reach their goal. They'll also have Pete's military benefits.

Suggestions: To stay disciplined, Casey and Pete need a "policy statement," says Jeffrey Rattiner, president of JR Financial Group, in Englewood, Colo. That means putting goals in writing, estimating the timing and amount of income and expenses, and agreeing to stick to a savings plan. Casey and Pete want Mackenzie's tuition fund to grow to $150,000 in 16 years. But assuming a $200-a-month investment in the 529 plan and an annual return of 7.5%, they'd accumulate only $80,000 in that time. (Casey's father is also saving for Mackenzie; that may make up for the shortfall.)

The other key issue: where to invest the $40,000 each year. With their long time horizon and the safety net of Pete's pension, the couple should place at least 70% of their investments in stocks or stock funds. They should put 20% in bonds, 5% in real estate securities and 5% in cash. Seven or eight good funds should suffice for now, though they can add some long-term growth stocks if they wish. Casey and Pete already have 15% of their long-term investments in **Dodge & Cox Stock**. We'd fill out the portfolio with 15% in **FMI Focus**, 10% each in **Legg Mason Opportunity**, **ABN Amro/ Montag & Caldwell Growth N** and **Aegis Value**, 5% in **Third Avenue Real Estate Value**, and the rest in either the **Artisan** or **Oakmark International** funds, or split between the two. A low-cost bond fund, such as **Vanguard Total Bond Market Index**, and cash complete the picture.

Source: Reprinted by permission from the April Issue of *Kiplinger's Personal Finance.* Copyright © 2004 The Kiplinger Washington Editors, Inc.

1. What actions did Casey and Pete take that reflect wise financial planning?

_____

_____

2. Describe actions you might take based on the experiences of Casey and Pete.

_____

_____

3. What information is available at www.kiplinger.com that might be of value when making personal financial decisions?

_____

_____

STEP 5 EXAMPLE

Carla has decided to reduce her course load and work longer hours in an effort both to reduce her debt level and to increase the amount she has in savings. What are the benefits and drawbacks of this choice?

_____

EXAMPLE FROM YOUR LIFE

_____

Step 6: Review and Revise Your Plan

Financial planning is a dynamic process that does not end when you take a particular action. You need to regularly assess your financial decisions. You should do a complete review of your finances at least once a year. Changing personal, social, and economic factors may require more frequent assessments.

When life events affect your financial needs, this financial planning process will provide a vehicle for adapting to those changes. Regularly reviewing this decision-making process will help you make priority adjustments that will bring your financial goals and activities in line with your current life situation.

STEP 6 EXAMPLE

Over the next 6 to 12 months, Carla Elliot should reassess her financial, personal, and educational situation. What types of circumstances might occur that could require that Carla take a different approach to her personal finances?

_____

EXAMPLE FROM YOUR LIFE

_____

Career Choice and Financial Planning

Have you ever wondered why some people find great satisfaction in their work while others only put in their time? As with other personal financial decisions, career selection and professional growth require planning. The average person changes jobs seven times during a lifetime. Most likely, therefore, you will reevaluate your choice of a job on a regular basis. The lifework you select is a key to your financial well-being and personal satisfaction.

Like other decisions, career choice and professional development alternatives have risks and opportunity costs. In recent years, many people have placed family and personal fulfillment above monetary reward and professional recognition. Career choices require periodic evaluation of trade-offs related to personal, social, and economic factors.

In addition, changing personal and social factors will require you to continually assess your work situation. The steps of the financial planning process can provide an approach to career planning, advancement, and career change. Your career goals will affect how you use this process. If you desire more responsibility on the job, for example, you may decide to obtain advanced training or change career fields. The appendix to this chapter provides a plan for obtaining employment and professional advancement.

**Sheet 3
Planning Your
Career**

YOUR CAREER PLANNING DECISIONS

Based on the your current or future career situation, describe how you might use the Financial Planning Process (Exhibit 1–4, p. 14) to plan and implement an employment decision.

_____

_____

✔ CONCEPTCHECK 1–4

1 What actions might a person take to identify alternatives when making a financial decision?

_____

_____

2 Why are career planning activities considered to be personal financial decisions?

_____

_____

3 For the following situations, identify the type of risk being described.

_____ Not getting proper rest and exercise.

_____ Not being able to obtain cash from a certificate of deposit before the maturity date.

_____ Taking out a variable rate loan when rates are expected to rise.

_____ Training for a career field with low potential demand in the future.

4 For the following main sources of personal finance information, list a specific Web site, organization, or person who you might contact in the future.

Type of information	Specific source	Contact information
Web site		
Financial Institution		
Media source		
Financial Specialist		

Back to Getting Personal

Redo the Getting Personal questions at the beginning of the chapter. Have any of your answers changed?

_____

_____

_____

_____

What did you learn in this chapter that might affect your answers to these questions in the future?

_____

_____

_____

_____

_____

Chapter Summary

Objective 1 Financial decisions are affected by a person's life situation (income, age, household size, health), personal values, and economic factors (prices, interest rates, and employment opportunities). The major elements of financial planning are obtaining, planning, saving, borrowing, spending, managing risk, investing, and retirement and estate planning.

Objective 2 Financial goals should (1) be realistic; (2) be stated in specific, measurable terms; (3) have a time frame; and (4) indicate the type of action to be taken.

Objective 3 Every decision involves a trade-off with things given up. Personal opportunity costs include time, effort, and health. Financial opportunity costs are based on the time value of money. Future value and present value calculations enable you to measure the increased value (or lost interest) that results from a saving, investing, borrowing, or purchasing decision.

Objective 4 Personal financial planning involves the following process: (1) determine your current financial situation; (2) develop financial goals; (3) identify alternative courses of action; (4) evaluate alternatives; (5) create and implement a financial action plan; and (6) review and revise the financial plan.

Key Terms

adult life cycle   2
bankruptcy   5
economics   4
financial plan   2

future value   10
inflation   4
opportunity cost   9
personal financial planning   2

present value   12
time value of money   10
values   4

Problems and Questions

1. In your opinion, what is the main benefit of wise financial planning?

2. Conduct Web research to obtain examples of economic statistics that might help you make wiser personal financial decisions.

3. Using the rule of 72, approximate the following amounts.
   a. If the value of land in an area is increasing 6 percent a year, how long will it take for property values to double?

   b. If you earn 10 percent on your investments, how long will it take for your money to double?

   c. At an annual interest rate of 5 percent, how long will it take for your savings to double?

4. A family spends $28,000 a year for living expenses. If prices increase by 4 percent a year for the next three years, what amount will the family need for their living expenses after three years?

5. Using time value of money tables (Exhibit 1–3 or Appendix A), calculate the following:
   a. The future value of $450 six years from now at 7 percent.

   b. The future value of $800 saved each year for 10 years at 8 percent.

   c. The amount a person would have to deposit today (present value) at a 6 percent interest rate to have $1,000 five years from now.

   d. The amount a person would have to deposit today to be able to take out $500 a year for 10 years from an account earning 8 percent.

6. What are possible drawbacks associated with seeking advice from a financial planning professional? How might these concerns be minimized?

7. Talk with several people about their career choices. How have their employment situations affected their financial planning activities?

8. Conduct a Web search for a financial planning topic on which you would like additional information. List the Web address and two key ideas you obtained from the Web site.

Internet Connection

RESEARCHING ECONOMIC CONDITIONS AFFECTING FINANCIAL DECISIONS

For these two major economic indicators, obtain current information and determine how the current trend might affect financial planning activities.

Inflation Web sources

_____

_____

Current findings:

_____

Possible influence on your financial decisions

_____

_____

Interest Rates Web sources

_____

_____

Current findings:

_____

Possible influence on your financial decisions

_____

_____

Case in Point

STUCK IN THE MIDDLE

Until recently, Fran and Ed Blake's personal finances ran smoothly. Both had well-paying jobs while raising two children. The Blakes have a daughter who is completing her freshman year of college and a son three years younger. Currently they have $22,000 in various savings and investment funds set aside for the children's education. With education costs increasing faster than inflation, they are uncertain whether this amount is adequate.

In recent months, Fran's mother has required extensive medical attention and personal care assistance. Unable to live alone, she is now a resident of a long-term care facility. The cost of this service is $2,050 a month, with annual increases of about 7 percent. While a major portion of the cost is covered by her Social Security and pension, Fran's mother is unable to cover the entire cost. Their desire to help adds to the Blakes' financial burden.

The Blakes are like millions of other Americans who have financial responsibilities for both dependent children and aging parents. Commonly referred to as the "sandwich generation," this group is squeezed on one side by the cost of raising and educating children and on the other side by the financial demands of caring for aging parents.

Finally, the Blakes, ages 47 and 43, are also concerned about saving for their own retirement. While they have consistently made annual deposits to a retirement fund, various current financial demands may force them to access some of this money.

Questions

1. What actions have the Blakes taken that would be considered wise financial planning choices?

2. What actions might be appropriate to address the concerns faced by the Blake household?

3. Conduct an Internet search to obtain additional information that might be of value to the Blakes.

Personal Financial Data

Financial Planning Activities: Complete the information request to provide a quick reference for vital household data.

Suggested Web Sites: www.money.com   www.kiplinger.com

Name	_____	_____
Birthdate	_____	_____
Marital Status	_____	_____
Address	_____	_____
Phone	_____	_____
e-mail	_____	_____
Social Security No.	_____	_____
Drivers License No.	_____	_____
Place of Employment	_____	_____
Address	_____	_____
Phone	_____	_____
Position	_____	_____
Length of Service	_____	_____
Checking Acct. No.	_____	_____
Financial Inst.	_____	_____
Address	_____	_____
Phone	_____	_____

Dependent Data

Name	Birthdate	Relationship	Social Security No.
_____	_____	_____	_____
_____	_____	_____	_____
_____	_____	_____	_____
_____	_____	_____	_____

What's Next for Your Personal Financial Plan?

- Identify financial planning experts (insurance agent, banker, investment adviser, tax preparer, others) you might contact for financial planning information or assistance.
- Discuss with other household members various financial planning priorities.

Setting Personal Financial Goals

Financial Planning Activities: Based on personal and household needs and values, identify specific goals that require action for your life.

Suggested Web Sites: www.financialplan.about.com   www.money.com

Short-Term Monetary Goals (less than two years)

Description	Amount needed	Months to achieve	Action to be taken	Priority
Example: pay off credit card debt	$850	12	Use money from pay raise	High

Intermediate and Long-Term Monetary Goals

Description	Amount needed	Months to achieve	Action to be taken	Priority

Nonmonetary Goals

Description	Time frame	Actions to be taken
Example: set up file for personal financial records and documents	next 2–3 months	locate all personal and financial records and documents; set up files for various spending, saving, borrowing categories

What's Next for Your Personal Financial Plan?

- Based on various financial goals, calculate the savings deposits necessary to achieve those goals.
- Identify current economic trends that might influence various saving, spending, investing, and borrowing decisions.

Planning Your Career

Financial Planning Activities: Research and plan various actions related to obtaining employment.

Suggested Web Sites: www.monster.com   www.careerjournal.com

Career area, job titles	
Useful career information sources—Web sites, books	
Career contacts (name, title, organization, address, phone, e-mail, organization Web site)	
Informational interview questions about the career field, industry	1. 2. 3.
Key items to include in my résumé	1. 2. 3.
Key points to emphasize in my cover letters	1. 2.
Interview questions I should practice answering	1. 2. 3.
Interview questions to ask the organization	1. 2.
Other career planning, job search ideas	

What's Next for Your Personal Financial Plan?

- Talk with various people who have worked in the career fields of interest to you.
- Outline a plan for long-term professional development and career advancement.

Your Personal Financial Plan

3

Appendix: A Career Search Strategy

The average person changes jobs seven times during a lifetime. Most likely, you will reevaluate your work situation on a regular basis. This appendix offers information to help you plan and manage your career.

Identifying Career Trends

While career opportunities have dwindled in some sectors of our economy, opportunities in other sectors have grown. Service industries that are expected to have the greatest employment potential include computer technology, health care, business services, social and government services, sales and retailing, hospitality and food services, management and human resources, education, and financial services.

Obtaining Employment Experience

A common concern among people seeking employment is a lack of work experience. The following opportunities offer work-related training:

1. *Part-time employment* can provide experience and knowledge for a career field.
2. *Volunteer work* in community organizations agencies can help you acquire skills, establish good work habits, and make contacts.
3. *Internships* allow you to gain experience needed to obtain employment in a field.
4. *Campus projects* offer work-related experiences to help you obtain career skills through campus organizations, course assignments, and research projects.

Identifying Job Opportunities

Job information can be found in many valuable sources.

1. *Job advertisements* in newspapers and professional periodicals are a common source. However, since over 60 percent of jobs may not be advertised to the public, also use other job search activities.
2. *Career fairs,* on campus and at convention centers, allow you to contact several firms in a short time. Be prepared to quickly communicate your potential contributions.
3. *Employment agencies* match job hunters with employers. Often the hiring company pays the fee. Be wary when asked to pay a fee in advance. Government employment services may be contacted through your state employment service or state department of labor.
4. *Business contacts* advise people about careers. Friends, relatives, and others are potential business contacts. *Networking* is the process of making and using contacts to obtain and update career information. Contacts can also help you obtain an *informational interview,* a meeting at which you gather information about a career or an organization.

5. *Job creation* involves developing a position that matches your skills with organizational needs. As you develop skills you enjoy, you may be able to create a demand for yourself.
6. *Other job search methods* include *(a)* visits to companies to make face-to-face contacts; *(b)* business directories and Web sites to obtain names of organizations that employ people with your qualifications; and *(c)* alumni who work in your field.

Developing a Résumé

Marketing yourself to prospective employers usually requires a résumé, or personal information sheet.

Résumé Elements

This summary of your education, training, experience, and other qualifications has these main components:

1. The *personal data section* presents your name, street address, telephone number, and e-mail address. Do not include your birth date, sex, height, and weight unless this information applies to a specific job qualification.
2. A *career objective* is designed to clearly focus you to a specific employment situation. Your career objective may be omitted from the résumé and communicated in your cover letter. Also, consider a *summary section* with a synopsis of your capabilities.
3. The *education section* should include dates, schools attended, fields of study, and degrees earned.
4. The *experience section* lists organizations, dates of involvement, and responsibilities for previous employment, relevant school activities, and community service. Highlight computer skills, technical abilities, and other specific competencies. Use action verbs such as *achieved, administered, coordinated, created, developed, implemented, managed, organized,* and *researched* to connect your experience to the needs of the organization. Focus this information on results and accomplishments.
5. The *related information section* may include honors, awards, and other activities related to your career field.
6. The *references section* lists people who can verify your skills. These individuals may be teachers, past employers, supervisors, or business colleagues. References are usually not included in a résumé; however, have this information available when requested.

Résumé Preparation

An effective résumé must be presented in a professional manner. Many candidates are disqualified by poor résumés. Limit your résumé to one page. Send a two-page résumé only if you have enough material to fill three pages; then use the most valid information to prepare an impressive two-page presentation.

Words and phrases that commonly impress prospective employers include "foreign language skills," "computer experience," "achievement," "research experience," "flexible," "team projects," and "overseas study or experience." For best results, seek assistance from counselors, the campus placement office, and friends to find errors and suggest improvements.

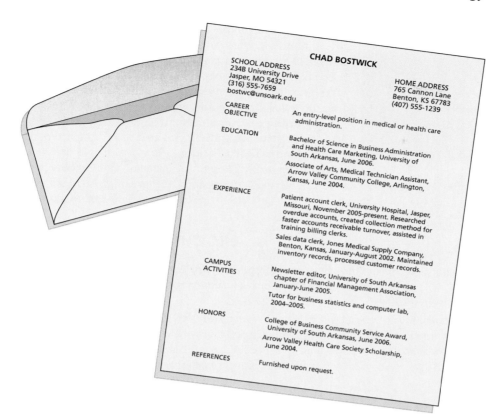

Exhibit [A-1]

Sample Résumé

E-résumés, used when applying for a job online, should be kept simple—avoid bold type, underlines, italics, and tabs. Do not use attached files that may be difficult to open. Beware that résumés posted on the Internet may be viewed by your current employer. Remember, an Internet résumé is less personal than a printed one or a phone call; most jobs are obtained offline through ads, job fairs, and networking.

Résumé Alternatives

Instead of a résumé, consider a *targeted application letter* describing your background, experience, and accomplishments. After researching a position and company, you can communicate how your specific skills will benefit the organization.

A *performance portfolio* provides tangible evidence of your experiences. This collection of materials could include:

- A résumé, sample interview answers, and a competency summary.
- Creative works—ads, product designs, packages, brand, promotions, and video clips.
- Class project samples—research findings, PowerPoint presentations, Web site designs, marketing plans, and photos of project activities.
- Employment accomplishments—published articles, sales results data, financial charts, and news articles of community activities.

Creation of a Web site with portfolio items can be effective. Be sure your home page is not cluttered and is organized to quickly find desired information. Consider sending a CD with your Web site files along with your résumé.

Exhibit [A-2]

Sample Cover Letter

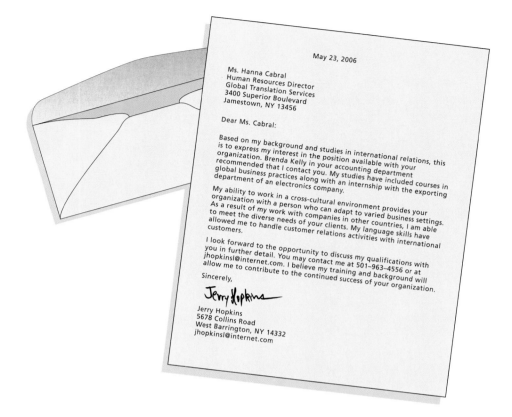

May 23, 2006

Ms. Hanna Cabral
Human Resources Director
Global Translation Services
3400 Superior Boulevard
Jamestown, NY 13456

Dear Ms. Cabral:

Based on my background and studies in international relations, this is to express my interest in the position available with your organization. Brenda Kelly in your accounting department recommended that I contact you. My studies have included courses in global business practices along with an internship with the exporting department of an electronics company.

My ability to work in a cross-cultural environment provides your organization with a person who can adapt to varied business settings. As a result of my work with companies in other countries, I am able to meet the diverse needs of your clients. My language skills have allowed me to handle customer relations activities with international customers.

I look forward to the opportunity to discuss my qualifications with you in further detail. You may contact me at 501–963–4556 or at jhopkinsl@internet.com. I believe my training and background will allow me to contribute to the continued success of your organization.

Sincerely,

Jerry Hopkins

Jerry Hopkins
5678 Collins Road
West Barrington, NY 14332
jhopkinsl@internet.com

Creating a Cover Letter

A *cover letter,* designed to express your interest in a specific job, accompanies your résumé and consists of three main sections:

1. The *introductory paragraph* gets the reader's attention. Indicate your reason for writing by referring to the employment position. Communicate what you have to offer the organization. If applicable, mention the name of the person who referred you.
2. The *development paragraphs* highlight aspects of your background that specifically qualify you for the position. At this point, elaborate on experiences and training. Connect your skills and competencies to specific organizational needs.
3. The *concluding paragraph* should request action. Ask for an interview to discuss your qualifications in detail. Include your contact information, such as telephone numbers and the times when available. Close your letter by summarizing your potential benefits to the organization.

Create a personalized cover letter for each position addressed to the appropriate person in the organization. A poorly prepared cover letter guarantees rejection.

Education and Training Questions

What education and training qualify you for this job?

Why are you interested in working for this company?

In addition to going to school, what activities have helped you to expand your interests and knowledge?

What did you like best about school?

What did you like least?

Work and Other Experience Questions

In what types of situations have you done your best work?

Describe the supervisors who motivated you most.

Which of your past accomplishments are you most proud of?

Have you ever had to coordinate the activities of several people?

Describe some people whom you have found difficult to work with.

Describe a situation in which your determination helped you achieve a specific goal.

What situations frustrate you?

Other than past jobs, what experiences have helped prepare you for this job?

What methods do you consider best for motivating employees?

Personal Qualities Questions

What are your major strengths?

What are your major weaknesses? What have you done to overcome your weaknesses?

What do you plan to be doing 5 or 10 years from now?

Which individuals have had the greatest influence on you?

What traits make a person successful?

How well do you communicate your ideas orally and in writing?

How would your teachers and your past employers describe you?

What do you do in your leisure time?

How persuasive are you in presenting ideas to others?

Exhibit [A-3]

Common Interview Questions

The Job Interview

The interview phase is limited to candidates who possess the desired qualifications.

Preparing for the Interview

Prepare by obtaining additional information about the organization. The best sources include the library, the Internet, observations during company visits, analysis of company products, informal conversations with employees, and discussions with people knowledgeable about the company or industry. Research the company's operations, competitors, recent successes, planned expansion, and personnel policies to help you discuss your potential contributions to the company.

Another preinterview activity is preparing questions you will ask, such as:

- What training opportunities are available to employees who desire advancement?
- What qualities do your most successful employees possess?
- What actions of competitors are likely to affect the company in the near future?

Successful interviewing requires practice. Use a video recorder or work with friends to develop confidence when interviewing. Organize ideas, speak clearly and calmly, and communicate enthusiasm. Prepare specific answers regarding your strengths. Campus organizations and career placement offices may offer opportunities for interview practice.

When interviewing, keep in mind that proper dress and grooming are vital. Dress more conservatively than employees. A business suit is usually appropriate. Avoid trendy and casual styles, and don't wear too much jewelry.

Confirm the time and location of the interview. Take copies of your résumé, your reference list, and paper for notes. Arrive about 10 minutes earlier than your appointed time.

The Interview Process

Interviews may include situations or questions to determine how you react under pressure. Remain calm. Answer clearly in a controlled manner.

Behavioral interviewing is frequently used to evaluate an applicant's on-the-job potential. In these questions, you might be asked how you would handle various work situations. Behavioral interview questions typically begin with "describe" or "tell me about . . ." to encourage interviewees to better explain their work style.

Most interviewers conclude by telling you when you can expect to hear from them. While waiting, do two things. First, send a follow-up letter within a day or two expressing your appreciation for the opportunity to interview. If you don't get the job, this thank-you letter can make a positive impression to improve your chances for future consideration.

Second, do a self-evaluation of your interview performance. Write down the areas to improve. Try to remember the questions you were asked that were different from what you expected. Remember, the more interviews you have, the better you will present yourself and the better the chance of being offered a job.

*Key Web Sites for Career
Planning*
www.careerjournal.com
www.ajb.dni.us
www.monster.com
www.bls.gov/oco
www.rileyguide.com
www.careerbuilder.com,
www.careerfairs.com/
www.businessweek.com/careers

2 Money Management Skills

Objectives

In this chapter, you will learn to:

1. Identify the main components of wise money management.
2. Create a personal balance sheet and cash flow statement.
3. Develop and implement a personal budget.
4. Connect money management activities with saving for personal financial goals.

Why is this important?

The average person in the United States saves about three cents of every dollar earned. This lack of saving results in not having adequate funds for long-term financial security. Effectively planning your spending and saving decisions provides a foundation for wise money management today and financial prosperity in the future.

 Getting Personal

What are your money management habits? For each of the following statements, circle the choice that best describes your current situation:

1. My system for organizing personal financial records could be described as
   a. Nonexistent . . . I have documents that are missing in action!
   b. Fairly efficient . . . I can find most stuff when I need to!
   c. Very efficient . . . better than the Library of Congress!

2. How often do you prepare a personal balance sheet?
   a. Every few months.
   b. Every year.
   c. Never.

3. The details of my cash flow statement are
   a. Simple . . . "money coming in" and "money going out."
   b. Appropriate for my needs . . . enough information for me.
   c. Very informative . . . I know where my money goes.

4. My budgeting activities could be described as
   a. "I don't have enough money to worry about where it goes."
   b. "I keep track of my spending in my checkbook."
   c. "I have a written plan for spending and paying my bills on time."

After studying this chapter, you will be asked to reconsider your responses to these items.

Key Web Sites

www.kiplinger.com   www.bls.gov/cex

www.money.com   www.asec.org

www.lifeadvice.com   www.betterbudgeting.com

Your Personal Financial Plan Sheets

4. Financial documents and records.
5. Creating a personal balance sheet.
6. Creating a personal cash flow statement.
7. Developing a personal budget.

A Successful Money Management Plan

OBJECTIVE 1

Identify the main components of wise money management.

money management Day-to-day financial activities necessary to manage current personal economic resources while working toward long-term financial security.

"Each month I have too much month and not enough money. If the month were only 20 days long, budgeting would be easy."

Daily spending and saving decisions are at the center of your financial planning activities. You must coordinate these decisions with your needs, goals, and personal situation. Maintaining financial records and planning your spending are essential skills for successful personal financial management. The time and effort you devote to these activities will yield many benefits. **Money management** refers to the day-to-day financial activities necessary to manage current personal economic resources while working toward long-term financial security.

Components of Money Management

As shown here, three major money management activities are interrelated:

3. Creating and implementing a plan for spending and saving (budgeting)

2. Creating personal financial statements (balance sheets and cash flow statements of income and outflows)

1. Storing and maintaining personal financial records and documents

First, personal financial records and documents are the foundation of systematic resource use. These provide written evidence of business transactions, ownership of property, and legal matters. Next, personal financial statements enable you to measure and assess your financial position and progress. Finally, your spending plan, or *budget,* is the basis for effective money management.

A System for Personal Financial Records

Invoices, credit card statements, insurance policies, and tax forms are the basis of financial recordkeeping and personal economic choices. An organized system of financial records provides a basis for (1) handling daily business activities, such as bill paying;

Exhibit [2-1]   Where to Keep Your Financial Records

Home File

1. Personal and Employment Records (Chapter 1)
- Current résumé
- Employee benefit information
- Social Security numbers
- Birth certificates

2. Money Management Records (Chapter 2)
- Current budget
- Recent personal financial statements (balance sheet, income statement)
- List of financial goals
- List of safe deposit box contents

3. Tax Records (Chapter 3)
- Paycheck stubs, W-2 forms, 1099 forms
- Receipts for tax-deductible items
- Records of taxable income
- Past income tax returns and documentation

4. Financial Services Records (Chapter 4)
- Checkbook, unused checks
- Bank statements, canceled checks
- Savings statements
- Location information and number of safe deposit box

5. Credit Records (Chapter 5)
- Unused credit cards
- Payment books
- Receipts, monthly statements
- List of credit account numbers and telephone numbers of issuers

6. Consumer Purchase & Automobile Records (Chapter 6)
- Warranties
- Receipts for major purchases
- Owner's manuals for major appliances
- Automobile service and repair records
- Automobile registration
- Automobile owner's manual

7. Housing Records (Chapter 7)
- Lease (if renting)
- Property tax records
- Home repair, home improvement receipts

8. Insurance Records (Chapters 8–10)
- Original insurance policies
- List of insurance premium amounts and due dates
- Medical information (health history, prescription drug information)
- Claim reports

9. Investment Records (Chapters 11–13)
- Records of stock, bond, and mutual fund purchases and sales
- List of investment certificate numbers
- Brokerage statements
- Dividend records
- Company annual reports

10. Estate Planning and Retirement Records (Chapter 14)
- Will
- Pension plan information
- IRA statements
- Social Security information
- Trust agreements

Safe Deposit Box

- Birth, marriage, and death certificates
- Citizenship papers
- Adoption, custody papers
- Military papers
- Serial numbers of expensive items
- Photographs or video of valuable belongings

- Certificates of deposit
- List of checking and savings account numbers and financial institutions
- Credit contacts
- List of credit card numbers and telephone numbers of issuers

- Mortgage papers, title deed
- Automobile title
- List of insurance policy numbers and company names
- Stock and bond certificates
- Rare coins, stamps, gems, and other collectibles
- Copy of will

Personal Computer System

- Current and past budgets
- Summary of checks written and other banking transactions
- Past income tax returns prepared with tax preparation software
- Account summaries and performance results of investments
- Computerized version of wills, estate plans, and other documents

(2) planning and measuring financial progress; (3) completing required tax reports; (4) making effective investment decisions; and (5) determining available resources for current and future spending.

As Exhibit 2–1 shows, most financial records are kept in one of three places: a home file, a safe deposit box, or a home computer. A home file should be used to keep records for current needs and documents with limited value. Your home file may be a series of folders, a cabinet with several drawers, or even a box. Whatever method you use, it is most important that your home file be organized to allow quick access to required documents and information.

Apply *Yourself!*

Objective 1

Working with two or three others in your class, develop a system for filing and maintaining personal financial records.

safe deposit box A private storage area at a financial institution with maximum security for valuables.

Important financial records and valuable articles should be kept in a location that provides better security than a home file. A **safe deposit box** is a private storage area at a financial institution with maximum security for valuables and difficult-to-replace documents. Items commonly kept in a safe deposit box include stock certificates, contracts, a list of insurance policies, and valuables such as rare coins and stamps.

The number of financial records and documents may seem overwhelming; however, they can easily be organized into 10 categories (see Exhibit 2–1). These groups correspond to the major topics covered in this book. You may not need to use all of these records and documents at present. As your financial situation changes, you will add others.

How long should you keep personal finance records? Records such as birth certificates, wills, and Social Security data should be kept permanently. Records on property and investments should be kept as long as you own these items. Federal tax laws dictate the length of time you should keep tax-related information. Copies of tax returns and supporting data should be saved for six years. Normally, an audit will go back only three years; however, under certain circumstances, the Internal Revenue Service may request information from six years back. Financial experts also recommend keeping documents related to the purchase and sale of real estate indefinitely.

DID YOU KNOW?

In the United States, people keep various documents and valuables in 30 million safe deposit boxes in banks and other financial institutions. While these boxes are usually very safe, each year a few people lose the contents of their safe deposit boxes through theft, fire, or natural disasters. Such losses are usually, but not always, covered by the financial institution's insurance.

Sheet 4
Financial
Documents
and Records

✔ CONCEPTCHECK 2–1

1 What are the three major money management activities?

_____

_____

2 What are the benefits of an organized system of financial records and documents?

_____

_____

3 For each of the following records, check the column to indicate the length of time the item should be kept. "Short time period" refers to less than five years.

Document	Short time period	Longer time period
Credit card statements		
Mortgage documents		
Receipts for furniture, clothing		
Retirement account information		
Will		

Personal Financial Statements

Every journey starts somewhere. You need to know where you are before you can go somewhere else. Personal financial statements tell you the starting point of your financial journey. Most financial documents come from financial institutions, businesses, or the government. However, two documents you create yourself are the personal balance sheet and the cash flow statement, also called *personal financial statements.*

These reports provide information about your current financial position and present a summary of your income and spending. The main purposes of personal financial statements are to (1) report your current financial position; (2) measure your progress toward financial goals; (3) maintain information about your financial activities; and (4) provide data for preparing tax forms or applying for credit.

OBJECTIVE 2
Create a personal balance sheet and cash flow statement.

Your Personal Balance Sheet: The Starting Point

The current financial position of an individual or family is a common starting point for financial planning. **A balance sheet,** also called a *net worth statement* or *statement of financial position,* reports what you own and what you owe. You prepare a personal balance sheet to determine your current financial position using the following process:

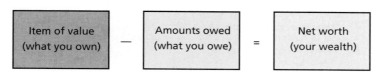

Item of value (what you own) − Amounts owed (what you owe) = Net worth (your wealth)

balance sheet A financial statement that reports what an individual or a family owns and owes; also called a *net worth statement* or *statement of financial position.*

For example, if your possessions are worth $4,500 and you owe $800 to others, your net worth is $3,700. As shown in Exhibit 2–2, preparation of a balance sheet involves three main steps.

STEP 1: LISTING ITEMS OF VALUE   Available cash and money in bank accounts combined with other items of value are the foundation of your current financial position. **Assets** are cash and other tangible property with a monetary value. The balance sheet for Sandra and Mark Scott lists their assets in four categories:

1. **Liquid assets** are cash and items of value that can easily be converted to cash. Money in checking and savings accounts is *liquid* and is available to the Scott family for current spending. The cash value of their life insurance may be borrowed if needed. While assets other than liquid assets can also be converted into cash, the process is not quite as easy.
2. *Real estate* includes a home, a condominium, vacation property, or other land that a person or family owns.
3. *Personal possessions* are a major portion of assets for most people. Included in this category are automobiles and other personal belongings. Although these items have value, they may be difficult to convert to cash. You may decide to list your possessions on the balance sheet at their original cost. However, these values probably need to be revised over time, since a five-year-old television set, for example, is worth less now than when it was new. Thus you may wish to list your possessions at their current value (also referred to as *market value*).
4. *Investment assets* are funds set aside for long-term financial needs. The Scott family will use their investments for such things as financing their children's education,

assets Cash and other property with a monetary value.

liquid assets Cash and items of value that can easily be converted to cash.

DID YOU KNOW?

According to the Bureau of the Census, U.S. Department of Commerce, the assets most frequently held by households are motor vehicles, homes, savings accounts, U.S. savings bonds, certificates of deposit, mutual funds, stocks, corporate bonds, and retirement accounts.

Exhibit [2-2]   Creating a Personal Balance Sheet

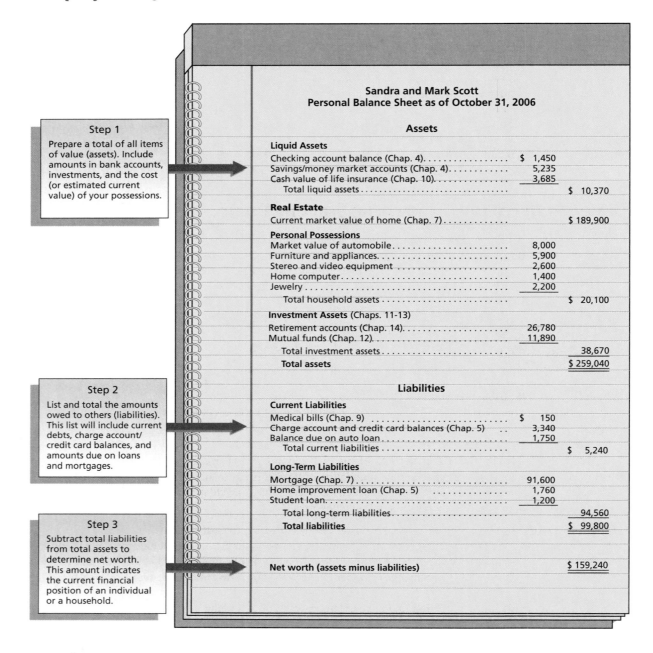

Step 1

Prepare a total of all items of value (assets). Include amounts in bank accounts, investments, and the cost (or estimated current value) of your possessions.

Step 2

List and total the amounts owed to others (liabilities). This list will include current debts, charge account/ credit card balances, and amounts due on loans and mortgages.

Step 3

Subtract total liabilities from total assets to determine net worth. This amount indicates the current financial position of an individual or a household.

Sandra and Mark Scott
Personal Balance Sheet as of October 31, 2006

Assets

Liquid Assets

Checking account balance (Chap. 4)	$ 1,450	
Savings/money market accounts (Chap. 4)	5,235	
Cash value of life insurance (Chap. 10)	3,685	
Total liquid assets		$ 10,370

Real Estate

Current market value of home (Chap. 7)	$ 189,900

Personal Possessions

Market value of automobile	8,000	
Furniture and appliances	5,900	
Stereo and video equipment	2,600	
Home computer	1,400	
Jewelry	2,200	
Total household assets		$ 20,100

Investment Assets (Chaps. 11-13)

Retirement accounts (Chap. 14)	26,780	
Mutual funds (Chap. 12)	11,890	
Total investment assets		38,670
Total assets		**$ 259,040**

Liabilities

Current Liabilities

Medical bills (Chap. 9)	$ 150	
Charge account and credit card balances (Chap. 5)	3,340	
Balance due on auto loan	1,750	
Total current liabilities		$ 5,240

Long-Term Liabilities

Mortgage (Chap. 7)	91,600	
Home improvement loan (Chap. 5)	1,760	
Student loan	1,200	
Total long-term liabilities		94,560
Total liabilities		**$ 99,800**

Net worth (assets minus liabilities)	**$ 159,240**

purchasing a vacation home, and planning for retirement. Since investment assets usually fluctuate in value, the amounts listed should reflect their value at the time the balance sheet is prepared.

STEP 2: DETERMINING AMOUNTS OWED   After looking at the total assets of the Scott family, you might conclude that they have a strong financial position. However, their debts must also be considered. **Liabilities** are amounts owed to others but do not include items not yet due, such as next month's rent. A liability is a debt you owe now, not something you may owe in the future. Liabilities fall into two categories:

1. **Current liabilities** are debts you must pay within a short time, usually less than a year. These liabilities include such things as medical bills, tax payments, insurance premiums, cash loans, and charge accounts.

liabilities Amounts owed to others.

current liabilities Debts that must be paid within a short time, usually less than a year.

2. **Long-term liabilities** are debts you do not have to pay in full until more than a year from now. Common long-term liabilities include auto loans, educational loans, and mortgages. A *mortgage* is an amount borrowed to buy a house or other real estate that will be repaid over a period of 15, 20, or 30 years.

long-term liabilities Debts that are not required to be paid in full until more than a year from now.

STEP 3: COMPUTING NET WORTH

Your **net worth** is the difference between your total assets and your total liabilities. This relationship can be stated as

$$\text{Assets} - \text{Liabilities} = \text{Net worth}$$

Net worth is the amount you would have left if all assets were sold for the listed values and all debts were paid in full. Also, total assets equal total liabilities plus net worth. The balance sheet of a business is commonly expressed as

$$\text{Assets} = \text{Liabilities} + \text{Net worth}$$

As Exhibit 2–2 shows, Sandra and Mark Scott have a net worth of $159,240. Since very few people, if any, liquidate all assets, the amount of net worth has a more practical purpose: It provides a measurement of your current financial position.

A person may have a high net worth but still have financial difficulties. Having many assets with low liquidity means not having the cash available to pay current expenses. **Insolvency** is the inability to pay debts when they are due; it occurs when a person's liabilities far exceed available assets.

Individuals and families can increase their net worth by (1) increasing their savings; (2) reducing spending; (3) increasing the value of investments and other possessions; and (4) reducing amounts owed. Remember, your net worth is *not* money available to use, but an indication of your financial position on a given date.

net worth The difference between total assets and total liabilities.

Sheet 5
Creating a
Personal
Balance Sheet

ApplyYourself!

Objective 2

Use the Web or library research to obtain information about the assets commonly held by households in the United States. How have the values of assets, liabilities, and net worth of U.S. consumers changed in recent years?

Your Cash Flow Statement: Inflows and Outflows

Each day, financial events can affect your net worth. When you receive a paycheck or pay living expenses, your total assets and liabilities change. **Cash flow** is the actual inflow and outflow of cash during a given time period. Income from employment will probably represent your most important *cash inflow;* however, other income, such as interest earned on a savings account, should also be considered. In contrast, payments for items such as rent, food, and loans are *cash outflows.*

A **cash flow statement,** also called a *personal income and expenditure statement* (Exhibit 2–3), is a summary of cash receipts and payments for a given period, such as a month or a year. This report provides data on your income and spending patterns, which will be helpful when preparing a budget.

A checking account can provide information for your cash flow statement. Deposits to the account are your *inflows;* checks written, cash withdrawals, and debit card payments are your *outflows.* Of course, in using this system, when you do not deposit entire amounts received, you must also note the spending of these nondeposited amounts in your cash flow statement.

The process for preparing a cash flow statement involves three steps:

insolvency The inability to pay debts when they are due because liabilities far exceed the value of assets.

cash flow The actual inflow and outflow of cash during a given time period.

cash flow statement A financial statement that summarizes cash receipts and payments for a given period; also called a *personal income and expenditure statement.*

| Total cash received during the time period | − | Cash outflows during the time period | = | Cash surplus or deficit |

STEP 1: RECORD INCOME

To create a cash flow statement, start by identifying the funds received. **Income** is the inflows of cash for an individual or a household.

income Inflows of cash to an individual or a household.

Figure It Out!

RATIOS FOR EVALUATING FINANCIAL PROGRESS

Financial ratios provide guidelines for measuring the changes in your financial situation. These relationships can indicate progress toward an improved financial position.

Ratio	Calculation	Example	Interpretation
Debt ratio	Liabilities divided by net worth	$25,000/$50,000 = 0.5	Shows relationship between debt and net worth; a low debt ratio is best.
Current ratio	Liquid assets divided by current liabilities	$4,000/$2,000 = 2	Indicates $2 in liquid assets for every $1 of current liabilities; a high current ratio is desirable to have cash available to pay bills.
Liquidity ratio	Liquid assets divided by monthly expenses	$10,000/$4,000 = 2.5	Indicates the number of months in which living expenses can be paid if an emergency arises; a high liquidity ratio is desirable.
Debt-payments ratio	Monthly credit payments divided by take-home pay	$540/$3,600 = 0.15	Indicates how much of a person's earnings goes for debt payments (excluding a home mortgage); most financial advisers recommend a debt/payments ratio of less than 20 percent.
Savings ratio	Amount saved each month divided by gross income	$648/$5,400 = 0.12	Financial experts recommend monthly savings of at least 10 percent.

Based on the following information, calculate the ratios requested:

- Liabilities $12,000
- Liquid assets $2,200
- Monthly credit payments $150
- Monthly savings $130

- Net worth $36,000
- Current liabilities $550
- Take-home pay $900
- Gross income $1,500

(1) Debt ratio _____

(2) Debt-payments ratio _____

(3) Current ratio _____

(4) Savings ratio _____

For most people, the main source of income is money received from a job. Other common income sources include commissions, self-employment income, interest, dividends, gifts, grants, scholarships, government payments, pensions, retirement income, alimony, and child support.

In Exhibit 2–3, notice that Kim Walker's monthly salary (or *gross income*) of $4,350 is her main source of income. However, she does not have use of the entire amount. **Take-home pay,** also called *net pay,* is a person's earnings after deductions for taxes and other items. Kim's deductions for federal, state, and Social Security taxes are $1,250. Her take-home pay is $3,100. This amount, plus earnings from savings and investments, is the income she has available for use during the current month.

Take-home pay is also called *disposable income,* the amount a person or household has available to spend. **Discretionary income** is money left over after paying for housing, food, and other necessities. Studies report that discretionary income ranges from less than 5 percent for people under age 25 to more than 40 percent for older people.

take-home pay Earnings after deductions for taxes and other items; also called *disposable income.*

discretionary income Money left over after paying for housing, food, and other necessities.

Exhibit [2-3]   Creating a Cash Flow Statement

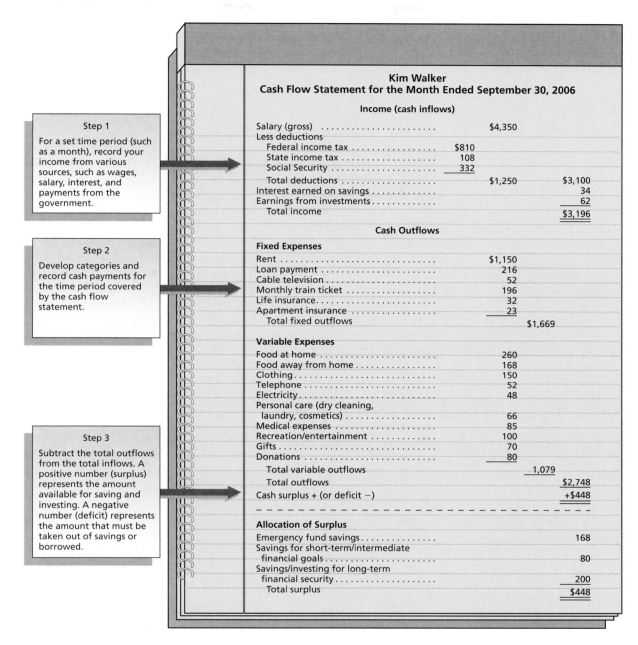

Step 1

For a set time period (such as a month), record your income from various sources, such as wages, salary, interest, and payments from the government.

Step 2

Develop categories and record cash payments for the time period covered by the cash flow statement.

Step 3

Subtract the total outflows from the total inflows. A positive number (surplus) represents the amount available for saving and investing. A negative number (deficit) represents the amount that must be taken out of savings or borrowed.

Kim Walker
Cash Flow Statement for the Month Ended September 30, 2006

Income (cash inflows)

Salary (gross)		$4,350	
Less deductions			
Federal income tax	$810		
State income tax	108		
Social Security	332		
Total deductions		$1,250	$3,100
Interest earned on savings			34
Earnings from investments			62
Total income			$3,196

Cash Outflows

Fixed Expenses

Rent	$1,150	
Loan payment	216	
Cable television	52	
Monthly train ticket	196	
Life insurance	32	
Apartment insurance	23	
Total fixed outflows		$1,669

Variable Expenses

Food at home	260	
Food away from home	168	
Clothing	150	
Telephone	52	
Electricity	48	
Personal care (dry cleaning, laundry, cosmetics)	66	
Medical expenses	85	
Recreation/entertainment	100	
Gifts	70	
Donations	80	
Total variable outflows	1,079	
Total outflows		$2,748
Cash surplus + (or deficit −)		+$448

Allocation of Surplus

Emergency fund savings	168
Savings for short-term/intermediate financial goals	80
Savings/investing for long-term financial security	200
Total surplus	$448

STEP 2: RECORD CASH OUTFLOWS   Cash payments for living expenses and other items make up the second component of a cash flow statement. Kim Walker divides her cash outflows into two major categories: fixed expenses and variable expenses. Every individual and household has different cash outflows, but these main categories, along with the subcategories Kim uses, can be adapted to most situations.

1. *Fixed expenses* are payments that do not vary from month to month. Rent or mortgage payments, installment loan payments, cable television service fees, and a monthly train ticket for commuting to work are examples of constant or fixed cash outflows. For Kim, another type of fixed expense is the amount she sets aside each month for payments due once or twice a year. For example, Kim

pays $384 every March for life insurance. Each month, she records a fixed outflow of $32 for deposit in a special savings account so that the money will be available when her insurance payment is due.

2. *Variable expenses* are flexible payments that change from month to month. Common examples of variable cash outflows are food, clothing, utilities (such as electricity and telephone), recreation, medical expenses, gifts, and donations. The use of a checkbook or some other recordkeeping system is necessary for an accurate total of cash outflows.

STEP 3: DETERMINE NET CASH FLOW   The difference between income and outflows can be either a positive (*surplus*) or a negative (*deficit*) cash flow. A deficit exists if more cash goes out than comes in during a given month. This amount must be made up by withdrawals from savings or by borrowing.

When you have a cash surplus, as Kim did (Exhibit 2–3), this amount is available for saving, investing, or paying off debts. Each month, Kim sets aside money for her *emergency fund* in a savings account that she would use for unexpected expenses or to pay living costs if she did not receive her salary. She deposits the rest of the surplus in savings and investment plans that have two purposes. The first is the achievement of short-term and intermediate financial goals, such as a new car, a vacation, or reenrollment in school; the second is long-term financial security—her retirement. A cash flow statement provides the foundation for preparing and implementing a spending, saving, and investment plan.

Sheet 6
Creating a
Personal
Cash Flow
Statement

✓ CONCEPTCHECK 2–2

1 What are the main purposes of personal financial statements?

2 What does a personal balance sheet tell you about your financial situation?

3 What information does a cash flow statement present?

4 Jan Franks has liquid assets of $6,300 and monthly expenses of $2,100. Based on the liquidity ratio, she has _____ months in which living expenses could be paid if an emergency arises.

A Plan for Effective Budgeting

OBJECTIVE 3
Develop and implement a personal budget.

A **budget,** or *spending plan,* is necessary for successful financial planning. The common financial problems of overusing credit, lacking a regular savings program, and failing to ensure future financial security can be minimized through budgeting. The main purposes

Exhibit [2-4]   Common Financial Goals

Personal Situation	Short-Term Goals (less than 2 years)	Intermediate Goals (2–5 years)	Long-Term Goals (over 5 years)
Single person	• Complete college • Pay off auto loan	• Take a vacation to Europe • Pay off education loan • Attend graduate school	• Buy a vacation home in the mountains • Provide for retirement income
Married couple (no children)	• Take an annual vacation • Buy a new car	• Remodel home • Build a stock portfolio	• Buy a retirement home • Provide for retirement income
Parent (young children)	• Increase life insurance • Increase savings	• Increase investments • Buy a new car	• Accumulate a college fund for children • Move to a larger home

of a budget are to help you live within your income, spend your money wisely, reach your financial goals, prepare for financial emergencies, and develop wise financial management habits. Budgeting may be viewed in seven main steps:

1. Set financial goals.
2. Estimate income.
3. Budget an emergency fund and savings.
4. Budget fixed expenses.
5. Budget variable expenses.
6. Record spending amounts.
7. Review spending and saving patterns.

budget A specific plan for spending income; also called a *spending plan.*

Step 1: Set Financial Goals

Future plans are an important dimension of your financial direction. Financial goals are plans for future activities that require you to plan your spending, saving, and investing. Exhibit 2–4 gives examples of common financial goals based on life situation and time.

Step 2: Estimate Income

As Exhibit 2–5 shows, after setting goals, you need to estimate available money for a given time period. A common budgeting period is a month, since many payments, such as rent or mortgage, utilities, and credit cards, are due each month. In determining available income, include only money that you are sure you'll receive. Bonuses, gifts, or unexpected income should not be considered until the money is actually received.

Budgeting income may be difficult if your earnings vary by season or your income is irregular, as with sales commissions. In these situations, estimate your income on the low side to help avoid overspending and other financial difficulties.

Step 3: Budget an Emergency Fund and Savings

To set aside money for unexpected expenses as well as future financial security, the Robinsons have budgeted several amounts for savings and investments (see Exhibit 2–5). Financial advisers suggest that an emergency fund representing three to six months of living expenses be established for use in periods of unexpected financial difficulty. This

Exhibit [2-5]   Developing a Monthly Budget

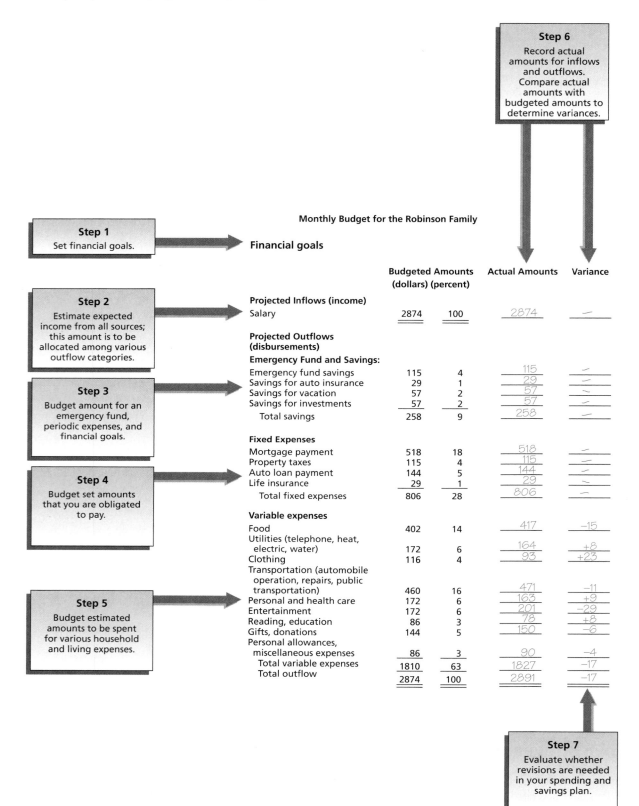

Step 6
Record actual amounts for inflows and outflows. Compare actual amounts with budgeted amounts to determine variances.

Step 1
Set financial goals.

Monthly Budget for the Robinson Family

Financial goals

Step 2
Estimate expected income from all sources; this amount is to be allocated among various outflow categories.

Step 3
Budget amount for an emergency fund, periodic expenses, and financial goals.

Step 4
Budget set amounts that you are obligated to pay.

Step 5
Budget estimated amounts to be spent for various household and living expenses.

	Budgeted Amounts (dollars) (percent)		Actual Amounts	Variance
Projected Inflows (income)				
Salary	2874	100	2874	—
Projected Outflows (disbursements)				
Emergency Fund and Savings:				
Emergency fund savings	115	4	115	—
Savings for auto insurance	29	1	29	—
Savings for vacation	57	2	57	—
Savings for investments	57	2	57	—
Total savings	258	9	258	—
Fixed Expenses				
Mortgage payment	518	18	518	—
Property taxes	115	4	115	—
Auto loan payment	144	5	144	—
Life insurance	29	1	29	—
Total fixed expenses	806	28	806	—
Variable expenses				
Food	402	14	417	−15
Utilities (telephone, heat, electric, water)	172	6	164	+8
Clothing	116	4	93	+23
Transportation (automobile operation, repairs, public transportation)	460	16	471	−11
Personal and health care	172	6	163	+9
Entertainment	172	6	201	−29
Reading, education	86	3	78	+8
Gifts, donations	144	5	150	−6
Personal allowances, miscellaneous expenses	86	3	90	−4
Total variable expenses	1810	63	1827	−17
Total outflow	2874	100	2891	−17

Step 7
Evaluate whether revisions are needed in your spending and savings plan.

amount will vary based on a person's life situation and employment stability.

The Robinsons also set aside an amount each month for their automobile insurance payment, which is due every six months. Both this amount and the emergency fund are put into a savings account.

A frequent budgeting mistake is to save the amount you have left at the end of the month. When you do that, you often have *nothing* left for savings. Since saving is vital for long-term financial security, remember to always "pay yourself first."

Step 4: Budget Fixed Expenses

Definite obligations make up this portion of a budget. As Exhibit 2–5 shows, the Robinsons have fixed expenses for housing, taxes, and loan payments. They make a monthly payment of $29 for life insurance. The budgeted total for their fixed expenses is $806, or 28 percent of estimated available income.

Assigning amounts to spending categories requires careful consideration. The amount you budget for various items will depend on your current needs and plans for the future. Exhibit 2–6 suggests budget allocations for different life situations. Although this information can be of value when creating budget categories, maintaining a detailed record of your spending for several months is a better source for your personal situation. However, don't become discouraged. Use a simple system, such as a notebook or your checkbook. This "spending diary" will help you know where your money is going.

Step 5: Budget Variable Expenses

Planning for variable expenses is not as easy as budgeting for savings or fixed expenses. Variable expenses will fluctuate by household situation, time of year, health, economic conditions, and a variety of other factors. A major portion of the Robinsons' planned spending—over 60 percent of their budgeted income—is for variable living costs. They base their estimates on past spending as well as expected changes in their cost of living.

Step 6: Record Spending Amounts

After having established a spending plan, you will need to keep track of your actual income and expenses. This process is similar to preparing a cash flow statement. In Exhibit 2–5, notice that the Robinsons estimated specific amounts for income and expenses. These are presented under "Budgeted Amounts." The family's actual spending was not always the same as planned. A **budget variance** is the difference between the amount budgeted and the actual amount received or spent. The total variance for the Robinsons was a $17 **deficit,** since their actual spending exceeded their planned spending by this amount. They would have had a **surplus** if their actual spending had been less than they had planned.

Variances for income should be viewed as the opposite of variances for expenses. Less income than expected would be a deficit, whereas more income than expected would be a surplus. Spending more than planned for an item may be justified by reducing spending for another item or putting less into savings. However, revising your budget and financial goals may be necessary.

budget variance The difference between the amount budgeted and the actual amount received or spent.

deficit The amount by which actual spending exceeds planned spending.

surplus The amount by which actual spending is less than planned spending.

DID YOU KNOW?

When people ages 25–45 were asked how financially prepared they are to deal with a setback, such as a serious illness, accident, or death, here's how they responded:

Very prepared	26%
Somewhat prepared	42%
Somewhat unprepared	14%
Very unprepared	11%

Source: *USA Today,* March 6, 2002, p. 18.

Exhibit [2-6] Typical After-Tax Budget Allocations

Budget Category	Student	Working Single (no dependents)	Couple (children under 18)	Single Parent (young children)	Parents (children over 18 in college)	Couple (over 55, no dependent children)
Housing (rent or mortgage payment; utilities; furnishings and appliances)	0–25%	30–35%	25–35%	20–30%	25–30%	25–35%
Transportation	5–10	15–20	15–20	10–18	12–18	10–18
Food (at home and away from home)	15–20	15–25	15–25	13–20	15–20	18–25
Clothing	5–12	5–15	5–10	5–10	4–8	4–8
Personal and health care (including child care)	3–5	3–5	4–10	8–12	4–6	6–12
Entertainment and recreation	5–10	5–10	4–8	4–8	6–10	5–8
Reading and education	10–30	2–4	3–5	3–5	6–12	2–4
Personal insurance and pension payments	0–5	4–8	5–9	5–9	4–7	6–8
Gifts, donations, and contributions	4–6	5–8	3–5	3–5	4–8	3–5
Savings	0–10	4–15	5–10	5–8	2–4	3–5

Sources: Bureau of Labor Statistics (http://stats.bls.gov); *American Demographics; Money; The Wall Street Journal.*

Step 7: Review Spending and Saving Patterns

Like most decision-making activities, budgeting is a circular, ongoing process. You will need to review and perhaps revise your spending plan on a regular basis.

REVIEW YOUR FINANCIAL PROGRESS   The results of your budget may be obvious: having extra cash in checking or falling behind in your bill payments. However, such obvious results may not always be present. Occasionally, you will have to review areas where spending has been more or less than expected. You can prepare an annual summary to compare actual spending with budgeted amounts for each month. A spreadsheet program can be useful for this purpose. This summary will help you see areas where changes in your budget may be necessary. This review process is vital to both successful short-term money management and long-term financial security.

REVISE YOUR GOALS AND BUDGET ALLOCATIONS   What should you cut first when a budget shortage occurs? This question doesn't have easy answers, and answers will vary for different households. The most common overspending areas are entertainment and food, especially away-from-home meals. Purchasing less expensive brand items,

Apply *Yourself!*

Objective 3

Ask two or three friends or relatives about their budgeting systems. Obtain information on how they maintain their spending records. Create a visual presentation (video or slide presentation) that communicates wise budgeting techniques.

Personal Finance in Practice

SELECTING A BUDGETING SYSTEM

Although your checkbook will give you a fairly complete record of your expenses, it does not serve the purpose of planning for spending. A budget requires that you outline how you will spend available income. Described below are various budgeting systems. For each, list a benefit and concern of this method, and explain who might use this system.

Type of budgeting system	What are the benefits? What are the concerns?	Who might use this system?
A *mental budget* exists only in a person's mind. This simple system may be appropriate if you have limited resources and minimal financial responsibilities.		
A *physical budget* involves envelopes, folders, or containers to hold the money or slips of paper. Envelopes would contain the amount of cash or a note listing the amount to be used for "Food," "Rent," "Auto Payment," and other expenses.		
A *written budget* can be kept on notebook paper or on specialized budgeting paper available in office supply stores.		
Computerized budgeting systems use a spreadsheet program or specialized software such as Microsoft Money (www.msn.com/money) or Quicken (www.quicken.com).		

What would you do? Describe your current budgeting system. Are there any recordkeeping activities you might do differently?

---

buying quality used products, and avoiding credit card purchases are common budget adjustment techniques. At this point in the budgeting process, you may also revise your financial goals. Are you making progress toward achieving your objectives? Have changes in personal or economic conditions affected the desirability of certain goals? Have new goals surfaced that should be given a higher priority? Addressing these issues while creating an effective saving method will help ensure accomplishment of your financial goals.

DID YOU KNOW?

For years, co-workers were amused by a woman who carried a brown bag to lunch each day. That woman later retired in financial comfort and lived her later years in beachfront property. A daily coffee and muffin can add up to over $1,300 a year.

CHARACTERISTICS OF SUCCESSFUL BUDGETING

Having a spending plan will not eliminate financial worries. A budget will work only if you follow it. Changes in income, living expenses, and goals will require changes in your spending plan. Successful budgets are commonly viewed as being:

- *Well planned.* A good budget takes time and effort to prepare and should involve everyone affected by it.
- *Realistic.* If you have a moderate income, don't immediately expect to save enough money for an expensive car. A budget is designed not to prevent you from enjoying life but to help you achieve what you want most.

Sheet 7
Developing a
Personal
Budget

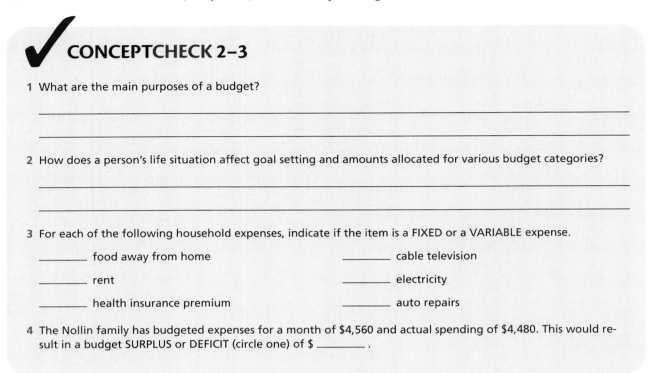

✔ CONCEPTCHECK 2–3

1 What are the main purposes of a budget?

_____

_____

2 How does a person's life situation affect goal setting and amounts allocated for various budget categories?

_____

_____

3 For each of the following household expenses, indicate if the item is a FIXED or a VARIABLE expense.

_____ food away from home   _____ cable television

_____ rent   _____ electricity

_____ health insurance premium   _____ auto repairs

4 The Nollin family has budgeted expenses for a month of $4,560 and actual spending of $4,480. This would result in a budget SURPLUS or DEFICIT (circle one) of $ _____ .

- *Flexible.* Unexpected expenses and life situation changes will require a budget that you can easily revise.
- *Clearly communicated.* Unless you and others involved are aware of the spending plan, it will not work. The budget should be written and available to all household members.

Money Management and Achieving Financial Goals

OBJECTIVE 4

Connect money management activities with saving for personal financial goals.

Your personal financial statements and budget allow you to achieve your financial goals with

1. Your balance sheet: reporting your current financial position—where you are now.
2. Your cash flow statement: telling you what you received and spent over the past month.
3. Your budget: planning spending and saving to achieve financial goals.

Many people prepare a balance sheet on a periodic basis, such as every three or six months. Between those points in time, your budget and cash flow statement help you plan and measure spending and saving activities. For example, you might prepare a balance sheet on January 1, June 30, and December 31. Your budget would serve to plan your spending and saving between these points in time, and your cash flow statement of income and outflows would document your actual spending and saving. This relationship may be illustrated in this way:

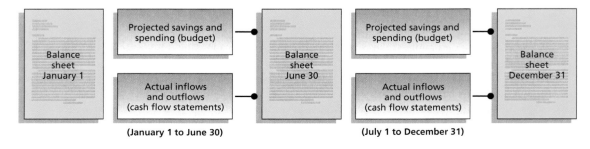

WEED OUT too much of a good thing

MARK AND Lori Bloomberg want to start married life on a firm financial footing. Mark, 36, develops electronic-order routing systems for Wall Street trading desks. Lori, 38, a marketing consultant, is the artsy member of the family, with a small candle-making business as a hobby.

The Bloombergs are beginning with a $200,000 collection of retirement accounts and individual stocks—a "ridiculous array," says Mark. Their mutual funds lack variety and tend toward high fees and inconsistent returns. The stocks are a mix of blue chips and broken-down tech companies. The couple also have $166,000 in cash, a safety net earmarked in part for the down payment on a house in the New York City suburbs.

Suggestions: Whether in business or matrimony, a successful merger requires consolidation. Between them, the Bloombergs have eight retirement accounts with some two-dozen funds—a mishmash of stellar performers and stinkers—as well as stock in Citigroup, Mark's former employer.

Although Mark's $7,000 stake in Citigroup dwarfs his other stocks, he should hang on—it's a good company,

Stumped by your investments? Write to us at portfoliodoc@kiplinger.com.

PHOTOGRAPH BY DANIELA STALLINGER

and he shouldn't surrender the tax break that comes with holding the stock in a qualified retirement plan. But Mark and Lori will do just fine with about half their present funds. Keepers include Ariel Appreciation and Dreyfus Mid-Cap Index (midsize companies), Vanguard 500 Index (large companies), Vanguard Windsor II (cheap stocks) and Evergreen International Equity. The purchase of Davis New York Venture B was unfortunate. When the back-end sales charge disappears in 2006, the couple should switch to its cheaper twin, Selected American Shares—but shouldn't take the hit to get out earlier.

Because the Bloombergs' funds are mostly in tax-deferred accounts, they

should clean house ruthlessly (we count 16 questionable funds) and use the proceeds to build positions in under-represented sectors. We recommend two low-cost exchange-traded funds—iShares MSCI EAFE (symbol EFA), which tracks an index of foreign stocks, and iShares Goldman Sachs Natural Resources (IGE), which tracks energy and other resource stocks at a time of rising demand.

In their taxable stock portfolio, selling losers generates a tax break. Nathan Gendelman at the Family Firm, in Bethesda, Md., figures they'll have $8,600 in losses to offset gains by dumping Travelers Property Casualty, Time Warner, JDS Uniphase, Corning and Qualcomm. They can use the $7,000 in proceeds to buy Vanguard Total Stock Market fund—which tracks the broadest possible index.

Lori's dad, who introduced her to dividend reinvestment plans, had the right idea. She has 13 DRIPs, in fine stocks such as Gannett and Yum Brands. DRIPs let you use dividends to buy more shares at low cost and encourage regular investing. If the Bloombergs solidify such habits now, they'll celebrate their silver anniversary in style. ◄

WEEDER COURTESY SMITH & HAWKEN

1. What effective money management actions have Mark and Lori taken?

_____

_____

2. Describe actions that are recommended for Mark and Lori to help them achieve financial goals.

_____

_____

3. Go to www.kiplinger.com to obtain additional information about budgeting and wise money management. Summarize your findings.

_____

_____

Apply *Yourself!*

Objective 4

Interview a young single person, a young couple, and a middle-aged person about their financial goals and savings habits. What actions do they take to determine and achieve various financial goals?

Changes in your net worth result from cash inflows and outflows. In periods when your outflows exceed your inflows, you must draw on savings or borrow (buy on credit). When this happens, lower assets (savings) or higher liabilities (due to the use of credit) result in a lower net worth. When inflows exceed outflows, putting money into savings or paying off debts will result in a higher net worth.

Selecting a Saving Technique

Traditionally, the United States ranks low among industrial nations in savings rate. Low savings affect personal financial situations. Studies reveal that the majority of Americans do not set aside an adequate amount for emergencies.

Since most people find saving difficult, financial advisers suggest these methods to make it easier:

1. Write a check each payday and deposit it in a savings account not readily available for regular spending. This savings deposit can be a percentage of income, such as 5 or 10 percent, or a specific dollar amount.
2. *Payroll deduction* is available at many places of employment. Under a *direct deposit* system, an amount is automatically deducted from your salary and deposited in savings.
3. Saving coins or spending less on certain items can help you save. Each day, put your change in a container. You can also increase your savings by taking a sandwich to work instead of buying lunch or by refraining from buying snacks or magazines.

How you save is far less important than making regular periodic savings deposits that will help you achieve financial goals. Small amounts of savings can grow faster than most people realize.

Exhibit [2-7]

Using Savings to Achieve Financial Goals

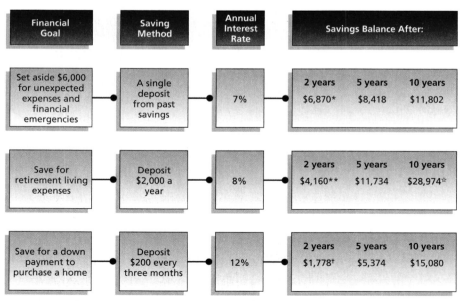

Financial Goal	Saving Method	Annual Interest Rate	Savings Balance After:		
			2 years	5 years	10 years
Set aside $6,000 for unexpected expenses and financial emergencies	A single deposit from past savings	7%	$6,870*	$8,418	$11,802
Save for retirement living expenses	Deposit $2,000 a year	8%	$4,160**	$11,734	$28,974☆
Save for a down payment to purchase a home	Deposit $200 every three months	12%	$1,778†	$5,374	$15,080

* Based on the future value of $1 tables in Chapter 1 and Appendix A.
** Based on the future value of a series of deposits tables in Chapter 1 and Appendix A.
☆ With annual $2,000 deposits, this same retirement account would grow to over $500,000 in 40 years.
† Based on quarterly compounding, explained in Chapter 4.

Calculating Savings Amounts

To achieve your financial objectives, you should convert your savings goals into specific amounts. Your use of a savings or investment plan is vital to the growth of your money. As Exhibit 2–7 shows, using the time value of money calculations, introduced in Chapter 1, can help you calculate progress toward achieving your financial goals.

✔ **CONCEPTCHECK 2–4**

1 What relationship exists among personal financial statements, budgeting, and achieving financial goals?

_____

_____

2 What are some suggested methods to make saving easy?

_____

_____

3 If you wanted to obtain the following types of information, check the box for the document that you would find most useful.

Financial information needed	Balance sheet	Cash flow statement	Budget
Amounts owed for medical expenses			
Spending patterns for the past few months			
Planned spending patterns for the next month			
Current value of investment accounts			
Amounts to deposit in savings accounts			

Back to **Getting Personal**

Review the Getting Personal items at the beginning of the chapter. Which of the items may require you to take different money management actions?

_____

_____

_____

_____

www.mhhe.com/kdh

Chapter Summary

Objective 1 Successful money management requires a coordination of personal financial records, personal financial statements, and budgeting activities. An organized system of financial records and documents should provide ease of access as well as security for financial documents that may be impossible to replace.

Objective 2 A personal balance sheet, also known as a *net worth statement,* is prepared by listing all items of value (assets) and all amounts owed to others (liabilities). The difference between your total assets and your total liabilities is your net worth. A cash flow statement, also called a *personal income and expenditure statement,* is a summary of cash receipts and payments for a given period, such as a month or a year.

Objective 3 The budgeting process consists of seven steps: (1) set financial goals; (2) estimate income; (3) budget an emergency fund and savings; (4) budget fixed expenses; (5) budget variable expenses; (6) record spending amounts; and (7) review spending and saving patterns.

Objective 4 The relationship among the personal balance sheet, cash flow statement, and budget provides the basis for achieving long-term financial security. Future value and present value calculations may be used to compute the increased value of savings for achieving financial goals

Key Terms

assets 39	deficit 47	long-term liabilities 41
balance sheet 39	discretionary income 42	money management 36
budget 45	income 41	net worth 41
budget variance 47	insolvency 41	safe deposit box 38
cash flow 41	liabilities 40	surplus 47
cash flow statement 41	liquid assets 39	take-home pay 42
current liabilities 40		

Problems and Questions

1. What do you believe to be the major characteristics of an effective system to keep track of financial documents and records?

2. Based on the following data, compute the total assets, total liabilities, and net worth:

   Liquid assets, $3,670 Investment assets, $8,340
   Current liabilities, $2,670 Household assets, $89,890
   Long-term liabilities, $76,230

   a. Total assets $ _____

   b. Total liabilities $ _____

   c. Net worth $ _____

3. Use the following items to determine the total assets, total liabilities, net worth, total cash inflows, and total cash outflows:

   Rent for the month, $650 Savings account balance, $1,890
   Spending for food, $345

   Current value of automobile, $7,800

   Credit card balance, $235

   Auto insurance, $230

   Stereo equipment, $2,350

   Lunches/parking at work, $180

   Home computer, $1,500

   Clothing purchase, $110

   Monthly take-home salary, $1,950

   Cash in checking account, $450

   Balance of educational loan, $2,160

   Telephone bill paid for month, $65

   Loan payment, $80

   Household possessions, $3,400

   Payment for electricity, $90

   Donations, $70

   Value of stock investment, $860

   Restaurant spending, $130

   a. Total assets $ _____

   b. Total liabilities $ _____

   c. Net worth $ _____

   d. Total cash inflows $ _____

   e. Total cash outflows $ _____

4. For each of the following situations, compute the missing amount:

   a. Assets $45,000; liabilities $16,000; net worth $ _____

   b. Assets $76,500; liabilities $ _____; net worth $18,700.

   c. Assets $34,280; liabilities $12,965; net worth $ _____

   d. Assets $ _____; liabilities $38,345; net worth $52,654

5. Fran Bowen created the following budget and reported the actual spending listed. Calculate the variance for each of these categories, and indicate whether it was a *deficit* or a *surplus*.

Item	Budgeted	Actual	Variance	Deficit/Surplus
Food	$350	$298	_____	_____
Transportation	320	337	_____	_____
Housing	950	982	_____	_____
Clothing	100	134	_____	_____
Personal	275	231	_____	_____

6. Discuss with several people how a budget might be changed if a household faced a decline in income. What spending areas might be reduced first?

7. Use future value and present value calculations (see tables in Appendix A) to determine the following:

   a. The future value of a $500 savings deposit after eight years at an annual interest rate of 7 percent.

   b. The future value of saving $1,500 a year for five years at an annual interest rate of 8 percent.

   c. The present value of a $2,000 savings account that will earn 6 percent interest for four years.

8. Ed Weston recently lost his job. Before unemployment occurred, the Weston household (Ed; wife, Alice; two children, ages 12 and 9) had a monthly take-home income of $3,165. Each month, the money went for the following items: $880 for rent, $180 for utilities, $560 for food, $480 for automobile expenses, $300 for clothing, $280 for insurance, $250 for savings, and $235 for personal and other items. After the loss of Ed's job, the household's monthly income is $1,550, from his wife's wages and his unemployment benefits. The Westons also have savings accounts, investments, and retirement funds of $28,000.

   a. What budget items might the Westons consider reducing to cope with their financial difficulties?

   b. How should the Westons use their savings and retirement funds during this financial crisis? What additional sources of funds might be available to them during this period of unemployment?

Internet Connection

COMPARING ONLINE MONEY MANAGEMENT ADVICE

Conduct an Internet search to locate two Web sites that provide information on budgeting and other money management activities. Compare the advice provided for the following categories:

Money management topic areas	Web site	Web site
1. What budget guidelines are provided for suggested spending amounts for food, housing, transportation, and other living expenses?		
2. How can a person avoid financial problems and money management difficulties?		
3. What suggestions are provided for saving and investing to achieve financial goals?		

What similarities and differences exist in the advice given by these Web sites? Which sites do you believe provide the most useful and reliable information?

Case in Point

A LITTLE BECOMES A LOT

Can you imagine saving 25 cents a week and having it grow to more than $30,000?

As hard as that may be to believe, that's exactly what Ken Lopez was able to do. Putting aside a quarter a week starting in second grade, he built up a small savings account. These funds were then invested in various stocks and mutual funds. While in college, Ken was able to pay for his education while continuing to save between $50 and $100 a month. He closely monitored spending. Ken realized that the few dollars here and there for snacks and other minor purchases quickly add up.

Today, at age 27, Ken works as a customer service manager for an online sales division of a retailing company. He lives with his wife, Alicia, and their two young children. The family's spending plan allows for all their needs and also includes regularly saving and investing for the children's education and for retirement. Recently, Ken was asked by a co-worker, Brian, "How come you and Alicia never seem to have financial stress in your household?"

Ken replied, "Do you know where your money is going each month?"

"Not really," was Brian's response.

"You'd be surprised by how much is spent on little things you might do without," Ken responded.

"I guess so, I just don't want to have to go around with a notebook writing down every amount I spend," Brian said in a troubled voice.

"Well, you have to take some action if you want your financial situation to change," Ken said in an encouraging voice.

Brian conceded with, "All right, what would you recommend?"

Questions

1. What money management behaviors did Ken practice that most people neglect?

2. Based on information at www.kiplinger.com, www.money.com, or www.asec.org, describe money management and financial planning advice that would be appropriate for Brian.

3. What additional goals might be appropriate for Ken, Alicia, and their children?

Name: _____ Date: _____

Financial Documents and Records

Financial Planning Activities: Indicate the location of the following records, and create files for the eight major categories of financial documents.

Suggested Web Sites: www.money.com   www.kiplinger.com

Item	Home file	Safe deposit box	Other (specify)
Money management records • budget, financial statements			
Personal/employment records • current résumé, social security card			
• educational transcripts			
• birth, marriage, divorce certificates			
• citizenship, military papers			
• adoption, custody papers			
Tax records **Financial services/consumer credit records** • unused, canceled checks			
• savings, passbook statements			
• savings certificates			
• credit card information, statements			
• credit contracts			
Consumer purchase, housing, and automobile records • warranties, receipts			
• owner's manuals			
• lease or mortgage papers, title deed, property tax info			
• automobile title			
• auto registration			
• auto service records			
Insurance records • insurance policies			
• home inventory			
• medical information (health history)			
Investment records • broker statements			
• dividend reports			
• stock/bond certificates			
• rare coins, stamps, and collectibles			
Estate planning and retirement • will			
• pension, social security info			

What's Next for Your Personal Financial Plan?

- Select a location for storing your financial documents and records.
- Decide if various documents may no longer be needed.

Creating a Personal Balance Sheet

5

Your Personal Financial Plan

Financial Planning Activities: List current values of the assets; amounts owed for liabilities; subtract total liabilities from total assets to determine net worth.

Suggested Web Sites: www.kiplinger.com   www.money.com

Balance sheet as of _____

Assets
Liquid assets
Checking account balance _____
Savings/money market accounts, funds _____
Cash value of life insurance _____
Other _____ _____
Total liquid assets _____

Household assets & possessions
Current market value of home _____
Market value of automobiles _____
Furniture _____
Stereo, video, camera equipment _____
Jewelry _____
Other _____ _____
Other _____ _____
Total household assets _____

Investment assets
Savings certificates _____
Stocks and bonds _____
Individual retirement accounts _____
Mutual funds _____
Other _____ _____
Total investment assets _____

Total Assets . . . . _____

Liabilities
Current liabilities
Charge account and credit card balances _____
Loan balances _____
Other _____ _____
Other _____ _____
Total current liabilities _____

Long-term liabilities
Mortgage _____
Other _____ _____
Total long-term liabilities _____

Total Liabilities . . . . _____

Net Worth (assets minus liabilities) _____

What's Next for Your Personal Financial Plan?

• Compare your net worth to previous balance sheets.
• Decide how often you will prepare a balance sheet.

Creating a Personal Cash Flow Statement

Financial Planning Activities: Record inflows and outflows of cash for a one- (or three-) month period.

Suggested Web Sites: www.quicken.com   www.money.com

For month ending _____

Cash Inflows
Salary (take-home) _____
Other income: _____
Other income: _____
Total Income _____

Cash Outflows
Fixed expenses
Mortgage or rent _____
Loan payments _____
Insurance _____
Other _____ _____
Other _____ _____
Total fixed outflows _____
Variable expenses _____
Food _____
Clothing _____
Electricity _____
Telephone _____
Water _____
Transportation _____
Personal care _____
Medical expenses _____
Recreation/entertainment _____
Gifts _____
Donations _____
Other _____ _____
Other _____ _____
Total variable outflows _____
Total Outflows _____
Surplus/Deficit _____

Allocation of surplus
Emergency fund savings _____
Financial goals savings _____
Other savings _____ _____

What's Next for Your Personal Financial Plan?

- Decide which areas of spending need to be revised.
- Evaluate your spending patterns for preparation of a budget.

Developing a Personal Budget

Financial Planning Activities: Estimate projected spending based on your cash flow statement, and maintain records for actual spending for these same budget categories.

Suggested Web Sites: www.quicken.com   www.betterbudgeting.com

	Budgeted amounts		Actual amounts	Variance
Income	**Dollar**	**Percent**		
Salary				
Other _____				
Total income		100%		
Expenses				
Fixed expenses Mortgage or rent				
Property taxes				
Loan payments				
Insurance				
Other _____				
Total fixed expenses				
Emergency fund/savings Emergency fund				
Savings for _____				
Savings for _____				
Total savings				
Variable expenses Food				
Utilities				
Clothing				
Transportation costs				
Personal care				
Medical and health care				
Entertainment				
Education				
Gifts/donations				
Miscellaneous				
Other _____				
Other _____				
Total variable expenses				
Total expenses		100%		

What's Next for Your Personal Financial Plan?

- Evaluate the appropriateness of your budget for your life situation.
- Assess whether your budgeting activities are helping you achieve your financial goals.

3 Taxes in Your Financial Plan

Objectives

In this chapter, you will learn to:

1. Identify the major taxes paid by people in our society.
2. Calculate taxable income and the amount owed for federal income tax.
3. Prepare a federal income tax return.
4. Select appropriate tax strategies for various life situations.

Why is this important?

Each year, more than 90 million American households receive an average tax refund of more than $1,600 for a total of over $144 billion. Invested at 5 percent for a year, these refunds represent about $7.2 billion in lost earnings. Planning and managing your tax activities is a frequently overlooked component of financial planning.

 Getting Personal

For each of the following statements, select "agree" or "disagree" to reflect your current behavior regarding these tax planning activities:

	Agree	Disagree
1. My tax records are organized to allow me to easily find needed information.	_____	_____
2. I have tax withheld from my pay to make sure I get a refund every year.	_____	_____
3. I am able to file my taxes on time each year.	_____	_____
4. My tax returns have never been questioned by the Internal Revenue Service.	_____	_____
5. Every few months, I learn new tax information to make filing easier and to reduce the amount of taxes owed.	_____	_____

After studying this chapter, you will be asked to reconsider your responses to these items.

Taxes in Your Financial Plan

> **OBJECTIVE 1**
> Identify the major taxes paid by people in our society.

Taxes are an everyday financial fact of life. You pay taxes when you get a paycheck or make a purchase. However, most people concern themselves with taxes only immediately before April 15.

Planning Your Tax Strategy

Each year, the Tax Foundation determines how long the average person works to pay taxes. In recent years, "Tax Freedom Day" came in early May. This means that the time that elapsed from January 1 until early May represents the portion of the year people work to pay their taxes.

Tax planning starts with knowing current tax laws. Next, maintain complete and appropriate tax records. Then, make purchase and investment decisions that can reduce your tax liability. Your primary goal should be to pay your fair share of taxes while taking advantage of appropriate tax benefits.

Apply *Yourself!*

Objective 1

Prepare a list of taxes that people commonly encounter in your geographic region.

Types of Tax

Most people pay taxes in four major categories: taxes on purchases, taxes on property, taxes on wealth, and taxes on earnings.

TAXES ON PURCHASES   You probably pay *sales tax* on many purchases. Many states exempt food and drugs from sales tax to reduce the financial burden on low-income households. In recent years, all but five states (Alaska, Delaware, Montana, New Hampshire, and Oregon) had a general sales tax. An **excise tax** is imposed by the federal and state governments on specific goods and services, such as gasoline, cigarettes, alcoholic beverages, tires, air travel, and telephone service.

excise tax A tax imposed on specific goods and services, such as gasoline, cigarettes, alcoholic beverages, tires, and air travel.

TAXES ON PROPERTY   *Real estate property tax* is a major source of revenue for local governments. This tax is based on the value of land and buildings. Some areas impose a *personal property tax* on the value of automobiles, boats, furniture, and farm equipment.

TAXES ON WEALTH   An **estate tax** is imposed on the value of a person's property at the time of death. This federal tax is based on the fair market value of the deceased person's investments, property, and bank accounts less allowable deductions and other taxes.

estate tax A tax imposed on the value of a person's property at the time of death.

Money and property passed on to heirs may be subject to a state tax. An **inheritance tax** is levied on the value of property bequeathed by a deceased person. This tax is paid for the right to acquire the inherited property.

Individuals are allowed to give money or items valued at $11,000 or less in a year to a person without being subject to taxes. Gift amounts greater than $11,000 are subject

inheritance tax A tax levied on the value of property bequeathed by a deceased person.

to federal tax. Amounts given for tuition payments or medical expenses are not subject to gift taxes.

TAXES ON EARNINGS The two main taxes on wages are Social Security and income taxes. Social Security taxes are used to finance the retirement, disability, and life insurance benefits of the federal government's Social Security program. Income tax is a major financial planning factor for most people. Most workers are subject to federal and state income taxes.

> **DID YOU KNOW?**
>
> According to the Tax Foundation (www.taxfoundation.org), Alaska, New Hampshire, Tennessee, Colorado, and South Dakota were the most "tax-friendly" states. In contrast, Maine, New York, Wisconsin, Vermont, and Hawaii had the highest taxes as a percentage of income.

 **CONCEPTCHECK 3–1**

1 What are the four major categories of taxes?

_____

_____

2 For each of the following situations, list the type of tax that is being described.

Financial planning situation	Type of tax
a. A tax on the value of a person's house.	
b. The additional charge for gasoline and air travel.	
c. Payroll deductions for federal government retirement benefits.	
d. Amount owed on property received from a deceased person.	
e. Payroll deductions for a direct tax on earnings.	

The Basics of Federal Income Tax

OBJECTIVE 2
Calculate taxable income and the amount owed for federal income tax.

Each year, millions of Americans are required to pay their share of income taxes to the federal government. As shown in Exhibit 3–1, this process involves several steps.

Step 1: Determining Adjusted Gross Income

This process starts with steps to determine **taxable income,** which is the net amount of income, after allowable deductions, on which income tax is computed.

TYPES OF INCOME Most, but not all, income is subject to taxation. Your gross, or total, income can consist of three main components:

1. **Earned income** is usually in the form of wages, salary, commission, fees, tips, or bonuses.
2. **Investment income** (sometimes referred to as *portfolio income*) is money received in the form of dividends, interest, or rent from investments.
3. **Passive income** results from business activities in which you do not actively participate, such as a limited partnership.

taxable income The net amount of income, after allowable deductions, on which income tax is computed.

earned income Money received for personal effort, such as wages, salary, commission, fees, tips, or bonuses.

investment income Money received in the form of dividends, interest, or rent from investments; also called *portfolio income.*

passive income Income resulting from business activities in which you do not actively participate.

Exhibit [3-1] Computing Taxable Income and Your Tax Liability

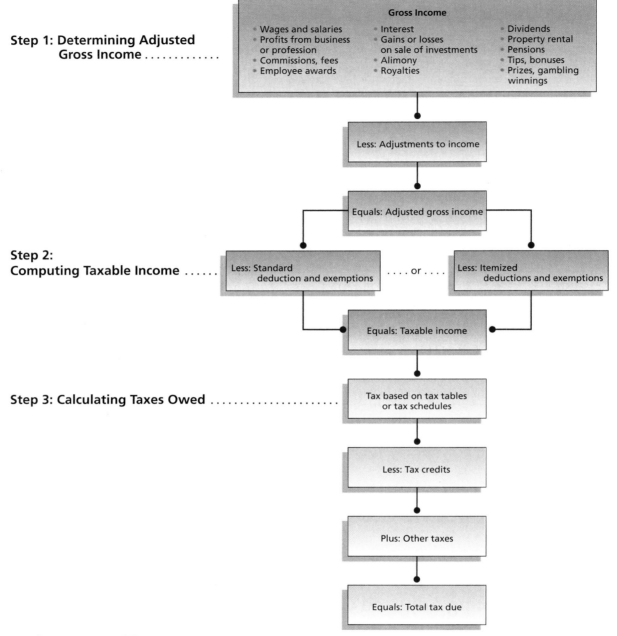

Step 1: Determining Adjusted Gross Income . . . .

Gross Income
- Wages and salaries
- Profits from business or profession
- Commissions, fees
- Employee awards
- Interest
- Gains or losses on sale of investments
- Alimony
- Royalties
- Dividends
- Property rental
- Pensions
- Tips, bonuses
- Prizes, gambling winnings

Less: Adjustments to income

Equals: Adjusted gross income

Step 2: Computing Taxable Income . . . . . .

Less: Standard deduction and exemptions . . . . or . . . . Less: Itemized deductions and exemptions

Equals: Taxable income

Step 3: Calculating Taxes Owed . . . .

Tax based on tax tables or tax schedules

Less: Tax credits

Plus: Other taxes

Equals: Total tax due

ApplyYourself!

Objective 2

Using library resources or an Internet search, determine the types of income that are exempt from federal income tax.

exclusion An amount not included in gross income.

Other types of income subject to federal income tax include alimony, awards, lottery winnings, and prizes. For example, cash and prizes won on television game shows are subject to both federal and state taxes.

Total income is also affected by exclusions. An **exclusion** is an amount not included in gross income. For example, the foreign income exclusion allows U.S. citizens working and living in another country to exclude a certain portion ($80,000) of their income from federal income taxes.

Exclusions may also be referred to as **tax-exempt income,** or income that is not subject to tax. For example, interest earned on most state and city bonds is exempt from federal income tax. **Tax-deferred income** is income that will be taxed at a later date.

ADJUSTMENTS TO INCOME   **Adjusted gross income (AGI)** is gross income after certain reductions have been made. These reductions, called *adjustments to income,* include contributions to an IRA or a Keogh retirement plan, penalties for early withdrawal of savings, and alimony payments. Adjusted gross income is used as the basis for computing various income tax deductions, such as medical expenses.

Step 2: Computing Taxable Income

DEDUCTIONS   A **tax deduction** is an amount subtracted from adjusted gross income to arrive at taxable income. Every taxpayer receives at least the **standard deduction,** a set amount on which no taxes are paid. As of 2004, single people receive a standard deduction of $4,850 (married couples filing jointly receive $9,700). Blind people and individuals 65 and older receive higher standard deductions.

Many people qualify for more than the standard deduction. **Itemized deductions** are expenses a taxpayer is allowed to deduct from adjusted gross income. Common itemized deductions include:

- *Medical and dental expenses*—physician fees, prescription medications, hospital expenses, medical insurance premiums, hearing aids, eyeglasses, and medical travel that has not been reimbursed or paid by others. The amount of this deduction is the medical and dental expenses that exceed 7.5 percent (as of 2004) of adjusted gross income.
- *Taxes*—state and local income tax, real estate property tax, and state or local personal property tax.
- *Interest*—mortgage interest, home equity loan interest, and investment interest expense up to an amount equal to investment income.
- *Contributions*—cash or property donated to qualified charitable organizations. Contribution totals greater than 20 percent of adjusted gross income are subject to limitations.
- *Casualty and theft losses*—financial losses resulting from natural disasters, accidents, or unlawful acts.
- *Moving expenses*—costs incurred for a change in residence associated with a new job that is at least 50 miles farther from your former home than your old main job location.
- *Job-related and other miscellaneous expenses*—unreimbursed job travel, union dues, required continuing education, work clothes or uniforms, investment expenses, tax preparation fees, safe deposit box rental (for storing investment documents), and so on. The total of these expenses must exceed 2 percent of adjusted gross income to qualify as a deduction.

The standard deduction *or* total itemized deductions, along with the value of your exemptions (see next section), are subtracted from adjusted gross income to obtain your taxable income.

You are required to maintain records to document tax deductions, such as a home filing system (Exhibit 3–2). Canceled checks and receipts serve as proof of payment for deductions such as charitable contributions, medical expenses, and business-related

tax-exempt income Income that is not subject to tax.

tax-deferred income Income that will be taxed at a later date.

adjusted gross income (AGI) Gross income reduced by certain adjustments, such as contributions to an individual retirement (IRA) and alimony payments.

DID YOU KNOW?

Each year, taxpayers are deceived with bogus opportunities such as a home-based business to qualify for a "home office" deduction, increased refunds for a "tax consultant" fee, prepayment for prizes you have won, and an offer to obtain a refund of Social Security taxes paid during your lifetime for a "paperwork" fee of $100. Information on these and other tax frauds are available at www.ustreas.gov/tigta.

---

tax deduction An amount subtracted from adjusted gross income to arrive at taxable income.

standard deduction A set amount on which no taxes are paid.

itemized deductions Expenses that can be deducted from adjusted gross income, such as medical expenses, real estate property taxes, home mortgage interest, charitable contributions, casualty losses, and certain work-related expenses.

Exhibit [3-2]

A Tax Recordkeeping System

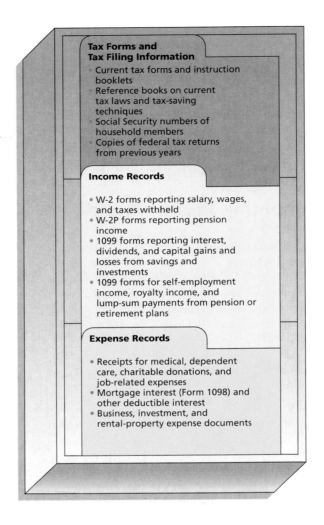

Tax Forms and Tax Filing Information

- Current tax forms and instruction booklets
- Reference books on current tax laws and tax-saving techniques
- Social Security numbers of household members
- Copies of federal tax returns from previous years

Income Records

- W-2 forms reporting salary, wages, and taxes withheld
- W-2P forms reporting pension income
- 1099 forms reporting interest, dividends, and capital gains and losses from savings and investments
- 1099 forms for self-employment income, royalty income, and lump-sum payments from pension or retirement plans

Expense Records

- Receipts for medical, dependent care, charitable donations, and job-related expenses
- Mortgage interest (Form 1098) and other deductible interest
- Business, investment, and rental-property expense documents

expenses. Travel expenses can be documented in a daily log with records of mileage, tolls, parking fees, and away-from-home costs.

Generally, you should keep tax records for three years from the date you file your return. However, you may be held responsible for providing back documentation up to six years. Records such as past tax returns and housing documents should be kept indefinitely.

exemption A deduction from adjusted gross income for yourself, your spouse, and qualified dependents.

EXEMPTIONS   An **exemption** is a deduction from adjusted gross income for yourself, your spouse, and qualified dependents. A dependent must not earn more than a set amount unless he or she is under age 19 or is a full-time student under age 24; you must provide more than half of the dependent's support; and the dependent must reside in your home or be a specified relative and must meet certain citizenship requirements. For 2004, taxable income was reduced by $3,100 for each exemption claimed. After deducting the amounts for exemptions, you obtain your taxable income, which is the amount used to determine taxes owed.

Step 3: Calculating Taxes Owed

Your taxable income is the basis for computing the amount of tax owed.

TAX RATES   Use your taxable income in conjunction with the appropriate tax table or tax schedule. For 2004, the six-rate system for federal income tax was as follows:

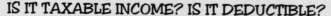

Personal Finance in Practice

IS IT TAXABLE INCOME? IS IT DEDUCTIBLE?

Certain financial benefits individuals receive are not subject to federal income tax. Indicate whether each of the following items would or would not be included in taxable income when you compute your federal income tax.

Indicate whether each of the following items would or would not be deductible when you compute your federal income tax.

Is it taxable income . . . ?	Yes	No
1. Lottery winnings	___	___
2. Child support received	___	___
3. Worker's compensation benefits	___	___
4. Life insurance death benefits	___	___
5. Municipal bond interest earnings	___	___
6. Bartering income	___	___

Is it deductible . . . ?	Yes	No
7. Life insurance premiums	___	___
8. Cosmetic surgery for improved looks	___	___
9. Fees for traffic violations	___	___
10. Mileage for driving to volunteer work	___	___
11. An attorney's fee for preparing a will	___	___
12. Income tax preparation fee	___	___

Note: These taxable income items and deductions are based on the 2004 tax year and may change due to changes in the tax code.

Answers: 1, 6, 10, 12—yes; 2, 3, 4, 5, 7, 8, 9, 11—no.

Rate on Taxable Income	Single Taxpayers	Married Taxpayers Filing Jointly	Heads of Households
10%	Up to $7,150	Up to $14,300	Up to $10,200
15	$7,150–$29,050	$14,300–$58,100	$10,200–$38,900
25	$29,050–$70,350	$58,100–$117,250	$38,900–$100,500
28	$70,350–$146,750	$117,250–$178,650	$100,500–$162,700
33	$146,750–$319,100	$178,650–$319,100	$162,700–$319,100
35	Over $319,100	Over $319,100	Over $319,100

A separate tax rate schedule also exists for married persons who file separate income tax returns.

The 10, 15, 27, 30, 35, and 38.6 percent rates are referred to as **marginal tax rates.** These rates are used to calculate tax on the last (and next) dollar of taxable income. After deductions and exemptions, a person in the 27 percent tax bracket pays 27 cents in taxes for every dollar of taxable income in that bracket.

In contrast, the **average tax rate** is based on the total tax due divided by taxable income. Except for taxpayers in the 10 percent bracket, this rate is less than a person's marginal tax rate. For example, a person with taxable income of $40,000 and a total tax bill of $4,200 would have an average tax rate of 10.5 percent ($4,200 ÷ $40,000).

Some taxpayers who receive special deductions may be subject to an additional tax. The *alternative minimum tax (AMT)* is designed to ensure that those who receive tax breaks also pay their fair share of taxes. Additional information about the AMT may be obtained at www.irs.gov.

marginal tax rate The rate used to calculate tax on the last (and next) dollar of taxable income.

average tax rate Total tax due divided by taxable income.

Figure It Out!

TAX CREDITS VERSUS TAX DEDUCTIONS

Many people confuse *tax credits* with *tax deductions*. Is one better than the other? A tax *credit,* such as eligible child care or dependent care expenses, results in a dollar-for-dollar reduction in the amount of taxes owed. A tax *deduction,* such as itemized deduction in the form of medical expenses, mortgage interest, or charitable contributions, reduces the taxable income on which your taxes are based.

Here is how a $100 tax credit compares with a $100 tax deduction:

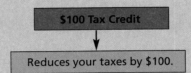

$100 Tax Credit

↓

Reduces your taxes by $100.

As your might expect, tax credits are less readily available than tax deductions. To qualify for a $100 child care tax credit, you may have to spend $500 in child care expenses. In some situations, spending on deductible items may be more beneficial than qualifying for a tax credit. A knowledge of tax law and careful financial planning will help you use both tax credits and tax deductions to maximum advantage.

$100 Tax Deduction

↓

Reduces your taxable income by $100. The amount of your tax reduction depends on your tax bracket. Your taxes will be reduced by $15 if you are in the 15 percent tax bracket and by $28 if you are in the 28 percent tax bracket.

CALCULATIONS

1. If a person in a 30 percent tax bracket received a $1,000 tax deduction, how much would the person's taxes be reduced? $_____

2. If a person in a 27 percent tax bracket received a $200 tax credit, how much would the person's taxes be reduced? $_____

---

tax credit An amount subtracted directly from the amount of taxes owed.

TAX CREDITS   The tax owed may be reduced by a **tax credit,** an amount subtracted directly from the amount of taxes owed. One example of a tax credit is the credit given for child care and dependent care expenses. Another tax credit for low-income workers is the *earned-income credit (EIC)*, for working parents with taxable income under a certain amount. Families that do not earn enough to owe federal income taxes are also eligible for the EIC and receive a check for the amount of their credit. A *tax credit* differs from a deduction in that a tax credit has a full dollar effect in lowering taxes, whereas a *deduction* reduces the taxable income on which the tax liability is computed.

Step 4: Making Tax Payments

You pay federal income taxes through either payroll withholding or estimated tax payments.

WITHHOLDING   The pay-as-you-go system requires an employer to deduct federal income tax from your pay. The withheld amount is based on the number of exemptions and the expected deductions claimed. For example, a married person with children would have less withheld than a single person with the same salary, since the married person will owe less tax.

After the end of the year, you will receive a W-2 form, which reports your annual earnings and the amounts deducted for taxes. The difference between the amount withheld and the tax owed is either the additional amount to pay or your refund. Students and low-income individuals may file for exemption from withholding if they paid no federal income tax last year and do not expect to pay any in the current year.

Many taxpayers view an annual tax refund as a "windfall," extra money they count on each year. These taxpayers are forgetting the opportunity cost of withholding excessive amounts. Others view their extra tax withholding as "forced savings." However, a payroll deduction plan for savings could serve the same purpose while also earning interest on your funds.

ESTIMATED PAYMENTS   Income from savings, investments, independent contracting, royalties, and pension payments is reported on Form 1099. People who receive such income may be required to make tax payments during the year (April 15, June 15, September 15, and January 15 as the last payment for the previous tax year). These payments are based on an estimate of taxes due at year-end. Underpayment or failure to make estimated payments can result in penalties and interest charges.

Step 5: Watching Deadlines and Avoiding Penalties

Most people are required to file a federal income tax return by April 15. If you are not able to file on time, you can use Form 4868 to obtain an automatic four-month extension.

This extension is for the 1040 form and other documents, but it does not delay your payment liability. You must submit the estimated amount owed along with Form 4868 by April 15. Failure to file on time can result in a penalty for being just one day late. Underpayment of quarterly estimated taxes may require paying interest on the amount you should have paid. Underpayment due to negligence or fraud can result in penalties of 50 to 75 percent.

The good news is that if you claim a refund several months or years late, the IRS will pay you interest. However, refunds must be claimed within three years of filing the return or within two years of paying the tax.

Sheet 8
Current
Income Tax
Estimate

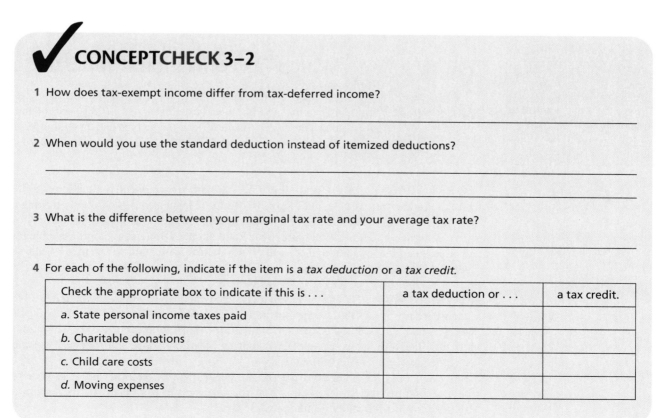

✔ CONCEPTCHECK 3–2

1 How does tax-exempt income differ from tax-deferred income?

_____

2 When would you use the standard deduction instead of itemized deductions?

_____

_____

3 What is the difference between your marginal tax rate and your average tax rate?

_____

4 For each of the following, indicate if the item is a *tax deduction* or a *tax credit*.

Check the appropriate box to indicate if this is . . .	a tax deduction or . . .	a tax credit.
a. State personal income taxes paid		
b. Charitable donations		
c. Child care costs		
d. Moving expenses		

Filing Your Federal Income Tax Return

OBJECTIVE 3
Prepare a federal income tax return.

As you prepare to do your taxes, you must first determine whether you are required to file a return. Next, you need to decide which tax form best serves you and if you are required to submit supplementary schedules or forms.

Who Must File?

Every citizen or resident of the United States and every U.S. citizen who is a resident of Puerto Rico is required to file a federal income tax return if his or her income is above a certain amount. The amount is based on the person's *filing status* and other factors such as age. For example, single persons under 65 had to file a return on April 15, 2005 (for tax year 2004), if their gross income exceeded $7,950. If your gross income is less than this amount but taxes were withheld, you should file a return to obtain your refund.

Your filing status is affected by marital status and dependents. The five filing status categories are:

- *Single*—never-married, divorced, or legally separated individuals with no dependents.
- *Married, filing joint return*—combines the spouses' incomes.
- *Married, filing separate returns*—each spouse is responsible for his or her own tax. Under certain conditions, a married couple can benefit from this filing status.
- *Head of household*—an unmarried individual or a surviving spouse who maintains a household (paying for more than half of the costs) for a child or a dependent relative.
- *Qualifying widow or widower*—an individual whose spouse died within the past two years and who has a dependent; this status is limited to two years after the death of the spouse.

In some situations, you may have a choice of filing status. In such cases, compute your taxes under the alternatives to determine the most advantageous filing status.

Apply *Yourself!*

Objective 3

Create a visual presentation (video or slide presentation) that demonstrates actions a person might take to reduce errors when filing a federal tax return.

Which Tax Form Should You Use?

Although more than 400 federal tax forms and schedules exist, you select from three basic forms when filing your income tax. Your decision will depend on the type and amount of your income, the number of deductions, and the complexity of your tax situation.

FORM 1040EZ   This form allows people with uncomplicated situations to file with minimal effort. You may use Form 1040EZ if (1) you are single or married filing a joint return, under age 65, and claim no dependents; (2) your income consisted only of wages, salaries, and tips and not more than $400 of taxable interest; (3) your taxable income is less than $50,000; and (4) you do not itemize deductions or claim any adjustments to income or any tax credits.

FORM 1040A   This form is used by people who have less than $50,000 in taxable income from wages, salaries, tips, unemployment compensation, interest, or dividends and who take the standard deduction. With Form 1040A, you can also take deductions for individual retirement account (IRA) contributions and a tax credit for child care and dependent care expenses.

If you qualify for either Form 1040EZ or Form 1040A, you may wish to use one of them to simplify the filing process. You will not want to use Form 1040EZ or Form 1040A if Form 1040 allows you to pay less tax.

FORM 1040   Form 1040 is an expanded version of Form 1040A that includes sections for all types of income. You are required to use this form if your income is over $50,000 or if you can be claimed as a dependent on your parents' return *and* you had interest or dividends over a set limit. Form 1040 allows you to itemize your deductions, which will reduce taxable income.

FORM 1040X   This form is used to amend a previously filed tax return. If you discovered income that was not reported, or if you found additional deductions, you may file Form 1040X to pay the additional tax or obtain a refund.

What Is the Process for Completing the Federal Income Tax Return?

The major sections of Form 1040 (see Exhibit 3–3) correspond to tax topics discussed in the previous sections of this chapter:

1. *Filing status and exemptions.* Your tax rate is determined by your filing status and allowances for yourself, your spouse, and each person you claim as a dependent.

Exhibit [3-3]   Federal Income Tax Return—Form 1040

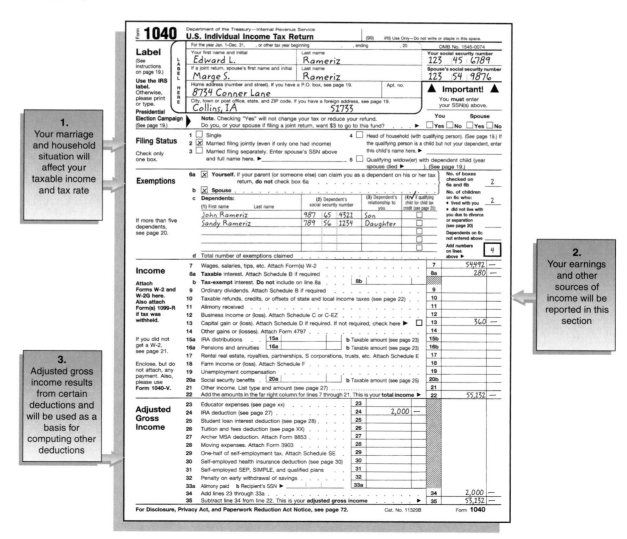

1. Your marriage and household situation will affect your taxable income and tax rate

2. Your earnings and other sources of income will be reported in this section

3. Adjusted gross income results from certain deductions and will be used as a basis for computing other deductions

Exhibit [3-3] (concluded)

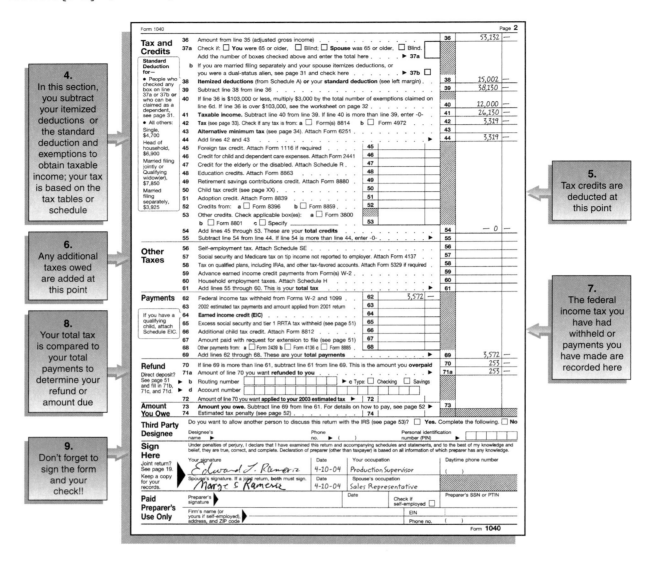

4. In this section, you subtract your itemized deductions or the standard deduction and exemptions to obtain taxable income; your tax is based on the tax tables or schedule

6. Any additional taxes owed are added at this point

8. Your total tax is compared to your total payments to determine your refund or amount due

9. Don't forget to sign the form and your check!!

5. Tax credits are deducted at this point

7. The federal income tax you have had withheld or payments you have made are recorded here

Note: These forms were used in a recent year; the current forms may not be exactly the same. Obtain current income tax forms and current tax information from your local IRS office, post office, public library, or at www.irs.gov.

2. *Income.* Earnings from your employment (as reported by your W-2 form) and other income, such as savings and investment income, are reported in this section of Form 1040.

3. *Adjustments to income.* As discussed later in the chapter, if you qualify, you may deduct contributions (up to a certain amount) to an individual retirement account (IRA) or other qualified retirement program.

4. *Tax computation.* In this section, your adjusted gross income is reduced by your itemized deductions (see Exhibit 3–4) or by the standard deduction for your tax situation. In addition, an amount is deducted for each exemption to arrive at your taxable income. That income is the basis for determining the amount of your tax (see Exhibit 3–5).

5. *Tax credits.* Any tax credits for which you qualify are subtracted at this point.

6. *Other taxes.* Any special taxes, such as self-employment tax, are included at this point.

7. *Payments.* Your total withholding and other payments are indicated in this section.

Exhibit [3-4]   Schedule A for Itemized Deductions—Form 1040

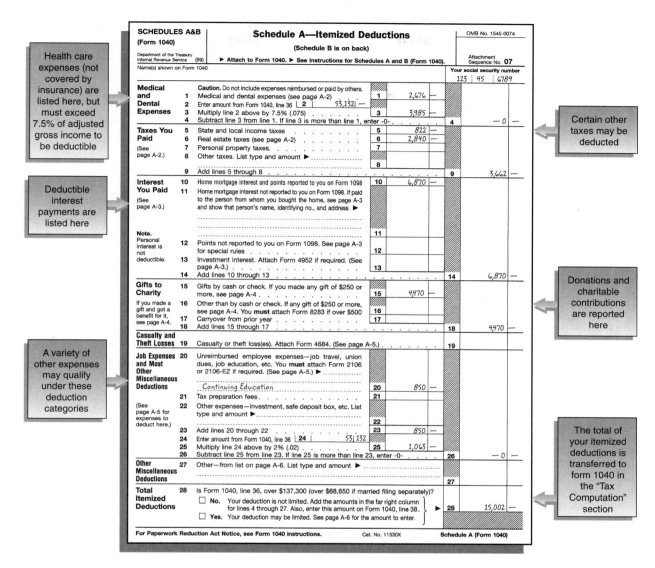

8. *Refund or amount you owe.* If your payments exceed the amount of income tax you owe, you are entitled to a refund. If the opposite is true, you must make an additional payment. Taxpayers who want their refunds sent directly to a bank can provide the necessary account information directly on Form 1040, 1040A, or 1040EZ.
9. *Your signature.* Forgetting to sign a tax return is one of the most frequent filing errors.

How Do I File My State Tax Return?

All but seven states (Alaska, Florida, Nevada, South Dakota, Texas, Washington, and Wyoming) have a state income tax. In most states, the tax rate ranges from 1 to 10 percent. For further information about the income tax in your state, contact the state department of revenue. States usually require income tax returns to be filed when the federal income tax return is due. For planning your tax activities, see Exhibit 3–6.

Exhibit [3-5] Tax Tables and Tax Rate Schedules

Tax Table

If taxable income is—		And you are—			
At least	But less than	Single	Married filing jointly *	Married filing separately	Head of a household
		Your tax is—			
26,000					
26,000	26,050	3,604	3,304	3,925	3,404
26,050	26,100	3,611	3,311	3,938	3,411
26,100	26,150	3,619	3,319	3,952	3,419
26,150	26,200	3,626	3,326	3,965	3,426
26,200	26,250	3,634	3,334	3,979	3,434
26,250	26,300	3,641	3,341	3,992	3,441
26,300	26,350	3,649	3,349	4,006	3,449
26,350	26,400	3,656	3,356	4,019	3,456
26,400	26,450	3,664	3,364	4,033	3,464
26,450	26,500	3,671	3,371	4,046	3,471
26,500	26,550	3,679	3,379	4,060	3,479
26,550	26,600	3,686	3,386	4,073	3,486
26,600	26,650	3,694	3,394	4,087	3,494
26,650	26,700	3,701	3,401	4,100	3,501
26,700	26,750	3,709	3,409	4,114	3,509
26,750	26,800	3,716	3,416	4,127	3,516
26,800	26,850	3,724	3,424	4,141	3,524
26,850	26,900	3,731	3,431	4,154	3,531
26,900	26,950	3,739	3,439	4,168	3,539
26,950	27,000	3,746	3,446	4,181	3,546

* This column must also be used by a qualifying widow(er).

Tax Rate Schedules

Schedule Y-1—Use if your filing status is **Married filing jointly** or **Qualifying widow(er)**

If the amount on Form 1040, line 41, is: Over—	But not over—	Enter on Form 1040, line 42	of the amount over—
$0	$12,000	.... 10%	$0
12,000	46,700	**$1,200.00 + 15%**	12,000
46,700	112,850	6,405.00 + 27%	46,700
112,850	171,950	24,265.50 + 30%	112,850
171,950	307,050	41,995.50 + 35%	171,950
307,050	....	89,280.50 + 38.6%	307,050

 Use **only** if your taxable income (Form 1040, line 41) is $100,000 or more. If less, use the **Tax Table.** Even though you cannot use the Tax Rate Schedules below if your taxable income is less than $100,000, all levels of taxable income are shown so taxpayers can see the tax rate that applies to each level.

Note: These were the federal income tax rates for a recent year. Current rates may vary due to changes in the tax code and adjustments for inflation. Obtain current income tax booklets from your local IRS office, post office, bank, public library, or at www.irs.gov.

How Do I File My Taxes Online?

Software packages such as *TaxCut* and *TurboTax* allow you to complete needed tax forms and schedules and either print for mailing or file online. Electronic filing of federal taxes now exceeds 60 million returns annually. With e-file, taxpayers usually receive their refunds within three weeks. The cost for this service is usually between $15 and $40.

DID YOU KNOW?

An IRS study of visits to its tax assistance centers found that 19 of 26 tax returns (83 percent) had been incorrectly prepared by IRS employees. The agency reported that 17 of the 19 inaccurately prepared fictitious returns would have resulted in incorrect refunds totaling nearly $32,000.

What Tax Assistance Sources Are Available?

As with other aspects of personal financial planning, many tax resources are available to assist you.

IRS SERVICES   If you prepare your own tax return or desire tax information, the IRS can assist in four ways:

1. *Publications.* The IRS offers hundreds of free booklets and pamphlets that can be obtained at a local IRS office, by mail request, or by telephone. Especially helpful is *Your Federal Income Tax* (IRS Publication 17). IRS publications and tax forms are available by phone at 1-800-TAX-FORM, online at www.irs.gov, or by fax at 703-368-9694.
2. *Recorded messages.* The IRS Tele-Tax system gives you 24-hour access to about 150 recorded tax tips at 1-800-829-4477.
3. *Phone hot line.* Information about specific problems is available through an IRS-staffed phone line at 1-800-829-1040.

Exhibit [3-6]   Tax-Planner Calendar

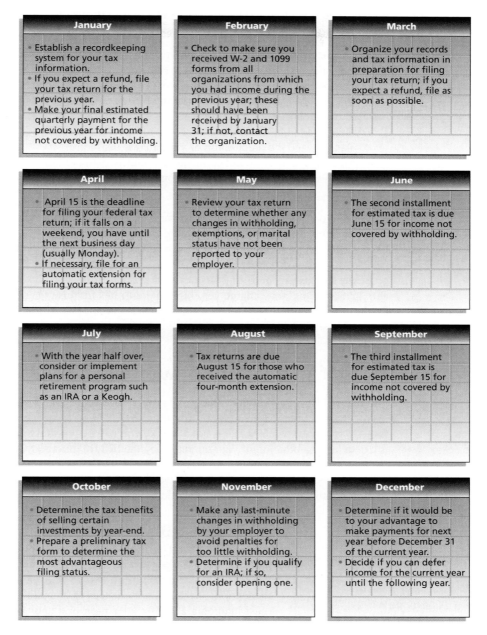

January	February	March
• Establish a recordkeeping system for your tax information. • If you expect a refund, file your tax return for the previous year. • Make your final estimated quarterly payment for the previous year for income not covered by withholding.	• Check to make sure you received W-2 and 1099 forms from all organizations from which you had income during the previous year; these should have been received by January 31; if not, contact the organization.	• Organize your records and tax information in preparation for filing your tax return; if you expect a refund, file as soon as possible.

April	May	June
• April 15 is the deadline for filing your federal tax return; if it falls on a weekend, you have until the next business day (usually Monday). • If necessary, file for an automatic extension for filing your tax forms.	• Review your tax return to determine whether any changes in withholding, exemptions, or marital status have not been reported to your employer.	• The second installment for estimated tax is due June 15 for income not covered by withholding.

July	August	September
• With the year half over, consider or implement plans for a personal retirement program such as an IRA or a Keogh.	• Tax returns are due August 15 for those who received the automatic four-month extension.	• The third installment for estimated tax is due September 15 for income not covered by withholding.

October	November	December
• Determine the tax benefits of selling certain investments by year-end. • Prepare a preliminary tax form to determine the most advantageous filing status.	• Make any last-minute changes in withholding by your employer to avoid penalties for too little withholding. • Determine if you qualify for an IRA; if so, consider opening one.	• Determine if it would be to your advantage to make payments for next year before December 31 of the current year. • Decide if you can defer income for the current year until the following year.

Note: Children born before the end of the year give you a full-year exemption, so plan accordingly!

4. *Walk-in service.* You can visit a local IRS office (400 are available) to obtain tax assistance.

TAX PUBLICATIONS   Each year, several tax guides are published and offered for sale. Publications such as *J. K. Lasser's Your Income Tax* and *The Ernst & Young Tax Guide* can be purchased online or at local stores.

THE INTERNET   As with other personal finance topics, extensive information may be found on Web sites such as those listed at the start of the chapter.

TAX PREPARATION SERVICES   More than 40 million U.S. taxpayers pay someone to prepare their taxes. The fee can range from $40 at a tax preparation service for a simple return to more than $2,000 for a certified public accountant. While many people do their own taxes, complications can occur, especially if you have income sources other than salary. The sources available for professional tax assistance include the following:

- Tax services range from local, one-person operations to national firms with thousands of offices, such as H&R Block.
- Enrolled agents—government-approved tax experts—prepare returns and provide tax advice. Information about the National Association of Enrolled Agents is available at www.naea.org.
- A certified public accountant (CPA) with special tax training can assist with tax planning and the preparation of your annual tax return.
- Attorneys usually do not complete tax returns; however, their services may be useful when a tax-related transaction or when a difference of opinion with the IRS occurs.

Even if you hire a professional tax preparer, you are responsible for supplying accurate and complete information. If you owe more tax because your return contains errors or you have made entries that are not allowed, it is your responsibility to pay that additional tax, plus any interest and penalties.

Beware of tax preparers and businesses that offer refunds in advance. These "refund anticipation loans" may charge very high interest rates for this type of consumer credit. Studies reveal interest rates on these short-term loans can exceed 500 percent (on an annualized basis).

What If Your Return Is Audited?

tax audit A detailed examination of your tax return by the Internal Revenue Service.

The Internal Revenue Service reviews all returns for completeness and accuracy. If you make an error, your tax is automatically refigured and you receive either a bill or a refund. If you make an entry that is not allowed, you will be notified by mail. A **tax audit** is a detailed examination of your tax return by the IRS. In most audits, the IRS requests more information to support your tax return. Be sure to keep accurate records. Receipts, canceled checks, and other evidence can verify amounts that you claim. Avoiding common filing mistakes helps to minimize your chances of an audit (see Exhibit 3–7).

DID YOU KNOW?

Electronically filed federal income tax returns have an accuracy rate of 99 percent, compared to 81 percent for paper returns. Most electronic filing programs do your calculations and signal potential errors before you file.

WHO GETS AUDITED?   About 0.6 percent of all tax filers—fewer than 1 million people—are audited each year. Although the IRS does not reveal its basis for auditing returns, several indicators are evident. People who claim large or unusual deductions increase their chances of an audit. Tax advisers suggest including a brief explanation or a copy of receipts for deductions that may be questioned.

TYPES OF AUDITS   The simplest and most frequent type of audit is the *correspondence audit*. This mail inquiry requires you to clarify or document minor questions. The *office audit* requires you to visit an IRS office to clarify some aspect of your tax return.

The *field audit* is more complex. An IRS agent visits you at your home, your business, or the office of your accountant so you have access to records. A field audit may be done to verify whether an individual has a home office if this is claimed.

The IRS also conducts more detailed audits for about 50,000 taxpayers. These range from random requests to document various tax return items to line-by-line reviews by IRS employees.

Exhibit [3-7]   How to Avoid Common Filing Errors

- Organize all tax-related information for easy access.

- Follow instructions carefully. Many people deduct total medical and dental expenses rather than the amount of these expenses that exceeds 7.5 percent of adjusted gross income.

- Use the proper tax rate schedule or tax table column.

- Be sure to claim the correct number of exemptions and correct amounts of standard deductions.

- Consider the alternative minimum tax that may apply to your situation. Be sure to pay self-employment tax and tax on early IRA withdrawals.

- Check your arithmetic several times.

- Sign your return (both spouses must sign a joint return), or the IRS won't process it.

- Be sure to include the correct Social Security number(s) and to record amounts on the correct lines.

- Attach necessary documentation such as your W-2 forms and required supporting schedules.

- Make the check payable to "U.S. Treasury."

- Put your Social Security number, the tax year, and a daytime telephone number on your check—and be sure to sign the check!

- Keep a photocopy of your return.

- Put the proper postage on your mailing envelope.

- Finally, check everything again—and file on time! Care taken when you file your income tax can result in "many happy returns."

YOUR AUDIT RIGHTS   When you receive an audit notice, you have the right to request time to prepare. Also, you can ask the IRS for clarification of items being questioned. When audited, follow these suggestions:

- Decide whether you will bring your tax preparer, accountant, or lawyer.
- Be on time for your appointment; bring only relevant documents.
- Present tax evidence in a logical, calm, and confident manner; maintain a positive attitude.
- Make sure the information you present is consistent with the tax law.
- Keep your answers aimed at the auditor's questions. Answer questions clearly and completely. Be as brief as possible. The five best responses to questions during an audit are "Yes," "No," "I don't recall," "I'll have to check on that," and "What specific items do you want to see?"

If you disagree with the results of an audit, you may request a conference at the Regional Appeals Office. Although most differences of opinion are settled at this stage, some taxpayers take their cases further. A person may go to the U.S. tax court, the U.S. claims court, or the U.S. district court. Some tax disputes have gone to the U.S. Supreme Court.

 **CONCEPTCHECK 3–3**

1 In what ways does your filing status affect preparation of your federal income tax return?

_____

_____

2 What are the main sources available to help people prepare their taxes?

_____

_____

3 What actions can reduce the chances of an IRS audit?

_____

_____

4 Which 1040 form should each of the following individuals use? (Check one for each situation.)

Tax situation	1040EZ	1040A	1040
a. A high school student with an after-school job and interest earnings of $480 from savings accounts.			
b. A college student who, because of ownership of property, is able to itemize deductions rather than take the standard deduction.			
c. A young, entry-level worker with no dependents and income only from salary.			

Selecting Tax Planning Strategies

OBJECTIVE 4
Select appropriate tax strategies for various life situations.

tax avoidance The use of legitimate methods to reduce one's taxes.

tax evasion The use of illegal actions to reduce one's taxes.

For people to pay their fair share of taxes—no more, no less—they should practice **tax avoidance,** the use of legitimate methods to reduce one's taxes. In contrast, **tax evasion** is the use of illegal actions to reduce one's taxes. To minimize taxes owed, follow these guidelines:

- If you expect to have the *same* or a *lower* tax rate next year, *accelerate deductions* into the current year. Pay real estate property taxes or make charitable donations by December 31.
- If you expect to have a *lower* or the *same* tax rate next year, *delay the receipt of income* until next year so the funds will be taxed at a lower rate or at a later date.
- If you expect to have a *higher* tax rate next year, consider *delaying deductions,* since they will have a greater benefit. A $1,000 deduction at 25 percent lowers your taxes $250; at 28 percent, your taxes are lowered $280.
- If you expect to have a *higher* tax rate next year, *accelerate the receipt of income* to have it taxed at the current lower rate.

When considering financial decisions in relation to your taxes, remember that purchasing, investing, and retirement planning are the areas most heavily affected by tax laws.

Consumer Purchasing

The buying decisions most directly affected by taxes are the purchase of a residence, the use of credit, and job-related expenses.

PLACE OF RESIDENCE   Owning a home is one of the best tax shelters. Both real estate property taxes and interest on the mortgage are deductible (as itemized deductions) and thus reduce your taxable income.

Figure It Out!

SHORT-TERM AND LONG-TERM CAPITAL GAINS

You will pay a lower tax rate on the profits from stocks and other investments if you hold the asset for more than 12 months. After May 5, 2003, a taxpayer in the 28 percent tax bracket would pay $280 in taxes on a $1,000 short-term capital gain (assets held for one year or less). However, that same taxpayer would pay only $150 on the $1,000 (a 15 percent capital gains tax) If the investment were held for more than a year.

	Short-Term Capital Gain (Assets held for one year or less)	Long-Term Capital Gain (Assets held for more than one year)
Capital Gain	$1,000	$1,000
Capital Gains Tax Rate	28%	15%
Capital Gains Tax	$ 280	$ 150
Tax Savings		$ 130

CONSUMER DEBT Current tax laws allow homeowners to borrow for consumer purchases. You can deduct interest on loans (of up to $100,000) secured by your primary or secondary home up to the actual dollar amount you have invested in it—the difference between the market value of the home and the amount you owe on it. These *home equity loans,* which are *second mortgages,* allow you to use that line of credit for various purchases. Some states place restrictions on home equity loans.

JOB-RELATED EXPENSES As previously mentioned, certain work expenses, such as union dues, some travel and education costs, business tools, and job search amounts, may be included as itemized deductions.

Investment Decisions

A major area of tax planning involves decisions related to investing.

TAX-EXEMPT INVESTMENTS Interest income from municipal bonds, which are issued by state and local governments, and other tax-exempt investments is not subject to federal income tax. Although municipal bonds have lower interest rates than other investments, the *after-tax* income may be higher. For example, if you are in the 27 percent tax bracket, earning $100 of tax-exempt income would be worth more to you than earning $125 in taxable investment income. The $125 would have an after-tax value of $91—$125 less $34 (27 percent of $125) for taxes.

TAX-DEFERRED INVESTMENTS Although tax-deferred investments, with income taxed at a later date, are less beneficial than tax-exempt investments, they give you the advantage of paying taxes in the future rather than now. Examples of tax-deferred investments include:

1. *Tax-deferred annuities,* usually issued by insurance companies, and
2. *Retirement plans,* such as IRA, Keogh, or 401(k) plans.

capital gains Profits from the sale of a capital asset such as stocks, bonds, or real estate.

Capital gains, profits from the sale of a capital asset such as stocks, bonds, or real estate, are also tax deferred; you do not have to pay the tax on these profits until the asset is sold. In recent years, *long-term* capital gains (on investments held more than a year) have been taxed at a lower rate.

The sale of an investment for less than its purchase price is, of course, a *capital loss.* Capital losses can be used to offset capital gains and up to $3,000 of ordinary income. Unused capital losses may be carried forward into future years to offset capital gains or ordinary income up to $3,000 per year.

SELF-EMPLOYMENT   Owning your own business can have tax advantages. Self-employed persons may deduct expenses such as health and certain life insurance as business costs. However, business owners have to pay self-employment tax (Social Security) in addition to the regular tax rate.

CHILDREN'S INVESTMENTS   A child under 14 with investment income of more than $1,500 is taxed at the parent's top rate. For investment income under $1,500, the child receives a deduction of $750 and the next $750 is taxed at his or her own rate, which is probably lower than the parent's rate. This restriction does not apply to children 14 and older.

Apply *Yourself!*

Objective 4

Survey friends and relatives about their tax planning strategies. Do most people get a federal tax refund or owe taxes each year? Is their situation (refund or payment) planned?

Retirement Plans

A major tax strategy of benefit to working people is the use of tax-deferred retirement plans such as individual retirement arrangements (IRAs), Keogh plans, and 401(k) plans.

TRADITIONAL IRA   The regular IRA deduction is available only to people who do not participate in employer-sponsored retirement plans and have an adjusted gross income under a certain amount. As of 2004, the IRA contribution limit was $3,000. Older workers, age 50 and over, were allowed to contribute up to $3,500 as a "catch up" to make up for lost time saving for retirement.

In general, amounts withdrawn from deductible IRAs are included in gross income. An additional 10 percent penalty is usually imposed on withdrawals made before age 59½ unless the withdrawn funds are on account of death or disability, for medical expenses, or for qualified higher education expenses.

ROTH IRA   The Roth IRA also allows a $3,000 annual contribution, which is not tax deductible; however, the earnings on the account are tax-free after five years. The funds from the Roth IRA may be withdrawn before age 59½ if the account owner is disabled, or for the purchase of a first home ($10,000 maximum). Like the regular IRA, the Roth IRA is limited to people with an adjusted gross income under a certain amount. While the Roth IRA does not have immediate benefits, the investment grows in value on a tax-free basis. Withdrawals from the Roth IRA are exempt from federal and state taxes.

In addition to the traditional IRA and the Roth IRA, self-employed people can make use of a SEP-IRA. A SEP (simplified employee pension plan) is an extended IRA that allows self-employed people to contribute greater amounts to their retirement as well as making contributions for employee retirement accounts.

EDUCATION IRA   The Education Savings Account is designed to assist parents in saving for the college education of children. Once again, the annual contribution (limited to $2,000) is not tax deductible and is limited to taxpayers with an adjusted gross income under a certain amount. However, as with the Roth IRA, the earnings accumulate tax-free and distributions are not taxed when used for qualified higher education expenses.

KEOGH PLAN   If you are self-employed and own your own business, you can establish a Keogh plan. This retirement plan, also called an HR10 plan, may combine a profit-sharing plan and a pension plan of other investments purchased by the employee. In general, with a Keogh, people may contribute 25 percent of their annual income, up to a maximum of $30,000, to this tax-deferred retirement plan.

401(k) PLAN   The part of the tax code called 401(k) authorizes a tax-deferred retirement plan sponsored by an employer. This plan allows you to contribute a greater tax-deferred amount (a maximum of $12,000 for 2003; gradually increasing to $15,000 in 2006) than you can contribute to an IRA. Older workers, age 50 and over, are allowed to contribute up to $14,000. However, most companies set a limit on your contribution, such as 15 percent of your salary.

Tax planners advise people to contribute as much as possible to a Keogh or 401(k) plan since (1) the increased value of the investment accumulates on a tax-free basis until the funds are withdrawn and (2) contributions reduce your adjusted gross income for computing your current tax liability.

Changing Tax Strategies

Each year, the IRS modifies the tax form and filing procedures. In addition, Congress frequently passes legislation that changes the tax code. These changes require that you regularly determine how to take best advantage of the tax laws for personal financial planning. Also, carefully consider changes in your personal situation and your income level. You should carefully monitor your personal tax strategies to best serve both your daily living needs and your long-term financial goals.

Sheet 9
Tax Planning
Activities

✔ **CONCEPTCHECK 3–4**

1 How does tax avoidance differ from tax evasion?

_____

_____

2 What common tax-saving methods are available to most individuals and households?

_____

_____

3 For the following tax situations, indicate if this item refers to tax-exempt income or tax-deferred income.

	Tax-exempt	Tax-deferred
a. Interest earned on municipal bonds		
b. Earnings on an individual retirement account		
c. Education IRA earnings used for college expenses		
d. Income of U.S. citizens working in another country		

TAXES | Save today for a better tomorrow and an immediate tax break. *By Mary Beth Franklin*

Give yourself **A BREAK**

Phyllis Garcia of Wethersfield, Conn., knows a good deal when she sees it. Last year, the former corporate-benefits manager found a way to save for retirement on a meager part-time salary and slash her federal income taxes by more than 20%—and she plans to do it again this year.

If you are single and earn $25,000 or less, or are married and have a joint income of $50,000 or less, you may also be able to take advantage of the saver's tax credit. Although it was created as an incentive for lower-income workers to save for retirement, the credit is a potential bonanza for part-time workers who fall within the income limits. You can claim a tax credit worth 10% to 50% of the amount you

SHUJI KOBAYASHI/GETTY IMAGES

contribute to your IRA or 401(k), up to a maximum credit of $1,000. The lower your income, the higher the percentage you get back via the credit.

Garcia, a widow, quit her full-time job a few years ago to stay at home with her son Robert Deffley, now 14. She collects social security survivors benefits (which are partially tax-free) and occasionally does clerical work at home. Last year, she earned only $1,700 but contributed $1,500 to a traditional IRA,

reducing her taxable income by the same amount. Together with her $150 saver's tax credit, Garcia's $1,500 IRA contribution saved nearly $600 on her taxes.

"It's a nice chunk of change that would otherwise go to Uncle Sam," says Garcia, 51.

The saver's tax credit is available only to taxpayers age 18 and older who are neither full-time students nor eligible to be claimed as a dependent on someone else's return. (That eliminates most 2003 college graduates, who can still be claimed on their parents' return. But the door could be open to 2002 grads struggling in low-paying jobs.)

If you are semiretired—working part-time and collecting social security benefits—you may also qualify for the credit. But if you receive payments from a pension, IRA, 401(k) or other retirement plan, those benefits will reduce or eliminate the tax credit (for more ways to save on taxes, see page 72). **K**

Source: Reprinted by permission from the December issue of *Kiplinger's Personal Finance.* Copyright © 2003 The Kiplinger Washington Editors, Inc.

1. What are the benefits of the "saver's tax credit"?

   _____
   _____
   _____
   _____
   _____

2. Locate and prepare a short summary of other current tax information at www.kiplinger.com.

   _____
   _____
   _____
   _____
   _____

Back to Getting Personal

Redo the Getting Personal questions at the beginning of the chapter. Have any of your answers changed?

_____

_____

_____

What did you learn in this chapter that might affect your answers to these questions in the future?

_____

_____

_____

Chapter Summary

Objective 1 Tax planning can influence spending, saving, borrowing, and investing decisions. An awareness of income taxes, sales taxes, excise taxes, property taxes, estate taxes, inheritance taxes, gift taxes, and Social Security taxes is vital for successful financial planning.

Objective 2 Taxable income is determined by subtracting adjustments to income, deductions, and allowances for exemptions from gross income. Your total tax liability is based on the published tax tables or tax schedules, less any tax credits.

Objective 3 The major sections of Form 1040 provide the basic framework for filing your federal income tax return. The main sources of tax assistance are IRS services and publications, other publications, the Internet, computer software, and professional tax preparers such as commercial tax services, enrolled agents, accountants, and attorneys.

Objective 4 You may reduce your tax burden through careful planning and making financial decisions related to consumer purchasing, and the use of debt, investments, and retirement planning.

Key Terms

adjusted gross income (AGI)   65

average tax rate   67

capital gains   80

earned income   63

estate tax   62

excise tax   62

exclusion   64

exemption   66

inheritance tax   62

investment income   63

itemized deductions   65

marginal tax rate   67

passive income   63

standard deduction   65

taxable income   63

tax audit   76

tax avoidance   78

tax credit   68

tax deduction   65

tax-deferred income   65

tax evasion   78

tax-exempt income   65

Problems and Questions

1. Thomas Franklin arrived at the following tax information:

   Gross salary, $41,780

   Dividend income, $80

   Itemized deductions, $3,890

   Interest earnings, $225

   One personal exemption, $2,650

   Adjustments to income, $1,150

   What amount would Thomas report as taxable income?

2. If Lola Harper had the following itemized deductions, should she use Schedule A or the standard deduction? The standard deduction for her tax situation is $6,050.

   Donations to church and other charities, $1,980

   Medical and dental expenses exceeding 7.5 percent of adjusted gross income, $430

   State income tax, $690

www.mhhe.com/kdh

Job-related expenses exceeding 2 percent of adjusted gross income, $1,610

3. What would be the average tax rate for a person who paid taxes of $4,864.14 on a taxable income of $39,870?

4. Based on the following data, would Ann and Carl Wilton receive a refund or owe additional taxes?

Adjusted gross income, $43,190

Itemized deductions, $11,420

Child care tax credit, $80

Federal income tax withheld, $6,784

Amount for personal exemptions, $7,950

Tax rate on taxable income, 15 percent

5. Using the tax table in Exhibit 3–5 (p. 74) determine the amount of taxes for the following situations:
   a. A head of household with taxable income of $26,210.

   b. A single person with taxable income of $26,888.

   c. A married person filing a separate return with taxable income of $26,272.

6. Use IRS publications and other reference materials to answer a specific tax question. Contact an IRS office to obtain an answer for the same question. What differences, if any, exist between the information sources?

7. Would you prefer a fully taxable investment earning 10.7 percent or a tax-exempt investment earning 8.1 percent? Why?

8. On December 30, you decide to make a $1,000 charitable donation.
   a. If you are in the 27 percent tax bracket, how much will you save in taxes for the current year?

   b. If you deposit that tax savings in a savings account for the next five years at 8 percent, what will be the future value of that account?

Internet Connection

COMPARING TAX INFORMATION SOURCES

Visit the Web sites of three commonly used tax information sources: (1) the Internal Revenue Service, (2) a tax preparation service, and (3) a financial planning information service, such as Kiplinger.com, Money.com, or Turbotax.com. Obtain information for the following items:

Areas of analysis	Internal Revenue Service	Tax preparation service	Financial planning service
Web site	www.irs.gov		
Major emphasis of information			
Availability of current tax forms			
Coverage of latest tax law changes			
Other information and services			
E-file information and cost			

Case in Point

A SINGLE FATHER'S TAX SITUATION

Ever since his wife's death, Eric Stanford has faced difficult personal and financial circumstances. His job provides him with a fairly good income but keeps him away from his daughters, ages 8 and 10, nearly 20 days a month. This requires him to use in-home child care services that consume a major portion of his income. Since the Stanfords live in a small apartment, this arrangement has been very inconvenient.

Due to the costs of caring for his children, Eric has only a minimal amount withheld from his salary for federal income taxes. Thus more money is available during the year, but for the last few years he has had to make a payment in April—another financial burden.

Although Eric has created an investment fund for his daughters' college education and for his retirement, he has not sought to select investments that offer tax benefits. Overall, he needs to look at several aspects of his tax planning activities to find strategies that will best serve his current and future financial needs.

Eric has assembled the following information for the current tax year:

Earnings from wages, $42,590

Interest earned on savings, $125

IRA deduction, $2,000

Checking account interest, $65

Three exemptions at $2,750 each

Current standard deduction for filing status, $6,350

Amount withheld for federal income tax, $3,178

Tax credit for child care, $400

Filing status: head of household

Questions

1. What are Eric's major financial concerns in his current situation?

2. In what ways might Eric improve his tax planning efforts?

3. Calculate the following
   a. What is Eric's taxable income? (Refer to Exhibit 3–1, page 64.)

   b. What is his total tax liability? (Use Exhibit 3–5, page 74.) What is his average tax rate?

   c. Based on his withholding, will Eric receive a refund or owe additional tax? What is the amount?

www.mhhe.com/kdh

Current Income Tax Estimate

Financial Planning Activities: Based on last year's tax return, estimates for the current year, and current tax regulations and rates, estimate your current tax liability.

Suggested Web Sites: www.irs.gov   www.taxlogic.com

Gross income (wages, salary, investment income, and other ordinary income		$
Less Adjustments to income (see current tax regulations)		– $
Equals Adjusted gross income		= $
Less Standard deduction **or**	Itemized deduction	
	medical expenses (exceeding 7.5% of AGI)	$
	state/local income, property taxes	$
	mortgage, home equity loan	$
	interest	$
	contributions	$
	casualty and theft losses	$
	moving expenses, job-related and miscellaneous expenses (exceeding 2% of AGI)	$
Amount – $	**Total**	– $
Less Personal exemptions	– $	
Equals Taxable income	= $	
Estimated tax (based on current tax tables or tax schedules)	$	
Less Tax credits	– $	
Plus Other taxes	+ $	
Equals Total tax liability	= $	
Less Estimated withholding and payments	– $	
Equals Tax due (or refund)	= $	

What's Next for Your Personal Financial Plan?

- Develop a system for filing and storing various tax records related to income, deductible expenses, and current tax forms.
- Using the IRS and other Web sites, identify recent changes in tax laws that may affect your financial planning decisions.

Name: _____ **Date:** _____

Tax Planning Activities

Financial Planning Activities: To determine which of the following actions are appropriate for your tax situation to prevent penalties and obtain tax savings.

Suggested Web Sites: www.turbotax.com   http://taxes.about.com

	Action to be taken (if applicable)	Completed
Filing status/withholding • Change filing status or exemptions due to changes in life situation		
• Change amount of withholding due to changes in tax situations		
• Plan to make estimated tax payments (due the 15th of April, June, September, and January)		
Tax records/documents • Organize home files for ease of maintaining and retrieving data		
• Send current mailing address and correct social security number to IRS, place of employment, and other income sources		
Annual tax activities • Be certain all needed data and current tax forms are available well before deadline		
• Research tax code changes and uncertain tax areas		
Tax-savings actions • Consider tax-exempt and tax-deferred investments		
• If you expect to have the same or lower tax rate next year, accelerate deductions into the current year		
• If you expect to have the same or lower tax rate next year, delay the receipt of income until next year		
• If you expect to have a higher tax rate next year, delay deductions since they will have a greater benefit		
• If you expect to have a higher tax rate next year, accelerate the receipt of income to have it taxed at the current lower rate		
• Start or increase use of tax-deferred retirement plans		
• Other		

What's Next for Your Personal Financial Plan?
- Identify saving and investing decisions that would minimize future income taxes.
- Develop a plan for actions to take related to your current and future tax situation.

4 Savings and Payment Services

Objectives

In this chapter, you will learn to:

1. Identify commonly used financial services.
2. Compare the types of financial institutions.
3. Assess various types of savings plans.
4. Evaluate different types of payment methods.

Why is this important?

ATM fees can range from nothing to $1 or $2 per cash withdrawal. If you are charged two $1 transaction fees a week and could invest your money at 5 percent, this convenience will cost you more than $570 over a five-year period.

 Getting Personal

What are your attitudes toward financial services? For each of the following statements, circle the choice that best describes your current situation.

1. The financial service about which I'm least informed is
   a. Online banking.
   b. Certificates of deposit and other savings plans.
   c. Checking accounts and other payment methods.

2. My primary financial service activities involve the use of
   a. A bank or credit union.
   b. Online payments and ATMs.
   c. A check-cashing outlet.

3. When selecting a savings plan, my main concern is
   a. Bank location and availability of cash machines.
   b. Federal deposit insurance coverage.
   c. Rate of return.

4. My checking account balance is
   a. Updated in my records after every check written and deposit made.
   b. Based on a rough estimate in my checkbook.
   c. Known only by my financial institution.

After studying this chapter, you will be asked to reconsider your responses to these items.

Key Web Sites		Your Personal Financial Plan Sheets
www.bankrate.com	www.fdic.gov	10. Planning the use of financial services.
www.banx.com	www.savingsbonds.gov	11. Comparing savings plans.
www.cuna.org	www.federalreserve.gov	12. Using savings plans to achieve financial goals.
		13. Comparing payment methods; bank reconciliation.

What Financial Services Do You Need?

OBJECTIVE 1
Identify commonly used financial services.

More than 20,000 banks, savings and loan associations, credit unions, and other financial institutions provide various payment, savings, and credit services. Today a trip to "the bank" may mean a visit to a credit union, a stop at an ATM at the mall, or a transfer of funds online. While some financial decisions relate directly to goals, your daily activities require different financial services. Exhibit 4–1 is an overview of financial services for managing cash flows and moving toward specific financial goals.

Meeting Daily Money Needs

Buying groceries, paying the rent, and completing other routine spending activities require a cash management plan. Cash, check, credit card, and automatic teller machine (ATM) card are the common payment choices. Mistakes made frequently when managing current cash needs include (1) overspending as a result of impulse buying and using credit; (2) having insufficient liquid assets to pay current bills; (3) using savings or borrowing to pay for current expenses; (4) failing to put unneeded funds in an interest-earning savings account or investment plan.

Exhibit [4-1]

Financial Services for Managing Cash Flow

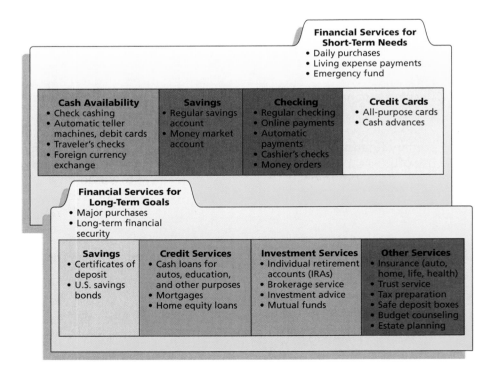

Financial Services for Short-Term Needs
• Daily purchases
• Living expense payments
• Emergency fund

Cash Availability	Savings	Checking	Credit Cards
• Check cashing • Automatic teller machines, debit cards • Traveler's checks • Foreign currency exchange	• Regular savings account • Money market account	• Regular checking • Online payments • Automatic payments • Cashier's checks • Money orders	• All-purpose cards • Cash advances

Financial Services for Long-Term Goals
• Major purchases
• Long-term financial security

Savings	Credit Services	Investment Services	Other Services
• Certificates of deposit • U.S. savings bonds	• Cash loans for autos, education, and other purposes • Mortgages • Home equity loans	• Individual retirement accounts (IRAs) • Brokerage service • Investment advice • Mutual funds	• Insurance (auto, home, life, health) • Trust service • Tax preparation • Safe deposit boxes • Budget counseling • Estate planning

Sources of Quick Cash

No matter how carefully you manage your money, at some time you will need more cash than you have available. To cope in that situation, you have two basic choices: liquidate savings or borrow. A savings account, certificate of deposit, mutual fund, or other investment may be accessed when you need funds. Or a credit card cash advance or a personal loan may be appropriate. Remember, however, that both using savings and increasing borrowing reduce your net worth and your potential to achieve long-term financial security.

Types of Financial Services

Banks and other financial institutions offer services to meet a variety of needs. These services fall into four main categories:

1. *Savings* provides safe storage of funds for future use. Commonly referred to as *time deposits,* money in savings accounts and certificates of deposit are examples of savings plans.
2. *Payment services* offer an ability to transfer money to others for daily business activities. Checking accounts and other payment methods are generally called *demand deposits.*
3. *Borrowing* is used by most people at some time during their lives. Credit alternatives range from short-term accounts, such as credit cards and cash loans, to long-term borrowing, such as a home mortgage.
4. *Other financial services* include insurance, investments, tax assistance, and financial planning. A **trust** is a legal agreement that provides for the management and control of assets by one party for the benefit of another. This type of arrangement is usually created through a commercial bank or a lawyer. Parents who want to set aside certain funds for their children's education may use a trust.

To simplify financial services, many financial businesses offer all-purpose accounts. An **asset management account,** also called a *cash management account,* provides a complete financial services program for a single fee. Investment companies and others offer this type of account, with checking, an ATM card, a credit card, online banking, and a line of credit as well as access for buying stocks, bonds, mutual funds, and other investments.

Electronic and Online Banking

Banking online and through electronic systems continues to expand (see Exhibit 4–2). While most traditional financial institutions offer online banking services, Web-only banks have also started. For example, E*Trade Bank (www.etradebank.com) operates online while also providing customers with access to ATMs. These "e-banks" and "e-branches" provide:

- *Direct deposit* of paychecks and government payments with funds automatically available for your use.
- *Automatic payments* to transfer funds to pay rent, mortgage, utilities, loans, and investment deposits.
- An **automatic teller machine (ATM),** also called a *cash machine,* allowing various banking activities and other types of transactions such as buying transit passes, postage stamps, and gift certificates. To minimize ATM

Apply *Yourself!*

Objective 1
Survey several people to determine awareness and use of various financial services such as online banking.

trust A legal agreement that provides for the management and control of assets by one party for the benefit of another.

asset management account An all-in-one account that includes savings, checking, borrowing, investing, and other financial services for a single fee; also called a *cash management account.*

automatic teller machine (ATM) A computer terminal used to conduct banking transactions; also called a *cash machine.*

DID YOU KNOW?

While paying bills online may have a cost, 80 percent of people who use various online payment services report not paying a fee for this convenience.

Exhibit [4-2] Electronic Banking Services

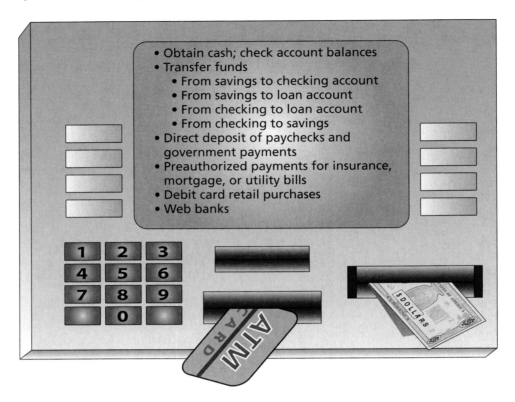

- Obtain cash; check account balances
- Transfer funds
  - From savings to checking account
  - From savings to loan account
  - From checking to loan account
  - From checking to savings
- Direct deposit of paychecks and government payments
- Preauthorized payments for insurance, mortgage, or utility bills
- Debit card retail purchases
- Web banks

debit card A plastic access card used in computerized banking transactions; also called a *cash card.*

fees, compare several financial institutions, use your own bank's ATM to avoid surcharges, and withdraw larger amounts to avoid fees on several small transactions.

- A **debit card,** or *cash card,* activates ATM transactions and may also be used to make purchases. A debit card is in contrast to a *credit card,* since you are spending your own funds rather than borrowing additional money. Today, debit cards are commonly used for retail purchases. In addition, card scanners are appearing on everything from soda machines to parking meters.

A lost or stolen debit card can be expensive. If you notify the financial institution within two days of losing the card, your liability for unauthorized use is $50. After that, you can be liable for up to $500 of unauthorized use for up to 60 days. Beyond that, your liability is unlimited. However, some card issuers use the same rules for lost or stolen debit cards as for credit cards: a $50 maximum. Of course, you are not liable for unauthorized use, such as a con artist using your account number to make a purchase. Remember to report the fraud within 60 days of receiving your statement to protect your right not to be charged for the transaction.

Financial Services and Economic Conditions

Sheet 10
Planning the
Use of
Financial
Services

Changing interest rates, rising consumer prices, and other economic factors influence financial services. For successful financial planning, be aware of the current trends and future prospects for interest rates (see Exhibit 4–3). You can learn about these trends and prospects by reading *The Wall Street Journal* (www.wsj.com), *The Financial Times* (www.ft.com), the business section of daily newspapers, and business periodicals such as *BusinessWeek* (www.businessweek.com), *Forbes* (www.forbes.com), and *Fortune* (www.fortune.com).

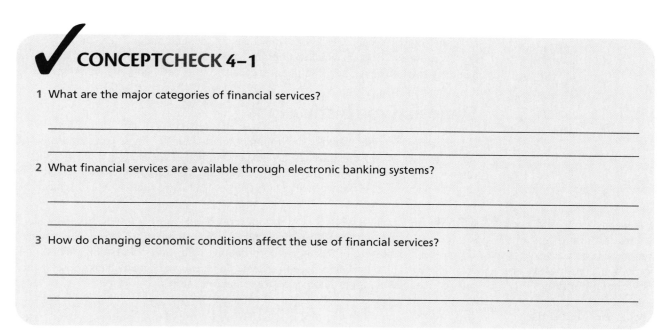

When interest rates are rising...

• Use long-term loans to take advantage of current low rates.
• Select short-term savings instruments to take advantage of higher rates when they mature.

• Use short-term loans to take advantage of lower rates when you refinance the loans.
• Select long-term savings instruments to "lock in" earnings at current high rates.

When interest rates are falling...

Exhibit [4-3]

Changing Interest Rates and Financial Service Decisions

✔ CONCEPTCHECK 4–1

1 What are the major categories of financial services?

_____

_____

2 What financial services are available through electronic banking systems?

_____

_____

3 How do changing economic conditions affect the use of financial services?

_____

_____

Selecting a Financial Institution

Many businesses, including insurance companies, investment brokers, and credit card companies, offer financial services that were once offered only by banks. Companies such as General Motors, Sears, and AT&T issue credit cards. Banks have also expanded their product line by providing investments, insurance, and real estate services.

OBJECTIVE 2
Compare the types of financial institutions.

Comparing Financial Institutions

The basic concerns of a financial services customer are simple:

• Where can I get the best return on my savings?
• How can I minimize the cost of checking and payments services?
• Will I be able to borrow money if I need it?

As you use financial services, decide what you want from the organization that will serve your needs. With the financial marketplace constantly changing, you must assess various services and other factors before selecting an organization (see Exhibit 4–4).

Exhibit [4-4]

How Should You Choose a
Financial Institution?

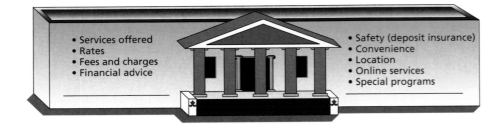

- Services offered
- Rates
- Fees and charges
- Financial advice

- Safety (deposit insurance)
- Convenience
- Location
- Online services
- Special programs

The services of a specific financial institution are likely to be a major factor in your decision. In addition, personal service is important to many customers. Convenience may be provided by business hours, branch offices, ATMs, and online access. Convenience and service have a cost, so be sure to compare fees and other charges at several financial institutions.

Finally, you should consider safety factors and interest rates. Obtain information about earnings you will receive on savings and checking accounts and the rate you will pay for borrowed funds. Most financial institutions have deposit insurance to protect customers against losses; however, not all of them are insured by federal government programs.

Deposit-Type Institutions

Despite changes in the banking environment, many familiar financial institutions still serve your needs. Most institutions have expanded their services. As Exhibit 4–5 shows, financial institutions fall into three major categories. Deposit-type financial institutions serve as intermediaries between suppliers (savers) and users (borrowers) of funds.

commercial bank A financial institution that offers a full range of financial services to individuals, businesses, and government agencies.

COMMERCIAL BANKS   A **commercial bank** offers a full range of financial services, including checking, savings, and lending, along with many other services. Commercial banks are organized as corporations, with investors (stockholders) contributing the capital the banks need to operate. In recent years, many banks have opened full-service branch offices in grocery stores and drug stores.

savings and loan association (S&L) A financial institution that traditionally specialized in savings accounts and mortgage loans.

SAVINGS AND LOAN ASSOCIATIONS   While the commercial bank traditionally served businesses and wealthy individuals, the **savings and loan association (S&L)** specialized in savings accounts and loans for mortgages. Today, these organizations have expanded their services to include checking accounts, specialized savings plans, loans to businesses, and investment services.

mutual savings bank A financial institution that is owned by depositors and specializes in savings accounts and mortgage loans.

MUTUAL SAVINGS BANKS   Another financial institution with an emphasis on individuals is the **mutual savings bank,** which is owned by depositors and also specializes in savings accounts and mortgage loans. Mutual savings banks are located mainly in the northeastern United States. Unlike the profits of other types of financial institutions, the profits of a mutual savings bank go to the depositors, paying higher rates on savings.

Exhibit [4-5]

Types of Financial
Institutions

Deposit-Type Institutions	Nondeposit Institutions	Problematic Financial Businesses
• Commercial banks • Savings and loan associations • Mutual savings banks • Credit unions	• Life insurance companies • Investment companies • Finance companies • Mortgage companies	• Pawnshops • Check-cashing outlets • Payday loans • Rent-to-own centers

CREDIT UNIONS   A **credit union** is a user-owned, nonprofit, cooperative financial institution. Traditionally, credit union members had to have a common bond such as work, church, or community affiliation. As the common bond restriction was loosened, the membership of credit unions increased. Today, more than 80 million people belong to over 9,500 credit unions in the United States. Each year, consumer surveys report lower fees for checking accounts, lower loan rates, and higher levels of user satisfaction for credit unions compared to other financial institutions. Most credit unions offer credit cards, mortgages, home equity loans, direct deposit, cash machines, safe deposit boxes, and investment services.

Apply *Yourself*

Objective 2

Using the Web site for the Credit Union National Association (www.cuna.org) or other sources, obtain information about joining a credit union and the services offered by this type of financial institution.

credit union A user-owned, nonprofit, cooperative financial institution that is organized for the benefit of its members.

Nondeposit Institutions

Financial services are also available from institutions such as life insurance companies, investment companies, finance companies, and mortgage companies.

LIFE INSURANCE COMPANIES   While the main purpose of life insurance is to provide financial security for dependents, many life insurance policies contain savings and investment features. In recent years, life insurance companies have expanded to include investment and retirement planning services.

INVESTMENT COMPANIES   Investment companies, also referred to as *mutual funds,* offer banking-type services. A common service of these organizations is the **money market fund,** a combination savings–investment plan in which the investment company uses your money to purchase a variety of short-term financial instruments. Your earnings are based on the interest the investment company receives. Unlike accounts at most banks, savings and loan associations, and credit unions, investment company accounts are not covered by federal deposit insurance.

money market fund A savings–investment plan offered by investment companies, with earnings based on investments in various short-term financial instruments.

FINANCE COMPANIES   Making loans to consumers and small businesses is the main function of finance companies. These loans have short and intermediate terms with higher rates than most other lenders charge. Most finance companies have also expanded their activities to offer other financial planning services.

MORTGAGE COMPANIES   Mortgage companies are organized primarily to provide loans for home purchases. Chapter 7 discusses the activities of mortgage companies.

Problematic Financial Businesses

Would you pay $8 to cash a $100 check? Or pay $20 to borrow $100 for two weeks? Many people without ready access to financial services (especially low-income consumers) use pawnshops, check-cashing outlets, loan stores, and rent-to-own centers.

PAWNSHOPS   Pawnshops make loans based on the value of tangible possessions such as jewelry or other valuable items. Many low- and moderate-income families use these organizations to obtain cash loans quickly. Pawnshops charge higher fees than other financial institutions. Thousands of consumers are increasingly in need of small loans— usually $50 to $75, to be repaid in 30 to 45 days. Pawnshops have become the "neighborhood bankers" and the "local shopping malls," since they provide both lending and retail shopping services, selling items that owners do not redeem. While states regulate the interest rates charged by pawnshops, 3 percent a month or higher is common.

CHECK-CASHING OUTLETS   Most financial institutions will not cash a check unless you have an account. The more than 6,000 check-cashing outlets (CCOs) charge anywhere from 1 to 20 percent of the face value of a check; the average cost is 2 to 3 percent. However, for a low-income family, that can be a significant portion of the total household budget. CCOs also offer services, including electronic tax filing, money orders, private postal boxes, utility bill payment, and the sale of transit tokens. A person can usually obtain most of these services for less at other locations.

PAYDAY LOANS   Many consumer organizations caution against using payday loans, also referred to as *cash advances, check advance loans, postdated check loans,* and *delayed deposit loans.* Desperate borrowers pay annual interest rates of as much as 780 percent and more to obtain needed cash from payday loan companies. These enterprises have increased to more than 8,000. The most frequent users of payday loans are workers who have become trapped by debts or who have been driven into debt by misfortune.

In a typical payday loan, a consumer writes a personal check for $115 to borrow $100 for 14 days. The payday lender agrees to hold the check until the next payday. This $15 finance charge for the 14 days translates into an annual percentage rate of 391 percent. Some consumers "roll over" their loans, paying another $15 for the $100 loan for the next 14 days. After a few rollovers, the finance charge can exceed the amount borrowed. The Chicago Department of Consumer Services has reported annual rates ranging from 659 to 1,300 percent for some payday loans.

RENT-TO-OWN CENTERS   Years ago, people who rented furniture and appliances found few deluxe items available. Today rental businesses offer big-screen televisions, seven-piece cherrywood bedroom sets, and personal computers. The rent-to-purchase industry is defined as stores that lease products to consumers who can own the item if they complete a certain number of monthly or weekly payments.

In Wisconsin, more than 10,000 customers of the Rent-A-Center chain became part of a class action lawsuit seeking refunds of finance charges for rented merchandise. The suit accused the rental chain of illegally charging interest rates as high as 100 percent to rent televisions and other appliances, often to customers in low-income areas.

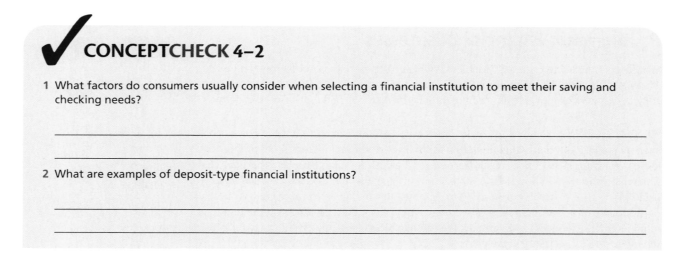

✔ CONCEPTCHECK 4–2

1 What factors do consumers usually consider when selecting a financial institution to meet their saving and checking needs?

_____

_____

2 What are examples of deposit-type financial institutions?

_____

_____

3 Match the following descriptions with the appropriate financial institution.

a. commercial bank   _____ Commonly used by people without a bank account.

b. credit union   _____ Investment services accompany main business focus.

c. life insurance company   _____ Traditionally provides widest range of financial services.

d. check-cashing outlet   _____ Offers lower fee costs for members.

Comparing Savings Plans

A savings plan is vital to attain financial goals. A range of savings alternatives exist (Exhibit 4–6). The many types of savings plans can be grouped into the following main categories.

> **OBJECTIVE 3**
> Assess various types of savings plans.

Regular Savings Accounts

Regular savings accounts, also called *passbook* or *statement accounts,* usually involve a low or no minimum balance and allow you to withdraw money as needed. Banks, savings and loan associations, and other financial institutions offer regular savings accounts. At a credit union, these savings plans are called *share accounts.*

Exhibit [4-6] Savings Alternatives

Type of Account	Benefits	Drawbacks
Regular savings accounts/ passbook accounts/share accounts	Low minimum balance Ease of withdrawal Insured	Low rate of return
Certificates of deposit (CDs)	Guaranteed rate of return for time of CD Insured	Possible penalty for early withdrawal Minimum deposit
Interest-earning checking accounts	Checking privileges Interest earned Insured	Service charge for going below minimum balance Cost or printing checks; other fees may apply
Money market accounts	Favorable rate of return (based on current interest rates) Allows some check writing Insured	Higher minimum balance than regular savings accounts No interest or service charge if below a certain balance
Money market funds	Favorable rate of return (based on current interest rates) Some check writing	Minimum balance Not insured
U.S. savings bonds	Fairly good rate of return (varies with current interest rates) Low minimum deposit Government guaranteed Exempt from state and local income taxes	Lower rate when redeemed before five years

Certificates of Deposit

certificate of deposit (CD) A savings plan requiring that a certain amount be left on deposit for a stated time period to earn a specified interest rate.

Higher earnings are available to savers when they leave money on deposit for a set time period. A **certificate of deposit (CD)** is a savings plan requiring that a certain amount be left on deposit for a stated time period (ranging from 30 days to five or more years) to earn a specific rate of return. These time deposits can be an attractive and a safe savings alternative. However, most financial institutions impose a penalty for early withdrawal of CD funds.

TYPES OF CDS   Financial institutions offer certificates of deposit with various features:

- *Rising-rate* or *bump-up CDs* have higher rates at various intervals. However, this rate may be in effect for only a couple of months.
- *Stock-indexed CDs* have earnings based on the stock market with higher earnings in times of strong stock performance. At other times, you may earn no interest and may even lose part of your savings.
- *Callable CDs* start with higher rates and long-term maturities. However, the bank may "call" the account after a stipulated period, such as one or two years, if interest rates drop. When the call option is exercised, the saver receives the original investment principal and any interest that has been earned.
- *Promotional CDs* attempt to attract savers with gifts or special rates. A Boulder, Colorado, bank offered Rolex watches, archery equipment, and Zodiac inflatable boats in lieu of interest. Compare the value of the item to the lost interest.

MANAGING CDS   When first buying or *rolling over* a CD (buying a new one at maturity), investigate potential earnings and costs. Do not allow your financial institution to automatically roll over your money into another CD for the same term. If interest rates have dropped, you might consider a shorter maturity. Or if you believe rates are at a peak and you won't need the money for some time, obtain a CD with a longer term.

Consider creating a CD *portfolio* with CDs maturing at different times, for example, $2,000 in a three-month CD, $2,000 in a six-month CD, $2,000 in a one-year CD, and $2,000 in a two-year CD. This will give you some degree of liquidity and flexibility when you reinvest your funds.

Interest-Earning Checking Accounts

Checking accounts frequently have a savings feature. These interest-earning accounts usually pay a low interest rate.

Money Market Accounts and Funds

money market account A savings account offered by banks, savings and loan associations, and credit unions that requires a minimum balance and has earnings based on market interest rates.

To provide savers with higher interest rates, a savings plan with a floating interest rate was created. A **money market account** is a savings account that requires a minimum balance and has earnings based on the changing market level of interest rates. Money market accounts may allow a limited number of checks to be written and generally impose a fee when the account balance goes below the required minimum, usually $1,000.

Both money market accounts and money market funds offer earnings based on current interest rates, and both have minimum-balance restrictions and allow check writing. The major difference is in safety. Money market *accounts* at banks and savings and loan associations are covered by federal deposit insurance. This is not true of money market *funds,* which are a product of investment and insurance companies. Since money market funds invest mainly in short-term (less than a year) government and corporate securities, however, they are usually quite safe.

U.S. Savings Bonds

In recent years, to attract more savers, the Treasury Department has used a floating interest rate on savings bonds. Earnings rise and fall based on the level of interest rates. Series EE bonds (called Patriot Bonds after September 11, 2001) may be purchased for amounts ranging from $25 to $5,000 (face values of $50 to $10,000, respectively). You must hold bonds at least five years to earn the stated rate. If you redeem bonds within five years of purchase, you earn a lower rate. Between the time the bond is six months and five years old, your money earns a slightly higher rate every six months. Series EE bonds continue to earn interest for 30 years, well beyond the time at which the face value is reached.

Series EE bonds have two main tax advantages: (1) the interest earned is exempt from state and local taxes and (2) you do not have to pay federal income tax on earnings until the bonds are redeemed.

EE bonds that have reached face value may be exchanged for Series HH bonds to defer the taxes. The taxes owed for interest earned on the EE bonds will not be due until the HH bonds are cashed in or reach maturity. Series HH bonds pay interest in cash twice a year. This interest is taxed as current income. The semiannual interest payments of HH bonds make them a popular source of retirement income.

Redeemed Series EE bonds may be exempt from federal income tax if the funds are used to pay tuition and fees at a college, university, or qualified technical school for yourself or a dependent. The bonds must be purchased by an individual who is at least 24 years old, and they must be issued in the names of one or both parents. These provisions have been designed to assist low- and middle-income households; people whose incomes exceed a certain amount do not qualify for the exemption.

Banks and other financial institutions sell U.S. savings bonds; they may also be purchased online. Lost, stolen, or destroyed savings bonds will be replaced by the government free of charge.

Apply Yourself!

Objective 3

Conduct online research to obtain past and current data on various interest rates (such as prime rate, T-bill rate, mortgage rate, corporate bond rate, and six-month CD rate). Information may be obtained at www.federalreserve.gov and other Web sites. How do these rates affect various personal financial decisions?

Key Web Site for Savings Bonds
www.savingsbonds.gov.

Evaluating Savings Plans

Selection of a savings plan is usually influenced by the rate of return, inflation, tax considerations, liquidity, safety, restrictions, and fees.

RATE OF RETURN   Earnings on savings can be measured by the **rate of return,** or *yield,* the percentage of increase in the value of your savings from earned interest. For example, a $100 savings account that earned $5 after a year would have a rate of return, or yield, of 5 percent. This rate of return was determined by dividing the interest earned ($5) by the amount in the savings account ($100). The yield on your savings usually will be greater than the stated interest rate.

Compounding refers to interest that is earned on previously earned interest. Each time interest is added to your savings, the next interest amount is computed on the new balance in the account. The more frequent the compounding, the higher your rate of return will be. For example, $100 in a savings account that earns 6 percent compounded annually will increase $6 after a year. But the same $100 in a 6 percent account compounded daily will earn $6.19 for the year. Although this difference may seem slight, large amounts held in savings for long periods of time will result in far higher differences (see Exhibit 4–7).

The *Truth in Savings Act* requires financial institutions to disclose the following information on savings account plans: (1) fees on deposit accounts; (2) the interest rate;

rate of return The percentage of increase in the value of savings as a result of interest earned; also called *yield.*

compounding A process that calculates interest based on previously earned interest.

Exhibit [4-7]

Compounding Frequency
Affects the Saving Yield

Shorter compounding periods result in higher yields. This chart shows the growth of
$10,000, earning a rate of 8 percent, but with different compounding methods.

End of year	COMPOUNDING METHOD			
	Daily	Monthly	Quarterly	Annually
1	$10,832.78	$10,830.00	$10,824.32	$10,800.00
2	11,743.91	11,728.88	11,716.59	11,664.00
3	12,712.17	12,702.37	12,682.41	12,597.12
4	13,770.82	13,756.66	13,727.85	13,604.89
5	14,917.62	14.898.46	14,859.46	14,693.28
Annual yield	8.33%	8.30%	8.24%	8.00%

annual percentage yield (APY)
The percentage rate
expressing the total amount
of interest that would be
received on a $100 deposit
based on the annual rate
and frequency of
compounding for a 365-day
period.

(3) the annual percentage yield (APY); and (4) other terms and conditions of the savings plan. Truth in Savings (TIS) defines **annual percentage yield (APY)** as the percentage rate expressing the total amount of interest that would be received on a $100 deposit based on the annual rate and frequency of compounding for a 365-day period. APY reflects the amount of interest a saver should expect to earn.

INFLATION   The rate of return you earn on your savings should be compared with the inflation rate. When inflation was over 10 percent, people with money in savings accounts earning 5 or 6 percent were experiencing a loss in the buying power of that money. In general, as the inflation rate increases, the interest rates offered to savers also increase.

TAXES   Like inflation, taxes reduce interest earned on savings. For example, a 10 percent return for a saver in a 28 percent tax bracket means a real return of 7.2 percent (the Figure It Out box shows how to compute the after-tax savings rate of return). As discussed in Chapter 3, several tax-exempt and tax-deferred savings plans and investments can increase your real rate of return.

LIQUIDITY   *Liquidity* allows you to withdraw your money on short notice without a loss of value or fees. Some savings plans impose penalties for early withdrawal or have other restrictions. With certain types of savings certificates and accounts, early withdrawal may be penalized by a loss of interest or a lower earnings rate. Consider the degree of liquidity you desire in relation to your savings goals. To achieve long-term financial goals, many people trade off liquidity for a higher return.

SAFETY   Most savings plans at banks, savings and loan associations, and credit unions are insured by agencies affiliated with the federal government. This protection prevents a loss of money due to the failure of the insured institution. While a few financial institutions have failed in recent years, savers with deposits covered by federal insurance have not lost any money. Depositors of failed organizations either have been paid the amounts in their accounts or have had the accounts taken over by a financially stable institution.

The Federal Deposit Insurance Corporation (FDIC) administers separate insurance funds: the Bank Insurance Fund and the Savings Association Insurance Fund (SAIF). Credit unions may obtain deposit insurance through the National Credit Union Association (NCUA). Some state-chartered credit unions have opted for a private insurance program.

SAVINGS | Banks can fail, and not all deposits are insured. *By Joan Goldwasser*

Watch your
BALANCE

T RY THIS QUIZ: What percentage of money in U.S. bank accounts is uninsured? a. 5%; b. 10%; c. 20%; d. 33%?

Considering that the federal government guarantees up to $100,000 for each depositor, you might be inclined to pick one of the lower figures. But in fact, $1.7 trillion of the $5.2 trillion residing in banks and thrifts—33%—is uninsured.

Although it's infrequent, banks do still fail, and depositors do lose money: Three banks went under in 2003. In one case—Southern Pacific Bank, in Torrance, Cal.—depositors lost about 25% of the $30 million in uninsured deposits. That's why you need to understand the rules.

The $100,000 cap is *per bank,* so if you spread your money among ten banks, your insured amount can reach $1 million. It is also possible to have more than $100,000 of insured deposits in a single bank: Deposits in accounts with different legal ownership are separately insured. For example, you could have an individual account, a joint account with your spouse, several testamentary or payable-on-death accounts for your children, plus a retirement account, all at the same bank, and each account would be insured for up to $100,000. If accrued interest pushes an account balance over $100,000, the excess is vulnerable if the bank fails. **K**

Source: Reprinted by permission from the March issue of *Kiplinger's Personal Finance,* Copyright © 2004 The Kiplinger Washington Editors, Inc.

1. What are some situations in which a person might have in a bank funds that are not covered by federal deposit insurance?

_____

_____

_____

_____

2. What actions can savers take to expand their deposit insurance beyond $100,000?

_____

_____

_____

3. Locate additional information about federal deposit insurance at www.kiplinger.com, www.fdic.gov, or from other Web sites.

_____

_____

_____

_____

Figure It Out!

AFTER-TAX SAVINGS RATE OF RETURN

The taxability of interest on your savings reduces your real rate of return. In other words, you lose some portion of your interest to taxes. This calculation consists of the following steps:

1. Determine your top tax bracket for federal income taxes.

2. Subtract this rate, expressed as a decimal, from 1.0.

3. Multiply the result by the yield on your savings account.

4. This number, expressed as a percentage, is your after-tax rate of return.

For example,

1. You are in the 28 percent tax bracket.

2. $1.0 - 0.28 = 0.72$.

3. If the yield on your savings account is 6.25 percent, $0.0625 \times 0.72 = 0.045$.

4. Your after-tax rate of return is 4.5 percent.

You may use the same procedure to determine the *real rate of return* on your savings based on inflation. For example, if you are earning 6 percent on savings and inflation is 5 percent, your real rate of return (after inflation) is 5.7 percent: $0.06 \times (1 - 0.05) = 0.057$.

CALCULATIONS

1. What would be the after-tax return for a person who is receiving 4 percent on savings and is in a 15 percent tax bracket? _____%

2. What would be the after-tax value of $100 earned in interest for a person who is in a 31 percent tax bracket? $_____

Sheet 11 Comparing Savings Plans

Sheet 12 Using Savings Plans to Achieve Financial Goals

The FDIC insures deposits of up to $100,000 per person per financial institution; a joint account is considered to belong proportionally to each name on the account. For example, if you have a $70,000 individual account and an $80,000 joint account with a relative in the same financial institution, $10,000 of your savings will not be covered by federal deposit insurance ($70,000 plus one-half of $80,000 exceeds the $100,000 limit). However, by using combinations of individual, joint, and trust accounts in different financial institutions, it is possible to have federal deposit insurance cover amounts that exceed $100,000. Remember, the maximum coverage of federal deposit insurance is based on each depositor, not on each account. The best advice is to never keep more than $100,000 in one financial institution. Be careful, however, since different branch offices count as the same institution. Also, mergers in the financial service industry may bring accounts from different banks together.

RESTRICTIONS AND FEES   Other limitations can affect your choice of a savings program. For example, there may be a delay between the time interest is earned and the time it is added to your account. This means the interest will not be available for your immediate use. Also, some institutions charge a transaction fee for each deposit or withdrawal. Some financial institutions offer a "free gift" when a certain savings amount is deposited. To receive this gift, you have to leave your money on deposit for a certain time period, or you may receive less interest, since some of the earnings are used to cover the cost of the "free" items.

✔ CONCEPTCHECK 4–3

1 What are the main types of savings plans offered by financial institutions?

_____

_____

2 How does a money market *account* differ from a money market *fund*?

_____

_____

3 What are the benefits of U.S. savings bonds?

_____

4 How do inflation and taxes affect earnings on savings?

_____

_____

5 In the following financial situations, check the box that is the major influence for the person when selecting a savings plan:

Financial planning situation	Rate of return	Inflation	Taxes	Liquidity	Safety
a. An older couple needs easy access to funds for living expenses.					
b. A person is concerned with loss of buying power of funds on deposit.					
c. A saver desires to maximize earnings from the savings plan.					
d. A middle-aged person wants assurance that the funds are safe.					

Comparing Payment Methods

While check writing is still a major portion of consumer transactions in our society, debit and credit cards are more frequently used for retail transactions.

Electronic Payments

Transactions not involving cash, checks, or credit cards have expanded with technology, improved security, and increased consumer acceptance.

DEBIT CARD TRANSACTIONS   Most retail stores, restaurants, and other businesses accept debit cards, also called check cards, issued by Visa and MasterCard. When the debit card transaction is processed, the amount of the purchase is deducted from your checking account. Most debit cards can be used two ways: (1) with your signature, like a credit card, or (2) with your personal identification number (PIN), like an ATM card.

ONLINE PAYMENTS   Banks and Internet companies are serving as third parties to facilitate online bill payments. Some of these Internet companies are www.paypal.com, www.checkfree.com, and www.paytrust.com. When using

OBJECTIVE 4
Evaluate different types of payment methods.

Apply *Yourself!*

Objective 4

Observe customers making payments in a retail store. How often are cash, checks, credit cards, or cash cards used?

these services, be sure to consider the monthly charge as well as online security and customer service availability. Also on the Web are "cyber cash" services creating their own *e-money* that serves as a medium of exchange for online transactions.

STORED-VALUE CARDS   Prepaid cards for telephone service, transit fares, highway tolls, laundry service, and school lunches are common. Some of these stored-value cards are disposable; others can be reloaded with an additional amount.

SMART CARDS   These "electronic wallets" are similar to other ATM cards. However, the imbedded microchip stores prepaid amounts as well as information with account balances, transaction records, insurance information, and medical history.

Checking Accounts

Despite increased use of electronic payment systems, a checking account is still a necessity for most people. Checking accounts fall into three major categories: regular checking accounts, activity accounts, and interest-earning checking accounts.

REGULAR CHECKING ACCOUNTS   *Regular checking accounts* usually have a monthly service charge that you may avoid by keeping a minimum balance in the account. Some financial institutions will waive the monthly fee if you keep a certain amount in savings. Avoiding the monthly service charge can be beneficial. For example, a monthly fee of $7.50 results in $90 a year. However, you lose interest on the minimum-balance amount in a non-interest-earning account.

ACTIVITY ACCOUNTS   *Activity accounts* charge a fee for each check written and sometimes a fee for each deposit in addition to a monthly service charge. However, you do not have to maintain a minimum balance. An activity account is most appropriate for people who write only a few checks each month and are unable to maintain the required minimum balance.

INTEREST-EARNING CHECKING   *Interest-earning checking accounts* usually require a minimum balance. If the account balance goes below this amount, you may not earn interest and will likely incur a service charge. These are called *share draft accounts* at credit unions.

Evaluating Checking Accounts

Would you rather have a checking account that pays interest and requires a $1,000 minimum balance or an account that doesn't pay interest and requires a $300 minimum balance? This decision requires evaluating factors such as restrictions, fees and charges, interest, and special services (see Exhibit 4–8).

RESTRICTIONS   The most common limitation on a checking account is the required amount that must be kept on deposit to earn interest or avoid a service charge. In the past, financial institutions placed restrictions on the holding period for deposited checks. A waiting period was usually required before you could access the funds. The Check Clearing for the 21st Century Act (known as Check 21) shortens the processing time. This law establishes the *substitute check,* which is a digital reproduction of the original paper check, and is considered a legal equivalent of the original check.

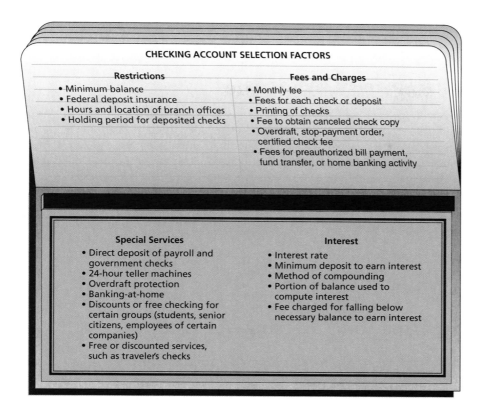

Exhibit [4-8]

Checking Account Selection Factors

FEES AND CHARGES   Nearly all financial institutions require a minimum balance or impose service charges for checking accounts. When using an interest-bearing checking account, compare your earnings with any service charge or fee. Also, consider the cost of lost or reduced interest resulting from maintaining the minimum balance. Checking account fees have increased in recent years. Items such as check printing, overdraft fees, and stop-payment orders have doubled or tripled in price at some financial institutions.

INTEREST   The interest rate, the frequency of compounding, and the interest computation method will affect the earnings on your checking account.

SPECIAL SERVICES   Many financial institutions attempting to reduce costs do not return canceled checks. Copies of a canceled check may be retrieved online by customers or by the financial institution from its microfilm file for a fee.

   Overdraft protection is an automatic loan made to checking customers for checks written in excess of their balance. This service is convenient but costly. Most overdraft plans make loans based on $50 or $100 increments. An overdraft of just $1 might trigger a $50 loan and corresponding finance charges of perhaps 18 percent. But overdraft protection can be less costly than the fee charged for a check you write when you do not have enough money on deposit to cover it. That fee may be $20 or more. Many financial institutions will allow you to cover checking account overdrafts with an automatic transfer from a savings account for a nominal fee.

   Beware of checking accounts packaged with several services (safe deposit box, traveler's checks, low-rate loans, and travel insurance) for a single monthly fee. This may

DID YOU KNOW?

A bounced check may result in not only a fee of $20 or more but also restrictions on the acceptance of your checks in the future. Some check-approval systems may keep your name on a "restricted" list for a period of six months to five years.

overdraft protection An automatic loan made to checking account customers to cover the amount of checks written in excess of the available balance in the checking account.

sound like a good value; however, financial experts observe that only a small group of people make use of all services in the package.

Other Payment Methods

A *certified check* is a personal check with guaranteed payment. The amount of the check is deducted from your balance when the financial institution certifies the check. A *cashier's check* is a check of a financial institution. You may purchase one by paying the amount of the check plus a fee. You may purchase a *money order* in a similar manner from financial institutions, post offices, and stores. Certified checks, cashier's checks, and money orders allow you to make a payment that the recipient knows is valid.

Traveler's checks allow you to make payments when you are away from home. This payment form requires you to sign each check twice. First, you sign the traveler's checks when you purchase them. Then, to identify you as the authorized person, you sign them again as you cash them. Electronic traveler's checks, in the form of a prepaid travel card, are also available. The card allows travelers visiting other nations to get local currency from an ATM.

Managing Your Checking Account

Obtaining and using a checking account involves several activities.

OPENING A CHECKING ACCOUNT   First, decide who the owner of the account is. Only one person is allowed to write checks on an *individual account*. A *joint account* has two or more owners. Both an individual account and a joint account require a signature card. This document is a record of the official signatures of the person or persons authorized to write checks on the account.

MAKING DEPOSITS   A *deposit ticket* is used for adding funds to your checking account. On this document, you list the amounts of cash and checks being deposited. Each check you deposit requires an *endorsement*—your signature on the back of the check—to authorize the transfer of the funds into your account. The three common endorsement forms are:

- A *blank endorsement* is just your signature, which should be used only when you are actually depositing or cashing a check, since a check may be cashed by anyone once it has been signed.
- A *restrictive endorsement* consists of the words *for deposit only,* followed by your signature, which is especially useful when you are depositing checks.
- A *special endorsement* allows you to transfer a check to someone else with the words *pay to the order of* followed by the name of the other person and then your signature.

WRITING CHECKS   Before writing a check, record the information in your check register and deduct the amount of the check from your balance. Many checking account customers use duplicate checks to maintain a record of their current balance.

The procedure for proper check writing has the following steps: (1) record the date; (2) write the name of the person or organization receiving the payment; (3) record the amount of the check in numerals; (4) write the amount of the check in words; checks for less than a dollar should be written as "only 79 cents," for example, and cross out the word *dollars* on the check; (5) sign the check; (6) note the reason for payment.

A *stop-payment order* may be necessary if a check is lost or stolen. Most banks do not honor checks with "stale" dates, usually six months old or older. The fee for a stop-

Personal Finance in Practice

ARE YOUR AVOIDING IDENTITY THEFT?

People who put their Social Security and driver's license numbers on their checks are making identity theft fairly easy. With one check, a con artist could know your Social Security, driver's license, and bank account numbers as well as your address, phone number, and perhaps even a sample of your signature.

An attorney had his wallet stolen. Within a week, the thieves ordered an expensive monthly cell phone package, applied for a Visa credit card, had a credit line approved to buy a Gateway computer, and received a PIN number from the Department of Motor Vehicles to change his driving record information online.

Identity fraud can range from passing bad checks and using stolen credit cards to theft of another person's total financial existence. The following quiz can help you avoid becoming one of the more than 1,000 people who each day have their identities stolen by con artists.

If you are a victim of identity theft, take the following actions:

- File a police report immediately in the area where the item was stolen. This proves you were diligent and is a first step toward an investigation (if there ever is one).

- Call the three national credit reporting organizations *immediately* to place a fraud alert on your name and Social Security number. The numbers are: Equifax, 1-800-525-6285; Experian (formerly TRW), 1-888-397-3742; and Trans Union, 1-800-680-7289.

- Contact the Social Security Administration fraud line at 1-800-269-0271.

Additional information on financial privacy and identity theft is available at www.identitytheft.org, www.idfraud.org, www.privacyrights.org, and www.pirg.org/calpirg/consumer/privacy.

Which of the following actions have you taken to avoid identity theft?	Yes	No	Action needed
1. I have only my initials and last name on my checks so a person will not know how I sign my checks.			
2. I do not put the full account number on my checks when paying a bill; I put only the last four numbers.			
3. I have my work phone and a P.O. box (if applicable) on my checks instead of home information.			
4. I don't put my Social Security number on any document unless it is legally required.			
5. I shred or burn financial information containing account or Social Security numbers.			
6. I use passwords other than maiden names.			
7. I do not mail bills from my home mailbox, especially if it is out by the street.			
8. I check my credit report once or twice a year to make sure it is correct.			
9. I ask to have my name removed from mailing lists operated by credit agencies and companies offering credit promotions.			
10. I have a photocopy of the contents of my wallet (both sides of each item) as a record to cancel accounts if necessary.			

payment commonly ranges from $10 to $20. If several checks are missing or you lose your checkbook, closing the account and opening a new one is likely to be less costly than paying several stop-payment fees.

RECONCILING YOUR CHECKING ACCOUNT
Each month you will receive a *bank statement* summarizing deposits, checks paid, ATM withdrawals, interest earned, and fees such as service charges and printing of checks. The balance reported on the statement will usually differ from the balance in your checkbook. Reasons for a

difference may include checks that have not yet cleared, deposits not received by the bank, and interest earned.

To determine the correct balance, prepare a *bank reconciliation,* to account for differences between the bank statement and your checkbook balance. This process involves the following steps:

1. Compare the checks written with those reported as paid on the statement. Use the canceled checks, or compare your check register with the check numbers reported on the bank statement. *Subtract* from the *bank statement balance* the total of the checks written but not yet cleared.
2. Determine whether any deposits made are not on the statement; *add* the amount of the outstanding deposits to the *bank statement balance.*
3. *Subtract* fees or charges on the bank statement and ATM withdrawals from your *checkbook balance.*
4. *Add* any interest earned to your *checkbook balance.*

Sheet 13
Comparing
Payment
Methods; Bank
Reconciliation

At this point, the revised balances for both the checkbook and the bank statement should be the same. If the two do not match, check your math; make sure every check and deposit was recorded correctly.

✔ CONCEPTCHECK 4–4

1 Are checking accounts that earn interest preferable to regular checking accounts? Why or why not?

_____

_____

2 What factors are commonly considered when selecting a checking account?

_____

_____

3 For the following situations, select and describe a payment method that would be appropriate for the needs of the person.

Payment situation	Suggested payment method
a. A need to send funds for a purchase from an organization that requires guaranteed payment.	
b. Traveling to Asia, you desire to be able to access funds in the local currencies of various countries.	
c. A desire to pay bills using your home computer instead of writing checks.	
d. You write only a few checks a month and you want to minimize your costs.	

4 Based on the following information, determine the true balance in your checking account.

Balance in your checkbook, $356   Balance on bank statement, $472

Service charge and other fees, $15   Interest earned on the account, $4

Total of outstanding checks, $187   Deposits in transit, $60

Back to Getting Personal

Reevaluate your Getting Personal responses at the beginning of the chapter. Which items might have different answers now or in the future as a result of studying this chapter?

_____

_____

_____

Chapter Summary

Objective 1 Financial products such as savings plans, checking accounts, loans, trust services, and electronic banking are used for managing daily financial activities.

Objective 2 Commercial banks, savings and loan associations, mutual savings banks, credit unions, life insurance companies, investment companies, finance companies, mortgage companies, pawnshops, and check-cashing outlets may be compared on the basis of services offered, rates and fees, safety, convenience, and special programs available to customers.

Objective 3 Commonly used savings plans include regular savings accounts, certificates of deposit, interest-earning checking accounts, money market accounts, money market funds, and U.S. savings bonds. Savings plans may be evaluated on the basis of rate of return, inflation, tax considerations, liquidity, safety, restrictions, and fees.

Objective 4 Debit cards, online payment systems, and stored-value cards are increasing in use for payment activities. Regular checking accounts, activity accounts, and interest-earning checking accounts can be compared with regard to restrictions (such as a minimum balance), fees and charges, interest, and special services.

Key Terms

annual percentage yield (APY)   100
asset management account   91
automatic teller machine (ATM)   91
certificate of deposit (CD)   98
commercial bank   94
compounding   99

credit union   95
debit card   92
money market account   98
money market fund   95
mutual savings bank   94

overdraft protection   105
rate of return   99
savings and loan association
   (S&L)   94
trust   91

Problems and Questions

1. What might be a savings goal for a person who buys a five-year CD paying 4.27 percent instead of an 18-month savings certificate paying 2.29 percent?

2. For each of the following situations, determine the savings amount. Use the time value of money tables in Chapter 1 (Exhibit 1–3) or Appendix A.

   a. What would be the value of a savings account started with $500, earning 6 percent (compounded annually) after 10 years?

   b. Brenda Young desires to have $10,000 eight years from now for her daughter's college fund. If she will earn

www.mhhe.com/kdh

7 percent (compounded annually) on her money, what amount should she deposit now? Use the present value of a single amount calculation.

c. What amount would you have if you deposited $1,500 a year for 30 years at 8 percent (compounded annually)?

3. What would be the annual percentage yield for a savings account that earned $56 in interest on $800 over the past 365 days?

4. With a 28 percent marginal tax rate, would a tax-free yield of 7 percent or a taxable yield of 9.5 percent give you a better return on your savings? Why?

5. Conduct Internet research to compare the rates received for various types of savings accounts at various financial institutions in different geographic regions. Prepare a summary of current rates of return for various savings accounts, money market accounts, and certificates of deposit of various lengths.

6. What is the annual opportunity cost of a checking account that requires a $350 minimum balance to avoid service charges? Assume an interest rate of 3 percent.

7. What would be the net *annual* cost of the following checking accounts?
  a. Monthly fee, $3.75; processing fee, 25 cents per check; checks written, an average of 22 a month.

  b. Interest earnings of 6 percent with a $500 minimum balance; average monthly balance, $600; monthly service charge of $15 for falling below the minimum balance, which occurs three times a year (no interest earned in these months).

8. What fees and deductions may be overlooked when balancing your checking account?

9. *a.* What are potential benefits of an "overdraft protection" service for your checking account?

  b. What costs should a person consider before deciding to use the overdraft protection service?

Internet Connection

COMPARING ONLINE PAYMENT SYSTEMS

Compare the online bill payment services for (1) a bank, (2) a bill payment service (such as www.bills.com or www.paytrust.com), and (3) money management software.

	Online bank	Internet payment service	Software (MS Money, Quicken)
Name, Web site			
Description of online payment services; types of payments			
Cost (per month or per transaction)			
Security measures			
Potential concerns			

Case in Point

BEWARE OF HIDDEN BANKING FEES

"Wow! My account balance is a little lower than I expected," commented Lisa Cross as she reviewed her monthly bank statement. "Wait a minute! There's nearly $20 in fees for ATM withdrawals and other service charges," she cried out.

Many people do not realize the amount they pay each month for various bank fees. These charges result from various services that give customers convenience, reliability, and safety.

"Oh no! I also went below the minimum balance required for my *free* checking account," Lisa groaned. "That cost me $7.50!"

Lisa is not alone in her frustration with fees paid for financial services. While careless money management caused many of these charges, others could be reduced or eliminated by comparing costs at various financial institutions.

Many consumers are also upset with slow customer service and long waits in lines. These drawbacks have caused many customers to consider the use of online banking services. Whether using the Internet services of your current financial institution or starting an account with a "Web bank," you can gain faster access to your account. Other benefits may also be present. Often, costs of online banking services are lower than those in traditional settings. Online banking can also offer access to an expanded array of financial services. For example, some online

bank accounts include low-cost online investment trading and instant loan approval.

Lisa believes that online banking services provide her with an opportunity to better control her financial service costs. However, she also has concerns about introductory low costs, privacy, and security of transaction information.

Questions

1. What benefits might Lisa gain when using online banking services?

2. Based on information at www.bankrate.com, describe how Lisa could reduce her checking account costs and other banking fees.

3. What concerns might be associated with using online banking services?

Planning the Use of Financial Services

Financial Planning Activities: List (1) currently used services with financial institution information (name, address, phone); and (2) services that are likely to be needed in the future.

Suggested Web Sites: www.bankrate.com   www.kiplinger.com

Types of financial services	Current financial services used	Additional financial services needed
Payment services (checking, ATM, online bill payment, money orders)	Financial Institution	
Savings services (savings account, money market account, certificate of deposit, savings bonds)	Financial Institution	
Credit services (credit cards, personal loans, mortgage)	Financial Institution	
Other financial services (investments, trust account, tax planning)	Financial Institution	

What's Next for Your Personal Financial Plan?

- Assess whether the current types and sources of your financial services are appropriate.
- Determine additional financial services you may wish to make use of in the future.

Name: _____ **Date:** _____

Comparing Savings Plans

Financial Planning Activities: Obtain information online and from various financial institutions to compare savings plans on the factors listed below.

Suggested Web Sites: www.bankrate.com   www.banx.com

Type of savings plan (regular passbook account, special accounts, savings certificate, money market account, other)			
Financial institution			
Address/phone			
Web site			
Annual interest rate			
Annual percentage yield (APY)			
Frequency of compounding			
Insured by FDIC, NCUA, other			
Maximum amount insured			
Minimum initial deposit			
Minimum time period savings must be on deposit			
Penalties for early withdrawal			
Service charges/transaction fees, other costs, fees			
Additional services, other information			

What's Next for Your Personal Financial Plan?

• Based on this savings plan analysis, determine the best types for your current and future financial situation.

• When analyzing savings plans, what factors should you carefully investigate?

Name: _____   **Date:** _____

Using Savings Plans to Achieve Financial Goals

Financial Planning Activities: Record savings plan information along with the amount of your balance or income on a periodic basis.

Suggested Web Sites: www.savingsbonds.gov   www.fdic.gov

Regular savings account

Acct. No. _____
Financial institution
_____
Address _____
_____
Phone _____

Savings goal/Amount needed/Date needed: _____

Initial deposit: Date _____ $ _____
Balance: Date _____ $ _____
Date _____ $ _____
Date _____ $ _____
Date _____ $ _____

Certificate of deposit

Acct. No. _____
Financial institution
_____
Address _____
_____
Phone _____

Savings goal/Amount needed/Date needed: _____

Initial deposit: Date _____ $ _____
Balance: Date _____ $ _____
Date _____ $ _____
Date _____ $ _____
Date _____ $ _____

Money market/fund acct.

Acct. No. _____
Financial institution
_____
Address _____
_____
Phone _____

Savings goal/Amount needed/Date needed: _____

Initial deposit: Date _____ $ _____
Balance: Date _____ $ _____
Date _____ $ _____
Date _____ $ _____
Date _____ $ _____

U.S. savings bonds

Purchase location _____
_____
Address _____
_____
Phone _____

Savings goal/Amount needed/Date needed: _____

Purchase date: _____   Maturity date: _____
Amount: _____   Maturity date: _____

Purchase date: _____   Maturity date: _____
Amount: _____   Maturity date: _____

Other savings

Acct. No. _____
Financial institution
_____
Address _____
_____
Phone _____

Savings goal/Amount needed/Date needed: _____

Initial deposit: Date _____ $ _____
Balance: Date _____ $ _____
Date _____ $ _____
Date _____ $ _____
Date _____ $ _____

What's Next for Your Personal Financial Plan?

- Assess your current progress toward achieving various savings goals. Evaluate existing and new savings goals.
- Plan actions to expand the amount you are saving toward various savings goals.

Comparing payment methods; bank reconciliation

Financial Planning Activities: Compare checking accounts and payment services at various financial institutions (banks, savings and loan associations, credit unions, Web banks).

Suggested Web Sites: www.bankrate.com   www.kiplinger.com

Institution name			
Address			
Phone			
Web site			
Type of account (regular checking, activity account, bill payment service)			
Minimum balance			
Monthly charge below balance			
"Free" checking for students?			
Online banking services			
Branch/ATM locations			
Banking hours			
Other fees/costs			
Printing of checks			
Stop-payment order			
Overdrawn account			
Certified check			
ATM, other charges			
Other information			

Checking Account Reconciliation

Statement date:	**Statement Balance:**		$_____
Step 1: Compare the checks written with those paid on statement. *Subtract* total of outstanding checks from the bank balance.	Check No.	Amount	−$_____
Step 2: Determine whether any deposits are not on the statement; *add* the amount of the outstanding deposits to the *bank statement balance*.	Deposit date	Amount	+$_____
	Adjusted Balance		=$_____
	Checkbook Balance		
Step 3: *Subtract* fees or charges on the bank statement and ATM withdrawals from your *checkbook balance*.	Item	Amount	−$_____
Step 4: *Add* interest or direct deposits earned to your *checkbook balance*.			+$_____
Note: The two adjusted balances should be the same; if not, carefully check your math and check to see that deposits and checks recorded in your checkbook and on your statement are for the correct amounts.	**Adjusted Balance**		=$_____

5 Consumer Credit: Advantages, Disadvantages, Sources, and Costs

Objectives

In this chapter, you will learn to:

1. Analyze advantages and disadvantages of using consumer credit.
2. Assess the types and sources of consumer credit.
3. Determine whether you can afford a loan and how to apply for credit.
4. Determine the cost of credit by calculating interest using various interest formulas.
5. Develop a plan to protect your credit and manage your debts.

Why is this important?

Understanding the advantages and disadvantages of consumer credit as well as the types of credit that are available will enable you to make wise decisions regarding credit now and in the future. Understanding the costs involved in obtaining credit will give you the tools to acquire the best source of credit.

 Getting Personal

Do you know how to use credit wisely? For each of the following statements, select "yes" or "no" to indicate your behavior regarding these statements:

	Yes	No
1. I always attempt to pay my bills when they are due.	_____	_____
2. If I need more money for my expenses, I will borrow it.	_____	_____
3. Repaying my debt in a timely manner is important to me.	_____	_____
4. I pay only the minimum balance on my credit card bills each month.	_____	_____
5. I check my credit report before applying for a loan.	_____	_____

After studying this chapter, you will be asked to reconsider your responses to these items.

Your Personal Financial Plan Sheets

14. Consumer credit usage patterns.
15. Credit card/charge account comparison.
16. Consumer loan comparison.

What Is Consumer Credit?

OBJECTIVE 1

Analyze advantages and disadvantages of using consumer credit.

credit An arrangement to receive cash, goods, or services now and pay for them in the future.

consumer credit The use of credit for personal needs (except a home mortgage).

Credit is an arrangement to receive cash, goods, or services now and pay for them in the future. **Consumer credit** refers to the use of credit for personal needs (except a home mortgage) by individuals and families, in contrast to credit used for business purposes.

Consumer credit is based on trust in people's ability and willingness to pay bills when due. It works because people by and large are honest and responsible. But how does consumer credit affect our economy, and how is it affected by our economy?

The Importance of Consumer Credit in Our Economy

Consumer credit dates back to colonial times. Although credit was originally a privilege of the affluent, farmers came to use it extensively. No direct finance charges were imposed; instead, the cost of credit was added to the prices of goods. With the advent of the automobile in the early 1900s, installment credit, in which the debt is repaid in equal installments over a specified period of time, exploded on the American scene.

All economists now recognize consumer credit as a major force in the American economy. Any forecast or evaluation of the economy includes consumer spending trends and consumer credit as a sustaining force. To paraphrase an old political expression, as the consumer goes, so goes the U.S. economy.

Uses and Misuses of Credit

Using credit to purchase goods and services may allow consumers to be more efficient or more productive or to lead more satisfying lives. Many valid reasons can be found for using credit. A medical emergency may leave a person strapped for funds. A homemaker returning to the workforce may need a car. An item may cost less money now than it will cost later. Borrowing for a college education is another valid reason. But borrowing for everyday living expenses or financing a Corvette on credit when a Ford Escort is all your budget allows is probably not reasonable.

Using credit increases the amount of money a person can spend to purchase goods and services now. But the trade-off is that it decreases the amount of money that will be available to spend in the future. However, many people expect their incomes to increase and therefore expect to be able to make payments on past credit purchases and still make new purchases.

Here are some questions you should consider before you decide how and when to make a major purchase, for example, a car:

- Do I have the cash I need for the down payment?
- Do I want to use my savings for this purchase?
- Does the purchase fit my budget?
- Could I use the credit I need for this purchase in some better way?
- Could I postpone the purchase?

Apply *Yourself!*

Objective 1

Using Web research and discussion with family members and friends, prepare a list of advantages and disadvantages of using credit.

- What are the opportunity costs of postponing the purchase (alternative transportation costs, a possible increase in the price of the car)?
- What are the dollar costs and the psychological costs of using credit (interest, other finance charges, being in debt and responsible for making a monthly payment)?

If you decide to use credit, make sure the benefits of purchasing now (increased efficiency or productivity, a more satisfying life, etc.) outweigh the costs (financial and psychological) of using credit. Thus, credit, when effectively used, can help you have more and enjoy more. When misused, credit can result in default, bankruptcy, and loss of creditworthiness.

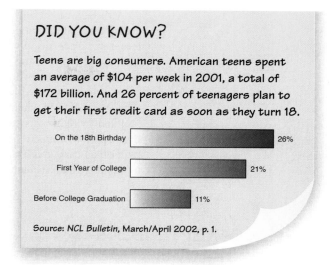

DID YOU KNOW?

Teens are big consumers. American teens spent an average of $104 per week in 2001, a total of $172 billion. And 26 percent of teenagers plan to get their first credit card as soon as they turn 18.

On the 18th Birthday	26%
First Year of College	21%
Before College Graduation	11%

Source: NCL Bulletin, March/April 2002, p. 1.

Advantages of Credit

Consumer credit enables people to enjoy goods and services now—a car, a home, an education, emergencies—and pay for them through payment plans based on future income.

Credit cards permit the purchase of goods even when funds are low. Customers with previously approved credit may receive other extras, such as advance notice of sales and the right to order by phone or to buy on approval. In addition, many shoppers believe that returning merchandise purchased on account is easier than returning cash purchases. Credit cards also provide shopping convenience and the efficiency of paying for several purchases with one monthly payment.

Credit is more than a substitute for cash. Many of the services it provides are taken for granted. Every time you turn on the water tap, click the light switch, or telephone a friend, you are using credit.

Using credit is safe, since charge accounts and credit cards let you shop and travel without carrying a large amount of cash. It offers convenience, since you need a credit card to make a hotel reservation, rent a car, and shop by phone or Internet. You may also use credit cards for identification when cashing checks, and the use of credit provides you with a record of expenses.

The use of credit cards can provide up to a 50-day "float," the time lag between when you make the purchase and when the lender deducts the balance from your checking account when payment is due. This float, offered by many credit card issuers, includes a grace period of 20 to 25 days. During the grace period, no finance charges are assessed on current purchases if the balance is paid in full each month within 25 days after billing.

Some corporations, such as General Electric Company and General Motors Corporation, issue their own Visa and MasterCard and offer rebates on purchases. In the late 1990s, however, some corporations began to eliminate these cards.

Finally, credit indicates stability. The fact that lenders consider you a good risk usually means you are a responsible individual. However, if you do not repay your debts in a timely manner, you will find that credit has many disadvantages.

Key Web Sites for
Money Management
www.moneymanagement.com
www.moneypage.com

Key Web Sites for
Consumer Credit
www.abcguides.com
www.lendingtree.com

Disadvantages of Credit

Perhaps the greatest disadvantage of using credit is the temptation to overspend, especially during periods of inflation. Buying today and paying tomorrow, using cheaper dollars, seems ideal. But continual overspending can lead to serious trouble.

Whether or not credit involves *security*—something of value to back the loan—failure to repay a loan may result in loss of income, valuable property, and your good reputation. It can even lead to court action and bankruptcy. Misuse of credit can create serious long-term financial problems, damage to family relationships, and a slowing of progress toward financial goals. Therefore, you should approach credit with caution and avoid using it more extensively than your budget permits.

Although credit allows immediate satisfaction of needs and desires, it does not increase total purchasing power. Credit purchases must be paid for out of future income; therefore, credit ties up the use of future income. Furthermore, if your income does not increase to cover rising costs, your ability to repay credit commitments will diminish. Before buying goods and services on credit, consider whether they will have lasting value, whether they will increase your personal satisfaction during present and future income periods, and whether your current income will continue or increase.

Finally, credit costs money. It is a service for which you must pay. Paying for purchases over a period of time is more costly than paying for them with cash. Purchasing with credit rather than cash involves one obvious trade-off: The items purchased will cost more due to monthly finance charges and the compounding effect of interest on interest.

✔ CONCEPTCHECK 5–1

1. What is consumer credit?

_____

_____

2. Why is consumer credit important to our economy?

_____

_____

3. For each of following situations, check "yes" if a valid reason to borrow, or "no" if not.

	Yes	No
a. A medical emergency.	_____	_____
b. Borrowing for college education.	_____	_____
c. Borrowing for everyday living expenses.	_____	_____
d. Borrowing to finance a luxury car.	_____	_____

4. For each of the following statements, check "yes" if an advantage, "no" if a disadvantage of using credit.

	Yes	No
a. It is easier to return merchandise if it is purchased on credit.	_____	_____
b. Credit cards provide shopping convenience.	_____	_____
c. Credit tempts people to overspend.	_____	_____
d. Failure to repay a loan may result in loss of income.	_____	_____

Types of Credit

OBJECTIVE 2

Assess the types and sources of consumer credit.

Two basic types of consumer credit exist: closed-end and open-end credit. With **closed-end credit,** you pay back one-time loans in a specified period of time and in payments

Closed-End Credit	Open-End Credit
• Mortgage loans • Automobile loans • Installment loans (installment sales contract, installment cash credit, single lump-sum credit)	• Cards issued by department stores, bank cards (Visa, MasterCard, American Express) • Travel and Entertainment (T&E) • Overdraft protection

Exhibit [5–1]

Examples of Closed-End and Open-End Credit

of equal amounts. With **open-end credit,** loans are made on a continuous basis and you are billed periodically for at least partial payment. Exhibit 5–1 shows examples of closed-end and open-end credit.

Closed-End Credit

Closed-end credit is used for a specific purpose and involves a specified amount. Mortgage loans, automobile loans, and installment loans for purchasing furniture or appliances are examples of closed-end credit. Generally, the seller holds title to the merchandise until the payments have been completed.

The three most common types of closed-end credit are installment sales credit, installment cash credit, and single lump-sum credit. *Installment sales credit* is a loan that allows you to receive merchandise, usually high-priced items such as large appliances or furniture. You make a down payment and usually sign a contract to repay the balance, plus interest and service charges, in equal installments over a specified period.

Installment cash credit is a direct loan of money for personal purposes, home improvements, or vacation expenses. You make no down payment and make payments in specified amounts over a set period.

Single lump-sum credit is a loan that must be repaid in total on a specified day, usually within 30 to 90 days. Lump-sum credit is generally, but not always, used to purchase a single item. As Exhibit 5–2 shows, consumer installment credit reached over $2 trillion in early 2004.

closed-end credit One-time loans that the borrower pays back in a specified period of time and in payments of equal amounts.

open-end credit A line of credit in which loans are made on a continuous basis and the borrower is billed periodically for at least partial payment.

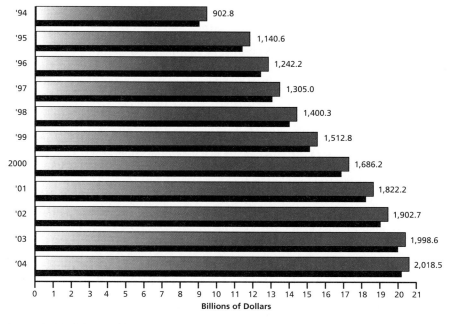

Exhibit [5–2]

Volume of Consumer Credit (as of February 2004)
All economists now recognize consumer credit as a major force in the American economy.

Year	Billions of Dollars
'94	902.8
'95	1,140.6
'96	1,242.2
'97	1,305.0
'98	1,400.3
'99	1,512.8
2000	1,686.2
'01	1,822.2
'02	1,902.7
'03	1,998.6
'04	2,018.5

Sources: *Statistical Abstract of the United States 2003,* Table 1190, p. 751, and http://www.federalreserve.gov, April 22, 2004.

Open-End Credit

Using a credit card issued by a department store, using a bank credit card (Visa, Master-Card) to make purchases at different stores, charging a meal at a restaurant, and using overdraft protection are examples of open-end credit. As you will soon see, you do not apply for open-end credit to make a single purchase, as you do with closed-end credit. Rather, you can use open-end credit to make any purchases you wish if you do not exceed your **line of credit,** the maximum dollar amount of credit the lender has made available to you. You may have to pay **interest,** a periodic charge for the use of credit, or other finance charges. Some creditors allow you a grace period of 20 to 25 days to pay a bill in full before you incur any interest charges.

Many retailers use open-end credit. Customers can purchase goods or services up to a fixed dollar limit at any time. Usually you have the option to pay the bill in full within 30 days without interest charges or to make set monthly installments based on the account balance plus interest.

Many banks extend **revolving check credit.** Also called a *bank line of credit,* this is a prearranged loan for a specified amount that you can use by writing a special check. Repayment is made in installments over a set period. The finance charges are based on the amount of credit used during the month and on the outstanding balance.

Sources of Consumer Credit

Many sources of consumer credit are available, including commercial banks and credit unions. Exhibit 5–3 summarizes the major sources of consumer credit. Study and compare the differences to determine which source might best meet your needs and requirements.

Loans

Loans involve borrowing money with an agreement to repay it, as well as interest, within a certain amount of time. If you were considering taking out a loan, your immediate thought might be to go to your local bank. However, you might want to explore some other options first.

INEXPENSIVE LOANS   Parents or other family members are often the source of the least expensive loans—loans with low interest. They may charge only interest they would have earned on the money if they had deposited it in a savings account. They may even give you a loan without interest. Be aware, however, that loans can complicate family relationships.

MEDIUM-PRICED LOANS   Often you can obtain medium-priced loans—loans with moderate interest—from commercial banks, savings and loan associations, and credit unions. Borrowing from credit unions has several advantages. They provide personalized service, and usually they're willing to be patient with borrowers who can provide good reasons for late or missed payments. However, you must be a member of a credit union in order to get a loan.

EXPENSIVE LOANS   The easiest loans to obtain are also the most expensive. Finance companies and retail stores that lend to consumers will frequently charge high interest rates, ranging from 12 to 25 percent. Banks also lend money to their credit card holders through cash advances—loans that are billed to the customer's credit card account. Most cards charge higher interest for a cash advance and charge interest from the

Exhibit [5–3]   Sources of Consumer Credit

Credit Source	Type of Loan	Lending Policies
Commercial banks	Single-payment loan Personal installment loans Passbook loans Check-credit loans Credit card loans Second mortgages	• Seek customers with established credit history • Often require collateral or security • Prefer to deal in large loans, such as vehicle, home improvement, and home modernization, with the exception of credit card and check-credit plans • Determine repayment schedules according to the purpose of the loan • Vary credit rates according to the type of credit, time period, customer's credit history, and the security offered • May require several days to process a new credit application
Consumer finance companies	Personal installment loans Second mortgages	• Often lend to consumers without established credit history • Often make unsecured loans • Often vary rates according to the size of the loan balance • Offer a variety of repayment schedules • Make a higher percentage of small loans than other lenders • Maximum loan size limited by law • Process applications quickly, frequently on the same day the application is made
Credit unions	Personal installment loans Share draft-credit plans Credit-card loans Second mortgages	• Lend to members only • Make unsecured loans • May require collateral or cosigner for loans over a specified amount • May require payroll deductions to pay off loan • May submit large loan applications to a committee of members for approval • Offer a variety of repayment schedules
Life insurance companies	Single-payment or partial-payment loans	• Lend on cash value of life insurance policy • No date or penalty on repayment • Deduct amount owed from the value of policy benefit if death or other maturity occurs before repayment
Federal savings banks (savings and loan associations)	Personal installment loans (generally permitted by state-chartered savings associations) Home improvement loans Education loans Savings account loans Second mortgages	• Will lend to all creditworthy individuals • Often require collateral • Loan rates vary depending on size of loan, length of payment, and security involved

Consumer credit is available from several types of sources. *Which sources seem to offer the widest variety of loans?*

day the cash advance is made. As a result, taking out a cash advance is much more expensive than charging a purchase to a credit card. Read the nearby Figure It Out box to learn why you should avoid such cash advances.

HOME EQUITY LOANS   A home equity loan is a loan based on your home equity—the difference between the current market value of your home and the amount you still owe on the mortgage. Unlike interest on most other types of credit,

Apply *Yourself!*

Objective 2

Research three credit card companies. List their fees and any advantages they offer. Record your findings.

Figure It Out!

CASH ADVANCES

A cash advance is a loan billed to your credit card. You can obtain a cash advance with your credit card at a bank or an automated teller machine (ATM) or by using checks linked to your credit card account.

Most cards charge a special fee when a cash advance is taken out. The fee is based on a percentage of the amount borrowed, usually about 2 or 3 percent.

Some credit cards charge a minimum cash advance fee, as high as $5. You could get $20 in cash and be charged $5, a fee equal to 25 percent of the amount you borrowed.

Most cards do not have a grace period on cash advances. This means you pay interest every day until you repay the cash advance, even if you do not have an outstanding balance from the previous statement.

On some cards, the interest rate on cash advances is higher than the rate on purchases. Be sure you check the details on the contract sent to you by the card issuer.

Here is an example of charges that could be imposed for a $200 cash advance that you pay off when the bill arrives:

Cash advance fee = $4 (2% of $200)

Interest for one month = $3 (18% APR on $200)

Total cost for one month = $7 ($4 + $3)

In comparison, a $200 purchase on a card with a grace period could cost $0 if paid off promptly in full.

The bottom line: It is usually much more expensive to take out a cash advance than to charge a purchase to your credit card. Use cash advances only for real emergencies.

the interest you pay on a home equity loan is tax-deductible. You should use these loans only for major items such as education, home improvements, or medical bills, and you must use them with care. If you miss payments on a home equity loan, the lender can take your home.

Credit Cards

Credit cards are extremely popular. The average cardholder has more than nine credit cards, including bank, retail, gasoline, and telephone cards. Cardholders who pay off their balances in full each month are often known as *convenience* users. Cardholders who do not pay off their balances every month are known as *borrowers*.

finance charge The total dollar amount paid to use credit.

Most credit card companies offer a grace period, a time period during which no finance charges will be added to your account. A **finance charge** is the total dollar amount you pay to use credit. Usually, if you pay your entire balance before the due date stated on your monthly bill, you will not have to pay a finance charge. Borrowers carry balances beyond the grace period and pay finance charges.

Key Web Sites for Credit Cards
www.cardratings.com
www.bankrate.com

The cost of a credit card depends on the type of credit card you have and the terms set forth by the lender. As a cardholder, you may have to pay interest or other finance charges. Some credit card companies charge cardholders an annual fee, usually about $20. However, many companies have eliminated annual fees in order to attract more customers. If you are looking for a credit card, be sure to shop around for one with no annual fee. The nearby Personal Finance in Practice box offers some other helpful hints for choosing a credit card.

DEBIT CARDS Don't confuse credit cards with debit cards. Although they may look alike, they're very different. A debit card electronically subtracts money from your savings or checking account to pay for goods and services. A credit card extends credit and delays your payment. Debit cards are most frequently used at automatic teller ma-

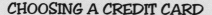

Personal Finance in Practice

CHOOSING A CREDIT CARD

When you choose a credit card, shopping around can yield big returns. Follow these suggestions to find the card that best meets your needs and to use it wisely:

1. Department stores and gasoline companies are good places to obtain your first credit card.

2. Bank credit cards are offered through banks and savings and loan associations. Annual fees and finance charges vary widely, so shop around.

3. If you plan on paying off your balance every month, look for a card that has a grace period and carries no annual fee or a low annual fee. You might have a higher interest rate, but you plan to pay little or no interest anyway.

4. Watch out for creditors that offer low or no annual fees but instead charge a transaction fee every time you use the card.

5. If you plan to carry a balance, look for a card with a low monthly finance charge. Be sure that you understand how the finance charge is calculated.

6. To avoid delays that may result in finance charges, follow the card issuer's instructions as to where, how, and when to make bill payments.

7. Beware of offers of easy credit. No one can guarantee to get you credit.

8. If your card offers a grace period, take advantage of it by paying off your balance in full each month. With a grace period of 25 days, you actually get a free loan when you pay bills in full each month.

9. If you have a bad credit history and have trouble getting a credit card, look for a savings institution that will give you a secured credit card. With this type of card, your line of credit depends on how much money you keep in a savings account that you open at the same time.

10. Travel and entertainment cards often charge higher annual fees than most credit cards. Usually, you must make payment in full within 30 days of receiving your bill, or no further purchases will be approved on the account.

11. Be aware that debit cards are not credit cards but simply a substitute for a check or cash. The amount of the sale is subtracted from your checking account.

12. Think twice before you make a telephone call to a 900 number to request a credit card. You will pay from $2 to $50 for the 900 call and may never receive a credit card.

Before you enter the world of credit, you need to understand the various options that are available to you. *Which of the preceding factors would be most important in your choice of a credit card?*

Sources: American Institute of Certified Public Accountants. U.S. Office of Consumer Affairs. Federal Trade Commission.

---

chines (ATMs). More and more, however, they are also used to purchase goods in stores and to make other types of payments.

SMART CARDS   Some lenders are starting to offer a new kind of credit card called a smart card. A smart card is a plastic card equipped with a computer chip that can store 500 times as much data as a normal credit card. Smart cards can combine credit card balances, a driver's license, health care identification, medical history, and other information all in one place. A smart card, for example, can be used to buy an airline ticket, store it digitally, and track frequent flyer miles.

TRAVEL AND ENTERTAINMENT CARDS   Travel and entertainment (T&E) cards are really not credit cards because the balance is due in full each month. However, most people think of T&E cards—such as Diners Club or American Express cards—as credit cards because they don't pay for goods or service when they purchase them.

> **DID YOU KNOW?**
>
> By senior year, the average undergraduate has racked up more than $3,200 in debt, spread out over six credit cards.
>
> Source: *U.S. News & World Report*, April 19, 2004, p. 62.

✔ CONCEPTCHECK 5–2

1 What are two types of consumer credit? _____   _____

2 Match the following key terms with the appropriate definition.

    a. closed-end credit   _____ A line of credit in which loans are made on a continuous basis.

    b. open-end credit   _____ One-time loan paid back in a specified time in payments of equal amounts.

    c. line of credit   _____ The dollar amount that a lender makes available to a borrower.

    d. interest   _____ The total dollar amount paid to use the credit.

    e. finance charge   _____ A periodic charge for the use of credit.

3 What are the major sources of:

Inexpensive loans	Medium-priced loans	Expensive loans
_____	_____	_____
_____	_____	_____
_____	_____	_____

4 What is the difference between a credit and a debit card?

_____

_____

Applying for Credit

OBJECTIVE 3
Determine whether you can afford a loan and how to apply for credit.

Can You Afford a Loan?

The only way to determine how much credit you can assume is to first learn how to make an accurate and sensible personal or family budget.

Before you take out a loan, ask yourself whether you can meet all of your essential expenses and still afford the monthly loan payments. You can make this calculation in two ways. One is to add up all your basic monthly expenses and then subtract this total from your take-home pay. If the difference will not cover the monthly payment and still leave funds for other expenses, you cannot afford the loan.

A second and more reliable method is to ask yourself what you plan to give up to make the monthly loan payment. If you currently save a portion of your income that is greater than the monthly payment, you can use these savings to pay off the loan. But if you do not, you will have to forgo spending on entertainment, new appliances, or perhaps even necessities. Are you prepared to make this trade-off? Although precisely measuring your credit capacity is difficult, you can follow certain rules of thumb.

General Rules of Credit Capacity

DEBT PAYMENTS-TO-INCOME RATIO The debt payments-to-income ratio is calculated by dividing your monthly debt payments (not including house payment, which is long-term liability) by your net monthly income. Experts suggest that you spend no more than 20 percent of your net (after-tax) income on consumer credit payments. Thus, as Exhibit 5–4 shows, a person making $1,068 per month after taxes should spend no more than $213 on credit payments per month.

The 20 percent is the maximum; however, 15 percent or less is much better. The 20 percent estimate is based on the average family, with average expenses; it does not take major emergencies into account. If you are just beginning to use credit, you should not consider yourself safe if you are spending 20 percent of your net income on credit payments.

DEBT-TO-EQUITY RATIO The debt-to-equity ratio is calculated by dividing your total liabilities by your net worth. In calculating this ratio, do not include the value of your home and the amount of its mortgage. If your debt-to-equity ratio is about 1—that is, if your consumer installment debt roughly equals your net worth (not including your home or the mortgage)—you have probably reached the upper limit of debt obligations.

None of the above methods is perfect for everyone; the limits given are only guidelines. Only you, based on the money you earn, your obligations, and your financial plans for the future, can determine the exact amount of credit you need and can afford. You must be your own credit manager.

DID YOU KNOW?

About 173 million people use more than 1.4 billion credit cards to buy goods and services.

Millions

Year	People with credit cards	Cards in circulation
1990	122	1,013
1997	149	1,387
2000	159	1,425
2005*	173	1,430

* Estimated.

Source: *Statistical Abstract of the United States 2003*, Table 1190, p. 751.

The Five Cs of Credit

When you're ready to apply for a loan or a credit card, you should understand the factors that determine whether a lender will extend credit to you.

Sheet 14
Consumer
Credit Usage
Patterns

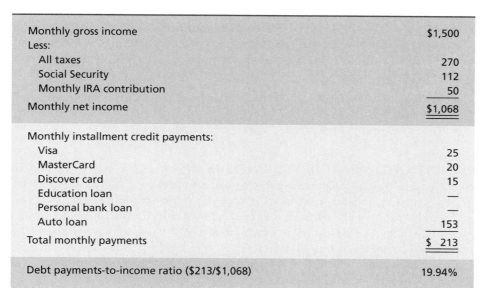

Monthly gross income	$1,500
Less:	
All taxes	270
Social Security	112
Monthly IRA contribution	50
Monthly net income	$1,068
Monthly installment credit payments:	
Visa	25
MasterCard	20
Discover card	15
Education loan	—
Personal bank loan	—
Auto loan	153
Total monthly payments	$ 213
Debt payments-to-income ratio ($213/$1,068)	19.94%

Exhibit 5–4

How to Calculate Debt Payments-to-Income Ratio

Spend no more than 20 percent of your net (after-tax) income on credit payments.

When a lender extends credit to consumers, it takes for granted that some people will be unable or unwilling to pay their debts. Therefore, lenders establish policies for determining who will receive credit. Most lenders build such policies around the "five Cs of credit": character, capacity, capital, collateral, and conditions.

CHARACTER: WILL YOU REPAY THE LOAN?

character The borrower's attitude toward his or her credit obligations.

Creditors want to know your **character**—what kind of person they are lending money to. They want to know that you're trustworthy and stable. They may ask for personal or professional references, and they may check to see whether you have a history of trouble with the law. Some questions a lender might ask to determine your character are:

- Have you used credit before?
- How long have you lived at your present address?
- How long have you held your current job?

CAPACITY: CAN YOU REPAY THE LOAN?

capacity The borrower's financial ability to meet credit obligations.

Your income and the debts you already have will affect your **capacity**—your ability to pay additional debts. If you already have a large amount of debt in proportion to your income, lenders probably won't extend more credit to you. Some questions a creditor may ask about your income and expenses are:

- What is your job, and how much is your salary?
- Do you have other sources of income?
- What are your current debts?

CAPITAL: WHAT ARE YOUR ASSETS AND NET WORTH?

capital The borrower's assets or net worth.

Assets are any items of value that you own, including cash, property, personal possessions, and investments. Your **capital** is the amount of your assets that exceed your liabilities, or the debts you owe. Lenders want to be sure that you have enough capital to pay back a loan. That way, if you lost your source of income, you could repay your loan from your savings or by selling some of your assets. A lender might ask:

- What are your assets?
- What are your liabilities?

*Apply*Yourself!

Objective 3

Talk to a person who has cosigned a loan. What experiences did this person have as a cosigner?

COLLATERAL: WHAT IF YOU DON'T REPAY THE LOAN?

collateral A valuable asset that is pledged to ensure loan payments.

Creditors look at what kinds of property or savings you already have, because these can be offered as **collateral** to secure the loan. If you fail to repay the loan, the creditor may take whatever you pledged as collateral. A creditor might ask:

- What assets do you have to secure the loan (such as a vehicle, your home, or furniture)?
- Do you have any other valuable assets (such as bonds or savings)?

CONDITIONS: WHAT IF YOUR JOB IS INSECURE?

conditions The general economic conditions that can affect a borrower's ability to repay a loan.

General economic **conditions,** such as unemployment and recession, can affect your ability to repay a loan. The basic question focuses on security—of both your job and the firm that employs you.

The information gathered from your application and the credit bureau establishes your credit rating. *A credit rating* is a measure of a person's ability and willingness to make credit payments on time. The factors that determine a person's credit rating are income, current debt, information about character, and how debts have been repaid in

Personal Finance in Practice

THE FIVE Cs OF CREDIT

Here is what lenders look for in determining your credit-worthiness.

CREDIT HISTORY

1. Character: Will you repay the loan?

	Yes	No
Do you have a good attitude toward credit obligations?	____	____
Have you used credit before?	____	____
Do you pay your bills on time?	____	____
Have you ever filed for bankruptcy?	____	____
Do you live within your means?	____	____

STABILITY

How long have you lived at your present address? _____ yrs.

Do you own your home? ____ ____

How long have you been employed by your present employer? _____ yrs.

INCOME

2. Capacity: Can you repay the loan?

Your salary and occupation? $_____ ; _____

Place of occupation? _____

How reliable is your income? Reliable ____ ; Not reliable ____

Any other sources of income? $_____

EXPENSES

Number of dependents? _____

Do you pay any alimony or child support? Yes _____ ; No _____

Current debts? $_____

NET WORTH

3. Capital: What are your assets and net worth?

What are your assets? $_____

What are your liabilities? $_____

What is your net worth? $_____

LOAN SECURITY

4. Collateral: What if you don't repay the loan?

What assets do you have to secure the loan? (Car, home, furniture?) _____

What sources do you have besides income? (Savings, stocks, bonds, insurance?) _____

JOB SECURITY

5. Conditions: What general economic conditions can affect your repayment of the loan?

How secure is your job? Secure _____ ; Not secure _____

How secure is the firm you work for? Secure _____ ; Not secure _____

Source: Adapted from William M. Pride, Robert J. Hughes, and Jack R. Kapoor, *Business,* 8th ed. (Boston: Houghton Mifflin, 2005), p. 590.

---

the past. If you always make your payments on time, you will probably have an excellent credit rating. If not, your credit rating will be poor, and a lender probably won't extend credit to you. A good credit rating is a valuable asset that you should protect.

Creditors use different combinations of the five Cs to reach their decisions. Some creditors set unusually high standards, and others simply do not offer certain types of loans. Creditors also use various rating systems. Some rely strictly on their own instincts and experience. Others use a credit scoring or statistical system to predict whether an applicant is a good credit risk. When you apply for a loan, the lender is likely to evaluate your application by asking questions such as those included in the checklist in the Personal Finance in Practice box.

You should also know what factors a lender cannot consider, according to the law. The *Equal Credit Opportunity Act* (ECOA) gives all credit applicants the same basic rights. It states that race, nationality, age, sex, marital status, and certain other factors may not be used to discriminate against you in any part of a credit dealing.

Other Factors Considered in Determining Creditworthiness

AGE The Equal Credit Opportunity Act is very specific about how a person's age may be used as a factor in credit decisions. A creditor may request that you state your age on an application, but if you're old enough to sign a legal contract (usually 18–21 years old, depending on state law), a creditor may not turn you down or decrease your credit because of your age. Creditors may not close your credit account because you reach a certain age or retire.

PUBLIC ASSISTANCE You may not be denied credit because you receive Social Security or public assistance. However, certain information related to this source of income can be considered in determining your creditworthiness.

HOUSING LOANS The ECOA also covers applications for mortgages or home improvement loans. In particular, it bans discrimination against you based on the race or nationality of the people in the neighborhood where you live or want to buy your home, a practice called *redlining.*

What If Your Application Is Denied?

If your credit application is denied, the ECOA gives you the right to know the reasons. If the denial is based on a credit report from the credit bureau, you're entitled to know the specific information in the report that led to the denial. After you receive this information, you can contact the credit bureau and ask for a copy of your credit report. The bureau cannot charge a fee for this service as long as you ask to see your files within 60 days of notification that your credit application has been denied. You're entitled to ask the bureau to investigate any inaccurate or incomplete information and correct its records (see Exhibit 5–5).

Your Credit Report

When you apply for a loan, the lender will review your credit history very closely. The record of your complete credit history is called your *credit report,* or *credit file.* Your credit records are collected and maintained by credit bureaus. Most lenders rely heavily on credit reports when they consider loan applications. Exhibit 5–6 provides a checklist for building and protecting your credit history.

CREDIT BUREAUS A credit bureau is an agency that collects information on how promptly people and businesses pay their bills. The three major credit bureaus are Experian, Trans Union, and Equifax. Each of these bureaus maintains more than 200 million credit files on individuals, based on information they receive from lenders. Several thousand smaller credit bureaus also collect credit information about consumers. These firms make money by selling the information they collect to creditors who are considering loan applications.

Credit bureaus get their information from banks, finance companies, stores, credit card companies, and other lenders. These sources regularly transmit information about the types of credit they extend to customers, the amounts and terms of the loans, and the

Exhibit [5–5]   What If You Are Denied Credit?

Steps you can take if you are denied credit

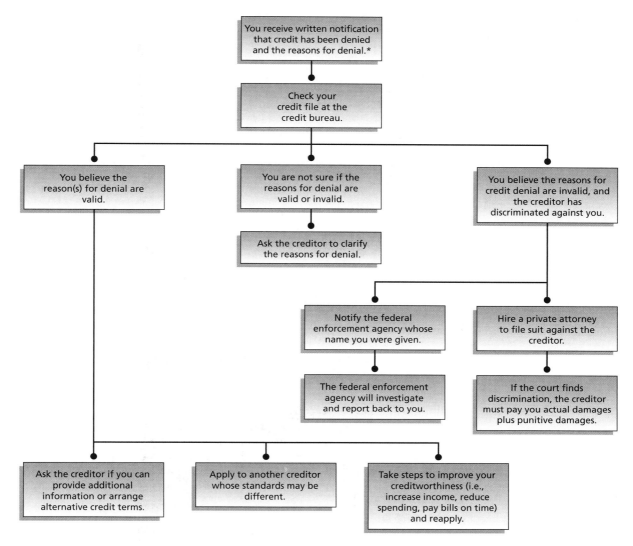

*If a creditor receives no more than 150 applications during a calendar year, the disclosures may be oral.
Source: Reprinted courtesy of Office of Public Information, Federal Reserve Bank of Minneapolis, Minneapolis, MN 55480.

customer's payment habits. Credit bureaus also collect some information from other sources, such as court records.

WHAT'S IN YOUR CREDIT FILES?   A typical credit bureau file contains your name, address, Social Security number, and birth date. It may also include the following information:

- Your employer, position, and income
- Your previous address
- Your previous employer
- Your spouse's name, Social Security number, employer, and income
- Whether you rent or own your home
- Checks returned for insufficient funds

Exhibit [5–6]   Checklist for Building and Protecting Your Credit History

It is simple and sensible to build and protect your own credit history. Here are some steps to get you started:

- Open a checking or savings account, or both.
- Apply for a local department store credit card.
- Take out a small loan from your bank. Make payments on time.

A Creditor Must . . .	**Remember that a Creditor Cannot . . .**
1. Evaluate all applicants on the same basis	1. Refuse you individual credit in your own name if you are creditworthy
2. Consider income from part-time employment	2. Require your spouse to cosign a loan. Any creditworthy person can be your cosigner if one is required
3. Consider the payment history of all joint accounts, if this accurately reflects your credit history	3. Ask about your family plans or assume that your income will be interrupted to have children
4. Disregard information on accounts if you can prove that it doesn't affect your ability or willingness to repay	4. Consider whether you have a telephone listing in your name

If you want a good credit rating, you must use credit wisely. *Why is it a good idea to apply for a local department store credit card or a small loan from your bank?*

Source: Reprinted by permission of the Federal Reserve Bank of Minneapolis.

In addition, your credit file contains detailed credit information. Each time you use credit to make a purchase or take out a loan of any kind, a credit bureau is informed of your account number and the date, amount, terms, and type of credit. Your file is updated regularly to show how many payments you've made, how many payments were late or missed, and how much you owe. Any lawsuits or judgments against you may appear as well. Federal law protects your rights if the information in your credit file is incorrect.

FAIR CREDIT REPORTING   Fair and accurate credit reporting is vital to both creditors and consumers. In 1971 the U.S. Congress enacted the Fair Credit Reporting Act, which regulates the use of credit reports. This law requires the deletion of out-of-date information and gives consumers access to their files as well as the right to correct any misinformation that the files may include. The act also places limits on who can obtain your credit report.

WHO CAN OBTAIN A CREDIT REPORT?   Your credit report may be issued only to properly identified persons for approved purposes. It may be supplied in response to a court order or by your own written request. A credit report may also be provided for use in connection with a credit transaction, underwriting of insurance, or some legitimate business need. Friends, neighbors, and other individuals cannot be given access to credit information about you. In fact, if they even request such information, they may be subject to a fine, imprisonment, or both.

Key Web Sites for Credit Reporting
www.experian.com
www.ftc.gov

TIME LIMITS ON UNFAVORABLE DATA   Most of the information in your credit file may be reported for only seven years. However, if you've declared personal bankruptcy, that fact may be reported for 10 years. A credit reporting agency can't disclose information in your credit file that's more than 7 or 10 years old unless you're being reviewed for a credit application of $75,000 or more, or unless you apply to purchase life insurance of $150,000 or more.

INCORRECT INFORMATION IN YOUR CREDIT FILE
Credit bureaus are required to follow reasonable procedures to ensure that the information in their files is correct. Mistakes can and do occur, however. If you think that a credit bureau may be reporting incorrect data from your file, contact the bureau to dispute the information. The credit bureau must check its records and change or remove the incorrect items. If you challenge the accuracy of an item on your credit report, the bureau must remove the item unless the lender can verify that the information is accurate.

If you are denied credit, insurance, employment, or rental housing based on the information in a credit report, you can get a free copy of your report. Remember to request it within 60 days of notification that your application has been denied.

WHAT ARE YOUR LEGAL RIGHTS?
You have legal rights to sue a credit bureau or creditor that has caused you harm by not following the rules established by the Fair Credit Reporting Act.

✓ CONCEPTCHECK 5–3

1 What are the two general rules of measuring credit capacity? How is it calculated?

_____

_____

2 Match the following key terms with the appropriate definition.

a. character   _____ An asset pledged to obtain a loan.

b. capacity   _____ The borrower's attitude toward credit obligations.

c. capital   _____ Financial ability to meet credit obligations.

d. collateral   _____ The borrower's assets or net worth.

e. conditions   _____ General economic conditions that affect your ability to repay a loan.

3 What are the three factors a lender cannot consider according to the law?

_____

4 What is a credit bureau? _____

5 Write the steps you should take if you are denied credit.

_____

_____

The Cost of Credit

If you are thinking of borrowing money or opening a credit account, your first step should be to figure out how much it will cost you and whether you can afford it. Then you should shop for the best terms. Two key concepts that you should remember are the finance charge and the annual percentage rate.

OBJECTIVE 4
Determine the cost of credit by calculating interest using various interest formulas.

Finance Charge and Annual Percentage Rate

annual percentage rate (APR)
The percentage cost (or relative cost) of credit on a yearly basis. The APR yields a true rate of interest for comparisons with other sources of credit.

Credit costs vary. If you know the finance charge and the annual percentage rate you can compare credit prices from different sources. The *finance charge* is the total dollar amount you pay to use credit. It includes interest costs and sometimes other costs such as service charges, credit-related insurance premiums, or appraisal fees.

For example, borrowing $100 for a year might cost you $10 in interest. If there is also a service charge of $1, the finance charge will be $11. The **annual percentage rate (APR)** is the percentage cost (or relative cost) of credit on a yearly basis. The APR is your key to comparing costs, regardless of the amount of credit or how much time you have to repay it.

Suppose you borrow $100 for one year and pay a finance charge of $10. If you can keep the entire $100 for one year and then pay it all back at once, you are paying an APR of 10 percent.

Amount Borrowed	Month Number	Payment Made	Loan Balance
$100	1	$ 0	$100
	2	0	100
	3	0	100
	.	.	.
	.	.	.
	.	.	.
	12	$100	0
		(plus $10 interest)	

On average, you had full use of $100 throughout the year. To calculate the average use, add the loan balance during the first and last month, then divide by 2:

$$\text{Average balance} = \frac{\$100 + \$100}{2} = \$100$$

But if you repay the $100 and the finance charge (a total of $110) in 12 equal monthly payments, you don't get use of $100 for the whole year. In fact, as shown next, you get use of increasingly less of that $100 each month. In this case, the $10 charge for credit amounts to an APR of 18.5 percent.

Amount Borrowed	Month Number	Payment Made	Loan Balance
$100	1	$ 0	$100.00
	2	8.33	91.67
	3	8.33	83.34
	4	8.33	75.01
	5	8.33	66.68
	6	8.33	58.35
	7	8.33	50.02
	8	8.33	41.69

Amount Borrowed	Month Number	Payment Made	Loan Balance
	9	8.33	33.36
	10	8.33	25.03
	11	8.33	16.70
	12	8.33	8.37

Note that you are paying 10 percent interest even though you had use of only $91.67 during the second month, not $100. During the last month, you owed only $8.37 (and had use of $8.37), but the $10 interest is for the entire $100. As calculated in the previous example, the average use of the money during the year is $100 + $8.37 ÷ 2, or $54.18.

Tackling the Trade-Offs

When you choose your financing, there are trade-offs between the features you prefer (term, size of payments, fixed or variable interest, or payment plan) and the cost of your loan. Here are some major trade-offs you should consider.

TERM VERSUS INTEREST COSTS   Many people choose longer term financing because they want smaller monthly payments, but the longer the term for a loan at a given interest rate, the greater the amount you must pay in interest charges. Consider the following analysis of the relationship between the term and interest costs.

Suppose you're buying a $7,500 used car. You put $1,500 down, and you need to borrow $6,000. Compare the following three credit arrangements:

	APR	Length of Loan	Monthly Payment	Total Finance Charge	Total Cost
Creditor A	14%	3 years	$205.07	$1,382.52	$7,382.52
Creditor B	14	4 years	163.96	1,870.08	7,870.08
Creditor C	15	4 years	166.98	2,015.04	8,015.04

How do these choices compare? The answer depends partly on what you need. The lowest cost loan is available from creditor A. If you are looking for lower monthly payments, you should repay the loan over a longer period of time. However, you would have to pay more in total costs. A loan from creditor B—also at a 14 percent APR, but for four years—would add about $488 to your finance charge.

If that four-year loan were available only from creditor C, the APR of 15 percent would add another $145 to your finance charges. Other terms, such as the size of the down payment, will also make a difference. Be sure to look at all the terms before you make your choice.

LENDER RISK VERSUS INTEREST RATE   You may prefer financing that requires low fixed payments with a large final payment or only a minimum of up-front cash. But both of these requirements can increase your cost of borrowing because they create more risk for your lender.

If you want to minimize your borrowing costs, you may need to accept conditions that reduce your lender's risk. Here are a few possibilities:

- *Variable interest rate.* A variable interest rate is based on fluctuating rates in the banking system, such as the prime rate. With this type of loan, you share the interest rate risks with the lender. Therefore, the lender may offer you a lower initial interest rate than it would with a fixed-rate loan.
- *A secured loan.* If you pledge property or other asset as collateral, you'll probably receive a lower interest rate on your loan.
- *Up-front cash.* Many lenders believe you have a higher stake in repaying a loan if you pay cash for a large portion of what you are financing. Doing so may give you a better chance of getting the other terms you want.
- *A shorter term.* As you have learned, the shorter the period of time for which you borrow, the smaller the chance that something will prevent you from repaying and the lower the risk to the lender. Therefore, you may be able to borrow at a lower interest rate if you accept a shorter-term loan, but your payments will be higher.

In the next section, you will see how the foregoing trade-offs can affect the cost of closed-end and open-end credit.

Calculating the Cost of Credit

The most common method of calculating interest is the simple interest formula. Other methods, such as simple interest on the declining balance and add-on interest, are variations of this formula.

simple interest Interest computed on principal only and without compounding.

SIMPLE INTEREST   **Simple interest** is the interest computed only on the principal, the amount that you borrow. It is based on three factors: the principal, the interest rate, and the amount of time for which the principal is borrowed. To calculate simple interest on a loan, multiply the principal by the interest rate and by the amount of time (in years) for which the money is borrowed. For example, suppose you convinced your aunt to lend you $1,000 to purchase a laptop computer. She agreed to charge only 5 percent simple interest and you agreed to repay the loan at the end of one year. How much interest will you pay for the year? Using the formula above, you simply multiply $1,000 by 5 percent and the term of one year ($1,000 \times 5\% \times 1 = \$50$).

Key Web Sites for Cost of Credit
www.pirg.org/consumer/credit
www.econsumer.equifax.com

SIMPLE INTEREST ON THE DECLINING BALANCE   When simple interest is paid back in more than one payment, the method of computing interest is known as the declining balance method. You pay interest only on the amount of principal that you have not yet repaid. The more often you make payments, the lower the interest you'll pay. Most credit unions use this method.

ADD-ON INTEREST   With the add-on interest method, interest is calculated on the full amount of the original principal, no matter how frequently you make payments. When you pay off the loan with one payment, this method produces the same annual percentage rate (APR) as the simple interest method. However, if you pay in installments, your actual rate of interest will be higher than the stated rate. Interest payments on this type of loan do not decrease as the loan is repaid. The longer you take to repay the loan, the more interest you'll pay.

COST OF OPEN-END CREDIT The Truth in Lending Act requires that open-end creditors inform consumers as to how the finance charge and the APR will affect their costs. For example, they must explain how they calculate the finance charge. They must also inform you when finance charges on your credit account begin to accrue, so that you know how much time you have to pay your bills before a finance charge is added.

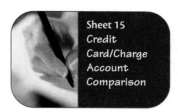

Sheet 15
Credit
Card/Charge
Account
Comparison

COST OF CREDIT AND EXPECTED INFLATION Inflation reduces the buying power of money. Each percentage point increase in inflation means a decrease of about 1 percent in the quantity of goods and services you can buy with the same amount of money. Because of this, lenders incorporate the expected rate of inflation when deciding how much interest to charge.

Remember the earlier example in which you borrowed $1,000 from your aunt at the bargain rate of 5 percent for one year? If the inflation rate was 4 percent that year, your aunt's actual rate of return on the loan would have been only 1 percent (5 percent stated interest minus 4 percent inflation rate). A professional lender who wanted to receive 5 percent interest on your loan might have charged you 9 percent interest (5 percent interest plus 4 percent anticipated inflation rate).

AVOID THE MINIMUM MONTHLY PAYMENT TRAP On credit card bills and with certain other forms of credit, the *minimum monthly payment* is the smallest amount you can pay and remain a borrower in good standing. Lenders often encourage you to make the minimum payment because it will then take you longer to pay off the loan. However, if you are paying only the minimum amount on your monthly statement, you need to plan your budget more carefully. The longer it takes for you to pay off a bill, the more interest you pay. The finance charges you pay on an item could end up being more than the item is worth.

Consider the following examples. In each example, the minimum payment is based on 1/36 of the outstanding balance or $20, whichever is greater.

Apply*Yourself!*

Objective 4

Use the Internet to obtain information about the costs of closed-end and open-end credit.

EXAMPLE 1

You are buying new books for college. If you spend $500 on textbooks using a credit card charging 19.8 percent interest and make only the minimum payment, it will take you more than 2½ years to pay off the loan, adding $150 in interest charges to the cost of your purchase. The same purchase on a credit card charging 12 percent interest will cost only $78 extra.

EXAMPLE 2

You purchase a $2,000 stereo system using a credit card with 19 percent interest and a 2 percent minimum payment. If you pay just the minimum every month, it will take you 265 months—over 22 years—to pay off the debt and will cost you nearly $4,800 in interest payments. Doubling the amount paid each month to 4 percent of the balance owed would allow you to shorten the payment time to 88 months from 265 months—or 7 years as opposed to 22 years—and save you about $3,680.

Sheet 16
Consumer
Loan
Comparison

✔ **CONCEPTCHECK 5–4**

1 What are the two key concepts to remember when you borrow money?

_____

2 What are the three major trade-offs you should consider as you take out a loan?

_____

3 Using terms from the following list, complete the sentences below. Write the term you have chosen in the space provided.

> finance charge
> annual percentage rate
> simple interest
> minimum monthly payment
> add-on interest method

a. The _____ is the cost of credit on a yearly basis expressed as a percentage.

b. The total dollar amount paid to use credit is the _____ .

c. The smallest amount a borrower can pay on a credit card bill and remain a borrower in good standing is the

_____ .

d. With the _____ , interest is calculated on the full amount of the original principal, no matter how often you make payments.

e. _____ is the interest computed only on the principal, the amount that you borrow.

Protecting Your Credit

> **OBJECTIVE 5**
> Develop a plan to protect your credit and manage your debts.

Have you ever received a bill for merchandise you never bought or that you returned to the store or never received? Have you ever made a payment that was not credited to your account or been charged twice for the same item? If so, you are not alone.

Billing Errors and Disputes

Fair Credit Billing Act (FCBA)
Sets procedures for promptly correcting billing mistakes, refusing to make credit card payments on defective goods, and promptly crediting payments.

The **Fair Credit Billing Act (FCBA),** passed in 1975, sets procedures for promptly correcting billing mistakes, refusing to make credit card or revolving credit payments on defective goods, and promptly crediting your payments.

Follow these steps if you think that a bill is wrong or want more information about it. First notify your creditor in writing, and include any information that might support your case. (A telephone call is not sufficient and will not protect your rights.) Then pay the portion of the bill that is not in question.

Your creditor must acknowledge your letter within 30 days. Then, within two billing periods (but not longer than 90 days), the creditor must adjust your account or tell you why the bill is correct. If the creditor made a mistake, you don't have to pay any finance charges on the disputed amount. If no mistake is found, the creditor must promptly send you an explanation of the situation and a statement of what you owe, including any finance charges that may have accumulated and any minimum payments you missed while you were questioning the bill.

PROTECTING YOUR CREDIT RATING

According to law, a creditor may not threaten your credit rating or do anything to damage your credit reputation while you're negotiating a billing dispute. In addition, the creditor may not take any action to collect the amount in question until your complaint has been answered.

DEFECTIVE GOODS AND SERVICES

Theo used his credit card to buy a new mountain bike. When it arrived, he discovered that some of the gears didn't work properly. He tried to return it, but the store would not accept a return. He asked the store to repair or replace the bike—but still he had no luck. According to the Fair Credit Billing Act, he may tell his credit card company to stop payment for the bike because he has made a sincere attempt to resolve the problem with the store.

Identity Crisis: What to Do If Your Identity Is Stolen

"I don't remember charging those items. I've never been in that store." Maybe you never charged those goods and services, but someone else did—someone who used your name and personal information to commit fraud. When imposters use your personal information for their own purposes, they are committing a crime.

The biggest problem? You may not know that your identity has been stolen until you notice that something is wrong: You may get bills for a credit card account you never opened, or you may see charges to your account for things that you didn't purchase.

If you think that your identity has been stolen and that someone is using it to charge purchases or obtain credit in some other way, the Federal Trade Commission recommends that you take the following three actions immediately:

1. *Contact the credit bureaus.* Tell them to flag your file with a fraud alert, including a statement that creditors should call you for permission before they open any new accounts in your name.
2. *Contact the creditors.* Contact the creditors for any accounts that have been tampered with or opened fraudulently. Follow up in writing.
3. *File a police report.* Keep a copy of the police report in case your creditors need proof of the crime. If you're still having identity problems, stay alert to new instances of identity theft. You can also contact the Privacy Rights Clearinghouse. Call 1-619-298-3396.

Protecting Your Credit from Theft or Loss

Some thieves will pick through your trash in the hope of coming across your personal information. You can prevent this from happening by tearing or shredding any papers that contain personal information before you throw them out.

If you believe that an identity thief has accessed your bank accounts, close the accounts immediately. If your checks have been stolen or misused, stop payment on them. If your debit card has been lost or stolen, cancel it and get another with a new personal identification number (PIN).

Lost credit cards are a key element in credit card fraud. To protect your card, you should take the following actions:

Key Web Sites for Protecting Credit
www.consumer-action.org
www.ftc.gov/.gc/stats.htm

Apply *Yourself!*

Objective 5

Use an Internet search engine to find branches of the Consumer Credit Counseling Service across the country. Choose one in your area and one in another part of the country. Visit the Web sites to find out who funds the offices.

Key Web Sites for Identity Theft
www.consumer.gov/idtheft/index
www.econsumer.equifax.com

- Be sure that your card is returned to you after a purchase. Unreturned cards can find their way into the wrong hands.
- Keep a record of your credit card number. You should keep this record separate from your card.
- Notify the credit card company immediately if your card is lost or stolen. Under the Consumer Credit Protection Act, the maximum amount that you must pay if someone uses your card illegally is $50. However, if you manage to inform the company before the card is used illegally, you have no obligation to pay at all.

Protecting Your Credit Information on the Internet

The Internet is becoming almost as important to daily life as the telephone and television. Increasing numbers of consumers use the Internet for financial activities, such as investing, banking, and shopping.

When you make purchases online, make sure that your transactions are secure, that your personal information is protected, and that your "fraud sensors" are sharpened. Although you can't control fraud or deception on the Internet, you can take steps to recognize it, avoid it, and report it. Here's how:

- Use a secure browser.
- Keep records of your online transactions.
- Review your monthly bank and credit card statements.
- Read the privacy and security policies of Web sites you visit.
- Keep your personal information private.
- Never give your password to anyone online.
- Don't download files sent to you by strangers.

Cosigning a Loan

If a friend or relative ever asks you to cosign a loan, think twice. *Cosigning* a loan means that you agree to be responsible for loan payments if the other party fails to make them. When you cosign, you're taking a chance that a professional lender will not take. The lender would not require a cosigner if the borrower were considered a good risk.

If you cosign a loan and the borrower does not pay the debt, you may have to pay up to the full amount of the debt as well as any late fees or collection costs. The creditor can even collect the debt from you without first trying to collect from the borrower. The creditor can use the same collection methods against you that can be used against the borrower. If the debt is not repaid, that fact will appear on your credit record.

Complaining about Consumer Credit

If you believe that a lender is not following the consumer credit protection laws, first try to solve the problem directly with the lender. If that fails, use formal complaint procedures. This section describes how to file a complaint with the federal agencies that administer credit protection laws.

DID YOU KNOW?

OPTING OUT
You can stop preapproved credit card offers by calling 1-888-567-8688.

Consumer Credit Protection Laws

If you have a particular problem with a bank in connection with any of the consumer credit protection laws, you can get advice and help from the Federal Reserve System. You don't need to have an account at the bank to file a complaint. You may also take

Six ways to clear your GOOD NAME

It can take months of phone calls and mountains of paperwork to clean up the mess after an identity thief wrecks your credit. Here's where to start.

File a report with your local police department. "That gives you victim status," says Tracey Thomas of the Identity Theft Resource Center. But it isn't always easy. Even in California, where the law *requires* a victim's local police department to take a report, victims are sometimes told they have to file reports wherever the crimes took place. Be persistent. You'll need to send a copy of the report to creditors when you dispute fraudulent charges.

File a complaint with the Federal Trade Commission at 877-382-4357 or www.consumer.gov/idtheft. Use the FTC's ID Theft Affidavit to notify creditors about fraudulent accounts in your name. This spares you the need to complete separate affidavits for each creditor.

Get reports from the major credit bureaus, Equifax (888-766-0008), Experian (888-397-3742) and TransUnion (800-680-7289), and request a fraud alert on your credit file. If you spot accounts that don't belong to you, contact the creditors directly (the credit bureaus should supply phone numbers). Also contact all creditors who have made non-promotional inquiries into your credit file. Such inquiries indicate applications for credit have been made in your name. Send all letters certified mail, return receipt requested.

Contact the fraud departments at the banks, credit-card companies and investment firms at which you have accounts. Ask them to require a PIN or password for all transactions or changes to your accounts. (Avoid using your mother's maiden name or the last four digits of your social security number.)

Get additional help on how to clear your name from the Privacy Rights Clearinghouse (www.privacyrights.org) and the Identity Theft Resource Center (www.idtheftcenter.org).

If necessary, find referrals to lawyers who specialize in Fair Credit Reporting Act issues through the National Association of Consumer Advocates (www.naca.net/resource.htm).
—**K.D.**

Source: Reprinted by permission from the January issue of *Kiplinger's Personal Finance*. Copyright © 2004 The Kiplinger Washington Editors, Inc.

1. What action gives you a victim status?

   _____

   _____

2. How can you avoid completing separate affidavits for each creditor?

   _____

   _____

3. Why should you send all letters by certified mail?

   _____

   _____

From the pages of . . . . Kiplinger's Personal Finance

legal action against a creditor. If you decide to file a lawsuit, you should be aware of the various consumer credit protection laws described below.

TRUTH IN LENDING AND CONSUMER LEASING ACTS If a creditor fails to disclose information as required under the Truth in Lending Act or the Consumer Leasing Act, or gives inaccurate information, you can sue for any money loss you suffer. You can also sue a creditor that does not follow rules regarding credit cards. In addition, the Truth in Lending Act and the Consumer Leasing Act permit class action of all the people who have suffered the same injustice.

EQUAL CREDIT OPPORTUNITY ACT (ECOA) If you think that you can prove that a creditor has discriminated against you for any reason prohibited by the ECOA, you may sue for actual damages plus punitive damages—a payment used to punish the creditor who has violated the law—up to $10,000.

Key Web Sites for Credit Protection Laws
www.federalreserve.gov
www.uschamber.com

FAIR CREDIT BILLING ACT A creditor that fails to follow the rules that apply to correcting any billing errors will automatically give up the amount owed on the item in question and any finance charges on it, up to a combined total of $50. This is true even if the bill was correct. You may also sue for actual damages plus twice the amount of any finance charges.

FAIR CREDIT REPORTING ACT You may sue any credit bureau or creditor that violates the rules regarding access to your credit records, or that fails to correct errors in your credit file. You're entitled to actual damages plus any punitive damages the court allows if the violation is proven to have been intentional.

CONSUMER CREDIT REPORTING REFORM ACT The Consumer Credit Reporting Reform Act of 1977 places the burden of proof for accurate credit information on the credit bureau rather than on you. Under this law, the creditor must prove that disputed information is accurate. If a creditor or the credit bureau verifies incorrect data, you can sue for damages.

Your Rights under Consumer Credit Laws

If you believe that you've been refused credit because of discrimination, you can take one or more of the following steps:

- Complain to the creditor. Let the creditor know that you are aware of the law.
- File a complaint with the government. You can report any violations to the appropriate government enforcement agency, as shown in Exhibit 5–7.
- If all else fails, sue the creditor. If you win, you can receive actual damages and punitive damages of up to $10,000. You can also recover reasonable attorneys' fees and court costs.

Managing Your Debts

A sudden illness or the loss of your job may prevent you from paying your bills on time. If you find you cannot make your payments, contact your creditors at once and try to work out a modified payment plan with them.

Exhibit [5–7]   Federal Government Agencies that Enforce the Consumer Credit Laws

If you think you've been discriminated against by:	You may file a complaint with the following agency:
A retailer, nonbank credit card issuer, consumer finance company, state-chartered credit union or bank, noninsured savings and loan institution	Federal Trade Commission (FTC) Equal Credit Opportunity Washington, DC 20580
A national bank	Comptroller of the Currency Consumer Affairs Division Washington, DC 20219
A Federal Reserve member bank	Board of Governors of the Federal Reserve System Director, Division of Consumer Affairs Washington, DC 20551
Other insured banks	Federal Deposit Insurance Corporation Office of Bank Customer Affairs Washington, DC 20429
Insured savings and loan institutions	Federal Home Loan Bank Board Equal Credit Opportunity Washington, DC 20552
The FHA mortgage program	Housing and Urban Development (HUD) Department of Health, Education and Welfare Washington, DC 20410
A federal credit union	National Credit Union Administration 2025 M Street, N.W. Washington, DC 20455

The law gives you certain rights as a consumer of credit. *What types of complaints about a creditor might you report to these government agencies?*

Warning Signs of Debt Problems

Chris is in his late 20s. A college graduate, he has a steady job and earns an annual income of $40,000. With the latest model sports car parked in the driveway of his new home, it would appear that Chris has the ideal life.

However, Chris is deeply in debt. He is drowning in a sea of bills. Almost all his income is tied up in debt payments. The bank has already begun foreclosure proceedings on his home, and several stores have court orders to repossess practically all of his new furniture and electronic gadgets. His current car payment is overdue, and he is behind in payments on all his credit cards. If he doesn't come up with a plan of action, he'll lose everything.

Chris's situation is all too common. Some people who seem to be wealthy are just barely keeping their heads above water financially. Generally, the problem they share is financial immaturity. They lack self-discipline and don't control their impulses. They use poor judgment or fail to accept responsibility for managing their money.

Chris and others like him aren't necessarily bad people. They simply haven't thought about their long-term financial goals. Someday you could find yourself in a situation similar to Chris's. Here are some warning signs that you may be in financial trouble:

- You make only the minimum monthly payment on credit cards.
- You're having trouble making even the minimum monthly payment on your credit card bills.

- The total balance on your credit cards increases every month.
- You miss loan payments or often pay late.
- You use savings to pay for necessities such as food and utilities.
- You receive second and third payment due notices from creditors.
- You borrow money to pay off old debts.
- You exceed the credit limits on your credit cards.
- You've been denied credit because of a bad credit bureau report.

If you are experiencing two or more of these warning signs, it's time for you to rethink your priorities before it's too late.

Debt Collection Practices

The Federal Trade Commission enforces the Fair Debt Collection Practices Act (FDCPA). This act prohibits certain practices by debt collectors—businesses that collect debts for creditors. The act does not erase the legitimate debts that consumers owe, but it does control the ways in which debt collection agencies may do business.

Financial Counseling Services

If you're having trouble paying your bills and need help, you have several options. You can contact your creditors and try to work out an adjusted repayment plan, or you can contact a nonprofit financial counseling program.

CONSUMER CREDIT COUNSELING SERVICES   The Consumer Credit Counseling Service (CCCS) is a nonprofit organization affiliated with the National Foundation for Consumer Credit (NFCC). Local branches of the CCCS provide debt-counseling services for families and individuals with serious financial problems. The CCCS is not a charity, a lending institution, or a government agency. CCCS counseling is usually free. However, when the organization supervises a debt repayment plan, it sometimes charges a small fee to help pay administrative costs.

According to the NFCC, millions of consumers contact CCCS offices each year for help with their personal financial problems. To find an office near you, check the white pages of your local telephone directory under Consumer Credit Counseling Service, or call 1-800-388-CCCS. All information is kept confidential.

Credit counselors know that most individuals who are overwhelmed with debt are basically honest people who want to clear up their unmanageable *indebtedness,* the condition of being deeply in debt. Too often, such problems arise from the lack of planning or a miscalculation of earnings. The CCCS is concerned with preventing problems as much as it is with solving them. As a result, its activities are divided into two parts:

- Aiding families with serious debt problems by helping them to manage their money better and set up a realistic budget.
- Helping people prevent indebtedness by teaching them the importance of budget planning, educating them about the pitfalls of unwise credit buying, and encouraging credit institutions to withhold credit from people who cannot afford it.

Key Web Sites for Credit Counseling
www.economagic.com/frbg
www.uscourts.gov

OTHER COUNSELING SERVICES   In addition to the CCCS, universities, credit unions, military bases, and state and federal housing authorities sometimes provide nonprofit credit counseling services. These organizations usually charge little or nothing for their assistance. You can also check with your bank or local consumer protection office to see whether it has a listing of reputable financial counseling services, such as the Debt Counselors of America.

Declaring Personal Bankruptcy

What if a debtor suffers from an extreme case of financial woes? Can there be any relief? The answer is bankruptcy proceedings. *Bankruptcy* is a legal process in which some or all of the assets of a debtor are distributed among the creditors because the debtor is unable to pay his or her debts. Bankruptcy may also include a plan for the debtor to repay creditors on an installment basis. Declaring bankruptcy is a last resort because it severely damages your credit rating.

Anita Singh illustrates the face of bankruptcy. A 43-year-old freelance photographer from California, she was never in serious financial trouble until she began running up big medical costs. She reached for her credit cards to pay the bills. Because Anita didn't have health insurance, her debt quickly mounted and soon reached $17,000—too much to pay off with her $25,000-a-year income. Her solution was to declare personal bankruptcy and enjoy the immediate freedom it would bring from creditors' demands.

In 1994 the U.S. Senate passed a bill that reduced the time and cost of bankruptcy proceedings. The bill strengthened creditor rights and enabled more individuals to get through bankruptcy proceedings without selling their assets. Today, legislators continue to propose new bankruptcy law reforms that are intended to end perceived abuses of the current bankruptcy system.

THE U.S. BANKRUPTCY ACT OF 1978   Exhibit 5–8 illustrates the rate of personal bankruptcy in the United States. The vast majority of bankruptcies in the United States, like Anita Singh's, are filed under a part of U.S. bankruptcy code known as Chapter 7. You have two choices in declaring personal bankruptcy: Chapter 7 (a straight bankruptcy) and Chapter 13 (a wage earner plan bankruptcy). Both choices are undesirable, and neither should be considered an easy way to get out of debt.

Chapter 7 Bankruptcy   In a Chapter 7 bankruptcy, an individual is required to draw up a petition listing his or her assets and liabilities. A person who files for relief under the bankruptcy code is called a *debtor.* The debtor submits the petition to a U.S. district court and pays a filing fee.

Chapter 7 is a straight bankruptcy in which many, but not all, debts are forgiven. Most of the debtor's assets are sold to pay off creditors. Certain assets, however, receive some protection. Among the assets usually protected are Social Security payments, unemployment compensation, and the net value of your home, vehicle, household goods and appliances, tools used in your work, and books.

Total Personal Bankruptcies

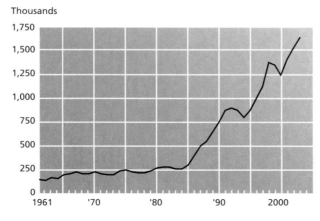

Exhibit [5–8]

U.S. Bankruptcies, 1961–2003

Sources: Administrative Office of the United States Courts; www.uscourts.gov/press_releases/fy03bk, April 22, 2004.

The release from debt does not affect alimony, child support, certain taxes, fines, certain debts arising from educational loans, or debts that you fail to disclose properly to the bankruptcy court. Furthermore, debts arising from fraud, driving while intoxicated, or certain other acts or crimes may also be excluded.

Chapter 13 Bankruptcy In Chapter 13 bankruptcy, a debtor with a regular income proposes a plan for using future earnings or assets to eliminate his or her debts over a period of time. In such a bankruptcy, the debtor normally keeps all or most of his or her property.

During the period when the plan is in effect, which can be as long as five years, the debtor makes regular payments to a Chapter 13 trustee, or representative, who then distributes the money to the creditors. Under certain circumstances, the bankruptcy court may approve a plan that permits the debtor to keep all property, even though he or she repays less than the full amount of the debts.

EFFECTS OF BANKRUPTCY People have varying experiences in obtaining credit after they file for bankruptcy. Some find the process more difficult, whereas others find it easier because they have removed the burden of prior debts or because creditors know that they cannot file another bankruptcy case for a certain period of time. Obtaining credit may be easier for people who file a Chapter 13 bankruptcy and repay some of their debts than for those who file a Chapter 7 bankruptcy and make no effort to repay any of their debts.

✔ CONCEPTCHECK 5–5

1 What steps might you take if there is a billing error in your monthly statement?

_____

_____

2 What steps would you take if someone stole your identity?

_____

_____

_____

3 How might you protect your credit information on the Internet?

_____

_____

4 What are some warning signs of debt problems?

_____

_____

_____

5 Distinguish between Chapter 7 and Chapter 13 bankruptcy.

_____

_____

_____

Back to   Getting Personal

Redo the Getting Personal questions at the beginning of this chapter. What did you learn in this chapter that might affect your answers to these questions in the future?

_____

_____

Chapter Summary

Objective 1   Consumer credit is the use of credit by individuals and families for personal needs. Among the advantages of using credit are the ability to purchase goods when needed and pay for them gradually, the ability to meet financial emergencies, convenience in shopping, and establishment of a credit rating. Disadvantages are that credit costs money, encourages overspending, and ties up future income.

Objective 2   Closed-end and open-end credit are two types of consumer credit. With closed-end credit, the borrower pays back a one-time loan in a stated period of time and with a specified number of payments. With open-end credit, the borrower is permitted to take loans on a continuous basis and is billed for partial payments periodically.

The major sources of consumer credit are commercial banks, savings and loan associations, credit unions, finance companies, life insurance companies, and family and friends. Each of these sources has unique advantages and disadvantages.

Parents or family members are often the source of the least expensive loans. They may charge you only the interest they would have earned had they not made the loan. Such loans, however, can complicate family relationships.

Objective 3   Two general rules for measuring credit capacity are the debt payments-to-income ratio and the debt-to-equity ratio. In reviewing your creditworthiness, a creditor seeks information from one of the three national credit bureaus or a regional credit bureau.

Creditors determine creditworthiness on the basis of the five Cs: character, capacity, capital, collateral, and conditions.

Objective 4   Compare the finance charge and the annual percentage rate (APR) as you shop for credit. Under the Truth in Lending Act, creditors are required to state the cost of borrowing so that you can compare credit costs and shop for credit.

Objective 5   If a billing error occurs on your account, notify the creditor in writing within 60 days. If the dispute is not settled in your favor, you can place your version of it in your credit file. You may also withhold payment on any defective goods or services you have purchased with a credit card as long as you have attempted to resolve the problem with the merchant.

If you have a complaint about credit, first try to deal directly with the creditor. If that fails, you can turn to the appropriate consumer credit law. These laws include the Truth in Lending Act, the Consumer Leasing Act, the Equal Credit Opportunity Act, the Fair Credit Billing Act, the Fair Credit Reporting Act, and the Consumer Credit Reporting Reform Act.

If you cannot meet your obligations, contact your creditors immediately. Also, contact your local Consumer Credit Counseling Service or other debt counseling organizations.

A debtor's last resort is to declare bankruptcy, permitted by the U.S. Bankruptcy Act of 1978. Consider the financial and other costs of bankruptcy before taking this extreme step. A debtor can declare Chapter 7 (straight) bankruptcy or Chapter 13 (wage earner plan) bankruptcy.

Key Terms

annual percentage rate (APR) 134	conditions 128	line of credit 122
capacity 128	consumer credit 118	open-end credit 121
capital 128	credit 118	revolving check credit 122
character 128	Fair Credit Billing Act (FCBA) 138	simple interest 136
closed-end credit 120	finance charge 124	
collateral 128	interest 122	

www.mhhe.com/kdh

1. Vicky is trying to decide whether to finance her purchase of a used Mustang convertible. What questions should Vicky ask herself before making her decision?

2. List advantages and disadvantages of using credit.

3. To finance a sofa for his new apartment, Caleb signed a contract to pay for the sofa in six equal installments. What type of consumer credit is Caleb using?

4. Alka plans to spend $5,000 on plasma television and a home theater system. She is willing to spend some of her $9,000 in savings. However, she wants to finance the rest and pay it off in small monthly installments out of the $400 a month she earns working part-time. How might she obtain a low interest rate and make low monthly payments?

5. Research two credit card companies. List their fees and any advantages they offer. Record your findings.

6. Bobby is trying to decide between two credit cards. One has no annual fee and an 18 percent interest rate, and the other has a $40 annual fee and an 8.9 percent interest rate. Should he take the card that's free or the one that costs $40?

7. Compile a list of places a person can call to report dishonest credit practices, get advice and help with credit problems, and check out a creditor's reputation before signing a contract.

8. Your friend is drowning in a sea of overdue bills and is being harassed by a debt collection agency. Prepare a list of the steps your friend should take if the harassment continues.

9. Visit a local office of the Consumer Credit Counseling Service. What assistance can debtors obtain from this office? What is the cost of this assistance, if any?

10. What factors would you consider in assessing the choices in declaring personal bankruptcy? Why should personal bankruptcy be the choice of last resort?

Internet Connection

COMPARING CREDIT SOURCES AND COSTS

Credit is available from many sources. Becoming aware of the differences among financial institutions related to borrowing costs and other factors while wisely managing your debt will help you avoid financial difficulties.

1. Using www.cardtrak.com and www.ramsearch.com, evaluate your current use of credit cards. Compare various credit card offers related to APR, annual fee, grace period, and other fees.

2. Using www.bankrate.com and www.banx.com, compare credit sources for loans related to various financial needs.

3. Using www.nfcc.org, www.dca.org, and www.nccs.org, investigate actions commonly taken to avoid debt problems.

4. Prepare a spending plan to minimize the use of credit, using www.centura.com/personal/calculators and www.finance-center.com.

Case in Point

FINANCING SUE'S HYUNDAI EXCEL

After shopping around, Sue Wallace decided on the car of her choice, a used Hyundai Excel. The dealer quoted her a total price of $8,000. Sue decided to use $2,000 of her savings as a down payment and borrow $6,000. The salesperson wrote this information on a sales contract that Sue took with her when she set out to find financing.

When Sue applied for a loan, she discussed loan terms with the bank lending officer. The officer told her that the bank's policy was to lend only 80 percent of the total price of a used car. Sue showed the officer her copy of the sales contract, indicating

that she had agreed to make a $2,000, or 25 percent, down payment on the $8,000 car, so this requirement caused her no problem. Although the bank was willing to make 48-month loans at an annual percentage rate of 15 percent on used cars, Sue chose a 36-month repayment schedule. She believed she could afford the higher payments, and she knew she would not have to pay as much interest if she paid off the loan at a faster rate. The bank lending officer provided Sue with a copy of the Truth-in-Lending Disclosure Statement shown here.

Truth-in-Lending Disclosure Statement (Loans)

Annual Percentage Rate	Finance Charge	Amount Financed	Total of Payments 36
The cost of your credit as a yearly rate.	The dollar amount the credit will cost you.	The amount of credit provided to you or on your behalf.	The amount you will have paid after you have made all payments as scheduled.
15%	$1,487.64	$6,000.00	$7,487.64

You have the right to receive at this time an itemization of the Amount Financed.

☒ I want an itemization.   ❏ I do not want an itemization.

Your payment schedule will be:

Number of Payments	Amount of Payments	When Payments Are Due
36	$207.99	1st of each month

Sue decided to compare the APR she had been offered with the APR offered by another bank, but the 20 percent APR of the second bank (bank B) was more expensive than the 15 percent APR of the first bank (bank A). Here is her comparison of the two loans:

	Bank A 15% APR	Bank B 20% APR
Amount financed	$6,000.00	$6,000.00
Finance charge	1,487.64	2,027.28
Total of payments	7,487.64	8,027.28
Monthly payments	207.99	222.98

The 5 percent difference in the APRs of the two banks meant Sue would have to pay $15 extra every month if she got her loan

from the second bank. Of course, she got the loan from the first bank.

Questions

1. What is perhaps the most important item shown on the disclosure statement? Why?

2. What is included in the finance charge?

3. What amount will Sue receive from the bank?

4. Should Sue borrow from bank A or bank B? Why?

Name: _____ Date: _____

Consumer Credit Usage Patterns

Financial Planning Activities: Record account names, numbers, and payments for current consumer debts.

Suggested Web Sites: www.finance-center.com   www.ftc.gov

Automobile, Education, Personal, and Installment Loans

Financial institution	Account number	Current balance	Monthly payment
_____	_____	_____	_____
_____	_____	_____	_____
_____	_____	_____	_____
_____	_____	_____	_____
_____	_____	_____	_____

Charge Accounts and Credit Cards

_____	_____	_____	_____
_____	_____	_____	_____
_____	_____	_____	_____
_____	_____	_____	_____
_____	_____	_____	_____

Other Loans (overdraft protection, home equity, life insurance loan)

_____	_____	_____	_____
_____	_____	_____	_____
_____	_____	_____	_____

Totals _____ _____

$$\text{Debt payment-to-income ratio} = \frac{\text{Total monthly payments}}{\text{net (after-tax) income}}$$

What's Next for Your Personal Financial Plan?

- Survey three or four individuals to determine their uses of credit.
- Talk to several people to determine how they first established credit.

Credit Card/Charge Account Comparison

Financial Planning Activities: Analyze ads and credit applications and contact various financial institutions to obtain the information requested below.

Suggested Web Sites: www.bankrate.com   www.banx.com

Type of credit/charge account			
Name of company/account			
Address/phone			
Web site			
Type of purchases that can be made			
Annual fee (if any)			
Annual percentage rate (APR) (interest calculation information)			
Credit limit for new customers			
Minimum monthly payment			
Other costs: • credit report • late fee • other _____			
Restrictions (age, minimum annual income)			
Other information for consumers to consider			
Frequent flyer or other bonus points			

What's Next for Your Personal Financial Plan?

- Make a list of the pros and cons of using credit or debit cards.
- Contact a local credit bureau to obtain information on the services provided and the fees charged.

Name: _____ **Date:** _____

Consumer Loan Comparison

Financial Planning Activities: Contact or visit a bank, credit union, and consumer finance company to obtain information on a loan for a specific purpose.

Suggested Web Sites: www.eloan.com   www.centura.com

Type of financial institution			
Name			
Address			
Phone			
Web site			
Amount of down payment			
Length of loan (months)			
What collateral is required?			
Amount of monthly payment			
Total amount to be repaid (monthly amount $\times$ number of months + down payment)			
Total finance charge/cost of credit			
Annual percentage rate (APR)			
Other costs • credit life insurance • credit report • other _____			
Is a cosigner required?			
Other information			

What's Next for Your Personal Financial Plan?

- Ask several individuals how they would compare loans at different financial institutions.
- Survey several friends and relatives to determine if they ever cosigned a loan. If yes, what were the consequences of cosigning?

6 Wise Buying of Motor Vehicles and Other Purchases

Objectives

In this chapter, you will learn to:

1. Identify strategies for effective consumer buying.
2. Implement a process for making consumer purchases.
3. Describe steps to take to resolve consumer problems.
4. Evaluate legal alternatives available to consumers.

Why is this important?

Unplanned and careless buying will reduce your potential for long-term financial security. Impulse buying activities of a few dollars a week can cost you thousands of dollars in just a couple of years.

 Getting Personal

For each of the following shopping behaviors, circle "agree," "neutral," or "disagree" to indicate your attitude toward this action.

1. Getting very good quality is very important to me.	Agree	Neutral	Disagree
2. Well-known national brands are best for me.	Agree	Neutral	Disagree
3. I buy as much as possible at "sale" prices.	Agree	Neutral	Disagree
4. I should plan my shopping more carefully than I do.	Agree	Neutral	Disagree
5. I have favorite brands I buy over and over.	Agree	Neutral	Disagree
6. Lower priced products are usually my choice.	Agree	Neutral	Disagree

After studying this chapter, you will be asked to reconsider your responses to these items.

Consumer Buying Activities

> **OBJECTIVE 1**
>
> Identify strategies for effective consumer buying.

Daily buying decisions involve a trade-off between current spending and saving for the future. A wide variety of economic, social, and personal factors affect daily buying habits. These factors are the basis for spending, saving, investing, and achieving personal financial goals. In very simple terms, the only way you can have long-term financial security is to not spend all of your current income. In addition, overspending leads to misuse of credit and financial difficulties.

Practical Purchasing Strategies

Comparison shopping is the process of considering alternative stores, brands, and prices. In contrast, *impulse buying* is unplanned purchasing, which can result in financial problems. Several buying techniques are commonly suggested for wise buying.

TIMING PURCHASES   Certain items go on sale the same time each year. You can obtain bargains by buying winter clothing in mid- or late winter, or summer clothing in mid- or late summer. Many people save by buying holiday items and other products at reduced prices in late December and early January.

STORE SELECTION   Your decision to use a particular retailer is probably influenced by location, price, product selection, and services available. Competition and technology have changed retailing with superstores, specialty shops, and online buying. This expanded shopping environment provides consumers with greater choice, potentially lower prices, and the need to carefully consider buying alternatives.

BRAND COMPARISON   Food and other products come in various brands. *National-brand* products are highly advertised items available in many stores. *Store-brand* and *private-label* products, sold by one chain of stores, are low-cost alternatives to famous-name products. Since store-brand products are frequently manufactured by the same companies that produce brand-name items, these lower cost alternatives can result in extensive savings.

LABEL INFORMATION   Certain label information is helpful; however, other information is nothing more than advertising. Federal law requires that food labels contain certain information. Product labeling for appliances includes information about operating costs to assist you in selecting the most energy-efficient models. *Open dating* describes the freshness or shelf life of a perishable product. Phrases such as "Use before May 2006" or "Not to be sold after October 8" appear on most grocery items.

PRICE COMPARISON   *Unit pricing* uses a standard unit of measurement to compare the prices of packages of different sizes. To calculate the unit price, divide the price of the item by the number of units of measurement, such as ounces, pounds, gallons, or number of sheets (for items such as paper towels and facial tissues). Then compare the unit prices for various sizes, brands, and stores.

Coupons and rebates also provide better pricing for wise consumers. A family saving about $8 a week on their groceries by using coupons will save $416 over a year and $2,080 over five years (not counting interest). Coupons are available online at www.coolsavings.com, www.centsoff.com, and www.couponsurfer.com. A *rebate* is a partial refund of the price of a product.

When comparing prices, remember that

- More store convenience (location, hours, sales staff) usually means higher prices.
- Ready-to-use products have higher prices.
- Large packages are usually the best buy; however, compare using unit pricing.
- "Sale" may not always mean saving money.

Exhibit 6–1 summarizes techniques that can assist you in your buying decisions.

Apply *Yourself!*

Objective 1

Conduct a survey regarding brand loyalty. For what products are people most brand loyal? What factors (price, location, information) may influence their selection of another brand?

Exhibit [6–1]

Wise Buying Techniques: A Summary

- ✓ Compare brands of similar products to determine which is best for your intended use.
- ✓ Compare stores and other sources of buying with regard to prices, services offered, product quality, and return privileges.
- ✓ Read and evaluate label information.
- ✓ Use coupons for products that you buy regularly or are trying out.
- ✓ Use unit pricing to compare packages of different sizes.
- ✓ Obtain "rain checks" for out-of-stock advertised specials that you can use for purchase later.
- ✓ Use open dating to determine the freshness and shelf life of perishable products.
- ✓ Use various consumer information sources to assist you with your buying decisions.
- ✓ Consider the nutritional value and health aspects of the foods you buy.
- ✓ Evaluate and compare the warranties of different brands.
- ✓ Read product testing reports to determine which items are the safest and of the highest quality.
- ✓ Plan your purchases to take advantage of sales and special offers.
- ✓ Consider the time and effort it takes to evaluate alternatives and go to different stores.

Warranties

warranty A written guarantee from the manufacturer or distributor of a product that specifies the conditions under which the product can be returned, replaced, or repaired.

Most products come with some guarantee of quality. A **warranty** is a written guarantee from the manufacturer or distributor that specifies the conditions under which the product can be returned, replaced, or repaired. An *express warranty,* usually in written form, is created by the seller or manufacturer and has two forms: the full warranty and the limited warranty. A *full warranty* states that a defective product can be fixed or replaced during a reasonable amount of time.

A *limited warranty* covers only certain aspects of the product, such as parts, or requires the buyer to incur part of the costs for shipping or repairs. An *implied warranty* covers a product's intended use or other basic understandings that are not in writing. For example, an implied *warranty of title* indicates that the seller has the right to sell the product. An implied *warranty of merchantability* guarantees that the product is fit for the ordinary uses for which it is intended: A toaster must toast bread, and a stereo must play CDs or tapes. Implied warranties vary from state to state.

USED-CAR WARRANTIES

The Federal Trade Commission (FTC) requires used cars to have a buyer's guide sticker telling whether the vehicle comes with a warranty and, if so, what protection the dealer will provide. If no warranty is offered, the car is sold "as is" and the dealer assumes no responsibility for any repairs, regardless of any oral claims. FTC used-car regulations do not apply to vehicles purchased from private owners.

While a used car may not have an express warranty, most states have implied warranties to protect used-car buyers. An implied warranty of merchantability means the product is guaranteed to do what it is supposed to do. The used car is guaranteed to run—at least for a while!

NEW-CAR WARRANTIES

New-car warranties provide buyers with an assurance of quality. These warranties vary in the time, mileage, and parts they cover. The main conditions of a new-car warranty are (1) coverage of basic parts against defects; (2) power train coverage for the engine, transmission, and drive train; and (3) the corrosion warranty, which usually applies only to holes due to rust, not to surface rust. Other important conditions of a warranty are a statement regarding whether the warranty is transferable to other owners of the car and details about the charges, if any, that will be made for major repairs in the form of a *deductible.*

service contract An agreement between a business and a consumer to cover the repair costs of a product.

SERVICE CONTRACTS

A **service contract** is an agreement between a business and a consumer to cover the repair costs of a product. Frequently called *extended warranties,* they are not warranties. For a fee, they insure the buyer against losses due to the cost of certain repairs. Automotive service contracts can cover repairs not included in the manufacturer's warranty. Service contracts range from $400 to more than $1,000; however, they do not always include everything you might expect. These contracts usually cover failure of the engine cooling system; however, some contracts exclude coverage of such failures if caused by overheating.

Because of costs and exclusions, service contracts may not be a wise financial decision. You can minimize your concern about expensive repairs by setting aside a fund of money to pay for them. Then, if you need repairs, the money to pay for them will be available.

Sheet 17
Consumer
Purchase
Comparison

✓ CONCEPTCHECK 6–1

1 What types of brands are commonly available to consumers?

_____

_____

2 In what situations can comparing prices help in purchasing decisions?

_____

_____

3 How does a service contract differ from a warranty?

_____

_____

4 Match the following descriptions with the warranties listed here. Write your answer in the space provided.

express warranty   limited warranty

full warranty   service contact

implied warranty

a. _____ covers only aspects of the item purchased.

b. _____ is commonly referred to as an extended warranty.

c. _____ usually is in a written form.

d. _____ covers a product's intended use; it may not be in writing.

e. _____ covers fixing or replacement of a product for a set time period.

Making Major Consumer Purchases: Buying Motor Vehicles

Shopping decisions should be based on a specific decision-making process. Exhibit 6–2 presents steps for effective purchasing of a motor vehicle.

OBJECTIVE 2
Implement a process for making consumer purchases.

Phase 1: Preshopping Activities

First define your needs and obtain relevant product information. These activities are the foundation for buying decisions to help you achieve your goals.

PROBLEM IDENTIFICATION   Effective decision making should start with an open mind. Some people always buy the same brand when another brand at a lower price would also serve their needs, or when another brand at the same price may provide better quality. A narrow view of the problem is a weakness in problem identification. You may think the problem is "I need to have a car" when the real problem is "I need transportation."

INFORMATION GATHERING   Information is power. The better informed you are, the better buying decisions you will make. Some people spend very little time gathering and evaluating buying information. At the other extreme are people who spend much time obtaining consumer information. While information is necessary for wise purchasing, too much information can create confusion and frustration. The following information sources are frequently helpful:

1. *Personal contacts* allow you to learn about product performance, brand quality, and prices from others.

Exhibit [6–2]   A Research-Based Approach for Purchasing a Motor Vehicle

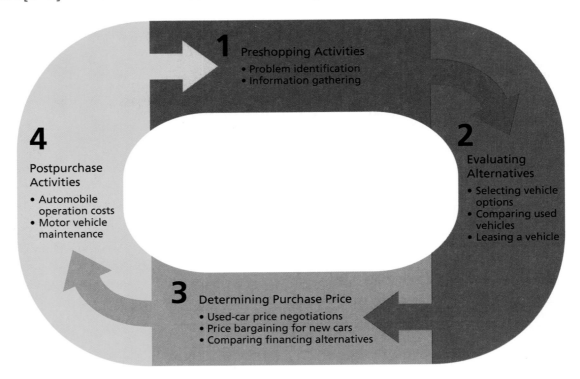

2. *Business organizations* offer advertising, product labels, and packaging that provide information about price, quality, and availability.
3. *Media information* (television, radio, newspapers, magazines, Web sites) can provide valuable information with purchasing advice.
4. *Independent testing organizations,* such as Consumers Union, provide information about the quality of products and services each month in *Consumer Reports.*
5. *Government agencies,* local, state, and federal, provide publications, toll-free telephone numbers, Web sites, and community programs.
6. *Online sources* offer extensive product information and shopping suggestions.

Phase 2: Evaluating Alternatives

Every purchasing situation usually has several acceptable alternatives. Ask yourself: Is it possible to delay the purchase or to do without the item? Should I pay for the item with cash or buy it on credit? Which brands should I consider? How do the price, quality, and service compare at different stores? Is it possible to rent the item instead of buying it? Considering such alternatives will result in more effective purchasing decisions.

Research shows that prices can vary for all types of products. For a camera, prices may range from under $100 to well over $500. The price of aspirin may range from less than $1 to over $3 for 100 five-grain tablets. While differences in quality and attributes may exist among the cameras, the aspirin are the same in quantity and quality.

Many people view comparison shopping as a waste of time. Although this may be true in certain situations, comparison shopping can be beneficial when (1) buying expensive or complex items; (2) buying items that you purchase often; (3) comparison shopping can be done easily, such as with

Apply *Yourself!*

Objective 2

Compare the prices charged by different automotive service locations for a battery, tune-up, oil change, and tires.

advertisements, catalogs, or online; (4) different sellers offer different prices and services; and (5) product quality or prices vary greatly.

SELECTING VEHICLE OPTIONS
Optional equipment for cars may be viewed in three categories: (1) mechanical devices to improve performance, such as a larger engine, the transmission, power steering, power brakes, and cruise control; (2) convenience options, including power seats, air conditioning, stereo systems, power locks, rear window defoggers, and tinted glass; and (3) aesthetic features that add to the vehicle's visual appeal, such as metallic paint, special trim, and upholstery.

COMPARING USED VEHICLES
The average used car costs about $10,000 less than the average new car. Common sources of used cars include:

- New-car dealers, which offer late-model vehicles and may give you a warranty. Prices usually are higher than at other sources.
- Used-car dealers, which usually have older vehicles. Warranties, if offered, will be limited. However, lower prices may be available.
- Individuals selling their own cars. This can be a bargain if the vehicle was well maintained, but few consumer protection regulations apply to private-party sales. Caution is suggested.
- Auctions and dealers that sell automobiles previously owned by businesses, auto rental companies, and government agencies.
- Used-car superstores, such as CarMax, which offer a large inventory of previously owned vehicles.

Certified preowned (CPO) vehicles are nearly new cars that come with the original manufacturer's guarantee of quality. The rigorous inspection and repair process means a higher price than other used vehicles. CPO programs were originally created to generate demand for the many low-mileage vehicles returned at the end of a lease.

The appearance of a used car can be deceptive. A well-maintained engine may be inside a body with rust; a clean, shiny exterior may conceal major operational problems. Therefore, conduct a used-car inspection as outlined in Exhibit 6–3. Have a trained and trusted mechanic of *your* choice check the car to estimate the costs of potential repairs. This service will help you avoid surprises.

LEASING A MOTOR VEHICLE
Leasing is a contractual agreement with monthly payments for the use of an automobile over a set time period, typically three, four, or five years. At the end of the lease term, the vehicle is usually returned to the leasing company.

Leasing offers several advantages: (1) only a small cash outflow may be required for the security deposit, whereas buying can require a large down payment; (2) monthly lease payments are usually lower than monthly financing payments; (3) the lease agreement provides detailed records for business purposes; and (4) you are usually able to obtain a more expensive vehicle, more often.

Leasing also has major drawbacks: (1) you have no ownership interest in the vehicle; (2) you must meet requirements similar to qualifying for credit; and (3) additional costs may be incurred for extra mileage, certain repairs, turning the car in early, or even a move to another state.

When leasing, you arrange for the dealer to sell the vehicle through a financing company. As a result, be sure you know the true cost, including

Sheet 18
Used Car
Purchase
Comparison

Key Web Sites for Used Cars
www.dealernet.com
www.americasautomall.com

Exhibit [6–3]   Checking Out a Used Car

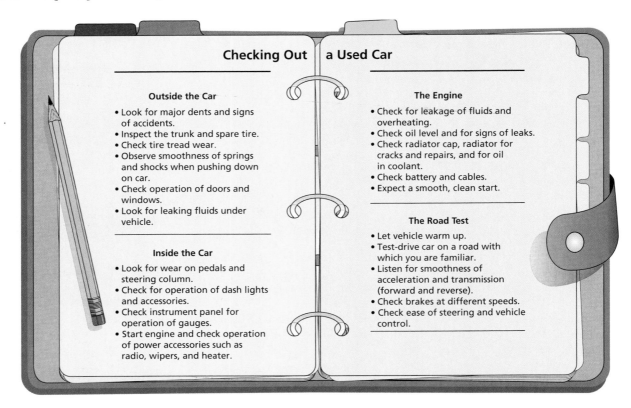

Checking Out a Used Car

Outside the Car

- Look for major dents and signs of accidents.
- Inspect the trunk and spare tire.
- Check tire tread wear.
- Observe smoothness of springs and shocks when pushing down on car.
- Check operation of doors and windows.
- Look for leaking fluids under vehicle.

Inside the Car

- Look for wear on pedals and steering column.
- Check for operation of dash lights and accessories.
- Check instrument panel for operation of gauges.
- Start engine and check operation of power accessories such as radio, wipers, and heater.

The Engine

- Check for leakage of fluids and overheating.
- Check oil level and for signs of leaks.
- Check radiator cap, radiator for cracks and repairs, and for oil in coolant.
- Check battery and cables.
- Expect a smooth, clean start.

The Road Test

- Let vehicle warm up.
- Test-drive car on a road with which you are familiar.
- Listen for smoothness of acceleration and transmission (forward and reverse).
- Check brakes at different speeds.
- Check ease of steering and vehicle control.

Sheet 19
Buying vs.
Leasing an
Automobile

1. The *capitalized cost,* which is the price of the vehicle. The average car buyer pays about 92 percent of the list price for a vehicle; the average leasing arrangement has a capitalized cost of 96 percent of the list price.
2. The *money factor,* which is the interest rate being paid on the capitalized cost.
3. The *payment schedule,* which is the amount paid monthly and the number of payments.
4. The *residual value,* or the expected value of the vehicle at the end of the lease.

After the final payment, you may return, keep, or sell the vehicle. If the current market value is greater than the residual value, you may be able to sell it for a profit. If the residual value is less than the market value (which is the typical case), returning the vehicle to the leasing company is usually the best decision.

Phase 3: Determining Purchase Price

Once you've done your research and evaluations, other activities and decisions may be appropriate. Products such as real estate or automobiles may be purchased using price negotiation. Negotiation may also be used in other buying situations to obtain a lower price or additional features. Two vital factors in negotiation are (1) having all the necessary information about the product and buying situation and (2) dealing with a person who has the authority to give you a lower price or additional features, such as the owner or store manager.

Key Web Sites for Used Car Prices
www.edmunds.com
www.kbb.com

USED-CAR PRICE NEGOTIATION   Begin to determine a fair price by checking newspaper ads for the prices of comparable vehicles. Other sources of current used-car prices are *Edmund's Used Car Prices* and the *Kelley Blue Book.*

Figure It Out!

BUYING VERSUS LEASING AN AUTOMOBILE

To compare the costs of purchasing and leasing a vehicle, use the following framework.

Purchase Costs	Example	Your Figures
Total vehicle cost, including sales tax ($22,000)		
Down payment (or full amount if paying cash)	$2,000	$ _____
Monthly loan payment: $469.70 × 48-month length of financing (this item is zero if vehicle is not financed)	22,545	_____
Opportunity cost of down payment (or total cost of the vehicle if bought for cash): $2,000 × 4 years of financing/ownership × 3 percent	240	_____
Less: Estimated value of vehicle at end of loan term/ownership period	−6,000	− _____
Total cost to buy	$18,785	_____

Leasing Costs	Example	Your Figures
Security deposit ($370)		
Monthly lease payments: $300 × 48-month length of lease	$17,760	$ _____
Opportunity cost of security deposit: $300 security deposit × 4 years × 3 percent	36	_____
End-of-lease charges (if applicable)*	800	_____
Total cost to lease	$18,596	_____

*With a closed-end lease, charges for extra mileage or excessive wear and tear; with an open-end lease, end-of-lease payment if appraised value is less than estimated ending value.

A number of factors influence the basic price of a used car. The number of miles the car has been driven, along with features and options, affect price. A low-mileage car will have a higher price than a comparable car with high mileage. The condition of the vehicle and the demand for the model also affect price.

PRICE BARGAINING FOR NEW CARS   An important new-car price information source is the *sticker price* label, printed on the vehicle with the suggested retail price. This label presents the base price of the car with costs of added features. The dealer's cost, or *invoice price,* is an amount less than the sticker price. The difference between the sticker price and the dealer's cost is the range available for negotiation. This range is larger for full-size, luxury cars; subcompacts usually do not have a wide negotiation range. Information about dealer's cost is available from sources such as *Edmund's New Car Prices* and *Consumer Reports*.

Set-price dealers use no-haggling car selling with the prices presented to be accepted or rejected as stated. *Car-buying services* are businesses that help buyers obtain a specific new car at a reasonable price. Also referred to as an *auto broker*, these businesses offer desired models with options for prices ranging between $50 and $200 over the dealer's cost. First, the auto broker charges a small fee for price information on desired models. Then, if you decide to buy a car, the auto broker arranges the purchase with a dealer near your home.

To prevent confusion in determining the true price of the new car, do not mention a trade-in vehicle until the cost of the new car has been settled. Then ask how much the

Key Web Sites for New Cars
www.edmunds.com
www.consumerreports.org

dealer is willing to pay for your old car. If the offer price is not acceptable, sell the old car on your own. A typical negotiating conversation might go like this:

Customer: "I'm willing to give you $15,600 for the car. That's my top offer."

Auto salesperson: "Let me check with my manager." After returning, "My manager says $16,200 is the best we can do."

Customer (who should be willing to walk out at this point): "I can go to $15,650."

Auto salesperson: "We have the car you want, ready to go. How about $15,700?"

If the customer agrees, the dealer has gotten $100 more than the customer's "top offer."

Other sales techniques you should avoid include:

- *Lowballing,* when quoted a very low price that increases when add-on costs are included at the last moment.
- *Highballing,* when offered a very high amount for a trade-in vehicle, with the extra amount made up by increasing the new-car price.
- The question "How much can you afford per month?" Be sure to also ask how many months.
- The offer to hold the vehicle for a small deposit only. Never leave a deposit unless you are ready to buy a vehicle or are willing to lose that amount.
- Unrealistic statements, such as "Your price is only $100 above our cost." Usually, hidden costs have been added in to get the dealer's cost.
- Sales agreements with preprinted amounts. Cross out numbers you believe are not appropriate for your purchase.

COMPARING FINANCING ALTERNATIVES   You may pay cash; however, most people buy cars on credit. Auto loans are available from banks, credit unions, consumer finance companies, and other financial institutions. Many lenders will *preapprove* you for a certain loan amount, which separates financing from negotiating the car price. Until the new-car price is set, you should not indicate that you intend to use the dealer's credit plan.

The lowest interest rate or the lowest payment does not necessarily mean the best credit plan. Also consider the loan length. Otherwise, after two or three years, the value of your car may be less than the amount you still owe; this situation is referred to as *upside-down* or *negative equity.* If you default on your loan or sell the car at this time, you will have to pay the difference.

Automobile manufacturers frequently present opportunities for low-interest financing. They may offer rebates at the same time, giving buyers a choice between a rebate and a low-interest loan. Carefully compare low-interest financing and the rebate. Special rebates are sometimes offered to students, teachers, credit union members, real estate agents, and other groups.

Phase 4: Postpurchase Activities

Maintenance and ownership costs are associated with most major purchases. Correct use can result in improved performance and fewer repairs. When you need repairs not covered by a warranty, follow a pattern similar to that used when making the original purchase. Investigate, evaluate, and negotiate a variety of servicing options.

In the past, when major problems occurred with a new car and the warranty didn't solve the difficulty, many consumers lacked a course of action. As a result, all 50 states and the District of Columbia enacted *lemon laws* that require a refund for the vehicle after the owner has made repeated attempts to obtain servicing. These laws apply to situations in which a person has made four attempts to get the same problem corrected or situations in which the vehicle has been out of service for more than 30 days within 12 months of purchase or the first 12,000 miles. The terms of the state laws vary.

Key Web Site for Lemon Laws
www.lemonlawamerica.com

AUTOMOBILE OPERATION COSTS   Over your lifetime, you can expect to spend more than $200,000 on automobile-related expenses. Your driving costs will vary based on two main factors: the size of your automobile and the number of miles you drive. These costs involve two categories:

Fixed Ownership Costs	Variable Operating Costs
Depreciation	Gasoline and oil
Interest on auto loan	Tires
Insurance	Maintenance and repairs
License, registration, taxes, and fees	Parking and tolls

The largest fixed expense associated with a new automobile is *depreciation,* the loss in the vehicle's value due to time and use. Since money is not paid out for depreciation, many people do not consider it an expense. However, this decreased value is a cost that owners incur. Well-maintained vehicles and certain high-quality, expensive models, such as BMW and Lexus, depreciate at a slower rate.

Costs such as gasoline, oil, and tires increase with the number of miles driven. Planning expenses is easier if the number of miles you drive is fairly constant. Unexpected trips and vehicle age will increase such costs.

MOTOR VEHICLE MAINTENANCE   People who sell, repair, or drive automobiles for a living stress the importance of regular care. While owner's manuals and articles suggest mileage or time intervals for certain servicing, more frequent oil changes or tune-ups can minimize major repairs and maximize vehicle life. Exhibit 6–4 suggests maintenance areas to consider.

AUTOMOBILE SERVICING SOURCES   The following businesses offer automobile maintenance and repair service:

- Car dealers provide a service department with a wide range of car care services. Service charges at a car dealer may be higher than those of other repair businesses.
- Service stations can provide convenience and reasonable prices for routine maintenance and repairs. However, the number of full-service stations has declined in recent years.
- Independent auto repair shops can service your vehicle at fairly competitive prices. Since the quality of these repair shops varies, talk with previous customers.
- Mass merchandise retailers, such as Sears and Wal-Mart, may emphasize sale of tires and batteries as well as brakes, oil changes, and tune-ups.
- Specialty shops offer brakes, tires, automatic transmissions, and oil changes at a reasonable price with fast service.

To avoid unnecessary expenses, be aware of the common repair frauds presented in Exhibit 6–5. Remember to deal with reputable auto service businesses. Be sure to get a written, detailed estimate in advance as well as a detailed, paid receipt for the service completed. Studies of consumer problems consistently rank auto repairs as one of the top consumer ripoffs. Many people avoid problems and minimize costs by working on their own vehicles.

Exhibit [6–4]

Extended Vehicle Life with Proper Maintenance

- Get regular oil changes.
- Check fluids (brake, power steering, transmission).
- Inspect hoses and belts for wear.
- Get a tune-up (new spark plugs, fuel filter, air filter) 12,000–15,000 miles.
- Check and clean battery cables and terminals.
- Check spark plug wires after 50,000 miles.
- Flush radiator and service transmission every 25,000 miles.
- Keep lights, turn signals, and horn in good working condition.
- Check muffler and exhaust pipes.
- Check tires for wear; rotate tires every 7,500 miles.
- Check condition of brakes.

Exhibit [6–5]

Common Automobile Repair Frauds

The majority of automobile servicing sources are fair and honest. Sometimes, however, consumers waste dollars when they fall prey to the following tricks:

- When checking the oil, the attendant puts the dipstick only partway down and then shows you that you need oil.
- An attendant cuts a fan belt or punctures a hose. Watch carefully when someone checks under your hood.
- A garage employee puts some liquid on your battery and then tries to convince you that it is leaking and you need a new battery.
- Removing air from a tire instead of adding air to it can make an unwary driver open to buying a new tire or paying for an unneeded patch on a tire that is in perfect condition.
- The attendant puts grease near a shock absorber or on the ground and then tells you your present shocks are dangerous and you need new ones.
- You are charged for two gallons of antifreeze with a radiator flush when only one gallon was put in.

Dealing with reputable businesses and a basic knowledge of your automobile are the best methods of avoiding deceptive repair practices.

✔ **CONCEPTCHECK 6–2**

1 What are the major sources of consumer information?

_____

_____

2 What actions are appropriate when buying a used car?

_____

_____

3 When might leasing a motor vehicle be appropriate?

_____

_____

4 What maintenance activities could reduce the life of your vehicle?

_____

_____

5 The following abbreviations appeared in an ad for selling used cars. Interpret these abbreviations.

AC _____   pwr mrrs _____

ABS _____   P/S _____

Resolving Consumer Complaints

Most customer complaints result from defective products, low quality, short product lives, unexpected costs, deceptive pricing, and poor repairs. Federal consumer agencies estimate annual consumer losses from fraudulent business activities at $10 billion to $40 billion for telemarketing and mail order, $3 billion for credit card fraud and credit "repair" scams, and $10 billion for investment swindles. In addition, consumers commonly encounter problems with motor vehicles, mail-order purchases, work-at-home opportunities, dry cleaning, travel services, magazine subscriptions, contests, and sweepstakes.

People do not anticipate problems with purchases but should be prepared for them. Exhibit 6–6 outlines the process for resolving differences. To help ensure success, keep a file of receipts, names of people you talked to, dates of attempted repairs, copies of letters you wrote, and costs incurred. An automobile owner kept detailed records and receipts for all gasoline purchases, oil changes, and repairs. When a warranty dispute occurred, the owner was able to prove proper maintenance and received a refund for the defective vehicle.

> **OBEJCTIVE 3**
> Describe steps to take to resolve consumer problems.

Apply *Yourself!*

> **Objective 3**
>
> Conduct online research to determine the most frequent sources of consumer complaints.

Step 1: Return to Place of Purchase

Most consumer complaints are resolved at the original sales location. As you talk with the salesperson, customer service person, or store manager, avoid yelling, threatening a lawsuit, or demanding unreasonable action. A calm, rational, yet persistent approach is recommended.

Key Web Site for Company Addresses www.consumeraction.gov

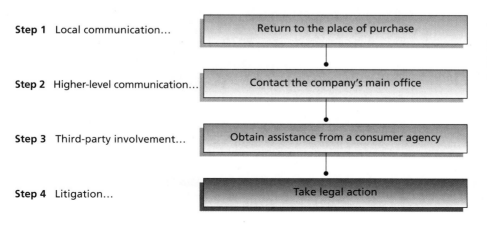

Step 1	Local communication...	Return to the place of purchase
Step 2	Higher-level communication...	Contact the company's main office
Step 3	Third-party involvement...	Obtain assistance from a consumer agency
Step 4	Litigation...	Take legal action

Exhibit [6–6]

Suggested Steps for Resolving Consumer Complaints

Step 2: Contact Company Headquarters

Express your dissatisfaction to the corporate level if a problem is not resolved at the local store. Use a letter or e-mail such as the one in Exhibit 6–7. You can obtain addresses of companies at www.consumeraction.gov or in reference books at your library. The Web sites of companies usually provide information for contacting the organization. You can obtain a company's consumer hotline number by calling 1-800-555-1212, the toll-free information number. Many companies print the toll-free hotline number and Web site information on product packages.

Exhibit [6–7]   Sample Complaint Letter

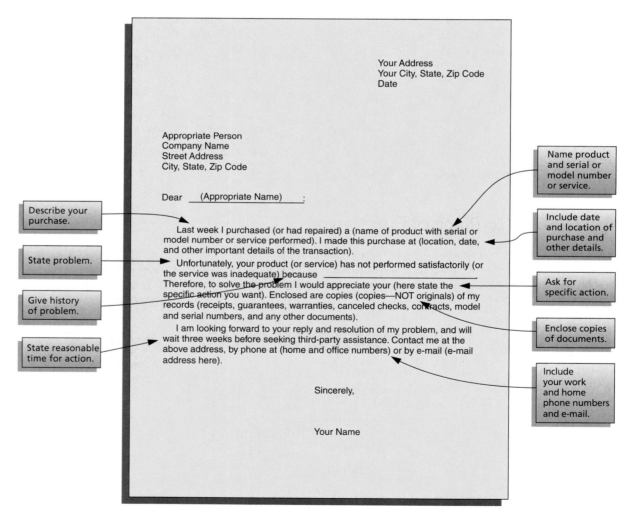

Note: Keep copies of your letter and all related documents and information.
Source: *Consumer's Resource Handbook* (www.pueblo.gsa.gov).

Step 3: Obtain Consumer Agency Assistance

If you do not receive satisfaction from the company, organizations are available to assist with automobiles, appliances, health care, and other consumer concerns. **Mediation** involves the use of a third party to settle grievances. In mediation, an impartial person—the *mediator*—tries to resolve a conflict between a customer and a business through discussion and negotiation. Mediation is a non-binding process. It can save time and money compared to other dispute settlement methods.

Arbitration is the settlement of a difference by a third party—the *arbitrator*—whose decision is legally binding. After both sides agree to arbitration, each side presents its case. Arbitrators are selected from volunteers trained for this purpose. Most major automobile manufacturers and many industry organizations have arbitration programs to resolve consumer complaints.

A vast network of government agencies is available. Problems with local restaurants or food stores may be handled by a city or county health department. Every state has agencies to handle problems involving deceptive advertising, fraudulent business practices, banking, insurance companies, and utility rates. Federal agencies are available to help with consumer concerns.

Step 4: Take Legal Action

The next section considers various legal alternatives available to resolve consumer problems.

> **DID YOU KNOW?**
>
> Without realizing it, many consumers sign contracts with provisions that stipulate arbitration as the method to resolve disputes. As a result, consumers face various risks, including rules vastly different from a jury trial, higher costs for the arbitrator's time, and selection of an arbitrator by the defendant.

mediation The attempt by an impartial third party to resolve a difference between two parties through discussion and negotiation.

arbitration The settlement of a difference by a third party whose decision is legally binding.

Key Web Site for Consumer Concerns www.consumer.gov

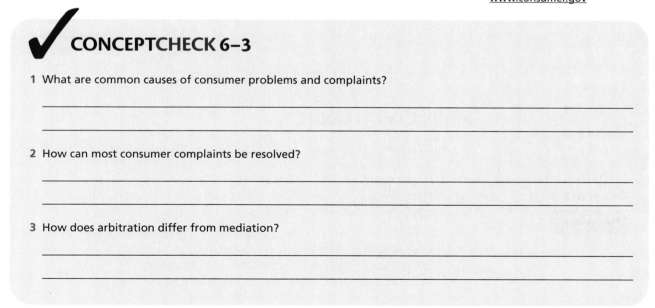

✔ CONCEPTCHECK 6–3

1 What are common causes of consumer problems and complaints?

_____

_____

2 How can most consumer complaints be resolved?

_____

_____

3 How does arbitration differ from mediation?

_____

_____

Legal Options for Consumers

If the previous actions fail to resolve your complaint, one of the following may be appropriate.

> **OBJECTIVE 4**
> Evaluate legal alternatives available to consumers.

Personal Finance in Practice

IS IT LEGAL?

The following situations are common problems for consumers. How would you respond to the question at the end of each situation?

	Yes	No
1. A store advertised a bottle of shampoo as "the $1.79 size, on sale for 99¢." If the store never sold the item for $1.79 but the manufacturer's recommended price was $1.79, was this a legitimate price comparison?	___	___
2. You purchase a stereo system for $650. Two days later, the same store offers the same item for $425. Is this legal?	___	___
3. You receive an unordered sample of flower seeds in the mail. You decide to plant them to see how well they will grow in your yard. A couple of days later, you receive a bill for the seeds. Do you have to pay for the seeds?	___	___
4. A store has a "going out of business sale—everything must go" sign in its window. After six months, the sign is still there. Is this a deceptive business practice?	___	___
5. A 16-year-old injured while playing ball at a local park is taken to a hospital for medical care. The parents refuse to pay the hospital since they didn't request the service. Can the parents be held legally responsible for the charges?	___	___
6. You purchase a shirt for a friend. The shirt doesn't fit, but when you return it to the store, you are offered an exchange since the store policy is no cash refunds. Is this legal?	___	___
7. A manufacturer refuses to repair a motorcycle that is still under warranty. The manufacturer can prove that the motorcycle was used improperly. If this is true, must the manufacturer honor the warranty?	___	___
8. An employee of a store incorrectly marks the price of an item at a lower amount. Is the store obligated to sell the item at the lower price?	___	___

Circumstances, interpretations of the law, and store policies, as well as state and local laws, can affect the above situations. The generally accepted answers are *no* for 1, 3, 7, and 8; *yes* for 2, 4, 5, and 6.

Small Claims Court

small claims court A court that settles legal differences involving amounts below a set limit and employs a process in which the litigants usually do not use a lawyer.

In **small claims court,** a person may file a claim involving amounts below a set dollar limit. The maximum varies from state to state, ranging from $500 to $10,000; most states have a limit of between $1,500 and $3,000. The process usually takes place without a lawyer, although in many states attorneys are allowed in small claims court. To effectively use small claims court, experts suggest that you:

- Become familiar with court procedures and filing fees (usually from $5 to $50).
- Observe other cases to learn about the process.
- Present your case in a polite, calm, and concise manner.
- Submit evidence such as photographs, contracts, receipts, and other documents.
- Use witnesses who can testify on your behalf.

Class-Action Suits

class-action suit A legal action taken by a few individuals on behalf of all the people who have suffered the same alleged injustice.

Occasionally a number of people have the same complaint. A **class-action suit** is a legal action taken by a few individuals on behalf of all the people who have suffered the same alleged injustice. These people are represented by one or more lawyers. Once a situation

INSURANCE | If a $2,000 legal bill would throw you for a loop, a prepaid legal plan can pay off. *By Ronaleen R. Roha*

LAWYERS on call

HERE'S A cheery thought: The odds are good that you or someone in your family will need a lawyer at some point this year. According to a study done for the American Bar Association, 70% of U.S. households may require help with a legal matter. Maybe you'll wind up in a dispute with your landlord or with a deficient home-repair company. Maybe you'll get one too many speeding tickets, jeopardizing your auto-insurance coverage. Or it may be time to revisit a child-support agreement. Chances are also good that you don't know a lawyer to call.

That's where a prepaid legal-services plan can help. For about $10 to $25 a month, such plans offer a menu of legal services from lawyers in your area. Just having a will drafted (a service included in most plans) is probably worth a year of premiums. "With a legal-services plan, you know where you stand with regard to fees before you have to pay them," says Alec Schwartz, executive director of the American Prepaid Legal Service Institute (APLSI), an affiliate of the American Bar Association.

But the most valuable feature may be having someone to call when you have a legal question. "Often just talking about a problem is all it takes," says Schwartz.

Prepaid plans were first offered as an employee benefit, and though some employers still pay as much as 25% to 50% of the cost, it's more likely today for employees to pay the full freight through payroll deductions. Still, an employer-based plan is your best bet if your company offers one because it's likely to be cheaper and more comprehensive than an individual plan. Group plans are also sold to members of affinity groups, such as American Express cardholders, bank customers and members of professional associations.

Legal-plan marketers are working hard to sell individual coverage to those who don't have access to a group plan. Among the companies that sell individual plans over the Internet are ARAG Group ($16 per month; www.aragdirect.com), GE Financial Services ($15 per month; www.legalhelpnow.com) and Hyatt Legal Plans ($395 per year; www.legalplans.com), which is the largest provider of group plans in the country and a wholly owned subsidiary of MetLife. Pre-Paid Legal Service Plans (starting at $16 per month; www.prepaidlegal.com) sells online and face to face.

What you get. Services offered by group and individual plans typically include simple wills, unlimited phone or office consultations, letter writing (for instance, to that landlord with whom you're arguing), and sometimes preparation of other documents, such as financial and health-care powers of attorney. Group plans tend to provide more assistance, such as drafting living trusts and, in some cases, even representing you in court.

Depending on the plan, you may pay extra for certain services. GE Financial's plan, for example, charges members $350 for an uncontested divorce and $300 for a residential real estate closing. Lawyers in some plans also agree to charge a fixed hourly fee—often below market rates—for work outside the scope of the plan. Like medical plans that limit coverage for preexisting conditions, plans may impose a waiting period before covering some services. ARAG's individual plans have a waiting period of 90 days to six months before lawyers will handle divorces, real estate closings and major trial work.

Do you need a plan? James Kraynik, vice-president of business development for ARAG, suggests that you "evaluate a legal plan just as you would an insurance program." If your savings or budget can withstand, for example, $2,000 in lawyer's fees, he says, then you may not need this insurance.

Get detailed descriptions of covered services and any extra charges that may crop up. Ask how long the sponsoring company has been in business, how long lawyers stay with the plan on average and the minimum experience a lawyer must have to join the plan. The APLSI Web site (www.aplsi.org) lists groups that sponsor plans for employers, affinity groups and individuals.
—*Reporter:* **JAY MARCUS**

1. What are the benefits of a prepaid legal service?

_____

_____

2. What legal services are commonly included in prepaid plans?

_____

_____

3. Go to www.kiplinger.com to obtain additional information on legal services and solving consumer complaints.

_____

_____

From the pages of . . . . Kiplinger's Personal Finance

DID YOU KNOW?

A class-action suit can be expensive. After winning $2.19 in back interest, Dexter J. Kamilewicz also noted a $91.33 "miscellaneous deduction" on his mortgage escrow account. This charge was his portion for lawyers he never knew he hired to win a class-action suit.

Apply Yourself!

Objective 4

Interview someone who has had a consumer complaint. What was the basis of the complaint? What actions were taken? Was the complaint resolved in a satisfactory manner?

legal aid society One of a network of publicly supported community law offices that provide legal assistance to consumers who cannot afford their own attorney.

Key Web Site for Legal Questions
www.nolo.com

Sheet 20
Legal Services
Cost
Comparison

qualifies as a class-action suit, all of the affected parties must be notified. A person may decide not to participate in the class-action suit and instead file an individual lawsuit. Recent class-action suits included auto owners who were sold unneeded replacement parts for their vehicles and a group of investors who sued a brokerage company for unauthorized buy-and-sell transactions that resulted in high commission charges.

Using a Lawyer

In some situations, you may seek the services of an attorney. Common sources of lawyers are referrals from friends, advertisements, and the local division of the American Bar Association.

In general, straightforward legal situations such as appearing in small claims court, renting an apartment, or defending yourself on a minor traffic violation may not need legal counsel. More complicated matters such as writing a will, settling a real estate purchase, or suing for injury damages will likely require the services of an attorney.

When selecting a lawyer, consider several questions: Is the lawyer experienced in your type of case? Will you be charged on a flat fee basis, at an hourly rate, or on a contingency basis? Is there a fee for the initial consultation? How and when will you be required to make payment for services?

Other Legal Alternatives

Legal services can be expensive. A **legal aid society** is one of a network of publicly supported community law offices that provide legal assistance to people who cannot afford their own attorney. These community agencies provide this assistance at a minimal cost or without charge.

Prepaid legal services provide unlimited or reduced-fee legal assistance for a set fee. Some programs provide basic services, such as telephone consultation and preparation of a simple will, for an annual fee. Prepaid legal programs are designed to prevent minor troubles from becoming complicated legal problems.

✔ CONCEPTCHECK 6–4

1 In what types of situations would small claims court and class-action suits be helpful?

_____

_____

2 Describe situations in which you might use the services of a lawyer.

_____

_____

3 For the following situations, identify the legal action that would be most appropriate to take.

a. _____ A low-income person wants to obtain the services of a lawyer to file a product-liability suit.

b. _____ A person is attempting to obtain a $150 deposit for catering that was never returned.

c. _____ A consumer wants to settle a dispute out of court with the use of a legally binding third party.

d. _____ A group of telephone customers were overcharged by $1.10 a month over the past 22 months.

Back to Getting Personal

Based on knowledge obtained in this chapter, how might you respond differently to the items in the Getting Personal feature at the beginning of the chapter?

_____

Chapter Summary

Objective 1   Timing purchases, comparing stores and brands, using label information, computing unit prices, and evaluating warranties are common strategies for effective purchasing.

Objective 2   A research-based approach to consumer buying involves (1) preshopping activities, such as problem identification and information gathering; (2) evaluating alternatives; (3) determining the purchase price; and (4) postpurchase activities, such as proper operation and maintenance.

Objective 3   Most consumer problems can be resolved by following these steps: (1) return to the place of purchase; (2) contact the company's main office; (3) obtain assistance from a consumer agency; and (4) take legal action.

Objective 4   Small claims court, class-action suits, the services of a lawyer, legal aid societies, and prepaid legal services are legal means for handling consumer problems that cannot be resolved through communication with the company involved or with help from a consumer protection agency.

Key Terms

arbitration   169

class-action suit   170

legal aid society   172

mediation   169

service contract   158

small claims court   170

warranty   158

Problems and Questions

1. Use advertisements, news articles, online sources, and personal observations to develop a list of shopping guidelines for your personal life situation.

2. John Walters is comparing the cost of credit to the cash price of an item. If John makes a $60 down payment and pays $32 a month for 24 months, how much more will that amount be than the cash price of $685?

3. Calculate the unit price of each of the following items:
   a. Motor oil: 2.5 quarts for
      $1.95 _____ cents/quart

   b. Cereal: 15 ounces for
      $2.17 _____ cents/ounce

   c. Canned fruit: 13 ounces
      for 89 cents _____ cents/ounce

   d. Facial tissue: 300 tissues
      for $2.25 _____ cents/100 tissues

4. You can purchase a service contract for all of your major appliances for $160 a year. If the appliances are expected to last for 10 years and you earn 5 percent on your savings, what would be the future value of the amount you will pay for the service contract? $_____

5. Based on financial and opportunity costs, which of the following do you believe would be the wiser purchase?
   Vehicle 1: A three-year-old car with 45,000 miles, costing $6,700 and requiring $385 of immediate repairs.

Vehicle 2: A five-year-old car with 62,000 miles, costing $4,500 and requiring $760 of immediate repairs.

6. Conduct research on the costs and potential concerns of obtaining furniture, appliances, and other items from rent-to-own businesses.

7. What is a "certified preowned" vehicle? What are the benefits and drawbacks of this type of purchase?

8. Conduct an Internet search to identify Web sites that could assist consumers with evaluating and comparing automobile prices.

OBTAINING CONSUMER PROTECTION ASSISTANCE

A variety of local, state, and federal government agencies provide consumer information and assistance. In addition, many other organizations provide consumer assistance. Conduct a Web search to locate a local, state, and federal agency or organization available to assist consumers.

Consumer assistance agency or organization	Local (city or county) agency	State agency	Federal agency
Name of agency or organization			
Phone			
Web address			
Main purpose, services provided			
Types of assistance provided; types of consumer problems			
Publications or information provided online			

Case in Point

BUYING ONLINE WITHOUT GOING OUT OF YOUR MIND

Amie Carver needed a birthday gift for her mother. She knew of several online sites with items her mother would like. Amie saw a sweater her mother would probably like. "This looks very nice," she thought. "And it's quite reasonably priced."

Amie placed an order online using her credit card. Within a week, she received the sweater. But when she opened the package, she noticed the style of the sweater was different than it looked online. "Oh no, this isn't what I wanted," she thought.

Amie called the company to find out how to return the item. The company told her to send the sweater back for a refund. While the company would pay the return postage, Amie was not refunded the original shipping and handling charges.

Later that day, Amie saw a table lamp for sale online. "This is a nice gift for Mother," she thought. After putting the item in her online shopping cart, she received a message notice that the item would not be available for four to six weeks.

With more than 70 percent of Internet users buying online, there will be problems. One study revealed that one in five survey respondents had a problem with online shopping. A major concern is getting something different from what was expected. While consumers have a strong concern about being charged for something they never agreed to, only a very small percentage of online shoppers have this problem.

Some online shopping Web sites charge a "restocking" fee for an item that is returned. Most will also make the consumer pay for the shipping when returning a product. Carefully check the company's return policies.

Questions

1. What benefits and drawbacks are associated with online shopping?

2. What actions might a consumer take before making an online purchase?

3. Conduct an Internet search to obtain suggestions for action to avoid online shopping problems.

Consumer Purchase Comparison

Financial Planning Activities: When considering the purchase of a major consumer item, use ads, catalogs, the Internet, store visits, and other sources to obtain the information below.

Suggested Web Sites: www.consumerreports.org   www.consumer.gov

Product

Exact description (size, model, features, etc.)

Research the item in consumer periodicals and online for information regarding your product

article/periodical _____ **Web site** _____

date/pages _____ **date** _____

What buying suggestions are presented in the articles?

Which brands are recommended in these articles? Why?

Contact or visit two or three stores that sell the product to obtain the following information:

	Store 1	Store 2	Store 3
Store, company name			
Address			
Phone/Web site			
Brand name/cost			
Product difference from item above			
Warranty (describe)			
Which brand and at which store would you buy this product? Why?			

What's Next for Your Personal Financial Plan?

- Which consumer information sources are most valuable for your future buying decisions?
- List guidelines to use in the future when making major purchases.

Used Car Purchase Comparison

Financial Planning Activities: When considering a used car purchase, use advertisements and visits to new- and used-car dealers to obtain the information below.

Suggested Web Sites: www.carbuyingtips.com   www.kbb.com

18

Your Personal Financial Plan

Automobile (year, make, model)			
Name			
Address			
Phone			
Web site (if applicable)			
Cost			
Mileage			
Condition of auto			
Condition of tires			
Radio			
Air conditioning			
Other options			
Warranty (describe)			
Items in need of repair			
Inspection items: • Rust, major dents?			
• Oil or fluid leaks?			
• Condition of brakes?			
• Proper operation of heater, wipers, other accessories?			
Other information			

What's Next for Your Personal Financial Plan?

- Maintain a record of automobile operating costs.
- Prepare a plan for regular maintenance of your vehicle.

Buying vs. Leasing an Automobile

Financial Planning Activities: Obtain cost information to compare leasing and buying a vehicle.

Suggested Web Sites: www.leasesource.com   www.kiplinger.com/tools

Purchase Costs

Total vehicle cost, including sales tax ($ _____)

Down payment (or full amount if paying cash) $ _____

Monthly loan payment: $ _____ times _____ month loan (this item is
zero if vehicle is not financed) $ _____

Opportunity cost of down payment (or total cost of the vehicle if bought for
cash):

$ _____ times number of years of financing/ownership times _____
percent (interest rate which funds could earn) $ _____

Less: estimated value of vehicle at end of loan term/ownership $ _____

Total cost to buy . . . . $ [   ]

Leasing Costs

Security deposit $ _____

Monthly lease payments: $ _____ times _____ months $ _____

Opportunity cost of security deposit: $ _____ times years
times _____ percent $ _____

End-of-lease charges (if applicable*) $ _____

Total cost to lease . . . . $ [   ]

*With a closed-end lease, charges for extra mileage or excessive wear and tear; with an open-end lease, end-of-lease payment if appraised value is less than estimated ending value.

What's Next for Your Personal Financial Plan?

- Prepare a list of future actions to use when buying, financing, and leasing a car.
- Maintain a record of operating costs and maintenance actions for your vehicle.

Legal Services Cost Comparison

Financial Planning Activities: Contact various sources of legal services (lawyer, prepaid legal service, legal aid society) to compare costs and available services.

Suggested Web Sites: www.nolo.com   www.abanet.org

Type of legal service			
Organization name			
Address			
Phone			
Web site			
Contact person			
Recommended by			
Areas of specialization			
Cost of initial consultation			
Cost of simple will			
Cost of real estate closing			
Cost method for other services—flat fee, hourly rate, or contingency basis			
Other information			

What's Next for Your Personal Financial Plan?

- Determine the best alternative for your future legal needs.
- Maintain a file of legal documents and other financial records.

7 Selecting and Financing Housing

Objectives

In this chapter, you will learn to:

1. Assess costs and benefits of renting.
2. Implement the home-buying process.
3. Determine costs associated with purchasing a home.
4. Develop a strategy for selling a home.

Why is this important?

While most people take out a 30-year mortgage, paying off the loan faster can save you thousands of dollars. Paying an additional $25 a month can shorten your loan by eight years or more and save you over $10,000.

 Getting Personal

What are your attitudes toward housing? For each of the following statements, circle the choice that best describes your current situation.

1. When selecting a place to live, what is most important for you?
   a. Being close to work or school.
   b. The costs involved.
   c. Flexibility for moving in the future.

2. A benefit of renting for me would be
   a. Ease of mobility.
   b. Low initial costs.
   c. No benefits of renting for me.

3. The housing I would purchase that would be best for me is
   a. A house.
   b. A condominium or townhouse.
   c. A mobile home.

4. The type of mortgage I am most likely to use is
   a. A fixed-rate, 30-year mortgage.
   b. An adjustable-rate mortgage.
   c. An FHA or VA mortgage.

After studying this chapter, you will be asked to reconsider your responses to these items.

Evaluating Renting and Buying Alternatives

OBJECTIVE 1
Assess costs and benefits of renting.

As you walk around various neighborhoods, you are likely to see a variety of housing types. When assessing housing alternatives, start by identifying factors that will influence your choice.

Your Lifestyle and Your Choice of Housing

Although the concept of *lifestyle*—how you spend your time and money—may seem intangible, it materializes in consumer purchases. Every buying decision is a statement about your lifestyle. Personal preferences are the foundation of a housing decision, but financial factors may modify the final choice.

Traditional financial guidelines suggest that "you should spend no more than 25 or 30 percent of your take-home pay on housing" or "your home should cost about 2½ times your annual income." Changes in various economic and social conditions have resulted in revised guidelines. Your budgeting activities and other financial records will provide information to determine an appropriate amount for your housing expenses.

Renting versus Buying Housing

The choice between renting and buying your residence should be analyzed based on lifestyle and financial factors. Mobility is a primary motivator of renters, whereas buyers usually want permanence (see Exhibit 7–1). As you can see in the Figure It Out box, the choice between renting and buying usually is not clear-cut. In general, renting is less costly in the short run, but home ownership usually has long-term financial advantages.

Exhibit [7–1] Comparing Renting and Buying of Housing

Advantages	Disadvantages
RENTING	
• Easy to move	• No tax benefits
• Fewer responsibilities for maintenance	• Limitations regarding remodeling
• Minimal financial commitment	• Restrictions regarding pets, other activities
BUYING	
• Pride of ownership	• Financial commitment
• Financial benefits	• Higher living expenses than renting
• Lifestyle flexibility	• Limited mobility

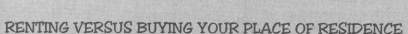

Figure It Out!

Comparing the costs of renting and buying involves consideration of a variety of factors. The following framework and example provide a basis for assessing these two housing alternatives. The apartment in the example has a monthly rent of $700, and the home costs $85,000. A 28 percent tax rate is assumed.

Although the numbers in this example favor buying, remember that in any financial decision, calculations provide only part of the answer. You should also consider your needs and values and assess the opportunity costs associated with renting and buying.

	Example	Your Figures
Rental Costs		
Annual rent payments	$ 8,400	$_____
Renter's insurance	170	_____
Interest lost on security deposit (amount of security deposit times after-tax savings account interest rate)	80	_____
Total annual cost of renting	$ 8,650	_____
Buying Costs		
Annual mortgage payments	$10,500	_____
Property taxes (annual costs)	2,000	_____
Homeowner's insurance (annual premium)	400	_____
Estimated maintenance and repairs (1%)	850	_____
After-tax interest lost on down payment and closing costs	1,030	_____
Less (financial benefits of home ownership):		
Growth in equity	−264	−_____
Tax savings for mortgage interest (annual mortgage interest times tax rate)	−2,866	−_____
Tax savings for property taxes (annual property taxes times tax rate)	−560	−_____
Estimated annual appreciation (3%)*	−2,550	−_____
Total annual cost of buying	$ 8,540	_____

*This is a nationwide average; actual appreciation of property will vary by geographic area and economic conditions.

Rental Activities

Are you interested in a "2-bd. garden apt, a/c, crptg, mod bath, lndry, sec $850"? Not sure? Translated, this means a two-bedroom garden apartment (at or below ground level) with air conditioning, carpeting, a modern bath, and laundry facilities. An $850 security deposit is required.

Sheet 21
Renting vs.
Buying
Housing

At some point in your life, you are likely to rent. As a tenant, you pay for the right to live in a residence owned by someone else. Exhibit 7–2 presents the activities involved in finding and living in a rental unit.

SELECTING A RENTAL UNIT   An apartment is the most common type of rental housing. Apartments range from modern, luxury units with extensive recreational facilities to simple one- and two-bedroom units in quiet neighborhoods. If you need more room, consider renting a house. If less space is needed, rent a room in a private house. The main information sources for rental units are newspaper ads, real estate and rental offices, and people you know. When comparing rental units, consider the factors in Exhibit 7–3.

Exhibit [7–2]   Housing Rental Activities

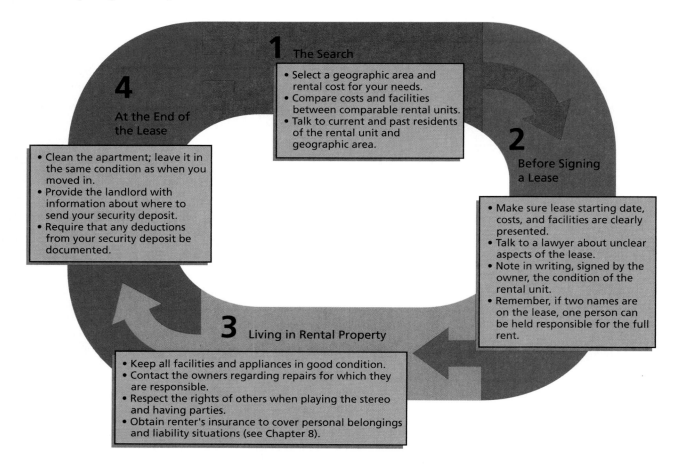

ADVANTAGES OF RENTING   Renting offers mobility when a location change is necessary or desirable. Renters have fewer responsibilities than homeowners since they usually do not have to be concerned with maintenance and repairs. Taking possession of a rental unit is less expensive than buying a home.

DISADVANTAGES OF RENTING   Renters do not enjoy the financial advantages of homeowners. Tenants cannot take tax deductions for mortgage interest and property taxes or benefit from the increased real estate value. Renters are generally limited in the types of activities they can pursue in their place of residence. Noise from a stereo system or parties may be monitored closely. Tenants are often subject to restrictions regarding pets and decorating.

lease A legal document that defines the conditions of a rental agreement.

LEGAL DETAILS   Most tenants sign a **lease,** a legal document that defines the conditions of a rental agreement. This document presents:

- A description of the property, including the address.
- The name and address of the owner/landlord (the *lessor*).
- The name of the tenant (the *lessee*).
- The effective date of the lease, and the length of the lease.

Apply *Yourself!*

Objective 1

Interview a tenant and a landlord to obtain their views about potential problems associated with renting. How do their views on tenant–landlord relations differ?

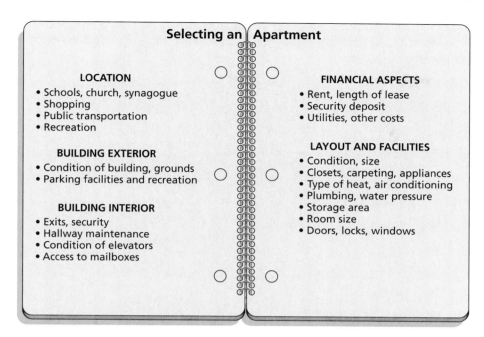

Exhibit [7–3]

Selecting an Apartment

Selecting an Apartment

LOCATION
- Schools, church, synagogue
- Shopping
- Public transportation
- Recreation

BUILDING EXTERIOR
- Condition of building, grounds
- Parking facilities and recreation

BUILDING INTERIOR
- Exits, security
- Hallway maintenance
- Condition of elevators
- Access to mailboxes

FINANCIAL ASPECTS
- Rent, length of lease
- Security deposit
- Utilities, other costs

LAYOUT AND FACILITIES
- Condition, size
- Closets, carpeting, appliances
- Type of heat, air conditioning
- Plumbing, water pressure
- Storage area
- Room size
- Doors, locks, windows

- The amount of the security deposit, and amount and due date of the monthly rent.
- The date and amount due of charges for late rent payments.
- A list of the utilities, appliances, furniture, or other facilities that are included in the rental amount.
- Restrictions regarding certain activities (pets, remodeling); tenant's right to sublet.
- Charges for damages or for moving out of the rental unit later (or earlier) than the lease expiration date.
- The conditions under which the landlord may enter the apartment.

Standard lease forms include conditions you may not want to accept. Negotiate with the landlord about lease terms you consider unacceptable. Some leases give you the right to *sublet* the rental unit. Subletting may be necessary if you must vacate the premises before the lease expires. Subletting allows you to have another person take over rent payments and live in the rental unit.

While most leases are written, oral leases are also valid. In those situations, one party must give a 30-day written notice to the other party before terminating the lease or imposing a rent increase. A lease provides protection to both landlord and tenant. The tenant is protected from rent increases unless the lease contains a provision allowing an increase. The lease gives the landlord the right to take legal action against a tenant for nonpayment of rent or destruction of property.

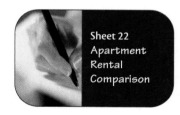

Sheet 22
Apartment
Rental
Comparison

COSTS OF RENTING A *security deposit*, frequently required when you sign a lease, is usually one month's rent. This money is held by the landlord to cover the cost of any damages. Some state and local laws may require that landlords pay interest on a security deposit if they own buildings with a certain number of rental units. After you vacate the rental unit, your security deposit should be refunded within a reasonable time. If money is deducted, you have the right to an itemized list of repair costs.

As a renter, you will incur other expenses. For many apartments, water is covered by the rent; however, other utilities may

DID YOU KNOW?

Renter's insurance is one of the most overlooked expenses of apartment dwellers. Damage or theft of personal property (clothing, furniture, stereo equipment, jewelry) usually is not covered by the landlord's insurance policy.

not be included. If you rent a house, you will probably pay for heat, electricity, water, telephone, and cable television. When you rent, be sure to obtain insurance coverage on your personal property.

✔ **CONCEPTCHECK 7–1**

1 What are the main benefits and drawbacks of renting a place of residence?

_____

_____

2 Which components of a lease are likely to be most negotiable?

_____

_____

3 For the following situations, would you recommend that the person rent or buy housing? (Circle your answer)

   a. A person who desires to reduce income taxes paid.   rent   buy

   b. A person who expects to be transferred for work soon.   rent   buy

   c. A person with few assets for housing expenses.   rent   buy

---

Home-Buying Activities

OBJECTIVE 2
Implement the home-buying process.

Many people dream of having a place of residence they can call their own. Home ownership is a common financial goal. Exhibit 7–4 presents the process for achieving this goal.

Step 1: Determine Home Ownership Needs

In the first phase of this process, consider the benefits and drawbacks of this major financial commitment. Also, evaluate the types of housing units and determine the amount you can afford.

EVALUATE HOME OWNERSHIP   Stability of residence and a personalized living location are important motives of many home buyers. One financial benefit is the deductibility of mortgage interest and real estate tax payments, reducing federal income taxes.

A disadvantage of home ownership is financial uncertainty. Obtaining money for a down payment and securing mortgage financing may be problems. Changing property values in an area can affect your financial investment. Home ownership does not provide ease of changing living location as does renting. If changes in your situation necessitate selling your home, doing so may be difficult.

Owning your place of residence can be expensive. The homeowner is responsible for maintenance and costs of repainting, repairs, and home improvements. Real estate taxes are a major expense of homeowners. Higher property values and increased tax rates mean higher real estate taxes.

TYPES OF HOUSING AVAILABLE   Home buyers generally choose from the following options:

Exhibit [7–4]   The Home-Buying Process

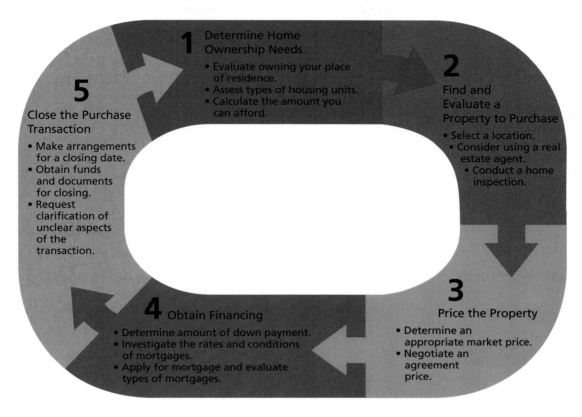

5 Close the Purchase Transaction
- Make arrangements for a closing date.
- Obtain funds and documents for closing.
- Request clarification of unclear aspects of the transaction.

1 Determine Home Ownership Needs
- Evaluate owning your place of residence.
- Assess types of housing units.
- Calculate the amount you can afford.

2 Find and Evaluate a Property to Purchase
- Select a location.
- Consider using a real estate agent.
- Conduct a home inspection.

3 Price the Property
- Determine an appropriate market price.
- Negotiate an agreement price.

4 Obtain Financing
- Determine amount of down payment.
- Investigate the rates and conditions of mortgages.
- Apply for mortgage and evaluate types of mortgages.

1. *Single-family dwellings* include previously owned houses, new houses, and custom-built houses.
2. *Multiunit dwellings* are dwellings with more than one living unit. A *duplex* is a building with separate homes. A *townhouse* may contain two, four, or six living units.
3. **Condominiums** are individually owned housing units in a building. Ownership does not include *common areas*, such as hallways, outside grounds, and recreational facilities. These areas are owned by the condominium association, which oversees the management and operation. Condominium owners pay a monthly fee for maintenance, repairs, improvements, and insurance of the building and common areas. A condominium is not the building structure; it is a legal form of home ownership.

    condominium An individually owned housing unit in a building with several such units.

4. **Cooperative housing** is a form of housing in which a building containing a number of units is owned by a nonprofit organization whose members rent the units. The living units of a co-op, unlike condominiums, are owned not by the residents but by the co-op. Rents in a co-op can increase quickly if living units become vacant, since the remaining residents must cover the maintenance costs of the building.

    cooperative housing A form of housing in which a building containing a number of housing units is owned by a nonprofit organization whose members rent the units.

5. *Manufactured homes* are assembled in a factory and then moved to the living site. *Prefabricated homes* have components built in a factory and then assembled at the housing site. *Mobile home* is not a completely accurate term since very few are moved from their original sites. Although typically smaller than 1,000 square feet, they can offer features such as a fully equipped kitchen, fireplace, cathedral ceiling, and whirlpool bath. The site for a mobile home may be either purchased or leased.

6. *Building a home* is for people who want certain specifications. Before starting such a project, be sure you possess the necessary knowledge, money, and perseverance. When choosing a contractor to coordinate the project, consider (*a*) the contractor's experience and reputation; (*b*) the contractor's relationship with the architect, materials suppliers, electricians, plumbers, carpenters, and other personnel; and (*c*) payment arrangements during construction. Your written contract should include a time schedule, cost estimates, a description of the work, and a payment schedule.

DETERMINE WHAT YOU CAN AFFORD   The amount you spend on housing is affected by funds available for a down payment, your income, and your current living expenses. Other factors you should consider are current mortgage rates, the potential future value of the property, and your ability to make monthly payments. To determine how much you can afford to spend on a home, have a loan officer at a mortgage company or other financial institution *prequalify* you. This service is provided without charge.

You may not get all the features you want in your first home, but financial advisers suggest getting into the housing market by purchasing what you can afford. As you move up in the housing market, your second or third home can include more of the features you want.

While the home you buy should be in good condition, you may wish to buy a *handyman's special*—a home that needs work and that you are able to get at a lower price. You will then need to put more money into the house for repairs and improvements or do some of the work yourself.

Step 2: Find and Evaluate a Home

Next, select a location, consider using the services of a real estate agent, and conduct a home inspection.

SELECT A LOCATION   Location is considered the most important factor when buying a home. You may prefer an urban, a suburban, or a rural setting. Or perhaps you want to live in a small town or in a resort area. Be aware of **zoning laws,** restrictions on how the property in an area can be used. The location of businesses and future construction projects may influence your decision.

zoning laws Restrictions on how the property in an area can be used.

If you have a family, assess the school system. Educators recommend that schools be evaluated on program variety, achievement level of students, percentage of students who go on to college, dedication of faculty members, facilities, school funding, and involvement of parents. Homeowners without children also benefit from strong schools, since the educational advantages of a community help maintain property values.

SERVICES OF REAL ESTATE AGENTS   Real estate agents have information about housing in areas of interest to you. Their main services include (1) showing you homes to meet your needs; (2) presenting your offer to the seller; (3) negotiating a settlement price; (4) assisting you in obtaining financing; and (5) representing you at the closing. A real estate agent may also recommend lawyers, insurance agents, home inspectors, and mortgage companies to serve your needs.

Apply *Yourself!*

Objective 2

Talk with a real estate agent about the process involved in selecting and buying a home. Ask about housing prices in your area and the services the agent provides.

Since the home seller usually pays the commission, a buyer may not incur a direct cost. However, this expense is reflected in the price paid for the home. In some states, the agent could be working for the seller. In others, the agent may be working for the buyer, the seller, or as a *dual agent,* working for both the

Ten steps to a **LOWER** tax bill

As Congress faces mounting deficits and state legislators struggle with shrinking coffers, local tax collectors have something to smile about: Rising property values can automatically push up property-tax revenues. Property-tax bills are based on two things: your home's assessed value and the local property-tax rate. As home values soar across the nation—the median price of existing homes jumped 10.1% between the third quarter of 2002 and the same period in 2003—property-tax bills increase even if tax rates don't. That's all the more reason to make sure you're not over-assessed.

1 | Look for obvious errors in the description of your house in the official records, such as incorrect age, square footage, condition or acreage. If you find a mistake, document it with blueprints, surveys, photographs and inspection reports.

2 | Compare the assessed value of your house with the assessments on similar homes in your neighborhood. This is public information and is available at Web sites such as www.domania.com or at your local property tax assessor's office.

3 | Ask a real estate agent or your assessor for a list of all sales within the past six months in your neighborhood. Identify three to six homes that are similar to yours and located near your property. Ask if any sales were the result of unusual circumstances, such as a property exchange or a sale among relatives (assessors might throw these comparisons out).

4 | Look for differences in lot size, floor plans, view and proximity to adverse factors (such as a noisy super-highway) that could influence value. Although only closed sales matter when determining comparable value, visit open houses regularly in your area so you know how they compare with yours.

5 | Take a copy of your purchase contract to any hearing and, if possible, copies of property-record cards for your house and comparable ones.

6 | Take photos of your house and comparables—and swallow your ego. You want to show your house's warts, such as foundation cracks or a sagging deck. Conversely, show what makes your neighbors' homes shine. But don't get carried away with photos, or you'll bore the board.

7 | Get a copy of your most recent home appraisal, which was probably done in connection with a mortgage.

If it was for a refinance, you might want to pay to have your house appraised again. In a refinance, some appraisers have been known to underestimate market values. Review boards know this.

8 | Check for special homestead exemptions or tax reductions for the disabled, senior citizens, veterans and low-income homeowners. Historic or energy-conserving buildings may get a break, too. Make sure you include all the breaks you deserve.

9 | Calculate and put in writing the reduction you believe you are entitled to, along with your reasons.

10 | Don't let a technicality doom your cause. Use whatever forms your jurisdiction requires and meet all deadlines. It's also a good idea to watch the review board in action in advance, so you get a feel for the kind of approach the members like and the evidence they require.

Source: Reprinted by permission from the March issue of *Kiplinger's Personal Finance,* Copyright © 2004 The Kiplinger Washington Editors, Inc.

1. What factors affect the property taxes for a home?

_____

_____

2. What actions might be taken to reduce property taxes?

_____

_____

3. Go to www.kiplinger.com to obtain additional information on property taxes and other home ownership costs.

_____

_____

From the pages of . . . Kiplinger's Personal Finance

Exhibit [7–5]   Conducting a Home Inspection

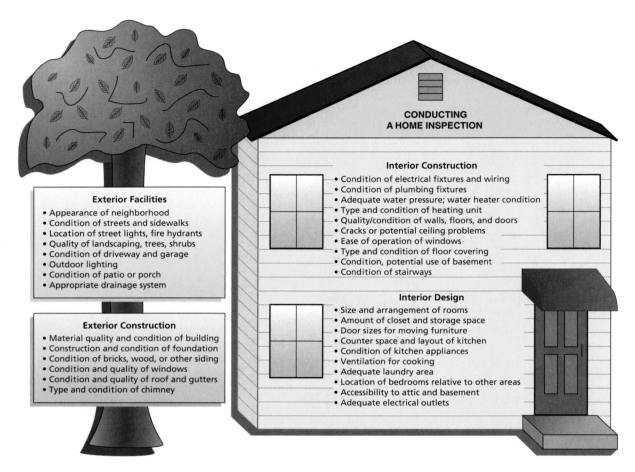

CONDUCTING A HOME INSPECTION

Interior Construction
- Condition of electrical fixtures and wiring
- Condition of plumbing fixtures
- Adequate water pressure; water heater condition
- Type and condition of heating unit
- Quality/condition of walls, floors, and doors
- Cracks or potential ceiling problems
- Ease of operation of windows
- Type and condition of floor covering
- Condition, potential use of basement
- Condition of stairways

Interior Design
- Size and arrangement of rooms
- Amount of closet and storage space
- Door sizes for moving furniture
- Counter space and layout of kitchen
- Condition of kitchen appliances
- Ventilation for cooking
- Adequate laundry area
- Location of bedrooms relative to other areas
- Accessibility to attic and basement
- Adequate electrical outlets

Exterior Facilities
- Appearance of neighborhood
- Condition of streets and sidewalks
- Location of street lights, fire hydrants
- Quality of landscaping, trees, shrubs
- Condition of driveway and garage
- Outdoor lighting
- Condition of patio or porch
- Appropriate drainage system

Exterior Construction
- Material quality and condition of building
- Construction and condition of foundation
- Condition of bricks, wood, or other siding
- Condition and quality of windows
- Condition and quality of roof and gutters
- Type and condition of chimney

buyer and the seller. When dual agency exists, some states require that buyers sign a disclosure acknowledging that they are aware the agent is working for both buyer and seller. Many states have *buyer agents* who represent the buyer's interests and may be paid by either the seller or the buyer.

THE HOME INSPECTION   An evaluation by a trained home inspector can minimize future problems. Being cautious will save you headaches and unplanned expenses. Exhibit 7–5 presents a detailed format for inspecting a home. Some states, cities, and lenders require inspection documents for pests, radon, or mold. The mortgage company will usually conduct an *appraisal,* which is not a home inspection but an assessment of the market value of the property.

Step 3: Price the Property

After selecting a home, determine an offer price and negotiate a final buying price.

DETERMINE THE HOME PRICE   The amount you offer will be affected by recent selling prices in the area, current demand for housing, the time the home has been on the market, the owner's need to sell, financing options, and features and condition

DID YOU KNOW?

A two-story addition, a remodeled bathroom, an updated kitchen, addition of a deck, and a refinished basement are the home upgrades most likely to add value to a home.

of the home. Each of these factors can affect your offer price. For example, you will have to offer a higher price in times of low interest rates and high demand for homes. On the other hand, a home that has been on the market for over a year could mean an opportunity to offer a lower price. Your offer will be in the form of a *purchase agreement,* or contract, which is your legal offer to purchase the home.

NEGOTIATE THE PURCHASE PRICE   If your initial offer is accepted, you have a valid contract. If your offer is rejected, you have several options. A *counteroffer* from the owner indicates a willingness to negotiate a price. If the counteroffer is only slightly lower than the asking price, you are expected to move closer to that price with your next offer. If the counteroffer is quite a bit off the asking price, you are closer to arriving at the purchase price. If no counteroffer is forthcoming, you may wish to make another offer to see whether the seller is willing to do any negotiating. Negotiations may involve things other than price, such as closing date or inclusion of existing items, such as appliances.

As part of the offer, the buyer must present **earnest money,** a portion of the purchase price deposited as evidence of good faith. At the closing of the home purchase, the earnest money is applied toward the down payment. This money is returned if the sale cannot be completed due to circumstances beyond the buyer's control.

earnest money A portion of the price of a home that the buyer deposits as evidence of good faith to indicate a serious purchase offer.

Home purchase agreements may contain a *contingency clause,* stating the agreement is binding only if a certain event occurs. For example, the contract may be valid only if the buyer obtains financing for the home purchase within a certain time period, or it may make the purchase of a home contingent on the sale of the buyer's current home.

✔ **CONCEPTCHECK 7–2**

1   What are the advantages and disadvantages of owning a home?
_____
_____

2   What guidelines can be used to determine the amount to spend for a home purchase?
_____
_____

3   How can the quality of a school system benefit even homeowners in a community who do not have school-age children?
_____
_____

The Finances of Home Buying

After you have decided to purchase a specific home and have agreed on a price, you will probably obtain a loan.

OBJECTIVE 3
Determine costs associated with purchasing a home.

Step 4: Obtain Financing

THE DOWN PAYMENT   The amount of cash available for a down payment affects the size of the mortgage required. If you can make a large down payment, say,

20 percent or more, you will obtain a mortgage relatively easily. Personal savings, pension plan funds, sales of investments or other assets, and assistance from relatives are common down payment sources. Parents can help their children purchase a home by giving them a cash gift or a loan.

Private mortgage insurance (PMI) is usually required if the down payment is less than 20 percent. This protects the lender from financial loss due to default. After building up 20 percent equity in a home, a home buyer should contact the lender to cancel PMI. The Homeowners Protection Act of 1998 requires that a PMI policy be terminated automatically when a homeowner's equity reaches 22 percent of the property value at the time the mortgage was executed. Homeowners can request termination earlier if they can provide proof that the equity in the home has grown to 20 percent of the current market value. Some home buyers apply for a second mortgage to obtain down payment funds and to avoid PMI.

Key Web Site for Private Mortgage Insurance
www.privateemi.com

mortgage A long-term loan on a specific piece of property such as a home or other real estate.

THE MORTGAGE   A **mortgage** is a long-term loan on a specific piece of property such as a home or other real estate. Payments on a mortgage are usually made over 15, 20, or 30 years. Applying for a mortgage involves three main phases:

1. You complete the mortgage application and meet with the lender to present evidence of employment, income, ownership of assets, and amounts of existing debts.
2. The lender obtains a credit report and verifies your application and financial status.
3. The mortgage is either approved or denied, with the decision based on your financial history and an evaluation of the home you want to buy.

This process will indicate the maximum mortgage for which you qualify. As shown in Exhibit 7–6, the major factors that affect the affordability of your mortgage are your income, other debts, the amount available for a down payment, the length of the loan,

Exhibit [7–6]   Housing Affordability and Mortgage Qualification Amounts

	Example A	Example B
Step 1: Determine your monthly gross income (annual income divided by 12).	$48,000 ÷ 12	$48,000 ÷ 12
Step 2: With a down payment of at least 10 percent, lenders use 33 percent of monthly gross income as a guideline for PITI (principal, interest, taxes, and insurance) and 38 percent of monthly gross income as a guideline for PITI plus other debt payments.	$ 4,000 × .38 $ 1,520	$ 4,000 × .33 $ 1,320
Step 3: Subtract other debt payments (e.g., payments on an auto loan) and an estimate of the monthly costs of property taxes and homeowner's insurance.	−380 −300	— −300
(a) Affordable monthly mortgage payment	$ 840	$ 1,020
Step 4: Divide this amount by the monthly mortgage payment per $1,000 based on current mortgage rates—an 8 percent, 30-year loan, for example (see Exhibit 7–7)—and multiply by $1,000.	÷ $ 7.34 × $ 1,000	÷ $ 7.34 × $ 1,000
(b) Affordable mortgage amount	$114,441	$138,965
Step 5: Divide your affordable mortgage amount by 1 minus the fractional portion of your down payment (e.g., 1 − .1 with a 10 percent down payment).	÷ .9	÷ .9
(c) Affordable home purchase price	$127,157	$154,405

Note: The two ratios lending institutions use (step 2) and other loan requirements may vary based on a variety of factors, including the type of mortgage. the amount of the down payment, your income level, and current interest rates.

and current mortgage rates. The results of this calculation are (*a*) the monthly mortgage payment you can afford, (*b*) the mortgage amount you can afford, and (*c*) the home purchase price you can afford.

These sample calculations are typical of those most financial institutions use; the actual qualifications for a mortgage may vary by lender and by the type of mortgage. The loan commitment is the financial institution's decision to provide the funds needed to purchase a specific property. The approved mortgage application usually *locks in* an interest rate for 30 to 90 days.

The mortgage loan for which you can qualify is larger when interest rates are low than when they are high. For example, a person who can afford a monthly mortgage payment of $700 will qualify for a 30-year loan of

Sheet 23
Housing
Affordability
and Mortgage
Qualification

$130,354 at 5 percent	$95,368 at 8 percent
$116,667 at 6 percent	$86,956 at 9 percent
$105,263 at 7 percent	$79,726 at 10 percent

As interest rates rise, fewer people are able to afford the cost of an average-priced home.

When comparing mortgage companies, remember that the interest rate you are quoted is not the only factor to consider. The required down payment and the points charged will affect the interest rate. **Points** are prepaid interest charged by the lender. Each *discount point* is equal to 1 percent of the loan amount and should be viewed as a premium you pay for obtaining a lower mortgage rate. In deciding whether to take a lower rate with more points or a higher rate with fewer points, consider the following:

points Prepaid interest charged by the lender.

- If you plan to live in your home a long time (over five years), the lower mortgage rate is probably the best action.
- If you plan to sell your home in the next few years, the higher mortgage rate with fewer discount points may be better.

Online research may be used to compare current mortgage rates, and you can apply for a mortgage online.

Term Rate	30 Years	25 Years	20 Years	15 Years
5.0%	$5.37	$5.85	$ 6.60	$ 7.91
5.5	5.68	6.14	6.88	8.17
6.0	6.00	6.44	7.16	8.43
6.5	6.32	6.67	7.45	8.71
7.0	6.65	7.06	7.75	8.98
7.5	6.99	7.39	8.06	9.27
8.0	7.34	7.72	8.36	9.56
8.5	7.69	8.05	8.68	9.85
9.0	8.05	8.39	9.00	10.14
9.5	8.41	8.74	9.32	10.44
10.0	8.78	9.09	9.65	10.75
10.5	9.15	9.44	9.98	11.05
11.0	9.52	9.80	10.32	11.37

Exhibit [7–7]

Mortgage Payment Factors (principal and interest factors per $1,000 of loan amount)

FIXED-RATE, FIXED-PAYMENT MORTGAGES As Exhibit 7–8 shows, fixed-rate, fixed-payment mortgages are a major type of mortgage. The *conventional mortgage* usually has equal payments over 15, 20, or 30 years based on a fixed interest rate. Mortgage payments are set to allow **amortization** of the loan; that is, the balance owed is reduced with each payment. Since the amount borrowed is large, the payments made during the early years of the mortgage are applied mainly to interest, with only small reductions in the loan principal. As the amount owed declines, the monthly payments have an increasing impact on the loan balance. Near the end of the mortgage term, almost all of each payment is applied to the balance.

amortization The reduction of a loan balance through payments made over a period of time.

For example, a $75,000, 30-year, 10 percent mortgage would have monthly payments of $658.18. The payments would be divided as follows:

	Interest		Principal	Remaining Balance
For the first month	$625.00	($75,000 × 0.10 × ½)	$ 33.18	$74,966.82 ($75,000 − $33.18)
For the second month	624.72	($74,966.82 × 0.10 × ½)	33.46	74,933.36 ($74,966.82 − $33.46)
For the 360th month	5.41		649.54	–0–

In the past, many conventional mortgages were *assumable*. This feature allowed a home buyer to continue with the seller's original agreement. Assumable mortgages were especially attractive if the mortgage rate was lower than market interest rates at the time of the sale. Today, due to volatile interest rates, assumable mortgages are seldom offered.

Apply *Yourself!*

Objective 3

Conduct Web research on various types of mortgages and current rates.

adjustable-rate mortgage (ARM) A home loan with an interest rate that can change during the mortgage term due to changes in market interest rates; also called a *flexible-rate mortgage* or a *variable-rate mortgage.*

DID YOU KNOW?

By taking out a 15-year instead of a 30-year mortgage, a home buyer borrowing $200,00 can save more than $150,000 in interest over the life of the loan. The faster equity growth with the shorter mortgage is also a benefit.

GOVERNMENT-GUARANTEED FINANCING PROGRAMS These include loans insured by the Federal Housing Authority (FHA) and loans guaranteed by the Veterans Administration (VA). These government agencies do not provide the mortgage money; rather, they help home buyers obtain low-interest, low-down-payment loans.

To qualify for an FHA-insured loan, a person must meet certain conditions related to the down payment and fees. Most low- and middle-income people can qualify for the FHA loan program. The VA-guaranteed loan program assists eligible armed services veterans with home purchases. As with the FHA program, the funds for VA loans come from a financial institution or a mortgage company, with the risk reduced by government participation. A VA loan can be obtained without a down payment.

ADJUSTABLE-RATE, VARIABLE-PAYMENT MORTGAGES The **adjustable-rate mortgage (ARM),** also referred to as a *flexible-rate mortgage* or a *variable-rate mortgage,* has an interest rate that increases or decreases during the life of the loan. ARMs usually have a lower initial interest rate than fixed-rate mortgages; however, the borrower, not the lender, bears the risk of future interest rate increases.

A *rate cap* restricts the amount by which the interest rate can increase or decrease during the ARM term. This limit prevents the borrower from having to pay an interest rate significantly higher than the one in the original agreement. A *payment cap* keeps the payments on an adjustable-rate mortgage at a given level or limits the amount to which those payments can rise. When mortgage payments do not rise but interest rates do, the amount owed can increase in months in which the mortgage payment does not cover the interest owed. This increased loan balance, called *negative amortization,* means the amount of the home equity is decreasing instead of increasing.

Consider several factors when evaluating adjustable-rate mortgages: (1) determine the frequency of and restrictions on allowed changes in interest rates; (2) consider the frequency of and restrictions on changes in the monthly payment; (3) investigate the possibility that the loan will be extended due to negative amortization, and find out if a limit exists on the amount of negative amortization; and (4) find out what index is used to set the mortgage interest rate.

Exhibit [7–8]   Types of Mortgages

Loan Type	Benefits	Drawback
FIXED-RATE, FIXED-PAYMENT		
1. Conventional 30-year mortgage.	• Fixed monthly payments for 30 years provide certainty of principal and interest payments.	• Higher initial rates than adjustables.
2. Conventional 15- or 20-year mortgage.	• Lower rate than 30-year fixed; faster equity buildup and quicker payoff of loan.	• Higher monthly payments.
3. FHA/VA fixed-rate mortgage (30-year and 15-year).	• Low down payment requirements and fully assumable with no prepayment penalties.	• May require additional processing time.
4. "Balloon" loan (3–10-year terms).	• May carry discount rates and other favorable terms, particularly when the home seller provides the loan.	• At the end of the 3- to 10-year term, the entire remaining balance is due in a lump-sum or "balloon" payment, forcing the borrower to find new financing.
ADJUSTABLE-RATE, VARIABLE-PAYMENT		
5. Adjustable-rate mortgage (ARM)—payment changes on 1-year, 3-year, and 5-year schedules.	• Lower initial rates than fixed-rate loans, particularly on the one-year adjustable. Generally assumable by new buyers. Offers possibility of future rate and payment decreases. Loans with rate "caps" may protect borrowers against increases in rates. Some may be convertible to fixed-rate plans.	• Shifts far greater interest rate risk onto borrowers than fixed-rate loans. May push up monthly payments in future years.
6. Graduated-payment mortgage (GPM)—payment increases by prearranged increments during first 5 to 7 years, then levels off.	• Allows buyers with marginal incomes to qualify. Higher incomes over next 5–7 years expected to cover gradual payment increases. May be combined with adjustable-rate mortgage to further lower initial rate and payment.	• May have higher annual percentage rate (APR) than standard fixed-rate or adjustable-rate loans. May involve negative amortization— increasing debt owed to lender. Income may not increase as expected.
7. Growing equity mortgage (GEM)—contributes rising portions of monthly payments to payoff of principal debt. Typically pays off in 15–18 years rather than 30.	• Lower up-front payments, quicker loan payoff than conventional fixed-rate or adjustable-rate loans.	• May have higher effective rates and higher down payments than other loans in the marketplace.

CREATIVE FINANCING   *Convertible ARMs* allow the home buyer to change an adjustable-rate mortgage to a fixed-rate mortgage during a certain period, such as the time between the second and fifth year of the loan. A conversion fee, typically between $250 and $500, must be paid to obtain a fixed rate, usually 0.25 to 0.50 percent higher than the current rates for conventional 30-year mortgages.

When mortgage rates are high, a *balloon mortgage,* with fixed monthly payments and a very large final payment, usually after three, five, or seven years, may be used. This financing plan is designed for people who expect to be able to refinance the loan or sell the home before or when the balloon payment is due. Most balloon mortgages allow conversion to a conventional mortgage (for a fee) if certain conditions are met.

A *graduated-payment mortgage (GPM)* is a financing agreement in which payments rise to different levels every 5 or 10 years during the term of the loan. In the early years, the loan payments could lead to a negative amortization with an increase in the amount owed. This type of mortgage is especially beneficial for people who anticipate increases in income in the future.

A *growing-equity mortgage (GEM)* provides for increases in payments that allow the amount owed to be paid off more quickly. With this mortgage, a person would be able to pay off a 30-year home loan in 15 to 18 years.

An *interest-only mortgage* allows a homebuyer to have lower payments for the first few years of the loan. During that time, none of the mortgage payment goes toward the loan amount. Once the interest-only period ends, the payment rises to include both principal and interest.

Sheet 24
Mortgage
Company
Comparison

OTHER FINANCING METHODS   A *buy-down* is an interest rate subsidy from a home builder or a real estate developer that reduces the mortgage payments during the first few years of the loan. This assistance is intended to stimulate sales among home buyers who cannot afford conventional financing. After the buy-down period, the mortgage payments increase to the level that would have existed without the financial assistance.

The *shared appreciation mortgage (SAM)* is an arrangement in which the borrower agrees to share the increased value of the home with the lender when the home is sold. This agreement provides the home buyer with a below-market interest rate and lower payments than a conventional loan.

A *second mortgage,* more commonly called a *home equity loan,* allows a homeowner to borrow on the paid-up value of the property. Lending institutions offer a variety of home equity loans, including a line of credit program that allows the borrower to obtain additional funds. You need to be careful when using a home equity line of credit. This revolving credit plan can keep you continually in debt as you request new cash advances. A home equity loan allows you to deduct the interest on consumer purchases on your federal income tax return. However, it creates the risk of losing the home if required payments on both the first and second mortgages are not made.

Reverse mortgages (also called *home equity conversion mortgages)* provide homeowners who are 62 or older with tax-free income in the form of a loan that is paid back (with interest) when the home is sold or the homeowner dies.

During the term of your mortgage, you may want to *refinance* your home, that is, obtain a new mortgage on your current home at a lower interest rate. Before taking this action, be sure the costs of refinancing do not offset the savings of a lower interest rate.

Another financing decision involves making extra payments on your mortgage. Since this amount will be applied to the loan principal, you will save interest and pay off the mortgage in a shorter time. Paying an additional $25 a month on a $75,000, 30-year, 10 percent mortgage will save you more than $34,000 in interest and enable you to pay off the loan in less than 25 years. Beware of organizations that promise to help

DID YOU KNOW?

A "portable" mortgage, offered by a few lenders, allows homebuyers to "move" their mortgages to a different home if they buy a different home within the term of the loan.

you make additional payments on your mortgage. You can do this on your own, without the fee they are likely to charge you.

Step 5: Close the Purchase Transaction

Before finalizing the transaction, a *walk-through* allows you to inspect the condition of the home. Use a camera or video recorder to collect evidence for any last-minute items you may need to negotiate.

The *closing* is a meeting of the buyer, seller, and lender of funds, or representatives of each party, to complete the transaction. Documents are signed, last-minute details are settled, and appropriate amounts are paid. A number of expenses are incurred at the closing. The **closing costs,** also referred to as *settlement costs,* are the fees and charges paid when a real estate transaction is completed; these commonly include:

title search fee	title insurance
attorney's fee	property survey
appraisal fee	recording fees; transfer taxes
credit report	termite inspection
lender's origination	reserves for home insurance, property taxes
points (if applicable)	real estate commission

interest paid in advance (from the closing date to the end of the month)

closing costs Fees and charges paid when a real estate transaction is completed; also called *settlement costs.*

Title insurance has two phases. First, the title company defines the boundaries of the property being purchased and conducts a search to determine whether the property is free of claims such as unpaid real estate taxes. Second, during the mortgage term, the title company protects the owner and the lender against financial loss resulting from future defects in the title and from other unforeseen property claims not excluded by the policy.

title insurance Insurance that, during the mortgage term, protects the owner or the lender against financial loss resulting from future defects in the title and from other unforeseen property claims not excluded by the policy.

Also due at closing time is the deed recording fee. The **deed** is the document that transfers ownership of property from one party to another. With a *warranty deed,* the seller guarantees the title is good. This document certifies that the seller is the true owner of the property, there are no claims against the title, and the seller has the right to sell the property.

The Real Estate Settlement Procedures Act (RESPA) helps home buyers understand the closing process and closing costs. This legislation requires that loan applicants be given an estimate of the closing costs before the actual closing. Obtaining this information early allows a home buyer to plan for the closing costs.

deed A document that transfers ownership of property from one party to another.

At the closing and when you make your monthly payments, you will probably deposit money to be used for home expenses. For example, the lender will require that you have property insurance. An **escrow account** is money, usually deposited with the lending institution, for the payment of property taxes and home insurance.

As a new home buyer, you might also consider purchasing an agreement that gives you protection against defects in the home. *Implied warranties* created by state laws may cover some problem areas; other repair costs can occur. Home builders and real estate sales companies offer warranties to buyers. Coverage offered usually provides protection against electrical, plumbing, heating, appliances, and other mechanical defects. Most home warranty programs have various limitations.

Key Web Site for RESPA
www.hud.gov

escrow account Money, usually deposited with the lending financial institution, for the payment of property taxes and homeowner's insurance.

Home Buying: A Summary

For most people, buying a home is the most expensive decision they will undertake. As a reminder, the Personal Finance in Practice feature provides an overview of the major elements to consider when making this critical financial decision.

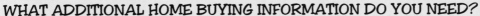

Personal Finance in Practice

WHAT ADDITIONAL HOME BUYING INFORMATION DO YOU NEED?

For each of the following main aspects of home buying, list questions, additional information, or actions you might need to take. Locate Web sites that provide information for these areas.

- **Location.** Consider the community and geographic region. A $150,000 home in one area may be an average-priced house, while in another part of the country it may be fairly expensive real estate. The demand for homes is largely affected by the economy and the availability of jobs.

  _____

- **Down payment.** While making a large down payment reduces your mortgage payments, you will also need the funds for closing costs, moving expenses, repairs, or furniture.

  _____

- **Mortgage application.** When applying for a home loan, you will usually be required to provide copies of recent tax returns, a residence and employment history, information about bank and investment accounts, a listing of debts, and evidence of auto and any real estate ownership.

  _____

- **Points.** You may need to select between a higher rate with no discount points and a lower rate requiring points paid at closing.

  _____

- **Closing costs.** Settlement costs can range from 2 to 6 percent of the loan amount. This means you could need as much as $6,000 to finalize a $100,000 mortgage; this amount is in addition to your down payment.

  _____

- **PITI.** Your monthly payment for principal, interest, taxes, and insurance is an important budget item. Beware of buying "too much house" and not having enough for other living expenses.

  _____

- **Maintenance costs.** As any homeowner will tell you, owning a home can be expensive. Set aside funds for repair and remodeling expenses.

  _____

Web sites to consult:

_____

_____

✔ CONCEPTCHECK 7–3

1 What are the main sources of money for a down payment?

_____

_____

2 What factors affect a person's ability to qualify for a mortgage?

_____

_____

3 How do changing interest rates affect the amount of mortgage a person can afford?

_____

_____

4 Under what conditions might an adjustable-rate mortgage be appropriate?

_____

_____

5 For the following situations, select the type of home financing action that would be most appropriate:

_a._ A mortgage for a person who desires to finance a home purchase at current interest rates for the entire term of the loan. _____

_b._ A homebuyer who wants to reduce the amount of monthly payments since interest rates have declined over the past year. _____

_c._ A homeowner who wants to access funds that could be used to remodel the home. _____

_d._ A person who served in the military, who does not have money for a down payment. _____

_e._ A retired person who wants to obtain income from the value of her home. _____

A Home-Selling Strategy

Most people who buy a home will eventually be on the other side of a real estate transaction. Selling your home requires preparing it for selling, setting a price, and deciding whether to sell it yourself or use a real estate agent.

> **OBJECTIVE 4**
> Develop a strategy for selling a home.

Preparing Your Home for Selling

The effective presentation of your home can result in a fast and financially favorable sale. Real estate salespeople recommend that you make needed repairs and paint worn exterior and interior areas. Clear the garage and exterior areas, and keep the lawn cut and the leaves raked. Keep the kitchen and bathroom clean. Remove excess furniture and dispose of unneeded items to make the house, closets, and storage areas look larger. When showing your home, open drapes and turn on lights. This effort will give your property a positive image and make it attractive to potential buyers.

Determining the Selling Price

Putting a price on your home can be difficult. You risk not selling it immediately if the price is too high, and you may not get a fair amount if the price is too low. An **appraisal,** an estimate of the current value of the property, can provide a good indication of the price you should set. An asking price is influenced by recent selling prices of comparable homes in your area, demand in the housing market, and current mortgage rates.

appraisal An estimate of the current value of a property.

The home improvements you have made may or may not increase the selling price. A hot tub or an exercise room may have no value for potential buyers. Among the most desirable improvements are energy-efficient features, a remodeled kitchen, an additional or remodeled bathroom, added rooms and storage space, a converted basement, a fireplace, and an outdoor deck or patio. Daily maintenance, timely repairs, and home improvements will increase the future sales price.

Sale by Owner

Each year, about 10 percent of home sales are made by the home's owners. If you sell your home without using a real estate agent, advertise in local newspapers and create a detailed information sheet. Distribute the sheet at stores and in other public areas. When selling your home on your own, obtain information about the availability of financing and financing requirements. This will help potential buyers determine whether a sale is possible. Use the services of a lawyer or title company to assist you with the contract, the closing, and other legal matters.

Require potential buyers to provide names, addresses, telephone numbers, and background information. Show your home only by appointment and only when two or more adults are at home. Selling your own home can save several thousand dollars in commission, but an investment of your time and effort is required.

Apply Yourself!

Objective 4

Visit a couple of homes for sale. What features do you believe would appeal to potential buyers? What efforts were made to attract potential buyers to the open houses?

Listing with a Real Estate Agent

If you sell your home with the assistance of a real estate agent, consider the person's knowledge of the community and the agent's willingness to actively market your home. A real estate agent will provide you with various services, such as suggesting a selling price, making potential buyers and other agents aware of your home, providing advice on features to highlight, conducting showings of your home, and handling the financial aspects of the sale. Marketing efforts are likely to include presentation of your home on various Web sites.

A real estate agent can also help screen potential buyers to determine whether they will qualify for a mortgage. Discount real estate brokers are available to assist sellers who are willing to take on certain duties and want to reduce selling costs.

✔ CONCEPTCHECK 7–4

1 What actions are recommended when planning to sell your home?

_____

_____

2 What factors affect the selling price of a home?

_____

_____

3 What should you consider when deciding whether to sell your home on your own or use the services of a real estate agent?

_____

_____

Back to Getting Personal

Reconsider your responses to the Getting Personal items at the start of the chapter. What factors in your life may affect your answers in the future?

_____

Chapter Summary

Objective 1   Assess renting and buying alternatives in terms of their financial and opportunity costs. The main advantages of renting are mobility, fewer responsibilities, and lower initial costs. The main disadvantages of renting are few financial benefits, a restricted lifestyle, and legal concerns.

Objective 2   Home buying involves five major stages: (1) determining home ownership needs, (2) finding and evaluating a property to purchase, (3) pricing the property, (4) financing the purchase, and (5) closing the real estate transaction.

Objective 3   The costs associated with purchasing a home include the down payment; mortgage origination costs; closing costs such as a deed fee, prepaid interest, attorney's fees, payment for title insurance, and a property survey; and an escrow account for homeowner's insurance and property taxes.

Objective 4   When selling a home, you must decide whether to make certain repairs and improvements, determine a selling price, and choose between selling the home yourself and using the services of a real estate agent.

Key Terms

adjustable-rate mortgage (ARM)   194

amortization   194

appraisal   199

closing costs   197

condominium   187

cooperative housing   187

deed   197

earnest money   191

escrow account   197

lease   184

mortgage   192

points   193

title insurance   197

zoning laws   188

Problems and Questions

1. What do you believe are the most important factors a person should consider when selecting housing?

2. Based on the following data, would you recommend buying or renting?

Rental Costs	Buying Costs
Annual rent, $7,380	Annual mortgage payments, $9,800 ($9,575 is interest)
Insurance, $145	Property taxes, $1,780
Security deposit, $650	Down payment/closing costs, $4,500
Insurance/maintenance, $1,050	Growth in equity, $225
	Estimated annual appreciation, $1,700

Assume an after-tax savings interest rate of 6 percent and a tax rate of 28 percent.

3. When Mark and Valerie Bowman first saw the house, they didn't like it. However, it was a dark, rainy day. They viewed the house more favorably on their second visit. Despite cracked ceilings, the need for a paint job, and a kitchen from the 1970s, the Bowmans saw a potential to create a place to call their own. How could the Bowmans benefit from buying a home that needed improvements?

4. Estimate the affordable monthly mortgage payment, the affordable mortgage amount, and the affordable home purchase price for the following situation (see Exhibit 7–6):

Monthly gross income, $2,950	Down payment to be made, 15 percent of purchase price
Other debt (monthly payment), $160	Monthly estimate for property taxes and insurance, $210

30-year loan at 8 percent

5. Based on Exhibit 7–7, what would be the monthly mortgage payments for each of the following situations?
   a. A $40,000, 15-year loan at 11.5 percent.

   b. A $76,000, 30-year loan at 9 percent.

   c. A $65,000, 20-year loan at 10 percent.

6. Which mortgage would result in higher total payments?
   Mortgage A: $985 a month for 30 years.
   Mortgage B: $780 a month for 5 years and $1,056 a month for 25 years.

7. Kelly and Tim Jones plan to refinance their mortgage to obtain a lower interest rate. They will reduce their mortgage payments by $56 a month. Their closing costs for refinancing will be $1,670. How long will it take them to cover the cost of refinancing?

8. Conduct a Web search for actions to take when selling your home.

COMPARING MORTGAGE RATES ONLINE

Using the three Web sites listed (or others of your choice), obtain the following information:

	www.bankrate.com	www.hsh.com	www.bestrate.com
What is the current rate for a 30-year, fixed-rate mortgage in your geographic area?			
What is the rate for a 15-year, fixed-rate mortgage?			
What is the rate for an adjustable-rate mortgage?			
What is the recent trend (up, down, stable) for mortgage rates?			
What do you believe to be the future prospect for mortgage rates (up, down, stable)?			
In addition to rate information, what additional services are provided on this Web site?			

www.mhhe.com/kdh

Case in Point

CAN YOU BUY A HOUSE ONLINE?

When Jamie Covington bought her first home, she did so without ever meeting in person with a mortgage broker or the title insurance representative. She was one of the first home buyers to conduct her real estate transaction completely online.

Jamie started the process by viewing homes on Web sites of various real estate companies and those listed online with various newspapers in her area. Later, Jamie went out to see several of the properties she was considering. The financing process involved several online activities, including:

- The prequalification process to determine the amount of mortgage for which Jamie was eligible.

- Comparing mortgage rates among various lenders both in her area and around the country.

- The mortgage application process in which Jamie was approved for her mortgage within a few hours.

The final negotiations involved a series of e-mail exchanges. Once the buyer and seller agreed on a price, next came the closing, which was conducted completely online. The bank providing Jamie's mortgage prepared the closing documents and sent them electronically over the Internet to the closing agent, who brought them up on a specially equipped computer screen. Jamie signed the documents on the screen. The deed was scanned and delivered by computer image. All completed documents were forwarded to the appropriate parties. Jamie received a CD-ROM with copies of all of the paperwork.

The Electronic Signature in Global and National Commerce Act allowed this process to take place. This law recognizes an *electronic signature* as "an electronic sound, symbol, or process, attached to or logically associated with a contract or other record and executed or adopted by a person with the intent to sign the record."

The time needed for the postclosing process is also reduced. The recording of documents and issuing of the title insurance policy usually takes 45 days. Online, the process was complete in about three hours. This process can result in lower closing costs. Various financial experts estimate that online closings could save businesses and home buyers about $750.

Questions

1. How has technology changed the home-buying process?

2. Based on information at www.homefair.com, describe some advice that should help a person buying a home.

3. What might be some concerns with online home-buying activities? Based on a Web search to obtain additional information on electronic home buying, what other advice would you offer when using the Internet for various phases of the home-buying process?

Renting vs. Buying Housing

Financial Planning Activities: To compare the cost of renting and buying your place of residence, obtain estimates for comparable housing units for the data requested below.

Suggested Web Sites: www.homefair.com   www.newbuyer.com/homes/

Rental costs

Annual rent payments (monthly rent $_____ × 12) $ _____

Renter's insurance $ _____

Interest lost on security deposit (deposit times after-tax savings account interest rate) $ _____

Total annual cost of renting $ _____

Buying Costs

Annual mortgage payments $ _____

Property taxes (annual costs) $ _____

Homeowner's insurance (annual premium) $ _____

Estimated maintenance and repairs $ _____

After-tax interest lost because of down payment/closing costs $ _____

Less: financial benefits of home ownership

Growth in equity $ – _____

Tax savings for mortgage interest (annual mortgage interest times tax rate) $ – _____

Tax savings for property taxes (annual property taxes times tax rate) $ – _____

Estimated annual depreciation $ – _____

Total annual cost of buying $ _____

What's Next for Your Personal Financial Plan?

- Determine if renting or buying is most appropriate for you at the current time.
- List some circumstances or actions that might change your housing needs.

Apartment Rental Comparison

Financial Planning Activities: Obtain the information requested below to compare costs and facilities of three apartments.

Suggested Web Sites: www.apartments.com   www.apartmentguide.com/

Name of renting person or apartment building			
Address			
Phone			
Monthly rent			
Amount of security deposit			
Length of lease			
Utilities included in rent			
Parking facilities			
Storage area in building			
Laundry facilities			
Distance to schools			
Distance to public transportation			
Distance to shopping			
Pool, recreation area, other facilities			
Estimated utility costs: • Electric • Telephone • Gas • Water			
Other costs			
Other information			

What's Next for Your Personal Financial Plan?

- Which of these rental units would best serve your current housing needs?
- What additional information should be considered when renting an apartment?

Housing Affordability and Mortgage Qualification

Financial Planning Activities: Enter the amounts requested to estimate the amount of affordable mortgage payment, mortgage amount, and home purchase price.

Suggested Web Sites: www.realestate.com   www.kiplinger.com/tools/

Step 1

Determine your monthly gross income (annual income divided by 12) $ _____

Step 2

With a down payment of at least 10 percent, lenders use 28 percent of monthly gross income as a guideline for TIPI (taxes, insurance, principal, and interest), 36 percent of monthly gross income as a guideline for TIPI plus other debt payments (enter 0.28 or 0.36)   × _____

Step 3

Subtract other debt payments (such as payments on an auto loan), if applicable   − _____

Subtract estimated monthly costs of property taxes and homeowners insurance   − _____

Affordable monthly mortgage payment $ _____

Step 4

Divide this amount by the monthly mortgage payment per $1,000 based on current mortgage rates (see Exhibit 7–7, text p. 193). For example, for a 10 percent, 30-year loan, the number would be $8.78.   ÷ _____

Multiply by $1,000   × _____$1,000_____

Affordable mortgage amount $ _____

Step 5

Divide your affordable mortgage amount by 1 minus the fractional portion of your down payment (for example, 0.9 for a 10 percent down payment).   ÷ _____

Affordable home purchase price $ _____

Note: The two ratios used by lending institutions (Step 2) and other loan requirements are likely to vary based on a variety of factors, including the type of mortgage, the amount of the down payment, your income level, and current interest rates. If you have other debts, lenders will calculate both ratios and then use the one that allows you greater flexibility in borrowing.

What's Next for Your Personal Financial Plan?

- Identify actions you might need to take to qualify for a mortgage.
- Discuss your mortgage qualifications with a mortgage broker or other lender.

Mortgage Company Comparison

Financial Planning Activities: Obtain the information requested below to compare the services and costs for different home mortgage sources.

Suggested Web Sites: www.hsh.com   www.eloan.com

Amount of mortgage:
$ _____   Down payment: $ _____   Years: _____

Company		
Address		
Phone		
Web site		
Contact person		
Application fee, credit report, property appraisal fees		
Loan origination fee		
Other fees, charges (commitment, title, tax transfer)		
Fixed-rate mortgage		
Monthly payment		
Discount points		
Adjustable-rate mortgage		
• Time until first rate charge • Frequency of rate charge		
Monthly payment		
Discount points		
Payment cap		
Interest rate cap		
Rate index used		
Commitment period		
Other information		

What's Next for Your Personal Financial Plan?

- What additional information should be considered when selecting a mortgage?
- Which of these mortgage companies would best serve your current and future needs?

8 Home and Automobile Insurance

Objectives

In this chapter, you will learn to:

1. Identify types of risks and risk management methods and develop a risk management plan.
2. Assess the insurance coverage and policy types available to homeowners and renters.
3. Analyze the factors that influence the amount of coverage and cost of home insurance.
4. Identify the important types of automobile insurance coverage.
5. Evaluate factors that affect the cost of automobile insurance.

Why is this important?

Recognizing the importance of insurance and learning how to develop an insurance program can protect you from financial loss. Understanding the factors that affect the cost of insurance will let you get the best insurance value for your money.

 Getting Personal

Do you understand the importance of purchasing insurance for your home and automobile? Read the numbered list of possible perils. Then, at the appropriate point along the continuum line following the list, write the number that corresponds to how likely you feel each peril is in your life.

1. You will own a home that will need to be protected against natural disasters, theft, and other adverse occurrences.
2. Your apartment will be robbed.
3. A tornado will destroy your home and automobile.
4. Someone will trip on your sidewalk and sue you.
5. A child of yours will accidentally break a neighbor's window.
6. Your dog will bite someone.
7. Your car will be involved in an accident causing physical injuries to passengers.
8. Your car will be hit by an uninsured motorist.

Most Likely   **Less Likely**

•——•

After studying this chapter, you will be asked to reconsider your priorities.

Key Web Sites

www.insure.com www.insweb.com
www.iii.com www.freeinsurancequotes.com
www.quicken.com/insurance www.ireweb.org

Your Personal Financial Plan Sheets

25. Current Insurance Policies and Needs
26. Home Inventory
27. Determining Needed Property Insurance
28. Apartment/Home Insurance Comparison
29. Automobile Insurance Cost Comparison

Insurance and Risk Management

> **OBJECTIVE 1**
> Identify types of risks and risk management methods and develop a risk management plan.

insurance Protection against possible financial loss.

insurance company A risk-sharing firm that assumes financial responsibility for losses that may result from an insured risk.

insurer An insurance company.

policy A written contract for insurance.

policyholder A person who owns an insurance policy.

premium The amount of money a policyholder is charged for an insurance policy.

coverage The protection provided by the terms of an insurance policy.

insured A person covered by an insurance policy.

Key Web Site for Insurance Company Ratings
www.ambest.com.

In today's world of the "strange but true," you can get insurance for just about anything. You might purchase a policy to protect yourself in the event that you're abducted by aliens. Some insurance companies will offer you protection if you think that you have a risk of turning into a werewolf. If you're a fast runner, you might be able to get a discount on a life insurance policy. Some people buy wedding disaster insurance just in case something goes wrong on the big day. You may never need these types of insurance, but you'll certainly need insurance on your home, your vehicle, and your personal property. The more you know about insurance, the better able you will be to make decisions about buying it.

What Is Insurance?

Insurance is protection against possible financial loss. You can't predict the future. However, insurance allows you to be prepared for the worst. It provides protection against many risks, such as unexpected property loss, illness, and injury. Many kinds of insurance exist, and they all share some common characteristics. They give you peace of mind, and they protect you from financial loss when trouble strikes.

An **insurance company**, or **insurer**, is a risk-sharing business that agrees to pay for losses that may happen to someone it insures. A person joins the risk-sharing group by purchasing a contract known as a **policy**. The purchaser of the policy is called a **policyholder**. Under the policy, the insurance company agrees to take on the risk. In return the policyholder pays the company a **premium**, or fee. The protection provided by the terms of an insurance policy is known as **coverage**, and the people protected by the policy are known as the **insured**.

Types of Risk

You face risks every day. You can't cross the street without some danger that a motor vehicle might hit you. You can't own property without running the risk that it will be lost, stolen, damaged or destroyed.

"Risk," "peril," and hazard" are important terms in insurance. In everyday use, these terms have almost the same meanings. In the insurance business, however, each has a distinct meaning.

Risk is the chance of loss or injury. In insurance it refers to the fact that no one can predict trouble. This means that an insurance company is taking a chance every time it issues a policy. Insurance companies frequently refer to the insured person or property as the risk.

Peril is anything that may possibly cause a loss. It's the reason someone takes out insurance. People buy policies for protection against a wide range of perils, including fire, windstorms, explosions, robbery, and accidents.

Hazard is anything that increases the likelihood of loss through some peril. For example, defective house wiring is a hazard that increases the chance that a fire will start.

The most common risks are personal risks, property risks, and liability risks. *Personal risks* involve loss of income or life due to illness, disability, old age, or unemployment. *Property risks* include losses to property caused by perils, such as fire or theft, and hazards. *Liability risks* involve losses caused by negligence that leads to injury or property damage. **Negligence** is the failure to take ordinary or reasonable care to prevent accidents from happening. If a homeowner doesn't clear the ice from the front steps of her house, for example, she creates a liability risk because visitors could fall on the ice.

Personal risks, property risks, and liability risks are types of *pure*, or *insurable, risk*. The insurance company will have to pay only if some event that the insurance covers actually happens. Pure risks are accidental and unintentional. Although no one can predict whether a pure risk will occur, it's possible to predict the costs that will accrue if one does.

A *speculative risk* is a risk that carries a chance of either loss or gain. Starting a small business that may or may not succeed is an example of speculative risk. Speculative risks are not insurable.

risk Chance or uncertainty of loss; also used to mean "the insured."

peril The cause of a possible loss.

hazard A factor that increases the likelihood of loss through some peril.

negligence Failure to take ordinary or reasonable care in a situation.

Risk Management Methods

Risk management is an organized plan for protecting yourself, your family, and your property. It helps reduce financial losses caused by destructive events. Risk management is a long-range planning process. Your risk management needs will change at various points in your life. If you understand how to manage risks, you can provide better protection for yourself and your family. Most people think of risk management as buying insurance. However, insurance is not the only way of dealing with risk. Four general risk management techniques are commonly used.

Apply *Yourself!*

Objective 1

Using Web research and discussion with others, develop a risk management plan that best suits your present need for insurance.

RISK AVOIDANCE   You can avoid the risk of a traffic accident by not driving to work. A car manufacturer can avoid the risk of product failure by not introducing new cars. These are both examples of risk avoidance. They are ways to avoid risks, but they require serious trade-offs. You might have to give up your job if you can't get there. The car manufacturer might lose business to competitors who take the risk of producing exciting new cars.

In some cases, though, risk avoidance is practical. By taking precautions in high-crime areas, you might avoid the risk that you will be robbed.

RISK REDUCTION   You can't avoid risks completely. However, you can decrease the likelihood that they will cause you harm. For example, you can reduce the risk of injury in an automobile accident by wearing a seat belt. You can reduce the risk of developing lung cancer by not smoking. By installing fire extinguishers in your home, you reduce the potential damage that could be caused by a fire. Your risk of illness might be lower if you eat properly and exercise regularly.

RISK ASSUMPTION   Risk assumption means taking on responsibility for the negative results of a risk. It makes sense to assume a risk if you know that the possible loss will be small. It also makes sense when you've taken all the precautions you can to avoid or reduce the risk.

Key Web Sites for Managing Risk
www.insure.com
www.insweb.com

When insurance coverage for a particular item is expensive, that item may not be worth insuring. For instance, you might decide not to purchase collision insurance on an older car. If an accident happens, the car may be wrecked, but it wasn't worth much anyway. *Self-insurance* is setting up a special fund, perhaps from savings, to cover the cost of a loss. Self-insurance does not eliminate risks, but it does provide a way of covering losses as an alternative to an insurance policy. Some people self-insure because they can't obtain insurance from an insurance company.

RISK SHIFTING   The most common method of dealing with risk is to shift it. That simply means to transfer it to an insurance company. In exchange for the fee you pay, the insurance company agrees to pay for your losses.

deductible The set amount that the policyholder must pay per loss on an insurance policy.

Most insurance policies include deductibles. Deductibles are a combination of risk assumption and risk shifting. A **deductible** is the set amount that the policyholder must pay per loss on an insurance policy. For example, if a falling tree damages your car, you may have to pay $200 toward the repairs. Your insurance company will pay the rest.

Exhibit 8–1 summarizes various risks and effective ways of managing them.

Exhibit [8–1]   Examples of Risks and Risk Management Strategies

RISKS		STRATEGIES FOR REDUCING FINANCIAL IMPACT		
Personal Events	**Financial Impact**	**Personal Resources**	**Private Sector**	**Public Sector**
Disability	Loss of one income Loss of services Increased expenses	Savings, investments Family observing safety precautions	Disability insurance	Disability insurance

Illness	Loss of one income
	Catastrophic hospital
	  expenses
		Health-enhancing
		  behavior
			Health insurance
			Health maintenance
			  organizations
				Military health care
				Medicare, Medicaid

Death	Loss of one income
	Loss of services
	Final expenses
		Estate planning
		Risk reduction
			Life insurance	Veteran's life
				  insurance
				Social Security
				  survivor's benefits

Retirement	Decreased income
	Unplanned living
	  expenses
		Savings
		Investments
		Hobbies, skills
			Retirement and/or
			  pensions
				Social Security
				Pension plan for
				  government
				  employees

Property loss	Catastrophic storm
	  damage to
	  property
	Repair or
	  replacement cost
	  of theft
		Property repair and
		  upkeep
		Security plans
			Automobile
			  insurance
			Homeowner's
			  insurance
			Flood insurance (joint
			  program with
			  government)
				Flood insurance (joint
				  program with
				  business)

Liability	Claims and
	  settlement costs
	Lawsuits and legal
	  expenses
	Loss of personal
	  assets and income
		Observing safety
		  precautions
		Maintaining property
			Homeowner's
			  insurance
			Automobile
			  insurance
			Malpractice insurance	

Planning an Insurance Program

Your personal insurance program should change along with your needs and goals. Dave and Tamara are a young couple. How will they plan their insurance program to meet their needs and goals?

Exhibit 8–2 outlines the steps in developing a personal insurance program.

STEP 1: SET INSURANCE GOALS   Dave and Tamara's main goal should be to minimize personal, property, and liability risks. They also need to decide how they will cover costs resulting from a potential loss. Income, age, family size, lifestyle, experience, and responsibilities will be important factors in the goals they set. The insurance they buy must reflect those goals. Dave and Tamara should try to come up with a basic risk management plan that achieves the following:

- Reduces possible loss of income caused by premature death, illness, accident, or unemployment.
- Reduces possible loss of property caused by perils, such as fire or theft, or hazards.
- Reduces possible loss of income, savings, and property because of personal negligence.

STEP 2: DEVELOP A PLAN TO REACH YOUR GOALS   Planning is a way of taking control of life instead of just letting life happen to you. Dave and Tamara need to determine what risks they face and what risks they can afford to take. They also have to determine what resources can help them reduce the damage that could be caused by serious risks.

Furthermore, they need to know what kind of insurance is available. The cost of different kinds of insurance and the way the costs vary among companies will be the key factors in their plan. Finally, this couple needs to research the reliability record of different insurance companies.

Dave and Tamara must ask four questions as they develop their risk management plan:

- What do they need to insure?
- How much should they insure it for?
- What kind of insurance should they buy?
- Who should they buy insurance from?

Key Web Sites for Insurance Planning Assistance
www.insuremarket.com
www.lifenet.com

STEP 3: PUT YOUR PLAN INTO ACTION   Once they've developed their plan, Dave and Tamara need to follow through by putting it into action. During this process they might discover that they don't have enough insurance protection. If that's the case, they could purchase additional coverage or change the kind of coverage they have. Another alternative would be to adjust their budget to cover the cost of additional insurance. Finally, Dave and Tamara might expand their savings or investment programs and use those funds in the case of an emergency.

The best risk management plans will be flexible enough to allow Dave and Tamara to respond to changing life situations. Their goal should be to create an insurance program that can grow or shrink as their protection needs change.

STEP 4: CHECK YOUR RESULTS   Dave and Tamara should take the time to review their plan every two or three years, or whenever their family circumstances change.

Until recently, Dave and Tamara were satisfied with the coverage provided by their insurance policies. However, when the couple bought a house six months ago, the

Sheet 25
Current
Insurance
Policies and
Needs

Exhibit [8–2] Creating a Personal Insurance Program

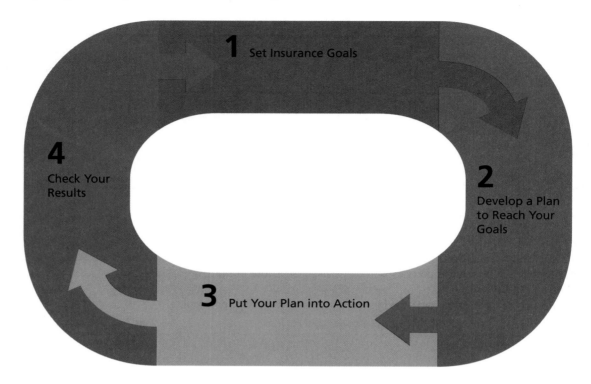

time had come for them to review their insurance plan. With the new house the risks became much greater. After all, what would happen if a fire destroyed part of their home?

The needs of a couple renting an apartment differ from those of a couple who own a house. Both couples face similar risks, but their financial responsibility differs greatly. When you're developing or reviewing a risk management plan, ask yourself if you're providing the financial resources you'll need to protect yourself, your family, and your property. The nearby Personal Finance in Practice feature suggests several guidelines to follow in planning your insurance programs.

Property and Liability Insurance in Your Financial Plan

claim A request for payment to cover financial losses.

Major natural disasters have caused catastrophic amounts of property loss in the United States and other parts of the world. In 1989 Hurricane Hugo caused $4.2 billion in damages. In 1992 Hurricane Andrew resulted in $15 billion worth of insurance **claims**, or requests for payment to cover financial losses. In the Midwest in 1993, floods caused more than $2 billion worth of damage.

Most people invest large amounts of money in their homes and motor vehicles. Therefore, protecting these items from loss is extremely important. Each year homeowners and renters in the United States lose billions of dollars from more than 3 million burglaries, 500,000 fires, and 200,000 cases of damage from other perils. The cost of injuries and property damage caused by vehicles is also enormous.

Think of the price you pay for home and motor vehicle insurance as an investment in protecting your most valuable possessions. The cost of such insurance may seem high. However, the financial losses from which it protects you are much higher.

Personal Finance in Practice

HOW CAN YOU PLAN AN INSURANCE PROGRAM?

Did you:	Yes	No
• Seek advice from a competent and reliable insurance adviser?	☐	☐
• Determine what insurance you need to provide your family with sufficient protection if you die?	☐	☐
• Consider what portion of the family protection is met by Social Security and by group insurance?	☐	☐
• Decide what other needs insurance must meet (funeral expenses, savings, retirement annuities, etc.)?	☐	☐
• Decide what types of insurance best meet your needs?	☐	☐
• Plan an insurance program and implement it except for periodic reviews of changing needs and changing conditions?	☐	☐
• Avoid buying more insurance than you need or can afford?	☐	☐
• Consider dropping one policy for another that provides the same coverage for less money?	☐	☐

Note: *Yes* answers reflect wise actions for insurance planning.

Two main types of risk are related to your home and your car or other vehicle. One is the risk of damage to or loss of your property. The second type involves your responsibility for injuries to other people or damage to their property.

POTENTIAL PROPERTY LOSSES People spend a great deal of money on their houses, vehicles, furniture, clothing, and other personal property. Property owners face two basic types of risk. The first is physical damage caused by perils such as fire, wind, water, and smoke. These perils can damage or destroy property. For example, a windstorm might cause a large tree branch to smash the windshield of your car. You would have to find another way to get around while it was being repaired. The second type of risk is loss or damage caused by criminal behavior such as robbery, burglary, vandalism, and arson.

LIABILITY PROTECTION You also need to protect yourself from liability. **Liability** is legal responsibility for the financial cost of another person's losses or injuries. You can be held legally responsible even if the injury or damage was not your fault. For example, suppose that Terry falls and gets hurt while playing in her friend Lisa's yard. Terry's family may be able to sue Lisa's parents even though Lisa's parents did nothing wrong. Similarly, suppose that Sanjay accidentally damages a valuable painting while helping Ed move some furniture. Ed may take legal action against Sanjay to pay the cost of the painting.

Usually, if you're found liable, or legally responsible, in a situation, it's because negligence on your part caused the mishap. Examples of such negligence include letting young children swim in a pool without supervision or cluttering a staircase with things that could cause someone to slip and fall.

liability Legal responsibility for the financial cost of another person's losses or injuries.

Key Web Sites for State Insurance Regulatory Agencies:
www.naic.org
www.ircweb.org

215

✓ CONCEPTCHECK 8–1

1 What are the three types of risk? Give an example for each.

_____

_____

_____

2 What are the four methods of managing risks? Give an example for each.

_____

_____

_____

_____

3 List the four steps in planning for your insurance program.

_____

_____

_____

_____

4 Give an example of each kind of risk—personal, property, and liability.

_____

_____

Home and Property Insurance

OBJECTIVE 2
Assess the insurance coverage and policy types available to homeowners and renters.

homeowner's insurance
Coverage for a place of residence and its associated financial risks.

Your home and personal belongings are probably a major portion of your assets. Whether you rent your dwelling or own a home, property insurance is vital. **Homeowner's insurance** is coverage for your place of residence and its associated financial risks, such as damage to personal property and injuries to others (see Exhibit 8–3).

Homeowner's Insurance Coverages

A homeowner's insurance policy provides coverage for the following:

- The building in which you live and any other structures on the property.
- Additional living expenses.
- Personal property.
- Personal liability and related coverage.
- Specialized coverage.

BUILDING AND OTHER STRUCTURES   The main purpose of homeowner's insurance is to protect you against financial loss in case your home is damaged or destroyed. Detached structures on your property, such as a garage or toolshed, are also covered. Homeowner's coverage even includes trees, shrubs, and plants.

ADDITIONAL LIVING EXPENSES   If a fire or other event damages your home, additional living expense coverage pays for you to stay somewhere else. For example,

Exhibit [8–3]   Home Insurance Coverage

| Building and other structures | Personal property | Loss of use/additional living expenses while home is uninhabitable | Personal liability and related coverages |

you may need to stay in a motel or rent an apartment while your home is being repaired. These extra living expenses will be paid by your insurance. Some policies limit additional living expense coverage to 10 to 20 percent of the home's coverage amount. They may also limit payments to a maximum of six to nine months. Other policies may pay additional living expenses for up to a year.

PERSONAL PROPERTY   Homeowner's insurance covers your household belongings, such as furniture, appliances, and clothing, up to a portion of the insured value of the home. That portion is usually 55, 70, or 75 percent. For example, a home insured for $80,000 might have $56,000 (70 percent) worth of coverage for household belongings.

Personal property coverage typically limits the payout for the theft of certain items, such as $1,000 for jewelry. It provides protection against the loss or damage of articles that you take with you when you are away from home. For example, items you take on vacation or use at college are usually covered up to the policy limit. Personal property coverage even extends to property that you rent, such as a rug cleaner, while it's in your possession.

Most homeowner's policies include optional coverage for personal computers, including stored data, up to a certain limit. Your insurance agent can determine whether the equipment is covered against data loss and damage from spilled drinks or power surges.

If something does happen to your personal property, you must prove how much it was worth and that it belonged to you. To make the process easier, you can create a household inventory. A **household inventory** is a list or other documentation of personal belongings, with purchase dates and cost information. You can get a form for such an inventory from an insurance agent. Exhibit 8–4 provides a list of items you might include if you decide to compile your own inventory. For items of special value, you should have receipts, serial numbers, brand names, and proof of value.

Your household inventory can include a video recording or photographs of your home and its contents. Make sure that the closet and storage area doors are photographed open. On the back of the photographs, indicate the date and the value of the objects. Update your inventory, photos, and related documents on a regular basis. Keep a copy of each document in a secure location, such as a safe deposit box.

If you own valuable items, such as expensive musical instruments, or need added protection for computers and related equipment, you can purchase a personal property floater. A **personal property floater** is additional property insurance that covers the damage or loss of a specific item of high value. The insurance company will require a detailed description of the item and its worth. You'll also need to have the item appraised, or evaluated by an expert, from time to time to make sure that its value hasn't changed.

household inventory A list or other documentation of personal belongings, with purchase dates and cost information.

personal property floater Additional property insurance to cover the damage or loss of a specific item of high value.

Sheet 26
Home
Inventory

Exhibit [8–4]   Household Inventory Contents

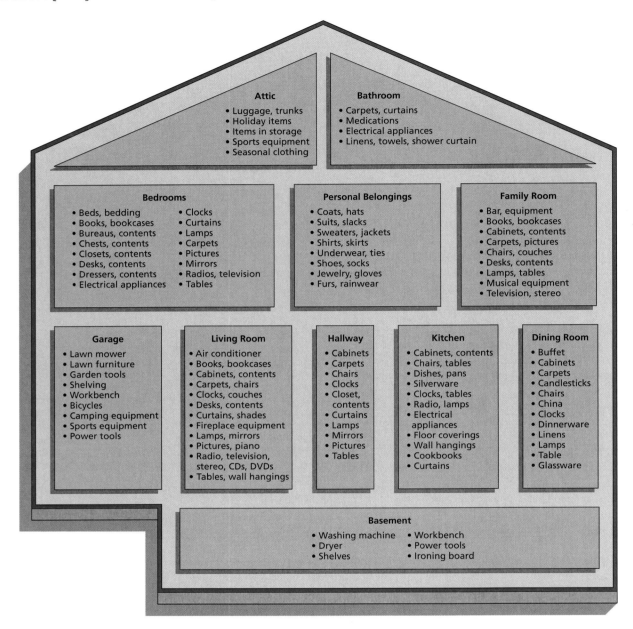

PERSONAL LIABILITY AND RELATED COVERAGE   Every day people face the risk of financial loss due to injuries to other people or their property. The following are examples of this risk:

- A guest falls on a patch of ice on the steps to your home and breaks his arm.
- A spark from the barbecue in your backyard starts a fire that damages a neighbor's roof.
- Your son or daughter accidentally breaks an antique lamp while playing at a neighbor's house.

In each of these situations, you could be held responsible for paying for the damage. The personal liability portion of a homeowner's policy protects you and members of your family if others sue you for injuries they suffer or damage to their property. This coverage includes the cost of legal defense.

Not all individuals who come to your property are covered by your liability insurance. Friends, guests, and babysitters are probably covered. However, if you have regular employees, such as a housekeeper, a cook, or a gardener, you may need to obtain worker's compensation coverage for them.

Most homeowner's policies provide basic personal liability coverage of $100,000, but often that's not enough. An **umbrella policy**, also called a *personal catastrophe policy,* supplements your basic personal liability coverage. This added protection covers you for all kinds of personal injury claims. For instance, an umbrella policy will cover you if someone sues you for saying or writing something negative or untrue or for damaging his or her reputation. Extended liability policies are sold in amounts of $1 million or more and are useful for wealthy people. If you are a business owner, you may need other types of liability coverage as well.

Medical payments coverage pays the cost of minor accidental injuries to visitors on your property. It also covers minor injuries caused by you, members of your family, or even your pets, away from home. Settlements under medical payments coverage are made without determining who was at fault. This makes it fast and easy for the insurance company to process small claims, generally up to $5,000. If the injury is more serious, the personal liability portion of the homeowner's policy covers it. Medical payments coverage does not cover injury to you or the other people who live in your home.

If you or a family member should accidentally damage another person's property, the supplementary coverage of homeowner's insurance will pay for it. This protection is usually limited to $500 or $1,000. Again, payments are made regardless of fault. If the damage is more expensive, however, it's handled under the personal liability coverage.

SPECIALIZED COVERAGE
Homeowner's insurance usually doesn't cover losses from floods and earthquakes. If you live in an area that has frequent floods or earthquakes, you need to purchase special coverage. In some places the National Flood Insurance Program makes flood insurance available. This protection is separate from a homeowner's policy. An insurance agent or the Federal Emergency Management Agency (FEMA) of the Federal Insurance Administration can give you additional information about this coverage.

You may be able to get earthquake insurance as an **endorsement**—addition of coverage—to a homeowners' policy or through a state-run insurance program. The most serious earthquakes occur in the Pacific Coast region. However, earthquakes can happen in other regions, too. If you plan to buy a home in an area that has high risk of floods or earthquakes, you may have to buy the necessary insurance in order to be approved for a mortgage loan.

umbrella policy
Supplementary personal liability coverage; also called a *personal catastrophe policy.*

medical payments coverage
Home insurance that pays the cost of minor accidental injuries on one's property.

DID YOU KNOW?

For $50 to $80 a year, homeowners can obtain $10,000 for sewage and drain backup damage. Heavy rains that clog a sewer line can cause damage to furniture and other items in a finished basement.

endorsement An addition of coverage to a standard insurance policy.

Renter's Insurance

For people who rent, home insurance coverage includes personal property protection, additional living expenses coverage, and personal liability and related coverage. Renter's insurance does not provide coverage on the building or other structures.

The most important part of renter's insurance is the protection it provides for your personal property. Many renters believe that they are covered under the landlord's insurance. In fact, that's only the case when the landlord is proved liable for some damage. For example, if bad wiring causes a fire and damages a tenant's property, the tenant may be able to collect money from the landlord. Renter's insurance is relatively inexpensive and provides many of the same kinds of protection as a homeowner's policy.

DID YOU KNOW?

While more than 9 out of 10 homeowners have property insurance, only about 4 out of 10 renters are covered.

Home Insurance Policy Forms

Home insurance policies are available in several forms. The forms provide different combinations of coverage. Some forms are not available in all areas.

The basic form (HO-1) protects against perils such as fire, lightning, windstorms, hail, volcanic eruptions, explosions, smoke, theft, vandalism, glass breakage, and riots.

The broad form (HO-2) covers an even wider range of perils, including falling objects and damage from ice, snow, or sleet.

The special form (HO-3) covers all basic- and broad-form risks, plus any other risks except those specifically excluded from the policy. Common exclusions are flood, earthquake, war, and nuclear accidents. Personal property is covered for the risks listed in the policy.

The tenant's form (HO-4) protects the personal property of renters against the risks listed in the policy. It does not include coverage on the building or other structures.

The comprehensive form (HO-5) expands the coverage of the HO-3. The HO-5 includes endorsements for items such as replacement cost coverage on contents and guaranteed replacement cost coverage on buildings.

Condominium owner's insurance (HO-6) protects personal property and any additions or improvements made to the living unit. These might include bookshelves, electrical fixtures, wallpaper, or carpeting. The condominium association purchases insurance on the building and other structures.

Manufactured housing units and mobile homes usually qualify for insurance coverage with conventional policies. However, some mobile homes may need special policies with higher rates because the way they are built increases their risk of fire and wind damage. The cost of mobile home insurance coverage depends on the home's location and the way it's attached to the ground. Mobile home insurance is quite expensive: A $40,000 mobile home can cost as much to insure as a $120,000 house.

In addition to the risks previously discussed, home insurance policies include coverage for:

- Credit card fraud, check forgery, and counterfeit money.
- The cost of removing damaged property.
- Emergency removal of property to protect it from damage.
- Temporary repairs after a loss to prevent further damage.
- Fire department charges in areas with such fees.

Not everything is covered by home insurance (see Exhibit 8–5).

Apply *Yourself!*

Objective 2

You are about to rent your first apartment. You have approximately $10,000 worth of personal belongings. Contact an insurance agent to find out the cost of renter's insurance.

DID YOU KNOW?

Computers and other equipment used in a home-based business are not usually covered by a home insurance policy. Contact your insurance agent to obtain needed coverage.

Exhibit [8–5]

Not Everything Is Covered

CERTAIN PERSONAL PROPERTY IS NOT COVERED BY HOMEOWNERS INSURANCE:	
• Items insured separately, such as jewelry, furs, boats, or expensive electronic equipment	• Aircraft and parts
• Animals, birds, or fish	• Property belonging to tenants
• Motorized vehicles not licensed for road use, except those used for home maintenance	• Property contained in a rental apartment
• Sound devices used in motor vehicles, such as radios and CD players	• Property rented by the homeowner to other people
	• Business property

Separate coverage may be available for personal property that is not covered by a homeowners insurance policy.

✔ CONCEPTCHECK 8–2

1 Define the following terms in the spaces below:

   a. Homeowner's insurance _____

   b. Household inventory _____

   c. Personal property floater _____

   d. Renter's insurance _____

2 Identify the choice that best completes the statement or answers the question:

   a. The personal liability portion of a homeowner's insurance policy protects the insured against financial loss when his or her (i) house floods, (ii) jewelry is stolen, (iii) guests injure themselves, (iv) reputation is damaged.

   b. Renter's insurance includes coverage for all of the following *except* (i) the building, (ii) personal property, (iii) additional living expenses, (iv) personal liability.

   c. The basic home insurance policy form protects against several perils, including (i) sleet, (ii) lightning, (iii) flood, (iv) earthquake.

3 Define the following terms in the spaces below:

   a. Umbrella policy _____

   b. Medical payments coverage _____

   c. Endorsement _____

4 List at least four personal property items that are *not* covered by a homeowner's insurance policy.

   _____

   _____

Home Insurance Cost Factors

How Much Coverage Do You Need?

You can get the best insurance value by choosing the right coverage amount and knowing the factors that affect insurance costs (See Exhibit 8–6). Your insurance should be based on the amount of money you would need to rebuild or repair your house, not the amount you paid for it. As construction costs rise, you should increase the amount of coverage. In fact, today most insurance policies automatically increase coverage as construction costs rise.

In the past, many homeowner's policies insured the building for only 80 percent of the replacement value. If the building were destroyed, the homeowner would have to pay for part of the cost of replacing it, which could be expensive. Today most companies recommend full coverage.

If you are borrowing money to buy a home, the lender will require that you have property insurance. Remember, too, that the amount of insurance on your home determines the coverage on your personal belongings. Coverage for personal belongings is usually from 55 to 75 percent of the insurance amount on your home.

OBJECTIVE 3
Analyze the factors that influence the amount of coverage and cost of home insurance.

Apply *Yourself!*

Objective 3

Research the Web to learn about the natural disasters that occur most frequently in your part of the country. How would you protect your home from such natural disasters?

Exhibit [8–6]

Determining the Amount of
Home Insurance You Need

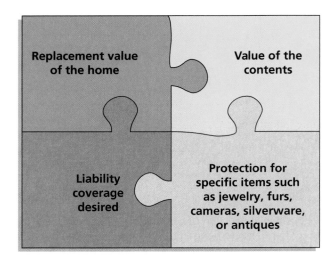

Replacement value of the home	Value of the contents
Liability coverage desired	Protection for specific items such as jewelry, furs, cameras, silverware, or antiques

actual cash value (ACV) A claim settlement method in which the insured receives payment based on the current replacement cost of a damaged or lost item, less depreciation.

replacement value A claim settlement method in which the insured receives the full cost of repairing or replacing a damaged or lost item.

Insurance companies base claim settlements on one or two methods. Under the **actual cash value (ACV)** method, the payment you receive is based on the replacement cost of an item minus depreciation. Depreciation is the loss of value of an item as it gets older. This means you would receive less for a five-year-old bicycle than you originally paid for it.

Under the **replacement value** method for settling claims, you receive the full cost of repairing or replacing an item. Depreciation is not considered. Many companies limit the replacement cost to 400 percent of the item's actual cash value. Replacement value coverage is more expensive than actual cash value coverage.

Factors That Affect Home Insurance Costs

The cost of your home insurance will depend on several factors, such as the location of the building and the type of building and construction materials. The amount of coverage and type of policy you choose will also affect the cost of home insurance. Furthermore, different insurance companies offer different rates.

Sheet 27
Determining
Needed
Property
Insurance

Key Web Sites for Comparing Coverage and Costs
www.quotesmith.com
www.accuquote.com

LOCATION OF HOME   The location of your home affects your insurance rates. Insurance companies offer lower rates to people whose homes are close to a water supply or fire hydrant or located in an area that has a good fire department. On the other hand, rates are higher in areas where crime is common. People living in regions that experience severe weather, such as tornadoes and hurricanes, may also pay more for insurance.

TYPE OF STRUCTURE   The type of home and its construction influence the price of insurance coverage. A brick house, for example, will usually cost less to insure than a similar structure made of wood. However, earthquake coverage is more expensive for a brick house than for a wood dwelling because a wooden house is more likely to survive an earthquake. Also, an older house may be more difficult to restore to its original condition. That means that it will cost more to insure.

COVERAGE AMOUNT AND POLICY TYPE   The policy and the amount of coverage you select affect the premium you pay. Obviously, it costs more to insure a $300,000 home than a $100,000 home.

The deductible amount in your policy also affects the cost of your insurance. If you increase the amount of your deductible, your premium will be lower because the company will pay out less in claims. The most common deductible amount is $250. Raising the deductible from $250 to $500 or $1,000 can reduce the premium you pay by 15 percent or more.

HOME INSURANCE DISCOUNTS   Most companies offer discounts if you take action to reduce risks to your home. Your premium may be lower if you have smoke detectors or a fire extinguisher. If your home has dead-bolt locks and alarm systems, which make a break-in harder for thieves, insurance costs may be lower. Some companies offer discounts to people who don't file any claims for a certain number of years.

COMPANY DIFFERENCES   You can save up to 25 percent on homeowner's insurance by comparing rates from several companies. Some insurance agents work for only one company. Others are independent agents who represent several different companies. Talk to both types of agent. You'll get the information you need to compare rates.

Don't select a company on the basis of price alone; also consider service and coverage. Not all companies settle claims in the same way. Suppose that all homes on Evergreen Terrace are dented on one side by large hail. They all have the same kind of siding. Unfortunately, the homeowners discover that this type of siding is no longer available so all the siding on all of the houses will need to be replaced. Some insurance companies will pay to replace all the siding. Others will pay only to replace the damaged parts.

State insurance commissions and consumer organizations can give you information about different insurance companies. *Consumer Reports* rates insurance companies on a regular basis.

Key Web Site for Flood Insurance
www.fema.gov/nfip

Sheet 28
Apartment/
Home
Insurance
Comparison

Key Web Sites for Home and Auto Insurance
www.independentagent.com
www.trustedchoice.com

✓ CONCEPTCHECK 8–3

1 In the space provided, write "T" if you believe the statement is true, "F" if the statement is false.

   a. Today most insurance policies automatically increase coverage as construction costs rise. _____

   b. In the past, many homeowner's policies insured the building for only 50 percent of the replacement value. _____

   c. Most mortgage lenders do not require that you buy home insurance. _____

   d. Coverage for personal belongings is usually from 55 to 75 percent of the insurance amount on your home. _____

2 What are the two methods insurance companies use in settling claims?

_____

(Continued)

Continued from page 223

3 List the five factors that affect home insurance costs.

_____

_____

_____

Automobile Insurance Coverages

> **OBJECTIVE 4**
>
> Identify the important types of automobile insurance coverage.

financial responsibility law
State legislation that requires drivers to prove their ability to cover the cost of damage or injury caused by an automobile accident.

Motor vehicle crashes cost more than $150 billion in lost wages and medical bills every year. Traffic accidents can destroy people's lives physically, financially, and emotionally. Buying insurance can't eliminate the pain and suffering that vehicle accidents cause. It can, however, reduce the financial impact.

Every state in the United States has a **financial responsibility law**, a law that requires drivers to prove that they can pay for damage or injury caused by an automobile accident. Recently, more than 45 states had laws requiring people to carry motor vehicle insurance. In the remaining states, most people buy motor vehicle insurance by choice. Very few people have the money they would need to meet financial responsibility requirements on their own.

The coverage provided by motor vehicle insurance falls into two categories. One is protection for bodily injury. The other is protection for property damage (see Exhibit 8–7).

Exhibit [8–7]   Two Major Categories of Automobile Insurance

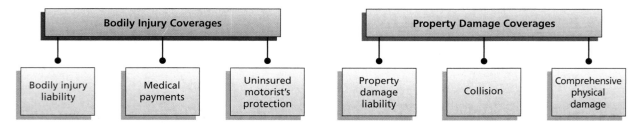

Buying bodily injury and property damage coverage can reduce the financial impact of an accident. *What type of expenses would be paid for by bodily injury liability coverage?*

Motor Vehicle Bodily Injury Coverages

bodily injury liability
Coverage for the risk of financial loss due to legal expenses, medical costs, lost wages, and other expenses associated with injuries caused by an automobile accident for which the insured was responsible.

Most of the money that motor vehicle insurance companies pay out in claims goes for legal expenses, medical expenses, and other costs that arise when someone is injured. The main types of bodily injury coverage are bodily injury liability, medical payments, and uninsured motorist's protection.

Bodily Injury Liability

Bodily injury liability is insurance that covers physical injuries caused by a vehicle accident for which you were responsible. If pedestrians, people in other vehicles, or pas-

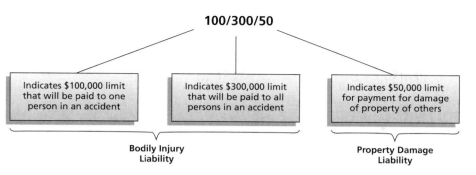

Exhibit [8–8]

Automobile Liability
Insurance Coverage

The three numbers used to describe liability coverage refer to the limits on different types of payments. *Why do you think the middle number is the highest?*

sengers in your vehicle are injured or killed, bodily injury liability coverage pays for expenses related to the crash.

Liability coverage is usually expressed by three numbers, such as 100/300/50. These amounts represent thousands of dollars of coverage. The first two numbers refer to bodily injury coverage. In the example above, $100,000 is the maximum amount that the insurance company will pay for the injuries of any one person in any one accident. The second number, $300,000, is the maximum amount the company will pay all injured parties (two or more) in any one accident. The third number, $50,000, indicates the limit for payment for damage to the property of others (see Exhibit 8–8).

MEDICAL PAYMENTS COVERAGE

Medical payments coverage is insurance that applies to the medical expenses of anyone who is injured in your vehicle, including you. This type of coverage also provides additional medical benefits for you and members of your family; it pays medical expenses if you or your family members are injured while riding in another person's vehicle or if any of you are hit by a vehicle.

medical payments coverage
Automobile insurance that covers medical expenses for people injured in one's car.

UNINSURED MOTORIST'S PROTECTION

Unfortunately, you cannot assume that everyone who is behind the wheel is carrying insurance. How can you guard yourself and your passengers against the risk of getting into an accident with someone who has no insurance? The answer is uninsured motorist's protection.

Uninsured motorist's protection is insurance that covers you and your family members if you are involved in an accident with an uninsured or hit-and-run driver. In most states it does not cover damage to the vehicle itself. Penalties for driving uninsured vary by state, but they generally include stiff fines and suspension of driving privileges.

Underinsured motorist's coverage protects you when another driver has some insurance, but not enough to pay for the injuries he or she has caused.

uninsured motorist's protection Automobile insurance coverage for the cost of injuries to a person and members of his or her family caused by a driver with inadequate insurance or by a hit-and-run driver.

Motor Vehicle Property Damage Coverage

One afternoon, during a summer storm, Carrie was driving home from her job as a hostess at a pancake house. The rain was coming down in buckets, and she couldn't see very well. As a result, she didn't realize that the car in front of her had stopped to make a left turn, and she hit the car. The crash totaled Carrie's new car. Fortunately, she had purchased property damage coverage. Property damage coverage protects you from financial loss if you damage someone else's property or if your vehicle is damaged. It includes property damage liability, collision, and comprehensive physical damage.

Apply Yourself!

Objective 4

Research the make and model of vehicles that are most frequently stolen, consequently resulting in higher insurance rates.

property damage liability
Automobile insurance coverage that protects a person against financial loss when that person damages the property of others.

collison Automobile insurance that pays for damage to the insured's car when it is involved in an accident.

PROPERTY DAMAGE LIABILITY   **Property damage liability** is motor vehicle insurance that applies when you damage the property of others. In addition, it protects you when you're driving another person's vehicle with the owner's permission. Although the damaged property is usually another car, the coverage also extends to buildings and to equipment such as street signs and telephone poles.

COLLISION   **Collision** insurance covers damage to your vehicle when it is involved in an accident. It allows you to collect money no matter who was at fault. However, the amount you can collect is limited to the actual cash value of your vehicle at the time of the accident. If your vehicle has many extra features, make sure that you have a record of its condition and value.

COMPREHENSIVE PHYSICAL DAMAGE   Comprehensive physical damage coverage protects you if your vehicle is damaged in a nonaccident situation. It covers your vehicle against risks such as fire, theft, falling objects, vandalism, hail, floods, tornadoes, earthquakes, and avalanches.

No-Fault Insurance

no-fault system An automobile insurance program in which drivers involved in accidents collect medical expenses, lost wages, and related injury costs from their own insurance companies.

To reduce the time and cost of settling vehicle injury cases, various states are trying a number of alternatives. Under the **no-fault system**, drivers who are involved in accidents collect money from their own insurance companies. It doesn't matter who caused the accident. Each company pays the insured up to the limits of his or her coverage. Because no-fault systems vary by state, you should investigate the coverage of no-fault insurance in your state.

Other Coverages

Several other kinds of motor vehicle insurance are available to you. *Wage loss insurance* pays for any salary or income you might have lost because of being injured in a vehicle accident. Wage loss insurance is usually required in states with a no-fault insurance system. In other states it's available by choice.

Emergency road service coverage pays for mechanical assistance in the event that your vehicle breaks down. This can be helpful on long trips or during bad weather. If necessary, you can get your vehicle towed to a service station. However, once your vehicle arrives at the repair shop, you are responsible for paying the bill. If you belong to an automobile club, your membership may include towing coverage. If that's the case, paying for emergency road service coverage could be a waste of money. *Rental reimbursement coverage* pays for a rental car if your vehicle is stolen or being repaired.

✔ **CONCEPTCHECK 8–4**

1 List the three main types of bodily injury coverage.

_____

_____

2 In the space provided, write "T" if the statement is true, "F" if it is false.

a. Financial responsibility law requires drivers to prove that they can pay for damage or injury caused by an automobile accident. _____

b. Insurance that covers physical injuries caused by a vehicle accident for which you were responsible is called uninsured motorist's protection. _____

c. Automobile liability coverage is usually expressed by three numbers 100/300/50. ____

d. The first two numbers in 100/300/50 refer to the limit for payment for damage to the property of others. ____

e. Uninsured motorist's protection is insurance that covers you and your family members if you are involved in an accident with an uninsured motorist or hit-and-run driver. ____

f. Collision insurance covers damage to your vehicle when it is involved in an accident. ____

3 What is no-fault insurance? What is its purpose?

_____

_____

4 List at least three other kinds of automobile insurance that are available to you.

_____

_____

Automobile Insurance Costs

Motor vehicle insurance is not cheap. The average household spends more than $1,000 for motor vehicle insurance yearly. The premiums are related to the amount of claims insurance companies pay out each year. Your automobile insurance cost is directly related to coverage amounts and factors such as the vehicle, your place of residence, and your driving record.

> **OBJECTIVE 5**
> Evaluate factors that affect the cost of automobile insurance.

Amount of Coverage

The amount you will pay for insurance depends on the amount of coverage you require. You need enough coverage to protect yourself legally and financially.

> Sheet 29
> Automobile Insurance Cost Comparison

LEGAL CONCERNS   As discussed earlier, most people who are involved in motor vehicle accidents cannot afford to pay an expensive court settlement with their own money. For this reason, most drivers buy liability insurance.

In the past, bodily injury liability coverage of 10/20 was usually enough. However, some people have been awarded millions of dollars in recent cases, so coverage of 100/300 is usually recommended.

PROPERTY VALUES   Just as medical expenses and legal settlements have increased, so has the cost of vehicles. Therefore, you should consider a policy with a limit of $50,000 or even $100,000 for property damage liability.

Motor Vehicle Insurance Premium Factors

Vehicle type, rating territory, and driver classification are three other factors that influence insurance costs.

VEHICLE TYPE   The year, make, and model of a vehicle will affect insurance costs. Vehicles that have expensive replacement parts and

> **DID YOU KNOW?**
>
> Foods and drinks that were reported as the most common distractions in auto accidents: coffee, hot soup, tacos, chili-covered foods, hamburgers, chicken, jelly- or cream-filled doughnuts, and soft drinks.

complicated repairs will cost more to insure. Also, premiums will probably be higher for vehicle makes and models that are frequently stolen.

RATING TERRITORY   In most states your rating territory is the place of residence used to determine your vehicle insurance premium. Different locations have different costs. For example, rural areas usually have fewer accidents and less frequent occurrences of theft. Your insurance would probably cost less there than if you lived in a large city.

DRIVER CLASSIFICATION   Driver classification is based on age, sex, marital status, driving record, and driving habits. In general, young drivers (under 25) and elderly drivers (over 70) have more frequent and more serious accidents. As a result these groups pay higher premiums. Your driving record will also influence your insurance premiums. If you have accidents or receive tickets for traffic violations, your rates will increase.

The cost and number of claims that you file with your insurance company will also affect your premium. If you file expensive claims, your rates will increase. If you have too many claims, your insurance company may cancel your policy. You will then have more difficulty getting coverage from another company. To deal with this problem, every state has an assigned risk pool. An **assigned risk pool** includes all the people who can't get motor vehicle insurance. Some of these people are assigned to each insurance company operating in the state. These policyholders pay several times the normal rates, but they do get coverage. Once they establish a good driving record, they can reapply for insurance at regular rates.

assigned risk pool Consists of people who are unable to obtain automobile insurance due to poor driving or accident records and must obtain coverage at high rates through a state program that requires insurance companies to accept some of them.

Reducing Vehicle Insurance Premiums

Two ways in which you can reduce your vehicle insurance costs are by comparing companies and taking advantage of discounts.

COMPARING COMPANIES   Rates and services vary among motor vehicle insurance companies. Even among companies in the same area, premiums can vary by as much as 100 percent. You should compare the service and rates of local insurance agents. Most states publish this type of information. Furthermore, you can check a company's reputation with sources such as *Consumer Reports* or your state insurance department.

Apply *Yourself!*

Objective 5

Using Web research, find the laws in your state regarding uninsured motorist's protection.

PREMIUM DISCOUNTS   The best way for you to keep your rates down is to maintain a good driving record by avoiding accidents and traffic tickets. In addition, most insurance companies offer various discounts. If you are under 25, you can qualify for reduced rates by taking a driver training program or maintaining good grades in college.

Furthermore, installing security devices will decrease the chance of theft and lower your insurance costs. Being a nonsmoker can qualify you for lower motor vehicle insurance premiums as well. Discounts are also offered for insuring two or more vehicles with the same company.

Increasing the amounts of deductibles will also lead to a lower premium. If you have an old car that's not worth much, you may decide not to pay for collision and comprehensive coverage. However, before you make this move, you should compare the value of your car for getting to college or work with the cost of these coverages. The nearby Figure It Out box presents motor vehicle insurance cost comparison.

Figure It Out!

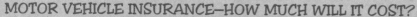

MOTOR VEHICLE INSURANCE—HOW MUCH WILL IT COST?

Before Mario bought the car he wanted, he needed to be sure he could afford the insurance for it. In this example he chose low liability, uninsured motorist coverage, and high deductibles to keep his insurance payments as low as possible. Clearly insurer B offered a lower price for the same coverage.

Investigating Insurance Companies		
	Insurer A	**Insurer B**
Bodily Injury Coverage:		
• Bodily injury liability $50,000 each person; $100,000 each accident	$472	$358
• Uninsured motorist's protection	208	84
• Medical payments coverage: $2,000 each person	48	46
Property Damage Coverage:		
• Property damage liability $50,000 each accident	182	178
• Collision with $500 deductible	562	372
• Comprehensive physical damage with $500 deductible	263	202
Car rental	40	32
Discounts: good driver, air bags, garage parking	(165)	
Annual total	$1,610	$1,272

RESEARCH

Identify a make, model, and year of a vehicle you might like to own. Research two insurance companies and get prices using this example. You can get their rates by telephone. Many also have Web sites. Using your workbook or on a separate sheet of paper, record your findings. How do they compare? Which company would you choose and why?

 **CONCEPTCHECK 8–5**

1 In the space provided, write "A" if you agree with the statement, "D" if you disagree.

a. Motor vehicle insurance is not cheap. ____

b. The average household spends less than $500 for motor vehicle insurance yearly. ____

c. Most people who are involved in an automobile accident can afford to pay an expensive court settlement with their own money. ____

d. Liability coverage of 100/300 is usually recommended. ____

e. You should consider a policy with a limit of $50,000 or even $100,000 for property damage liability. ____

f. The year, make, and model of a vehicle do not affect insurance costs. ____

g. Your automobile insurance would probably cost more in rural areas than if you lived in a large city. ____

Continued

Continued from page 229

2 List the five factors that determine driver classification.

_____

_____

3 What are the two ways by which you can reduce your vehicle insurance costs?

_____

_____

Back to Getting Personal

Based on your responses at the beginning of the chapter, what are your priority insurance needs or which insurance policies do you need to reevaluate?

_____

_____

Chapter Summary

Objective 1 The main types of risk are personal risk, property risk, and liability risk. Risk management methods include avoidance, reduction, assumption, and shifting.

Planning an insurance program is a way to manage risks.

Property and liability insurance protect your homes and motor vehicles against financial loss.

Objective 2 A homeowner's policy provides coverage for buildings and other structures, additional living expenses, personal property, personal liability and related coverages, and specialized coverages.

Renter's insurance provides many of the same kinds of protection as homeowner's policies.

Objective 3 The factors that affect home insurance coverage and costs include the location, the type of structure, the coverage amount and policy type, discounts, and the choice of insurance company.

Objective 4 Motor vehicle bodily injury coverages include bodily injury liability, medical payments coverage, and uninsured motorist's protection.

Motor vehicle property damage coverages include property damage liability, collision, and comprehensive physical damage.

Objective 5 Motor vehicle insurance costs depend on the amount of coverage you need as well as vehicle type, rating territory, and driver classification.

Key Terms

actual cash value (ACV)   222
assigned risk pool   228
bodily injury liability   224
claim   214
collision   226

coverage   210
deductible   212
endorsement   219
financial responsibility law   224
hazard   211

homeowner's insurance   216
household inventory   217
insurance   210
insurance company   210
insured   210

Problems and Questions

1. Survey friends and relatives to determine the types of insurance coverage they have. Also obtain information about the process used to select the coverage.

2. Explain how developing an insurance program can help you manage risk.

3. Conduct Web research to obtain useful information for selecting and comparing various insurance coverage.

4. Outline a personal insurance plan with the following phases:
   a. Identify personal, financial, and property risks.

   b. Set goals you might achieve when obtaining needed insurance coverage.

   c. Describe actions you might take to achieve these insurance goals.

5. Talk to an insurance agent about the financial difficulties faced by people who lack adequate home and auto insurance. What common coverage do many people overlook?

6. Contact two or three insurance agents to obtain information about home or renter's insurance. Compare the coverage and cost.

7. Examine a homeowner's or renter's insurance policy. What coverage does the policy include?

   Does the policy include unclear conditions or wording?

8. Talk to several homeowners about the actions they take to reduce the cost of their home insurance.

   Locate Web sites that offer information about reducing home insurance costs.

9. Survey several people to determine the types and amounts of automobile insurance coverage they have. Do most of them have adequate coverage?

10. Search the World Wide Web to obtain suggestions for reducing automobile insurance costs. List the Web sites used.

www.mhhe.com/kdh

CREATING AN INSURANCE PLAN (INCLUDING APPROPRIATE COVERAGE FOR YOUR HOME, PERSONAL PROPERTY, AND MOTOR VEHICLES)

For these three major insurance coverages, obtain current information and determine how you can get the appropriate coverage at the best rates.

Home/Renter's Insurance

Web sources: _____

_____

Current findings: _____

_____

Possible influence on your insurance decision: _____

_____

Automobile Insurance

Web sources: _____

_____

Current findings: _____

_____

Possible influence on your insurance decision: _____

_____

Case in Point

WE RENT, SO WHY DO WE NEED INSURANCE?

"Have you been down in the basement?" Nathan asked his wife, Erin, as he entered their apartment.

"No, what's up?" responded Erin.

"It's flooded because of all that rain we got last weekend!" he exclaimed.

"Oh no! We have the extra furniture my mom gave us stored down there. Is everything ruined?" Erin asked.

"The couch and coffee table are in a foot of water; the loveseat was the only thing that looked OK. Boy, I didn't realize the basement of this building wasn't waterproof. I'm going to call our landlady to complain."

As Erin thought about the situation, she remembered that when they moved in last fall, Kathy, their landlady, had informed them that her insurance policy covered the building but not the property belonging to each tenant. Because of this, they had purchased renter's insurance. "Nathan, I think our renter's insurance will cover the damage. Let me give our agent a call."

When Erin and Nathan purchased their insurance, they had to decide whether they wanted to be insured for cash value or for replacement costs. Replacement was more expensive, but it meant they would collect enough to go out and buy new household items at today's prices. If they had opted for cash value, the couch for which Erin's mother had paid $1,000 five years ago would be worth less than $500 today.

Erin made the call and found out their insurance did cover the furniture in the basement, and at replacement value after

they paid the deductible. The $300 they had invested in renter's insurance last year was well worth it!

Not every renter has as much foresight as Erin and Nathan. Fewer than 4 in 10 renters have renter's insurance. Some aren't even aware they need it. They may assume they are covered by the landlord's insurance, but they aren't. This mistake can be costly.

Think about how much you have invested in your possessions and how much it would cost to replace them. Start with your stereo equipment or the color television and DVD that you bought last year. Experts suggest that people who rent start thinking about these things as soon as they move into their first apartment. Your policy should cover your personal belongings and provide funds for living expenses if you are dispossessed by a fire or other disaster.

Questions

1. Why is it important for people who rent to have insurance?

2. Does the building owner's property insurance ever cover the tenant's personal property?

3. What is the difference between cash value and replacement value?

4. When shopping for renter's insurance, what coverage features should you look for?

Current Insurance Policies and Needs

Financial Planning Activities: Establish a record of current and needed insurance coverage. List current insurance policies and areas where new or additional coverage is needed.

Suggested Web Sites: www.insure.com   www.insweb.com

Current Coverage	Needed Coverage
Property _____	
Company _____	
Policy No. _____	
Coverage amounts _____	
Deductible _____	
Annual premium _____	
Agent _____	
Address _____	
Phone _____	
Web site _____	
Automobile Insurance	
Company _____	
Policy No. _____	
Coverage amounts _____	
Deductible _____	
Annual premium _____	
Agent _____	
Address _____	
Phone _____	
Web site _____	
Disability Income Insurance	
Company _____	
Policy No. _____	
Coverage _____	
Contact _____	
Phone _____	
Web site _____	
Health Insurance	
Company _____	
Policy No. _____	
Policy provisions _____	
Contact _____	
Phone _____	
Web site _____	
Life Insurance	
Company _____	
Policy No. _____	
Type of policy _____	
Amount of coverage _____	
Cash value _____	
Agent _____	
Phone _____	
Web site _____	

What's Next for Your Personal Financial Plan?

- Talk with friends and relatives to determine the types of insurance coverage they have.
- Locate Web sites that provide additional useful information for company various insurance coverages.

Home Inventory

Financial Planning Activities: Create a record of personal belongings for use when settling home insurance claims. For areas of the home, list your possessions including a description (model, serial number), cost, and date of acquisition.

Suggested Web Sites: www.ireweb.com   www.money.com

Item, Description	Cost	Date Acquired
Attic		
Bathroom		
Bedrooms		
Family room		
Living room		
Hallways		
Kitchen		
Dining room		
Basement		
Garage		
Other items		

What's Next for Your Personal Financial Plan?

- Survey others about the areas of insurance they have and other coverages they are considering.
- Talk to a local insurance agent to point out the areas of protection that many people tend to overlook.

Determining Needed Property Insurance

Financial Planning Activities: Determine property insurance needed for a home or apartment. Estimate the value and your needs for the categories below.

Suggested Web Sites: www.iii.com   www.quicken.com

Real Property (this section not applicable to renters)

Current replacement value of home $ _____

Personal Property

Estimated value of appliances, furniture, clothing and other household $ _____
items (conduct an inventory)

Type of coverage for personal property (check one)

Actual cash value [   ]

Replacement value [   ]

Additional coverage for items with limits on standard personal property coverage such as jewelry, firearms, silverware, and photographic, electronic, and computer equipment

Item	Amount
_____	_____
_____	_____
_____	_____

Personal Liability

Amount of additional personal liability coverage desired for possible $ _____
personal injury claims

Specialized Coverages

If appropriate, investigate flood or earthquake coverage excluded from $ _____
home insurance policies

Note: Use Sheet 28 to compare companies, coverages, and costs for apartment or home insurance.

What's Next for Your Personal Financial Plan?

- Outline the steps involved in planning an insurance program.
- Outline special types of property and liability insurance such as personal computer insurance, trip cancellation insurance, and liability insurance.

Apartment/Home Insurance Comparison

Financial Planning Activities: Research and compare companies, coverages, and costs for apartment or home insurance. Contact three insurance agents to obtain the information requested below.

Suggested Web Sites: www.freeinsurancequotes.com   www.insure.com

Type of building: ☐ apartment ☐ home ☐ condominium

Location: _____

Type of construction _____ Age of building _____

Company name			
Agent's name, address, and phone			
Coverage: Dwelling $ Other structure $ (does not apply to apartment/condo coverage)	**Premium**	**Premium**	**Premium**
Personal property $			
Additional living expenses $			

Personal liability
  Bodily injury
  $
  Property damage
  $			

Medical payments
  Per person
  $
  Per accident
  $			

Deductible amount			
Other coverage $			
Service charges or fees			
Total Premium			

What's Next for Your Personal Financial Plan?

- Talk to an insurance agent or claim adjuster to determine the type of documentation required for a claim settlement.
- List the reasons most commonly given by renters for not having renter's insurance.

Automobile Insurance Cost Comparison

Financial Planning Activities: Research and compare companies, coverages, and costs for auto insurance. Contact three insurance agents to obtain the information requested below.

Suggested Web Sites: www.autoinsuranceindepth.com   www.progressive.com/home

Automobile (year, make, model, engine size) _____

Driver's age _____ Sex _____ Total miles driven in a year _____

Full- or part-time driver? _____ Total miles driven in a year _____

Driver's education completed? _____

Accidents or violations within the past three years? _____

Company name			
Agent's name, address, and phone			
Policy length (6 months, 1 year)			
Coverage: Bodily injury liability Per person $ Per accident $	Premium	Premium	Premium
Property damage liability per accident $			
Collision deductible $			
Comprehensive deductible $			
Medical payments per person $			
Uninsured motorist liability Per person $ Per accident $			
Other coverage			
Service charges			
Total Premium			

What's Next for Your Personal Financial Plan?

- Make a list of some arguments in favor of and against mandatory auto insurance.
- Talk to friends, relatives, and insurance agents to determine methods of reducing the cost of auto insurance.

Your Personal Financial Plan

29

9 Health and Disability Income Insurance

Objectives

In this chapter, you will learn to:

1. Recognize the importance of health insurance in financial planning.
2. Analyze the costs and benefits of various types of health insurance coverage as well as major provisions in health insurance policy.
3. Assess the trade-offs of different health insurance plans.
4. Evaluate the differences among health care plans offered by private companies and by the government.
5. Explain the importance of disability income insurance in financial planning and identify its sources.

Why is this important?

Knowing how to determine the type of health and disability income insurance that you need can help you meet your financial goals even when dealing with unexpected medical costs and inability to work.

Getting Personal

Should you be concerned about health insurance? Disability income insurance? For each of the following statements, select "yes" or "no" to indicate your behavior regarding these health insurance and disability insurance statements.

	Yes	No
1. Since I am a young adult, I don't really need health insurance.	_____	_____
2. Since I am a healthy adult, I don't need to worry about disability income insurance.	_____	_____
3. If my employer does not provide health insurance, I can easily and inexpensively purchase my own insurance.	_____	_____
4. I am aware of some of the trade-offs of different health insurance policies.	_____	_____
5. I am aware of health care plans offered by private companies and by the government.	_____	_____

After studying this chapter, you will be asked to reassess health and disability income insurance and to reconsider your responses to these items.

Key Web Sites

www.healthinsuranceinfo.net

www.dol.gov/ebsa

www.insurancefraud.org

www.naic.org

www.healthcare-choices.org

www.BestDoctors.com

www.ncqa.org

www.ehealthinsurance.com

www.national-healthcouncil.org

www.jcaho.org

Your Personal Financial Plan Sheets

30 Assessing Current and Needed Health Care Insurance.

31 Disability Income Insurance Needs.

Health Insurance and Financial Planning

> **OBJECTIVE 1**
>
> Recognize the importance of health insurance in financial planning.

What Is Health Insurance?

Health insurance is a form of protection that eases the financial burden people may experience as a result of illness or injury. You pay a *premium,* or fee, to the insurer. In return the company pays most of your medical costs. Although plans vary in what they cover, they may reimburse you for hospital stays, doctors' visits, medications, and sometimes vision and dental care.

Health insurance includes both medical expense insurance, as discussed above, and disability income insurance. *Medical expense insurance* typically pays only the actual medical costs. *Disability income insurance* provides payments to make up for some of the income of a person who cannot work as a result of injury or illness. In this chapter the term "health insurance" refers to medical expense insurance.

Health insurance plans can be purchased in several different ways: group health insurance, individual health insurance, and COBRA.

GROUP HEALTH INSURANCE Most people who have health insurance are covered under group plans. Typically, these plans are employer sponsored. This means that the employer offers the plans and usually pays some or all of the premiums. Other organizations, such as labor unions and professional associations, also offer group plans. Group insurance plans cover you and your immediate family. The Health Insurance Portability and Accountability Act of 1996 set new federal standards to ensure that workers would not lose their health insurance if they changed jobs. As a result, a parent with a sick child, for example, can move from one group health plan to another without a lapse in coverage. Moreover, the parent will not have to pay more for coverage than other employees do.

The cost of group insurance is relatively low because many people are insured under the same *policy*—a contract with a risk-sharing group, or insurance company. However, group insurance plans vary in the amount of protection that they provide. For example, some plans limit the amount that they will pay for hospital stays and surgical procedures. If your plan does not cover all of your health insurance needs, you have several choices.

If you are married, you may be able to take advantage of a coordination of benefits (COB) provision, which is included in most group insurance plans. This provision allows you to combine the benefits from more than one insurance plan. The benefits received from all the plans are limited to 100 percent of all allowable medical expenses. For example, a couple could use benefits from one spouse's group plan and from the other spouse's plan up to 100 percent.

If this type of provision is not available to you, or if you are single, you can buy individual health insurance for added protection.

Apply *Yourself!*

Objective 1

Ask someone in a human resources office of an organization to obtain information on the health insurance provided as an employee benefit.

INDIVIDUAL HEALTH INSURANCE   Some people do not have access to an employer-sponsored group insurance plan because they are self-employed. Others are simply dissatisfied with the coverage that their group plan provides. In these cases individual health insurance may be the answer. You can buy individual health insurance directly from the company of your choice. Plans usually cover you as an individual or cover you and your family. Individual plans can be adapted to meet your own needs. You should comparison shop, however, because rates can vary.

> **DID YOU KNOW?**
>
> You can receive *A Consumer Guide for Getting and Keeping Health Insurance* for your state from Georgetown University Health Policy Institute. Visit www.healthinsuranceinfo.net.

COBRA   Hakeem had a group insurance plan through his employer, but he was recently laid off. He wondered how he would be able to get medical coverage until he found a new job. Fortunately for Hakeem, the Consolidated Omnibus Budget Reconciliation Act of 1986, known as COBRA, allowed him to keep his former employer's group coverage for a set period of time. He had to pay the premiums himself, but at least the coverage wasn't canceled. When he found a new job, he was then able to switch to that employer's group plan with no break in coverage.

Not everyone qualifies for COBRA. You have to work for a private company or state or local government to benefit.

Key Web Sites for Health Insurance Information
www.insure.com
www.life-line.org

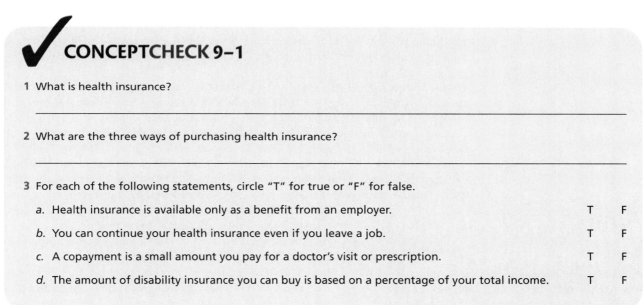

✔ CONCEPTCHECK 9–1

1 What is health insurance?

_____

2 What are the three ways of purchasing health insurance?

_____

3 For each of the following statements, circle "T" for true or "F" for false.

  a. Health insurance is available only as a benefit from an employer.   T   F

  b. You can continue your health insurance even if you leave a job.   T   F

  c. A copayment is a small amount you pay for a doctor's visit or prescription.   T   F

  d. The amount of disability insurance you can buy is based on a percentage of your total income.   T   F

Health Insurance Coverage

Several types of health insurance coverage are available, either through a group plan or through individual purchase. Some benefits are included in nearly every health insurance plan; other benefits are seldom offered.

Types of Health Insurance Coverage

BASIC HEALTH INSURANCE COVERAGE   **Basic health insurance coverage** includes hospital expense coverage, surgical expense coverage, and physician expense coverage.

> **OBJECTIVE 2**
>
> Analyze the costs and benefits of various types of health insurance coverage as well as major provisions in health insurance policy.

basic health insurance coverage Hospital expense insurance, surgical expense insurance, and physician expense insurance.

hospital expense insurance Pays part or all of hospital bills for room, board, and other charges.

Hospital Expense   **Hospital expense coverage** pays for some or all of the daily costs of room and board during a hospital stay. Routine nursing care, minor medical supplies, and the use of other hospital facilities are covered as well. For example, covered expenses would include anesthesia, laboratory fees, dressings, X-rays, local ambulance service, and the use of an operating room.

Be aware, though, that most policies set a maximum amount they will pay for each day you are in the hospital. They may also limit the number of days they will cover. Recall from Chapter 8 that many policies require a deductible. A **deductible** is a set amount that the policyholder must pay toward medical expenses before the insurance company pays benefits.

deductible An amount the insured must pay before benefits become payable by the insurance company.

surgical expense insurance Pays part or all of the surgeon's fees for an operation.

Surgical Expense   **Surgical expense coverage** pays all or part of the surgeon's fees for an operation, whether it is done in a hospital or in the doctor's office. Policies often have a list of the services that they cover, which specifies the maximum payment for each type of operation. For example, a policy might allow $500 for an appendectomy. If the entire surgeon's bill is not covered, the policyholder has to pay the difference. People often buy surgical expense coverage in combination with hospital expense coverage.

physician expense insurance Provides benefits for doctors' fees for nonsurgical care, X-rays, and lab tests.

Physician Expense   **Physician expense coverage** meets some or all the costs of physician care that do not involve surgery. This form of health insurance covers treatment in a hospital, a doctor's office, or even a patient's home. Plans may cover routine doctor visits, X-rays, and lab tests. Like surgical expense, physician expense specifies maximum benefits for each service. Physician expense coverage is usually combined with surgical and hospital coverage in a package called basic health insurance.

Major Medical Expense Insurance Coverage   Most people find that basic health insurance meets their usual needs. The cost of a serious illness or accident, however, can quickly go beyond the amounts that basic health insurance will pay. Chen had emergency surgery, which meant an operation, a two-week hospital stay, a number of lab tests, and several follow-up visits. He was shocked to discover that his basic health insurance paid less than half of the total bill, leaving him with debts of more than $10,000.

Chen would have been better protected if he had had major medical expense insurance. This coverage pays the large costs involved in long hospital stays and multiple surgeries. In other words, it takes up where basic health insurance coverage leaves off. Almost every type of care and treatment prescribed by a physician, in and out of a hospital, is covered. Maximum benefits can range from $5,000 to more than $1 million per illness per year.

Of course, this type of overage isn't cheap. To control premiums, most major medical plans require a deductible. Some plans also include a coinsurance provision. **Coinsurance** is the percentage of the medical expenses the policyholder must pay in addition to the deductible amount. Many policies require policyholders to pay 20 or 25 percent of expenses after they have paid the deductible.

Apply*Yourself!*

Objective 2

Raj is thinking about buying major medical insurance to supplement his basic health insurance from work. Describe a situation in which Raj would need major medical.

coinsurance A provision under which both the insured and the insurer share the covered losses.

Ariana's policy includes an $800 deductible and a coinsurance provision requiring her to pay 20 percent of all bills. If her bill total is $3,800, for instance, the company will first exclude $800 from coverage, which is Ariana's deductible. It will then pay 80 percent of the remaining $3,000, or $2,400. Therefore, Ariana's total costs are $1,400 ($800 for the deductible and $600 for the coinsurance).

stop-loss A provision under which an insured pays a certain amount, after which the insurance company pays 100 percent of the remaining covered expenses.

Some major medical policies contain a stop-loss provision. **Stop-loss** is a provision that requires the policyholder to pay all costs up to a certain amount, after which the insurance company pays 100 percent of the remaining expenses, as long as they are covered in the policy. Typically, the policyholder will pay between $3,000 and $5,000 in out-of-pocket expenses before the coverage begins.

Figure It Out!

Major medical expense insurance may be offered as a single policy with basic health insurance coverage, or it can be bought separately. Comprehensive major medical insurance is a type of complete insurance that helps pay hospital, surgical, medical, and other bills. It has a low deductible, usually $400 to $800. Many major medical policies set limits on the benefits they will pay for certain expenses, such as surgery and hospital room and board. The nearby Figure It Out box offers an example.

HOSPITAL INDEMNITY POLICIES A hospital indemnity policy pays benefits when you're hospitalized. Unlike most of the other plans mentioned, however, these policies don't directly cover medical costs. Instead you are paid in cash, which you can spend on medical or nonmedical expenses as you choose. Hospital indemnity policies are used as a supplement to—and not a replacement for—basic health or major medical policies. The average person who buys such a policy, however, usually pays much more in premiums that he or she receives in payments.

DENTAL EXPENSE INSURANCE Dental expense insurance provides reimbursement for the expenses of dental services and supplies. It encourages preventive dental care. The coverage normally provides for oral examinations (including X-rays and cleanings), fillings, extractions, oral surgery, dentures, and braces. As with other insurance plans, dental insurance may have a deductible and a coinsurance provision, stating that the policyholder pays from 20 to 50 percent after the deductible.

VISION CARE INSURANCE An increasing number of insurance companies are including vision care insurance as part of group plans. Vision care insurance may cover eye examinations, glasses, contact lenses, eye surgery, and the treatment of eye diseases.

DREAD DISEASE POLICIES Dread disease, trip accident, death insurance, and cancer policies are usually sold through the mail, in newspapers and magazines, or by door-to-door salespeople. These kinds of policy play upon unrealistic fears, and they are illegal in many states. They cover only specific conditions, which are already fully covered if you are insured under a major medical plan.

LONG-TERM CARE INSURANCE **Long-term care insurance (LTC)** provides coverage for the expense of daily help that you may need if you become seriously ill or disabled and are unable to care for yourself. It is useful whether you require a lengthy stay in a nursing home or just need help at home with daily activities such as dressing, bathing, and household chores. Annual premiums range from less than $900 up to $15,000, depending on your age and extent of the coverage. The nearby Personal Finance in Practice box can help you compare the features of long-term care policies.

long-term care insurance (LTC) Provides day-in, day-out care for long-term illness or disability.

Key Web Site for Long-Term Care
www.longtermcareinsurance.org

Personal Finance in Practice

LONG-TERM CARE POLICY CHECKLIST

The following checklist will help you compare LTC policies you may be considering:

	Policy A	Policy B			Policy A	Policy B
1. What services are covered?			**8.** Are Alzheimer's disease and other organic mental and nervous disorders covered?		_____	_____
Skilled care	_____	_____				
Intermediate care	_____	_____	**9.** Does this policy require:			
Custodial care	_____	_____	Physician certification of need?		_____	_____
Home health care	_____	_____	An assessment of activities of daily living?		_____	_____
Adult day care	_____	_____	A prior hospital stay for:			
Other	_____	_____	Nursing home care?		_____	_____
2. How much does the policy pay per day?			Home health care?		_____	_____
For skilled care	_____	_____	A prior nursing home stay for home health care coverage?		_____	_____
For intermediate care	_____	_____	Other?		_____	_____
For custodial care	_____	_____	**10.** Is the policy guaranteed renewable?		_____	_____
For home health care	_____	_____				
For adult day care	_____	_____	**11.** What is the age range of enrollment?		_____	_____
3. How long will benefits last?			**12.** Is there a waiver-of-premium provision:			
In a nursing home for:			For nursing home care?		_____	_____
Skilled nursing care	_____	_____	For home health care?		_____	_____
Intermediate nursing care	_____	_____	**13.** How long must I be confined before premiums are waived?		_____	_____
Custodial care	_____	_____				
At home:	_____	_____	**14.** Does the policy offer an inflation adjustment feature? If so:			
4. Does the policy have a maximum lifetime benefit? If so, what is it?			What is the rate of increase?		_____	_____
For nursing home care	_____	_____	How often is it applied?		_____	_____
For home health care	_____	_____	For how long?		_____	_____
5. Does the policy have a maximum length of coverage for each period of confinement? If so, what is it?			Is there an additional cost?		_____	_____
For nursing home care	_____	_____	**15.** What does the policy cost:			
For home health care	_____	_____	Per year?			
6. How long must I wait before pre-existing conditions are covered?		_____	_____	With inflation feature		_____	_____
			Without inflation feature		_____	_____
7. How many days must I wait before benefits begin?			Per month?			
For nursing home care	_____	_____	With inflation feature		_____	_____
For home health care	_____	_____	Without inflation feature		_____	_____
			16. Is there a 30-day free look?		_____	_____

Source: *Guide to Long-Term Care Insurance* (Washington, DC: Health Insurance Association of America, 1994), pp. 11–12.

Major Provisions in a Health Insurance Policy

All health insurance policies have certain provisions in common. You have to be sure that you understand what your policy covers. What are the benefits? What are the limits? The following are details of provisions that are usually found in health insurance policies:

- *Eligibility:* The people covered by the policy must meet specified eligibility requirements, such as family relationship and, for children, a certain age.
- *Assigned benefits:* You are reimbursed for payments when you turn in your bills and claim forms. When you assign benefits, you let your insurer make direct payments to your doctor or hospital.
- *Internal limits:* A policy with internal limits sets specific levels of repayment for certain services. Even if your hospital room costs $400 a day, you won't be able to get more than $250 if an internal limit specifies that maximum.
- *Copayment:* A **copayment** is a flat fee that you pay every time you receive a covered service. The fee is usually between $5 and $15, and the insurer pays the balance of the cost of the service. This is different from coinsurance, which is the percentage of your medical costs for which you are responsible after paying your deductible.
- *Service benefits:* Policies with this provision list coverage in terms of services, not dollar amounts: You're entitled to X-rays, for instance, not $40 worth of X-rays per visit. Service benefits provisions are always preferable to dollar amount coverage because the insurer will pay all the costs.
- *Benefit limits:* This provision defines a maximum benefit, either in terms of a dollar amount or in terms of number of days spent in the hospital.
- *Exclusions and limitations:* This provision specifies services that the policy does not cover. It may include preexisting conditions (a condition you were diagnosed with before your insurance plan took effect), cosmetic surgery, or more.
- *Guaranteed renewable:* This provision means that the insurer can't cancel the policy unless you fail to pay the premiums. It also forbids insurers to raise premiums unless they raise all premiums for all members of your group.
- *Cancellation and termination:* This provision explains the circumstances under which the insurer can cancel your coverage. It also explains how you can convert your group contract into an individual contract.

copayment A provision under which the insured pays a flat dollar amount each time a covered medical service is received after the deductible has been met.

✔ **CONCEPTCHECK 9–2**

1 What three types of coverage are included in the basic health insurance?

_____

2 What benefits are provided by

   a. Hospital expense coverage? _____

_____

   b. Surgical expense coverage? _____

_____

   c. Physician expense coverage? _____

_____

Continued

Continued from page 245

3 Match the following terms with an appropriate statement.

coinsurance

a. Requires the policyholder to pay all costs up to a certain amount. _____

stop-loss

b. The percentage of the medical expenses you must pay. _____

hospital indemnity policy

c. A policy used as a supplement to basic health or major medical policies.
_____

exclusion and limitations

d. Defines who is covered by the policy. _____

copayment

e. Specifies services that the policy does not cover. _____

eligibility

f. A flat fee that you pay every time you receive a covered service. _____

Health Insurance Trade-Offs

> **OBJECTIVE 3**
> Assess the trade-offs of different health insurance plans.

Different health insurance policies may offer very different benefits. As you decide which insurance plan to buy, consider the following trade-offs.

REIMBURSEMENT VERSUS INDEMNITY   A reimbursement policy pays you back for actual expenses. An indemnity policy provides you with specific amounts, regardless of how much the actual expenses may be.

Katie and Seth are both charged $200 for an office visit to the same specialist. Katie's reimbursement policy has a deductible of $300. Once she has met the deductible, the policy will cover the full cost of such a visit. Seth's indemnity policy will pay him $125, which is what his plan provides for a visit to any specialist.

INTERNAL LIMITS VERSUS AGGREGATE LIMITS   A policy with internal limits will cover only a fixed amount for an expense, such as the daily cost of room and board during a hospital stay. A policy with aggregate limits will limit only the total amount of coverage (the maximum dollar amount paid for all benefits in a year), such as $1 million in major expense benefits, or it may have no limits.

Apply *Yourself!*

Objective 3

Prepare a list of trade-offs that are important to you in a health insurance policy.

DEDUCTIBLES AND COINSURANCE   The cost of a health insurance policy can be greatly affected by the size of the deductible (the set amount that the policyholder must pay toward medical expenses before the insurance company pays benefits). It can also be affected by the terms of the *coinsurance provision* (which states what percentage of the medical expenses the policyholder must pay in addition to the deductible amount).

OUT-OF-POCKET LIMITS   Some policies limit the amount of money you must pay for the deductible and coinsurance. After you have reached that limit, the insurance company covers 100 percent of any additional costs. Out-of-pocket limits help you lower your financial risk, but they also increase your premiums.

BENEFITS BASED ON REASONABLE AND CUSTOMARY CHARGES
Some policies consider the average fee for a service in a particular geographical area. They then use the amount to set a limit on payments to policyholders. If the standard

A health insurance plan should:

- Offer basic coverage for hospital and doctor bills

- Provide at least 120 days' hospital room and board in full

- Provide at least a $1 million lifetime maximum for each family member

- Pay at least 80 percent for out-of-hospital expenses after a yearly deductible of $500 per person or $1,000 per family

- Impose no unreasonable exclusions

- Limit your out-of-pocket expenses to no more than $3,000 to $5,000 a year, excluding dental, vision care, and precription costs

Although health insurance plans vary greatly, all plans should have the same basic features. *Would you add anything to this list of must-haves?*

Exhibit [9–1]

Health Insurance Must-Haves

cost of a certain procedure is $1,500 in your part of the country, then your policy won't pay more than that amount.

Which Coverage Should You Choose?

Now that you are familiar with the available types of health insurance and some of their major provisions, how do you choose one? The type of coverage you choose will be affected by the amount you can afford to spend on the premiums and the level of benefits that you feel you want and need. It may also be affected by the kind of coverage your employer offers, if you are covered through your employer.

You can buy basic health coverage, major medical coverage, or both basic and major medical coverage. Any of these three choices will take care of at least some of your medical expenses. Ideally, you should get a basic plan and a major medical supplement. Another option is to purchase a comprehensive major medical policy that combines the value of both plans in a single policy. Exhibit 9–1 describes the most basic features you should look for.

DID YOU KNOW?

The Employee Benefits Security Administration (EBSA) provides Health Benefits Education for Consumers and Health Insurance Tips. Call toll-free 866-444-3272 or visit www.dol.gov/ebsa.

Sheet 30 Assessing Current and Needed Health Care Insurance.

✔ CONCEPTCHECK 9–3

1 As you decide which health insurance plan to buy, what trade-offs would you consider?

_____

_____

2 Match the following terms with an appropriate statement.

reimbursement   a. A policy that will cover only a fixed amount of an expense. _____

indemnity   b. A policy that pays you back for actual expenses. _____

internal limits   c. A policy that provides you with specific amounts, regardless of how much the actual expenses may be. _____

Continued

Continued from page 247

deductible	*d.* After you have reached a certain limit, the insurance company covers 100 percent of any additional cost. _____
out-of-pocket limit	*e.* The set amount that you must pay toward medical expenses before the insurance company pays benefits. _____

3 What basic features should be included in your health insurance plan?

_____

_____

Private Health Care Plans and Government Health Care Programs

OBJECTIVE 4
Evaluate the differences among health care plans offered by private companies and by the government.

Blue Cross An independent nonprofit membership corporation that provides protection against the cost of hospital care.

Blue Shield An independent nonprofit membership corporation that provides protection against the cost of surgical and medical care.

managed care Prepaid health plans that provide comprehensive health care to members.

Private Health Care Plans

Most health insurance in the United States is provided by private organizations rather than by the government. Private health care plans may be offered by a number of sources: private insurance companies; hospital and medical service plans; health maintenance organizations; preferred provider organizations; home health care agencies; and employer self-funded health plans.

PRIVATE INSURANCE COMPANIES Several hundred private insurance companies are in the health insurance business. They provide mostly group health plans to employers, which in turn offer them to their employees as a benefit. Premiums may be fully or partially paid by the employer, with the employee paying any remainder. These policies typically pay you for medical costs you incur, or they send the payment directly to the doctor, hospital, or lab that provides the services.

HOSPITAL AND MEDICAL SERVICE PLANS Blue Cross and Blue Shield are statewide organizations similar to private health insurance companies. Each state has its own Blue Cross and Blue Shield. The "Blues" provide health insurance to millions of Americans. **Blue Cross** provides hospital care benefits. **Blue Shield** provides benefits for surgical and medical services performed by physicians.

HEALTH MAINTENANCE ORGANIZATIONS Rising health care costs have led to an increase in managed care plans. According to a recent industry survey, 23 percent of employed Americans are enrolled in some form of managed care. **Managed care** refers to prepaid health plans that provide comprehensive health care to their members. Managed care is designed to control the cost of health care services by controlling how they are used. Managed care is offered by health maintenance organizations (HMOs), preferred provider organizations (PPOs), and point-of-service plans (POSs).

Health maintenance organizations are an alternative to basic health insurance and major medical expense insurance. A **health maintenance organization (HMO)** is a health insurance plan that directly employs or contracts with selected physicians and other medical professionals to provide health care services in exchange for a fixed, prepaid monthly premium.

DID YOU KNOW?

The National Association of Insurance Commissioners provides a useful brochure, *Protect Yourself against Illegal Health Plans.* Visit www.naic.org/pressroom/consumer_alerts/.

HMOs are based on the idea that preventive services will minimize future medical problems. Therefore, these plans typically cover routine immunizations and checkups, screening programs, and diagnostic tests. They also provide customers with coverage for surgery, hospitalization, and emergency care. If you have an HMO, you will usually pay a small copayment for each covered service. Supplemental services may include vision care and prescription services, which are typically available for an additional fee.

When you first enroll in an HMO, you must choose a plan physician from a list of doctors provided by the HMO. The physician provides or arranges for all of your health care services. You must receive care through your plan physician; if you don't, you are responsible for the cost of the service. The only exception to this rule is in the case of a medical emergency. If you experience a sudden illness or injury that would threaten your life or health if not treated immediately, you may go to the emergency room of the nearest hospital. All other care must be provided by hospitals and doctors under contract with the HMO.

HMOs are not for everyone. Many HMO customers complain that their HMO denies them necessary care. Others feel restricted by the limited choice of doctors.

Exhibit 9–2 provides some tips on using and choosing an HMO: Because HMOs require you to use only certain doctors, you should make sure that these doctors are near your home or office. You should also be able to change doctors easily if you don't like your first choice. Similarly, second opinions should always be available at the HMO's

health maintenance organization (HMO) A health insurance plan that provides a wide range of health care services for a fixed, prepaid monthly premium.

Key Web Sites for Health Insurance Articles
www.money.com
www.kiplinger.com

Exhibit [9–2]   Tips on Using and Choosing an HMO

How to Use an HMO
When you first enroll in an HMO, you must choose a plan physician (family practitioner, internist, pediatrician, or obstetrician-gynecologist) who provides or arranges for all of your health care services. It is extremely important that you receive your care through the plan physician. If you don't, you are responsible for the cost of the service rendered.

The only exceptions to the requirement that care be received through the plan physician are medical emergencies. A medical emergency is a sudden onset of illness or a sudden injury that would jeopardize your life or health if not treated immediately. In such instances, you may use the facilities of the nearest hospital emergency room. All other care must be provided by hospitals and doctors under contract with the HMO.

How to Choose an HMO
If you decide to enroll in an HMO, you should consider these additional factors:

1. *Accessibility.* Since you must use plan providers, it is extremely important that they be easily accessible from your home or office.

2. *Convenient office hours.* Your plan physician should have convenient office hours.

3. *Alternative physicians.* Should you become dissatisfied with your first choice of a physician, the HMO should allow you the option to change physicians.

4. *Second opinions.* You should be able to obtain second opinions.

5. *Type of coverage.* You should compare the health care services offered by various HMOs, paying particular attention to whether you will incur out-of-pocket expenses or copayments.

6. *Appeal procedures.* The HMO should have a convenient and prompt system for resolving problems and disputes.

7. *Price.* You should compare the prices various HMOs charge to ensure that you are getting the most services for your health care dollar.

What to Do When an HMO Denies Treatment or Coverage

- *Get it in writing.* To better defend your case, ask for a letter detailing the clinical reasons your claim was denied and the name and medical expertise of the HMO staff member responsible.

- *Know your rights.* The plan document or your HMO's member services department will tell you how experimental treatments are defined and covered and how the appeals process works.

- *Keep records.* Make copies of any correspondence, including payments and any reimbursements. Also, keep a written log of all conversations relevant to your claim.

- *Find advocates.* Enlist the help of your doctor, employer, and state insurance department to lobby your case before the HMO.

Source: Reprinted from the May 18, 1997, issue of *BusinessWeek* by special permission. © 1999 McGraw-Hill Companies, Inc.

expense, and you should be able to appeal any case in which the HMO denies care. Finally, look at the costs and benefits: Will you incur out-of-pocket expenses or copayments? What services will the plan provide?

PREFERRED PROVIDER ORGANIZATIONS   A variation on the HMO is a **preferred provider organization (PPO)**, a group of doctors and hospitals that agree to provide specified medical services to members at prearranged fees. PPOs offer these discounted services to employers either directly or indirectly through an insurance company. The premiums for PPOs are slightly higher than the premiums for HMOs.

PPO plan members often pay no deductibles and may make minimal copayments. Whereas HMOs require members to receive care from HMO providers only, PPOs allow members greater flexibility. Members can either visit a preferred provider (a physician whom you select from a list, as in an HMO) or go to their own physicians. Patients who decide to use their own doctors do not lose coverage as they would with an HMO. Instead they must pay deductibles and larger copayments.

Increasingly, the difference between PPOs and HMOs is becoming less clear. A **point-of-service (POS) plan** combines features of both HMOs and PPOs. POSs use a network of participating physicians and medical professionals who have contracted to provide services for certain fees. As with your HMO, you choose a plan physician who manages your care and controls referrals to specialists. As long as you receive care from a plan provider, you pay little or nothing, just as you would with an HMO. However, you're allowed to seek care outside the network at a higher charge, as with a PPO.

HOME HEALTH CARE AGENCIES   Rising hospital costs, new medical technology, and the increasing number of elderly people have helped make home care one of the fastest growing areas of the health care industry. Home health care consists of home health agencies; home care aide organizations; and hospices, facilities that care for the terminally ill. These providers offer medical care in a home setting in agreement with a medical order, often at a fraction of the cost hospitals would charge for a similar service.

EMPLOYER SELF-FUNDED HEALTH PLANS   Some companies choose to self-insure. The company runs its own insurance plan, collecting premiums from employees and paying medical benefits as needed. However, these companies must cover any costs that exceed the income from premiums. Unfortunately, not all corporations have the financial assets necessary to cover these situations, which can mean a financial disaster for the company and its employees.

Government Health Care Programs

The health insurance coverage discussed thus far is normally purchased through private companies. Some consumers, however, are eligible for health insurance coverage under programs offered by federal and state governments.

MEDICARE   Perhaps the best-known government health program is Medicare. *Medicare* is a federally funded health insurance program available mainly to people over 65 and to people with disabilities. Medicare has two parts: hospital insurance (Part A) and medical insurance (Part B). Medicare hospital insurance is funded by part of the Social Security payroll tax. Part A helps pay for inpatient hospital care, inpatient care in a skilled nursing facility, home health care, and hospice care. Program participants pay a single annual deductible.

---

preferred provider organization (PPO) A group of doctors and hospitals that agree to provide health care at rates approved by the insurer.

point-of-service (POS) plan A network of selected contracted, participating providers; also called an *HMO-PPO hybrid* or *open-ended HMO*.

Key Web Sites for Health Insurance Information
www.healthfinder.gov
www.achoo.com

Apply *Yourself!*

Objective 4

Talk to several people covered by Medicare and Medicaid to obtain information on the coverage provided and the difficulties sometimes faced.

Part B helps pay for doctors' services and a variety of other medical services and supplies not covered or not fully covered by Part A. Part B has a deductible and a 20 percent coinsurance provision. Medicare medical insurance is a supplemental program paid for by individuals who feel that they need it. A regular monthly premium is charged. The federal government matches this amount.

Medicare is constantly in financial trouble. Health care costs continue to grow, and the proportion of senior citizens in society is rising. This situation puts Medicare in danger of running out of funds. According to projections in 2003, the program will be bankrupt by the year 2026 if no changes are made.

The Balanced Budget Act of 1997 created the new Medicare Choice program. This program allows many Medicare members to choose a managed care plan in addition to their Medicare coverage. For some additional costs, members can receive greater benefits. Exhibit 9–3 compares features of different Medicare options.

Exhibit [9–3]

A Comparison of Various Medicare Plans

	Current Options	New Options (Medicare and Choice)	Plan Description
Original Medicare	✔	✔	• You choose your health care providers. • Medicare pays your providers for covered services. • Most beneficiaries choose Medicare supplemental insurance to cover deductible and copayments.
Medicare health maintenance organization (HMO)	✔	✔	• You must live in the plan's service area. • You agree to use the plan network of doctors, hospitals, and other health providers, except in an emergency. • Medicare pays the HMO to provide all medical services.
Preferred provider organization (PPO)		✔	• Works like an HMO, except you have the choice to see a health provider out of the network. • If you do see an out-of-network provider, you will pay a higher cost.
Provider-sponsored organization (PSO)		✔	• Works like a Medicare HMO, except the networks are managed by health care providers (doctors and hospitals) rather than an insurance company.
Private fee for service		✔	• Medicare pays a lump sum to a private insurance health plan. • Providers can bill more than what the plan pays; you are responsible for paying the balance. • The plan may offer more benefits than original Medicare.
Medical savings account (MSA)		✔	• A test program is limited to 390,000 Medicare beneficiaries. • Medicare MSAs are a special type of savings account that can be used to pay medical bills. • CMS will make an annual lump-sum deposit into enrollee's account (only Medicare can deposit funds into this account). • MSAs work with a special private insurance company and carry a very high deductible. • Funds withdrawn for nonmedical purposes are taxable and subject to a penalty.

Source: *Medicare & You* (Washington, DC: The Centers for Medicare and Medicaid Services, 2004).

What Is Not Covered by Medicare?   Although Medicare is very helpful for meeting medical costs, it does not cover everything. In addition to the deductibles and coinsurance payments, Medicare will not cover some medical expenses at all. These are certain types of skilled or long-term nursing care, out-of-hospital prescription drugs, routine checkups, dental care, and most immunizations. Medicare also severely limits the types of services it will cover and the amount it will pay for those services. If your doctor does not accept Medicare's approved amount as payment in full, you're responsible for the difference.

MEDIGAP   Those eligible for Medicare who would like more coverage may buy **MEDIGAP (MedSup) insurance**. MEDIGAP insurance supplements Medicare by filling the gap between Medicare payments and medical costs not covered by Medicare. It is offered by private companies.

MEDICAID   The other well-known government health program is *Medicaid*, a medical assistance program offered to certain low-income individuals and families. Medicaid is administered by states, but it is financed by a combination of state and federal funds. Unlike Medicare, Medicaid coverage is so comprehensive that people with Medicaid do not need supplemental insurance. Typical Medicaid benefits include physicians' services, inpatient and outpatient hospital services, lab services, skilled nursing and home health services, prescription drugs, eyeglasses, and preventive care for people under the age of 21.

GOVERNMENT CONSUMER HEALTH INFORMATION WEB SITES
The Department of Health and Human Services operates more than 60 Web sites with a wealth of reliable information related to health and medicine. For example,

- *Healthfinder:* Healthfinder includes links to more than 1,000 Web sites operated by government and nonprofit organizations. It lists topics according to subject (www.hhs.gov).
- *MedlinePlus:* Medline Plus is the world's largest collection of published medical information. It was originally designed for health professionals and researchers, but it's also valuable for students and others who are interested in health care and medical issues (www.nlm.nih.gov/medlineplus).
- *NIH Health Information Page:* The National Institutes of Health (NIH) operates a Web site called the NIH Health Information Page, which can direct you to the consumer health information in NIH publications and on the Internet (www.nih.gov).
- *FDA:* The Food and Drug Administration (FDA) also runs a Web site. This consumer protection agency's site provides information about the safety of various foods, drugs, cosmetics, and medical devices (www.fda.gov).

Key Web Site for Medicare Information www.ssa.gov

medigap (MedSup) insurance Supplements Medicare by filling the gap between Medicare payments and medical costs not covered by Medicare.

CONCEPTCHECK 9–4

1 What are the six sources of private health plans?

_____

_____

2 Match the following terms with an appropriate statement.

Blue Cross   *a.* A medical assistance program offered to certain low-income individuals and families. _____

Blue Shield

b. Combines features of both HMOs and PPOs. _____

HMOs

c. A statewide organization that provides hospital care benefits. _____

PPOs

d. A federally funded health insurance program available mainly to people over 65 and to people with disabilities. _____

point of service (POS)

e. A health insurance plan that directly employs or contracts with selected physicians to provide health services in exchange for a fixed, prepaid monthly premium. _____

Medicare

f. A statewide organization that provides benefits for surgical and medical services performed by physicians. _____

Medicaid

g. A group of doctors and hospitals that agree to provide specified medical services to members at prearranged fees. _____

3 What health care services are not covered by Medicare?

_____

_____

Disability Income Insurance

The Need for Disability Income

Before disability insurance existed, people who were ill lost more money from missed paychecks than from medical bills. Disability income insurance was set up to protect against such loss of income. This kind of coverage is very common today, and several hundred insurance companies offer it.

Disability income insurance provides regular cash income when you're unable to work because of a pregnancy, a non-work-related accident, or an illness. It protects your earning power, your most valuable resource.

The exact definition of a disability varies from insurer to insurer. Some insurers will pay you when you are unable to work at your regular job. Others will pay only if you are so ill or badly hurt that you can't work at any job. A violinist with a hand injury, for instance, might have trouble doing his or her regular work but might be able to perform a range of other jobs. A good disability income insurance plan pays you if you can't work at your regular job. A good plan will also pay partial benefits if you are able to work only part-time.

Many people make the mistake of ignoring disability insurance, not realizing that it's very important insurance to have. Disability can cause even greater financial problems than death. Disabled persons lose their earning power but still have to meet their living expenses. In addition, they often face huge costs for the medical treatment and special care that their disabilities require.

Sources of Disability Income

Before you buy disability income insurance from a private insurance company, remember that you may already have some form of insurance of this kind. This coverage may be available through worker's compensation if you're injured on the job. Disability benefits may also be available through your employer or through Social Security in case of a long-term disability.

OBJECTIVE 5

Explain the importance of disability income insurance in financial planning and identify its sources.

disability income insurance Provides payments to replace income when an insured person is unable to work.

Building a **GOOD POLICY**

D isability insurance is expensive. Some agents figure you need to spend 3% to 6% of your salary to buy comprehensive coverage. Cheap policies are so full of holes that they often aren't worth it. For a small, restricted benefit, such as $3,000 a month, a 35-year-old male lawyer in excellent health might pay $720 a year, and a woman hundreds of dollars more. Professionals such as certified public accountants, lawyers and engineers are considered better risks than doctors, pilots and blue-collar applicants. In any event, make sure you get a policy that fits your needs and will pay off if you need it.

You want your policy to replace at least 60% of your income. (Benefits from policies you buy yourself are tax-free, so you don't need to replace 100% of your income to be whole.) And you don't want the insurer to try to force you into a different job so that it can deny benefits, as happened to Joan Hangarter and Randall Chapman, whose cases are described in the accompanying story.

Your own occupation. To start, insist on the definition of disability as the inability to perform "the material and substantial duties" of your occupation. Again, that's no absolute protection against a claims denial. But weaker language like "anything for which you are reasonably fitted by education, training and experience" leaves you open to more grief. Under those terms, if you have a master's or doctorate, an insurance company might say you can teach or "do research." Never mind if the job market and the salary scale for teachers are awful.

If "own occupation to age 65" is too expensive, look at "modified own occupation." This offers two to five years of full benefits if you can't do your actual job and then, unless you're completely disabled, you'll have to work something out with the insurance company. Since the odds are against a disability lasting five years, you can live with a shorter term unless yours is a strenuous occupation in which pain or long-lasting injury could sideline you indefinitely.

Noncancelable. Disability policies are "noncancelable" or "guaranteed renewable." Noncancelable is what you want. It means the company can't raise the premiums. Guaranteed renewable lets the company raise rates if, for example, you're an architect and the company finds itself paying big claims to other architects.

Expandable. You want the right to buy more insurance as your income rises without new medical screening.

Inflation-protected. Take a cost-of-living rider that bumps up your benefits by 3%, 4% or 6% after you begin collecting. It's cheap.

Longer waiting period. One way to shave the premium is to extend the period before you can collect benefits to six months. You may have sick leave, short-term benefits from work or savings to get by for six months.

What to avoid. Skip anything intended to feed retirement plans while you're on claim. This costs a lot, and you might not be free to invest where you like. Instead, you may be given choices with the insurance company's investment affiliates.

Source: Reprinted by permission from the February issue of *Kiplinger's Personal Finance*. Copyright © 2004 The Kiplinger Washington Editors, Inc. Joan Goldwasser, "Building a Good Policy."

1. Why should one consider purchasing a "modified own occupation" disability income policy?

   _____

   _____

2. What features should you consider in purchasing a disability income insurance policy?

   _____

   _____

3. What information is available at www.kiplinger.com that might be helpful when purchasing disability income insurance?

   _____

   _____

WORKER'S COMPENSATION   If your disability is a result of an accident or illness that occurred on the job, you may be eligible to receive worker's compensation benefits in your state. Benefits will depend on your salary and your work history.

EMPLOYER PLANS   Many employers provide disability income insurance through group insurance plans. In most cases your employer will pay part or all of the cost of such insurance. Some policies may provide continued wages for several months only, whereas others will give you long-term protection.

SOCIAL SECURITY   Social Security may be best known as a source of retirement income, but it also provides disability benefits. If you're a worker who pays into the Social Security system, you're eligible for Social Security funds if you become disabled. How much you get depends on your salary and the number of years you've been paying into Social Security. Your dependents also qualify for certain benefits. However, Social Security has very strict rules. Workers are considered disabled if they have a physical or mental condition that prevents them from working and that is expected to last for at least 12 months or to result in death. Benefits start at the sixth full month the person is disabled. They stay in effect as long as the disability lasts.

PRIVATE INCOME INSURANCE PROGRAMS   Privately owned insurance companies offer many policies to protect people from loss of income resulting from illness or disability. Disability income insurance gives weekly or monthly cash payments to people who cannot work because of illness or accident. The amount paid is usually 40 to 60 percent of a person's normal income. Some plans, however, pay as much as 75 percent.

Disability Income Insurance Trade-Offs

As with the purchase of health insurance, you must make certain trade-offs when you decide among different private disability insurance policies. Keep the following in mind as you look for a plan that is right for you.

WAITING OR ELIMINATION PERIOD   Benefits won't begin the day you become disabled. You'll have to wait anywhere between one and six months before you can begin collecting. The span of time is called an elimination period. Usually a policy with a longer elimination period charges lower premiums.

DURATION OF BENEFITS   Every policy names a specified period during which benefits will be paid. Some policies are valid for only a few years. Others are automatically canceled when you turn 65. Still others continue to make payments for life. You should look for a policy that pays benefits for life. If your policy stops payments when you turn 65, then permanent disability could be a major financial as well as physical loss.

AMOUNT OF BENEFITS   You should aim for a benefit amount that, when added to other sources of income, will equal 70 to 80 percent of your take-home pay. Of course, the greater the benefit, the greater the cost, or premium.

Apply *Yourself!*

Objective 5

Contact an insurance agent to obtain cost information for an individual disability income insurance policy.

ACCIDENT AND SICKNESS COVERAGE   Some disability policies pay only for accidents. Coverage for sickness is important, though. Accidents are not the only cause of disability.

GUARANTEED RENEWABILITY   If your health becomes poor, your disability insurer may try to cancel your coverage. Look for a plan that guarantees coverage as long as you continue to pay your premiums. The cost may be higher, but it's worth the extra security and peace of mind. You may even be able to find a plan that will stop charging the premiums if you become disabled, which is an added benefit.

Your Disability Income Needs

Sheet 31
Disability
Income
Insurance
Needs.

Once you have found out what your benefits from the numerous public and private sources would be, you should determine whether those benefits would meet your disability income needs. Ideally, you'll want to replace all the income you otherwise would have earned. This should enable you to pay your day-to-day expenses while you're recovering. You won't have work-related expenses and your taxes will be lower during the time you are disabled. In some cases you may not have to pay certain taxes at all. Use Exhibit 9–4 to determine how much income you will have available if you become disabled.

Exhibit [9–4]

Calculating Disability Income

How much income will you have available if you become disabled?

	Monthly Amount	After Waiting:	For a Period of:
Sick leave or short-term disability	_____	_____	_____
Group long-term disability	_____	_____	_____
Social Security	_____	_____	_____
Other government programs	_____	_____	_____
Individual disability insurance	_____	_____	_____
Credit disability insurance	_____	_____	_____
Other income:	_____	_____	_____
Savings	_____	_____	_____
Spouse's income	_____	_____	_____
Total monthly income while disabled:	$ _____		

CONCEPTCHECK 9–5

1 What is the purpose of disability income insurance?

_____

_____

2 What are the four sources of disability income?

_____

_____

3 Match the following terms with an appropriate statement.

waiting or elimination period   *a.* A specified period during which benefits are paid. _____

duration of benefits   *b.* A plan that guarantees coverage as long as you continue to pay your premiums. _____

guaranteed renewability   *c.* A period of one to six months that must elapse before benefits can be collected. _____

Back to   **Getting Personal**

www.mhhe.com/kdh

Reevaluate your Getting Personal responses at the beginning of the chapter. Which statements might have different responses now or in the future as a result of studying this chapter?

_____

_____

Chapter Summary

Objective 1   Health insurance is protection that provides payments of benefits for a covered sickness or injury. Health insurance should be a part of your overall insurance program to safeguard your family's economic security. Health insurance plans can be purchased through group health insurance, individual health insurance, and COBRA.

Objective 2   Four basic types of health insurance are available under group and individual policies: hospital expense insurance, surgical expense insurance, physician's expense insurance, and major medical expense insurance.

Major provisions of a health insurance policy include eligibility requirements, assigned benefits, internal limits, copayment, service benefits, benefit limits, exclusions and limitations, guaranteed renewability, and cancellation and termination.

Objective 3   Health insurance policy trade-offs include reimbursement versus indemnity, internal limits versus aggregate limits, deductibles and coinsurance, out-of-pocket limits, and benefits based on reasonable and customary charges.

Objective 4   Health insurance and health care are available from private insurance companies, hospital and medical service plans such as Blue Cross/Blue Shield, health maintenance organizations (HMOs), preferred provider organization (PPOs), point-of-service plans (POSs), home health care agencies, and employer self-funded health plans.

The federal and state governments offer health coverage in accordance with laws that define the premiums and benefits. Two well-known government health programs are Medicare and Medicaid.

Objective 5   Disability income insurance provides regular cash income lost by employees as the result of an accident, illness, or pregnancy. Sources of disability income insurance include the employer, Social Security, worker's compensation, and private insurance companies.

Key Terms

basic health insurance coverage   241

Blue Cross   248

Blue Shield   248

coinsurance   242

copayment   245

deductible   242

disability income insurance   253

health maintenance organization
   (HMO)   249

hospital expense insurance   242

long-term care insurance (LTC)   243

managed care   248

medigap (MedSup) insurance   252

physician expense insurance   242

point-of-service (POS) plan   250

preferred provider organization
   (PPO)   250

stop-loss   242

surgical expense insurance   242

Problems and Questions

1. Larry and Liz are a young couple both working full time and earning about $50,000 a year. They recently purchased a house and took out a large mortgage. Since both of them work, they own two cars and are still making payments on them. Liz has major medical health insurance through her employer, but Larry's coverage is inadequate. They have no children, but they hope to start a family in about three years. Liz's employer provides disability income insurance, but Larry's employer does not. Analyze the need for health and disability insurance for Liz and Larry.

2. Pam is 31 and recently divorced, with children ages 3 and 6. She earns $28,000 a year as a secretary. Her employer provides her with basic health insurance coverage. She receives child support from the children's father, but he misses payments often and is always behind in payments. Her ex-husband, however, is responsible for the children's medical bills. Analyze the need for health and disability insurance for Pam.

3. The Kelleher family has health insurance coverage that pays 80 percent of out-of-hospital expenses after a $500 deductible per person. If one family member has doctor and prescription medication expenses of $1,100, what amount would the insurance company pay?

4. A health insurance policy pays 65 percent of physical therapy costs after a $200 deductible. In contrast, an HMO charges $15 per visit for physical therapy. How much would a person save the HMO if he or she had 10 physical therapy sessions costing $50 each?

5. List the benefits included in your employee benefit package, such as health insurance, disability income insurance, and life insurance. Discuss the importance of such a benefit package to the consumer.

6. Visit the Social Security Administration's Web page to determine your approximate monthly Social Security disability benefits should you become disabled in the current year. Or call your Social Security office to request the latest edition of *Social Security: Understanding the Benefits*.

7. Obtain sample health insurance policies from insurance agents or brokers, and analyze the policies for definitions, coverage, exclusions, limitations on coverage, and amounts of coverage. In what ways are the policies similar? In what ways do they differ?

8. Visit the following Web sites to gather information about various types of health insurance coverage. Prepare a summary report on how this information may be useful to you.

a. Healthfinder (http://www.healthfinder.gov).

b. Medline (http://www.medline.gov).

9. Visit the National Health Information Center's Web page (http://www.health.gov/nhic). The NHIC is an online directory of more than 1,400 health-related organizations that can provide health care information. Report the types of health insurance and health care available to consumers.

10. Write to the Centers for Medicare and Medicaid Services, Baltimore, MD 21207, and ask for the latest edition of *Guide to Health Insurance for People with Medicare*. On the basis of the information contained in this source, describe the changes that have been made in the hospital insurance and medical insurance provided by Medicare.

11. Georgia Braxton, a widow, has take-home pay of $600 a week. Her disability insurance coverage replaces 70 percent of her earnings after a four-week waiting period. What amount would she receive in disability benefits if an illness kept Georgia off work for 16 weeks?

Internet Connection

www.mhhe.com/kdh

RESEARCHING HEALTH INSURANCE STATISTICS

The U.S. Census Bureau collects a wide variety of data about the people and economy of the United States. Health insurance coverage is one of the many surveys the bureau completes each year.

Locate the Health Insurance section of the U.S. Census Bureau Web site. Complete the worksheet below and answer the questions that follow.

Results	
U.S. Census Bureau Web site address	
For what year is the most recent health insurance coverage survey presented?	
In the most recent health insurance survey, how many people in the United States were without health insurance coverage?	
What populations (age or race) are less likely to have health insurance?	
How many children under the age of 18 have no health insurance according to the most recent health insurance survey?	

Case in Point

BUYING ADEQUATE HEALTH INSURANCE COVERAGE

Kathy Jones was a junior at Glenbard High School. She had two younger brothers. Her father, the manager of a local supermarket, had take-home pay of $3,000 a month. He had a group health insurance policy and a $30,000 life insurance policy. He said that he could not afford to buy additional insurance. All of his monthly salary was used to meet current expenses, including car and house payments, food, clothing, transportation, children's allowances, recreation and entertainment, and vacation trips.

One evening, Kathy was talking with her father about insurance, which she was studying in an economics course. She asked what kind of insurance program her father had for their family. The question started Mr. Jones thinking about how well he was planning for his wife and children. Since the family had always been in good health, Mr. Jones felt that additional health and life insurance was not essential. Maybe after he received a raise in his salary and after his daughter was out of high school, he could afford to buy more insurance.

Questions

1. Do you think Kathy's father was planning wisely for the welfare of his family? Can you suggest ways in which this family could have cut monthly expenses and thus set aside some money for more insurance?

2. Although Mr. Jones's salary was not big enough to buy insurance for all possible risks, what protection do you think he should have had at this time?

3. Suppose Mr. Jones had been seriously injured and unable to work for at least one year. What would his family have done? How might this situation have affected his children?

Assessing Current and Needed Health Care Insurance

Financial Planning Activities: Assess current and needed medical and health care insurance. Investigate your existing medical and health insurance, and determine the need for additional coverages.

Suggested Web Sites: www.insure.com   www.life-line.org

Insurance company

Address

Type of coverage   ☐ individual health policy   ☐ group health policy

           ☐ HMO   ☐ PPO   ☐ other

Premium amount (monthly/quarter/semiannual/annual)

Main coverages

Amount of coverage for

- Hospital costs

- Surgery costs

- Physician's fees

- Lab tests

- Outpatient expenses

- Maternity

- Major medical

Other items covered/amounts

Policy restrictions (deductible, coinsurance, maximum limits)

Items not covered by this insurance

Of items not covered, would supplemental coverage be appropriate for your personal situation?

What actions related to your current (or proposed additional) coverage are necessary?

What's Next for Your Personal Financial Plan?

- Talk to others about the impact of their health insurance on other financial decisions.
- Contact an insurance agent to obtain cost information for an individual health insurance plan.

Name: _____   **Date:** _____

Disability Income Insurance Needs

Financial Planning Activities: Determine financial needs and insurance coverage related to employment disability situations. Use the categories below to determine your potential income needs and disability insurance coverage.

Suggested Web Sites: www.ssa.gov   www.insuremarket.com

Monthly Expenses

	Current	When Disabled
Mortgage (or rent)	$ _____	$ _____
Utilities	$ _____	$ _____
Food	$ _____	$ _____
Clothing	$ _____	$ _____
Insurance payments	$ _____	$ _____
Debt payments	$ _____	$ _____
Auto/transportation	$ _____	$ _____
Medical/dental care	$ _____	$ _____
Education	$ _____	$ _____
Personal allowances	$ _____	$ _____
Recreation/entertainment	$ _____	$ _____
Contributors, donations	$ _____	$ _____
Total monthly expenses when disabled		$ _____

Substitute Income   **Monthly Benefit***

	Monthly Benefit*
Group disability insurance	$ _____
Social Security	$ _____
State disability insurance	$ _____
Worker's compensation	$ _____
Credit disability insurance (in some auto loan or home mortgages)	$ _____
Other income (investments, etc.)	$ _____
Total projected income when disabled	$ _____

If projected income when disabled is less than expenses, additional disability income insurance should be considered.

*Most disability insurance programs have a waiting period before benefits start, and they may have a limit as to how long benefits are received.

What's Next for Your Personal Financial Plan?

- Survey several people to determine if they have disability insurance.
- Talk to an insurance agent to compare the costs of disability income insurance available from several insurance companies.

10 Financial Planning with Life Insurance

Objectives

In this chapter, you will learn to:

1. Define life insurance and determine your life insurance needs.
2. Distinguish between the types of life insurance companies and analyze various life insurance policies these companies issue.
3. Select important provisions in life insurance contracts and create a plan to buy life insurance.
4. Recognize how annuities provide financial security.

Why is this important?

Life insurance helps protect the people who depend on you. Deciding whether you need it and choosing the right policy take time, research, and careful thought.

 Getting Personal

Should you be concerned about life insurance? For each of the following statements, select "yes" or "no" to indicate your behavior regarding these life insurance statements.

	Yes	No
1. My life insurance premiums will be lower if I buy a policy at a younger age.	_____	_____
2. I can determine my average life expectancy with some certainty.	_____	_____
3. I am aware of several different types of life insurance.	_____	_____
4. I can decide who receives the benefits of my life insurance policy.	_____	_____
5. I am aware of the key provisions in a life insurance policy.	_____	_____
6. With an annuity, I can arrange to continue receiving payments as long as I live.	_____	_____

After studying this chapter, you will be asked to use what you learned about the purpose of life insurance and types of life insurance policies to reconsider your responses to these items.

What Is Life Insurance?

OBJECTIVE 1
Define life insurance and determine your life insurance needs.

beneficiary A person designated to receive something, such as life insurance proceeds, from the insured.

Even though putting a price on your life is impossible, you probably own some life insurance—through a group plan where you work, as a veteran, or through a policy you bought. Life insurance is one of the most important and expensive purchases you may ever make. Deciding whether you need it and choosing the right policy from dozens of options take time, research, and careful thought. This chapter will help you make decisions about life insurance. It describes what life insurance is and how it works, the major types of life insurance coverage, and how you can use life insurance to protect your family.

When you buy life insurance, you're making a contract with the company issuing the policy. You agree to pay a certain amount of money—the premium—periodically. In return the company agrees to pay a death benefit, or a stated sum of money upon your death, to your beneficiary. A **beneficiary** is a person named to receive the benefits from an insurance policy.

The Purpose of Life Insurance

Most people buy life insurance to protect the people who depend on them from financial losses caused by their death. Those people could include a spouse, children, an aging parent, or a business partner or corporation. Life insurance benefits may be used to:

Apply *Yourself!*

Objective 1

Interview relatives and friends to determine why they purchased life insurance. Summarize your findings.

- Pay off a home mortgage or other debts at the time of death.
- Provide lump-sum payments through an endowment for children when they reach a specified age.
- Provide an education or income for children.
- Make charitable donations after death.
- Provide a retirement income.
- Accumulate savings.
- Establish a regular income for survivors.
- Set up an estate plan.
- Pay estate and gift taxes.

The Principle of Life Insurance

No one can say with any certainty how long a particular person will live. Still, insurance companies are able to make some educated guesses. Over the years they've compiled tables that show about how long people live. Using these tables, the company will make a rough guess about a person's life span and charge him or her accordingly. The sooner a person is likely to die, the higher the premiums he or she will pay.

How Long Will You Live?

If history is a guide, you'll live longer than your ancestors did. In 1900 an American male could be expected to live 46.3 years. By 2000, in contrast, life expectancy had risen to 74 years for men and 80 for women. Exhibit 10–1 shows about how many years a person can be expected to live today. For instance, a 30-year-old woman can be expected to live another 50.6 years. That doesn't mean that she has a high probability of dying at age 80.6. This just means that 50.6 is the average number of additional years a 30-year-old woman may expect to live.

> **DID YOU KNOW?**
>
> Japan spends more per capita on life insurance than any other nation. Next: Switzerland, the United States, Great Britain, and the Netherlands.

Do You Need Life Insurance?

Before you buy life insurance, you'll have to decide whether you need it at all. Generally, if your death would cause financial hardship for somebody, then life insurance is a wise purchase. Households with children usually have the greatest need for life insurance. Single people who live alone or with their parents, however, usually have little or no need for life insurance.

Estimating Your Life Insurance Requirements

There are four general methods for determining the amount of insurance you may need: the easy method, the DINK method, the "nonworking" spouse method, and the "family need" method.

THE EASY METHOD   Simple as this method is, it is remarkably useful. It is based on the insurance agent's rule of thumb that a "typical family" will need approximately 70 percent of your salary for seven years before they adjust to the financial consequences of your death. In other words, for a simple estimate of your life insurance needs, just multiply your current gross income by 7 (7 years) and 0.70 (70 percent).

Exhibit [10–1]   Life Expectancy Tables, All Races, 2000

Age	Both Sexes	Male	Female	Age	Both Sexes	Male	Female
0	76.9	74.1	79.5	45	34.4	32.2	36.3
1	76.4	73.7	79.0	50	30.0	27.9	31.8
5	72.5	69.8	75.1	55	24.7	23.8	27.4
10	67.6	64.9	70.1	60	21.6	19.9	23.1
15	62.6	59.9	65.2	65	17.9	16.3	19.2
20	57.8	55.2	60.3	70	14.4	13.0	15.5
25	53.1	50.6	55.4	75	11.3	10.1	12.1
30	48.3	45.9	50.6	50	8.6	7.6	9.1
35	43.6	41.3	45.8	85	6.3	5.6	6.7
40	38.9	36.7	41.0				

This table helps insurance companies determine insurance premiums. *Use the table to find the average number of additional years a 15-year-old male and female are expected to live.*

EXAMPLE

$30,000 current income × 7 = $210,000 × 0.70 = $147,000

EXAMPLE FROM YOUR LIFE

$ _____ current income × 7 = $ _____ × 0.70 = $ _____

This method assumes your family is "typical." You may need more insurance if you have four or more children, if you have above-average family debt, if any member of your family suffers from poor health, or if your spouse has poor employment potential. On the other hand, you may need less insurance if your family is smaller.

THE DINK (DUAL INCOME, NO KIDS) METHOD   If you have no dependents and your spouse earns as much or more than you do, you have very simple insurance needs. Basically, all you need to do is ensure that your spouse will not be unduly burdened by debts should you die. Here is an example of the DINK method:

EXAMPLE

	Example	Your Figures
Funeral expenses	$ 5,000	$ _____
One-half of mortgage	60,000	_____
One-half of auto loan	7,000	_____
One-half of credit card balance	1,500	_____
One-half of personal debt	1,500	_____
Other debts	1,000	_____
Total insurance needs	$76,000	$ _____

This method assumes your spouse will continue to work after your death. If your spouse suffers poor health or is employed in an occupation with an uncertain future, you should consider adding an insurance cushion to see him or her through hard times.

THE "NONWORKING" SPOUSE METHOD   Insurance experts have estimated that extra costs of up to $10,000 a year may be required to replace the services of a homemaker in a family with small children. These extra costs may include the cost of a housekeeper, child care, more meals out, additional carfare, laundry services, and so on. They do not include the lost potential earnings of the surviving spouse, who often must take time away from the job to care for the family.

To estimate how much life insurance a homemaker should carry, simply multiply the number of years before the youngest child reaches age 18 by $10,000:

EXAMPLE

10 years × $10,000 = $100,000

EXAMPLE FROM YOUR LIFE

_____ years × $10,000 = $ _____

Figure It Out!

A WORKSHEET TO CALCULATE YOUR LIFE INSURANCE NEEDS

1. Five times your personal yearly income	_____ (1)
2. Total approximate expenses above and beyond your daily living costs for you and your dependents (e.g., tuition, care for a disabled child or parent) amount to =	_____ (2)
3. Your emergency fund (3 to 6 months of living expenses) amounts to =	_____ (3)
4. Estimated amount for your funeral expenses (U.S. average is $5,000 to $10,000)	+ _____ (4)
5. Total estimate of your family's financial needs (add lines 1 through 4)	= _____ (5)
6. Your total liquid assets (e.g., savings accounts, CDs, money market funds, existing life insurance both individual and group, pension plan death benefits, and Social Security benefits	− _____ (6)
7. Subtract line 6 from line 5 and enter the difference here.	= _____ (7)

The net result (line 7) is an estimate of the shortfall your family would face upon your death. Remember, these are just rules of thumb. For a complete analysis of your needs, consult a professional.

Sources: *About Life Insurance,* Metropolitan Life Insurance Company, February 1997, p. 3; *The TIAA Guide to Life Insurance Planning for People in Education* (New York: Teachers Insurance and Annuity Association, January 1997), p. 3.

If there are teenage children, the $10,000 figure can be reduced. If there are more than two children under age 13, or if anyone in the family suffers poor health or has special needs, the $10,000 figure should be adjusted upward.

THE "FAMILY NEED" METHOD The first three methods assume you and your family are "typical" and ignore important factors such as Social Security and your liquid assets. The nearby Figure It Out box provides a detailed worksheet for making a thorough estimate of your life insurance needs.

Although this method is quite thorough, if you believe it does not address all of your special needs, you should obtain further advice from an insurance expert or a financial planner.

As you determine your life insurance needs, don't forget to consider the life insurance you may already have. You may have ample coverage through your employer and through any mortgage and credit life insurance you purchased.

Sheet 32
Determining
Life Insurance
Needs

*Key Web Sites for Life
Insurance Planning*
www.ircweb.org
www.iiaa.com

✔ CONCEPTCHECK 10–1

1 What is life insurance? What is its purpose?

_____

_____

2 For each of the following statements, indicate your response by writing "T" or "F".

   a. Life insurance is one of the least important and inexpensive purchases. _____

   b. A beneficiary is a person named to receive the benefits from the insurance policy. _____

Continued

Continued from page 267

    c. Life insurance benefits may be used to pay off a home mortgage or other debts at the time of death. ____

    d. The sooner a person is likely to die, the higher the premiums he or she will pay. ____

    e. All people need to purchase a life insurance policy. ____

3 What are the four methods of determining life insurance needs?

_____

_____

Types of Life Insurance Companies and Policies

OBJECTIVE 2

Distinguish between the types of life insurance companies and analyze various types of life insurance policies these companies issue.

nonparticipating policy Life insurance that does not provide policy dividends; also called a *nonpar policy.*

participating policy Life insurance that provides policy dividends; also called a *par policy.*

Types of Life Insurance Companies

You can purchase the new or extra life insurance you need from two types of life insurance companies: stock life insurance companies, owned by shareholders, and mutual life insurance companies, owned by policyholders. About 95 percent of the U.S. life insurance companies are stock companies, and about 5 percent are mutual.

Stock companies generally sell **nonparticipating** (or *nonpar*) **policies,** while mutual companies specialize in the sale of **participating** (or *par*) **policies.** A participating policy has a somewhat higher premium than a nonparticipating policy, but a part of the premium is refunded to the policyholder annually. This refund is called the *policy dividend.*

A long debate about whether stock companies or mutual companies offer less expensive life insurance has been inconclusive. You should check with both stock and mutual companies to determine which type offers the best policy for your particular needs at the lowest price.

If you wish to pay exactly the same premium each year, you should choose a nonparticipating policy with its guaranteed premiums. However, you may prefer life insurance whose annual price reflects the company's experience with its investments, the health of its policyholders, and its general operating costs, that is, a participating policy.

Nevertheless, as with other forms of insurance, price should not be your only consideration in choosing a life insurance policy. You should consider the financial stability of and service provided by the insurance company.

Types of Life Insurance Policies

Both mutual insurance companies and stock insurance companies sell two basic types of life insurance: temporary and permanent insurance. Temporary insurance can be term, renewable term, convertible term, or decreasing term insurance. Permanent insurance is known by different names, including whole life, straight life, ordinary life, and cash value life insurance. As you will learn in the next section, permanent insurance can be limited payment, variable, adjustable, or universal life insurance. Other types of insurance policies—group life and credit life insurance—are generally temporary forms of insurance. Exhibit 10–2 lists major types and subtypes of life insurance.

Exhibit [10–2]

Major Types and Subtypes
of Life Insurance

Term (temporary)	Whole, Straight, or Ordinary Life	Other Types
• Term	• Limited payment	• Group life
• Renewable term	• Variable life	• Credit life
• Multiyear level term	• Adjustable life	• Endowment life
• Convertible term	• Universal life	
• Decreasing term		

Exhibit [10–2]

Major Types and Subtypes
of Life Insurance

TERM LIFE INSURANCE

Term insurance, sometimes called *temporary life insurance,* provides protection against loss of life for only a specified term, or period of time. A term insurance policy pays a benefit only if you die during the period it covers, which may be 1, 5, 10, or 20 years, or up to age 70. If you stop paying the premiums, your coverage stops. Term insurance is often the best value for customers. You need insurance coverage most while you are raising children. As your children become independent and your assets increase, you can reduce your coverage. Term insurance comes in many different forms. Here are some examples.

term insurance Life insurance protection for a specified period of time; sometimes called *temporary life insurance.*

Renewable Term   The coverage of term insurance ends at the conclusion of the term, but you can continue it for another term—five years, for example—if you have a renewable option. However, the premium will increase because you will be older. It also usually has an age limit; you cannot renew after you reach a certain age.

Multiyear Level Term   A multiyear level term, or *straight term,* policy guarantees that you will pay the same premium for the duration of your policy.

Conversion Term   This type of policy allows you to change from term to permanent coverage. This will have a higher premium.

Decreasing Term   Term insurance is also available in a form that pays less to the beneficiary as time passes. The insurance period you select might depend on your age or on how long you decide that the coverage will be needed. For example, if you have a mortgage on a house, you might buy a 25-year decreasing term policy as a way to make sure that the debt could be paid if you died. The coverage would decrease as the balance on the loan decreased.

WHOLE LIFE INSURANCE

The other major type of life insurance is known as whole life insurance (also called a *straight life policy,* a *cash-value policy,* or an *ordinary life policy*). **Whole life insurance** is a permanent policy for which you pay a specified premium each year for the rest of your life. In return the insurance company pays your beneficiary a stated sum when you die. The amount of your premium depends mostly on the age at which you purchase the insurance.

whole life insurance An insurance plan in which the policyholder pays a specified premium each year for as long as he or she lives; also called a *straight life policy,* a *cash-value life policy,* or an *ordinary life policy.*

cash value The amount received after giving up a life insurance policy.

Whole life insurance can also serve as an investment. Part of each premium you pay is set aside in a savings account. When and if you cancel the policy, you are entitled to the accumulated savings, which is known as the **cash value.** Whole life policies are popular because they provide both a death benefit and a savings component. You can borrow from your cash value if necessary, although you must pay interest on the loan. Cash-value policies may make sense for people who intend to keep the policies for the

DID YOU KNOW?

A Harris interactive poll reported 8 percent of Americans bought more disability insurance and 6 percent bought or increased their life insurance within one month of September 11, 2001.

long term or for people who want a more structured way to save. However, the Consumer Federation of America Insurance Group suggests that you explore other savings and investment strategies before investing your money in a permanent policy.

The premium of a term insurance policy will increase each time you renew your insurance. In contrast, whole life policies have a higher annual premium at first, but the rate remains the same for the rest of your life. Several types of whole life policies have been developed to meet the needs of different customers. These include the limited payment policy, the variable life policy, the adjustable life policy and universal life insurance.

Limited Payment Policy   Limited payment policies charge premiums for only a certain length of time, usually 20 or 30 years or until the insured reaches a certain age. At the end of this time, the policy is "paid up," and the policyholder remains insured for life. When the policyholder dies, the beneficiary receives the full death benefit. The annual premiums are higher for limited payment policies because the premiums have to be paid within a shorter period of time.

Variable Life Policy   With a variable life policy, your premium payments are fixed. As with a cash value policy, part of your premium is placed in a separate account; this money is invested in a stock, bond, or money market fund. The death benefit is guaranteed, but the cash value of the benefit can vary considerably according to the ups and downs of the stock market. Your death benefit can also increase, depending on the earnings of that separate fund.

Apply *Yourself!*

Objective 2

Choose one stock and one mutual life insurance company. Obtain and compare premiums for $50,000 term, whole life, and universal life insurance.

Adjustable Life Policy   An adjustable life policy allows you to change your coverage as your needs change. For example, if you want to increase or decrease your death benefit, you can change either the premium payments or the period of coverage.

universal life insurance A whole life policy that combines term insurance and investment elements.

Universal Life   **Universal life insurance** is essentially a term policy with a cash value. Part of your premium goes into an investment account that grows and earns interest. You are able to borrow or withdraw your cash value. Unlike a traditional whole life policy, a universal life policy allows you to change your premium without changing your coverage.

OTHER TYPES OF LIFE INSURANCE POLICIES
Other types of life insurance policies include group life insurance, credit life insurance, and endowment life insurance.

Group Life Insurance   Group life insurance is basically a variation of term insurance. It covers a large number of people under a single policy. The people included in the group do not need medical examinations to get the coverage. Group insurance is usually offered through employers, who pay part or all of the costs for their employees, or through professional organizations, which allow members to sign up for the coverage. Group plans are easy to enroll in, but they can be much more expensive than similar term policies.

Credit Life Insurance   Credit life insurance is used to pay off certain debts, such as auto loans or mortgages, in the event that you die before they are paid in full. These types of policies are not the best buy for the protection that they offer. Decreasing term insurance is a better option.

Key Web Sites for Life Insurance Information
www.iii.org
www.insweb.com

Endowment Life Insurance   Endowment is life insurance that provides coverage for a specific period of time and pays an agreed-upon sum of money to the policyholder if he or she is still living at the end of the endowment period. If the policyholder dies before that time, the beneficiary receives the money.

✔ **CONCEPTCHECK 10–2**

1 What are the two types of life insurance companies?

_____

2 For each of the following statements, indicate your response by writing "T" or "F".

a. Stock life insurance companies generally sell participating (or par) policies. ____

b. Mutual life insurance companies specialize in the sale of nonparticipating (nonpar) policies. ____

c. If you wish to pay exactly the same premium each year, you should choose a nonpar policy. ____

d. Permanent insurance is also known as whole life, straight life, ordinary life, and cash-value life insurance. ____

e. Term life insurance is the most expensive type of policy. ____

3 What are the four forms of term insurance?

_____

_____

4 What are the four forms of whole life insurance?

_____

_____

5 Define the following types of life insurance policies:

a. Group life insurance _____

b. Credit life insurance _____

c Endowment life insurance _____

Selecting Provisions and Buying Life Insurance

Key Provisions in a Life Insurance Policy

Study the provisions in your policy carefully. The following are some of the most common features.

> **OBJECTIVE 3**
> Select important provisions in life insurance contracts and create a plan to buy life insurance.

NAMING YOUR BENEFICIARY You decide who receives the benefits of your life insurance policy: your spouse, your child, or your business partner, for example. You can also name contingent beneficiaries, those who will receive the money if your primary beneficiary dies before or at the same time as you do. Update your list of beneficiaries as your needs change.

INCONTESTABILITY CLAUSE The incontestability clause says that the insurer can't cancel the policy if it's been in force for a specified period, usually two years. After that time the policy is considered valid during the lifetime of the insured. This is true even if the policy was gained through fraud. The incontestability clause protects the beneficiaries from financial loss in the event that the insurance company refuses to meet the terms of the policy.

THE GRACE PERIOD   When you buy a life insurance policy, the insurance company agrees to pay a certain sum of money under specified circumstances and you agree to pay a certain premium regularly. The *grace period* allows 28 to 31 days to elapse, during which time you may pay the premium without penalty. After that time, the policy lapses if you have not paid the premium.

POLICY REINSTATEMENT   A lapsed policy can be put back in force, or reinstated, if it has not been turned in for cash. To reinstate the policy, you must again qualify as an acceptable risk, and you must pay overdue premiums with interest. There is a time limit on reinstatement, usually one or two years.

NONFORFEITURE CLAUSE   One important feature of the whole life policy is the **nonforfeiture clause.** This provision prevents the forfeiture of accrued benefits if you choose to drop the policy. For example, if you decide not to continue paying premiums, you can exercise specified options with your cash value.

nonforfeiture clause A provision that allows the insured not to forfeit all accrued benefits.

MISSTATEMENT OF AGE PROVISION   The misstatement of age provision says that if the company finds out that your age was incorrectly stated, it will pay the benefits your premiums would have bought if your age had been correctly stated. The provision sets forth a simple procedure to resolve what could otherwise be a complicated legal matter.

Apply *Yourself!*

Objective 3

Examine your life insurance policies and the policies of other members of your family. Note the contractual provisions of each policy. What does the company promise to do in return for premiums?

POLICY LOAN PROVISION   A loan from the insurance company is available on a whole life policy after the policy has been in force for one, two, or three years, as stated in the policy. This feature, known as the *policy loan provision,* permits you to borrow any amount up to the cash value of the policy. However, a policy loan reduces the death benefit by the amount of the loan plus interest if the loan is not repaid.

SUICIDE CLAUSE   In the first two years of coverage, beneficiaries of someone who dies by suicide receive only the amount of the premiums paid. After two years beneficiaries receive the full value of death benefits.

RIDERS TO LIFE INSURANCE POLICIES   An insurance company can change the conditions of a policy by adding a rider to it. A **rider** is a document attached to a policy that changes its terms by adding or excluding specified conditions or altering its benefits.

rider A document attached to a policy that modifies its coverage.

Waiver of Premium Disability Benefit   One common rider is a waiver of premium disability benefit. This clause allows you to stop paying premiums if you're totally and permanently disabled before you reach a certain age, usually 60. The company continues to pay the premiums at its own expense.

double indemnity A benefit under which the company pays twice the face value of the policy if the insured's death results from an accident.

Accidental Death Benefit   Another common rider to life insurance is an accidental death benefit, sometimes called **double indemnity.** Double indemnity pays twice the value of the policy if you are killed in an accident. Again, the accident must occur before a certain age, generally 60 to 65. Experts counsel against adding this rider to your coverage. The benefit is very expensive, and your chances of dying in an accident are slim.

Guaranteed Insurability Option   A third important rider is known as a guaranteed insurability option. This rider allows you to buy a specified additional amount of life insurance at certain intervals without undergoing medical exams. This is a good option for people who anticipate needing more life insurance in the future.

Cost-of-Living Protection   This special rider is designed to help prevent inflation from eroding the purchasing power of the protection your policy provides. A *loss, reduction,* or *erosion of purchasing power* refers to the impact inflation has on a fixed amount of money. As inflation increases the cost of goods and services, that fixed amount will not buy as much in the future as it does today. Exhibit 10–3 shows the effects of inflation on a $100,000 life insurance policy. However, your insurance needs are likely to be smaller in later years.

Accelerated Benefits   *Accelerated benefits,* also know as *living benefits,* are life insurance policy proceeds paid to the policyholder who is terminally ill before he or she dies. The benefits may be provided for directly in the policies, but more often they are added by riders or attachments to new or existing policies. A representative list of insurers that offer accelerated benefits is available from the National Insurance Consumer Helpline (NICH) at 800-942-4242. Although more than 150 companies offer some form of accelerated benefits, not all plans are approved in all states. NICH cannot tell you whether a particular plan is approved in any given state. For more information, check with your insurance agent or your state department of insurance.

Second-to-Die Option   A *second-to-die life insurance policy,* also called *survivorship life,* insures two lives, usually husband and wife. The death benefit is paid when the second spouse dies. Usually a second-to-die policy is intended to pay estate taxes when both spouses die. However, some attorneys claim that with the right legal advice, you can minimize or avoid estate taxes completely.

Now that you know the various types of life insurance policies and the major provisions of and riders to such policies, you are ready to make your buying decisions.

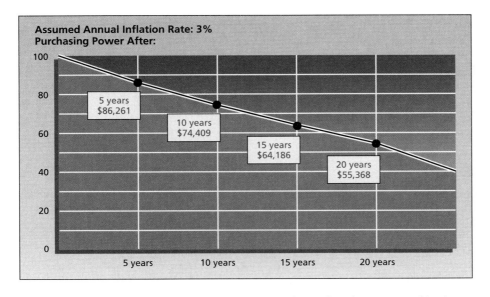

Assumed Annual Inflation Rate: 3%
Purchasing Power After:

5 years $86,261
10 years $74,409
15 years $64,186
20 years $55,368

Exhibit [10–3]

Effects of Inflation on a $100,000 Life Insurance Policy

Source: *The TIAA Guide to Life Insurance Planning for People in Education* (New York: Teachers Insurance and Annuity Association, January 1997), p. 8.

Buying Life Insurance

You should consider a number of factors before buying life insurance. As discussed earlier in this chapter, these factors include your present and future sources of income, other savings and income protection, group life insurance, group annuities (or other pension benefits), Social Security, and, of course, the financial strength of the company.

FROM WHOM TO BUY?   Look for insurance coverage from financially strong companies with professionally qualified representatives. It is not unusual for a relationship with an insurance company to extend over a period of 20, 30, or even 50 years. For that reason alone you should choose carefully when deciding on an insurance company or an insurance agent. Fortunately, you have a choice of sources.

Sources   Protection is available from a wide range of private and public sources, including insurance companies and their representatives; private groups such as employers, labor unions, and professional or fraternal organizations; government programs such as Medicare and Social Security; and financial institutions and manufacturers offering credit insurance.

Exhibit [10–4]

Rating Systems of Major Rating Agencies: You Should Deal with Companies Rated Superior or Excellent

	A. M. Best	Standard & Poor's Duff & Phelps	Moody's	Weiss Research
Superior	A++	AAA	Aaa	A+
	A+			
Excellent	A	AA+	Aa1	A
	A−	AA	Aa2	A−
		AA−	Aa3	B+
Good	B++	A+	A1	B
	B+	A	A2	B−
		A−	A3	C+
Adequate	B	BBB+	Baa1	C
	B−	BBB	Baa2	C−
		BBB−	Baa3	D+
Below average	C++	BB+	Ba1	D
	C+	BB	Ba2	D−
		BB−	Ba3	E+
Weak	C	B+	B1	E
	C−	B	B2	E−
	D	B−	B3	
Nonviable	E	CCC	Caa	F
	F	CC	Ca	
		C, D	C	

Personal Finance in Practice

CHECKLIST FOR CHOOSING AN INSURANCE AGENT

	Yes	No
1. Is your agent available when needed? Clients sometimes have problems that need immediate answers.	☐	☐
2. Does your agent advise you to have a financial plan? Each part of the plan should be necessary to your overall financial protection.	☐	☐
3. Does your agent pressure you? You should be free to make your own decisions about insurance coverage.	☐	☐
4. Does your agent keep up with changes in the insurance field? Agents often attend special classes or study on their own so that they can serve their clients better.	☐	☐
5. Is your agent happy to answer questions? Does he or she want you to know exactly what you are paying for with an insurance policy?	☐	☐

Rating Insurance Companies   Some of the strongest, most reputable insurance companies in the nation provide excellent insurance coverage at reasonable costs. In fact, the financial strength of an insurance company may be a major factor in holding down premium costs for consumers.

Locate an insurance company by checking the reputations of local agencies. Ask members of your family, friends, or colleagues about the insurers they prefer. Exhibit 10–4 describes the rating systems used by A. M. Best and the other big four rating agencies.

Choosing Your Insurance Agent   An insurance agent handles the technical side of insurance. However, that's only the beginning. The really important part of the agent's job is to apply his or her knowledge of insurance to help you select the proper kind of protection within your financial boundaries.

Choosing a good agent is among the most important steps in building your insurance program. How do you find an agent? One of the best ways to begin is by asking your parents, friends, neighbors, and others for their recommendations. The nearby Personal Finance in Practice feature offers guidelines for choosing an insurance agent.

COMPARING POLICY COSTS
Each life insurance company designs the policies it sells to make them attractive and useful to many policyholders. One policy may have features another policy doesn't; one company may be more selective than another company; one company may get a better return on its investments than another company. These and other factors affect the prices of life insurance policies.

In brief, five factors affect the price a company charges for a life insurance policy: the company's cost of doing business, the return on its investments, the mortality rate it expects among its policyholders, the features the policy contains, and competition among companies with comparable policies.

Ask your agent to give you interest-adjusted indexes. An **interest-adjusted index** is a method of evaluating the cost of life insurance by taking into account the time value of money. Highly complex mathematical calculations and formulas combine premium payments, dividends, cash-value buildup, and present value analysis into an index number that makes possible a fairly accurate cost comparison among insurance companies.

DID YOU KNOW?

Life insurance salespeople who pass examinations and meet other requirements are awarded the Chartered Life Underwriter (CLU) designation.

DID YOU KNOW?

Buying a $4.00 pack of cigarettes every day for 15 years will cost you about $22,000 and almost double your life insurance premiums.

Key Web Sites for Insurance Company Ratings
www.standardandpoor.com
http://infoseek.go.com/

interest-adjusted index A method of evaluating the cost of life insurance by taking into account the time value of money.

Figure It Out!

DETERMINING THE COST OF INSURANCE

In determining the cost of insurance, don't overlook the time value of money. You must include as part of that cost the interest (opportunity cost) you would earn on money if you did not use it to pay insurance premiums. For many years, insurers did not assign a time value to money in making their sales presentations. Only recently has the insurance industry widely adopted interest-adjusted cost estimates.

If you fail to consider the time value of money, you may get the false impression that the insurance company is giving you something for nothing. Here is an example. Suppose you are 35 and have a $10,000 face amount, 20-year, limited-payment, participating policy. Your annual premium is $210, or $4,200 over the 20-year period. Your dividends over the 20-year payment period total $1,700, so your total net premium is $2,500 ($4,200 − $1,700). Yet the cash value of your policy at the end of 20 years is $4,600. If you disregard the interest your premiums could otherwise have earned, you might get the impression that the insurance company is giving you $2,100 more than you paid ($4,600 − $2,500). But if you consider the time value of money (or its opportunity cost), the insurance company is

not giving you $2,100. What if you had invested the annual premiums in a conservative stock mutual fund? At an 8 percent annual yield, your account would have accumulated to $6,180 in 20 years. Therefore, instead of having received $2,100 from the insurance company, you have paid the company $1,580 for 20 years of insurance protection:

Premiums you paid over 20 years	$4,200	
Time value of money	1,980	($6,180 − $4,200)
Total cost	6,180	
Cash value	4,600	
Net cost of insurance	1,580	($6,180 − $4,600)

Be sure to request interest-adjusted indexes from your agent; if he or she doesn't give them to you, look for another agent. As you have seen in the example, you can compare the costs among insurance companies by combining premium payments, dividends, cash value buildup, and present value analysis into an index number.

*Key Web Sites for
Comparing Rates*
www.accuquote.com
www.iquote.com

The lower the index number, the lower the cost of the policy. The nearby Figure It Out box shows how to use an interest-adjusted index to compare the costs of insurance.

OBTAINING AND EXAMINING A POLICY A life insurance policy is issued after you submit an application for insurance and the insurance company accepts the application. The company determines your insurability by means of the information in your application, the results of a medical examination, and the inspection report. When you receive a life insurance policy, read every word of the contract and, if necessary, ask your agent for a point-by-point explanation of the language. Many insurance companies have rewritten their contracts to make them more understandable. These are legal documents, and you should be familiar with what they promise, even though they use technical terms.

After you buy new life insurance, you have a 10-day "free-look" period during which you can change your mind. If you do so, the company will return your premium without penalty.

CHOOSING SETTLEMENT OPTIONS Selecting the appropriate settlement option is an important part of designing a life insurance program. The most common settlement options are lump-sum payment, limited installment payment, life income option, and proceeds left with the company.

Lump-Sum Payment The insurance company pays the face amount of the policy in one installment to the beneficiary or to the estate of the insured. This form of settlement is the most widely used option.

Limited Installment Payment This option provides for payment of the life insurance proceeds in equal periodic installments for a specified number of years after your death.

LIFE INSURANCE | Rates are falling even for those not in the best of health. *By Kimberly Lankford*

New hope for lower PREMIUMS

CHANGES IN the way insurers decide who gets coverage and how much it costs is good news for those who have diabetes, asthma, heart disease and hepatitis C, and for those who have lost weight, stopped smoking or haven't had cancer treatments for at least three years. If you've had trouble finding a good deal on life insurance—or any coverage at all—now's a good time to shop again.

Not only have premiums been dropping for healthy people, but several companies have been cutting rates for folks who aren't in the best of health—often because medical advances have improved life expectancy for people with certain conditions. The result can be hundreds of dollars in savings.

Ray Kelly, a swimming-pool designer in Suwanee, Ga., isn't the model of perfect health. "I have borderline diabetes, a heart problem, a lung problem, and I'm 46 years old," he says. "I wouldn't insure me."

And neither would most life-insurance companies when he shopped for a policy a decade ago. He finally found a $100,000 term policy with a price tag that kept increasing every year. He's paying about $700 this year. "I was resigned to the fact that the $100,000 policy was the only one I'd be able to get unless I had it through my job," he says. That strategy worked until he switched jobs and his former firm wanted $6,840 a year to keep his $300,000 coverage.

Kelly called insurance brokerage AccuQuote to seek alternatives, but he didn't have high hopes. Based on Kelly's health, an agent told him that he might qualify for a $300,000, 20-year term policy for $2,470 per year. He applied and got a big surprise: U.S. Financial Life offered him a $300,000 policy for just $991 per year.

"He got a much better deal than we could have expected," says Byron Udell, the head of AccuQuote. U.S. Financial Life gave Kelly a nonsmoker rate even though he had not been off cigarettes more than a year, the typical requirement. The company also tends to offer decent deals to people who successfully control their illnesses, even though other insurers may reject them.

How to get the best deal. It's essential to shop around because the price range can be huge. When Larry Achter, a 51-year-old accountant from Oakton, Va., began shopping last winter, two companies quoted him about $2,000 for a $500,000, 20-year term policy. But after learning more about his medical history, including the fact that he'd had a stent inserted in a blocked artery in November 2002, the price quotes jumped to more than $5,000. U.S. Financial Life, however, offered him a policy for $2,400. "Don't give up hope," Achter says. "Be persistent."

It's best to work with a broker who deals with many companies and knows which ones tend to offer the best rates for someone with your health problem. Members of the Risk Appraisal Forum, for example, specialize in finding insurance for high-risk people. (For contact information, see www.kiplinger.com/magazine/links/html.) These experts know how to strengthen your case with information about how you control your condition.

Healthy premiums. Improving your blood pressure or cholesterol level can cut your premium. And taking drugs to control these problems won't necessarily mark you as high risk. "If you are taking medication to control cholesterol, and the drug is controlling it, you may get preferred coverage," says Rich Boutilier, vice-president of underwriting for John Hancock.

Many companies have lowered rates for people with certain forms of diabetes, "particularly noninsulin dependent, if well controlled by diet or oral medications," says Boutilier. And people with prostate cancer can get a better rate if they have certain Gleason and PSA scores, two measurements of the cancer's severity. Even if you do have to pay extra, you may get a price break two or three years after your last treatment for many types of cancer, says Bob Littell, president of Second Opinion Insurance Services in Atlanta, which finds coverage for high-risk people.

—*Reporter:* **JOAN GOLDWASSER**

1. Why is now a good time for people in less than perfect health to shop again for life insurance?

   _____

   _____

2. What is the best way to get a good deal on life insurance?

   _____

   _____

3. Why is working with a knowledgeable insurance broker important?

   _____

   _____

Personal Finance in Practice

TEN GOLDEN RULES OF BUYING LIFE INSURANCE

Remember that your need for life insurance coverage will change over time. Your income may go up or down, or your family size might change. Therefore, it is wise to review your coverage periodically to ensure that it keeps up with your changing needs.

Follow these rules when buying life insurance	Done
1. Understand and know what your life insurance needs are before you make any purchase, and make sure the company you choose can meet those needs.	☐
2. Buy your life insurance from a company that is licensed in your state.	☐
3. Select an agent who is competent, knowledgeable, and trustworthy.	☐
4. Shop around and compare costs.	☐
5. Buy only the amount of life insurance you need and can afford.	☐
6. Ask about lower premium rates for nonsmokers.	☐
7. Read your policy and make sure you understand it.	☐
8. Inform your beneficiaries about the kinds and amount of life insurance you own.	☐
9. Keep your policy in a safe place at home, and keep your insurance company's name and your policy number in a safe deposit box.	☐
10. Check your coverage periodically, or whenever your situation changes, to ensure that it meets your current needs.	☐

Source: American Council of Life Insurance, 1001 Pennsylvania Avenue NW, Washington, DC 20004-2599.

Sheet 33
Life Insurance
Policy
Comparison

Key Web Sites for Life Insurance Information
www.accuquote.com
www.quickquote.com

Life Income Option   Under the life income option, payments are made to the beneficiary for as long as she or he lives. The amount of each payment is based primarily on the sex and attained age of the beneficiary at the time of the insured's death.

Proceeds Left with the Company   The life insurance proceeds are left with the insurance company at a specified rate of interest. The company acts as trustee and pays the interest to the beneficiary. The guaranteed minimum interest rate paid on the proceeds varies among companies.

SWITCHING POLICIES   Think twice if your agent suggests that you replace the whole life or universal life insurance you already own. Before you give up this protection, make sure you are still insurable (check medical and any other qualification requirements). Ask your agent or company for an opinion about the new proposal to get both sides of the argument. The nearby Personal Finance in Practice feature presents 10 important guidelines for purchasing life insurance.

✔ CONCEPTCHECK 10–3

1 What are the key provisions in a life insurance policy?

_____

_____

Continued

2 What is a rider?

_____

_____

3 What are the various riders in a life insurance policy?

_____

_____

4 What factors do you consider in choosing an insurance agent?

_____

_____

5 What are the four most common settlement options?

_____

_____

6 Match the following terms with the appropriate definition:

endowment   *a.* A person named to receive the benefits from an insurance policy. _____

beneficiary   *b.* Provides coverage for a specific period of time and pays an agreed-upon sum of money to the policyholder if he or she is still living at the end of the period.

_____

whole life insurance   *c.* A permanent policy for which the policyholder pays a specified premium for the rest of his or her life. _____

double indemnity   *d.* A rider to a life insurance policy that pays twice the value of the policy if the policyholder is killed in an accident. _____

Financial Planning with Annuities

As you have seen so far, life insurance provides a set sum of money at your death. However, if you want to enjoy benefits while you are still alive, you might consider annuities. An annuity protects you against the risk of outliving your assets.

An **annuity** is a financial contract written by an insurance company that provides you with regular income. Generally, you receive the income monthly, often with payments arranged to continue for as long as you live. The payments may begin at once (*immediate annuity*) or at some future date (*deferred annuity*).

As with the life insurance principle, discussed earlier, the predictable mortality experience of a large group of individuals is fundamental to the annuity principle. By determining the average number of years a large number of persons in a given age group will live, the insurance company can calculate the annual amounts to pay to each person in the group over his or her entire life.

Because the annual payouts per premium amount are determined by average mortality experience, annuity contracts are more attractive for people whose present health, living habits, and family mortality experience suggest that they are likely to live longer than average. As a general rule, annuities are not advisable for people in poor health, although exceptions to this rule exist.

OBJECTIVE 4
Recognize how annuities provide financial security

annuity A contract that provides a regular income for as long as the person lives.

Why Buy Annuities?

A primary reason for buying an annuity is to give you retirement income for the rest of your life. You should fully fund your IRAs, Keoghs, and 401(k)s before considering annuities. We discuss retirement income in Chapter 14.

Although people have been buying annuities for many years, the appeal of variable annuities increased during the mid-1990s due to a rising stock market. A *fixed annuity* states that the annuitant (the person who is to receive the annuity) will receive a fixed amount of income over a certain period or for life. With a *variable annuity,* the monthly payments vary because they are based on the income received from stocks or other investments.

Some of the growth in the use of annuities can be attributed to the passage of the Employee Retirement Income Security Act (ERISA) of 1974. Annuities are often purchased for individual retirement accounts (IRAs), which ERISA made possible. They may also be used in Keogh-type plans for self-employed people. As you will see in Chapter 14, contributions to both IRA and Keogh plans are tax deductible up to specified limits.

Apply *Yourself!*

Objective 4

Interview friends, relatives, and others who have bought annuities. Which type of annuity did they purchase, and why?

Tax Considerations

When you buy an annuity, the interest on the principal, as well as the interest compounded on that interest, builds up free of current income tax. The Tax Reform Act of 1986 preserves the tax advantage of annuities (and insurance) but curtails deductions for IRAs. With an annuity, there is no maximum annual contribution. Also, if you die during the accumulation period, your beneficiary is guaranteed no less than the amount invested.

Exhibit 10–5 shows the difference between an investment in an annuity and an investment in a certificate of deposit (CD). Remember, federal income tax on an annuity is deferred, whereas the tax on interest earned on a CD must be paid currently.

Exhibit [10–5]

Tax-Deferred Annuity versus Taxable CD (a 30-year projection of performance; single deposit of $30,000.)

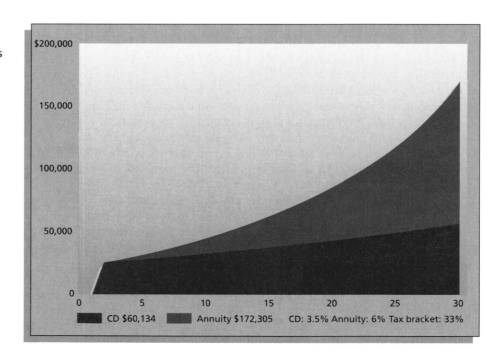

CD $60,134   Annuity $172,305   CD: 3.5% Annuity: 6% Tax bracket: 33%

As with any other financial product, the advantages of annuities are tempered by drawbacks. In the case of variable annuities, these drawbacks include reduced flexibility and fees that lower investment return.

✔ CONCEPTCHECK 10–4

1 What is an annuity?

_____

_____

2 What is the difference between an immediate and a deferred annuity?

_____

_____

3 As a general rule, are annuities advisable for people in poor health?

_____

Why or why not? _____

4 What are fixed and variable annuities?

_____

_____

Back to **Getting Personal**

Reevaluate your Getting Personal responses at the beginning of the chapter. Which statements might have different responses now or in the future as a result of studying this chapter?

_____

Chapter Summary

Objective 1   Life insurance protects the people who depend on you from financial losses caused by your death. You can use the easy method, the DINK method, the "nonworking" spouse method, or the "family need" method to determine your life insurance need.

Objective 2   Two types of insurance companies—stock and mutual—sell nonparticipating and participating policies. Both sell two basic types of insurance: term life and whole life. Many variations and combinations of these types are available.

Objective 3   Most life insurance policies have standard features. An insurance company can change the conditions of a policy by adding a rider to it.

Before buying life insurance, consider all your present and future sources of income, then compare the costs and choose appropriate settlement options.

Objective 4   An annuity pays while you live, whereas life insurance pays when you die. With a fixed annuity, you receive a fixed amount of income over a certain period or for life. With a variable annuity, the monthly payments vary because they are based on the income received from stocks or other investments.

Key Terms

Problems and Questions

1. Choose a current issue of *Money, Kiplinger's Personal Finance Magazine, Consumer Reports,* or *Worth* and summarize an article that provides information on human life expectancy and how life insurance may provide financial security.

2. Analyze the four methods of determining life insurance requirements. Which method is best, and why?

3. You are the wage earner in a "typical family," with $30,000 gross annual income. Use the easy method to determine how much insurance you should carry.

4. You and your spouse are in good health and have reasonably secure careers. Each of you makes about $28,000 annually. You own a home with an $80,000 mortgage, and you owe $10,000 on car loans, $5,000 in personal debts, and $3,000 on credit card loans. You have no other debts. You have no plans to increase the size of your family in the near future. Estimate your total insurance needs using the DINK method.

5. Tim and Allison are married and have two children, ages 4 and 7. Allison is a "nonworking" spouse who devotes all of her time to household activities. Estimate how much life insurance Tim and Allison should carry.

6. Obtain premium rates for $25,000 whole life, universal life, and term life policies from local insurance agents. Compare the costs and provisions of these policies.

7. Visit a few Web sites of companies such as Metropolitan Life, New York Life, Transamerica Life, Lincoln Benefit Life, or others of your choice. Then summarize the various types of insurance coverage available from these companies.

8. Contact your state insurance department to get information about whether your state requires interest-adjusted cost disclosure. Summarize your findings.

9. Review the settlement options on your family's life insurance policies, and discuss with your family which option would be the best choice for them at this time.

www.mhhe.com/kdh

BUYING LIFE INSURANCE

Providing for the financial needs of dependents is the primary goal of a life insurance program. Comparing policy types, coverage amounts, and other provisions will help you meet this financial purpose. Visit Web sites of two reputable insurance companies of your choice and compare the following:

Company A Web address _____

Company B Web address _____

Type of Policy	Company A	Company B
20-year term insurance $100,000		
Monthly premium		
Total premiums, 20 years		
Cash value at 20 years	None	None
Whole life insurance $100,000		
Monthly premium		
Total premiums, 20 years		
Cash value at 20 years		

1. Which is less expensive, term insurance or whole life insurance?

   _____ term   _____ whole life

2. Which company would you select for your purchase of life insurance? Why?

   _____

   _____

   _____

   _____

www.mhhe.com/kdh

LIFE INSURANCE FOR THE YOUNG MARRIED

Jeff and Ann are both 28 years old. They have been married for three years, and they have a son who is almost 2. They expect their second child in a few months.

Jeff is a teller in a local bank. He has just received a $30-a-week raise. His income is $480 a week, which, after taxes, leaves him with $1,648 a month. His company provides $20,000 of life insurance, a medical/hospital/surgical plan, and a major medical plan. All of these group plans protect him as long as he stays with the bank.

When Jeff received his raise, he decided that part of it should be used to add to his family's protection. Jeff and Ann talked to their insurance agent, who reviewed the insurance Jeff obtained through his job. Under Social Security, they also had some basic protection against the loss of Jeff's income if he became totally disabled or if he died before the children were 18.

But most of this protection was only basic, a kind of floor for Jeff and Ann to build on. For example, monthly Social Security payments to Ann would be approximately $1,250 if Jeff died leaving two children under age 18. Yet the family's total expenses would soon be higher after the birth of the second baby. Although the family's expenses would be lowered if Jeff died, they would be at least $250 a month more than Social Security would provide.

Questions

1. What type of policy would you suggest for Jeff and Ann? Why?

2. In your opinion do Jeff and Ann need additional insurance? Why or why not?

Determining Life Insurance Needs

Financial Planning Activities: Estimate life insurance coverage needed to cover expected expenses and future family living costs.

Subbested Web Sites: www.insure.com   www.kiplinger.com/tools/

Household expenses to be covered

Final expenses (funeral, estate taxes, etc.)	1	$ _____
Payment of consumer debt amounts	2	$ _____
Emergency fund	3	$ _____
College fund	4	$ _____

Expected living expenses:

Average living expense	$ _____
Spouse's income after taxes	$ – _____
Annual Social Security benefits	$ – _____
Net annual living expenses	$ _____
Years until spouse is 90	$ _____
Investment rate factor (see below)	$ _____

Total living expenses

(net annual expenses times investment rate factor)	5	$ _____
Total monetary needs (1 + 2 + 3 + 4 + 5)		$ _____
Less: Total current investments		$ _____
Life insurance needs		$ _____

Investment rate factors

Years until spouse is 90	25	30	35	40	45	50	55	60
Conservative investment	20	22	25	27	30	31	33	35
Aggressive investment	16	17	19	20	21	21	22	23

Note: Use Sheet 33 to compare life insurance policies.

What's Next for Your Personal Financial Plan?

- Survey several people to determine their reasons for buying life insurance.
- Talk to an insurance agent to compare the rates charged by different companies and for different age categories.

Name: _____ **Date:** _____

Life Insurance Policy Comparison

Financial Planning Activities: Research and compare companies, coverages, and costs for different life insurance policies. Analyze ads and contact life insurance agents to obtain the information requested below.

Suggested Web Sites: www.quotesmith.com   www.accuquote.com

Age:			
Company			
Agent's name, address, and phone			
Type of insurance (term, straight/whole, limited payment, endowment, universal)			
Type of policy (individual, group)			
Amount of coverage			
Frequency of payment (monthly, quarterly, semiannual, annual)			
Premium amount			
Other costs: • Service charges • Physical exam			
Rate of return (annual percentage increase in cash value; not applicable for term policies)			
Benefits of insurance as stated in ad or by agent			
Potential problems or disadvantages of this coverage			

What's Next for Your Personal Financial Plan?

- Talk to a life insurance agent to obtain information on the methods they suggest for determining the amount of life insurance a person should have.
- Research the differences in premium costs between a mutual and a stock company.

11 Investing Basics and Evaluating Bonds

Objectives

In this chapter, you will learn to

1. Explain why you should establish an investment program.
2. Describe how safety, risk, income, growth, and liquidity affect your investment program.
3. Identify the factors that can reduce investment risk.
4. Recognize why investors purchase bonds and other conservative investments.
5. Evaluate bonds when making an investment.

Why is this important?

While many people dream of being rich, dreaming doesn't make anything happen. You have to want to establish an investment program—especially since no one is going to make you save the money you need to fund an investment plan.

Getting Personal

Why invest? For each of the following statements, select "yes" or "no" to indicate your behavior regarding these investing activities:

	Yes	No
1. My investment goals are written down.	_____	_____
2. I have enough money to begin an investment program.	_____	_____
3. I am aware of various risk factors that may affect my investment program.	_____	_____
4. When making investment decisions, I understand how asset allocation can affect the choice of investments.	_____	_____
5. I know why people invest in bonds and other conservative investments.	_____	_____

After studying this chapter, you will be asked to reconsider your responses to these items.

Preparing for an Investment Program

OBJECTIVE 1

Explain why you should establish an investment program.

The old saying goes "I've been rich and I've been poor, but believe me, rich is better." While being rich doesn't guarantee happiness, the accumulation of money does provide financial security. And yet, just dreaming of being rich doesn't make it happen. In fact, it takes planning, research, and continued evaluation of existing investments to establish and maintain an investment program that will help you accomplish your goals. By studying the material in this chapter, along with the information on stocks and mutual funds in Chapters 12 and 13, you can create an investment plan that is custom-made for you.

The decision to establish an investment plan is an important first step to accomplishing your long-term financial goals. Like other decisions, the decision to start an investment plan is one you must make for yourself. No one is going to make you save the money you need to fund an investment plan. In fact, the *specific* goals you want to accomplish must be the driving force behind your investment plan.

Establishing Investment Goals

Sheet 34
Setting
Investment
Goals

Some financial planners suggest that investment goals be stated in terms of money: By December 31, 2010, I will have total assets of $120,000. Other financial planners believe investors are more motivated to work toward goals that are stated in terms of the particular things they desire: By January 1, 2011, I will have accumulated enough money to purchase a second home in the mountains. To be useful, investment goals must be specific and measurable. They must also be tailored to your particular financial needs. The following questions will help you establish valid investment goals:

1. What will you use the money for?
2. How much money do you need to satisfy your investment goals?
3. How will you obtain the money?
4. How long will it take you to obtain the money?
5. How much risk are you willing to assume in an investment program?
6. What possible economic or personal conditions could alter your investment goals?
7. Considering your economic circumstances, are your investment goals reasonable?
8. Are you willing to make the sacrifices necessary to ensure that you meet your investment goals?
9. What will the consequences be if you don't reach your investment goals?

Your investment goals are always oriented toward the future. In Chapter 1, we classified goals as short term (less than two years), intermediate (two to five years), or long term (over five years). These same classifications are also useful in planning your investment program. For example, you may establish a short-term goal of accumulating $5,000 in a savings account over the next 24 months. You may then use the $5,000 to purchase stocks or mutual funds to help you obtain your intermediate or long-term investment goals.

The SEDUCTIVE lure of luxury

AS A SOMETIME procrastinator, I'm all too aware of the wisdom of Parkinson's Law, which posits that "work expands to fill the time available for its completion." And as a longtime observer of how people handle their money, I've come to believe that there is a financial corollary to Parkinson's Law: "Household spending expands to consume rising income."

This law explains why so many people who make a very comfortable living, with steadily rising income, can't seem to accumulate any wealth. They're always vowing to start saving some real money someday—as soon as their income rises a bit more. Their problem, of course, isn't how much they earn, but how much they spend. And their overspending is likely rooted in an inability to distinguish between needs and wants.

I need, I want. The blurring of this needs/wants distinction helps fuel our consumer society. After all, the whole point of marketing is to convince consumers that things they once considered to be optional luxuries are now typical necessities of the good life.

The success of this process over the past two decades has resulted in what I call the democratizing of luxury. Today as never before, American households at virtually every income level seek products whose price, quality and prestige clearly exceed the functional need to be met.

Rising personal income—especially in highly educated, dual-income households—made this splurging possible. But much of it isn't truly affordable, because it's being financed by a surging tide of consumer debt. And it's crowding out saving for future needs, especially retirement.

Okay, some examples: Production of luxury cars keeps soaring, thanks in part to easy financing with short-term leases. The 27-inch color TV is being replaced by elaborate home theaters with giant flat screens and throbbing sound. Middle-class preteens get their nails done professionally. High school kids are ferried in rented, stretch limousines to proms held in hotel ballrooms. Elegant plumbing fixtures, granite and marble kitchen counters, and oriental rugs are on display at the home-and-hardware superstores.

A generation ago, before luxury went mass market, many solidly middle-class consumers prided themselves on living simply. They knew the difference between needs and wants. They were proud that their savings were quietly growing, and that their increasing net worth wasn't evident to all the world. Not surprisingly, America's personal-savings rate was a lot higher a generation ago than the historic lows of recent years.

By holding fast to these values, many Americans accumulated surprising levels of wealth. They are the people described in *The Millionaire Next Door,* the eye-opening book by Thomas Stanley and William Danko that was published in 1996. As these marketing professors demonstrate, conspicuous consumption may denote a high level of income, but it's rarely a reliable indicator of net worth.

Pay yourself first. I know that everyone has a soft spot for certain indulgences, and I don't begrudge anyone his or her personal passion. The trick is to be selective in your luxury-buying, without abandoning your savings plan. If you're one of those people who say they never have anything left over after paying their bills, try the time-honored technique of paying yourself first. Make that first check you write each month a deposit into your investment account. Better yet, set up an automatic payroll-deduction plan with your employer and a mutual fund. If you come up short after trying to pay all your bills, you'll know what needs to be trimmed—some of those wants that you redefined as needs.

> **❝ Many people who make a very comfortable living, with steadily rising income, can't seem to accumulate any wealth. ❞**

Columnist Knight Kiplinger is editor in chief of this magazine and of The Kiplinger Letter *and* Kiplinger.com.

1. How would you define a need? A want?

_____

2. Based on your current life situation and income, list three needs and three wants.

   Needs: _____

   Wants: _____

3. Describe how the "pay yourself first" technique could help you accumulate wealth.

_____

From the pages of . . . Kiplinger's Personal Finance

Performing a Financial Checkup

Before beginning an investment program, your personal financial affairs should be in good shape. In this section, we examine several factors you should consider before making your first investment.

Apply *Yourself!*

Objective 1

Visit the Consumer Credit Counseling Service Web site (www.cccs.net) and describe the services available to individuals who need help managing their finances.

WORK TO BALANCE YOUR BUDGET   Many individuals regularly spend more than they make. They purchase items on credit and then must make monthly installment payments and pay finance charges ranging between 12 and 18 percent or higher. With this situation, it makes no sense to start an investment program until credit card and installment purchases, along with the accompanying finance charges, are reduced or eliminated. Therefore, you should limit credit purchases to only the necessities or to purchases required to meet emergencies. A good rule of thumb is to limit consumer credit payments to 20 percent of your net (after-tax) income. Eventually, the amount of cash remaining after the bills are paid will increase and can be used to start a savings program or finance investments. A word of caution: Corrective measures take time.

OBTAIN ADEQUATE INSURANCE PROTECTION   We discussed insurance in detail in Chapters 8, 9, and 10 and will not cover that topic again here. However, it is essential that you consider insurance needs before beginning an investment program. The types of insurance and the amount of coverage will vary from one person to the next. Before you start investing, examine the amount of your insurance coverage for life insurance, hospitalization, your home and other real estate holdings, automobiles, and any other assets that may need coverage.

START AN EMERGENCY FUND   Most financial planners suggest that an investment program should begin with the accumulation of an emergency fund. An **emergency fund** is an amount of money you can obtain quickly in case of immediate need. This money should be deposited in a savings account paying the highest available interest rate or in a money market mutual fund that provides immediate access to cash if needed.

emergency fund An amount of money you can obtain quickly in case of immediate need.

The amount of money to be put away in the emergency fund varies from person to person. However, most financial planners agree that an amount equal to three to nine months' living expenses is reasonable. For example, if your monthly expenses total $1,800, before you can begin investing, you must save at least $5,400 ($1,800 × 3 months = $5,400) in a savings account or other near-cash investments to meet emergencies.

HAVE ACCESS TO OTHER SOURCES OF CASH FOR EMERGENCY NEEDS   You may also want to establish a line of credit at a commercial bank, savings and loan association, credit union, or credit card company. A **line of credit** is a short-term loan that is approved before you actually need the money. Because the paperwork has already been completed and the loan has been preapproved, you can later obtain the money as soon as you need it. The cash advance provision offered by major credit card companies can also be used in an emergency. However, both lines of credit and credit cards have a ceiling, or maximum dollar amount, that limits the amount of available credit. If you have already exhausted both of these sources of credit on everyday expenses, they will not be available in an emergency.

line of credit   A short-term loan that is approved before the money is actually needed.

Getting the Money Needed to Start an Investment Program

Once you have established your investment goals and completed your financial checkup, it's time to start investing—assuming you have enough money to finance your investments. Unfortunately, the money doesn't automatically appear. In today's world, you must work to accumulate the money you need to start any investment program.

PRIORITY OF INVESTMENT GOALS   How badly do you want to achieve your investment goals? Are you willing to sacrifice some purchases to provide financing for your investments? The answers to both questions are extremely important. Take Rita Johnson, a 32-year-old nurse in a large St. Louis hospital. As part of a divorce settlement in 2001, she received a cash payment of almost $55,000. At first, she was tempted to spend this money on a new BMW and new furniture. But after some careful planning, she decided to save $25,000 in a certificate of deposit and invest the remainder in a conservative mutual fund. On May 31, 2004, these investments were valued at $79,000.

DID YOU KNOW?

The more money you make, the more challenging your investment goals can be. Here are household income levels for U.S. families.

14% Over $75,000
29% $50,000 to $75,000
28% $25,000 to $50,000
29% Under $25,000

Source: *Statistical Abstract of the United States 2003*, U.S. Bureau of the Census Web site (www.census.gov), May 1, 2004 (Washington, DC: U.S. Government Printing Office), p. 456.

As pointed out earlier in this chapter, no one can make you save money to finance your investment program. You have to *want* to do it. And *you* may be the most important part of a successful investment program. What is important to you? What do you value? Each of these questions affects your investment goals. At one extreme are people who save or invest as much of each paycheck as they can. The satisfaction they get from attaining their intermediate and long-term investment goals is more important than the more immediate satisfaction of spending a large part of their paychecks on new clothes, a meal at an expensive restaurant, or a weekend getaway. At the other extreme are people who spend everything they make and run out of money before their next paycheck. Most people find either extreme unacceptable and take a more middle-of-the-road approach. These people often spend money on the items that make their lives more enjoyable and still save enough to fund an investment program. Suggestions to help you obtain the money you need to fund an investment program are listed in the nearby Personal Finance in Practice feature.

The Value of Long-Term Investment Programs

Many people never start an investment program because they have only small sums of money. But even small sums grow over a long period of time. Mary and Peter Miller, for example, began their investment program by investing $2,000 *each year* when they were in their 20s; yet they expect their investment portfolio to be worth more than $1.5 million by the time Peter reaches age 65. How did they do it? Simple: They took advantage of the time value of money. You can achieve the same type of result. For instance, if you invest $2,000 each year for 40 years at a 5 percent annual rate of return, your investment will grow to $241,600. The rate of return and the length of time your money is invested *do* make a difference. Exhibit 11–1 shows how much your investment portfolio will be worth at the end of selected time periods and with different rates of return.

Notice that the value of your investments increases each year because of two factors. First, it is assumed you will invest another $2,000 each year. For example, at

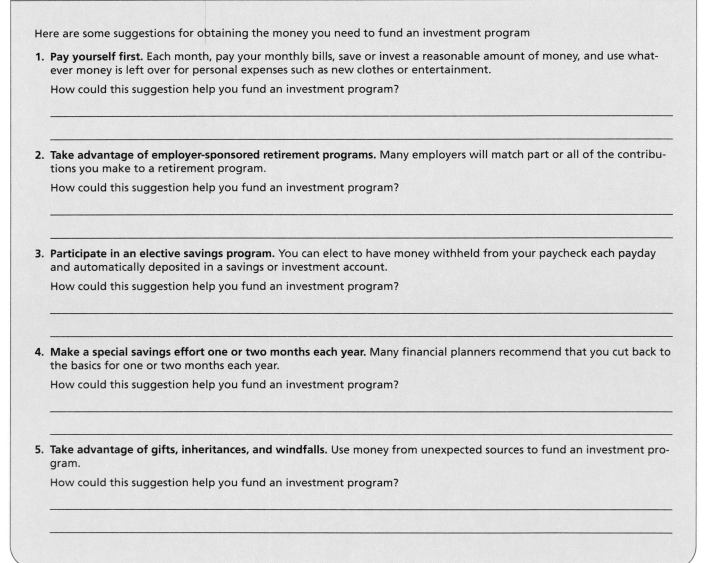

Personal Finance in Practice

Here are some suggestions for obtaining the money you need to fund an investment program

1. **Pay yourself first.** Each month, pay your monthly bills, save or invest a reasonable amount of money, and use whatever money is left over for personal expenses such as new clothes or entertainment.

   How could this suggestion help you fund an investment program?

   _____

   _____

2. **Take advantage of employer-sponsored retirement programs.** Many employers will match part or all of the contributions you make to a retirement program.

   How could this suggestion help you fund an investment program?

   _____

   _____

3. **Participate in an elective savings program.** You can elect to have money withheld from your paycheck each payday and automatically deposited in a savings or investment account.

   How could this suggestion help you fund an investment program?

   _____

   _____

4. **Make a special savings effort one or two months each year.** Many financial planners recommend that you cut back to the basics for one or two months each year.

   How could this suggestion help you fund an investment program?

   _____

   _____

5. **Take advantage of gifts, inheritances, and windfalls.** Use money from unexpected sources to fund an investment program.

   How could this suggestion help you fund an investment program?

   _____

   _____

the end of 40 years, you will have invested a total of $80,000 ($2,000 × 40 years). Second, all investment earnings are allowed to accumulate and are added to your yearly deposits. In the above example, you earned $161,600 ($241,600 total return − $80,000 yearly contributions = $161,600 accumulated earnings). Thus, the totals illustrated in Exhibit 11–1 are a result of continuous yearly deposits *plus* earnings on your investments.

Also, notice that if investments earn a higher rate of return, total portfolio values increase dramatically. For example, a $2,000 annual investment that earns 6 percent a year is worth $309,520 at the end of 40 years. But if the same $2,000 annual investment earns 12 percent each year, your investment portfolio value increases to $1,534,180 at the end of the same 40-year period. The search for higher returns is one reason many investors choose stocks and mutual funds that offer higher potential returns compared to certificates of deposit or savings accounts.

	BALANCE AT END OF YEAR					
Rate of Return	1	5	10	20	30	40
2%	$2,000	$10,408	$21,900	$48,594	$81,176	$ 120,804
3	2,000	10,618	22,928	53,740	95,150	150,802
4	2,000	10,832	24,012	59,556	112,170	190,052
5	2,000	11,052	25,156	66,132	132,878	241,600
6	2,000	11,274	26,362	73,572	158,116	309,520
7	2,000	11,502	27,632	81,990	188,922	399,280
8	2,000	11,734	28,974	91,524	226,560	518,120
9	2,000	11,970	30,386	102,320	272,620	675,780
10	2,000	12,210	31,874	114,550	328,980	885,180
11	2,000	12,456	33,444	128,406	398,040	1,163,660
12	2,000	12,706	35,098	144,104	482,660	1,534,180

Exhibit [11–1]

Growth Rate for $2,000 Invested at the End of Each Year at Various Rates of Return for Different Time Periods

✔ **CONCEPTCHECK 11–1**

1 Why should an individual develop specific investment goals?

_____

_____

2 What factors should you consider when performing a financial checkup?

_____

_____

3 Below are suggestions that you can use to help you accumulate the money needed to fund an investment program. Beside each suggestion, indicate if this is an action that seems logical given your current financial condition. Then explain your answer in the space provided.

Suggestion	Helpful		Explanation
Pay yourself first	Yes	No	
Employer-sponsored retirement programs	Yes	No	
Elective savings programs	Yes	No	
Special savings efforts one or two months each year	Yes	No	
Gifts, inheritances, and windfalls	Yes	No	

Continued

4 In your own words, describe the time value of money concept and how it could affect your investment program.

_____

_____

Factors Affecting the Choice of Investments

OBJECTIVE 2

Describe how safety, risk, income, growth, and liquidity affect your investment program.

Millions of Americans buy stocks, bonds, or mutual funds, purchase gold and silver, or make similar investments. And they all have reasons for investing their money. Some people want to supplement their retirement income when they reach age 65, while others want to become millionaires before age 40. Although each investor may have specific, individual goals for investing, all investors must consider a number of factors before choosing an investment alternative.

Safety and Risk

The safety and risk factors are two sides of the same coin. You cannot evaluate any investment without assessing how safety relates to risk. Safety in an investment means minimal risk or loss. On the other hand, risk in an investment means a measure of uncertainty about the outcome. Investments range from very safe to very risky. At one end of the investment spectrum are very safe investments that attract conservative investors. Investments in this category include government bonds, savings accounts, certificates of deposit, certain corporate bonds, stocks, and mutual funds. Real estate may also be a very safe investment. Investors pick such investments because they know there is very little chance that investments of this kind will become worthless. Although anyone can choose investments like those just listed, someone who chooses conservative investments usually has a specific reason. Many investors choose conservative investments because of the individual life situations in which they find themselves. As people approach retirement, for example, they usually choose more conservative investments with less chance of losing a large part of their nest egg. Some people choose to invest one-time windfalls or inheritances in a conservative investment because they know it may be impossible to replace the money if it is lost. Finally, some investors simply dislike the risk associated with investments that promise larger returns.

Sheet 35
Assessing
Risk for
Investments

speculative investment A high-risk investment made in the hope of earning a relatively large profit in a short time.

At the other end of the investment spectrum are speculative investments. A **speculative investment** is a high-risk investment made in the hope of earning a relatively large profit in a short time. Such investments offer the possibility of a larger dollar return, but if they are unsuccessful, you may lose most or all of your initial investment. Speculative stocks, certain bonds, some mutual funds, and some real estate, commodities, options, precious metals, precious stones, and collectibles are risk-oriented investments.

From an investor's standpoint, one basic rule sums up the relationship between the factors of safety and risk: _The potential return on any investment should be directly related to the risk the investor assumes._ For example, Ana Luna was injured in a work-related accident three years ago. After a lengthy lawsuit, she received a legal settlement totaling $420,000. As a result of the injury, she was no longer qualified to perform her old job as an assembler for an electronics manufacturer. When she thought about the future, she knew she needed to get a job, but realized she would be forced to acquire new employment skills. She also realized she had received a great deal of money that could be invested to provide a steady source of income not only for the next two years while she obtained job training but also for the remainder of her life. Having never invested before, she quickly realized her tolerance for risk was minimal. She had to conserve her $420,000 settlement. Eventually, after much discussion with professionals and her own research, she chose to save about half of her money in federally insured certificates of deposit. For the remaining half, she chose three stocks that offered a 3 percent average dividend, a potential for growth, and a high degree of safety because of the financial stability of the corporations that issued the stocks. A more risk-oriented investor might have criticized Ana's decisions as too conservative. In fact, this second type of investor might have chosen to invest in more speculative stocks that offer a greater potential for growth and increase in market value.

Often beginning investors are afraid of the risk associated with many investments. But remember that without the risk, obtaining the larger returns that really make an investment program grow is impossible. The key is to determine how much risk you are willing to assume, and then choose quality investments that offer higher returns without an unacceptably high risk. To help you determine how much risk you are willing to assume, take the test for risk tolerance presented in Exhibit 11–2.

Exhibit [11–2]   A Quick Test to Measure Investment Risk

The following quiz, adapted from one prepared by the T. Rowe Price group of mutual funds, can help you discover how comfortable you are with varying degrees of risk. Other things being equal, your risk tolerance score is a useful guide in deciding how heavily you should weight your portfolio toward safe investments versus more risk-oriented, speculative investments.

1. You're the winner on a TV game show. Which prize would you choose?
   - ☐ $2,000 in cash (1 point).
   - ☐ A 50 percent chance to win $4,000 (3 points).
   - ☐ A 20 percent chance to win $10,000 (5 points).
   - ☐ A 2 percent chance to win $100,000 (9 points).

2. You're down $500 in a poker game. How much more would you be willing to put up to win the $500 back?
   - ☐ More than $500 (8 points).
   - ☐ $500 (6 points).
   - ☐ $250 (4 points).
   - ☐ $100 (2 points).
   - ☐ Nothing—you'll cut your losses now (1 point).

3. A month after you invest in a stock, it suddenly goes up 15 percent. With no further information, what would you do?
   - ☐ Hold it, hoping for further gains (3 points).
   - ☐ Sell it and take your gains (1 point).
   - ☐ Buy more—it will probably go higher (4 points).

4. Your investment suddenly goes down 15 percent one month after you invest. Its fundamentals still look good. What would you do?
   - ☐ Buy more. If it looked good at the original price, it looks even better now (4 points).

- ☐ Hold on and wait for it to come back (3 points).
- ☐ Sell it to avoid losing even more (1 point).

5. You're a key employee in a start-up company. You can choose one of two ways to take your year-end bonus. Which would you pick?
   - ☐ $1,500 in cash (1 point).
   - ☐ Company stock options that could bring you $15,000 next year if the company succeeds, but will be worthless if it fails (5 points).

Your total score: _____

Scoring

5–18 points You are a more conservative investor. You prefer to minimize financial risks. The lower your score, the more cautious you are. When you choose investments, look for high credit ratings, well-established records, and an orientation toward stability. In stocks, bonds, and real estate, look for a focus on income.

19–30 points You are a less conservative investor. You are willing to take more chances in pursuit of greater rewards. The higher your score, the bolder you are. When you invest, look for high overall returns. You may want to consider bonds with higher yields and lower credit ratings, the stocks of newer companies, and real estate investments that use mortgage debt.

A primer on the ABCs of investing is available from T. Rowe Price, 100 E. Pratt St., Baltimore, MD 21202 (800-638-5660).

Components of the Risk Factor

The risk factor associated with a specific investment does change from time to time. For example, the stock of Computer-Tabulating-Recording Company was once considered a high-risk investment. Then this company changed its name to IBM and eventually became a leader in the computer industry. By the early 1980s, many conservative investors were purchasing IBM stock because of its safety and earnings potential. But in the early 1990s, many of these same investors sold their IBM stock because changes in the computer industry had brought financial problems for IBM. IBM was once again considered too risky for many investors. In the late 1990s, as a result of solving many of its financial problems, IBM was once again considered an excellent choice for most investors. Today, many conservative investors have sold their IBM stock because of the uncertainty associated with firms in the computer and technology industries. At the same time, many more risk-oriented investors are purchasing IBM stock because of potential larger gains as the computer industry begins to rebound.

When choosing an investment, you must carefully evaluate changes in the risk factor. In fact, the overall risk factor can be broken down into four components.

INFLATION RISK As defined in Chapter 1, inflation is a rise in the general level of prices. During periods of high inflation, there is a risk that the financial return on an investment will not keep pace with the inflation rate. To see how inflation reduces your buying power, let's assume you have deposited $10,000 in the bank at 3 percent interest. At the end of one year, your money will have earned $300 in interest ($10,000 × 3% = $300). Assuming an inflation rate of 5 percent, it will cost you an additional $500 ($10,000 × 5% = $500), or a total of $10,500, to purchase the same amount of goods you could have purchased for $10,000 a year earlier. Thus, even though you earned $300, you lost $200 in purchasing power. And after paying taxes on the $300 interest, your loss of purchasing power is even greater.

INTEREST RATE RISK The interest rate risk associated with preferred stocks or government or corporate bonds is the result of changes in the interest rates in the economy. The value of preferred stocks, government bonds, or corporate bonds decreases when overall interest rates increase. In contrast, the value of these same investments rises when overall interest rates decrease. For example, suppose you purchase a $1,000 corporate bond issued by AMR, the parent company of American Airlines, that matures in 2016 and pays 9 percent interest until maturity. If bond interest rates for comparable bonds increase to 11 percent, the market value of your 9 percent bond will decrease. No one will be willing to purchase your bond at the price you paid for it, since a comparable bond that pays 11 percent can be purchased for $1,000. As a result, you will have to sell your bond for less than $1,000 or hold it until maturity.

Of course, if overall interest rates declined, your bond would increase in value. Let's assume that interest rates on comparable corporate bonds declined to 7 percent. As a result, the value of your AMR bond that pays 9 percent would increase in value.

BUSINESS FAILURE RISK The risk of business failure is associated with investments in stock and corporate bonds. With each of these investments, you face the possibility that bad management, unsuccessful products, competition, or a host of other factors will cause the business to be less profitable than originally anticipated. Lower profits usually mean lower dividends or no dividends at all. If the business continues to operate at a loss, even interest payments and repayment of bonds may be questionable. The business may even fail and be forced to file for bankruptcy, in which case your investment may become totally worthless. Before ignoring the possibility of business failure, consider the plight of employees and investors who owned stock in Enron. Of course, the best way to protect yourself against such losses is to carefully evaluate the companies that issue the stocks and bonds you purchase and then continue to evaluate your investment after the purchase. Purchasing stock in more than one company, and thus diversifing your investments, also protects against losses.

MARKET RISK   The prices of stocks, bonds, mutual funds, and other investments may fluctuate because of the behavior of investors in the marketplace. As a result, economic growth is not as systematic and predictable as most investors might believe. Generally, a period of rapid expansion is followed by a period of recession. During periods of recession, it may be quite difficult to sell investments such as real estate. Fluctuations in the market price for stocks and bonds may have nothing to do with the fundamental changes in the financial health of corporations. Such fluctuations may be caused by political or social conditions. For example, the price of petroleum stocks may increase or decrease as a result of political activity in the Middle East. Certainly, the tragic events of September 11, 2001, and the war on terrorism have caused the value of many investments to decline.

Investment Income

Investors sometimes purchase certain investments because they want a predictable source of income. The safest investments—passbook savings accounts, certificates of deposit, and securities issued by the United States government—are also the most predictable sources of income. With these investments, you know exactly what the interest rate is and how much income will be paid on a specific date.

If investment income is a primary objective, you can also choose government bonds, corporate bonds, preferred stocks, utility stocks, or selected common stock issues. When purchasing stocks or corporate bonds for potential income, most investors are concerned about the issuing corporation's overall profits, earnings projections, and dividend policies.

Other investments that may provide income potential are mutual funds and real estate rental property. Although the income from mutual funds is not guaranteed, you can choose funds whose primary objective is income. Income from rental property is not guaranteed because the possibility of either vacancies or unexpected repair bills always exists.

Investment Growth

To investors, *growth* means their investments will increase in value. Often the greatest opportunity for growth is an investment in common stock. During the 1990s, investors found that stocks issued by corporations in the electronics, technology, energy, and health care industries provided the greatest growth potential. And yet, many corporations in those same industries encountered financial problems, lower profits, or even losses during the first part of the 21st century. In fact, many firms—especially dot-coms and technology firms—failed during this same time period. Now the U.S. economy appears to be weathering the storm and shows signs of stability and even improvement. While many analysts still debate whether the recent recession is over, one factor is certain: Investors still like the potential that is offered by growth investments.

When purchasing growth stocks, investors often sacrifice immediate cash dividends in return for greater dollar value in the future. Companies with earnings potential, sales revenues that are increasing, and managers who can solve the problems associated with rapid expansion are often considered to be growth companies. These same companies generally pay little or no dividends. For most growth companies, profits that would normally be paid to stockholders in the form of dividends are reinvested in the companies in the form of *retained earnings*. The money the companies keep can provide at least part of the financing they need for future growth and expansion and control the cost of borrowing money. As a result, they grow at an even faster pace. Growth financed by retained earnings normally increases the dollar value of a share of stock for the investor.

Other investments that may offer growth potential include mutual funds and real estate. For example, many mutual funds are referred to as growth funds or aggressive growth funds because of the growth potential of the individual securities included in the fund.

Apply *Yourself!*

Objective 2

Why would an investor choose an investment for income? Why would an investor choose an investment for growth?

Investment Liquidity

liquidity The ability to buy or sell an investment quickly without substantially affecting the investment's value.

Liquidity is the ability to buy or sell an investment quickly without substantially affecting the investment's value. Investments range from near-cash investments to frozen investments from which it is virtually impossible to get your money. Checking and savings accounts are very liquid because they can be quickly converted to cash. Certificates of deposit impose penalties for withdrawing money before the maturity date.

With other investments, you may be able to sell quickly, but market conditions, economic conditions, or many other factors may prevent you from regaining the amount you originally invested.

✔ CONCEPTCHECK 11–2

1 Why are safety and risk two sides of the same coin?

_____

_____

2 In your own words, describe each of the four components of the risk factor?

Inflation risk:	
Interest rate risk:	
Business failure risk:	
Market risk:	

3 How do income, growth, and liquidity affect the choice of an investment?

_____

_____

Factors that Reduce Investment Risk

OBJECTIVE 3

Identify the factors that can reduce investment risk.

By now, you are probably thinking, how can I choose the right investment for me? Good question. To help answer that question, consider the following: Since 1900—more than 100 years—stocks have returned approximately 10 percent a year. During the same period, U.S. Treasury bills and bonds earned 4 percent.[1] And projections by well-respected

[1]Motley Fool Web site (www.fool.com), April 22, 2004, The Motley Fool, 123 N. Pitt Street, Alexandria, VA 22314.

Roger Ibbotson (chairman of Ibbotson Associates, the investment consulting, software, and research firm) indicate that these same investments will perform at about the same pace between now and the year 2025.[2] These facts and projections suggest that everyone should invest in stocks because they offer the largest returns. In reality, many stocks have a place in your investment portfolio, but establishing an investment program is more than just picking a bunch of stocks. Before making the decision to purchase stocks, consider the factors of portfolio management and asset allocation, the time period that your investments will work for you, and your age.

Portfolio Management and Asset Allocation

Earlier in this chapter, we examined how safety, risk, income, growth, and liquidity affect your investment choices. Now let's compare the factors that affect the choice of investments with each investment alternative. Exhibit 11–3 ranks each alternative in terms of safety, risk, income, growth, and liquidity. More information on each investment alternative is provided in this chapter and Chapters 12 and 13.

ASSET ALLOCATION   **Asset allocation** is the process of spreading your assets among several different types of investments to lessen risk. The term *asset allocation* is a fancy way of saying you need to diversify and avoid the pitfall of putting all your eggs in one basket—a common mistake made by investors. Asset allocation is often expressed in percentages. For example, what percentage of my assets do I want to put in stocks and mutual funds? What percentage do I want to put in bonds or certificates of deposit? The answers to these questions are often tied to your tolerance for risk. Remember the basic rule presented earlier in this chapter: *The potential return on any investment should be directly related to the risk the investor assumes.* Consider what happened when Susan Vaughn invested over $20,000 in stocks and mutual funds during the summer of 2001. She chose quality stock and mutual fund investments that should have done well over a long period of time. But after the tragic events of September 11, the value of her investment portfolio dropped 30 percent within a three-week period. That's when she called her broker and sold her investments. Later, she admitted that she wasn't comfortable with the risk associated with investments in stocks and mutual funds. In short, the amount of risk that you are comfortable with is a very important factor when choosing where to allocate your investment dollars.

asset allocation The process of spreading your assets among several different types of investments to lessen risk.

	FACTORS TO BE EVALUATED				
Type of Investment	**Safety**	**Risk**	**Income**	**Growth**	**Liquidity**
Common stock	Average	Average	Average	High	Average
Preferred stock	Average	Average	High	Average	Average
Corporate bonds	Average	Average	High	Low	Average
Government bonds	High	Low	Low	Low	High
Mutual funds	Average	Average	Average	Average	Average
Real estate	Average	Average	Average	Average	Low

Exhibit [11–3]

Factors Used to Evaluate Traditional Investment Alternatives

[2]Roger G. Ibbotson, "Predictions of the Past and Forecasts for the Future: 1976–2025," Ibbotson Associates Web site (www.Ibbotson.com), April 22, 2004, Ibbotson Associates, 225 North Michigan Avenue, Chicago, IL 60601.

THE TIME FACTOR The amount of time that your investments have to work for you is another important factor when managing your investment portfolio. Recall the investment returns presented above. Since 1900, stocks have returned approximately 10 percent a year and returned more than other investment alternatives. And yet, during the same period, there were years when stocks decreased in value.[3] The point is that if you invested at the wrong time and then couldn't wait for the investment to recover, you would lose money. Remember Susan Vaughn's decision to sell her stocks and mutual funds at a loss. Had she been willing to wait for her stock and mutual fund investments to recover, she would not have lost 30 percent of her original investment.

The amount of time you have before you need your investment money is crucial. If you can leave your investments alone and let them work for you for 5 to 10 years or more, then you can invest in stocks and mutual funds. On the other hand, if you need your investment money in two years or less, you should probably invest in short-term government bonds, highly rated corporate bonds, or certificates of deposit. By taking a more conservative approach for short-term investments, you reduce the possibility of having to sell your investments at a loss because of depressed market value or a staggering economy.

YOUR AGE A final factor to consider when choosing an investment is your age. As mentioned earlier in this chapter, younger investors tend to invest a large percentage of their nest egg in growth-oriented investments. If their investments take a nosedive, they have time to recover. On the other hand, older investors tend to be more conservative and invest in government bonds, high-quality corporate bonds, and very safe corporate stocks or mutual funds. As a result, a smaller percentage of their nest egg is placed in growth-oriented investments. How much of your portfolio should be in growth-oriented investments? Well-known personal financial expert Suze Orman suggests that you subtract your age from 110, and the difference is the percentage of your assets that should be invested in growth investments. For example, if you are 40 years old, subtract 40 from 110, which gives you 70. Therefore, 70 percent of your assets should be invested in growth-oriented investments while the remaining 30 percent should be kept in safer, conservative investments.[4]

Apply Yourself!

Objective 3

Use the Suze Orman method to determine the percentage of your investments that should be invested in growth investments.

Your Role in the Investment Process

Successful investors continually evaluate their investments. They never sit back and let their investments manage themselves. Some factors to consider when choosing different investments are described next.

EVALUATE POTENTIAL INVESTMENTS Let's assume you have $25,000 to invest. Also assume your investment will earn a 10 percent return the first year. At the end of one year, you will have earned $2,500 and your investment will be worth $27,500. Not a bad return on your original investment! Now ask yourself: How long would it take to earn $2,500 if I had to work for this amount of money at a job? For some people, it might take a month; for others, it might take longer. The point is that if you want this type of return, you should be willing to work for it, but the work takes a different form than a job. When choosing an investment, the work you invest is the time needed to research different investments so that you can make an informed decision.

---

[3]Motley Fool Web site (www.fool.com), April 22, 2004, The Motley Fool, 123 N. Pitt Street, Alexandria, VA 22314.
[4]Suze Orman, *The Road to Wealth* (New York: Riverbend Books, 2001), p. 371.

Figure It Out!

CHARTING THE VALUE OF YOUR INVESTMENT

To monitor the value of their investments, many investors use a simple chart like the one illustrated here. To construct a chart like this one, place the original purchase price of your investment in the middle on the side of the chart. Then use price increments of a logical amount to show increases and decreases in dollar value.

Place individual dates along the bottom of the chart. For stocks, bonds, mutual funds, and similar investments, you may want to graph every two weeks and chart current values on, say, a Friday. For longer term investments like real estate, you can chart current values every six months. It is also possible to use computer software to chart the value of your investments.

A WORD OF CAUTION

If an investment is beginning to have a large increase or decrease in value, you should watch that investment more closely. You can still continue to chart at regular intervals, but you may want to check dollar values more frequently—in some cases, daily.

PRACTICE MAKES PERFECT!

Using the dates and dollar amounts below, construct a graph to illustrate the price movements for a share of stock issued by Chesapeake Manufacturing.

Date	Price
June 1	$19
June 15	$16
June 29	$17
July 13	$20
July 27	$24
August 10	$25
August 24	$23

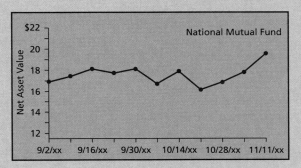

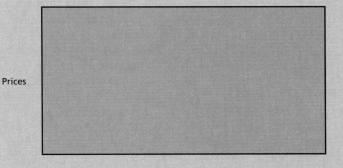

Prices

Some people invest large sums of money and never research the investments they purchase. Obviously, this is a flawed approach that can lead to large dollar losses. On the other hand, an informed investor has a much better chance of choosing the types of investments that will increase in value. Later in this chapter, and then in Chapters 12 and 13, you will learn how to evaluate bond, stock, and mutual fund investments.

MONITOR THE VALUE OF YOUR INVESTMENTS Would you believe that some people invest large sums of money and don't know what their investments are worth? They don't know if their investments have increased or decreased in value. They don't know if they should sell their investments or continue to hold them. A much better approach is to monitor the value of your investments. If you choose to invest in stocks, bonds, mutual funds, commodities, or options, you can determine the value of your holdings by looking at the price quotations reported on the Internet, on cable financial news programs, and in newspapers. Your real estate holdings may be compared with similar properties currently for sale in the surrounding area. Finally, you can determine the value of your precious metals, gemstones, and collectibles by checking with reputable dealers and investment firms. Regardless of which type of investment you choose, close surveillance will keep you informed of whether your investment increases or decreases in value. The nearby Figure It Out box presents further information on monitoring the value of your investments.

KEEP ACCURATE AND CURRENT RECORDS Accurate recordkeeping can help you spot opportunities to maximize profits or reduce dollar losses when you sell your investments. Accurate recordkeeping can also help you decide whether you want to invest additional funds in a particular investment. At the very least, you should keep purchase records for each of your investments that include the actual dollar cost of the investment, plus any commissions or fees you paid. It is also useful to keep a list of the sources of information (Internet addresses, business periodicals, research publications, etc.), along with copies of the material you used to evaluate each investment. Then, when it is time to reevaluate an existing investment, you will know where to begin your search for current information. Accurate recordkeeping is also necessary for tax purposes.

OTHER FACTORS THAT IMPROVE INVESTMENT DECISIONS To achieve their financial goals, many people seek professional help. In many cases, they turn to stockbrokers, lawyers, accountants, bankers, or insurance agents. However, these professionals are specialists in one specific field and may not be qualified to provide the type of advice required to develop a thorough financial plan. Another source of investment help is a financial planner who has had training in securities, insurance, taxes, real estate, and estate planning. For more information on choosing a financial planner and on the financial planning process, you may want to review the material in Chapter 1.

Whether you are making your own decisions or have professional help, you must consider the tax consequences of selling your investments. Taxes were covered in Chapter 3, and it is not our intention to cover them again. And yet, it is your responsibility to determine how taxes affect your investment decisions. You may want to review the material on dividend, interest, and rental income and on capital gains and capital losses that result from selling an investment. You may also want to read the material on tax-deferred investment income and retirement planning presented in Chapter 14.

✔ CONCEPTCHECK 11–3

1 Assume you must choose an investment that will help you obtain your investment goals. Rank the following investments from 1 (low) to 6 (high) and then justify your choice for your investment portfolio. (See Exhibit 11–3 for help evaluating each investment.)

Investment	Rank (1 = low; 6 = high)	Justification
Common stocks		
Preferred stocks		
Corporate bonds		
Government bonds		
Mutual funds		
Real estate		

2 Why should investors be concerned with asset allocation and the time their investments have to work for them?

_____

_____

Continued

3 Why should you monitor the value of your investments?

_____

_____

Conservative Investment Options

As noted in the last section, stocks have outperformed other investment alternatives over the past 100 years. Nevertheless, smart investors sometimes choose other investments. Answer the following questions to see if conservative investments, including certificates of deposit, government bonds, and corporate bonds, may be right for you:

Question	Yes	No
1. Stocks seem to be overpriced and will probably go down in the next 12 to 18 months.	_____	_____
2. I need to convert my investments to cash in a short period of time.	_____	_____
3. I'm afraid I will lose the money invested in speculative investments.	_____	_____
4. At my age, replacing the money invested in stocks or mutual funds if they should decline in value would be hard if not impossible.	_____	_____

If you answered yes to any of these questions, you may want to consider the more conservative investments described in this section. Before investing, you may also want to review the concepts of asset allocation and portfolio management described earlier in this chapter.

As discussed in Chapter 4, savings accounts, certificates of deposit, money market accounts, and savings bonds provide a safe place to invest your money. Unfortunately, with interest rates at or near all-time lows, they don't offer a lot of growth or income potential. Other conservative investments that may offer more potential include government bonds and corporate bonds.

Government Bonds and Debt Securities

The U.S. government and state and local governments issue bonds to obtain financing. A **government bond** is a written pledge of a government or a municipality to repay a specified sum of money, along with interest. In this section, we discuss bonds issued by each level of government and look at why investors purchase these bonds.

U.S. TREASURY BILLS, NOTES, AND BONDS
The main reason investors choose U.S. government securities is that most investors consider them risk free. Because they are backed by the full faith and credit of the U.S. government and carry a decreased risk of default, they offer lower interest rates than corporate bonds. Today, the U.S. Treasury Department issues three principal types of securities: Treasury bills, Treasury notes, and U.S. government savings bonds. (Although still available in the secondary market,

government bond The written pledge of a government or a municipality to repay a specified sum of money, along with interest.

another type of security—long-term Treasury bonds—is no longer issued by the Treasury Department.) Treasury bills, notes, and savings bonds can be purchased through Treasury Direct offices in Boston, Minneapolis, and Dallas. Treasury Direct conducts auctions to sell Treasury bills and notes. Buyers interested in purchasing these securities at such auctions may bid competitively or noncompetitively. If they bid competitively, they must specify the rate or interest yield they are willing to accept. If they bid noncompetitively, they are willing to accept the interest rate or yield determined at auction. For more information about Treasury Direct, visit the Web site at www.treasurydirect.gov. Treasury securities may also be purchased through banks or brokers, which charge a commission.

U.S. government securities can be held until maturity or sold/redeemed before maturity. Interest paid on U.S. government securities is taxable for federal income tax purposes but is exempt from state and local taxation.

Treasury Bills   A *Treasury bill,* sometimes called a *T-bill,* is sold in a minimum unit of $1,000 with additional increments of $1,000 above the minimum. Although the maturity for T-bills may be as long as 1 year, the Treasury Department currently only sells T-bills with 4-week, 13-week, and 26-week maturities. T-bills are discounted securities, and the actual purchase price you pay is less than the maturity value of the T-bill.

Treasury Notes   A *Treasury note* is issued in $1,000 units with a maturity of more than 1 year but not more than 10 years. Typical maturities are 2, 3, 5, and 10 years. Interest rates for Treasury notes are slightly higher than those for Treasury bills, because investors must wait longer to get their money back and therefore demand higher interest. Interest for Treasury notes is paid every six months.

Treasury Bonds   As mentioned earlier in this section, the Treasury Department no longer issues Treasury bonds. However, many are still in existence and may be purchased in the secondary market through a broker or other financial institution. Therefore, basic information about Treasury bonds is provided below. A *Treasury bond* is issued in minimum units of $1,000 that have maturities ranging from 10 to 30 years. Interest rates for Treasury bonds are generally higher than those for either Treasury bills or Treasury notes. Again, the primary reason for the higher interest rates is the length of time investors must hold Treasury bonds. Like interest on Treasury notes, interest on Treasury bonds is paid every six months.

FEDERAL AGENCY DEBT ISSUES   In addition to the bonds and securities issued by the Treasury Department, debt securities are issued by federal agencies and quasi-federal agencies, which include the Federal National Mortgage Association (sometimes referred to as Fannie Mae), the Federal Housing Administration (FHA), the Government National Mortgage Association (sometimes referred to as Ginnie Mae), and the Federal Home Loan Mortgage Corporation (which somehow became known as Freddie Mac).

Although these debt issues are, for practical purposes, risk free, they offer a slightly higher interest rate than government securities issued by the Treasury Department. The minimum investment may be as high as $25,000. Securities issued by federal agencies usually have maturities ranging from 15 to 30 years, with an average life of about 12 years.

municipal bond A debt security issued by a state or local government.

STATE AND LOCAL GOVERNMENT SECURITIES   A **municipal bond,** sometimes called a *muni,* is a debt security issued by a state or local government. Such securities are used to finance the ongoing activities of state and local governments and major projects such as airports, schools, toll roads, and toll bridges, and may be purchased directly from the government entity that issued them or through account executives.

general obligation bond A bond backed by the full faith, credit, and unlimited taxing power of the government that issued it.

State and local securities are classified as either general obligation bonds or revenue bonds. A **general obligation bond** is backed by the full faith, credit, and unlimited taxing power of the government that issued it. A **revenue bond** is repaid from the income generated by the project it is designed to finance. Although both general obligation and revenue bonds are relatively safe, defaults have occurred in recent years.

revenue bond A bond that is repaid from the income generated by the project it is designed to finance.

If the risk of default worries you, you can purchase insured municipal bonds. A number of states offer to guarantee payments on selected securities. Three large private insurers—MBIA, Inc. (Municipal Bond Insurance Association); the Financial Security Assurance Corporation (FSA); and AMBAC, Inc. (American Municipal Bond Assurance Corporation)—also issue insured bonds.

Even if a municipal bond issue is insured, however, financial experts worry about the insurer's ability to pay off in the event of default on a large bond issue. Most advise investors to determine the underlying quality of a bond whether or not it is insured. Also, guaranteed municipal securities usually carry a slightly lower interest rate than uninsured bonds because of the reduced risk of default.

One of the most important features of municipal bonds is that the interest on them may be exempt from federal taxes. Whether or not the interest on municipal bonds is tax exempt often depends on how the funds obtained from their sale are used. *You are responsible, as an investor, to determine whether or not interest on municipal bonds is taxable.* Municipal bonds exempt from federal taxation are generally exempt from state and local taxes only in the state where they are issued. Although the interest on municipal bonds may be exempt from taxation, a *capital gain* that results when you sell a municipal bond before maturity and at a profit may be taxable just like capital gains on other investments sold at a profit.

Because of their tax-exempt status, the interest rates on municipal bonds are lower than those on taxable bonds. By using the following formula, you can calculate the *taxable equivalent yield* for a municipal security:

$$\text{Taxable equivalent yield} = \frac{\text{Tax-exempt yield}}{1.0 - \text{Your tax rate}}$$

For example, the taxable equivalent yield on a 5 percent, tax-exempt municipal bond for a person in the 28 percent tax bracket is 6.94 percent, as follows:

$$\text{Taxable equivalent yield} = \frac{0.05}{1.0 - 0.28} = 0.0694, \text{ or } 6.94 \text{ percent}$$

If this taxpayer had been in the 35 percent tax bracket, the taxable equivalent yield for a 5 percent, tax-exempt investment would increase to 7.69 percent. Once you have calculated the taxable equivalent yield, you can compare the return on tax-exempt securities with the return on taxable investments. Exhibit 11–4 illustrates the yields for tax-exempt investments and their taxable equivalent yields.

Exhibit 11–4

Yields for Tax-Exempt Investments

The following information can be used to compare the return on tax-exempt investments with the returns offered by taxable investments. Note: Additional tax rate reductions have been approved by Congress and will be phased in by 2010.

| Tax-Exempt Yield | EQUIVALENT YIELDS FOR TAXABLE INVESTMENTS | | | | |
	15% Tax Rate	25% Tax Rate	28% Tax Rate	33% Tax Rate	35% Tax Rate
4%	4.71%	5.33%	5.56%	5.97%	6.15%
5	5.88	6.67	6.94	7.46	7.69
6	7.06	8.0	8.33	8.96	9.23
7	8.24	9.33	9.72	10.45	10.77
8	9.41	10.67	11.11	11.94	12.31
9	10.59	12.0	12.5	13.43	13.85

Characteristics of Corporate Bonds

corporate bond A corporation's written pledge to repay a specified amount of money with interest.

face value The dollar amount the bondholder will receive at the bond's maturity.

A **corporate bond** is a corporation's written pledge to repay a specified amount of money with interest. The **face value** is the dollar amount the bondholder will receive at the bond's maturity. The usual face value of a corporate bond is $1,000. Between the time of purchase and the maturity date, the corporation pays interest to the bondholder. For example, assume you purchase a $1,000 bond issued by Ford Motor Corporation. The interest rate for this bond is 6⅜ percent. Using the following formula, you can calculate the annual interest amount for this Ford corporate bond:

$$\text{Amount of annual interest} = \text{Face value} \times \text{Interest rate}$$
$$= \$1,000 \times 6.375 \text{ percent}$$
$$= \$1,000 \times 0.06375$$
$$= \$63.75$$

Typically, the interest is paid semiannually, or every six months, in $31.88 ($63.75 ÷ 2 = $31.875) installments until the bond matures.

maturity date For a corporate bond, the date on which the corporation is to repay the borrowed money.

The **maturity date** of a corporate bond is the date on which the corporation is to repay the borrowed money. On the maturity date, the bondholder returns the bond to the corporation and receives cash equal to the bond's face value. Maturity dates for bonds generally range from 1 to 30 years after the date of issue.

bond indenture A legal document that details all of the conditions relating to a bond issue.

trustee A financially independent firm that acts as the bondholders' representative.

The actual legal conditions for a corporate bond are described in a bond indenture. A **bond indenture** is a legal document that details all of the conditions relating to a bond issue. Since corporate bond indentures are very difficult for the average person to read and understand, a corporation issuing bonds appoints a trustee. The **trustee** is a financially independent firm that acts as the bondholders' representative. Usually the trustee is a commercial bank or some other financial institution. If the corporation fails to live up to all the provisions in the indenture agreement, the trustee may bring legal action to protect the bondholders' interests.

Why Corporations Sell Corporate Bonds

Corporations borrow when they don't have enough money to pay for major purchases—much as individuals do. Bonds can also be used to finance a corporation's ongoing business activities. In addition, corporations often sell bonds when it is difficult or impossible to sell stock. The sale of bonds can also improve a corporation's financial leverage—the use of borrowed funds to increase the corporation's return on investment. Finally, the interest paid to bond owners is a tax-deductible expense and thus can be used to reduce the taxes the corporation must pay to the federal and state governments.

While a corporation may use both bonds and stocks to finance its activities, there are important distinctions between the two. Corporate bonds are a form of *debt financing,* whereas stock is a form of *equity financing.* Bond owners must be repaid at a future date; stockholders do not have to be repaid. Interest payments on bonds are required; dividends are paid to stockholders at the discretion of the board of directors. Finally, in the event of bankruptcy, bondholders have a claim to the assets of the corporation prior to that of stockholders.

Before issuing bonds, a corporation must decide what type of bond to issue and how the bond issue will be repaid.

debenture A bond that is backed only by the reputation of the issuing corporation.

TYPES OF BONDS   Most corporate bonds are debentures. A **debenture** is a bond that is backed only by the reputation of the issuing corporation. If the corporation fails to make either interest payments or repayment at maturity, debenture bondholders become general creditors, much like the firm's suppliers.

To make a bond issue more appealing to conservative investors, a corporation may issue a mortgage bond. A **mortgage bond** (sometimes referred to as a *secured bond*) is a corporate bond secured by various assets of the issuing firm. Because of this added security, interest rates on mortgage bonds are usually lower than interest rates on unsecured debentures.

mortgage bond A corporate bond secured by various assets of the issuing firm.

CONVERTIBLE BONDS   A special type of bond a corporation may issue is a convertible bond. A **convertible bond** can be exchanged, at the owner's option, for a specified number of shares of the corporation's common stock. This conversion feature allows investors to enjoy the lower risk of a corporate bond but also take advantage of the speculative nature of common stock. For example, Kerr-McGee Corporation's $1,000 bond issue with a 2010 maturity date is convertible. Each bond can be converted to 16.373 shares of the company's common stock. This means you could convert the bond to common stock whenever the price of the company's common stock is $61.08 ($1,000 ÷ 16.373 = $61.08) or higher.

convertible bond A bond that can be exchanged, at the owner's option, for a specified number of shares of the corporation's common stock.

In reality, there is no guarantee that Kerr-McGee bondholders will convert to common stock even if the market value of the common stock does increase to $61.08 or higher. The reason for choosing not to exercise the conversion feature in this example is quite simple. As the market value of the common stock increases, the market value of the convertible bond *also* increases. By not converting to common stock, bondholders enjoy the added safety of the bond and interest income in addition to the increased market value of the bond caused by the price movement of the common stock. Generally, the interest rate on a convertible bond is 1 to 2 percent lower than that on traditional bonds. Convertible bonds, like all potential investments, must be carefully evaluated. Remember, not all convertible bonds are quality investments.

PROVISIONS FOR REPAYMENT   Today most corporate bonds are callable. A **call feature** allows the corporation to call in, or buy, outstanding bonds from current bondholders before the maturity date. In most cases, corporations issuing callable bonds agree not to call them for the first 5 to 10 years after the bonds have been issued. When a call feature is used, the corporation may have to pay the bondholders a premium, an additional amount above the face value of the bond. The money needed to call a bond may come from the firm's profits, the sale of additional stock, or the sale of a new bond issue that has a lower interest rate.

call feature A feature that allows the corporation to call in, or buy, outstanding bonds from current bondholders before the maturity date.

A corporation may use one of two methods to ensure that it has sufficient funds available to redeem a bond issue at maturity. First, the corporation may establish a sinking fund. A **sinking fund** is a fund to which annual or semiannual deposits are made for the purpose of redeeming a bond issue.

sinking fund A fund to which annual or semiannual deposits are made for the purpose of redeeming a bond issue.

Second, a corporation may issue serial bonds. **Serial bonds** are bonds of a single issue that mature on different dates. For example, Seaside Productions used a 20-year, $100 million bond issue to finance its expansion. None of the bonds mature during the first 10 years. Thereafter, 10 percent of the bonds mature each year until all the bonds are retired at the end of the 20-year period.

serial bonds Bonds of a single issue that mature on different dates.

Detailed information about provisions for repayment, along with other vital information (including maturity date, interest rate, bond rating, call provisions, trustee, and details about security), is available from Moody's Investors Service, Standard & Poor's Corporation, and other financial service companies. Take a look at the information provided by Mergent's *Public Utility Manual* for the Cincinnati Gas & Electric Company bond illustrated in the nearby Personal Finance in Practice feature.

Why Investors Purchase Corporate Bonds

Investors often consider many corporate and government bonds a safer investment when compared to stocks or mutual funds. Bonds are also considered a "safe harbor" in

Personal Finance in Practice

THE "HOW TO" OF RESEARCHING A BOND

How do you find out whether or not a corporate bond is callable? Where can you find out who the trustee for a specific bond issue is? These are only two of the multitude of questions that concern investors who are trying to evaluate bond investments. Fortunately, the answers are easy to obtain if you know where to look.

Today the most readily available source of detailed information about a corporation, including information about its bond issues, is Mergent's *Manuals*. Individual subscriptions to this series of publications are too expensive for most investors, but the series is available at both college and public libraries. It includes individual manuals on industrial companies, public utilities, banks and financial institutions, and transportation companies. Each manual contains detailed information on major companies in the United States, including the company's history, operations, products, and bond issues.

The following data on a corporate bond issued by Cincinnati Gas & Electric Company will give you an idea of the contents of the "Long-Term Debt" section of a Mergent's report.

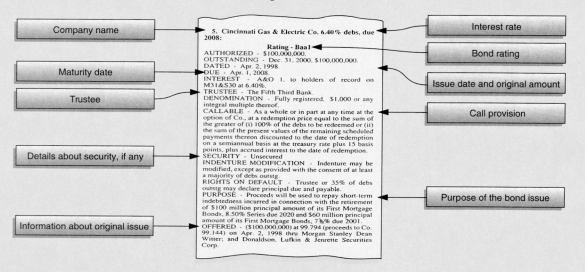

Company name		Interest rate
Maturity date		Bond rating
Trustee		Issue date and original amount
Details about security, if any		Call provision
Information about original issue		Purpose of the bond issue

5. Cincinnati Gas & Electric Co. 6.40% debs, due 2008:

Rating - Baa1
AUTHORIZED - $100,000,000.
OUTSTANDING - Dec. 31, 2000. $100,000,000.
DATED - Apr. 2, 1998.
DUE - Apr. 1, 2008.
INTEREST - A&O 1. to holders of record on M31&S30 at 6.40%.
TRUSTEE - The Fifth Third Bank.
DENOMINATION - Fully registered. $1,000 or any integral multiple thereof.
CALLABLE - As a whole or in part at any time at the option of Co., at a redemption price equal to the sum of the greater of (i) 100% of the debs to be redeemed or (ii) the sum of the present values of the remaining scheduled payments thereon discounted to the date of redemption on a semiannual basis at the treasury rate plus 15 basis points, plus accrued interest to the date of redemption.
SECURITY - Unsecured
INDENTURE MODIFICATION - Indenture may be modified, except as provided with the consent of at least a majority of debs outstg.
RIGHTS ON DEFAULT - Trustee or 35% of debs outstg may declare principal due and payable.
PURPOSE - Proceeds will be used to repay short-term indebtedness incurred in connection with the retirement of $100 million principal amount of its First Mortgage Bonds, 8.50% Series due 2020 and $60 million principal amount of its First Mortgage Bonds, 7⅞% due 2001.
OFFERED - ($100,000,000) at 99.794 (proceeds to Co. 99.144) on Apr. 2, 1998 thru Morgan Stanley Dean Witter; and Donaldson, Lufkin & Jenrette Securities Corp.

Source: The information for the Cincinnati Gas & Electric Company corporate bond was taken from Mergent's *Public Utility Manual* (New York: Mergent, 2003), p. 917.

troubled economic times. For example, many stock investors lost money during the period from 2000 to 2002 because of the economic downturn and the terrorist attacks on the United States. As an alternative to leaving your money in stocks, assuming that you thought the stock market was headed for a period of decline, you could have moved money into corporate or government bonds. That's exactly what Joe Goode did in January 2000. Although his friends thought he was crazy for taking such a conservative approach, he actually avoided a prolonged downturn in the stock market. Now many of his friends wish they had made the same decision. According to Joe, he earned interest on his bond investments while preserving his investment funds for a return to the stock market when the economy rebounds. Basically, investors purchase corporate bonds for three reasons: (1) interest income, (2) possible increase in value, and (3) repayment at maturity.

INTEREST INCOME As mentioned earlier in this section, bondholders normally receive interest payments every six months. Because interest income is so important to bond investors, let's review this calculation. If IBM issues a 7 percent bond with a face value of $1,000, the investor will receive $70 ($1,000 × 7% = $70) a year, paid in installments of $35 at the end of each six-month period.

The method used to pay bondholders their interest depends on whether they own registered bonds, registered coupon bonds, bearer bonds, or zero-coupon bonds. A **registered bond** is registered in the owner's name by the issuing company. Interest checks for registered bonds are mailed directly to the bondholder of record. A variation of a registered bond is the registered coupon bond. A **registered coupon bond** is registered for principal only, not for interest. To collect interest payments on a registered coupon bond, the owner must present one of the detachable coupons to the issuing corporation or the paying agent.

A third type of bond is a **bearer bond,** which is not registered in the investor's name. As with a registered coupon bond, the owner of a bearer bond must detach a coupon and present it to the issuing corporation or the paying agent to collect interest payments. *Be warned:* If you own a bearer bond, you can be out of luck if it is lost or stolen. While some bearer bonds are still in circulation, U.S. corporations no longer issue them. Bearer bonds are generally issued by corporations in foreign countries.

A **zero-coupon bond** is sold at a price far below its face value, makes no annual or semiannual interest payments, and is redeemed for its face value at maturity. With a zero-coupon bond, the buyer receives a return based on the bond's increased market value as its maturity date approaches. For example, assume you purchased a Waste Management zero-coupon bond for $350 in 1995 and Waste Management will pay you $1,000 when the bond matures in 2012.

Before investing in zero-coupon bonds, you should consider at least two factors. First, even though all of the interest on these bonds is paid at maturity, the IRS requires you to report interest each year—that is, as you earn it, not when you actually receive it. Second, zero-coupon bonds are more volatile than other types of bonds.

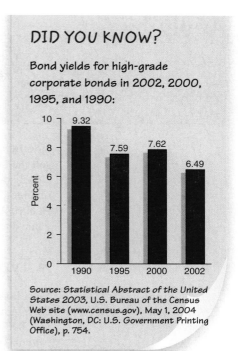

DID YOU KNOW?

Bond yields for high-grade corporate bonds in 2002, 2000, 1995, and 1990:

Source: *Statistical Abstract of the United States 2003,* U.S. Bureau of the Census Web site (www.census.gov), May 1, 2004 (Washington, DC: U.S. Government Printing Office), p. 754.

DOLLAR APPRECIATION OF BOND VALUE

Most beginning investors think that a $1,000 bond is always worth $1,000. In reality, the price of a corporate bond may fluctuate until the maturity date. Changes in overall interest rates in the economy are the primary cause of most bond price fluctuations. Changing bond prices that result from changes in overall interest rates in the economy are an example of interest rate risk, discussed earlier in this chapter. When IBM issued the bond mentioned earlier, the 7 percent interest rate was competitive with the interest rates offered by other corporations issuing bonds at that time. If overall interest rates fall, the IBM bond will go up in market value due to its higher, 7 percent, interest rate. On the other hand, if overall interest rates rise, the market value of the IBM bond will fall due to its lower, 7 percent, interest rate.

When a bond is selling for less than its face value, it is said to be selling at a *discount.* When a bond is selling for more than its face value, it is said to be selling at a *premium.* It is possible to approximate a bond's market value using the following formula:

$$\text{Approximate market value} = \frac{\text{Dollar amount of annual interest}}{\text{Comparable interest rate}}$$

For example, assume you purchase a Verizon New York bond that pays annual interest of $48.75 and has a face value of $1,000. Also assume new corporate bond issues of comparable quality are currently paying 6 percent. The approximate market value is $812.50, as follows:

$$\text{Approximate market value} = \frac{\text{Dollar amount of annual interest}}{\text{Comparable interest rate}} = \frac{\$48.75}{6\%}$$

$$= \$812.50$$

registered bond A bond that is registered in the owner's name by the issuing company.

registered coupon bond A bond that is registered for principal only, and not for interest.

bearer bond A bond that is not registered in the investor's name.

zero-coupon bond A bond that is sold at a price far below its face value, makes no annual or semiannual interest payments, and is redeemed for its face value at maturity.

Apply *Yourself!*

Objective 4

Why would investors choose government or corporate bonds for an investment program?

The market value of a bond may also be affected by the financial condition of the company or government unit issuing the bond, the factors of supply and demand, an upturn or downturn in the economy, and the proximity of the bond's maturity date.

BOND REPAYMENT AT MATURITY Corporate bonds are repaid at maturity. After you purchase a bond, you have two options: You may keep the bond until maturity and then redeem it, or you may sell the bond at any time to another investor. In either case, the value of your bond is closely tied to the corporation's ability to repay its bond indebtedness. For example, the retailer Color Tile and Carpet filed for reorganization under the provisions of the U.S. Bankruptcy Act. As a result, the bonds issued by Color Tile immediately dropped in value due to questions concerning the prospects for bond repayment at maturity.

A Typical Bond Transaction

Most bonds are sold through full-service brokerage firms, discount brokerage firms, or the Internet. If you use a full-service brokerage firm, your account executive should provide both information and advice about bond investments. Your account executive's role is to make suggestions and provide information that may enable you to make a more informed decision. As with other investments, the chief advantage of using a discount brokerage firm or trading online is lower commissions, but you must do your own research. As you will see later in this chapter, many sources of information can be used to evaluate bond investments.

Generally, if you purchase a $1,000 bond through an account executive or brokerage firm, you should expect to pay a minimum commission of between $10 and $35. If you purchase more bonds, the commission usually drops to $5 to $20 per bond. You should also expect to pay commissions when you sell bonds.

✔ CONCEPTCHECK 11–4

1 What is the difference between a treasury bill, a treasury note, and federal agency debt issues?

_____

_____

2 Explain the difference between a general obligation bond and a revenue bond.

_____

_____

3 Calculate the taxable equivalent yield in the following situations:

Tax-Exempt Yield	Equivalent Yield for a Taxpayer in the 25% Tax Bracket	Equivalent Yield for a Taxpayer in the 28% Tax Bracket	Equivalent Yield for a Taxpayer in the 33% Tax Bracket
4.5%			
5.5%			

Continued

4 Calculate the annual interest and the semiannual interest payment for corporate bond issues with a face value of $1,000.

Annual Interest Rate	Annual Interest	Semiannual Interest Payment
6%		
6.5%		
7%		
7.5%		

5 In your own words, describe why corporations issue corporate bonds.

_____

_____

6 List the three reasons investors purchase corporate bonds.

_____

_____

The Decision to Buy or Sell Bonds

One basic principle we have stressed throughout this text is the need to evaluate any potential investment. Certainly corporate *and* government bonds are no exception. As you will see in this section, a number of sources of information can be used to evaluate bond investments.

OBJECTIVE 5
Evaluate bonds when making an investment

The Internet

By accessing a corporation's Web page and locating the topics "financial information," "annual report," or "investor relations," you can find many of the answers to the questions asked in Your Personal Financial Plan Sheet 36. As an added bonus, a corporation may provide more than one year's annual report on its Web site, so you can make comparisons from one year to another.

Apply*Yourself!*

Objective 5

Visit one of the bond Web sites listed in this section and describe the type of information available to investors.

When investing in bonds, you can use the Internet in three other ways. First, you can obtain price information on specific bond issues to track your investments. Especially if you live in a small town or rural area without access to newspapers that provide bond coverage, the Internet can be a welcome source of current bond prices. Second, it is possible to trade bonds online and pay lower commissions than you would pay a full-service or discount brokerage firm. Third, you can get research about a corporation and its bond issues (including recommendations to buy or sell) by accessing specific bond Web sites. *Be warned:* Bond Web sites are not as numerous as Web sites that provide information on stocks, mutual funds, or personal financial planning. And many of the better bond Web sites charge a fee for their research and recommendations.

Sheet 36
Evaluating
Corporate
Bonds

You may want to visit the Moody's Web site (www.moodys.com) and the Standard & Poor's Web site (www.standardpoors.com) to obtain detailed information about both corporate and government bonds.

How to Read the Bond Section of the Newspaper

Not all local newspapers contain bond quotations, but *The Wall Street Journal, Barron's,* and many metropolitan newspapers publish complete information on this subject. In bond quotations, prices are given as a percentage of the face value, which is usually $1,000. Thus, to find the actual market price for a bond, you must multiply the face value ($1,000) by the newspaper quote. For example, a price quoted as 84 means a selling price of $1,000 × 84% = $840. In addition to price information, most newspaper coverage also provides information on the interest rate, current yield, volume, maturity date, and net change. Similar information is also available on the Internet.

For government bonds, most financial publications include two price quotations. The first price quotation, or the *bid price,* is the price a dealer is willing to pay for a government security. The bid price represents the amount that a seller could receive for a government bond. The second price quotation, or the *asked price,* represents the price at which a dealer is willing to sell a government security. The asked price represents the amount for which a buyer could purchase the security.

Bond Ratings

To determine the quality and risk associated with bond issues, investors rely on the bond ratings provided by Moody's Investors Service, Inc., and Standard & Poor's Corporation. Both companies rank thousands of corporate and municipal bonds.

As Exhibit 11–5 illustrates, bond ratings generally range from AAA (the highest) to D (the lowest). For both Moody's and Standard & Poor's, the first four individual categories represent investment-grade securities. Investment-grade securities are suitable for conservative investors who want a safe investment that provides a predictable source of income. Bonds in the next two categories are considered speculative in nature. Finally, the C and D categories are used to rank bonds where there are poor prospects of repayment or even continued payment of interest. Bonds in these categories may be in default.

Generally, U.S. government securities issued by the Treasury Department and various federal agencies are not graded because they are risk free for practical purposes. The rating of long-term and short-term municipal bonds is similar to that of corporate bonds.

Bond Yield Calculations

yield The rate of return earned by an investor who holds a bond for a stated period of time.

current yield Determined by dividing the yearly dollar amount of income generated by an investment by the investment's current market value.

For a bond investment, the **yield** is the rate of return earned by an investor who holds a bond for a stated period of time. The **current yield** is determined by dividing the yearly dollar amount of income generated by an investment by the investment's current market value. For bonds, the following formula may help you complete this calculation:

$$\text{Current yield} = \frac{\text{Annual income amount}}{\text{Current market value}}$$

For example, assume you own an AT&T corporate bond that pays 7.5 percent interest on an annual basis. This means that each year you will receive $75 ($1,000 × 7.5% = $75). Also assume the current market price of the AT&T bond is $1,040. Because the current market value is more than the bond's face value, the current yield decreases to 7.2 percent, as follows:

$$\text{Current yield} = \frac{\$75}{\$1,040}$$

$$= 0.072 = 7.2\%$$

Exhibit [11–5]   Description of Bond Ratings Provided by Moody's Investors Service and Standard & Poor's Corporation

Quality	Moody's	Standard & Poor's	Description
High-grade	Aaa	AAA	Bonds that are judged to be of the best quality.
	Aa	AA	Bonds that are judged to be of high quality by all standards. Together with the first group, they comprise what are generally known as *high-grade* bonds.
Medium-grade	A	A	Bonds that possess many favorable investment attributes and are to be considered upper-medium-grade obligations.
	Baa	BBB	Bonds that are considered medium-grade obligations; i.e., they are neither highly protected nor poorly secured.
Speculative	Ba	BB	Bonds that are judged to have speculative elements; their future cannot be considered well assured.
	B	B	Bonds that generally lack characteristics of the desirable investment.
Default	Caa	CCC	Bonds that are of poor standing.
	Ca	CC	Bonds that represent obligations that are highly speculative.
	C		Bonds that are regarded as having extremely poor prospects of attaining any real investment standing.
		C	Standard & Poor's rating given to bonds where a bankruptcy petition has been filed.
		D	Bond issues in default.

Sources: Moody's Web site (www.moodys.com), July 13, 2002, Moody's Investors Service, 99 Church St., New York, NY 10007; and Standard & Poor's Web site (www.standardpoors.com), July 13, 2002, Standard & Poor's Corporation, 25 Broadway, New York, NY 10004.

This calculation allows you to compare the yield on a bond investment with the yields of other investment alternatives, which include savings accounts, certificates of deposit, common stock, preferred stock, and mutual funds. Naturally, the higher the current yield, the better! A current yield of 9 percent is better than a current yield of 7.2 percent.

Other Sources of Information

Investors can use two additional sources of information to evaluate potential bond investments. First, business periodicals can provide information about the economy and interest rates and detailed financial information about a corporation or government entity that issues bonds. You can locate many of these periodicals at your college or public library or on the Internet.

Second, a number of federal agencies provide information that may be useful to bond investors in either printed form or on the Internet. Reports and research published by the Federal Reserve System, the U.S. Treasury, and the Department of Commerce may be used to assess the nation's economy. You can also obtain information that corporations have reported to the Securities and Exchange Commission by accessing the SEC Web site. Finally, state and local governments will provide information about specific municipal bond issues.

Key Web Sites for Bond Investors
www.federalreserve.gov
www.treasury.gov
www.commerce.gov
www.sec.gov

CONCEPTCHECK 11–5

1 What type of information is found on a corporation's Web page? How could this information be used to evaluate a bond issue?

_____

_____

2 Calculate the current market value for the following bonds:

Face Value	Newspaper Quotation	Current Market Value
$1,000	84	
$1,000	92	
$1,000	77.5	

3 Explain what the following bond ratings mean for investors.

Bond Rating	Explanation
Aaa	
BBB	
B	
CC	

Back to   Getting Personal

Reevaluate your Getting Personal answers at the beginning of the chapter. Then answer the following questions.

1. How can you obtain the money needed to establish an emergency fund and an investment program?

_____

_____

2. How do asset allocation and age affect your investment program?

_____

_____

3. Would you consider either government bonds or corporate bonds for your investment program? Explain your answer.

_____

_____

Chapter Summary

Objective 1   Investment goals must be specific and measurable. In addition to developing investment goals, you must make sure your personal financial affairs are in order. The next step is the accumulation of an emergency fund equal to three to nine months' living expenses. Then, and only then, is it time to save the money needed to establish an investment program.

Objective 2   Although each investor may have specific, individual reasons for investing, all investors must consider the factors of safety, risk, income, growth, and liquidity. Especially important is the relationship between safety and risk. Basically, this relationship can be summarized as follows: The potential return for any investment should be directly related to the risk the investor assumes.

Objective 3   Before making the decision to purchase an investment, you should consider the factors of asset allocation, the time your investments will work for you, and your age. Asset allocation is the process of spreading your assets among several different types of investments to lessen risk. In addition to asset allocation, the amount of time before you need your money is a critical component in the type of investments you choose. Finally, your age is a factor that influences investment choices. Younger investors tend to invest a large percentage of their nest egg in growth-oriented investments. On the other hand, older investors tend to be more conservative. You can also improve your investment returns by evaluating all potential investments, monitoring the value of your investments, and keeping accurate and current records.

Objective 4   Conservative investments include savings accounts, certificates of deposit, money market accounts, savings bonds, and government and corporate bonds. Generally, U.S. government bonds are chosen because most investors consider them risk free. Although the level of risk can be higher for federal agency debt issues and municipal bonds, they are also chosen as a conservative investment. Bonds are also issued by corporations to raise capital. Investors purchase corporate bonds for interest income, dollar appreciation of bond value, and repayment at maturity.

Objective 5   Today it is possible to obtain information and trade bonds online via the Internet. In addition to the Internet, *The Wall Street Journal, Barron's,* and some local newspapers provide investors with information they need to evaluate a bond issue. To determine the quality of a bond issue, most investors study the ratings provided by Standard & Poor's and Moody's. Investors can also calculate a current yield to evaluate a decision to buy or sell bond issues.

Key Terms

asset allocation 299	face value 306	registered coupon bond 309
bearer bond 309	general obligation bond 304	revenue bond 304
bond indenture 306	government bond 303	serial bonds 307
call feature 307	line of credit 290	sinking fund 307
convertible bond 307	liquidity 298	speculative investment 294
corporate bond 306	maturity date 306	trustee 306
current yield 312	mortgage bond 307	yield 312
debenture 306	municipal bond 304	zero-coupon bond 309
emergency fund 290	registered bond 309	

Problems and Questions

1. Choose a current issue of *Kiplinger's Personal Finance Magazine, Money,* or *Consumer Reports* and summarize an article that provides suggestions on how you could use your money more effectively.

2. Jane and Bill Collins have total take-home pay of $3,900 a month. Their monthly expenses total $2,800. Calculate the minimum amount this couple needs to establish an emergency fund. How did you calculate this amount?

3. List three personal factors that might lead some investors to emphasize income rather than growth in their investment planning.

4. List three personal factors that might lead some investors to emphasize growth rather than income in their investment planning.

5. How can portfolio management and asset allocation help reduce investment risk? Explain why your age and how the time factor affect the choice of investments for your portfolio.

March	$17.20
April	$18.90
May	$19.80
June	$16.50

September	$15.20
October	$16.70
November	$18.40
December	$19.80

6. Based on the following information, construct a graph that illustrates price movement for a share of the Washington Utilities Bond Fund.

January	$16.60	July	$14.00
February	$15.50	August	$13.10

7. Use the following table to compare U.S. Treasury bills, Treasury notes, and Treasury bonds:

	Minimum Amount	Maturity Range	How Interest Is Paid
Treasury bill			
Treasury note			
Treasury bond			

8. Assume you are in the 35 percent tax bracket and purchase a 5¼ percent municipal bond. Use the formula presented in this chapter to calculate the taxable equivalent yield for this investment.

9. In your own words, explain how each of the following factors is a reason to invest in bonds:

Interest income:	
Dollar appreciation:	
Repayment at maturity:	

10. Assume that three years ago you purchased a corporate bond that pays 6.5 percent. The purchase price was $1,000. Also assume that three years after your bond investment, comparable bonds are paying 8 percent.
    a. What is the annual dollar amount of interest that you receive from your bond investment?

    b. Assuming that comparable bonds are paying 8 percent, what is the approximate dollar price for which you could sell your bond?

    c. In your own words, explain why your bond increased or decreased in value.

11. Choose a corporate bond that you would consider purchasing. Then, using information obtained on the Internet or in the library, answer the questions in Your Personal Financial Plan Sheet 36. Based on your research, would you still purchase this bond?

12. Determine the current yield on a corporate bond investment that has a face value of $1,000, pays 7 percent interest, and has a current market value of $820.

RESEARCHING INVESTMENT PLANNING AND CONSERVATIVE INVESTMENTS

Use the Internet to research the following topics, determine the type of information that is available, and determine how it might affect your investment decisions.

Investment Planning

Web Sources _____

Type of information available _____

_____

Possible influence on your investment decisions _____

_____

Corporate and Government Bonds

Web Sources _____

Type of information available _____

_____

Possible influence on your investment decisions _____

_____

www.mhhe.com/kdh

Case in Point

YOU'D BE A FOOL IF YOU DIDN'T USE THE MOTLEY FOOL WEB SITE!

Ten years ago, Penny and Jim Tilson opened a brokerage account, and each month they contributed what they could afford. Over the years, they had managed to invest almost $30,000 in high-tech dot-com companies. Because their investments increased in value, the value of their investment portfolio had grown to just over $100,000 by January 2000. And yet, by January 2003, the value of their investments had dropped to a little less than $55,000. They had lost almost half the value of their investments in just three years. What happened?

To answer that question, you must understand that the Tilsons were like a lot of people investing in the high-tech surge. They chose high-tech stocks because they offered great returns. Computers were popular, and who would even dream that the bubble would eventually burst? Now the Tilsons admit that they didn't know how to research stocks, mutual funds, or other potential investments. In fact, they didn't even bother to open the statements that their brokerage firm sent out each month. They just assumed that their investments would keep increasing in value. Unfortunately, their wake-up call came when they opened their January 2003 statement in order to obtain some information they needed to file their tax return. That's when they realized how much money they had lost. That's also when they decided that if they were going to continue to invest their money, they needed to learn how to invest.

The Tilsons began their search for educational materials by using their home computer to find investment Web sites. According to Penny, there were many sites offering investment information, but they chose the Motley Fool Web site because they felt pretty foolish after losing so much money. Started by David and Tom Gardner, the goal of the Motley Fool is to help average people make the best decisions about every dollar that they spend, save, and invest. Although just one of many investment Web sites, the Motley Fool is an excellent choice for beginning investors like the Tilsons as well as more experienced investors.

While the Tilsons looked at other Web sites, they kept coming back to the Motley Fool because this site offered investment advice that the average person could understand. According to Jim, learning about the investments was not only rewarding, but also fun. For the first time since they began their investment program, they actually knew how to evaluate their investment options.

Questions

1. The Tilsons lost almost half of the value of their investment portfolio in just three years. What did they do wrong.

2. Visit the Motley Fool Web site at www.fool.com. Describe the type of investment information that is available.

3. If you were beginning an investment program, would you use the information provided by the Motley Fool or similar Web sites? Explain your answer.

Setting Investment Goals

Financial Planning Activities : Determine specific goals for an investment program. Based on short- and long-term objectives for your investment efforts, enter the items requested below.

Suggested Web Sites: www.fool.com   www.americanbank.com

Description of financial need	Amount	Date needed	Investment goal (safety, growth, income)	Level of risk (high, medium, low)	Possible investments to achieve this goal

Note: Sheets 36, 37, and 40 may be used to implement specific investment plans to achieve these goals.

What's Next for Your Personal Financial Plan?
- Use the suggestions listed in this chapter to perform a financial checkup.
- Discuss the importance of investment goals and financial planning with other household members.

Assessing Risk for Investments

Financial Planning Activities: Assess the risk of various investments in relation to your personal risk tolerance and financial goals. List various investments you are considering based on the type and level of risk associated with each.

Suggested Web Sites: www.investor.nasd.com   www.fool.com

Type of Investment	Loss of market value (market risk)	Type of Risk		
		Inflation risk	Interest rate risk	Liquidity risk
High risk				
Moderate risk				
Low risk				

What's Next for Your Personal Financial Plan?

- Identify current economic trends that might increase or decrease the risk associated with your choice of investments.
- Based on the risk associated with the investments you chose, which investment would you choose to obtain your investment goals?

Evaluating Corporate Bonds

Financial Planning Activities: No checklist can serve as a foolproof guide for choosing a corporate or government bond. However, the following questions will help you evaluate a potential bond investment. Use bond Web sites on the Internet and/or library materials to answer these questions about a corporate bond that you believe could help you obtain your investment goals.

Suggested Web Sites: http://bonds.yahoo.com   www.bondsonline.com

Category 1: Information about the Corporation

1. What is the corporation's name? _____

2. What are the corporation's address and telephone number? _____

3. What type of products or services does this firm provide? _____

4. Briefly describe the prospects for this company. (Include significant factors like product development, plans for expansion, plans for mergers, etc.) _____

Category 2: Bond Basics

5. What type of bond is this? _____
6. What is the face value for this bond? _____
7. What is the interest rate for this bond? _____
8. What is the dollar amount of annual interest for this bond? _____
9. When are interest payments made to bondholders? _____
10. Is the corporation currently paying interest as scheduled?   ☐ Yes ☐ No
11. What is the maturity date for this bond? _____
12. What is Moody's rating for this bond? _____
13. What is Standard & Poor's rating for this bond? _____

14. What do these ratings mean? _____

15. What was the original issue date? _____

16. Who is the trustee for this bond issue? _____

17. Is the bond callable? If so, when? _____

18. Is the bond secured with collateral? If so, what? ☐ Yes ☐ No _____

19. How did the corporation use the money from this bond issue? _____

Category 3: Financial Performance

20. What are the firm's earnings per share for the last year? _____
21. Have the firm's earnings increased over the past five years? _____
22. What is the firm's current price-earnings ratio? _____

23. Describe trends for the firm's price-earnings ratio over the past three years. Do these trends show improvement (lower PE ratio) or decline in investment value (higher PE ratio). _____

24. What are the firm's projected earnings for the next year? _____
25. Have sales increased over the last five years? _____

26. Do the analysts indicate that this is a good time to invest in this company? _____

continued

Evaluating Corporate Bonds (continued)

27. Briefly describe any other information that you obtained from Moody's, Standard & Poor's, or other sources of information.

_____

_____

A Word of Caution:

When you use a checklist, there is always a danger of overlooking important relevant information. The above checklist is not a cure-all, but it does provide some very sound questions that you should answer before making a decision to invest in bonds. Quite simply, it is a place to start. If you need other information, *you* are responsible for obtaining it and for determining how it affects your potential investment.

What's Next for Your Personal Financial Plan?

- Talk with various people who have invested in government, municipal, or corporate bonds.
- Discuss with other household members why government, municipal, or corporate bonds might be a logical choice for your investment program.

12 Investing in Stocks

Objectives

In this chapter, you will learn to:

1. Identify the most important features of common and preferred stock.
2. Explain how you can evaluate stock investments.
3. Analyze the numerical measures that cause a stock to increase or decrease in value.
4. Describe how stocks are bought and sold.
5. Explain the trading techniques used by long-term investors and short-term speculators.

Why is this important?

Today, financial planners recommend that investors who want their investments to grow choose stocks or mutual funds that contain growth-oriented stocks. This chapter provides the information you need to become a better stock investor.

 Getting Personal

Why invest in stocks? For each of the following statements, select "yes" or "no" to indicate your behavior regarding these investing activities:

	Yes	No
1. I understand the reasons corporations raise money by selling stocks.	_____	_____
2. I understand the three ways investors can profit from stock investments.	_____	_____
3. My investment plan includes some growth stocks.	_____	_____
4. I know how to evaluate a stock issue.	_____	_____
5. I know the difference between a long-term and short-term investment technique.	_____	_____

After studying this chapter, you will be asked to reconsider your responses to these questions.

Key Web Sites

www.fool.com
www.money.com
www.Kiplinger.com

www.smartmoney.com
www.businessweek.com
http://finance.yahoo.com

Common and Preferred Stock

OBJECTIVE 1

Identify the most important features of common and preferred stock.

Many beginning investors face two concerns when they begin an investment program. First, they don't know where to get the information they need to evaluate potential investments. In reality, more information is available than most investors can read. Yet, as crazy as it sounds, some investors invest in stocks without doing any research at all. Unfortunately, these same uninformed investors often lose money on their investments. As we begin this chapter, you should know that there is no substitute for quality information about a potential investment. *Simply put, good investors know something about the company before they invest their money in the company's stock.*

Second, beginning investors sometimes worry that they won't know what the information means when they do find it. Yet common sense goes a long way when evaluating potential investments. For example, consider the following questions:

1. Is an increase in sales revenues a healthy sign for a corporation? (Answer: yes)
2. Should a firm's net income increase or decrease over time? (Answer: increase)
3. Should a corporation's earnings per share increase or decrease over time? (Answer: increase)

Although the answers to these questions are obvious, you will find more detailed answers to these and other questions in this chapter. In fact, that's what this chapter is all about. We want you to learn how to evaluate a stock and to make money from your investment decisions.

Investors provide the money; the corporation uses the money to generate sales and earn profits; and the stockholders earn a return on their investment. Today a lot of people buy and sell stocks. Why? The most obvious answer is simple: They want larger returns than those more conservative investments offer. As pointed out in the last chapter, significant differences exist between the rates of return offered by stock investments compared to those of U.S. Treasury bills and bonds. Although stocks have returned on average about 10 percent a year since 1900—substantially more than U.S. Treasury bills or bonds—there are periods when stocks have declined in value. For proof, just ask any long-term investor what happened for the three-year period beginning in 2000. And yet, projections by well-respected Roger Ibbotson, chairman of Ibbotson Associates, the investment consulting, software, and research firm, indicate that stock investments will still grow at about 10 percent a year between now and the year 2025.[1] The key to success with any investment program is often the opportunity to allow your investments to work for you over a long period of time. In short, a long-term investment program allows you to ride through the rough times and enjoy the good times. However, before you decide to invest in stocks, you should realize that this type of investment involves more risk and greater potential for loss.

[1] Roger G. Ibbotson, "Predictions of the Past and Forecasts for the Future: 1976–2025," Ibbotson Associates Web site (www.Ibbotson.com), April 22, 2004, Ibbotson Associates, 225 North Michigan Avenue, Chicago, IL 60601.

Since common stockholders are the actual owners of the corporation, they share in its success. But before investing your money, it helps to understand why corporations issue common stock and why investors purchase that stock.

Why Corporations Issue Common Stock

Corporations issue common stock to finance their business start-up costs and help pay for expansion and their ongoing business activities. Corporate managers prefer selling common stock as a method of financing for several reasons.

A FORM OF EQUITY   *Important point:* Stock is equity financing and corporations don't have to repay the money obtained from selling stock. Generally, a stockholder may sell his or her stock to another individual. The selling price is determined by how much a buyer is willing to pay for the stock. Simply put, if the demand for a particular stock increases, the market value of the stock will increase. If the demand for a particular stock decreases, the market value of the stock will decrease. Demand for a stock changes when information about the firm or its future prospects is released to the general public. For example, information about expected sales revenues, earnings, expansions or mergers, or other important developments within the firm can increase or decrease the demand for, and ultimately the market value of, the firm's stock.

DIVIDENDS NOT MANDATORY   *Important point:* Dividends are paid out of profits, and dividend payments must be approved by the corporation's board of directors. Dividend policies vary among corporations, but most firms distribute between 30 and 70 percent of their earnings to stockholders. However, some corporations follow a policy of smaller or no dividend distributions to stockholders. In general, these are rapidly growing firms, like Amazon (online sales), that retain a large share of their earnings for research and development, expansion, or major projects. On the other hand, utility companies, such as Duke Energy, and other financially secure enterprises may distribute 80 to 90 percent of their earnings. Always remember that if a corporation has had a bad year, dividend payments may be reduced or omitted.

VOTING RIGHTS AND CONTROL OF THE COMPANY   In return for the financing provided by selling common stock, management must make concessions to stockholders that may restrict corporate policies. For example, corporations are required by law to have an annual meeting at which stockholders have a right to vote, usually casting one vote per share of stock. Stockholders may vote in person or by proxy. A **proxy** is a legal form that lists the issues to be decided at a stockholders' meeting and requests that stockholders transfer their voting rights to some individual or individuals. The common stockholders elect the board of directors and must approve major changes in corporate policies.

proxy A legal form that lists the issues to be decided at a stockholders' meeting and requests that stockholders transfer their voting rights to some individual or individuals.

Why Investors Purchase Common Stock

How do you make money by buying common stock? Basically, there are three ways: income from dividends, dollar appreciation of stock value, and the possibility of increased value from stock splits.

INCOME FROM DIVIDENDS   While the corporation's board members are under no legal obligation to pay dividends, most board members like to keep stockholders happy (and prosperous). Few things will unite stockholders into a powerful opposition

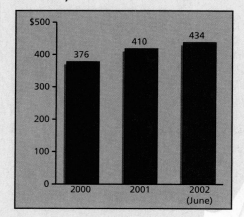

Source: Statistical Abstract of the United States, 2003, U.S. Bureau of the Census Web site (www.census.gov), May 14, 2004 (Washington, DC: U.S. Government Printing Office), p. 520.

record date The date on which a stockholder must be registered on the corporation's books in order to receive dividend payments.

force more rapidly than omitted or lowered dividends. Therefore, board members usually declare dividends if the corporation's after-tax profits are sufficient for them to do so. Since dividends are a distribution of profits, investors must be concerned about future after-tax profits. In short, how secure is the dividend?

Corporate dividends for common stock may take the form of cash, additional stock, or company products. However, the last type of dividend is extremely unusual. If the board of directors declares a cash dividend, each common stockholder receives an equal amount per share. Although dividend policies vary, most corporations pay dividends on a quarterly basis.

Notice in Exhibit 12–1 that Chicago Rivet and Machine Company has declared a quarterly dividend of $0.18 per share to stockholders who own the stock on the record date of June 4, 2004. The **record date** is the date on which a stockholder must be registered on the corporation's books in order to receive dividend payments. When a stock is traded around the record date, the company must determine whether the buyer or the seller is entitled to the dividend. To solve this problem, this rule is followed: *Dividends remain with the stock until two business days before the record date.* On the second day before the record date, the stock begins selling *ex-dividend.* Investors who purchase an ex-dividend stock are not entitled to receive dividends for that quarter, and the dividend is paid to the previous owner of the stock.

For example, Chicago Rivet and Machine declared a quarterly dividend of $0.18 per share to stockholders who owned its stock on Friday, June 4. The stock went ex-dividend on Wednesday, June 2, two *business* days before the June 4 date. A stockholder who purchased the stock on June 2 or after was not entitled to this quarterly dividend payment. The actual dividend payment was paid on June 18 to stockholders who owned the stock on the record date. Investors are generally very conscious of the date on which a stock goes ex-dividend, and the dollar value of the stock may go down by the value of the quarterly dividend.

DOLLAR APPRECIATION OF STOCK VALUE   In most cases, you purchase stock and then hold onto that stock for a period of time. If the market value of the stock increases, you must decide whether to sell the stock at the higher price or continue to hold it. If you decide to sell the stock, the dollar amount of difference between the purchase price and the selling price represents your profit.

Let's assume that on October 28, 2002, you purchased 100 shares of General Motors stock at a cost of $35 a share. Your cost for the stock was $3,500 plus $55 in commission charges, for a total investment of $3,555. (Note: Commissions, a topic covered later in this chapter, are charged when you purchase stock *and* when you sell stock.) Let's also assume you held your 100 shares until May 10, 2004, and then sold them for $45 a share. During the investment period you owned General Motors, the company paid dividends totaling $3.00 a share. Exhibit 12–2 shows your return on the investment. In this case, you made money because of dividend distributions and through an increase in stock value from $35 to $45 per share. As Exhibit 12–2 shows, your total return is $1,190. Of course, if the stock's value should decrease, or if the firm's board of directors reduces or votes to omit dividends, your return may be less than the original investment. For help in deciding if it's time to sell stock, read the nearby Personal Finance in Practice feature.

Corporate Dividend News				
DIVIDENDS REPORTED MAY 11				
Company	**Period**	**AMT**	**Payable Date**	**Record Date**
Regular				
Blackrock Inc. A	Q	.25	6-23-04	6-07
CP Ships Ltd	Q	.04	6-04-04	5-20
Chicago Rivet	Q	.18	6-18-04	6-04
Ensco Int'l	Q	.025	6-16-04	5-28
Fin'l Sec Quibs	Q	.429688	6-15-04	5-31
Jinpan Int'l Ltd	—	t.10	7-16-04	7-06
PXRE Grp	Q	t.06	6-01-04	5-17
Scottish Re Grp	Q	t.05	6-02-04	5-19
TV Azteca ADS	—	t.1724	5-24-04	5-17
Tatneft (AO) ADS	—	t.2072	—	5-17
UBS Pfd 7.25%pf	Q	t.45313	6-15-04	5-31

Source: Republished with permission of Dow Jones, Inc., from *The Wall Street Journal,* May 12, 2004; permission conveyed through Copyright Clearance Center, Inc.

Exhibit [12–1]

Typical Information on Corporate Dividends as Presented in *The Wall Street Journal*

Assumptions			
100 shares of common stock purchased October 28, 2002, sold May 10, 2004; dividends of $3.00 per share for the investment period.			
Costs when purchased		**Return when sold**	
100 shares @ $35 =	$3,500	100 shares @ $45 =	$4,500
Plus commission	+ 55	Minus commission	− 55
Total investment	$3,555	Total return	$4,445
Transaction summary			
Total return		$4,445	
Minus total investment		− 3,555	
Profit from stock sale		$ 890	
Plus dividends		+ 300	
Total return for the transaction		$1,190	

Exhibit [12–2]

Sample Stock Transaction for General Motors

Personal Finance in Practice

Here are some suggestions for deciding when you should sell a stock.

1. *Follow your stock's value.* Too often, investors purchase a stock and then forget about it. A much better approach is to graph the dollar value of your stock on a weekly basis.

   How could this suggestion help you decide if it is time to sell a stock?

   _____

   _____

2. *Watch the company's financials.* Smart investors evaluate a stock investment before they make it. The smartest investors use all the available information to continuously evaluate their stocks.

   How could this suggestion help you decide if it is time to sell a stock?

   _____

   _____

3. *Track the firm's product line.* If the firm's products become obsolete and the company fails to introduce state-of-the-art new products, its sales—and, ultimately, profits—may take a nosedive. The failure to introduce new products may destroy the firm's ability to compete.

   How could this suggestion help you decide if it is time to sell a stock?

   _____

   _____

4. *Monitor economic developments.* An economic recession or an economic recovery may cause the value of a stock investment to increase or decrease. Also, watch the unemployment rate, inflation rate, interest rates, productivity rates, and similar economic indicators that may affect the value of stocks in your investment portfolio.

   How could this suggestion help you decide if it is time to sell a stock?

   _____

   _____

5. *Be patient.* The secret of success for making money with stocks is time. As pointed out earlier in this chapter, stocks have returned approximately 10 percent before adjusting for inflation each year since 1900. Assuming you purchase quality stocks, your investments will eventually increase in value.

   How could this suggestion help you decide if it is time to sell a stock?

   _____

   _____

Apply *Yourself!*

Objective 1

Use the Internet to identify a stock split. Then graph the price of the stock each day for a week before the split and each day for a week after the split. Describe your findings.

stock split A procedure in which the shares of stock owned by existing stockholders are divided into a larger number of shares.

POSSIBILITY OF INCREASED VALUE FROM STOCK SPLITS

Investors can also increase potential profits through a stock split. A **stock split** is a procedure in which the shares of stock owned by existing stockholders are divided into a larger number of shares. In 2004, for example, the board of directors of Yahoo!, the well-known search engine, approved a 2-for-1 stock split. After the stock split, a stockholder who had previously owned 100 shares now owned 200 shares. The most common stock splits are 2-for-1, 3-for-1, and 4-for-1.

Why do corporations split their stock? In many cases, a firm's management has a theoretical ideal price range for the firm's stock. If the market value of the stock rises above the ideal range, a stock split brings the market value back in line. In the case of Yahoo!, the 2-for-1 stock split reduced the market value to one-half of the stock's value on the day prior to the split. The lower market value for each share of stock was the result of dividing the dollar value of the company by a larger number of shares of common stock. Also, a decision to split a company's stock and the resulting lower market value make the stock more attractive to the investing public. This attraction is based on the belief that most corporations split their stock only when their financial future is improving and on the upswing.

Be warned: There are no guarantees that a stock's market value will go up after a split. This is important to understand, because investors often think that a stock split leads to immediate profits. Nothing could be further from the truth. Here's why. The total market capitalization—the value of the company's stock multiplied by the number of shares outstanding—does not change because a corporation splits its stock. A company that has a market capitalization of $100 million before a 2-for-1 stock split is still worth $100 million after the split. Simply put, there is twice as much stock, but each share is worth half of its previous value before the stock split occurred. If a stock's value does increase after a stock split, it increases because of the firm's financial performance after the split and not just because there are more shares of stock.

Preferred Stock

In addition to or instead of purchasing common stock, you may purchase preferred stock. The most important priority an investor in preferred stock enjoys is receiving cash dividends *before* common stockholders are paid any cash dividends. Unlike the amount of the dividend on common stock, the dollar amount of the dividend on preferred stock is known before the stock is purchased. The dividend amount is either a stated amount of money for each share of preferred stock or a certain percentage of the par value of the stock. The **par value** is an assigned (and often arbitrary) dollar value that is printed on a stock certificate. For example, if the par value for a preferred stock issue is $50 and the dividend rate is 4 percent, the dollar amount of the dividend is $2 ($50 × 4% = $2).

par value An assigned (and often arbitrary) dollar value that is printed on a stock certificate.

Preferred stocks are often referred to as "middle" investments because they represent an investment midway between common stock (an ownership position for the stockholder) and corporate bonds (a creditor position for the bondholder). When compared to corporate bonds, the yield on preferred stocks is often smaller than the yield on bonds. When compared to common stocks, preferred stocks are safer investments that offer more secure dividends. They are often purchased by individuals who need a predictable source of income greater than offered by common stock investments. They are also purchased by other corporations, because corporations receive a tax break on the dividend income from preferred stock. For all other investors, preferred stocks lack the growth potential that common stocks offer and the safety of many corporate bond issues. As a result, preferred stocks are generally considered a poor investment for most individuals.

While preferred stock does not represent a legal debt that must be repaid, if the firm is dissolved or declares bankruptcy, preferred stockholders do have first claim to the corporation's assets after creditors (including bondholders).

When compared to corporations selling common stock, preferred stock is used less often by only a few corporations, yet it is an alternative method of financing that may attract investors who do not wish to buy common stock. Preferred stock, like common stock, is equity financing that does not have to be repaid. And dividends on preferred stock, as on common stock, may be omitted by action of the board of directors. To make preferred stock issues more attractive, some corporations may offer two additional features.

If the corporation's board of directors believes that omitting dividends is justified, it can vote to omit both the dividends paid to common stockholders and the dividends paid to preferred stockholders. One way preferred stockholders can protect themselves against omitted dividends is to purchase cumulative preferred stock. *Cumulative preferred stock* is stock whose unpaid dividends accumulate and must be paid before any cash dividend is paid to the common stockholders. If a corporation does not pay dividends to the cumulative preferred stockholders during one dividend period, the amount of the missed dividends is added to the following period's preferred dividends. If you own noncumulative preferred stock, an omitted dividend will not be made up later.

The second feature that makes preferred stock attractive is the conversion feature. *Convertible preferred stock* can be exchanged, at the stockholder's option, for a specified number of shares of common stock. The conversion feature provides the investor with the added safety of preferred stock and the possibility of greater speculative gain through conversion to common stock.

All the information relating to the number of shares of common stock that may be obtained through conversion of preferred stock is stated in the corporate records and is usually printed on the preferred stock certificate. For example, assume Martin & Martin Manufacturing Corporation has issued a convertible preferred stock. Each share of preferred stock in this issue is convertible into two shares of common stock. Assume the market price of Martin & Martin's convertible preferred stock is $24 and the stock pays an annual dividend of $1.60 a share. Also assume the market price of the company's common stock is $9 and the common stock currently pays an annual dividend of $0.54 a share. Under these circumstances, you would keep the preferred stock. If the market price of the common stock increased to above $12 a share, however, you would have an incentive to exercise the conversion option.

The decision to convert preferred stock to common stock is complicated by three factors. First, the dividends paid on preferred stock are more secure than the dividends paid on common stock. Second, the amount of the dividend for preferred stock is generally higher than the amount of the dividend for common stock. Third, because of the conversion option, the market value of convertible preferred stock usually increases as the market value of common stock increases.

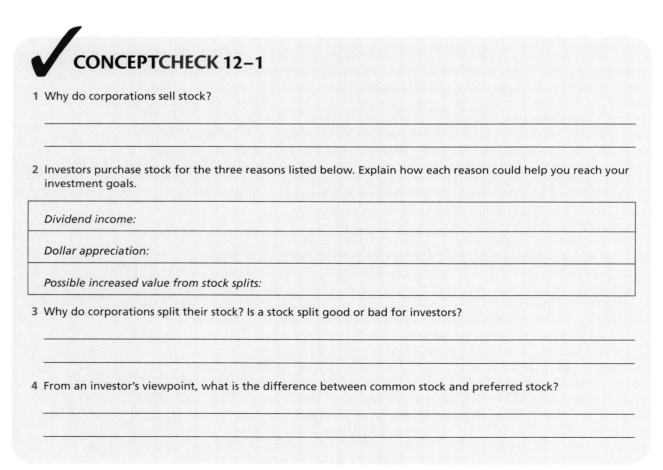

✔ CONCEPTCHECK 12–1

1 Why do corporations sell stock?

_____

_____

2 Investors purchase stock for the three reasons listed below. Explain how each reason could help you reach your investment goals.

Dividend income:	
Dollar appreciation:	
Possible increased value from stock splits:	

3 Why do corporations split their stock? Is a stock split good or bad for investors?

_____

_____

4 From an investor's viewpoint, what is the difference between common stock and preferred stock?

_____

_____

Evaluating a Stock Issue

Many investors expect to earn a 10 percent or higher return on their investments, yet they are unwilling to spend the time required to become a good investor. In fact, many people purchase investments without doing *any* research. They wouldn't buy a car without a test drive or purchase a home without comparing different houses, but for some unknown reason they invest without doing their homework. The truth is that there is no substitute for a few hours of detective work when choosing an investment. This section explains how to evaluate a potential stock investment. A wealth of information is available to stock investors, and a logical place to start the evaluation process for stock is with the classification of different types of stock investments described in Exhibit 12–3. Once you have identified a type of stock that may help you obtain your investment goals, you may want to use the Internet to evaluate a potential investment.

OBJECTIVE 2
Explain how you can evaluate stock investments.

The Internet

In this section, we examine some Web sites that are logical starting points when evaluating a stock investment, but there are many more than those described. Let's begin with information about the corporation that is available on the Internet.

Today most corporations have a Web site, and the information these pages provide is especially useful. First, it is easily accessible. All you have to do is type in the corporation's URL address or use a search engine to locate the corporation's home page. Second, the information on the Web site may be more up to date and thorough than printed material obtained from the corporation or outside sources. Look at the financial information on the investor page for General Electric displayed in Exhibit 12–4. By clicking on a button, you can access General Electric's latest annual report, information on the firm's earnings, and other financial factors that could affect the value of the company's stock.

Exhibit [12–3]

Evaluating Stocks

When evaluating a stock investment, investors often classify stocks into the following eight categories.

Type of Stock	Characteristics of This Type of Investment
Blue chip	A safe investment that generally attracts conservative investors.
Income	An investment that pays higher-than-average dividends.
Growth	A stock issued by a corporation that has the potential of earning profits above the average profits of all firms in the economy.
Cyclical	A stock that follows the business cycle of advances and declines in the economy.
Defensive	A stock that remains stable during declines in the economy.
Large cap	A stock issued by a corporation that has a large amount of capitalization in excess of $5 billion.
Small cap	A stock issued by a company that has a capitalization of $500 million or less.
Penny	A stock that typically sells for less than $1 per share.

Exhibit [12–4]   Financial Information Available on General Electric's Investor Relations Web Page

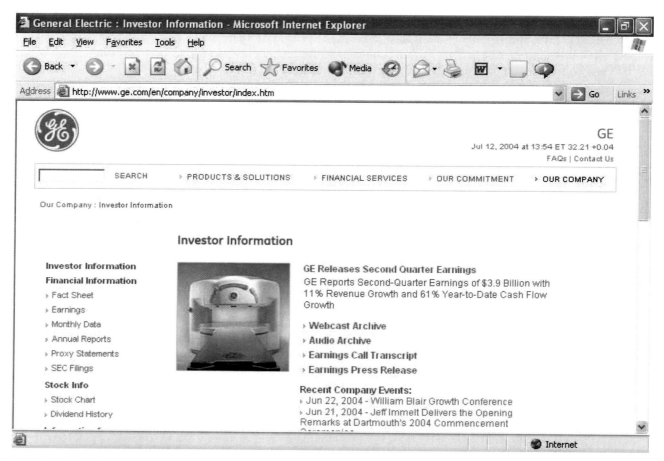

You can also use Web sites like Yahoo! and other search engines to obtain information about stock investments. Take a look at a small portion of the opening page of the Yahoo! Finance Web site (http://finance.yahoo.com) in Exhibit 12–5. The entire Web site provides a wealth of information. For example, under the stock research category, there is a stock screener that will help you pick stock investments. You can also get current market values by entering a corporation's stock symbol and clicking on the Go button at the top of the page. If you don't know the symbol, just click on Symbol Lookup and follow the directions. In addition to the current market value, the Yahoo! Finance Web site provides even more specific information about a particular company. By clicking on the buttons for the quotes, charts, company, and financial topics that are part of the screen for each corporation, you can obtain even more information. How about picking a company like Texas Instruments (symbol TXN) or Procter & Gamble (symbol PG) and going exploring on the Internet? To begin, enter the Web address for Yahoo! Finance. Then enter the symbol for one of the above corporations in the Quotes section. You'll be surprised at the amount of information you can obtain with a click of your mouse.

In addition, you can use professional advisory services like Standard & Poor's Financial Information Services (www.standardpoors.com), Mergent Online (www.fisonline.com), and Value Line (www.valueline.com). While some of the information provided by these services is free, there is a charge for the more detailed information you may need to

Exhibit [12–5]   A Portion of the Opening Page for the Yahoo! Finance Web site

Source: Reproduced with permission of Yahoo! Inc. © 2004 by Yahoo! Inc. Yahoo! and Yahoo! logo are trademarks of Yahoo! Inc.

evaluate a stock investment. For more information about professional advisory services and the type of information they provide, read the next section.

Stock Advisory Services

In addition to the Internet, sources of information you can use to evaluate potential stock investments are the printed materials provided by stock advisory services. The information ranges from simple alphabetical listings to detailed financial reports.

Standard & Poor's reports, Value Line, and Mergent are three widely used advisory services that provide detailed research for stock investors. Here we will examine a detailed report for Reebok International, Ltd., a worldwide manufacturer and distributor of athletic footwear, fitness equipment, and apparel, that is published in *Mergent's Handbook of Common Stocks* (see Exhibit 12–6).

The basic report illustrated in Exhibit 12–6 consists of six main sections. The top section provides information about stock prices and capitalization, earnings, and dividends. The Business Summary describes the company's major operations in detail. The next section, Recent Developments, provides current information about the company's net income and sales revenue. The Prospects section describes the company's outlook. The Annual Financial Data section provides important data on the company for the past 10 years. Among the topics included in this section are total revenues, percent of operating

Key Web Sites for Investing Advice
www.standardpoors.com
www.fisonline.com
www.valueline.com

Exhibit [12–6]

Mergent's Report for
Reebok International, Ltd.

REEBOK INTERNATIONAL, LTD.

Exchange	Symbol	Price	52Wk Range	Yield	P/E
NYS	RBK	$37.81 (2/20/2004)	37.81–37.81	0.79	17.92

*7 Year Price Score 138.7   *NYSE Composite Index=100   *12 Month Price Score 102.7

Interim Earnings (per Share)

Qtr.	Mar	Jun	Sep	Dec
2000	0.56	0.19	0.56	0.09
2001	0.68	0.24	0.66	0.08
2002	0.58	0.39	0.81	0.26
2003	0.63	0.41	0.96	...

Interim Dividends (per Share)

Amt	Decl	Ex	Rec	Pay
0.075S	2/15/1996	3/8/1996	3/12/1996	4/2/1996
0.075S	5/7/1996	6/7/1996	6/11/1996	7/2/1996
0.075S	7/25/1996	9/9/1996	9/11/1996	10/2/1996
0.15S	7/29/2003	8/15/2003	8/19/2003	9/3/2003

Indicated Div: $0.30

Valuation Analysis

		Institutional Holding	
Forecast P/E	15.50	No of Institutions	
Trailing P/E	17.92	30	
Market Cap	$2.3 Billion	Shares	
Book Value	927.7 Million	999,895	
Price/Book	2.15	% Held	
Price/Sales	0.61	–	

Business Summary – Rubber Products (MIC: 11.6 SIC: 3021 NAIC:316211)

Reebok International is engaged primarily in the design and marketing of sports and fitness products, including footwear and apparel. Co. has four major brand groups. The Reebok Division designs, produces and markets sports, fitness and casual footwear, apparel and accessories under the *Reebok*®brand. Rockport designs, produces and distributes comfort footwear under the *Rockport*® brand. Ralph Lauren Footwear, a subsidiary of Co., is responsible for footwear and certain apparel sold under the *Ralph Lauren*®and *Polo Sport*®brands. The Greg Norman Division produces a range of men's apparel and accessories marketed under the *Greg Norman* name and logo.

Recent Developments

For the quarter ended Sep 30 2003, net income advanced 17.4% to $62.7 million from $53.4 million in the prior-year quarter. Net sales increased 14.2% to $1.04 billion from $911.6 million the previous year. Net sales benefited from growth in sales of licensed sports apparel, as well as favorable foreign currency exchange rates. In the U.S., footwear sales increased 16.0% to $279.1 million, while apparel sales climbed 31.1% to $207.9 million. International footwear sales increased 11.0% to $207.4 million, while international apparel sales grew 11.8% to $203.2 million. Rockport sales declined 8.3% to $96.6 million. Other brand sales improved 21.0% to $46.6 million.

Prospects

Going forward, Co. should benefit from the investments it is making in product marketing and infrastructure improvements, despite difficult retail conditions in many of its key markets. In an effort to drive growth, Co. will build upon the performance of the *Reebok* brand, leveraging its strength in sports and its partnerships with the NBA and NFL. In addition to the *RBk* and *Vector* footwear performance products, Co. plans to promote its Reebok Classic products. Moreover, Co. will strive to expand the reach of its sports licensed products, and with the NFL season under way and the NBA season kicking off, it is well positioned to have another successful year.

Annual Financial Data

(US$ in Thousands)	12/31/2002	12/31/2001	12/31/2000	12/31/1999	12/31/1998	12/31/1997	12/31/1996	12/31/1995	12/31/1994	12/31/1993
Earnings Per Share	2.04	1.66	1.40	0.20	0.42	2.32	2.00	2.07	3.02	2.53
Cash Flow Per Share	3.29	2.69	3.17	4.98	2.66	2.17	4.08	2.12	2.04	1.61
Tang. Book Val. Per Share	13.57	10.89	9.45	8.17	8.05	8.26	5.57	11.10	11.04	8.98
Dividends Per Share	...	...	...	...	...	...	0.30	0.30	0.30	0.30
Dividend Payout %	...	...	...	...	...	...	15.00	14.4928	9.9338	11.8577
Income Statement										
Total Revenues	3,127,872	2,992,878	2,865,240	2,891,237	3,205,425	3,637,441	3,482,929	3,484,576	3,287,583	2,893,933
Total Indirect Exp.	954,596	913,941	915,387	977,128	1,046,631	1,073,590	1,069,202	1,003,798	893,935	779,796
Depreciation & Amort.	32,033	36,619	46,201	48,643	48,017	47,423	42,927	39,579	37,400	35,553
Operating Income	215,449	184,440	170,167	130,195	121,329	269,802	269,305	366,694	427,510	394,268
Income Taxes	60,570	48,300	49,000	10,093	11,925	12,490	84,083	99,753	153,994	139,832
Equity Earnings/Minority Int.	(3,289)	(4,780)	(5,927)	(6,900)	(1,178)	(10,476)	(14,635)	(11,423)	(8,896)	(8,261)
Net Income	126,458	102,726	80,878	11,045	23,927	135,119	138,950	164,798	254,478	223,415
Average Shs. Outstg.	68,013	65,495	57,724	56,530	57,029	58,309	69,619	79,487	84,311	88,348
Balance Sheet										
Cash & Cash Equivalents	642,367	413,281	268,665	281,744	180,070	209,766	232,365	80,393	83,936	79,347
Total Current Assets	1,613,567	1,294,695	1,225,205	1,243,118	1,361,796	1,464,820	1,463,088	1,342,929	1,337,444	1,127,115
Net Property	134,767	133,952	141,833	178,111	172,585	156,959	185,292	192,033	164,848	130,607
Total Assets	1,860,772	1,543,173	1,463,046	1,564,128	1,739,624	1,756,097	1,786,184	1,656,223	1,649,461	1,391,711
Total Current Liabilities	579,920	449,406	488,139	623,903	612,284	577,453	516,961	431,948	505,588	396,358
Long-Term Obligations	353,329	351,210	345,015	370,302	554,432	639,355	854,099	254,178	131,799	134,207
Net Stockholders' Equity	884,570	719,938	607,863	528,816	524,377	507,157	381,234	895,289	990,505	846,617
Net Working Capital	1,033,647	845,289	737,066	619,215	749,512	887,367	946,127	910,981	831,856	730,757
Year-end Shs. Outstg.	60,224	59,038	57,492	56,269	56,590	53,375	55,840	74,804	80,945	83,691
Statistical Record										
Operating Profit Margin %	6.88	6.16	5.93	4.50	3.78	7.41	7.73	10.52	13.00	13.62
Return on Equity %	14.90	14.30	13.30	2.10	4.60	26.60	36.44	18.40	25.69	26.38
Return on Assets %	7.10	6.70	5.50	0.70	1.40	7.70	7.77	9.95	15.42	16.05
Debt/Total Assets %	18.98	22.75	23.58	23.67	31.87	36.40	47.81	15.34	7.99	9.64
Price Range	29.69-21.70	34.44-18.86	27.44-7.09	22.52-7.84	32.85-12.57	52.20-27.99	44.02-25.31	37.57-24.58	38.41-27.26	35.78-21.70
P/E Ratio	14.55-10.64	20.75-11.36	19.60-5.06	112.60-39.20	78.21-29.93	22.50-12.06	22.01-12.66	18.15-11.87	12.72-9.03	14.14-8.58
Average Yield %	N/A	N/A	N/A	N/A	N/A	N/A	0.93	0.91	0.92	1.04

Address: 1895 J.W. Foster Boulevard, Canton, MA 02021, United States **Telephone:** (781) 401–5000 **Fax:** (781) 401–7402 **Web Site:** www.reebok.com	**Officers:** Paul B. Fireman – Chmn., C.E.O. Jay M. Margolis – Pres., C.O.O. Kenneth I. Watchmaker – Exec. V.P., C.F.O. David A. Perdue – Exec. V.P. Martin Coles – Exec. V.P.	**Transfer Agents:** American Stock Transfer &Trust Company, New York, NY **Auditors:** Ernst &Young LLP **Investor Contact:** Neil Kerman, 781–401–7152 **Legal Counsel:** Ropes &Gray

728

Source: *Mergent's Handbook of Common Stocks,* Winter 2003–2004 (New York: Mergent, 2004).

Apply *Yourself!*

Objective 2

Go to the library and use Standard & Poor's, Value-Line, or Mergent to research a stock that you think would help you obtain your investment goals.

profit, return on equity, and net income. The final section of the report states, among other things, who its auditors are, where its principal office is located, who its transfer agent is, and who its main corporate officers are. While other stock advisory services provide basically the same types of information as that in Exhibit 12–6, it is the investor's job to interpret such information and decide whether the company's stock is a good investment.

How to Read the Financial Section of the Newspaper

The Wall Street Journal and most metropolitan newspapers contain information about stocks listed on the New York Stock Exchange, the American Stock Exchange, other major stock exchanges, and the over-the-counter market. Although not all newspapers print exactly the same information, they usually provide the basic information. Stocks are listed alphabetically, so your first task is to move down the table to find the stock you're interested in. Then, to read the stock quotation, you simply read across the table. In addition to current and historical prices, most newspapers provide information on dividends, yield percentage, price-to-earnings ratio, volume, and net change.

If a corporation has more than one stock issue, the common stock is always listed first. Then the preferred stock issues are listed and indicated by the letters *pf* behind the firm's name.

Corporate News

The federal government requires corporations selling new issues of securities to disclose in a prospectus information about corporate earnings, assets and liabilities, products or services, and the qualifications of top management. In addition to a prospectus, all publicly owned corporations send their stockholders an annual report that contains detailed financial data. Even if you're not a stockholder, you can obtain an annual report from the corporation. For most corporations, all it takes is a call to a toll-free phone number, a written request to the corporation's headquarters, or a visit to a corporation's Web site.

In addition to corporate publications, you can access the Securities and Exchange Commission Web site (www.sec.gov) to obtain financial and other important information that a corporation has supplied to the federal government. Finally, many periodicals, including *Business Week, Fortune, Forbes, Money, Kiplinger's Personal Finance Magazine,* and similar publications contain information about stock investing.

 CONCEPTCHECK 12-2

1 Assume that you are considering a $2,500 investment in common stock issued by Microsoft. How would you go about researching your potential investment?

_____

_____

2 Describe how each of the following sources of investment information could help you evaluate a stock investment.

Source of Information	Type of Information	How Could This Help
The Internet		
A newspaper		
Advisory services		
Government publications		
Business periodicals		

Continued

3 What is the difference between a prospectus and an annual report?

_____

_____

4 Describe other sources of information that could be used to obtain information about a corporation.

_____

_____

Numerical Measures That Influence Investment Decisions

OBJECTIVE 3

Analyze the numerical measures that cause a stock to increase or decrease in value.

How do you determine whether the time is right to buy or sell a particular stock? Good question! Unfortunately, there is no simple answer. In addition to the material in the last section, Evaluating a Stock Issue, many investors rely on numerical measures that include current earnings, projected earnings, current yield, and similar calculations to decide when to invest in a stock. These same calculations can also help investors decide if it is time to sell a stock. We begin this section by examining the relationship between a stock's price and a corporation's earnings.

Why Corporate Earnings Are Important

Many analysts believe that a corporation's ability or inability to generate earnings in the future may be one of the most significant factors that account for an increase or decrease in the value of a stock. Simply put, higher earnings generally equate to higher stock value. Unfortunately, the reverse is also true. If a corporation's earnings decline, generally the stock's value will also decline. Corporate earnings are reported in the firm's annual report. You can also obtain information about a corporation's current earnings by using one of the professional advisory services or accessing the Yahoo! Finance Web site described in the last section.

In addition, many investors also calculate earnings per share to evaluate the financial health of a corporation. **Earnings per share** are a corporation's after-tax earnings divided by the number of outstanding shares of a firm's common stock. For example, assume that in 2004, XYZ Corporation has after-tax earnings of $2,500,000. Also assume that XYZ has 1,000,000 shares of common stock. This means XYZ's earnings per share are $2.50, as illustrated below.

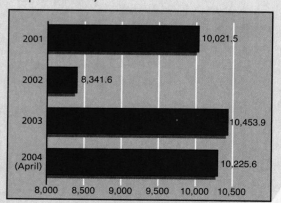

DID YOU KNOW?

The Dow Jones Industrial Average measures 30 different stocks that are considered leaders in the economy. (Closing values as of end of December, except as noted.)

Year	Value
2001	10,021.5
2002	8,341.6
2003	10,453.9
2004 (April)	10,225.6

8,000 8,500 9,000 9,500 10,000 10,500

Sources: _Statistical Abstract of the United States, 2003,_ U.S. Bureau of the Census Web site (www.census.gov), May 14, 2004 (Washington, DC: U.S. Government Printing Office), p. 758, and Yahoo! Finance Web site (http://finance.yahoo.com), May 14, 2004, Yahoo!, Inc., 201 First Avenue, Sunnyvale, CA 94089.

$$\text{Earnings per share} = \frac{\text{After-tax income}}{\text{Number of shares outstanding}}$$

$$= \frac{\$2,500,000}{1,000,000}$$

$$= \$2.50$$

Most stockholders consider the amount of earnings per share important because it is a measure of the company's profitability. No meaningful average for this measure exists, mainly because the number of shares of a firm's stock is subject to change via stock splits and stock dividends. *As a general rule, however, an increase in earnings per share is a healthy sign for any corporation and its stockholders.*

Another calculation, the price-earnings ratio, can be used to evaluate a potential stock investment. The **price-earnings (PE) ratio** is the price of a share of stock divided by the corporation's earnings per share of stock. For example, assume XYZ Corporation's common stock is selling for $50 a share. As determined earlier, XYZ's earnings per share are $2.50. XYZ's price-earnings ratio is, therefore, 20, as illustrated below.

earnings per share A corporation's after-tax earnings divided by the number of outstanding shares of a firm's common stock.

price-earnings (PE) ratio The price of a share of stock divided by the corporation's earnings per share of stock.

$$\text{Price-earnings (PE) ratio} = \frac{\text{Price per share}}{\text{Earnings per share}}$$

$$= \frac{\$50.00}{\$2.50}$$

$$= 20$$

The price-earnings ratio is a key factor that serious investors use to evaluate stock investments. *A low price-earnings ratio indicates that a stock may be a good investment, and a high price-earnings ratio indicates that it may be a poor investment.* Generally, you should study the price-earnings ratio for a corporation over a period of time. For example, if XYZ's price-earnings ratio has ranged from 17 to 45 over the past five years, its current ratio of 20 indicates that it is a potentially good investment. If XYZ's current price-earnings ratio was 45—at the high end of the range—it might be a poor investment at this time. It is also possible to use price-earnings ratios to compare firms within the same industry. Generally, the firm with the lowest PE ratio is the better investment.

Both earnings per share and the price-earnings ratio are based on historical numbers. In other words, this is what the company has done in the past—not what it will do in the future. With this fact in mind, many investors will also look at earnings estimates for a corporation. The Yahoo! Finance Web site or similar financial Web sites provide earnings estimates for major corporations. At the time of publication, for example, Yahoo! Finance provided the following earnings estimates for Home Depot, the world's largest home improvement store.[2]

Apply *Yourself!*

Objective 3

Use the Yahoo Finance Web site (http://finance.yahoo.com) to locate the projected earnings for Microsoft, Procter & Gamble, and GE. (*Hint:* Look for a button marked Analyst's Estimates.)

Home Depot	This Year	Next Year
Yearly earnings estimates	$2.09 per share	$2.41 per share

From an investor's standpoint, a projected increase in earnings from $2.09 per share to $2.41 per share is a good sign. In the case of Home Depot, these estimates were determined by surveying more than 20 different analysts who track the Home Depot Corporation. By using the same projected earnings amount, it is possible to calculate a projected price-earnings ratio or a projected price per share of stock. Of course, you should remember that these are estimates and are not "etched in stone." An increase or decrease in interest rates, higher or lower unemployment rates, terrorist attacks, and changes that affect the economy or the company's sales and profit amounts could cause analysts to revise the above estimates.

[2]Yahoo! Finance Web site (http://finance.yahoo.com), May 13, 2004, Yahoo!, Inc., 701 First Avenue, Sunnyvale, CA 94089.

Figure It Out!

CALCULATIONS CAN IMPROVE INVESTMENT DECISIONS!

Numbers, numbers, numbers! The truth is that if you are going to be a good investor, you must learn the numbers game. As mentioned in the text, many calculations can help you gauge the value of a potential stock investment. These same calculations can help you decide if the time is right to sell a stock investment.

Now it's your turn. Use the following financial information for Bozo Oil Company to calculate the earnings per share, price-earnings (PE) ratio, and current yield:

After-tax income, $6,250,000
Dividend amount, $1.20
Price per share, $30
Number of shares outstanding, 5,000,000

Calculation	Calculation Formula	Your Answer	Indications
Earnings per share			
Price-earnings (PE) ratio			
Current yield			

Other Factors That Influence the Price of a Stock

current yield The yearly dollar amount of income generated by an investment divided by the investment's current market value.

One of the calculations investors use most frequently to monitor the value of their investments is the current yield. The **current yield** is the yearly dollar amount of income generated by an investment divided by the investment's current market value. For example, assume you purchase stock in Ford Motor Company. Also assume Ford pays an annual dividend of $0.40 per share and is currently selling for $15 a share. The current dividend yield is 2.7 percent, calculated as follows:

$$\text{Current yield} = \frac{\text{Annual income amount}}{\text{Current market value}}$$

$$= \frac{\$0.40}{\$15}$$

$$= 0.027, \text{ or } 2.7 \text{ percent}$$

As a general rule, an increase in current yield is a healthy sign for any investment. A current yield of 4 percent is better than a 2.7 percent current yield.

Although the current yield calculation is useful, you should also consider whether the investment is increasing or decreasing in dollar value. **Total return** is a calculation that includes not only the yearly dollar amount of income but also any increase or decrease in the original purchase price of the investment. The following formula is used to calculate total return:

total return A calculation that includes the yearly dollar amount of income as well as any increase or decrease in the original purchase price of the investment.

$$\text{Total return} = \text{Current return} + \text{Capital gain}$$

While this concept may be used for any investment, let's illustrate it by using the assumptions for Ford stock presented in the preceding example. Assume, in addition, that you own 100 shares of the stock that you purchased for $15.00 a share and hold your stock for two years before deciding to sell it at the current market price of $24.00 a share. Your total return for this investment would be $980, calculated as follows:

$$\text{Total return} = \text{Current return} + \text{Capital gain}$$

$$\$980 = \$80 + \$900$$

Sheet 37
Evaluating
Corporate
Stocks

The current return of $80 results from the payment of dividends for two years ($0.40 per-share dividend $\times$ 100 shares $\times$ 2 years). The capital gain of $900 results from the increase in the stock price from $15 a share to $24 a share ($9 per-share increase $\times$ 100 shares = $900). (Of course, commissions to buy and sell your stock, a topic covered in the next section, would reduce your total return.)

Although little correlation may exist between the market value of a stock and its book value, book value is widely reported in financial publications. Therefore, it deserves mention. The **book value** for a share of stock is determined by deducting all liabilities from the corporation's assets and dividing the remainder by the number of outstanding shares of common stock. For example, assume XYZ Corporation has assets of $60 million and liabilities of $30 million and has issued 1,000,000 shares of common stock. In this situation, the book value for a share of XYZ stock is $30 per share, as follows:

book value Determined by deducting all liabilities from the corporation's assets and dividing the remainder by the number of outstanding shares of common stock.

$$\text{Book value} = \frac{\text{Assets} - \text{Liabilities}}{\text{Shares outstanding}}$$

$$= \frac{\$60,000,000 - \$30,000,000}{1,000,000 \text{ shares of stock}} = \$30 \text{ per share}$$

Some investors believe they have found a bargain when a stock's market value is about the same as or lower than its book value. *Be warned:* Book value calculations may be misleading, because the dollar amount of assets used in the above formula may be understated or overstated on the firm's financial statements. From a practical standpoint, most financial experts suggest that book value is just one piece of the puzzle and you must consider other factors along with book value when evaluating a possible stock investment.

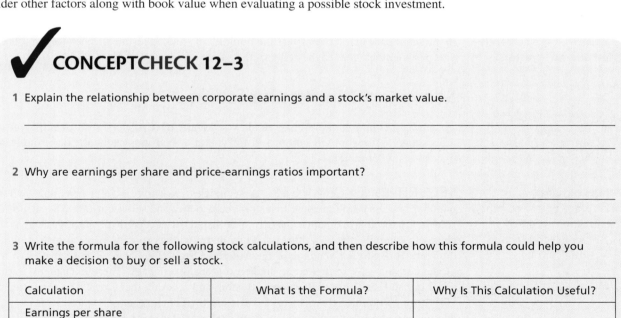

✔ **CONCEPTCHECK 12–3**

1 Explain the relationship between corporate earnings and a stock's market value.

_____

_____

2 Why are earnings per share and price-earnings ratios important?

_____

_____

3 Write the formula for the following stock calculations, and then describe how this formula could help you make a decision to buy or sell a stock.

Calculation	What Is the Formula?	Why Is This Calculation Useful?
Earnings per share		
Price-earnings (PE) ratio		
Current yield		
Total return		
Book value		

Buying and Selling Stocks

> **OBJECTIVE 4**
> Describe how stocks are bought and sold.

primary market A market in which an investor purchases financial securities, via an investment bank or other representative, from the issuer of those securities.

investment bank A financial firm that assists corporations in raising funds, usually by helping to sell new security issues.

initial public offering (IPO) Occurs when a corporation sells stock to the general public for the first time.

secondary market A market for existing financial securities that are currently traded among investors.

To purchase a pair of Levi Strauss jeans, you simply walk into a store that sells Levi's, choose a pair, and pay for your purchase. To purchase common or preferred stock, you generally have to work through a brokerage firm. In turn, your brokerage firm must buy the stock in either the primary or secondary market. In the **primary market,** you purchase financial securities, via an investment bank or other representative, from the issuer of those securities. An **investment bank** is a financial firm that assists corporations in raising funds, usually by helping to sell new security issues.

New security issues sold through an investment bank can be issued by corporations that have sold stocks and bonds before and need to sell new issues to raise additional financing. The new securities can also be initial public offerings. An **initial public offering (IPO)** occurs when a corporation sells stock to the general public for the first time. Companies that have used IPOs to raise capital include Home Depot, Microsoft, and United Parcel Service. Investors bought these stocks through brokerage firms acting as agents for an investment banking firm, and the money they paid for common stock flowed to the corporations that issued the stock. Because these companies used the financing obtained through IPOs wisely, they have grown and prospered, and investors have profited from their IPO investments. However, not all companies that use IPOs to raise capital are good investments.

Be warned: The promise of quick profits often lures investors to purchase IPOs. An IPO is generally classified as a high-risk investment—one made in the hope of earning a relatively large profit in a short time. Depending on the corporation selling the new security, IPOs are usually too speculative for most people.

After a stock has been sold through the primary market, it is traded through the secondary market. The **secondary market** is a market for existing financial securities that are currently traded among investors. Once the stocks are sold in the primary market, they can be sold time and again in the secondary market. The fact that stocks can be sold in the secondary market improves the liquidity of stock investments because the money you pay for stock goes to the seller of the stock.

Secondary Markets for Stocks

To purchase common or preferred stock, you usually have to work with an employee of a brokerage firm who will buy or sell for you at a securities exchange or through the over-the-counter market.

securities exchange A marketplace where member brokers who represent investors meet to buy and sell securities.

SECURITIES EXCHANGES A **securities exchange** is a marketplace where member brokers who represent investors meet to buy and sell securities. The securities sold at a particular exchange must first be listed, or accepted for trading, at that exchange. Generally, the securities issued by nationwide corporations are traded at either the New York Stock Exchange or the American Stock Exchange. The securities of regional corporations are traded at smaller, regional exchanges. These exchanges are located in San Francisco, Philadelphia, Boston, and several other cities. The securities of very large corporations may be traded at more than one exchange. American firms that do business abroad may also be listed on foreign securities exchanges—in Tokyo, London, or Paris, for example.

The New York Stock Exchange (NYSE) is one of the largest securities exchanges in the world. This exchange lists stocks for about 3,000 corporations with a total market value of about $12 trillion.[3] The NYSE has 1,366 members, or *seats.* Most of these members represent brokerage firms that charge commissions on security trades made by their representatives for their customers. Other members are called *specialists* or *spe-*

---

[3]New York Stock Exchange Web site (www.nyse.com), May 13, 2004.

cialist firms. A **specialist** buys *or* sells a particular stock in an effort to maintain an orderly market.

Before a corporation's stock is approved for listing on the NYSE, the corporation must meet specific listing requirements. The American Stock Exchange (AMEX) and various regional exchanges also have listing requirements, but typically these are less stringent than the NYSE requirements. The stock of corporations that cannot meet the NYSE requirements, find it too expensive to be listed on the NYSE, or choose not to be listed on the NYSE is often traded on the American Stock Exchange, on one of the regional exchanges, or through the over-the-counter market.

specialist Buys or sells a particular stock in an effort to maintain an orderly market.

THE OVER-THE-COUNTER MARKET Not all securities are traded on organized exchanges. Stocks issued by several thousand companies are traded in the over-the-counter market. The **over-the-counter (OTC) market** is a network of dealers who buy and sell the stocks of corporations that are not listed on a securities exchange. Today these stocks are not really traded over the counter. The term was coined more than 100 years ago when securities were sold "over the counter" in stores and banks.

Most over-the-counter securities are traded through Nasdaq (pronounced "nazz-dack"). **Nasdaq** is an electronic marketplace for stocks issued by 3,300 different companies.[4] In addition to providing price information, this computerized system allows investors to buy and sell shares of companies traded on Nasdaq. When you want to buy or sell shares of a company that trades on Nasdaq—say, Microsoft—your account executive sends your order into the Nasdaq computer system, where it shows up on the screen with all the other orders from people who want to buy or sell Microsoft. Then a Nasdaq dealer (sometimes referred to as a *market maker*) sitting at a computer terminal matches buy and sell orders for Microsoft. Once a match is found, your order is completed.

Begun in 1971 and regulated by the National Association of Securities Dealers, Nasdaq is known for its innovative, forward-looking growth companies. Although many securities are issued by smaller companies, some large firms, including Intel, Microsoft, and Cisco Systems, also trade on Nasdaq.

over-the-counter (OTC) market A network of dealers who buy and sell the stocks of corporations that are not listed on a securities exchange.

Nasdaq An electronic marketplace for stocks issued by 3,300 different companies.

Apply Yourself!

Objective 4

Prepare a list of at least five questions that could help you interview a prospective account executive.

Brokerage Firms and Account Executives

An **account executive,** or *stockbroker,* is a licensed individual who buys or sells securities for his or her clients. (Actually, *account executive* is the more descriptive title because such individuals handle all types of securities, not just stocks.) While all account executives can buy or sell stock for clients, most investors expect more from their account executives. Ideally, an account executive should provide information and advice to be used in evaluating potential investments. Many investors begin their search for an account executive by asking friends or business associates for recommendations. This is a logical starting point, but remember that some account executives are conservative while others are more risk oriented.

Before choosing an account executive, you should have already determined your short-term and long-term financial objectives. Then you must be careful to communicate those objectives to the account executive so that he or she can do a better job of advising you. Needless to say, account executives may err in their investment recommendations. To help avoid a situation in which your account executive's recommendations are automatically implemented, you should be *actively* involved in the decisions of your investment program and you should never allow your account executive to use his or her discretion without your approval. Watch your account for signs of churning. **Churning** is excessive buying and selling of securities to generate commissions. From a total dollar return standpoint, this practice usually leaves the client worse off or at least

account executive A licensed individual who buys or sells securities for clients; also called a *stockbroker.*

Sheet 38
Investment
Broker
Comparison

churning Excessive buying and selling of securities to generate commissions.

[4]The Nasdaq Web site (www.nasdaq.com), May 13, 2004.

no better off. Churning is illegal under the rules established by the Securities and Exchange Commission; however, it may be difficult to prove. Finally, keep in mind that account executives generally are not liable for client losses that result from their recommendations. In fact, most brokerage firms require new clients to sign a statement in which they promise to submit any complaints to an arbitration board. This arbitration clause generally prevents a client from suing an account executive or a brokerage firm.

Should You Use a Full-Service or a Discount Brokerage Firm?

Today a healthy competition exists between full-service brokerage firms and discount brokerage firms. While the most obvious difference between full-service and discount firms is the amount of the commissions they charge when you buy or sell stock and other securities, there are at least three other factors to consider. First, consider how much research information is available and how much it costs. Both types of brokerage firms offer excellent research materials, but you are more likely to pay extra for information if you choose a discount brokerage firm.

Second, consider how much help you need when making an investment decision. Many full-service brokerage firms argue that you need a professional to help you make important investment decisions. While this may be true for some investors, most account executives employed by full-service brokerage firms are too busy to spend unlimited time with you on a one-on-one basis, especially if you are investing a small amount. On the other side, many discount brokerage firms argue that you alone are responsible for making your investment decisions. They are quick to point out that the most successful investors are the ones involved in their investment programs. And they argue that they have both personnel and materials dedicated to helping you learn how to become a better investor.

Finally, consider how easy it is to buy and sell stock and other securities when using either a full-service or discount brokerage firm. Questions to ask include:

1. Can I buy or sell stocks over the phone?
2. Can I trade stocks online?
3. Where is your nearest office located?
4. Do you have a toll-free telephone number for customer use?
5. How often do I get statements?
6. Is there a charge for statements, research reports, and other financial reports?
7. Are there any fees in addition to the commissions I pay when I buy or sell stocks?

Computerized Transactions

Many people still prefer to use telephone orders to buy and sell stocks, but a growing number are using computers to complete security transactions. To meet this need, discount brokerage firms and many full-service brokerage firms allow investors to trade online.

As a rule of thumb, the more active the investor is, the more sense it makes to use computers to trade online. Other reasons that justify using a computer include

1. The size of your investment portfolio.
2. The ability to manage your investments closely.
3. The capability of your computer and the software package.

While computers can make the investment process easier and faster, you should realize that *you* are still responsible for analyzing the information and making the final decision to buy or sell a security. All the computer does is provide more information and, in most cases, complete transactions more quickly and economically.

A Sample Stock Transaction

Once you and your account executive have decided on a particular transaction, it is time to execute an order to buy or sell. Let's begin by examining four types of orders used to trade stocks.

A **market order** is a request to buy or sell a stock at the current market value. Since the stock exchange is an auction market, the account executive's representative will try to get the best price available and the transaction will be completed as soon as possible. Payment for stocks is generally required within three business days of the transaction. Then, in about four to six weeks, a stock certificate is sent to the purchaser of the stock, unless the securities are left with the brokerage firm for safekeeping. Today it is common practice for investors to leave stock certificates with a brokerage firm. Because the stock certificates are in the broker's care, transfers when the stock is sold are much easier. The phrase "left in the street name" is used to describe investor-owned securities held by a brokerage firm.

market order A request to buy or sell a stock at the current market value.

A **limit order** is a request to buy or sell a stock at a specified price. When you purchase stock, a limit order ensures that you will buy at the best possible price but not above a specified dollar amount. When you sell stock, a limit order ensures that you will sell at the best possible price, but not below a specified dollar amount. For example, if you place a limit order to buy General Motors common stock for $40 a share, the stock will not be purchased until the price drops to $40 a share or lower. Likewise, if your limit order is to sell General Motors for $40 a share, the stock will not be sold until the price rises to $40 a share or higher. *Be warned:* Limit orders are executed if and when the specified price or better is reached and *all* other previously received orders have been fulfilled.

limit order A request to buy or sell a stock at a specified price.

Many stockholders are certain they want to sell their stock if it reaches a specified price. A limit order does not guarantee this will be done. With a limit order, as mentioned above, orders by other investors may be placed ahead of your order. If you want to guarantee that your order will be executed, you place a special type of limit order known as a stop order. A **stop order** (sometimes called a *stop-loss order*) is an order to sell a particular stock at the next available opportunity after its market price reaches a specified amount. This type of order is used to protect an investor against a sharp drop in price and thus stop the dollar loss on a stock investment. For example, assume you purchased General Motors common stock at $40 a share. Two weeks after you made that investment, General Motors is facing multiple product liability lawsuits. Fearing that the market value of your stock will decrease, you enter a stop order to sell your General Motors stock at $33. This means that if the price of the stock decreases to $33 or lower, the account executive will sell it. While a stop order does not guarantee that your stock will be sold at the price you specified, it does guarantee that it will be sold at the next available opportunity. Both limit and stop orders may be good for one day, one week, one month, or good until canceled (GTC).

stop order An order to sell a particular stock at the next available opportunity after its market price reaches a specified amount.

You can also choose to place a discretionary order. A **discretionary order** is an order to buy or sell a security that lets the account executive decide when to execute the transaction and at what price. Financial planners advise against using a discretionary order for two reasons. First, a discretionary order gives the account executive a great deal of authority. If the account executive makes a mistake, it is the investor who suffers the dollar loss. Second, financial planners argue that only investors (with the help of their account executives) should make investment decisions.

discretionary order An order to buy or sell a security that lets the account executive decide when to execute the transaction and at what price.

Commission Charges

Most brokerage firms have a minimum commission ranging from $7 to $55 for buying and selling stock. Additional commission charges are based on the number of shares and the value of stock bought and sold.

Exhibit 12–7 shows typical commissions charged by online brokerage firms. Generally, full-service and discount brokerage firms charge higher commissions than those charged by online brokerage firms. As a rule of thumb, full-service brokers may charge as much as 1 to 2 percent of the transaction amount. In return for charging higher commissions,

Exhibit [12–7]

Typical Commission Charges
for Online Stock
Transactions

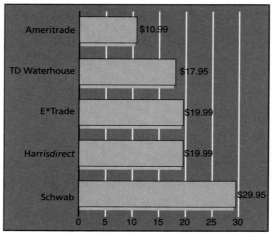

Internet Trading: 1,000 Shares

Source: Ameritrade Web site (www.ameritrade.com), May 13, 2004, Ameritrade, Inc., 4211 South 102nd Street, Omaha, NE 68127.

full-service brokers usually spend more time with each client, help make investment decisions, and provide free research information.

Although full-service brokerage firms usually charge higher commissions, on some occasions a discount brokerage firm may charge higher commissions. This generally occurs when the transaction is small, involving a total dollar amount of less than $1,000, and the investor is charged the discount brokerage firm's minimum commission charge.

✔ CONCEPTCHECK 12–4

1 What is the difference between the primary market and the secondary market? What is an initial public offering (IPO)?

_____

_____

2 Explain the difference between a securities exchange and the over-the-counter market.

_____

_____

3 Assume you want to purchase stock. Would you use a full-service broker or a discount broker? Would you ever trade stocks online?

_____

_____

4 Explain the important characteristics of each of the following types of stock transaction orders:

Market order:	
Limit order:	
Stop order:	
Discretionary order:	

Long-Term and Short-Term Investment Strategies

Once you purchase stock, the investment may be classified as either long term or short term. Generally, individuals who hold an investment for a long period of time are referred to as *investors*. Typically, long-term investors hold their investments for at least a year or longer. Individuals who routinely buy and then sell stocks within a short period of time are called *speculators* or *traders*.

Long-Term Techniques

In this section, we discuss the long-term techniques of buy and hold, dollar cost averaging, direct investment programs, and dividend reinvestment programs.

BUY-AND-HOLD TECHNIQUE   Many long-term investors purchase stock and hold onto it for a number of years. When they do this, their investment can increase in value in three ways. First, they are entitled to dividends if the board of directors approves dividend payments to stockholders. Second, the price of the stock may go up. Third, the stock may be split. Although there are no guarantees, stock splits may increase the future value of a stock investment over a long period of time.

DOLLAR COST AVERAGING   **Dollar cost averaging** is a long-term technique used by investors who purchase an equal dollar amount of the same stock at equal intervals. Assume you invest $2,000 in Johnson & Johnson's common stock each year for a period of three years. The results of your investment program are illustrated in Exhibit 12–8. Notice that when the price of the stock increased in 2003 and 2004, you purchased fewer shares. The average cost for a share of stock, determined by dividing the total investment ($6,000) by the total number of shares, is $46.69 ($6,000 ÷ 128.5 = $46.69). Other applications of dollar cost averaging occur when employees purchase shares of their company's stock through a payroll deduction plan or as part of an employer-sponsored retirement plan over an extended period of time.

Investors use dollar cost averaging to avoid the common pitfall of buying high and selling low. In the situation shown in Exhibit 12–8, you would lose money only if you sold your stock at less than the average cost of $46.69. Thus, with dollar cost averaging, you can make money if the stock is sold at a price higher than the average cost for a share of stock.

DIRECT INVESTMENT AND DIVIDEND REINVESTMENT PLANS
Today a large number of corporations offer direct investment plans. A **direct investment plan** allows you to purchase stock directly from a corporation without having to use an account executive or a brokerage firm. Similarly, a **dividend reinvestment plan** allows you the option to reinvest your cash dividends to purchase stock of the corporation. For stockholders, the chief advantage of both types of plans is that these plans enable them to purchase stock without paying a commission charge to a brokerage firm. As an added

dollar cost averaging A long-term technique used by investors who purchase an equal dollar amount of the same stock at equal intervals.

direct investment plan A plan that allows stockholders to purchase stock directly from a corporation without having to use an account executive or a brokerage firm.

dividend reinvestment plan A plan that allows current stockholders the option to reinvest or use their cash dividends to purchase stock of the corporation.

Year	Investment	Stock Price	Shares Purchased
2002	$2,000	$40	50.0
2003	2,000	50	40.0
2004	2,000	52	38.5
Total	$6,000		128.5

Exhibit [12–8]

Dollar Cost Averaging for Johnson & Johnson

STOCKS | SanDisk is a bet on the burgeoning popularity of digital cameras and cell phones. *By David Landis*

Cash in on their **CHIPS**

SANDISK isn't exactly a semiconductor company, but lately its stock sure has been acting as if it were. Despite a recent surge, its shares are down 10% from their January highs, tracking the moves in chip stocks. That's a strange way for investors to treat a company whose products—flash-memory cards—are key components of some of today's hottest consumer devices, including digital cameras, cell-phone cameras and digital-music players.

Michael Gray, SanDisk's chief financial officer, says the disconnect doesn't surprise him. "Wall Street sometimes struggles because it's not sure whether to view us as a semiconductor company or a consumer company," he says. The fact, though, is that SanDisk (symbol SNDK) derives 92% of its sales from buyers of consumer electronics. Its flash-memory cards are used to store digitized media, such as photos and music. The cards are sold in more than 50,000 electronics stores; a new, $15 "Shoot & Store" card, aimed at digital-camera owners who don't have a computer, will extend SanDisk's reach into grocery and drug stores.

Pretty picture. Riding a surge in digital-camera sales, SanDisk's earnings

---

SANDISK

- **Market capitalization:** $5.3 billion
- **Earnings per share:** 2003: $1.02; 2004: $1.33 (estimate)
- **Annual revenues:** $1.1 billion
- **Number of patents held:** 242 (U.S.); 97 (foreign)
- **Shareholder services:** 408-542-0500

SOURCES: SanDisk, Thomson First Call

---

more than tripled last year. In January, the company said 2004 earnings could rise as much as 60%. Given that explosive growth, why is the stock, recently $33, trading at just 25 times 2004 profit forecasts?

A major reason is that supply and demand for flash memory is erratic. As demand rises, companies rush to add new manufacturing capacity. Eventually, supply exceeds demand, sending prices plummeting. In January, SanDisk set off alarm bells by forecasting that a key profit-margin number would fall in the second half of the year. But some analysts say SanDisk's forecasts are overly conservative. "The company substantially beat its estimates in every quarter last year," says Eric Gomberg, of Thomas Weisel Partners, who rates the shares "outperform."

Besides, to some degree SanDisk and other manufacturers can offset the effects of additional supply by offering more memory storage for the same price. So, although the price per megabyte of memory plunged 40% last year, the average capacity of a memory card sold by SanDisk in the fourth quarter was 184 MB, up from 100 MB a year earlier. That dynamic, and a growing consumer demand for digital media, allowed SanDisk and Samsung (the largest maker of flash memory) to each boost megabytes sold last year by more than 200% without overwhelming the market.

Huge potential. Regardless of what happens to supply, analysts see no letup in demand. Michael McConnell, of investment bank Pacific Crest Securities, estimates that digital-camera sales will grow an average of 36% annually over the next three years. Experts also see great demand for camera phones with removable memory cards. International Data Corp. predicts sales of 330 million units in 2006, up from 26 million in 2002. Key-chain-size flash-memory devices that plug in to personal computers will be another big market.

Given an expected annual-earnings growth rate of 50% over the next few years, McConnell thinks SanDisk should trade at 30 times earnings. Applying that P/E ratio to the average analyst earnings estimate for 2004 of $1.33 per share implies a stock price of $40. —*Reporter:* **JOAN GOLDWASSER**

Source: David Landis, "Cash in on Their Chips." Reprinted by permission from the June issue of *Kiplinger's Personal Finance*. Copyright © 2004 The Kiplinger Washington Editors, Inc.

---

1. In this chapter, we discuss many factors that could cause a stock's price to increase or decrease. Based on the information in this article, do you think the price of SanDisk will increase or decrease in the next three years? Explain your answer.

_____

_____

2. On May 14, 2004, a share of SanDisk stock was selling for $23.86. Use the Internet or library sources to answer the following questions:
   a. Have there been any stock splits since May 14, 2004? _____
   b. What is the current price for a share of SanDisk stock? _____
   c. If you had purchased SanDisk stock on May 14, 2004, would your SanDisk investment have been profitable? Explain your answer.

_____

_____

incentive, some corporations even offer their stock at a small discount to encourage the use of their direct investment and dividend reinvestment plans. Also, with the dividend reinvestment plan, you can take advantage of dollar cost averaging, discussed in the last section. For corporations, the chief advantage of both types of plans is that they provide an additional source of capital. As an added bonus, they are providing a service to their stockholders.

Short-Term Techniques

In addition to the long-term techniques presented in the preceding section, investors sometimes use more speculative, short-term techniques. In this section, we discuss buying stock on margin, selling short, and trading in options. *Be warned:* The methods presented in this section are risky; do not use them unless you fully understand the underlying risks. Also, you should not use them until you have experienced success using the more traditional long-term techniques described above.

BUYING STOCK ON MARGIN   When buying stock on **margin,** you borrow part of the money needed to buy a particular stock. The margin requirement is set by the Federal Reserve Board and is subject to periodic change. The current margin requirement is 50 percent and a $2,000 minimum. This requirement means you may borrow up to half of the total stock purchase price as long as you have at least $2,000 in your brokerage firm account. Although margin is regulated by the Federal Reserve, margin requirements and the interest charged on the loans used to fund margin transactions may vary among brokers and dealers. Usually the brokerage firm either lends the money or arranges the loan with another financial institution.

margin A speculative technique whereby an investor borrows part of the money needed to buy a particular stock.

Investors buy on margin because the financial leverage created by borrowing money can increase the return on an investment. Because they can buy up to twice as much stock by buying on margin, they can earn larger returns. Suppose you expect the market price of a share of Boeing to increase in the next three to four months. Let's say you have enough money to purchase 100 shares of the stock. However, if you buy on margin, you can purchase an additional 100 shares for a total of 200 shares. If the price of Boeing's stock increases by $7 a share, your profit will be $700 ($7 × 100 shares = $700) if you pay cash. But it will be $1,400 ($7 × 200 shares = $1,400) if you buy on margin. That is, buying more shares on margin, you will earn double the profit (less the interest you pay on the borrowed money and customary commission charges).

If the value of a margined stock decreases to approximately one-half of the original price, you will receive a *margin call* from the brokerage firm. After the margin call, you must pledge additional cash or securities to serve as collateral for the loan. If you don't have acceptable collateral or cash, the margined stock is sold and the proceeds are used to repay the loan. The exact price at which the brokerage firm issues the margin call is determined by the amount of money you borrowed when you purchased the stock. Generally, the more money you borrow, the sooner you will receive a margin call if the value of the margined stock drops.

In addition to facing the possibility of larger dollar losses, you must pay interest on the money borrowed to purchase stock on margin. Most brokerage firms charge 1 to 3 percent above the prime rate. Normally, economists define the prime rate as the interest rate that the best business customers must pay. Interest charges can absorb the potential profits if the value of margined stock does not increase rapidly enough and the margined stocks must be held for long periods of time.

SELLING SHORT   Your ability to make money by buying and selling securities is related to how well you can predict whether a certain stock will increase or decrease in market value. Normally, you buy stocks and assume they will increase in value, a procedure referred to as *buying long*. But not all stocks increase in value. In fact, the value of a stock may decrease for many reasons, including lower sales, lower profits,

selling short Selling stock that has been borrowed from a brokerage firm and must be replaced at a later date.

reduced dividends, product failures, increased competition, and product liability lawsuits. With this fact in mind, you may use a procedure called *selling short* to make money when the value of a stock is expected to decrease in value. **Selling short** is selling stock that has been borrowed from a brokerage firm and must be replaced at a later date. When you sell short, you sell today, knowing you must buy or *cover* your short transaction at a later date. To make money in a short transaction, you must take these steps:

1. Arrange to *borrow a stock certificate* for a certain number of shares of a particular stock from a brokerage firm.
2. *Sell the borrowed* stock, assuming it will drop in value in a reasonably short period of time.
3. *Buy the stock at a lower price* than the price it sold for in step 2.
4. Use the stock purchased in step 3 to *replace the stock borrowed from the brokerage firm* in step 1.

When selling short, your profit is the difference between the amount received when the stock is sold in step 2 and the amount paid for the stock in step 3. For example, assume that you think Walt Disney stock is overvalued at $23 a share. You also believe the stock will decrease in value over the next four to six months. You call your broker and arrange to borrow 100 shares of Walt Disney stock (step 1). The broker then sells your borrowed Disney stock for you at the current market price of $23 a share (step 2). Also assume that four months later Disney stock drops to $15 a share. You instruct your broker to purchase 100 shares of Disney stock at the current lower price (step 3). The newly purchased Disney stock is given to the brokerage firm to repay the borrowed stock (step 4). In this example, you made $800 profit by selling short ($2,300 selling price − $1,500 purchase price = $800 profit). Remember, the $800 profit must be reduced by the commissions you paid to the broker for buying and selling the Disney stock.

There is usually no special or extra brokerage charge for selling short, since the brokerage firm receives its regular commission when the stock is bought and sold. Before selling short, consider two factors. First, since the stock you borrow from your broker is actually owned by another investor, you must pay any dividends the stock earns before you replace the stock. After all, you borrowed the stock and then sold the borrowed stock. Eventually, dividends can absorb the profits from your short transaction if the price of the stock does not decrease rapidly enough. Second, to make money selling short, you must be correct in predicting that a stock will decrease in value. If the value of the stock increases, you lose.

option The right to buy or sell a stock at a predetermined price during a specified period of time.

TRADING IN OPTIONS An **option** gives you the right to buy or sell a stock at a predetermined price during a specified period of time. Options are usually available for three-, six-, or nine-month periods. If you think the market price of a stock will increase during a short period of time, you may decide to purchase a call option. A *call option* is sold by a stockholder and gives the purchaser the right to *buy* 100 shares of a stock at a guaranteed price before a specified expiration date.

It is also possible to purchase a put option. A *put option* is the right to sell 100 shares of a stock at a guaranteed price before a specified expiration date. With both call and put options, you are betting that the price of the stock will increase or decrease in value before the expiration date. If this price movement does not occur before the expiration date, you lose the money you paid for your option.

Because of the increased risk involved in option trading, a more detailed discussion of how you profit or lose money with options is beyond the scope of this book. *Be warned:* Amateurs and beginning investors should stay away from options unless they fully understand all of the risks involved. For the rookie, the lure of large profits over a short period of time may be tempting, but the risks are real.

Apply *Yourself!*

Objective 5

In a short paragraph, describe why you would use a long-term technique or a short-term technique to achieve your investment goals.

✔ CONCEPTCHECK 12–5

1 In your own words, describe the difference between an investor and a speculator.

_____

_____

2 In the space provided, describe how each of the following investment techniques could help an investor experience success.

Buy and hold:	
Dollar cost averaging:	
Direct investment:	
Dividend reinvestment:	
Margin:	
Selling short:	
Options:	

3 Based on your tolerance for risk, pick two of the investment techniques that you would use in your investment program. Then explain why these techniques match your tolerance for risk.

_____

_____

www.mhhe.com/kdh

Back to Getting Personal

Reevaluate your Getting Personal answers at the beginning of the chapter. Then answer the following questions.

1. In your own words, describe why corporations sell stock to obtain financing. Why do investors purchase stock?

_____

2. Why is it important for your investment portfolio to include some growth stocks?

_____

_____

3. A number of different long-term and short-term investment techniques were described in this chapter. Indicate below which techniques you would use to obtain your investment goals. Then explain why you made each decision.

Continued

Investment Technique	Long-Term or Short-Term Technique	Would I Use This Technique?	Explanation for My Choice
Buy and hold			
Dollar cost averaging			
Direct investment			
Dividend reinvestment			
Margin			
Selling short			
Options			

Chapter Summary

Objective 1   Corporations sell stock to finance their business start-up costs and help pay for their ongoing business activities. In return for providing the money needed to finance the corporation, stockholders have the right to elect the board of directors. They must also approve major changes to corporate policies.

People invest in stock because of dividend income, appreciation of value, and the possibility of gain through stock splits. In addition to common stock, a few corporations may issue preferred stock. The most important priority an investor in preferred stock enjoys is receiving cash dividends before any cash dividends are paid to common stockholders. Still, dividend distributions to both preferred and common stockholders must be approved by the board of directors.

Objective 2   A number of factors can make a share of stock increase or decrease in value. When evaluating a particular stock issue, most investors begin with the information on the Internet. Information is also available from professional advisory services, the newspaper, business and personal finance periodicals, and government publications.

Objective 3   Many analysts believe that a corporation's ability or inability to generate earnings in the future may be one of the most significant factors that account for an increase or decrease in the value of a stock. Generally, higher earnings equate to higher stock value, and lower earnings equate to lower stock value. In addition to the total amount of earnings reported by the corporation, investors can calculate earnings per share and a price-earnings ratio to evaluate a stock investment. Whereas both earnings per share

and price-earnings ratio are historical numbers based on what a corporation has already done, investors can obtain earnings estimates for most corporations. Other calculations that help evaluate stock investments include current yield, total return, and book value.

Objective 4   A corporation may sell a new stock issue with the help of an investment banking firm. Once the stock has been sold in the primary market, it can be sold time and again in the secondary market. In the secondary market, investors purchase stock listed on a securities exchange or traded in the over-the-counter market. Many securities transactions are made through an account executive who works for a brokerage firm, but a growing number of investors are completing security transactions online. Whether you trade online or not, you must decide if you want to use a market, limit, stop, or discretionary order to buy or sell stock. Most brokerage firms charge a minimum commission for buying or selling stock. Additional commission charges are based on the number and value of the stock shares bought or sold and if you use a full-service or discount broker or trade online.

Objective 5   Purchased stock may be classified as either a long-term investment or a speculative investment. Long-term investors typically hold their investments for at least a year or longer; speculators (sometimes referred to as traders) usually sell their investments within a shorter time period. Traditional trading techniques long-term investors use include the buy-and-hold technique, dollar cost averaging, direct investment plans, and dividend reinvestment plans. More speculative techniques include buying on margin, selling short, and trading in options.

Key Terms

Problems and Questions

1. In your own words, describe how an investment in common or preferred stock could help you obtain your investment goals.

2. Jamie and Peter Dawson own 250 shares of IBM common stock. IBM's quarterly dividend is $0.18 per share. What is the amount of the dividend check the Dawson couple will receive for this quarter?

3. In March, stockholders of Avon Products approved a 2-for-1 stock split. After the split, how many shares of Avon stock will an investor have if she or he owned 360 shares before the split?

4. Wallace Martin owns Ohio Utility preferred stock. If this preferred stock issue pays 3.5 percent based on a par value of $50, what is the dollar amount of the dividend for one share of Ohio Utility?

5. Wanda Sotheby purchased 100 shares of All-American Manufacturing stock at $29.50 a share. One year later, she sold the stock for $38 a share. She paid her broker a $34 commission when she purchased the stock and a $42 commission when she sold it. During the 12 months she owned the stock, she received $108 in dividends. Calculate Wanda's total return on this investment.

6. Assume you have $5,000 to invest and that you are trying to decide between investing in Ford Motor Company or Coca Cola. Pick two of the sources of information that were described in this chapter and explain how each source could help you decide which investment is the right one for you.

7. As a stockholder of Kentucky Gas and Oil, you receive its annual report. In the financial statements, the firm has reported after-tax earnings of $1,200,000 and 1,500,000 shares of common stock. The stock is currently selling for $24 a share.

   a. Calculate the earnings per share for Kentucky Gas and Oil.

   b. Calculate the price-earnings (PE) ratio for Kentucky Gas and Oil.

8. Prepare a list of questions you could use to interview an account executive about career opportunities in the field of finance.

9. Prepare a chart that describes the similarities and differences among the buy-and-hold investment technique, dollar cost averaging, and dividend reinvestment.

10. Why would a speculator use margin? Why would a speculator sell short?

www.mhhe.com/kdh

Internet Connection

RESEARCHING STOCK INVESTMENTS

Visit the following Web sites and describe the type of information provided by each site.

Sponsor	Web Site	Type of Information	How Could This Site Help Me Invest?
Hoover's	www.hoovers.com		
Motley Fool	www.fool.com		
Nasdaq	www.nasdaq.com		
New York Stock Exchange	www.nyse.com		
Yahoo! Finance	http://finance.yahoo.com		

Case in Point

RESEARCH INFORMATION AVAILABLE FROM MERGENT

This chapter stressed the importance of evaluating potential investments. Now it's your turn to try your skill at evaluating a potential investment in Reebok International, Ltd. Assume you could invest $10,000 in the common stock of this company. To help you evaluate this potential investment, carefully examine Exhibit 12–6, which reproduces the research report on Reebok International from the *Mergent's Handbook of Common Stocks*. The report was published in the winter of 2003.

Questions

1. Based on the research provided by Mergent, would you buy Reebok International stock? Justify your answer.

2. What other investment information would you need to evaluate Reebok International common stock? Where would you obtain this information?

3. On March 2, 2004, Reebok International common stock was selling for $39.92 a share. Using the Internet or a newspaper, determine the current price for a share of Reebok. Based on this information, would your Reebok investment have been profitable? (*Hint:* Reebok stock is listed on the New York Stock Exchange and its stock symbol is RBK.)

4. Assuming you purchased Reebok International stock on March 2, 2004, and based on your answer to question 3, how would you decide if you want to hold or sell your Reebok stock? Explain your answer.

Evaluating Corporate Stocks

Financial Planning Activities: No checklist can serve as a foolproof guide for choosing a common or preferred stock. However, the following questions will help you evaluate a potential stock investment. Use stock Web sites on the Internet and/or use library materials to answer these questions about a corporate stock that you believe could help you obtain your investment goals.

Suggested Web Sites: http://finance.yahoo.com   www.smartmoney.com

Category 1: The Basics

1. What is the corporation's name? _____
_____

2. What are the corporation's address and telephone number? _____
_____

3. Have you requested the latest annual report and quarterly report?   ☐ Yes ☐ No

4. What information about the corporation is available on the Internet? _____
_____

5. Where is the stock traded? _____
_____

6. What types of products or services does this firm provide? _____
_____

7. Briefly describe the prospects for this company. (Include significant factors like product development, plans for expansion, plans for mergers, etc.)
_____

Category 2: Dividend Income

8. Is the corporation currently paying dividends? If so, how much? _____
_____

9. What is the current yield for this stock? _____
_____

10. Has the dividend payout increased or decreased over the past five years? _____
_____

11. How does the yield for this investment compare with those for other potential investments?
_____

Category 3: Financial Performance

12. What are the firm's earnings per share for the last year? _____
_____

13. Have the firm's earnings increased over the past five years? _____
_____

14. What is the firm's current price-earnings ratio?
_____

15. How does the firm's current price-earnings ratio compare with firms in the same industry?
_____

16. Describe trends for the firm's price-earnings ratio over the past three years. Do these trends show improvement (lower PE ratio) or decline in investment value (higher PE ratio)? _____
_____

17. What are the firm's projected earnings for the next year? _____
_____

18. Have sales increased over the last five years?
_____

19. What is the stock's current price? _____

20. What are the 52-week high and low for this stock?
_____

21. Do the analysts indicate that this is a good time to invest in this stock? _____
_____

22. Briefly describe any other information that you obtained from Mergent, Value Line, Standard & Poor's, or other sources of information.

A Word of Caution

When you use a checklist, there is always a danger of overlooking important relevant information. This checklist is not all-inclusive, but it does provide some very sound questions that you should answer before making a decision to invest in stock. Quite simply, it is a place to start. If you need other information, *you* are responsible for obtaining it and for determining how it affects your potential investment.

What's Next for Your Personal Financial Plan?

- Identify additional factors that may affect your decision to invest in this corporation's stock.
- Develop a plan for monitoring an investment's value once a stock(s) is purchased.

Your Personal Financial Plan

37

Investment Broker Comparison

Financial Planning Activities: To compare the benefits and costs of different investment brokers, compare the services of an investment broker based on the factors listed below.

Suggested Web Sites: www.scottrade.com   www.placeatrade.com

Broker's name		
Organization		
Address		
Phone		
Web site		
Years of experience		
Education and training		
Areas of specialization		
Certifications held		
Professional affiliations		
Employer's stock exchange and financial market affiliations		
Information services offered		
Minimum commission charge		
Commission on 100 shares of stock at $50/share		
Fees for other investments: • Corporate bonds • Mutual funds • Stock options		
Other fees: • Annual account fee • Inactivity fee • Other		

What's Next for Your Personal Financial Plan?

- Using the information you obtained, choose a brokerage firm that you feel will help you obtain your investment goals.
- Access the Web site for the brokerage firm you have chosen and answer the questions on page 342 in your text.

13 Investing in Mutual Funds

Objectives

In this chapter, you will learn to:

1. Describe the characteristics of mutual fund investments.
2. Classify mutual funds by investment objective.
3. Evaluate mutual funds.
4. Describe how and why mutual funds are bought and sold.

Why is this important?

For many investors, mutual funds have become the investment of choice. Yet even though mutual funds offer professional management and diversification, investors still need to evaluate mutual funds before investing their money.

 Getting Personal

Why invest in mutual funds? For each of the following statements, select "yes" or "no" to indicate your behavior regarding these investment activities.

	Yes	No
1. I understand the reasons investors choose mutual funds.	_____	_____
2. I understand the different charges and fees associated with mutual fund investments.	_____	_____
3. I can identify the type of mutual fund that will help me achieve my investment goals.	_____	_____
4. I know how to evaluate a mutual fund.	_____	_____
5. I understand the purchase and withdrawal options for mutual funds.	_____	_____

After studying this chapter, you will be asked to reconsider your responses to these questions.

Key Web Sites

www.businessweek.com   www.morningstar.com

www.ici.org   www.mutualfund.com

www.mfea.com   www.smartmoney.com

mutual fund An investment chosen by people who pool their money to buy stocks, bonds, and other financial securities selected by professional managers who work for an investment company.

investment company A firm that invests the pooled funds of investors in securities appropriate to its stated investment objective.

If you ever thought about buying stocks or bonds but decided not to, your reasons were probably like most other people's: You didn't know enough to make a good decision, and you lacked enough money to diversify your investments among several choices. These same two reasons explain why people invest in mutual funds. By pooling your money with money from other investors, a mutual fund can do for you what you can't do on your own. Specifically, a **mutual fund** is an investment chosen by people who pool their money to buy stocks, bonds, and other financial securities selected by professional managers who work for investment companies. The Investment Company Institute defines an **investment company** as a firm that invests the pooled funds of investors in securities appropriate to its stated investment objective.[1] Mutual funds are an excellent choice for many individuals. In many cases, they can also be used for retirement accounts, including 401(k), 403(b), traditional individual retirement accounts, and Roth IRAs.

An investment in mutual funds is based on the concept of opportunity costs, which we have discussed throughout this text. Simply put, you have to be willing to take some chances if you want to get larger returns on your investments. Before deciding whether mutual funds are the right investment for you, read the material presented in the next section.

Why Investors Purchase Mutual Funds

OBJECTIVE 1

Describe the characteristics of mutual fund investments.

In the 1990s, people loved their mutual funds. With a few exceptions, investors expected and got big returns each year until the end of the 1990s. Then the bubble burst. Since 2000, many people have firsthand knowledge that the value of mutual fund shares can decline. And yet the following statistics illustrate how important mutual fund investments are to both individuals and the nation's economy:

1. An estimated 91 million individuals own 77 percent of the mutual funds in the United States.[2]
2. The number of mutual funds grew from 361 in 1970 to over 8,100 in 2003.[3]
3. In 2003, the last year for which complete totals are available, the combined value of assets owned by mutual funds in the United States totaled $7.4 trillion. This amount is expected to continue to increase based on long-term performance.[4]

No doubt about it, the mutual fund industry is big business. And yet, you may be wondering why so many people invest in mutual funds.

The major reasons investors purchase mutual funds are *professional management* and *diversification*. Most investment companies do everything possible to convince you that they can do a better job of picking securities than you can. Sometimes these

---

[1]Investment Company Institute Web site (www.ici.org), May 24, 2004, Investment Company Institute, 1401 H Street, NW, Washington, DC 20005.

[2]Ibid.

[3]Ibid.

[4]Ibid.

Portfolio Composition by Sector*	
Consumer discretionary	12.0%
Consumer staples	8.8
Energy	4.0
Financials	20.8
Health care	14.7
Industrials	7.8
Information technology	24.5
Materials	1.5
Telecommunication services	1.6
Utilities	1.6
Top Ten Equity Holdings (as of date: 03/31/2004)†	
1 Citigroup Inc.	3.76%
2 Microsoft Corp.	3.10
3 Pfizer Inc.	2.93
4 Cisco Systems Inc.	2.88
5 Wal-Mart Stores Inc.	2.86
6 General Electric Co.	2.72
7 Exxon Mobil Corp.	2.48
8 American International Group Inc.	2.36
9 Procter & Gamble Co.	2.22
10 JP Morgan Chase & Co.	2.08

Exhibit [13–1]

Types of Securities Included in the Portfolio of the AIM Blue Chip Fund

*Excludes money market funds.

†Holdings are subject to change.

Source: The AIM Investments Company Web site (www.aiminvestments.com), May 24, 2004, AIM Family of Funds, 11 Greenway Plaza, Suite 100, Houston, TX 77046.

claims are true, and sometimes they are just so much hot air. Still, investment companies do have professional fund managers with years of experience who devote large amounts of time to picking just the "right" securities for their funds' portfolios. *Be warned:* Even the best portfolio managers make mistakes. So you, the investor, must be careful!

The diversification mutual funds offer spells safety, because an occasional loss incurred with one investment contained in a mutual fund is usually offset by gains from other investments in the fund. For example, consider the diversification provided in the portfolio of the AIM Blue Chip Fund, shown in Exhibit 13–1. An investment in the $3 billion AIM Blue Chip Fund represents ownership in at least 10 different industries, as seen at the top of Exhibit 13–1. In addition, the companies in the fund's portfolio are often market leaders, as seen at the bottom of the exhibit. With a total of more than 80 different companies included in the fund's investment portfolio, investors enjoy diversification coupled with AIM's stock-selection expertise. Note that the information contained in Exhibit 13–1 was taken from the fund's promotional materials at the end of May 2004. If you want more up-to-date information on the composition of investments within the fund or other information about the fund, visit its Web site at www.aiminvestments.com.

Characteristics of Mutual Funds

Today mutual funds may be classified as closed-end funds, exchange-traded funds, or open-end funds.

CLOSED-END, EXCHANGE-TRADED, OR OPEN-END MUTUAL FUNDS

closed-end fund A mutual fund whose shares are issued by an investment company only when the fund is organized.

Approximately 6 percent of all mutual funds are closed-end funds offered by investment companies. A **closed-end fund** is a mutual fund whose shares are issued by an investment company only when the fund is organized. As a result, only a certain number of shares are available to investors. After all the shares originally issued have been sold, an investor can purchase shares only from another investor who is willing to sell. Closed-end funds are actively managed by professional fund managers and shares are traded on the floors of stock exchanges, including the New York Stock Exchange, or in the over-the-counter market (Nasdaq). Like the prices of stocks, the prices of shares for closed-end funds are determined by the factors of supply and demand, by the value of stocks and other investments contained in the fund's portfolio, and by investor expectations. A special section of *The Wall Street Journal* provides information about closed-end funds.

exchange-traded fund (ETF) A fund that invests in the stocks contained in a specific stock index, like the Standard & Poor's 500 stock index, and whose shares are traded on a stock exchange or over the counter.

An **exchange-traded fund (ETF)** is a fund that invests in the stocks contained in a specific stock index, like the Standard & Poor's 500 stock index, and whose shares are traded on a stock exchange or over the counter. With both a closed-end fund and an exchange-traded fund, an investor can purchase as little as one share of a fund, because both types are traded on a stock exchange or over-the-counter market like individual corporate stock issues. Although exchange-traded funds are similar to closed-end funds, there is an important difference. Most closed-end funds are actively managed, with portfolio managers making the selection of stocks and other securities contained in a closed-end fund. An exchange-traded fund, on the other hand, invests in the stocks included in a specific stock index. Exchange-traded funds tend to mirror the performance of the index, moving up or down as the individual stocks contained in the index move up or down. Therefore, there is less need for a portfolio manager to make investment decisions. Although increasing in popularity, there are only about 150 exchange-traded funds. Like closed-end funds, ETFs are reported in a special section of *The Wall Street Journal*.

open-end fund A mutual fund whose shares are issued and redeemed by the investment company at the request of investors.

Approximately 93 percent of all mutual funds are open-end funds. An **open-end fund** is a mutual fund whose shares are issued and redeemed by the investment company at the request of investors. Investors are free to buy and sell shares at the net asset value. The **net asset value (NAV)** per share is equal to the current market value of securities contained in the mutual fund's portfolio minus the mutual fund's liabilities divided by the number of shares outstanding:

net asset value (NAV) The current market value of the securities contained in the mutual fund's portfolio minus the mutual fund's liabilities divided by the number of shares outstanding.

$$\text{Net asset value} = \frac{\text{Value of the fund's portfolio} - \text{Liabilities}}{\text{Number of shares outstanding}}$$

For example, assume the portfolio of all investments contained in the New American Frontiers Mutual Fund has a current market value of $244 million. The fund also has liabilities totaling $4 million. If this mutual fund has 12 million shares outstanding, the net asset value per share is $20:

$$\text{Net asset value} = \frac{\text{Value of the fund's portfolio} - \text{Liabilities}}{\text{Number of shares outstanding}}$$

$$= \frac{\$244 \text{ million} - \$4 \text{ million}}{12 \text{ million shares}}$$

$$= \$20 \text{ per share}$$

For most mutual funds, the net asset value is calculated at the close of trading each day.

In addition to buying and selling shares on request, most open-end funds provide their investors with a wide variety of services, including payroll deduction programs, automatic reinvestment programs, automatic withdrawal programs, and the option to change shares in one fund to another fund within the same fund family—all topics discussed later in this chapter.

LOAD FUNDS AND NO-LOAD FUNDS

Before investing in mutual funds, you should compare the cost of this type of investment with the cost of other investment alternatives, such as stocks or bonds. With regard to cost, mutual funds are classified as load funds or no-load funds. A **load fund** (sometimes referred to as an *A fund*) is a mutual fund in which investors pay a commission every time they purchase shares. The commission, sometimes referred to as the *sales charge,* may be as high as 8.5 percent of the purchase price for investments under $10,000. (Typically, this fee declines for investments over $10,000.)

Many exceptions exist, but the average load charge for mutual funds is between 3 and 5 percent. Let's assume you decide to invest $10,000 in the Davis New York Venture mutual fund. This fund charges a sales load of 4.75 percent that you must pay when you purchase shares. The dollar amount of the sales charge on your $10,000 investment is $475 ($10,000 × 4.75% = $475). After paying the $475, the amount available for investment is reduced to $9,525 ($10,000 − $475 = $9,525). The "stated" advantage of a load fund is that the fund's sales force (account executives, financial planners, or brokerage divisions of banks and other financial institutions) will explain the mutual fund to investors and offer advice as to when shares of the fund should be bought or sold.

A **no-load fund** is a mutual fund in which the individual investor pays no sales charge. No-load funds don't charge commissions when you buy shares because they have no salespeople. If you want to buy shares of a no-load fund, you must deal directly with the investment company. The usual means of contact is by telephone, the Internet, or mail. You can also purchase shares in a no-load fund from many discount brokers, including Charles Schwab, Ameritrade, TD Waterhouse Securities, and E*Trade.

As an investor, you must decide whether to invest in a load fund or a no-load fund. Some investment salespeople have claimed that load funds outperform no-load funds. But many financial analysts suggest there is generally no significant difference between mutual funds that charge commissions and those that do not.[5] *Since no-load funds offer the same investment opportunities load funds offer, you should investigate them further before deciding which type of mutual fund is best for you.* Although the sales commission should not be the decisive factor, the possibility of saving a load charge of up to 8.5 percent is a factor to consider.

Instead of charging investors a fee when they purchase shares in a mutual fund, some mutual funds charge a **contingent deferred sales load** (sometimes referred to as a *back-end load,* a *B fund,* or a *redemption fee*). These fees range from 1 to 5 percent, depending on how long you own the mutual fund before making a withdrawal. For example, assume you withdraw $5,000 from B shares that you own in the AIM Balance mutual fund within a year of your original purchase date. You must pay a 5 percent contingent

load fund A mutual fund in which investors pay a commission (as high as 8.5 percent) every time they purchase shares.

no-load fund A mutual fund in which the individual investor pays no sales charge.

contingent deferred sales load A 1 to 5 percent charge that shareholders pay when they withdraw their investment from a mutual fund.

[5]The Mutual Fund Education Alliance Web site (www.mfea.com), May 24, 2004, Mutual Fund Education Alliance, 100 NW Englewood, Suite 130, Kansas City, MO 64418.

deferred sales fee. Your fee is $250 ($5,000 × 5% = $250). After the fee is deducted from your $5,000 withdrawal, you will receive $4,750 ($5,000 − $250 = $4,750). *Generally,* the contingent deferred sales load declines until there is no withdrawal charge if you own the shares in the fund for more than five years.

MANAGEMENT FEES AND OTHER CHARGES

In evaluating a specific mutual fund, you should consider management fees and a number of other charges. The investment companies that sponsor mutual funds charge management fees. This fee, which is disclosed in the fund's prospectus, is a fixed percentage of the fund's net asset value on a predetermined date. Today annual management fees range between 0.25 and 2 percent of the fund's net asset value. While fees vary considerably, the average is 0.5 to 1.25 percent of the fund's net asset value.

> **12b-1 fee** A fee that an investment company levies to defray the costs of advertising and marketing a mutual fund.

The investment company may also levy a **12b-1 fee** (sometimes referred to as a *distribution fee*) to defray the costs of advertising and marketing a mutual fund and commissions paid to a broker who sold you shares in the mutual fund. Approved by the Securities and Exchange Commission, annual 12b-1 fees are calculated on the value of a fund's assets and are approximately 1 percent of a fund's assets per year.

Unlike the one-time sales load fees that mutual funds charge to purchase or sell shares, the 12b-1 fee is often an ongoing fee that is charged on an annual basis. Note that 12b-1 fees can cost you a lot of money over a period of years. Assuming there is no difference in performance offered by two different mutual funds, one of which charges a 12b-1 fee while the other doesn't, choose the latter fund. The 12b-1 fee is so lucrative for investment companies that a number of them have begun selling Class C shares that charge a higher 12b-1 fee and no sales load or contingent deferred sales fee to attract new investors. When compared to Class A shares (commissions charged when shares are purchased) and Class B shares (commissions charged when withdrawals are made over the first five years), Class C shares, with their ongoing, higher 12b-1 fees, may be more expensive over a long period of time.

> **expense ratio** The amount that investors pay for all of a mutual fund's management fees and operating costs.

Together, all the different management fees and fund's operating costs are often referred to as an **expense ratio.** Many financial planners recommend that you choose a mutual fund with an expense ratio of 1 percent or less.

By now, you are probably asking yourself, "Should I purchase Class A shares, Class B shares, or Class C shares?" There are no easy answers, but your professional financial adviser or broker can help you determine which class of shares of a particular mutual fund best suits your financial needs. You can also do your own research to determine which fund is right for you. Factors to consider include whether you want to invest in a load fund or no-load fund, management fees, and expense ratios. As you will see later in this chapter, a number of sources of information can help you evaluate investment decisions.

The investment company's prospectus must provide all details relating to management fees, sales fees, 12b-1 fees, and other expenses. Exhibit 13–2 reproduces the summary of expenses (sometimes called a *fee table*) taken from the Davis New York Venture Fund. Notice that this fee table has three separate parts. The first part describes shareholder transaction expenses. For this fund, the maximum sales charge is 4.75 percent. The second part describes the fund's annual operating expenses. For this fund, the expense ratio is 0.95 percent for Class A shares. The third part illustrates the total fees and expenses you would pay on a $10,000 investment, assuming a 5 percent annual return and redemption at the end of 1, 3, 5, and 10 years.

Exhibit 13–3 summarizes information for load charges, no-load charges, and Class A, Class B, and Class C shares. In addition, it reports typical management fees, contingent deferred sales loads, and 12b-1 charges.

Apply *Yourself!*

Objective 1

Use the Internet to find a fund you are interested in for investment purposes. Then determine the fund's load charge (if any), management fee, and expense ratio.

	Class A Shares	Class B Shares	Class C Shares
Fees You May Pay as a Davis Fund Shareholder *(paid directly from your investment)*			
Maximum sales charge (load) imposed on purchases (as a percentage of offering price)*	4.75%	None	None
Maximum deferred sales charge (load) imposed on redemptions (as a percentage of the lesser of the net asset value of the shares redeemed or the total cost of such shares)	0.75%	4.00%	1.00%
Maximum sales charge (load) imposed on reinvested dividends	None	None	None
Exchange fee	None	None	None
Davis New York Venture Fund Annual Operating Expenses *(deducted from the fund's assets)*			
Management fees	0.52%	0.52%	0.52%
Distribution (12b-1) fees	0.24%	1.00%	1.00%
Other expenses	0.19%	0.25%	0.22%
Total annual operating expenses	0.95%	1.77%	1.74%

Expenses may vary in future years.

Example

This example is intended to help you compare the cost of investing in the fund with the cost of investing in other mutual funds.

The example assumes that you invest $10,000 in the fund for the time periods indicated. The example also assumes that your investment has a 5% return each year and that the fund's operating expenses remain the same. Although your actual costs may be higher or lower, your costs, based on these assumptions, would be:

If You Sell Your Shares in:	1 Year	3 Years	5 Years	10 Years
Class A shares	$567	$763	$976	$1586
Class B shares	$580	$857	$1159	$1868*
Class C shares	$277	$548	$944	$2052

If You Still Hold Your Shares after:	1 Year	3 Years	5 Years	10 Years
Class A shares	$567	$763	$976	$1586
Class B shares	$180	$557	$959	$1868*
Class C shares	$177	$548	$944	$2052

Exhibit [13–2]

Summary of Expenses Paid to Invest in the Davis New York Venture Fund

*Class B shares' expenses for the 10-year period include 2 years of Class A shares' expenses since Class B shares automatically convert to Class A shares after 8 years.

Source: Excerpted from the Davis New York Venture Fund Prospectus, Davis New York Venture Web site (www.davisfunds.com), May 24, 2002, Davis Funds, P.O. Box 8406, Boston, MA 02266.

Exhibit 13–3

Typical Fees Associated with
Mutual Fund Investments

Type of Fee or Charge	Customary Amount
Load fund	Up to 8.5 percent of the purchase.
No-load fund	No sales charge.
Contingent deferred sales load	1 to 5 percent of withdrawals, depending on how long you own shares in the fund before making a withdrawal.
Management fee	0.25 to 2 percent per year of the fund's net asset value on a predetermined date.
12b-1 fee	Approximately 1 percent of the fund's assets per year.
Class A shares	Commission charge when shares are purchased.
Class B shares	Commission charge when money is withdrawn during the first five years.
Class C shares	No commission to buy or sell shares of a fund, but higher, ongoing 12b-1 fees.

✔ CONCEPTCHECK 13–1

1 In what ways could mutual funds help you obtain your investment goals?

_____

_____

2 Closed-end, exchange-traded, or open-end mutual funds are available today. Describe the differences between each type of fund.

Closed-end fund:
Exchange-traded fund:
Open-end fund:

3 What is the net asset value (NAV) for a mutual fund that has assets totaling $365 million, liabilities totaling $5 million, and 12 million shares outstanding?

_____

_____

4 In the table below, indicate the typical charges for each type of mutual fund fee and how often the fee is assessed.

Fee	Typical Charge	How Often Assessed?
Front-end sales load		
Contingent deferred sales load		
Management fee		
12b-1 fee		

5 What is an expense ratio? Why is it important?

_____

_____

Classifications of Mutual Funds

The managers of mutual funds tailor their investment portfolios to the investment objectives of their customers. Usually a fund's objectives are plainly disclosed in its prospectus. For example, the objectives of the Fundamental Investors Mutual Fund are described as follows:

> The fund's investment objective is to achieve long-term growth of capital and income. The fund invests primarily in common stocks or securities convertible into common stocks and may invest significantly in securities of issuers domiciled outside the United States and not included in the Standard & Poor's 500 Composite Index.[6]

Although categorizing the 8,100-plus mutual funds may be helpful, note that different sources of investment information may use different categories for the same mutual fund. In most cases, the name of the category gives a pretty good clue to the types of investments included within the category. The *major* fund categories are described in alphabetical order as follows:

Stock Funds

- *Aggressive growth funds* seek rapid growth by purchasing stocks whose prices are expected to increase dramatically in a short period of time. Turnover within an aggressive growth fund is high because managers are buying and selling stocks of small, growth companies. Investors in these funds experience wide price swings because of the underlying speculative nature of the stocks in the fund's portfolio.
- *Equity income funds* invest in stocks issued by companies with a long history of paying dividends. The major objective of these funds is to provide income to shareholders. These funds are attractive investment choices for conservative or retired investors.
- *Global stock funds* invest in stocks of companies throughout the world, including the United States.
- *Growth funds* invest in companies expecting higher-than-average revenue and earnings growth. While similar to aggressive growth funds, growth funds tend to invest in larger, well-established companies. As a result, the prices for shares in a growth fund are less volatile compared to aggressive growth funds.
- *Index funds* invest in the same companies included in an index like the Standard & Poor's 500 stock index or Russell 3000 Index. Since fund managers pick the

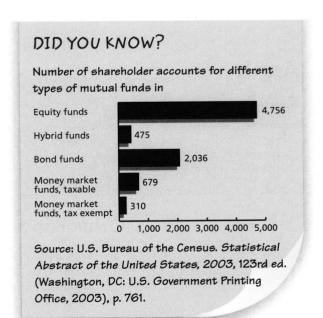

OBJECTIVE 2
Classify mutual funds by investment objective.

DID YOU KNOW?

Number of shareholder accounts for different types of mutual funds in

Equity funds	4,756
Hybrid funds	475
Bond funds	2,036
Money market funds, taxable	679
Money market funds, tax exempt	310

Source: U.S. Bureau of the Census. *Statistical Abstract of the United States, 2003*, 123rd ed. (Washington, DC: U.S. Government Printing Office, 2003), p. 761.

[6]Prospectus for the Fundamental Investors Mutual Fund, American Funds Web site (www.americanfunds.com), May 25, 2004, American Funds, P.O. Box 25065, Santa Ana, CA 92799.

stocks issued by the companies included in the index, an index fund should provide approximately the same performance as the index. Also, since index funds are cheaper to manage, they often have lower management fees and expense ratios.

- *International funds* invest in foreign stocks sold in securities markets throughout the world; thus, if the economy in one region or nation is in a slump, profits can still be earned in others. Unlike global funds, which invest in stocks issued by companies in both foreign nations and the United States, a true international fund invests outside the United States.
- *Midcap funds* invest in companies with total capitalization of at least $500 million whose stocks offer more security than small-cap funds and more growth potential than funds that invest in large corporations.
- *Regional funds* seek to invest in stock traded within one specific region of the world, such as the European region, the Latin American region, and the Pacific region.
- *Sector funds* invest in companies within the same industry. Examples of sectors include Health and Biotech, Science & Technology, and Natural Resources.
- *Small-cap funds* invest in smaller, lesser-known companies with a total capitalization of less than $500 million. Because these companies are small and innovative, these funds offer higher growth potential. They are more speculative than funds that invest in larger, more established companies.

Bond Funds

- *High-yield (junk) bond funds* invest in high-yield, high-risk corporate bonds.
- *Intermediate corporate bond funds* invest in investment-grade corporate debt with maturities between 5 and 10 years.
- *Intermediate U.S. bond funds* invest in U.S. Treasury notes with maturities between 5 and 10 years.
- *Long-term corporate bond funds* invest in investment-grade corporate bond issues with maturities in excess of 10 years.

Apply *Yourself!*

Objective 2

Use *The Wall Street Journal, BusinessWeek,* or *Kiplinger's Personal Finance Magazine* to identify one stock fund, one bond fund, and a balanced fund or asset allocation fund.

- *Long-term (U.S.) bond funds* invest in U.S. Treasury bonds with maturities in excess of 10 years.
- *Municipal bond funds* invest in municipal bonds that provide investors with tax-free interest income.
- *Short-term corporate bond funds* invest in investment-grade bond issues with maturities between 1 and 5 years.
- *Short-term (U.S.) government bond funds* invest in U.S. Treasury issues with maturities between 1 and 5 years.

Other Funds

- *Asset allocation funds* invest in various asset classes, including stocks, bonds, fixed-income securities, and money market instruments. These funds seek high total return by maintaining precise amounts within each type of asset.
- *Balanced funds* invest in both stocks and bonds with the primary objectives of conserving principal, providing income, and providing long-term growth. Often the percentage of stocks and bonds is stated in the fund's prospectus.
- *Money market funds* invest in certificates of deposit, government securities, and other safe and highly liquid investments.

family of funds A group of mutual funds managed by one investment company.

A **family of funds** exists when one investment company manages a group of mutual funds. Each fund within the family has a different financial objective. For instance, one fund may be a long-term government bond fund and another a growth stock fund. Most investment companies offer exchange privileges that enable shareholders to switch among the mutual funds in a fund family. For example, if you own shares in the Franklin growth fund, you may, at your discretion, switch to the Franklin income fund. Generally, investors may give instructions to switch from one fund to another within the same family in writing, over the telephone, or via the Internet. The family-of-funds concept makes it convenient for shareholders to switch their investments among funds as different funds offer more potential, financial reward, or security. Charges for exchanges, if any, generally are small for each transaction. For funds that do charge, the fee may be as low as $5 per transaction.

✔ CONCEPTCHECK 13–2

1 How important is the investment objective as stated in a mutual fund's prospectus?

_____

_____

2 Identify one mutual fund in each of the three categories (stocks, bonds, and other) and describe the characteristics of the fund you select and the type of investor who would invest in that type of fund.

General Fund Type	Specific Fund Type	Characteristics of Fund	Typical Investor
Stock			
Bond			
Other			

3 Explain the family-of-funds concept. How is it related to shareholder exchanges?

_____

_____

How to Make a Decision to Buy or Sell Mutual Funds

Often the decision to buy or sell shares in mutual funds is "too easy" because investors assume they do not need to evaluate these investments. Why question what the professional portfolio managers decide to do? Yet professionals do make mistakes. The responsibility for choosing the right mutual fund rests with *you*. After all, you are the only one who knows how much risk you are willing to assume and how a particular mutual fund can help you achieve your goals.

Fortunately, a lot of information is available to help you evaluate a specific mutual fund. Unfortunately, you can get lost in all the facts and figures and forget your ultimate goal: to choose a mutual fund that will help you achieve your financial goals. To help you sort out all the research, statistics, and information about mutual funds and give you some direction as to what to do first, answer the questions in the nearby Personal Finance in Practice feature. Then answer one basic question: Do you want a managed fund or an index fund?

> **OBJECTIVE 3**
> Evaluate mutual funds.

Managed Funds versus Index Funds

Most mutual funds are managed funds. In other words, there is a professional fund manager (or team of managers) that chooses the securities that are contained in the fund. The

Reset your PENSION plan

IN 1998, John Macari's employer, the state of Michigan, made a one-time offer he could not refuse. John, a psychologist at a state prison in Ypsilanti, said yes to the irrevocable opportunity to give up his traditional pension (based on salary and years of service) and switch to a defined-contribution plan, which offered the hope for larger long-term gains. "I got sucked in to the 1990s boom, chasing performance," John says. He's worried now because, at age 41, and after three bad years in a technology-heavy portfolio, he has $102,000 in the plan—much less than he anticipated. Assuming 3% annual raises, the traditional pension stood to pay as much as $90,000 a year at retirement after 37 years of employment. But that's gone.

John, married and the father of three, has a goal of accumulating $1.5 million to retire on in 2023, at age 60. His $102,000 is 40% in a stable-value fund that yields 4.5%, and 20% each in a Standard & Poor's 400 midsize-company index fund, a Russell 2000 small-company index fund and Dodge & Cox Stock fund. All are among the choices in his state employee plan.

Suggestions: First, is $1.5 million a sensible target? Perhaps. A 60-year-old man in Michigan today needs $1.4 million to buy an income annuity that pays $90,000 a year and guarantees 25 years of benefits to him or his widow. But to reach $1.5 million from here would be a stretch, says Louis Kokernak, a financial planner in Austin, Tex. He says John should count on just $900,000 in 20 years. That's if he invests an average of $12,000 annually, up from $10,500 today (counting the state's contribution) and earns 7%. (Our estimate of 8% would bring John to a hair over $1 million.)

To reach $1.5 million, John would need to put aside much more—which he says he cannot afford until he's in his fifties—or earn between 10% and 11%. That's on the high side, but not impossible. To even get close, John must dial up the risk, which he's been slow to do because of lingering fear from the stock market's collapse. He knows 40% in a stable-value fund (which pays higher income than a money-market fund but with a constant share price) is too much. We'd slash that to 10% and deploy the rest as follows: 20% in an **S&P 500** index fund, 15% in an **S&P 400** fund, 15% in a **Russell 2000** fund, and 10% each in **Artisan Mid Cap Value**, **Columbia Acorn**, **Dodge & Cox Stock** and **Templeton Foreign** (all available in his plan). He should also try to find more money to contribute.

Source: "Reset Your Pension Plan." Reprinted by permission from the April issue of *Kiplinger's Personal Finance*. Copyright © 2004 The Kiplinger Washington Editors, Inc.

1. John Macari, the Michigan prison psychologist described in this article, chose to give up a traditional pension (based on salary and years of service) and switch to a plan that allowed him to choose different mutual funds with the potential for larger returns. Would you have made the same choice? Explain your answer.

_____

_____

2. One way for John Macari to reach his retirement goal is to choose mutual fund investments that return between 10 and 11 percent. According to the article, that's not impossible, but he must "dial up the risk." When investing in mutual funds, what is the relationship between risk and reward?

_____

_____

3. The last recommendation in the article is for John to find more money to contribute. Assuming you were 41 years old and in this situation, how would you go about identifying money that could be invested for your retirement?

_____

_____

Personal Finance in Practice

Here are some suggestions for beginning a mutual fund investment program.

1. *Perform a financial checkup.* Before investing, you should make sure your budget is balanced, you have adequate insurance protection, and you have established an emergency fund.

   How could this suggestion help you prepare for an investment program?

   _____

   _____

2. *Obtain the money you need to purchase mutual funds.* Although the amount will vary, $250 to $3,000 or more is usually required to open an account with a brokerage firm or an investment company.

   How can I obtain the money needed to fund my investment program?

   _____

   _____

3. *Determine your investment goals.* Without investment goals, you cannot know what you want to accomplish. For more information on the importance of goals, review the material in Chapter 11.

   How could this suggestion help you establish a mutual fund investment program?

   _____

   _____

4. *Find a fund with an objective that matches your objective. The Wall Street Journal, Barron's,* and personal finance magazines may help you identify funds with objectives that match your investment objectives.

   Why is a "match" between your investment objective and a fund's objective important?

   _____

   _____

5. *Evaluate, evaluate, and evaluate any mutual fund before buying or selling.* Possible sources of information include the Internet, professional advisory services, the fund's prospectus, the fund's annual report, financial publications, and newspapers—all sources described in the remainder of this section.

   Since mutual funds provide professional management, why is evaluation important?

   _____

   _____

fund manager also decides when to buy and sell securities in the fund. *Caution: Don't forget the role of the fund manager in determining a fund's success.* One important question is how long the present fund manager has been managing the fund. If a fund has performed well under its present manager over a 5-year, 10-year, or longer period, there is a strong likelihood that it will continue to perform well under that manager in the future. On the other hand, if the fund has a new manager, his or her decisions may affect the performance of the fund. The decisions made by a new manager are often untested and may or may not stand the test of time. Ultimately, the fund manager is responsible for the fund's success. Managed funds may be open-end funds or closed-end funds.

Instead of investing in a managed fund, some investors choose to invest in an index fund. Why? The answer to that question is simple: Over many years, index funds have outperformed almost 85 percent of all managed funds.[7] Simply put: It's hard to beat an index like the Standard & Poor's 500. If the individual securities included in an index increase in value, the index goes up. Because an index mutual fund is a mirror image of a specific index, the dollar value of a share in an index fund also increases when the index increases. Unfortunately, the reverse is true. If the index goes down, the value of a share in an index fund goes down. Index funds, sometimes called

[7]Suze Orman, *The Road to Wealth* (New York: Riverhead Books, 2001), p. 393.

"passive" funds, have managers, but they simply buy the stocks or bonds contained in the index. A second reason why investors choose index funds is the lower expense ratio charged by these passively managed funds. Typical expense ratios for an index fund are 0.50 percent or less. Index funds may be open-end funds, closed-end funds, or exchange-traded funds.

Which type of fund is best? Good question. The answer depends on which managed mutual fund you choose. If you pick a managed fund that has better performance than an index, then you made the right choice. If, on the other hand, the index (and the index fund) outperforms the managed fund—which happens almost 85 percent of the time— an index fund is a better choice. With both investments, the key is how well you can research a specific investment alternative using the sources of information that are described in the remainder of this section.

The Internet

Many investors have found a wealth of information about mutual fund investments on the Internet. Basically, you can access information three ways. First, you can obtain current market values for mutual funds by using one of the Internet search engines, such as Yahoo!. The Yahoo! Finance page (http://finance.yahoo.com) has a box where you can enter the symbol of the mutual fund you want to research. If you don't know the symbol, you can enter in the name of the mutual fund in the symbol lookup box. The Yahoo! Finance Web site will respond with the correct symbol. In addition to current market values, you can obtain a price history for a mutual fund, a profile including research information about current holdings, performance data, and comparative data.

Apply *Yourself!*

Objective 3

Use the Yahoo! Finance Web site (http://finance.yahoo.com) to locate a mutual fund with a five-star Morningstar rating. What does the five-star rating mean?

Second, most investment companies that sponsor mutual funds have a Web page. To obtain information, all you have to do is access one of the Internet search engines and type in the name of the fund or enter the investment company's URL in your computer. Before reading on, take a look at Exhibit 13–4, the opening page for the American Funds Investment Company. Generally, statistical information about individual funds, procedures for opening an account, promotional literature, and different investor services are provided. *Be warned:* Investment companies want you to become a shareholder. As a result, the Web sites for *some* investment companies read like a sales pitch. Read between the glowing descriptions and look at the facts before investing your money.

Finally, professional advisory services, covered in the next section, offer online research reports for mutual funds. A sample of the information available from the Morningstar Web site for the Dodge and Cox Balanced Fund is illustrated in Exhibit 13–5. Note that information about the fund symbol, current NAV, Morningstar Rating, and past returns is provided. You can also obtain more detailed information by clicking on the appropriate button on the left side of the Web site. Many investors have found that the research reports provided by companies like Morningstar, Inc. (www.morningstar.com) and Lipper Analytical Services, Inc. (www.lipperweb.com) are well worth the $5 to $10 fee charged for online services. While the information is basically the same as that in the printed reports described later in this section, the ability to obtain up-to-date information quickly without having to wait for research materials to be mailed or to make a trip to the library is a real selling point.

Key Web Sites for Investing Advice
www.morningstar.com
www.lipperweb.com
www.valueline.com
www.standardpoors.com

Professional Advisory Services

A number of subscription services provide detailed information on mutual funds. Standard and Poor's Corporation, Lipper Analytical Services, Morningstar, Inc., and Value Line are four widely used sources of such information. Exhibit 13–6 illustrates the type of information provided by Morningstar, Inc., for the T. Rowe Price Growth Stock Fund.

Exhibit [13–4]   Opening Page of the Web Site for the American Family of Mutual Funds

Source: American Funds Web site (www.americanfunds.com), May 31, 2004, American Funds, P.O. Box 25065, Santa Ana, CA 92799.

Although the Morningstar report is just one page long, it provides a wealth of information designed to help you decide if this is the right fund for you. Notice that the information is divided into various sections. At the top, a small box entitled "Historical Profile" contains information about financial return, risk, and rating. Notice that T. Rowe Price Growth Stock Fund is rated five stars, Morningstar's highest rating. The report also provides statistical information over the past 12 years. The middle section of the report provides information about the fund's performance, risk analysis, and portfolio analysis. The last section at the very bottom describes the investment philosophy of the fund. Generally, the "Morningstar's Take" section summarizes the analyst's research.

As you can see, the research information for this fund is pretty upbeat. However, other research firms like Standard & Poor's, Lipper Analytical Services, and Value Line, as well as Morningstar, Inc., will also tell you if a fund is a poor performer that offers poor investment potential.

In addition, various mutual fund newsletters provide financial information to subscribers for a fee. All of these sources are rather expensive, but their reports may be available from brokerage firms or libraries.

The Mutual Fund Prospectus

An investment company sponsoring a mutual fund must give potential investors a prospectus. You can also request a prospectus by mail, by calling a toll-free phone number, or by accessing the investment company Web site.

Exhibit [13–5]   Information about the Dodge and Cox Balanced Fund Available from the Morningstar Web Site

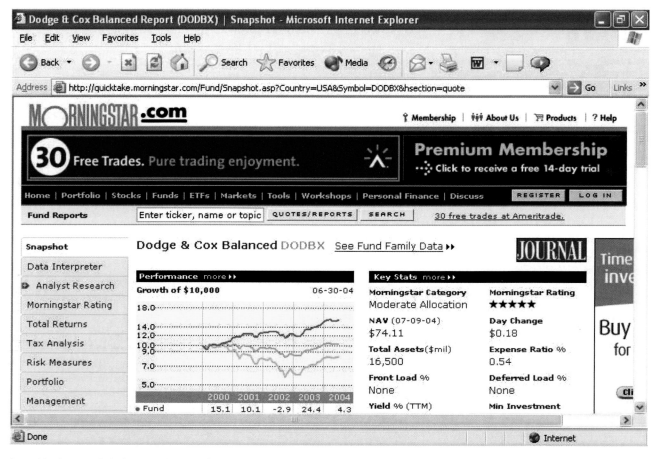

Source: Morningstar Web site (www.morningstar.com), June 1, 2004, Morningstar, Inc., 225 W. Wacker Drive, Chicago, IL 60606.

According to financial experts, the prospectus is usually the first piece of information investors receive, and they should read it completely before investing. Although it may look foreboding, a commonsense approach to reading a fund's prospectus can provide valuable insights. In fact, most investors find that a fund's prospectus offers a wealth of information. As pointed out earlier, the prospectus summarizes the fund's objective. Also, the fee table summarizes the fees a fund charges. In addition to information about objectives and fees, the prospectus should provide the following:

- A statement describing the risk factor associated with the fund.
- A description of the fund's past performance.
- A statement describing the type of investments contained in the fund's portfolio.
- Information about dividends, distributions, and taxes.
- Information about the fund's management.
- Information on limitations or requirements the fund must honor when choosing investments.
- The process investors can use to buy or sell shares in the fund.
- A description of services provided to investors and fees for services, if any.
- Information about how often the fund's investment portfolio changes (sometimes referred to as its *turnover ratio*).

Exhibit [13–6]   Mutual Fund Research Information Provided by Morningstar, Inc.

T. Rowe Price Gr Stk

	Ticker	Load	NAV	Yield	Total Assets	Mstar Category
	PRGFX	None	$23.18	0.2%	$4,686 mil	Large Growth

Management

Portfolio Manager(s)

Bob Smith has been at the helm of this offering since 1997. He's supported by T. Rowe Price's deep analyst bench domestically and overseas. Smith says he keeps about 70% of his investment holdings split between this fund and his other charge, T. Rowe Price Global Stock Fund, which he's helped run since 1995.

Strategy

Bob Smith uses a growth-at-a-reasonable-price approach, paying particular attention to financially sound companies with strong management teams and ample free cash flows. His growth leanings push the fund into the large-growth camp, but the fund is more diversified by sector than its typical peer. Smith also gives more attention to foreign blue chips than most of his rivals do: The fund often has 10% to 15% of assets invested abroad, considerably above the category norm.

Historical Profile
Return High
Risk Below Avg
Rating ★★★★★ Highest

Investment Style: Equity, Stock %
92% 96% 92% 94% 97% 95% 97% 98% 96%

Growth of $10,000
▬ Investment Values of Fund
— Investment Values of S&P 500
38.0 / 31.0 / 24.0 / 17.0 / 10.0

▼ Manager Change ▽ Partial Manager Change

Performance Quartile (within Category)

	1992	1993	1994	1995	1996	1997	1998	1999	2000	2001	2002	11-03	History
NAV	18.66	20.42	18.75	23.35	26.18	28.99	32.07	33.27	27.20	24.18	18.58	23.18	NAV
	5.99	15.56	0.89	30.97	21.70	26.57	27.41	22.15	0.27	-9.79	-23.00	24.76	Total Return %
	-1.63	5.50	-0.42	-6.56	-1.25	-6.78	-1.17	1.11	9.37	2.09	-0.91	2.50	+/-S&P 500
	1.02	12.66	-1.77	-6.22	-1.42	-3.91	-11.29	-11.01	22.69	10.63	4.89	-0.66	+/-Russ 1000Gr
	0.96	0.75	0.88	1.23	0.81	0.76	0.86	0.31	0.21	0.29	0.17	0.20	Income Return %
	5.03	14.81	0.01	29.74	20.89	25.81	26.55	21.84	0.06	-10.08	-23.17	24.56	Capital Return %
	58	26	22	56	32	51	68	83	7	6	19	42	Total Rtn % Rank Cat
	0.18	0.14	0.18	0.23	0.19	0.20	0.25	0.10	0.07	0.08	0.04	0.05	Income $
	1.03	0.99	1.66	0.97	2.06	3.87	4.27	5.42	6.28	0.27	0.00	0.00	Capital Gains $
	0.83	0.82	0.81	0.80	0.77	0.75	0.74	0.74	0.73	0.77	0.77	—	Expense Ratio %
	0.94	0.86	0.91	1.09	0.74	0.74	0.67	0.31	0.20	0.34	0.23	—	Income Ratio %
	27	35	54	42	49	41	55	56	74	64	47	—	Turnover Rate %
	1,946	2,051	2,068	2,762	3,431	3,988	5,041	5,672	5,428	4,685	3,728	4,656	Net Assets $mil

Performance 11-30-03

	1st Qtr	2nd Qtr	3rd Qtr	4th Qtr	Total
1999	2.40	6.00	-5.75	19.39	22.15
2000	8.60	-0.42	1.08	-8.28	0.27
2001	-14.96	8.86	-14.81	14.39	-9.79
2002	-1.41	-14.97	-15.15	8.25	-23.00
2003	-1.61	16.36	2.59	—	—

Trailing	Total Return%	+/- S&P 500	+/- Russ 1000Gr	%Rank Cat	Growth of $10,000
3 Mo	5.12	-0.33	-0.47	45	10,512
6 Mo	10.80	0.00	-1.64	57	11,080
1 Yr	17.50	2.42	0.75	35	11,750
3 Yr Avg	-3.73	1.79	7.61	7	8,922
5 Yr Avg	2.64	3.11	6.75	16	11,392
10 Yr Avg	11.19	0.56	2.16	9	28,884
15 Yr Avg	12.16	0.20	0.89	23	55,920

Tax Analysis	Tax-Adj Rtn%	%Rank Cat	Tax-Cost Rat	%Rank Cat
3 Yr Avg	-5.36	10	1.69	70
5 Yr Avg	0.35	19	2.23	79
10 Yr Avg	8.73	13	2.21	66

Potential Capital Gain Exposure: 12% of assets

Rating and Risk

Time Period	Load-Adj Return %	Morningstar Rtn vs Cat	Morningstar Risk vs Cat	Morningstar Risk-Adj Rating
1 Yr	17.50			
3 Yr	-3.73	High	Avg	★★★★★
5 Yr	2.64	+Avg	-Avg	★★★★★
10 Yr	11.19	High	-Avg	★★★★★
Incept	9.29			

Other Measures	Standard Index S&P 500	Best Fit Index Russ 1000
Alpha	2.5	1.7
Beta	1.05	1.05
R-Squared	97	97
Standard Deviation	18.86	
Mean	-3.73	
Sharpe Ratio	-0.32	

Portfolio Analysis 09-30-03

Share change since 06-03 Total Stocks:109

Sector		PE	YTD Ret%	% Assets
⊕ Citigroup	Financial	17.1	40.79	4.09
⊕ Microsoft	Software	29.7	6.77	3.31
⊕ UnitedHealth Group	Health	22.2	34.30	3.02
⊖ Pfizer	Health	60.1	14.23	2.67
First Data	Business	21.9	9.68	2.41
⊕ American International G	Financial	26.1	12.06	2.23
⊖ Target	Consumer	20.8	27.66	1.92
⊖ Cisco Systems	Hardware	41.7	81.60	1.61
⊖ General Electric	Ind Mtrls	21.8	29.53	1.57
⊕ Clear Channel Communicat	Media	39.7	23.88	1.53
⊕ Fannie Mae	Financial	14.3	12.50	1.52
⊕ Affiliated Computer Serv	Business	24.2	1.08	1.45
Vodafone Grp	Telecom	—	—	1.40
⊖ Viacom B	Media	31.2	5.19	1.40
⊖ Merrill Lynch & Company	Financial	18.5	52.08	1.35
⊕ Home Depot	Consumer	21.4	49.46	1.34
⊕ Comcast Corporatio	Media	—	—	1.33
State Str	Financial	22.6	31.37	1.30
⊖ Tyco International	Ind Mtrls	—	47.51	1.29
⊕ Amgen	Health	35.5	27.95	1.29

Current Investment Style

Value Blnd Growth — Large Mid Small

	Market Cap %
Giant	40.9
Large	51.5
Mid	7.6
Small	0.0
Micro	0.0
Avg $mil:	37,512

Value Measures		Rel Category
Price/Earnings	20.24	0.88
Price/Book	3.13	0.91
Price/Sales	1.90	0.89
Price/Cash Flow	8.67	0.86
Dividend Yield %	0.89	1.20

Growth Measures	%	Rel Category
Long-Term Erngs	13.71	0.97
Book Value	11.16	0.95
Sales	8.98	1.17
Cash Flow	18.97	1.19
Historical Erngs	13.55	1.21

Profitability	%	Rel Category
Return on Equity	15.93	1.04
Return on Assets	6.61	0.86
Net Margin	9.83	0.99

Sector Weightings

	% of Stocks	Rel S&P 500	3 Year High Low	
↻ Info	24.79	1.04		
Software	5.48	1.19	9	4
Hardware	5.35	0.45	22	4
Media	10.39	2.55	11	5
Telecom	3.57	1.07	10	2
☞ Service	59.42	1.26		
Health	16.42	1.26	22	10
Consumer	13.22	1.41	13	7
Business	9.28	2.37	12	4
Financial	20.50	0.98	23	13
☐ Mfg	15.78	0.55		
Goods	7.50	0.79	8	4
Ind Mtrls	4.46	0.40	7	4
Energy	3.82	0.69	6	4
Utilities	0.00	0.00	1	0

Composition
- Cash 3.9
- Stocks 96.1
- Bonds 0.0
- Other 0.0
- Foreign 8.8 (% of Stock)

Morningstar's Take by Christopher Davis 12-15-03

T. Rowe Price Growth Stock Fund's restrained style continues to serve investors well.

Relative to the large-growth competition, this offering is more conservative than most. Manager Bob Smith keeps the portfolio well diversified by sector and generally goes light on growth-oriented technology and health-care stocks. For instance, hardware and software stocks account for just 11% of assets; the typical large-growth fund's combined stake in both sectors is 26%. Even with little exposure to racier fare, the fund isn't limited to slow growers. In fact, its holdings' average growth rates near or exceed those of its average peer. Smith avoids paying up for that growth, though, as the fund's below-average price multiples attest.

By and large, 2003 hasn't been a banner year for conservative large-growth funds, but this one has bucked the trend. Through Dec. 12, the fund has gained 27% for the year to date, placing in the category's top third and comfortably ahead of the S&P 500 Index. Names like Cisco Systems and Yahoo!, which Smith scooped up at depressed prices in 2002, have notched handsome gains, as have retail and financial picks such as Target and Citigroup.

These days, Smith has turned to firms he thinks will benefit from a recovery in the economy but haven't had a big runup in their stock prices this year. As examples, he cites top-10 holdings Microsoft and American International Group, which have notched tepid gains in the 2003 rally. Smith has also looked overseas for bargains, scooping up Credit Suisse Group and Samsung Electronics.

All told, we continue to like this offering. Smith has delivered solid results in rallies while capably protecting shareholders from excessive downside risk, resulting in a terrific long-term record. The fund's modest 0.77% expense ratio also gives Smith a significant advantage. Those expecting chart-topping gains in the raciest environments may be disappointed, but long-term investors should fare well here.

Address:	100 East Pratt Street Baltimore MD 21202 800-638-5660	Minimum Purchase:	$2500	Add: $100	IRA: $1000
		Min Auto Inv Plan:	$100	Add: $50	
Web Address	www.troweprice.com	Sales Fees:	No-load		
Inception:	04-11-50	Management Fee:	0.57%		
Advisor:	T. Rowe Price Associates, Inc.	Actual Fees:	Mgt:0.57%	Dist:	
Subadvisor	None	Expense Projections:	3Yr:$246	5Yr:$428	10Yr:$954
		Income Distrib:	Annually		
NTF Plans:	TD Waterhouse Ins NT				

Source: *Morningstar Mutual Funds,* January 6, 2004, p. 463, Morningstar, Inc., 225 W. Wacker Drive, Chicago, IL 60606.

Exhibit [13–7] Portion of the 2004 Mutual Fund Survey by *BusinessWeek* Magazine

Equity Fund Scoreboard

How to Use the Tables

BUSINESSWEEK RATINGS Overall ratings are based on five-year, risk-adjusted returns. They are calculated by subtracting a fund's risk-of-loss factor (see RISK) from historical pretax total return. Category ratings are based on risk-adjusted returns of the funds in that category. The ratings:

A SUPERIOR	**C- BELOW AVERAGE**
B+ VERY GOOD	**D POOR**
B ABOVE AVERAGE	**F VERY POOR**
C AVERAGE	

These tables list A-rated funds. For others go to http://bwnt.businessweek.com/mutual_fund

MANAGEMENT CHANGES ⬥ indicates the fund's manager has held the job at least 10 years; a ⬥ indicates a change since Dec. 31, 2002.

S&P 500 COMPARISON The pretax total returns for the Standard & Poor's 500-stock index are as follows: 2003, 28.7%; three-year average (2001-2003), –4.0%; five-year average (1999-2003), –0.6%; 10-year average (1994-2003), 9.8%.

CATEGORY Each U.S. diversified fund is classified by market capitalization of the stocks in the portfolio and by the nature of those stocks. If the average market cap is greater than $10 billion, the fund is large-cap; from $2 billion to $10 billion, mid-cap; less than $2 billion, small-cap. All-cap

funds are those that don't follow a fixed-capitalization policy. "Value" funds are those whose stocks have price-to-earnings and price-to-book ratios lower than the average of the stocks in their market capitalizations. "Growth" funds have higher than average p-e and p-b ratios. "Blend" funds are those in which the ratios are about average. Hybrids mix stocks and bonds, and possibly other assets. World funds generally include U.S. stocks; foreign funds do not. Sector and regional foreign funds are as indicated.

SALES CHARGE The cost of buying a fund. Many funds take this "load" out of the initial investment, and for ratings purposes, returns are reduced by these charges. Loads may be levied on withdrawals.

FUND/SYMBOL	OVERALL RATING (COMPARES RISK-ADJUSTED PERFORMANCE OF EACH FUND AGAINST ALL FUNDS)	CATEGORY (COMPARES RISK-ADJUSTED PERFORMANCE OF FUND WITHIN CATEGORY)	RATING	SIZE ASSETS $MIL.	% CHG. 2002-2003	FEES SALES CHARGE (%)	EXPENSE RATIO (%)	2003 RETURNS (%) PRE-TAX	AFTER-TAX	YIELD
ABN AMRO VEREDUS AGGRESSIVE GROWTH N VERDX	A	Small-cap Growth	B+	473.3	48	No load	1.40 *	44.5	44.5	0.0
AFBA FIVE STAR U.S.A. GLOBAL INSTITUTIONAL AFGLX	B	Large-cap Growth	A	39.4	21	No load	1.08	37.5	37.5	0.0
AIM BASIC VALUE A GTVLX	B+	Large-cap Value	A	3544.9	32	5.50 **	1.33 *	33.8	33.8	0.0
AIM OPPORTUNITIES I A ASCOX	A	Small-cap Growth	B+	250.1	33	5.50 **	0.72 *	39.2	39.2	0.0
AIM OPPORTUNITIES II A AMCOX	B+	Mid-cap Growth	A	92.2	-3	5.50 **	1.07 *	29.6	29.6	0.0
AIM REAL ESTATE A IARAX	A	Real Estate	B	253.3	146	4.75 **	1.72 *	39.2	38.0	2.3
AXP PRECIOUS METALS A INPMX	A	Precious Metals	C-	79.8	90	5.75 **	1.57 *	59.6	56.3	6.5
AEGIS VALUE AVALX	A	Small-cap Value	B+	425.0	144	No load	1.50	35.8	35.1	0.0
ALPINE REALTY INCOME & GROWTH Y AIGYX	A	Real Estate	A	199.2	257	No load	1.46	33.8	31.6	4.6
ALPINE U.S. REAL ESTATE EQUITY Y EUEYX ⬥	A	Real Estate	A	138.1	308	No load	1.72	82.0	80.5	0.0

Finally, the prospectus provides information about how to open a mutual fund account with the investment company.

The Mutual Fund Annual Report

If you are a prospective investor, you can request an annual report by mail, a toll-free telephone number, or the Internet. Once you are a shareholder, the investment company will send you an annual report. A fund's annual report contains a letter from the president of the investment company, from the fund manager, or both. The annual report also contains detailed financial information about the fund's assets and liabilities, statement of operations, and statement of changes in net assets. Next, the annual report includes a schedule of investments. Finally, the fund's annual report should include a letter from the fund's independent auditors that provides an opinion as to the accuracy of the fund's financial statements.

Financial Publications

Investment-oriented magazines like *BusinessWeek, Forbes, Kiplinger's Personal Finance Magazine,* and *Money* are other sources of information about mutual funds. Each

EXPENSE RATIO This counts expenses as a percentage of average net assets for the fund's most recent fiscal year. It measures how much shareholders pay for management. Footnotes indicate the inclusion of a 12(b)-1 plan, which spends shareholder money on marketing. The average is 1.44%.

PRETAX TOTAL RETURN A fund's net gain to investors, including reinvestment of dividends and capital gains at month-end prices.

AFTERTAX TOTAL RETURN Pretax return adjusted for federal taxes. Assumes ordinary income is taxed at the 30.5% tax rate. Capital gains are assumed long-term and taxed at 20%.

YIELD Income distributions as a percent of net asset value, adjusted for capital-gains distributions.

HISTORY A fund's returns relative to all other equity funds for five one-year periods, which, from left to right, are 1999, 2000, 2001, 2002, and 2003. The numbers designate which quintile the fund was in during the period: **1** for the top quintile, **2** for the second, and so on. No number indicates that there is no data for that period.

TURNOVER Trading activity, the lesser of purchases or sales divided by average monthly assets.

CASH Portion of fund assets not invested in stocks or bonds. A negative number means the fund has borrowed to buy securities.

UNTAXED GAINS Percentage of assets in portfolio that are unrealized and undistributed capital gains. A negative figure indicates losses that may offset future gains.

P-E RATIO The average price-earnings ratio of the fund derived from each stock price divided by reported per-share earnings.

TOP 10 STOCKS The percentage of fund assets that represents the 10 largest holdings. The higher the number, the more concentrated the fund, and the more dependent on the performance of a relatively small number of stocks.

LARGEST HOLDING Comes from the latest available fund reports.

RISK Potential for losing money in a fund, or risk-of-loss factor. For each fund, the three-month Treasury bill return is subtracted from the monthly total return for each of the 60 months in the ratings period. When a fund has not performed as well as Treasury bills, the monthly result is negative. The sum of these negative numbers is divided by the number of months. The result is a negative number, and the greater its magnitude, the higher the risk of loss. This number is the basis for BusinessWeek ratings, category ratings, and the RISK column.

BEST AND WORST QUARTERS Highest and lowest quarterly returns of the past five years.

AVERAGE ANNUAL TOTAL RETURNS (%)						HISTORY	PORTFOLIO DATA						RISK					TELEPHONE
3 YEARS		5 YEARS		10 YEARS		RESULTS VS.	TURNOVER	CASH	UNTAXED	P-E	TOP 10	LARGEST HOLDING	LEVEL	BEST		WORST		
PRETAX	AFTERTAX	PRETAX	AFTERTAX	PRETAX	AFTERTAX	ALL FUNDS		%	GAINS%	RATIO	STKS.%	COMPANY (% ASSETS)		QTR	%RET	QTR	%RET	
−11.1	−11.1	14.3	13.1	NA	NA	1 1 4 5 1	High	6	−13	22	32	Hovnanian Enterprises Class A (4)	High	Q4 99	44.7	Q3 02	−21.7	800-992-8151
−3.5	−3.5	5.3	5.1	NA	NA	2 2 3 4 2	Very Low	9	−7	28	37	Aflac (4)	Average	Q4 99	19.5	Q3 02	−21.9	800-243-9865
1.0	1.0	10.3	10.3	NA	NA	2 1 2 4 3	Low	4	5	25	30	Computer Associates International (4)	Average	Q2 99	21.1	Q3 02	−20.8	800-347-4246
−1.7	−1.7	16.6	14.4	NA	NA	1 1 3 4 2	High	9	13	28	21	Russell 2000 Futures (2)	High	Q4 99	38.0	Q3 02	−18.1	800-347-4246
−6.9	−6.9	14.9	14.4	NA	NA	1 2 5 3 3	High	4	−84	29	15	Agco (2)	Average	Q4 99	31.4	Q1 01	−19.1	800-347-4246
18.6	17.5	15.9	14.6	NA	NA	5 1 1 1 2	High	1	19	24	48	General Growth Properties (7)	Very Low	Q2 00	12.3	Q3 99	−7.3	800-347-4246
39.5	38.0	19.2	18.4	5.6	5.0	5 4 1 1 1	High	NA	15	34	NA	Buena Ventura (5)	High	Q1 02	34.8	Q1 00	−13.6	800-862-7919
25.2	24.6	19.8	18.0	NA	NA	4 1 1 1 2	Low	32	15	27	42	Scpie Holdings (3)	Very Low	Q2 03	21.0	Q3 02	−9.2	800-528-3780
20.1	17.9	18.6	16.4	NA	NA	5 1 1 1 3	High	16	17	23	41	Prime Group Realty Tr. Pfd. Ser. B % (4)	Very Low	Q2 00	16.0	Q3 99	−6.8	888-785-5578
32.9	32.6	18.8	18.6	13.8	13.0	5 1 1 1 1	High	6	19	14	52	Ryland Group (7)	Average	Q2 03	34.2	Q3 02	−19.0	888-785-5578

of these publications provides an annual survey of mutual funds and ranks them on a number of important investment criteria. Exhibit 13–7 illustrates a portion of *Business-Week*'s mutual fund survey for 2004.

A fund's past long-term performance is no guarantee of future success, but it is a valid predictor. To gauge this variable, most annual surveys include information about a fund's total return. In Exhibit 13–7, total returns for 1 year, 3 years, 5 years, and 10 years are reported for each fund included in the survey. Also included in the *Business-Week* survey is information about

- The fund's overall rating when compared with *all* other funds.
- The fund's rating when compared with funds in the same category.
- The size of the fund.
- The sales charge and expense ratio for each fund.
- Portfolio data, including turnover, percentage of cash, untaxed gains, PE ratio, and largest holdings.
- Risk of loss factor for each fund.
- A toll-free telephone number for each fund.

In addition to annual surveys like the *BusinessWeek* survey, a number of mutual fund guidebooks are available at your local bookstore or public library.

Sheet 39
Evaluating
Mutual Fund
Investment
Information

Sheet 40
Evaluation of a
Mutual Fund

Newspapers

Most large, metropolitan newspapers, *The Wall Street Journal,* and *Barron's* provide information about mutual funds. Typical coverage includes information about net asset value, net change, the fund family and fund name, and total return over selected time periods. Much of this same information is also available on the Internet.

The letters beside the name of a specific fund can be very informative. You can find out what they mean by looking at the footnotes that accompany the newspaper's mutual fund quotations. Generally, "p" means a 12b-1 distribution fee is charged, "r" means a redemption charge may be made, "t" means both the p and r footnotes apply, and "s" means the fund has had a stock split or paid a dividend.

The newspaper coverage described in this section is a good means of monitoring the value of your mutual fund investments. However, other sources of information provide a more complete basis for evaluating mutual fund investments.

✔ CONCEPTCHECK 13–3

1 In your own words, describe the difference between a managed fund and an index fund. Which one do you think could help you achieve your investment goals?

_____

_____

2 Assume you are considering a $5,000 investment in a growth mutual fund. How would you go about researching your potential mutual fund investment?

_____

_____

3 Describe how each of the following sources of investment information could help you evaluate a mutual fund investment.

Source of Information	Type of Information	How This Could Help
The Internet		
Professional advisory services		
Mutual fund prospectus		
Mutual fund annual report		
Financial publications		
Newspapers		

The Mechanics of a Mutual Fund Transaction

For many investors, mutual funds have become the investment of choice. In fact, you probably either own shares or know someone who owns shares in a mutual fund—they're that popular! They may be part of a 401(k) or 403(b) retirement account, a

SEP IRA, a Roth IRA, or a traditional IRA retirement account, all topics discussed in Chapter 14. They can also be owned outright by purchasing shares through a brokerage firm or an investment company that sponsors a mutual fund. As you will see later in this section, it's easy to purchase shares in a mutual fund. For $250 to $3,000 or more, you can open an account and begin investing. And there are other advantages that encourage investors to purchase shares in funds. Unfortunately, there are also disadvantages. Exhibit 13–8 summarizes the advantages and disadvantages of mutual fund investments.

One advantage of any investment is the opportunity to make money on it. In the next section, we examine how you can make money by investing in closed-end funds, exchange-traded funds, or open-end funds. We consider how taxes affect your mutual fund investments. Then we look at the options used to purchase shares in a mutual fund. Finally, we examine the options used to withdraw money from a mutual fund.

Return on Investment

As with other investments, the purpose of investing in a closed-end fund, exchange-traded fund, or open-end fund is to earn a financial return. Shareholders in such funds can receive a return in one of three ways. First, all three types of funds pay income dividends. **Income dividends** are the earnings a fund pays to shareholders from its dividend and interest income. Second, investors may receive capital gain distributions. **Capital gain distributions** are the payments made to a fund's shareholders that result from the sale of securities in the fund's portfolio. Both amounts generally are

OBJECTIVE 4
Describe how and why mutual funds are bought and sold.

income dividends The earnings a fund pays to shareholders from its dividend and interest income.

capital gain distributions The payments made to a fund's shareholders that result from the sale of securities in the fund's portfolio.

Exhibit [13–8]

Advantages and Disadvantages of Investing in Mutual Funds

Advantages

- Diversification.
- Professional management.
- Ease of buying and selling shares.
- Multiple withdrawal options.
- Distribution or reinvestment of dividends and capital gains.
- Switching privileges within the same fund family.
- Services that include toll-free telephone numbers, complete records of all transactions, and savings and checking accounts.

Disadvantages

- Purchase/withdrawal costs.
- Ongoing management fees and 12b-1 fees.
- Poor performance that may not match the Standard & Poor's 500 stock index or some other index.
- Inability to control when capital gain distributions occur and complicated tax-reporting issues.
- Potential market risk associated with all investments.
- Some sales personnel are aggressive and/or unethical.

Figure It Out!

CALCULATING TOTAL RETURN FOR MUTUAL FUNDS

In Chapter 12, we defined total return as a calculation that includes not only the yearly dollar amount of income but also any increase or decrease in market value from the original purchase price of an investment. For mutual funds, you can use the following calculation to determine the dollar amount of total return:

> Income dividends
> + Capital gain distributions
> + Change in share market value when sold
> ———————————————————
> Dollar amount of total return

For example, assume you purchased 100 shares of Majestic Growth Fund for $12.20 per share for a total investment of $1,220. During the next 12 months, you received income dividends of $0.45 a share and capital gain distributions of $0.90 a share. Also, assume you sold your investment at the end of 12 months for $14.40 a share. As illustrated below, the dollar amount for total return is $355:

Income dividends = 100 × $0.45 =	$ 45
Capital gain distributions = 100 × $0.90 =	+ 90
Change in share value = $14.40 − $12.20 = $2.20 × 100 =	+ 220
Dollar amount of total return	$ 355

To calculate the percentage of total return, divide the dollar amount of total return by the original cost of your mutual fund investment. The percentage of total return for the above example is 29.1 percent, as follows:

$$\text{Percent of total return} = \frac{\text{Dollar amount of total return}}{\text{Original cost of your investment}}$$

$$= \frac{\$355}{\$1,220}$$

$$= 0.291, \text{ or } 29.1\%$$

Now it's your turn. Use the following financial information for the Northeast Utility fund to calculate the dollar amount of total return and percent of total return over a 12-month period.

> Number of shares, 100
> Purchase price, $14.00 a share
> Income dividends, $0.30 a share
> Capital gain distribution, $0.60 a share
> Sale price, $15.25 a share

Calculation	Calculation Formula	Your Answer
Dollar amount of total return		
Percent of total return		

paid once a year. Note: Exchange-traded funds don't usually pay end-of-the-year capital gain distributions. Third, as with stock and bond investments, you can buy shares in funds at a low price and then sell them after the price has increased. For example, assume you purchased shares in the Fidelity Stock Selector Fund at $21.00 per share and sold your shares two years later at $23.50 per share. In this case, you made $2.50 ($23.50 selling price minus $21.00 purchase price) per share. With this financial information and the dollar amounts for income dividends and capital gain distributions, you can calculate a total return for your mutual fund investment. Before completing this section, you may want to examine the actual procedure used to calculate the dollar amount of total return and percentage of total return in the nearby Figure It Out box.

When shares in a mutual fund are sold, the profit that results from an increase in value is referred to as a *capital gain.* Note the difference between a capital gain distribution and a capital gain. A capital gain distribution occurs when *the fund* distributes profits that result from *the fund* selling securities in the portfolio at a profit. On the other hand, a capital gain is the profit that results when *you* sell your shares in the mutual fund for more than you paid for them. Of course, if the price of a fund's shares goes down between the time of your purchase and the time of sale, you incur a capital loss.

Taxes and Mutual Funds

Income dividends, capital gain distributions, and financial gains and losses from the sale of closed-end, exchange-traded, or open-end funds are subject to taxation. At the end of each year, investment companies are required to send each shareholder a statement specifying how much he or she received in dividends and capital gain distributions. Although investment companies may provide this information as part of their year-end statement, most funds use IRS Form 1099 DIV.

The following information provides general guidelines on how mutual fund transactions are taxed:

- Income dividends are reported, along with all other dividend amounts you have received, on your federal tax return and are taxed as regular income
- Capital gain distributions that result from the fund selling securities in the fund's portfolio at a profit are reported on Schedule D as part of your federal tax return and on the 1040.
- Capital gains or losses that result from your selling shares in a mutual fund are reported on Schedule D and the 1040. How long you hold the shares determines if your gains or losses are taxed as a short-term or long-term capital gain. (See Chapter 3 for more information on capital gains and capital losses.)

DID YOU KNOW?

Who owns mutual funds?

3% Less than 25 years old
17% 25 to 34 years old
25% 35 to 44 years old
24% 45 to 54 years old
15% 55 to 64 years old
16% Over 65 years old

Source: U.S. Bureau of the Census, Statistical Abstract of the United States, 2003, 123rd ed. (Washington, DC: U.S. Government Printing Office, 2003), p. 761.

Two specific problems develop with taxation of mutual funds. First, almost all investment companies allow you to reinvest income dividends and capital gain distributions from the fund to purchase additional shares instead of receiving cash. Even though you didn't receive cash because you chose to reinvest such distributions, they are still taxable and must be reported on your federal tax return as current income. Second, when you purchase shares of stock, corporate bonds, or other investments and use the buy-and-hold technique described in Chapter 12, you decide when you sell. Thus, you can pick the tax year when you pay tax on capital gains or deduct capital losses. Mutual funds, on the other hand, buy and sell securities within the fund's portfolio on a regular basis during any 12-month period. At the end of the year, profits that result from the mutual fund's buying and selling activities are paid to shareholders in the form of capital gain distributions. Unlike the investments that you manage, you have no control over when the mutual fund sells securities and when you will be taxed on capital gain distributions. To ensure having all of the documentation you need for tax reporting purposes, it is essential that *you* keep accurate records. The same records will help you monitor the value of your mutual fund investments and make more intelligent decisions with regard to buying and selling these investments.

Purchase Options

You can buy shares of a closed-end fund or exchange-traded fund through a stock exchange or in the over-the-counter market. You can purchase shares of an open-end, no-load fund by contacting the investment company that manages the fund. You can purchase shares of an open-end, load fund through a salesperson who is authorized to sell them, through an account executive of a brokerage firm, or directly from the investment company that sponsors the fund.

You can also purchase both no-load and load funds from mutual fund supermarkets available through brokerage firms. A mutual fund supermarket offers at least two advantages. First, instead of dealing with numerous investment companies that sponsor mutual funds, you can make one toll-free phone call to obtain information, purchase shares, and sell shares in a large number of mutual funds. Second, you receive one statement from the brokerage firm instead of receiving a statement from each investment company you deal with. One statement can be a real plus because it provides the information you need to monitor the value of your investments in one place and in the same format.

Because of the unique nature of open-end fund transactions, we will examine how investors buy and sell shares in this type of mutual fund from an investment company.

To purchase shares in an open-end mutual fund from an investment company, you may use four options: regular account transactions, voluntary savings plans, contractual savings plans, and reinvestment plans. The most popular and least complicated method of purchasing shares in an open-end fund is through a regular account transaction. When you use a regular account transaction, you decide how much money you want to invest and when you want to invest, and simply buy as many shares as possible.

The chief advantage of the voluntary savings plan is that it allows you to make smaller purchases than the minimum purchases required by the regular account method described above. At the time of the initial purchase, you declare an intent to make regular minimum purchases of the fund's shares. Although there is no penalty for not making purchases, most investors feel an "obligation" to make purchases on a periodic basis, and, as pointed out throughout this text, small monthly investments are a great way to save for long-term objectives. For most voluntary savings plans, the minimum purchase ranges from $25 to $100 for each purchase after the initial investment. Funds try to make investing as easy as possible. Most offer payroll deduction plans, and many will deduct, upon proper shareholder authorization, a specified amount from a shareholder's bank account. Also, many investors can choose mutual funds as a vehicle to invest money that is contributed to a 401(k), 403(b), or individual retirement account. As mentioned earlier, Chapter 14 provides more information on the tax advantages of different types of retirement accounts.

Contractual savings plans require you to make regular purchases over a specified period of time, usually 10 to 15 years. These plans are sometimes referred to as *front-end load plans* because almost all of the commissions are paid in the first few years of the contract period. You will incur penalties if you do not fulfill the purchase requirements. For example, if you drop out of a contractual savings plan before completing the purchase requirements, you sacrifice the prepaid commissions. Many financial experts and government regulatory agencies are critical of contractual savings plans. As a result, the Securities and Exchange Commission and many states have imposed new rules on investment companies offering contractual savings plans.

You may also purchase shares in an open-end fund by using the fund's reinvestment plan. A **reinvestment plan** is a service provided by an investment company in which income dividends and capital gain distributions are automatically reinvested to purchase additional shares of the fund. Most reinvestment plans allow shareholders to use reinvested money to purchase shares without having to pay additional sales charges or commissions. *Reminder:* When your dividends or capital gain distributions are reinvested, you must still report these transactions as taxable income.

All four purchase options allow you to buy shares over a long period of time. As a result, you can use the principle of *dollar cost averaging,* which was explained in Chapter 12. Dollar cost averaging allows you to average many individual purchase prices over a long period of time. This method helps you avoid the problem of buying high and selling low. With dollar cost averaging, you can make money if you sell your mutual fund shares at a price higher than their *average* purchase price.

Withdrawal Options

Because closed-end funds and exchange-traded funds are listed on stock exchanges or traded in the over-the-counter market, an investor may sell shares in such a fund to another

ApplyYourself!

Objective 4

In a short paragraph, describe which purchase option and which withdrawal option appeal to you. Explain your answer.

reinvestment plan A service provided by an investment company in which shareholder income dividends and capital gain distributions are automatically reinvested to purchase additional shares of the fund.

investor. Shares in an open-end fund can be sold on any business day to the investment company that sponsors the fund. In this case, the shares are redeemed at their net asset value. All you have to do is give proper notification and the fund will send you a check. With some funds, you can even write checks to withdraw money from the fund.

In addition, most funds have provisions that allow investors with shares that have a minimum net asset value (usually at least $5,000) to use four options to systematically withdraw money. First, you may withdraw a specified, fixed dollar amount each investment period until your fund has been exhausted. Normally, an investment period is three months.

A second option allows you to liquidate or "sell off" a certain number of shares each investment period. Since the net asset value of shares in a fund varies from one period to the next, the amount of money you receive will also vary.

A third option allows you to withdraw a fixed percentage of asset growth. For example, assume you arrange to receive 60 percent of the asset growth of your investment, and the asset growth of your investment amounts to $1,200 in a particular investment period. For that period, you will receive a check for $720 ($1,200 × 60% = $720). If no asset growth occurs, no payment is made to you. Under this option, your principal remains untouched.

A final option allows you to withdraw all income dividends and capital gain distributions earned by the fund during an investment period. Under this option, your principal remains untouched.

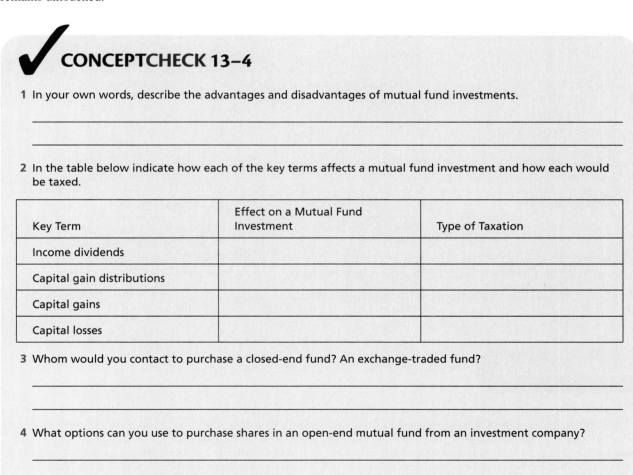

✔ CONCEPTCHECK 13–4

1 In your own words, describe the advantages and disadvantages of mutual fund investments.

_____

_____

2 In the table below indicate how each of the key terms affects a mutual fund investment and how each would be taxed.

Key Term	Effect on a Mutual Fund Investment	Type of Taxation
Income dividends		
Capital gain distributions		
Capital gains		
Capital losses		

3 Whom would you contact to purchase a closed-end fund? An exchange-traded fund?

_____

_____

4 What options can you use to purchase shares in an open-end mutual fund from an investment company?

_____

_____

Continued

5 What options can you use to withdraw money from an open-end mutual fund?

_____

_____

Back to   **Getting Personal**

Reevaluate your Getting Personal answers at the beginning of the chapter. Then answer the following questions.

1. In your own words, describe why you would choose mutual funds to help you obtain your investment goals.

_____

_____

2. Mutual funds charge investors a number of different fees and charges. In the table below indicate the typical fee or charge and when it is assessed.

Charge or Fee	Typical Fee	When Assessed
Front-end load		
Contingent deferred sales load		
12b-l fee		
Management fee		

3. In this chapter, mutual funds were divided into three different categories: stock funds, bond funds, and other funds. Choose a specific type of fund described in one of the three categories. Then explain how that fund seems to match your investment goals.

_____

_____

Chapter Summary

Objective 1   The major reasons investors choose mutual funds are professional management and diversification. Mutual funds are also a convenient way to invest money. There are three types of mutual funds: closed-end funds, exchange-traded funds, and open-end funds. A closed-end fund is a mutual fund whose shares are issued only when the fund is organized. An exchange-traded fund (ETF) is a fund that invests in the stocks contained in a specific stock index like the Standard & Poor's 500 stock index. Both closed-end and exchange-traded funds are traded on a stock ex-change or in the over-the-counter market. An open-end fund is a mutual fund whose shares are sold and redeemed by the investment company at the net asset value (NAV) at the request of investors.

Mutual funds can also be classified as A shares (commissions charged when shares are purchased), B shares (commissions charged when money is withdrawn during the first five years), and C shares (no commission to buy or sell shares, but higher, on-going 12b-l fees). Other possible fees include management fees and 12b-l fees.

Objective 2 The major categories of stock mutual funds, in terms of the types of securities in which they invest, are aggressive growth, equity income, global, growth, index, international, midcap, regional, sector, and small cap. There are also bond funds that include high-yield (junk), intermediate corporate, intermediate U.S. government, long-term corporate, long-term U.S. government, municipal, short-term corporate, and short-term U.S. government. Finally, other funds invest in a mix of different stocks, bonds, and other investment securities that include asset allocation funds, balanced funds, and money market funds. Today many investment companies use a family-of-funds concept, which allows shareholders to switch among funds as different funds offer more potential, financial reward, or security.

Objective 3 The responsibility for choosing the "right" mutual fund rests with you, the investor. Fortunately, a lot of information is available to help you evaluate a specific mutual fund. Often, the first question investors must answer is whether they want a managed fund or an index fund. With a managed fund, a professional fund manager (or team of managers) chooses the securities that are contained in the fund. Some investors choose to invest in an index fund, because over many years, index funds have outperformed almost 85 percent of all managed funds. If the individual securities included in an index increase in value, the index goes up. On the other hand, if the securities included in the index go down, the index goes down. Because an index mutual fund is a mirror image of a specific index, the dollar value of a share in an index fund also increases or decreases when the index increases or decreases. To help evaluate different mutual funds, investors can use the information on the Internet, from professional advisory services, from the fund's prospectus and annual report, in financial publications, and in newspapers.

Objective 4 The advantages and disadvantages of mutual funds have made mutual funds the investment of choice for many investors. For $250 to $3,000 or more, you can open an account and begin investing. The shares of a closed-end fund or exchange-traded fund are bought and sold on organized stock exchanges or the over-the-counter market. The shares of an open-end fund may be purchased through a salesperson who is authorized to sell them, through an account executive of a brokerage firm, from a mutual fund supermarket, or from the investment company that sponsors the fund. The shares in an open-end fund can be sold to the investment company that sponsors the fund. Shareholders in mutual funds can receive a return in one of three ways: income dividends, capital gain distributions when the fund buys and sells securities in the fund's portfolio at a profit, and capital gains when the shareholder sells shares in the mutual fund at a higher price than the price paid. A number of purchase and withdrawal options are available for mutual fund investors.

Key Terms

capital gain distributions 375	family of funds 364	net asset value (NAV) 358
closed-end fund 358	income dividends 375	no-load fund 359
contingent deferred sales load 359	investment company 356	open-end fund 358
exchange-traded fund (ETF) 358	load fund 359	reinvestment plan 378
expense ratio 360	mutual fund 356	12b-1 fee 360

Problems and Questions

1. Given the following information, calculate the net asset value for the Boston Equity mutual fund:
   Total assets, $225,000,000
   Total liabilities, $5,000,000
   Total number of shares, 4,400,000

2. Jan Throng invested $15,000 in the AIM Charter Mutual Fund. The fund charges a 5.50 percent commission when shares are purchased. Calculate the amount of commission Jan must pay.

3. Mary Canfield purchased the New Dimensions bond fund. This fund doesn't charge a front-end load, but it does charge a contingent deferred sales load of 4 percent for any withdrawals during the first five years. If Mary withdraws $6,000 during the second year, how much is the contingent deferred sales load?

4. Mike Jackson invested a total of $8,500 in the ABC Mutual Fund. The management fee for this particular fund is 0.70 percent of the total asset value. Calculate the management fee Mike must pay this year.

5. This chapter explored a number of different classifications of mutual funds.
   a. Based on your age and current financial situation, which type of mutual fund seems appropriate for your investment needs? Explain your answer.

b. As people get closer to retirement, their investment goals often change. Assume you are now 45 and have accumulated $110,000 in a retirement account. In this situation, what type of mutual fund would you choose? Why?

c. Assume you are now 60 years of age and have accumulated $400,000 in a retirement account. Also assume you would like to retire when you are 65. What type of mutual funds would you choose to help you reach your investment goals? Why?

6. Choose either the AIM Charter (symbol CHTRX) mutual fund or the AIM Basic Value (symbol GTVLX) mutual fund. Then describe how each of the following sources of information could help you evaluate one of these mutual funds.
a. The Internet.

b. Professional advisory services.

c. The fund's prospectus.

d. The fund's annual report.

e. Financial publications.

f. Newspapers.

7. Visit the Yahoo! Finance Web site and evaluate one of the following mutual funds. To complete this activity, follow these steps:
a. Go to http://finance.yahoo.com.
b. Choose one of the following three funds, enter its symbol, and click on the "Go" button: Oakmark I Fund (OAKMX), Scudder Growth A Fund (KGRAX), and American Funds Washington Mutual A Fund (AWSHX).
c. Print out the information for the mutual fund that you chose to evaluate.
d. Based on the information included in this research report, would you invest in this fund? Explain your answer.

8. Assume that one year ago, you bought 100 shares of a mutual fund for $15 per share, you received a $0.75 per-share capital gain distribution during the past 12 months, and the market value of the fund is now $18.
a. Calculate the total return for your $1,500 investment.

b. Calculate the percentage of total return for your $1,500 investment.

9. Obtain a mutual fund prospectus to determine the options you can use to purchase and redeem shares.
a. Which purchase option would appeal to you? Why?

b. Assuming you are now of retirement age, which withdrawal option would appeal to you?

Internet Connection

RESEARCHING MUTUAL FUND INVESTMENTS

Visit the following Web sites and describe the types of information provided by each site. Then describe how this site could help you invest.

Sponsor	Web Site	Type of Information	How Could This Site Help Me Invest?
Bloomberg	www.Bloomberg.com		
CNNMoney	www.money.com		
Motley Fool	www.fool.com		
Kiplinger	www.kiplinger.com		
SmartMoney	www.smartmoney.com		

Case in Point

RESEARCH INFORMATION AVAILABLE FROM MORNINGSTAR

This chapter stressed the importance of evaluating potential investments. Now it is your turn to try your skill at evaluating a potential investment in the T. Rowe Price Growth Stock Fund. Assume you could invest $10,000 in shares of this fund. To help you evaluate this potential investment, carefully examine Exhibit 13–6, which reproduces the Morningstar research report for the T. Rowe Price Growth Stock Fund. The report was published January 6, 2004.

Questions

1. Based on the research provided by Morningstar, would you buy shares in the T. Rowe Price Growth Stock Fund? Justify your answer.

2. What other investment information would you need to evaluate this fund? Where would you obtain this information?

3. On June 2, 2004, shares in the T. Rowe Price Growth Stock Fund were selling for $24.58 per share. Using the Internet or a newspaper, determine the current price for a share of this fund. Based on this information, would your investment have been profitable? (*Hint:* The symbol for this fund is PRGFX.)

4. Assuming you purchased shares in the T. Rowe Price Growth Stock Fund on June 2, 2004, and based on your answer to question 3, how would you decide if you want to hold or sell your shares? Explain your answer.

Name: _____ Date: _____

Evaluating Mutual Fund Investment Information

Financial Planning Activities: To identify and assess the value of various investment information sources, obtain samples of several items of investment information that you might consider to guide you in your investment decisions.

Suggested Web Sites: www.morningstar.com   www.mfea.com

Criteria Evaluation	Item 1	Item 2	Item 3
Location (address, phone)			
Web site			
Overview of information provided (main features)			
Cost			
Ease of access			
Evaluation • Reliablility • Clarity • Value of information compared to cost			

What's Next for Your Personal Financial Plan?
- Talk with friends and relatives to determine what sources of information they use to evaluate mutual funds.
- Choose one source of information and describe how the information could help you obtain your investment goals.

Your Personal Financial Plan

Evaluation of a Mutual Fund

Financial Planning Activities: No checklist can serve as a foolproof guide for choosing a mutual fund. However, the following questions will help you evaluate a potential investment in such a fund. Use mutual fund Web sites on the Internet and/or library materials to answer these questions about a mutual fund that you believe could help you obtain your investment goals.

Suggested Web Sites: www.morningstar.com   http://finance.yahoo.com

Category 1: Fund Characteristics

1. What is the fund's name?

   _____

2. What is this fund's Morningstar rating?

   _____

3. What is the minimum investment?

   _____

4. Does the fund allow telephone or Internet exchanges?   ☐ Yes ☐ No

5. Is there a fee for exchanges?   ☐ Yes ☐ No

Category 2: Costs

6. Is there a front-end load charge? If so, how much is it?

   _____

7. Is there a redemption fee? If so, how much is it?

   _____

8. How much is the annual management fee?

   _____

9. Is there a 12b-1 fee? If so, how much is it?

   _____

10. What is the fund's expense ratio?

    _____

Category 3: Diversification

11. What is the fund's objective?

    _____

12. What types of securities does the fund's portfolio include?

    _____

13. How many different securities does the fund's portfolio include?

    _____

14. How many types of industries does the fund's portfolio include?

    _____

15. What are the fund's five largest holdings?

    _____

Category 4: Fund Performance

16. How long has the fund manager been with the fund?

    _____

17. How would you describe the fund's performance over the past 12 months?

    _____

18. How would you describe the fund's performance over the past five years?

    _____

19. How would you describe the fund's performance over the past 10 years?

    _____

20. What is the current net asset value for this fund?

    _____

21. What is the high net asset value for this fund over the last 12 months?

    _____

22. What is the low net asset value for this fund over the last 12 months?

    _____

23. What do the experts say about this fund?

    _____

Category 5: Conclusion

24. Based on the above information, do you think an investment in this fund will help you achieve your investment goals?   ☐ Yes ☐ No

25. Explain your answer to question 24.

    _____

A Word of Caution

When you use a checklist, there is always a danger of overlooking important relevant information. This checklist is not a cure-all, but it does provide some very sound questions that you should answer before making a mutual fund investment decision. Quite simply, it is a place to start. If you need other information, *you* are responsible for obtaining it and for determining how it affects your potential investment.

What's Next for Your Personal Financial Plan?

- Identify additional factors that may affect your decision to invest in this fund.
- Develop a plan for monitoring an investment's value once a mutual fund(s) is purchased.

14 Retirement and Estate Planning

Objectives

In this chapter, you will learn to:

1. Analyze your current assets and liabilities for retirement and estimate your retirement living costs.
2. Determine your planned retirement income and develop a balanced budget based on your retirement income.
3. Analyze the personal and legal aspects of estate planning.
4. Distinguish among various types of wills and trusts.

Why is this important?

Retirement planning is important because you'll probably spend many years in retirement. Properly estimating your retirement living costs and housing needs will enable you to save or invest enough money to live comfortably during retirement.

Identifying various kinds of wills and trusts will help you devise an estate plan that protects your interests as well as those of your family. Creating an effective estate plan will allow you to prosper during retirement and provide for your loved ones when you die.

 Getting Personal

What are your attitudes toward retirement and estate planning? For each of the following statements, select "agree" or "disagree" to indicate your behavior regarding the following statements:

	Agree	Disagree
1. I have plenty of time to start saving for retirement.	_____	_____
2. My living expenses will drop when I retire.	_____	_____
3. I can depend on Social Security and my company pension to pay for my retirement living expenses.	_____	_____
4. Since I am not married now, I don't need a will.	_____	_____
5. I believe estate planning is only for the rich and famous.	_____	_____
6. I can free myself from managing my assets by setting up a trust.	_____	_____

After studying this chapter, you will be asked to reconsider your responses to these questions.

Planning for Retirement

OBJECTIVE 1

Analyze your current assets and liabilities for retirement and estimate your retirement living costs.

Your retirement years may seem a long way off right now. However, the fact is, it's never too early to start planning for retirement. Planning can help you cope with sudden changes that may occur in your life and give you a sense of control over your future.

If you haven't done any research on the subject of retirement, you may hold some outdated beliefs about your "golden years." Some common mistaken beliefs include:

- You have plenty of time to start saving for retirement.
- Saving just a little bit won't help.
- You'll spend less money when you retire.
- Your retirement will only last about 15 years.
- You can depend on Social Security and a company pension plan to pay your basic living expenses.
- Your pension benefits will increase to keep pace with inflation.
- Your employer's health insurance plan and Medicare will cover all your medical expenses when you retire.

Some of these statements were once true but are no longer true today. You may live for many years after you retire. If you want your retirement to be a happy and comfortable time of your life, you'll need enough money to suit your lifestyle. You can't count on others to provide for you. That's why you need to start planning and saving as early as possible. It's never too late to start saving for retirement, but the sooner you start, the better off you'll be.

Suppose that you want to have at least $1 million when you retire at age 65. If you start saving for retirement at age 25, you can meet that goal by putting about $127 per month into investment funds that grow at a rate of about 11 percent each year. If you wait until you're 50, the monthly amount skyrockets to $2,244.

As you think about your retirement years, consider your long-range goals. What does retirement mean to you? Maybe it will simply be a time to stop working, sit back, and relax. Perhaps you imagine traveling the world, developing a hobby, or starting a second career. Where do you want to live after you retire? What type of lifestyle would you like to have? Once you've pondered these questions, you have to determine your current financial situation. That requires you to analyze your current assets and liabilities.

Apply *Yourself!*

Objective 1

Survey friends, relatives, and other people to get their views on retirement planning. Prepare a written report of your findings.

Key Web Sites for Retirement Planning
www.isrplan.org/
www.asec.org

Conducting a Financial Analysis

As you learned in Chapter 2, an asset is any item of value that you own—cash, property, personal possessions, and investments—including cash in checking and savings accounts, a house, a car, a television, and so on. It also includes the current value of any stocks,

	Sample Figures	Your Figures
Assets: What We Own		
Cash:		
Checking account	$ 800	_____
Savings account	4,500	_____
Investments:		
U.S. savings bonds		
(current cash-in value)	5,000	_____
Stocks, mutual funds	4,500	_____
Life insurance:		
Cash value, accumulated dividends	10,000	_____
Company pension rights:		
Accrued pension benefit	20,000	_____
Property:		
House (resale value)	50,000	_____
Furniture and appliances	8,000	_____
Collections and jewelry	2,000	_____
Automobile	3,000	_____
Other:		
Loan to brother	1,000	_____
Gross assets	$108,800	_____
Liabilities: What We Owe		
Current unpaid bills	600	_____
Home mortgage (remaining balance)	9,700	_____
Auto loan	1,200	_____
Property taxes	1,100	_____
Home improvement loan	3,700	_____
Total liabilities	$ 16,300	_____

Exhibit [14–1]

Review Your Assets, Liabilities, and Net Worth

Reviewing your assets to ensure they are sufficient for retirement is a sound idea.

Net worth: Assets of $108,000 minus liabilities of $16,300 equals $92,500.

bonds, and other investments that you may have as well as the current value of any life insurance and pension funds.

Your liabilities, on the other hand, are the debts you owe: the remaining balance on a mortgage or automobile loan, credit card balances, unpaid taxes, and so on. If you subtract your liabilities from your assets, you get your net worth. Ideally, your net worth should increase each year as you move closer to retirement. The Exhibit 14–1 checklist is an example of how you might analyze your assets and liabilities.

It's a good idea to review your assets on a regular basis. You may need to make adjustments in your saving, spending, and investment in order to stay on track. As you review your assets, consider the following factors: housing, life insurance, and other investments. Each will have an important effect on your retirement income.

HOUSING   A house will probably be your most valuable asset. However, if you buy a home with a large mortgage that prevents you from saving, you put your ability to meet your retirement goal at risk. In that case you might consider buying a smaller, less expensive place to live. Remember that a smaller house is usually easier and cheaper to maintain. You can use the money you save to increase your retirement fund.

LIFE INSURANCE   At some point in the future, you may buy life insurance to provide financial support for your children in case you die while they are still young. As you near retirement, though, your children will probably be self-sufficient. When that time comes, you might reduce your premium payments by decreasing your life insurance coverage. This would give you extra money to spend on living expenses or to invest for additional income.

OTHER INVESTMENTS   When you review your assets, you'll also want to evaluate any other investments you have. When you originally chose these investments, you may have been more interested in making your money grow than in getting an early return from them. When you are ready to retire, however, you may want to use the income from those investments to help cover living expenses instead of reinvesting it.

Estimating Retirement Living Expenses

Next you should estimate how much money you'll need to live comfortably during your retirement years. (See the nearby Personal Finance in Practice feature.) You can't predict exactly how much money you'll need when you retire. You can, however, estimate what your basic needs will be. To do this, you'll have to think about your spending patterns and how your living situation will change when you retire. For instance, you probably spend more money on recreation, health insurance, and medical care in retirement than you do now. At the same time, you may spend less on transportation and clothing. Your federal income taxes may be lower. Also, some income from various retirement plans may be taxed at a lower rate or not at all. As you consider your retirement living expenses, remember to plan for emergencies. Look at Exhibit 14–2 for an example of retirement spending patterns.

Exhibit [14–2]

How an "Average" Older (65+) Household Spends Its Money
Retired families spend a greater share of their income for food, housing, and medical care than nonretired families.

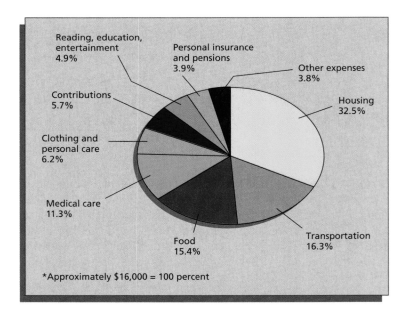

Source: U.S. Bureau of Labor Statistics.

Personal Finance in Practice

YOUR RETIREMENT HOUSING

The place where you choose to live during retirement can have a significant impact on your financial needs. Use vacations in the years before you retire to explore areas you think you might enjoy. If you find a place you really like, go there at different times of the year. That way you'll know what the climate is like. Meet people who live in the area and learn about activities, transportation, and taxes.

Consider the downside of moving to a new location. You may find yourself stuck in a place you really don't like after all. Moving can also be expensive and emotionally draining. You may miss your children, your grandchildren, and the friends and relatives you leave behind. Be realistic about what you'll have to give up as well as what you'll gain if you move after you retire.

AVOIDING RETIREMENT RELOCATION PITFALLS

Some retired people move to the location of their dreams and then discover that they've made a big mistake financially. Here are some tips from retirement specialists on how to uncover hidden taxes and other costs before you move to a new area:

- Contact the local chamber of commerce to get details on area property taxes and the local economy.

- Contact the state tax department to find out about income, sales, and inheritance taxes as well as special exemptions for retirees.

- Read the Sunday edition of the local newspaper of the city where you're thinking of moving.

- Check with local utility companies to get estimates on energy costs.

- Visit the area in different seasons, and talk to local residents about the various costs of living.

- Rent for a while instead of buying a home immediately.

What are your findings?

_____

_____

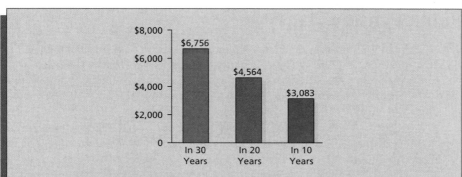

This chart shows you what $10,000 today will be worth in 10, 20, and 30 years assuming a fairly conservative 4 percent rate of inflation.

The prices of goods and services rarely remain the same for any significant period of time because of inflation. *How much will $10,000 be worth in 30 years, assuming a 4 percent rate of inflation? What can you do to counteract the effects of inflation?*

Exhibit [14–3]

The Effects of Inflation over Time

Don't forget to take inflation into account. Estimate high when calculating how much the prices of goods and services will rise by the time you retire (see Exhibit 14–3). Even a 3 percent rate of inflation will cause prices to double every 24 years.

✔ **CONCEPTCHECK 14–1**

1 The three assets you should review on a regular basis during retirement are:

_____

_____

2 What expenses are likely to increase during retirement?

_____

_____

3 What expenses are likely to decrease during retirement?

_____

_____

Your Retirement Income

OBJECTIVE 2

Determine your planned retirement income and develop a balanced budget based on your retirement income.

The four major sources of retirement income are public pension plans, employer pension plans, personal retirement plans, and annuities.

Public Pension Plans

A pension plan is a retirement plan that is funded, at least in part, by an employer. One source of retirement income is Social Security, a public pension plan established by the U.S. government in 1935. The government agency that manages the program is called the Social Security Administration.

SOCIAL SECURITY   Social Security is an important source of retirement income for most Americans. The program covers 97 percent of all workers, and almost one out of every six Americans currently collects some form of Social Security benefit. Social Security is actually a package of protection that provides benefits to retirees, survivors, and disabled persons. The package protects you and your family while you are working and after you retire. Nevertheless, you should not rely on Social Security to cover all of your retirement expenses. Social Security was never intended to provide 100 percent of your retirement income.

Who Is Eligible for Social Security Benefits? The amount of retirement benefits you receive from Social Security is based on your earnings over the years. The more you work and the higher your earnings, the greater your benefits, up to a certain maximum amount.

The Social Security Administration provides you an annual history of your earnings and an estimate of your future monthly benefits. The statement includes an estimate, in today's dollars, of how much you will get each

DID YOU KNOW?

This chart shows the percentage of final earnings Social Security is estimated to replace. Will you have enough to make up the difference?

Your Retirement "Gap"

Preretirement Salary	Percent of Income Replaced by Social Security	The "Gap" You and Your Employer Must Fill
$ 20,000	45%	35%
30,000	40	40
40,000	33	47
60,000	25	55
$100,000	15	65

Source: TIAA-CREF.

month from Social Security when you retire—at age 62, 65, or 70—based on your earnings to date and your projected future earnings.

To qualify for retirement benefits you must earn a certain number of credits. These credits are based on the length of time you work and pay into the system through the Social Security tax, or contribution, on your earnings. You and your employer pay equal amounts of the Social Security tax. Your credits are calculated on a quarterly basis. The number of quarters you need depends on your year of birth. People born after 1928 need 40 quarters to qualify for benefits.

Certain dependents of a worker may receive benefits under the Social Security program. They include a wife or dependent husband aged 62 or older; unmarried children under 18 (or under 19 if they are full-time students no higher than grade 12); and unmarried, disabled children aged 18 or older. Widows or widowers can receive Social Security benefits earlier.

Social Security Retirement Benefits   Most people can begin collecting Social Security benefits at age 62. However, the monthly amount at age 62 will be less than it would be if the person waits until full retirement age. This reduction is permanent.

In the past, people could receive full retirement benefits at age 65. However, because of longer life expectancies, the full retirement age is being increased in gradual steps. For people born in 1960 and later, the full retirement age will be 67. If you postpone applying for benefits beyond your full retirement age, your monthly payments will increase slightly for each year you wait, but only up to age 70.

Social Security Information   For more information about Social Security, you can visit the Social Security Web site. It provides access to forms and publications and gives links to other valuable information. To learn more about the taxability of Social Security benefits, contact the Internal Revenue Service at 800-829-3676 and ask for Publication 554, *Social Security and Equivalent Railroad Retirement Benefits.*

Key Web Sites for Retirement Income
www.quicken.com/retirement
www.moneymag.com

OTHER PUBLIC PENSION PLANS   Besides Social Security, the federal government provides several other special retirement plans for federal government workers and railroad employees. Employees covered under these plans are not covered by Social Security. The Veterans Administration provides pensions for survivors of people who died while in the armed forces. It also offers disability pensions for eligible veterans. Many state and local governments provide retirement plans for their employees as well.

Employer Pension Plans

Another possible source of retirement income is an employer pension plan offered by the company for which you work. With this type of plan, your employer contributes to your retirement benefits, and sometimes you contribute too. (See the nearby Figure It Out feature.) These contributions and earnings remain tax-deferred until you start to withdraw them in retirement.

Private employer pension plans vary. If the company you work for offers one, you should know when you become eligible to receive pension benefits. You'll also need to know what benefits you'll receive. Most employer plans are one of two basic types: defined-contribution plans or defined-benefit plans.

DEFINED-CONTRIBUTION PLAN   A **defined-contribution plan**, sometimes called an *individual account plan*, consists of an individual account of each employee to which the employer contributes a specific amount annually. This type of retirement plan does not guarantee any particular benefit. When you retire and become eligible for benefits, you simply receive the total amount of funds (including investment earnings) that have been placed in your account.

defined-contribution plan A plan—profit sharing, money purchase, Keogh, or 401(k)—that provides an individual account for each participant; also called an *individual account plan*.

Figure It Out!

SAVING FOR RETIREMENT

Calculate how much you would have in 10 years if you saved $2,000 a year at an annual compound interest rate of 10 percent, with the company contributing $500 a year.

	Contributions	10% Interest	Total
Annual contribution of 10% of a $20,000 salary	$2,000.00		
Company annual contribution matching $0.50 of 5% of the salary	500.00		
1st Year			
2nd Year			
3rd Year			
4th Year			
5th Year			
6th Year			
7th Year			
8th Year			
9th Year			
10th Year			
Total			

401(k) plan A plan under which employees can defer current taxation on a portion of their salary; also called a *salary-reduction plan.*

Apply *Yourself!*

Objective 2

Read newspaper or magazine articles to determine what expenses are likely to increase and decrease during retirement. How might this information affect your retirement-planning decisions?

Several types of defined-contribution plans exist. With a money-purchase plan, your employer promises to set aside a certain amount of money for you each year. The amount is generally a percentage of your earnings. Under a stock bonus plan, your employer's contribution is used to buy stock in the company for you. The stock is usually held in trust until you retire. Then you can either keep your shares or sell them. Under a profit-sharing plan, you employer's contribution depends on the company's profits.

In a **401(k) plan**, also known as a *salary-reduction plan,* you set aside a portion of your salary from each paycheck to be deducted from your gross pay and placed in a special account. Your employer will often match your contribution up to a specific dollar amount or percentage of your salary. The funds in 401(k) plans are invested in stocks, bonds, and mutual funds. As a result you can accumulate a significant amount of money in this type of account if you begin contributing to it early in your career. In addition, the money that accumulates in your 401(k) plan is tax-deferred, meaning that you don't have to pay taxes on it until you withdraw it.

If you're employed by a tax-exempt institution, such as a hospital or a nonprofit organization, the salary-reduction plan is called a Section 403(b) plan. As in 401(k) plan, the funds in a 403(b) plan are tax-deferred. The 401(k) and 403(b) plans are often referred to as *tax-sheltered annuity*

(TSA) plans. The amount that can be contributed annually to 401(k) and 403(b) plans is limited by law, as is the amount of annual contributions to money-purchase plans, stock bonus plans, and profit-sharing plans.

Employee contributions to a pension plan belong to you, the employee, regardless of the amount of time that you are with a particular employer. What happens to the contributions that the employer has made to your account if you change jobs and move to another company before you retire? One of the most important aspects of such plans is vesting. **Vesting** is the right to receive the employer's pension plan contributions that you've gained, even if you leave the company before retiring. After a certain number of years with the company, you will become *fully vested,* or entitled to receive 100 percent of the company's contributions to the plan on your behalf. Under some plans, vesting may occur in stages. For example, you might become eligible to receive 20 percent of your benefits after three years and gain another 20 percent each year until you are fully vested.

DEFINED-BENEFIT PLAN

A **defined-benefit plan** specifies the benefits you'll receive at retirement age, based on your total earnings and years on the job. The plan does not specify how much the employer must contribute each year. Instead your employer's contributions are based on how much money will be needed in the fund as each participant in the plan retires. If the fund is inadequate, the employer will have to make additional contributions.

CARRYING BENEFITS FROM ONE PLAN TO ANOTHER

Some pension plans allow *portability,* which means that you can carry earned benefits from one pension plan to another when you change jobs. Workers are also protected by the Employee Retirement Income Security Act of 1974 (ERISA), which sets minimum standards for pensions plans. Under this act the federal government insures part of the payments promised by defined-benefit plans.

Personal Retirement Plans

In addition to public and employer retirement plans, many people choose to set up personal retirement plans. Such plans are especially important to self-employed people and other workers who are not covered by employer pension plans. Among the most popular personal retirement plans are individual retirement accounts (IRAs) and Keogh accounts.

INDIVIDUAL RETIREMENT ACCOUNTS

An **individual retirement account (IRA)** is a special account in which the person sets aside a portion of income for retirement. Several types of IRAs are available:

- **Regular IRA:** A regular (traditional or classic) IRA lets you make annual contributions until age 70½. You can contribute up to $4,000 per year through 2007. The contribution limit increases to $5,000 in 2008 and after. Depending on your tax filing status and income, the contribution may be fully or partially tax-deductible. The tax deductibility of a traditional IRA also depends on whether you belong to an employer-provided retirement plan.
- **Roth IRA:** Annual contributions to a Roth IRA are not tax-deductible, but the earnings accumulate tax-free. You may contribute the amounts discussed above if you're a single taxpayer with an adjusted gross income (AGI) of less than $95,000. For married couples the combined AGI must be less than $150,000. You can continue to make annual contributions to a Roth IRA even after age 70½. If you have a Roth IRA, you can withdraw money from the account tax-free and penalty-free after five years if you are at least 59½ years old or plan to use the money to help buy your first home. You may convert a regular IRA to a Roth IRA. Depending on your situation, one type of account may be better for you than the other.

vesting An employee's right to at least a portion of the benefits accrued under an employer pension plan, even if the employee leaves the company before retiring.

defined-benefit plan A plan that specifies the benefits the employee will receive at the normal retirement age.

Key Web Sites for Personal Retirement Plans
www.financialengines.com
www.401k.com

individual retirement account (IRA) A special account in which the employee sets aside a portion of his or her income; taxes are not paid on the principal or interest until money is withdrawn from the account.

- **Simplified Employee Pension (SEP) Plan:** A simplified employee pension (SEP) plan, also known as a SEP IRA, is an individual retirement account funded by an employer. Each employee sets up an IRA account at a bank or other financial institution. Then the employer makes an annual contribution of up to $40,000. The employee's contributions, which can vary from year to year, are fully tax-deductible, and earnings are tax-deferred. The SEP IRA is the simplest type of retirement plan if a person is self-employed.
- **Spousal IRA:** A spousal IRA lets you make contributions on behalf of your non-working spouse if you file a joint tax return. The contributions are the same as for the traditional and Roth IRAs. As with a traditional IRA, this contribution may be fully or partially tax-deductible, depending on your income. This also depends on whether you belong to an employer-provided retirement plan.
- **Rollover IRA:** A rollover IRA is a traditional IRA that lets you roll over, or transfer, all or a portion of your taxable distribution from a retirement plan or other IRA. You may move your money from plan to plan without paying taxes on it. To avoid taxes, however, you must follow certain rules about transferring the money from one plan to another. If you change jobs or retire before age 59½, a rollover IRA may be just what you need. It will let you avoid the penalty you would otherwise have to pay on early withdrawals.
- **Education IRA:** An education IRA, also known as a Coverdell Education Savings Account, is a special IRA with certain restrictions. It allows individuals to contribute up to $2,000 per year toward the education of any child under age 18. The contributions are not tax-deductible. However, they do provide tax-free distributions for education expenses.

Exhibit [14–4]

Various Types of IRA

Type of IRA	IRA Features
Regular IRA	• Tax-deferred interest and earnings • Annual limit on individual contributions • Limited eligibility for tax-deductible contributions • Contributions do not reduce current taxes
Roth IRA	• Tax-deferred interest and earnings • Annual limit on individual contributions • Withdrawals are tax-free in specific cases • Contributions do not reduce current taxes
Simplifed Employee Pension Plan (SEP IRA)	• "Pay yourself first" payroll rreduction contributions • Pre-tax contributions • Tax-deferred interest and earnings
Spousal IRA	• Tax-deferred interest and earnings • Both working spouse and nonworking spouse can contribute up to the annual limit • Limited eligibility for tax-deductible contributions • Contributions do not reduce current taxes
Rollover IRA	• Traditional IRA that accepts rollovers of all or a portion of your taxable distribution from a retirement plan • You can roll over to a Roth IRA
Education IRA	• Tax-deferred interest and earnings • 10% early withdrawal penalty is waived when money is used for higher-education expenses • Annual limit on individual contributions • Contributions do not reduce current taxes

IRAs can be a good way to save money for retirement. *What are the features of the Education IRA?*

Exhibit 14–4 summarizes the various types of IRA.

Whether or not you're covered by another type of pension plan, you can still make IRA contributions that are not tax-deductible. All of the income your IRA earns will compound tax-deferred, until you begin making withdrawals. Remember, the biggest benefit of an IRA lies in its tax-deferred earnings growth. The longer the money accumulates tax-deferred, the bigger the benefit, as shown in Exhibit 14–5.

IRA Withdrawals   When you retire, you can withdraw the money from your IRA by one of several methods. You can take out all of the money at one time, but the entire amount will be taxed as income. If you decide to withdraw the money from your IRA in installments, you will have to pay tax only on the amount that you withdraw. A final alternative would be to place the money that you withdraw in an annuity that guarantees payments over your lifetime. See the discussion of annuities later in this section for further information about this option.

KEOGH PLANS   A **Keogh plan**, also known as an *H.R. 10 plan* or a *self-employed retirement plan,* is a retirement plan specially designed for self-employed people and their employees. Keogh plans have limits on the amount of annual tax-deductible contributions as well as various other restrictions. Keogh plans can be complicated to administer, so you should get professional tax advice before using this type of personal retirement plan.

Keogh plan A plan in which tax-deductible contributions fund the retirement of self-employed people and their employees; also called an *H.R. 10 plan* or a *self-employed retirement plan.*

LIMITS ON PERSONAL RETIREMENT PLANS   With the exception of Roth IRAs, you cannot keep money in most tax-deferred retirement plans forever. When you retire, or by age 70½ at the latest, you must begin to receive "minimum lifetime distributions," withdrawals from the funds you accumulated in the plan. The amount of the distributions is based on your life expectancy at the time the distributions begin. If you don't withdraw the minimum distributions from a retirement account, the IRS will charge you a penalty.

Sheet 41
Retirement
Plan
Comparison

Annuities

What do you do if you have funded your 401(k), 403(b), Keogh, and profit-sharing plans up to the allowable limits and you want to put away more money for retirement? The answer may be an annuity. You will recall from Chapter 10, an *annuity* is a contract

Exhibit [14–5]   Benefits of Starting a Retirement Plan Early

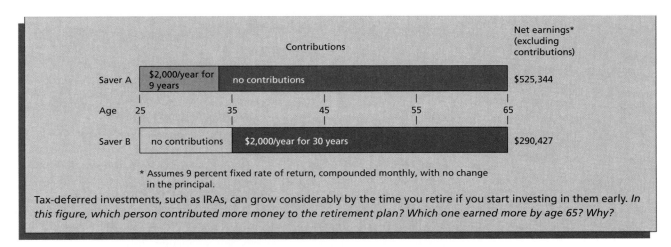

Tax-deferred investments, such as IRAs, can grow considerably by the time you retire if you start investing in them early. *In this figure, which person contributed more money to the retirement plan? Which one earned more by age 65? Why?*

Source: *The Franklin Investor* (San Mateo, CA: Franklin Distributors, Inc.), January 1989.

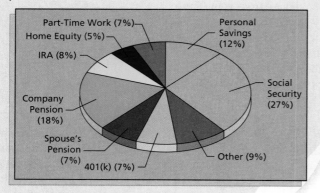

DID YOU KNOW?

Social Security provides only 27 percent of the average retiree's annual income. On average, pension income accounts for about 19 percent, slightly less than that provided by Social Security.

Part-Time Work (7%)
Home Equity (5%)
IRA (8%)
Company Pension (18%)
Spouse's Pension (7%)
401(k) (7%)
Personal Savings (12%)
Social Security (27%)
Other (9%)

SOURCES OF INCOME IN RETIREMENT

purchased from an insurance company that provides for a sum of money to be paid to a person at regular intervals for a certain number of years or for life.

You might purchase an annuity with the money you receive from an IRA or company pension. You can simply buy an annuity to supplement the income you'll receive from either of these types of plans.

You can choose to purchase an annuity that has a single payment or installment payments. You will also need to decide whether you want the insurance company to send the income from your annuity to you immediately or begin sending it to you at a later date. The payments you receive from an annuity are taxed as ordinary income. However, the interest you earn from the annuity accumulates tax-free until payments begin.

Living on Your Retirement Income

As you plan for retirement, you'll estimate a budget or spending plan. When the time to retire arrives, however, you may find that your expenses are higher than you expected. If that's the case, you'll have some work to do.

First, you'll have to make sure that you're getting all the income to which you're entitled. Are there other programs or benefits for which you might qualify? You'll also need to think about any assets or valuables you might be able to convert to cash or sources of income.

You may have to confront the trade-off between spending and saving again. For example, perhaps you can use your skills and time instead of money. Instead of spending money on an expensive vacation, take advantage of free and low-cost recreation opportunities, such as public parks, museums, libraries, and fairs. Retirees often receive special discounts on movie tickets, meals, and more.

Sheet 42
Forecasting
Retirement
Income

WORKING DURING RETIREMENT   Some people decide to work part-time after they retire. Some even take new full-time jobs. Work can provide a person with a greater sense of usefulness, involvement, and self-worth. It may also be a good way to add to your retirement income.

DIPPING INTO YOUR NEST EGG   When should you take money out of your savings during retirement? The answer depends on your financial circumstances, your age, and how much you want to leave to your heirs. (Your *heirs* are the people who will have the legal right to your assets when you die.) Your savings may be large enough to allow you to live comfortably on the interest alone. On the other hand, you may need to make regular withdrawals to help finance your retirement. Dipping into savings isn't wrong. However, you must do so with caution.

If you dip into your retirement nest egg, you should consider one important question: How long will your savings last if you make regular withdrawals? For example, if you have $10,000 in savings that earns 5.5 percent interest, compounded quarterly, you could take out $68 every month for 20 years before reducing those savings to zero. If you have $40,000, you could withdraw $224 every month for 30 years. Whatever your situation is, once your nest egg is gone, it's gone.

✔ **CONCEPTCHECK 14–2**

1 What are four major sources of retirement income?

_____

_____

2 What are the two basic types of employer pension plans?

_____

_____

3 What are the most popular personal retirement plans?

_____

_____

4 What is the major difference between a regular IRA and a Roth IRA?

_____

_____

5 What might you do if your expenses during retirement are higher than you expected?

_____

_____

Estate Planning

The Importance of Estate Planning

Many people think of estates as belonging only to the rich or elderly. The fact is, however, everyone has an estate. Simple defined, your **estate** consists of everything you own. During your working years your financial goal is to acquire and accumulate money for both your current and future needs. Many years from now, as you grow older, your point of view will change. Instead of working to acquire assets, you'll start to think about what will happen to your hard-earned wealth after you die. In most cases you'll want to pass that wealth along to your loved ones. That is where estate planning becomes important.

What Is Estate Planning?

Estate planning is the process of creating a detailed plan for managing your assets so that you can make the most of them while you're alive and ensure that they're distributed wisely after your death. It's not pleasant to think about your own death. However, it is a part of estate planning. Without a good estate plan, the assets you

OBJECTIVE 3
Analyze the personal and legal aspects of estate planning.

estate Everything one owns.

estate planning A definite plan for the administration and disposition of one's property during one's lifetime and at one's death.

accumulate during your lifetime might be greatly reduced by various taxes when you die.

Estate planning is an essential part of both retirement planning and financial planning. It has two phases. First, you build your estate through savings, investments, and insurance. Second, you ensure that your estate will be distributed as you wish at the time of your death. If you're married, your estate planning should take into account the needs of your spouse and children. If you are single, you still need to make sure that your financial affairs are in order for your beneficiaries. Your *beneficiary* is a person you've named to receive a portion of your estate after your death.

When you die, your surviving spouse, children, relatives, and friends will face a period of grief and loneliness. At the same time, one or more of these people will probably be responsible for settling your affairs. Make sure that important documents are accessible, understandable, and legally proper.

Legal Documents

An estate plan typically involves various legal documents, one of which is usually a will. When you die, the person who is responsible for handling your affairs will need access to these and other important documents. The documents must be reviewed and verified before your survivors can receive the money and other assets to which they're entitled. If no one can find the necessary documents, your heirs may experience emotionally painful delays. They may even lose part of their inheritance. The important papers you need to collect and organize include:

- Birth certificates for you, your spouse, and your children.
- Marriage certificates and divorce papers.
- Legal name changes (especially important to protect adopted children).
- Military service records.
- Social Security documents.
- Veteran's documents.
- Insurance policies.
- Transfer records of joint bank accounts.
- Safe-deposit box records.
- Automobile registration.
- Titles to stock and bond certificates.

Apply *Yourself!*

Objective 3

Contact several lawyers in your area to find out how much they would charge to prepare your simple will. Are their fees about the same?

Sheet 43
Estate
Planning
Activities

✔ **CONCEPTCHECK 14–3**

1 What is estate planning?

_____

_____

2 What are the two stages in planning your estate?

_____

_____

Continued

3 List some important documents you will need to collect and organize.

_____

_____

Legal Aspects of Estate Planning

Wills

One of the most important documents that every adult should have is a written will. A **will** is the legal document that specifies how you want your property to be distributed after your death. If you die **intestate**—without a valid will—your legal state of residence will step in and control the distribution of your estate without regard for any wishes you may have had.

You should avoid the possibility of dying intestate. The simplest way to do that is to make sure that you have a written will. By having an attorney help you draft your will, you may forestall many difficulties for your heirs. Legal fees for drafting a will vary with the size of your estate and your family situation. A standard will costs between $200 and $350. Make sure that you find an attorney who has experience with wills and estate planning.

Types of Wills

You have several options in preparing a will. The four basic types of wills are the simple will, the traditional marital share will, the exemption trust will, and the stated amount will. The differences among them can affect how your estate will be taxed.

SIMPLE WILL   A simple will leaves everything to your spouse. Such a will is generally sufficient for people with small estates. However, if you have a large or complex estate, a simple will may not meet your objectives. It may also result in higher overall taxation, since everything you leave to your spouse will be taxed as part of his or her estate.

TRADITIONAL MARITAL SHARE WILL   The traditional marital share will leaves one-half of the adjusted gross estate (the total value of the estate minus debts and costs) to the spouse. The other half of the estate may go to children or other heirs. It can also be held in trust for the family. A **trust** is an arrangement by which a designated person, known as a _trustee,_ manages assets for the benefit of someone else. A trust can provide a spouse with a lifelong income and would not be taxed at his or her death.

EXEMPTION TRUST WILL   With an exemption trust will, all of your assets go to your spouse except for a certain amount, which goes into a trust. This amount, plus any interest it earns, can provide your spouse with lifelong income that will not be taxed. The tax-free aspect of this type of will may become important if your property value increases considerably after you die.

OBJECTIVE 4
Distinguish among various types of wills and trusts.

will The legal declaration of a person's mind as to the disposition of his or her property after death.

intestate Without a valid will.

Key Web Sites for Estate Planning
www.law.cornell.edu
www.nolo.com/lawcenter

trust A legal arrangement through which one's assets are held by a trustee.

DID YOU KNOW?

According to a recent American Association of Retired Persons (AARP) survey, over 40 percent of Americans age 45 or older have not drawn up a will.

Source: AARP Bulletin, March 2004, p. 16.

STATED AMOUNT WILL The stated amount will allows you to pass on to your spouse any amount that satisfies your family's financial goals. For tax purposes you could pass the exempted amount of $1.5 million (in 2005). However, you might decide to pass on a stated amount related to your family's future income needs or to the value of personal items.

WILLS AND PROBATE The type of will that is best for your particular needs depends on many factors, including the size of your estate, inflation, your age, and your objectives. No matter what type of will you choose, it's best to avoid probate. **Probate** is the legal procedure of proving a valid or invalid will. It's the process by which your estate is managed and distributed after your death, according to the provisions of your will. A special probate court generally validates wills and makes sure that your debts are paid. You should avoid probate because it's expensive, lengthy, and public. As you read later, a living trust avoids probate and is also less expensive, quicker, and private.

probate The legal procedure of proving a valid or invalid will.

Formats of Wills

Wills may be either holographic or formal. A *holographic will* is a handwritten will that you prepare yourself. It should be written, dated, and signed entirely in your own handwriting. No printed or typed information should appear on its pages. Some states do not recognize holographic wills as legal.

A *formal will* is usually prepared with the help of an attorney. It may be typed, or it may be a preprinted form that you fill out. You must sign the will in front of two witnesses; neither person can be a beneficiary named in the will. The witnesses must then sign the will in front of you.

A *statutory will* is prepared on a preprinted form, available from lawyers or stationery stores. Using preprinted forms to prepare your will presents serious risks. The form may include provisions that are not in the best interests of your heirs. Therefore, it is best to seek a lawyer's advice when you prepare your will.

Sheet 44
Will Planning
Sheet

Writing Your Will

Writing a will allows you to express exactly how you want your property to be distributed to your heirs. If you're married, you may think that all the property owned jointly by you and your spouse will automatically go to your spouse after your death. This is true of some assets, such as your house. Even so, writing a will is the only way to ensure that all of your property will end up where you want it.

executor Someone willing and able to perform the tasks involved in carrying out your will.

SELECTING AN EXECUTOR An **executor** is someone who is willing and able to perform the tasks involved in carrying out your will. These tasks include preparing an inventory of your assets, collecting any money due, and paying off your debts. Your executor must also prepare and file all income and estate tax returns. In addition, he or she will be responsible for making decisions about selling or reinvesting assets to pay off debt and provide income for your family while the estate is being settled. Finally, your executor must distribute the estate and make a final accounting to your beneficiaries and to the probate court.

guardian A person who assumes responsibility for providing children with personal care and managing the deceased's estate for them.

SELECTING A GUARDIAN If you have children, your will should also name a guardian to care for them in the event that you and your spouse die at the same time and the children cannot care for themselves. A **guardian** is a person who accepts the responsibility of providing children with personal care after their parents' death and managing the parents' estate for the children until they reach a certain age.

DID YOU KNOW?

Who can be an executor? Any U.S. citizen over 18 who has not been convicted of a felony can be named the executor of a will.

ALTERING OR REWRITING YOUR WILL   Sometimes you'll need to change the provisions of your will because of changes in your life or in the law. Once you've made a will, review it frequently so that it remains current. Here are some reasons to review your will:

- You've moved to a new state that has different laws.
- You've sold property that is mentioned in the will.
- The size and composition of your estate have changed.
- You've married, divorced, or remarried.
- Potential heirs have died, or new ones have been born.

Don't make any written changes on the pages of an existing will. Additions, deletions, or erasures on a will that has been signed and witnessed can invalidate the will. If you want to make only a few minor changes, adding a codicil may be the best choice. A **codicil** is a document that explains, adds, or deletes provisions in your existing will.

codicil A document that modifies provisions in an existing will.

A Living Will

At some point in your life you may become physically or mentally disabled and unable to act on your own behalf. (See the nearby feature From the Pages of . . . *Kiplinger's Personal Finance.*) If that happens, you'll need a living will. A **living will** is a document in which you state whether you want to be kept alive by artificial means if you become terminally ill and unable to make such a decision. Many states recognize living wills. Exhibit 14–6 is an example of a typical living will.

living will A document that enables an individual, while well, to express the intention that life be allowed to end if he or she becomes terminally ill.

Exhibit [14–6]   A Living Will

Living Will Declaration

Declaration made this _____ day of _____ (month, year)

I, _____, being of sound mind, willfully and voluntarily make known my desire that my dying shall not be artificially prolonged under the circumstances set forth below, do hereby declare

If at any time I should have an incurable injury, disease, or illness regarded as a terminal condition by my physician and if my physician has determined that the application of life-sustaining procedures would serve only to artificially prolong the dying process and that my death will occur whether or not life-sustaining procedures are utilized, I direct that such procedures be withheld or withdrawn and that I be permitted to die with only the administration of medication or the performance of any medical procedure deemed necessary to provide me with comfort care.

In the absence of my ability to give directions regarding the use of such life-sustaining procedures, it is my intention that this declaration shall be honored by my family and physician as the final expression of my legal right to refuse medical or surgical treatment and accept the consequences from such refusal. I understand the full import of this declaration, and I am emotionally and mentally competent to make this declaration.

Signed _____

City, County, and State of Residence _____

The declarant has been personally known to me, and I believe him or her to be of sound mind.

Witness _____

Witness _____

Some people who becme terminally ill cannot make decisions on their own behalf. *What is the basic purpose of a living will?*

ESTATE PLANNING | A Florida family's tragedy shows how much you need a living will. *By Ronaleen R. Roha*

Your **WILL** be done

THE PERSONAL and political firestorm surrounding Terri Schiavo—the 40-year-old, brain-damaged Florida woman who has been tube-fed for almost 14 years—makes heartbreakingly clear the need to do more than write a will to divvy up your assets. You also need a medical advance directive that specifies something even more important: what you want to happen to yourself.

Had Schiavo made clear, in writing, the medical treatments she did or did *not* want in the event she was unable to speak for herself, and had she designated a person she wished to make medical decisions for her, her name might be known only to her loved ones.

Advance directives take two basic forms, and you need both, says Martin Shenkman, an estate-planning attorney and author of *Living Wills and Health Care Proxies*. The book—written in response to the Schiavo case—includes detailed sample forms (available through www.healthcareinstructions.com; $26.95 plus $3.50 shipping).

The first advance directive, a *durable power of attorney for health care*, appoints a person to be your health-care agent or proxy to make medical decisions for you if you can't do so yourself. It ap-plies any time you become incapacitated (for instance, if you were to be rendered unconscious as the result of a car accident), not just at the end of life. It should grant broad powers to maintain flexibility, says Shenkman, "because you can never conceive of all eventualities."

For example, your agent should have the right to arrange for hospice or other kinds of care. If it becomes necessary to move you to another state in order to honor your wishes, your agent should be empowered to make that decision and make sure that the new state's laws apply to you.

The second, a *living will*, spells out the kinds of medical treatment you do and do not want if you are unable to speak for yourself. It generally applies only if a person is terminally ill and faces imminent death—or if he or she is in a persistent vegetative state. Although this can be a contentious issue, it's much more likely that your wishes will be followed—and that no legislature or governor will intervene—if you have a living will.

"Unforeseen events often happen in the wee hours of the morning with no doctor or family around," says Patti Klein, a physician in Teaneck, N.J. "If there's a living will in a patient's hospi-tal chart, decisions may be made a lot easier."

Advance directives should be tailored to your needs. Many simple, do-it-yourself documents are insufficient. For instance, a document may provide that "no heroic measures" be used to keep you alive. "But in some states," Shenkman says, "the definition of 'heroic measures' may not include feeding tubes and hydration." Ask your doctor to define what it really means to be tube-fed, resuscitated, in a persistent vegetative state or on a respirator.

Talk, and then talk some more. You may be closemouthed about who'll get which assets under your will, but advance-directive planning is no time for secrets, says Shenkman. Talking with your lawyer isn't enough, either. Make sure your agent, family and doctor are all part of the discussion. Consider including your rabbi, pastor or priest. You want to make sure that anyone who could be involved in a crisis knows your wishes. To help start the dialogue, download the *Consumer's Tool Kit for Health Care Advance Planning* from the American Bar Association Commission on Law and Aging (available free at www.abanet.org/aging).

Cost should not be an excuse. Shenkman says an estate-planning lawyer might charge $100 to $500 to memorialize your wishes. And it's never too early: Terri Schiavo was only 26 when her ordeal began. —*Reporter:* **AMY ESBENSHADE**

1. What can one learn from one Florida family's tragedy?

_____

_____

2. What is the purpose of a durable power of attorney for health care?

_____

_____

3. Why should one consider preparing a living will?

_____

_____

4. How old was Terri Schiavo when her unfortunate ordeal began and how could it have been avoided?

_____

_____

POWER OF ATTORNEY   Related to the idea of a living will is power of attorney. A **power of attorney** is a legal document that authorizes someone to act on your behalf. If you become seriously ill or injured, you'll probably need someone to take care of your needs and personal affairs. This can be done through a power of attorney.

power of attorney A legal document authorizing someone to act on one's behalf.

LETTER OF LAST INSTRUCTION   In addition to a traditional will, it is a good idea to prepare a letter of last instruction. This document is not legally binding, but it can provide your heirs with important information. It should contain your wishes for your funeral arrangements as well as the names of the people who are to be informed of your death.

Trusts

Basically, a trust is a legal arrangement that helps manage the assets of your estate for your benefit or that of your beneficiaries. The creator of the trust is called the *trustor,* or *grantor.* The *trustee* might be a person or institution, such as a bank, that administers the trust. A bank charges a small fee for its services in administering a trust. The fee is usually based on the value of the assets in the trust.

Individual circumstances determine whether establishing a trust makes sense. Some of the common reasons for setting up a trust are to:

- Reduce or otherwise provide payment of estate taxes.
- Avoid probate and transfer your assets immediately to your beneficiaries.
- Free yourself from managing your assets while you receive a regular income from the trust.
- Provide income for a surviving spouse or other beneficiary.
- Ensure that your property serves a desired purpose after your death.

Key Web Sites for Trusts
www.webtrust.com
www.netplanning.com

Types of Trusts

There are many types of trusts, some of which are described in detail below. You'll need to choose the type of trust that's most appropriate for your particular situation. An estate attorney can advise you about the right type of trust for your personal and family needs.

All trusts are either revocable or irrevocable. A *revocable trust* is one in which you have the right to end the trust or change its terms during your lifetime. An *irrevocable trust* is one that cannot be changed or ended. Revocable trusts avoid the lengthy process of probate, but they do not protect assets from federal or state estate taxes. Irrevocable trusts avoid probate and help reduce estate taxes. However, by law you cannot remove any assets from an irrevocable trust, even if you need them at some later point in your life.

Objective 4

Discuss with your attorney the possibility of establishing a trust as a means of managing your estate.

CREDIT-SHELTER TRUST   A credit-shelter trust is one that enables the spouse of a deceased person to avoid paying federal taxes on a certain amount of assets left to him or her as part of an estate. Perhaps the most common estate planning trust, the credit-shelter trust has many other names: bypass trust, "residuary" trust, A/B trust, exemption equivalent trust, or family trust.

DISCLAIMER TRUST   A disclaimer trust is appropriate for couples who do not yet have enough assets to need a credit-shelter trust but may have in the future. With a disclaimer trust, the surviving spouse is left everything, but he or she has the right to disclaim, or deny, some portion of the estate. Anything that is disclaimed goes into a credit-shelter trust. This approach allows the surviving spouse to protect wealth from estate taxes.

LIVING TRUST   A living trust, also known as an inter vivos trust, is a property management arrangement that goes into effect while you're alive. It allows you, as a trustor, to receive benefits during your lifetime. To set up a living trust, you simply transfer some of your assets to a trustee. Then you give the trustee instructions for managing the trust while you're alive and after your death. A living trust has several advantages:

- It ensures privacy. A will is a public record; a trust is not.
- The assets held in trust avoid probate at your death. This eliminates probate costs and delays.
- It enables you to review your trustee's performance and make changes if necessary.
- It can relieve you of management responsibilities.
- It's less likely than a will to create arguments between heirs upon your death.
- It can guide your family and doctors if you become terminally ill or unable to make your own decisions.

Setting up a living trust costs more than creating a will. However, depending on your particular circumstances, a living trust can be a good estate planning option.

Sheet 45
Trust
Comparison
Sheet

TESTAMENTARY TRUST   A testamentary trust is one established by your will that becomes effective upon your death. Such a trust can be valuable if your beneficiaries are inexperienced in financial matters. It may also be your best option if your estate taxes will be high. A testamentary trust provides many of the same advantages as a living trust.

Taxes and Estate Planning

Federal and state governments impose various types of taxes that you must consider in estate planning. The four major types of taxes are estate taxes, estate and trust federal income taxes, inheritance taxes, and gift taxes.

ESTATE TAXES   An estate tax is a federal tax collected on the value of a person's property at the time of his or her death. The tax is based on the fair market value of the deceased person's investments, property, and bank accounts, less an exempt amount of $1.5 million in 2005. This tax is due nine months after a death.

ESTATE AND TRUST FEDERAL INCOME TAXES   In addition to the federal estate tax return, estates and certain trusts must file federal income tax returns with the Internal Revenue Service. Taxable income for estates and trusts is computed in the same manner as taxable income for individuals. Trusts and estates must pay quarterly estimated taxes.

INHERITANCE TAXES   Your heirs might have to pay a tax for the right to acquire the property that they have inherited. An inheritance tax is a tax collected on the property left by a person in his or her will.

Only state governments impose inheritance taxes. Most states collect an inheritance tax, but state laws differ widely as to exemptions and rates of taxation. A reasonable average for state inheritance taxes would be 4 to 10 percent of whatever the heir receives.

GIFT TAXES   Both the state and federal governments impose a gift tax, a tax collected on money or property valued at more than $11,000 given by one person to another in a single year. One way to reduce the tax liability of your estate is to reduce the size of the estate while you're alive by giving away portions of it as gifts. You're free to make such gifts to your spouse, children, or anyone else at any time. (Don't give away assets if you need them in your retirement!)

✓ **CONCEPTCHECK 14–4**

1 What is a will?

_____

_____

2 What are the four basic types of wills?

_____

_____

3 What are the responsibilities of an executor?

_____

_____

4 Why should you name a guardian?

_____

_____

5 What is the difference between a revocable and an irrevocable trust?

_____

_____

6 What are the four major types of trusts?

_____

_____

7 What are the four major types of taxes to consider in estate planning?

_____

_____

Back to **Getting Personal**

Reconsider your Getting Personal answers at the beginning of the chapter. Then answer the following questions.

1. When should one start planning for retirement?

_____

_____

2. Can you depend on Social Security and a company pension plan to pay for your basic living expenses? Explain.

_____

_____

Chapter Summary

Objective 1 The difference between your assets and your liabilities is your net worth. Review your assets to ensure they are sufficient for retirement. Then estimate your living expenses. Some expenses are likely to decrease while others will increase.

Objective 2 Your possible sources of income during retirement include public pension plans, employer pension plans, personal retirement plans, and annuities. If your income approximates your expenses, you are in good shape; if not, determine additional income needs and sources.

Objective 3 The personal aspects of estate planning depend on whether you are single or married. Never having been married

does not eliminate the need to organize your financial affairs. Every adult should have a written will. A will is a way to transfer your property according to your wishes after you die.

Objective 4 The four basic types of wills are the simple will, the traditional marital share will, the exemption trust will, and the stated amount will. Types of trusts include the credit-shelter trust, the disclaimer trust, the living trust, and the testamentary trust.

Federal and state governments impose various types of estate taxes; you can prepare a plan for paying these taxes.

Key Terms

codicil 403
defined-benefit plan 395
defined-contribution plan 393
estate 399
estate planning 399
executor 402

401(k) plan 394
guardian 402
individual retirement
   account (IRA) 395
intestate 401
Keogh plan 397

living will 403
power of attorney 405
probate 402
trust 401
vesting 395
will 401

Problems and Questions

1. Prepare your net worth statement using the guidelines presented in Exhibit 14–1.

2. How will your spending patterns change during your retirement years? Compare your spending patterns with those shown in Exhibit 14–2.

3. Obtain Form SSA-7004 from your local Social Security office. Complete and mail the form to receive a personal earnings and benefits statement. Use the information in this statement to plan your retirement.

4. Outline the steps you must take to live on your retirement income and balance your retirement budget.

5. Prepare a written report of personal information that would be helpful to you and your heirs. Be sure to include the location of family records, your military service file, and other important papers; medical records; bank accounts;

charge accounts; location of your safe-deposit box; U.S. savings bonds, stocks, bonds, and other securities; property owned; life insurance; annuities; and Social Security information.

6. Visit Metropolitan Life Insurance Company's Web page at http://www.lifeadvice.com. Using this information, prepare a report on the following: (*a*) Who needs a will? (*b*) What are the elements of a will (naming a guardian, naming an executor, preparing a will, updating a will, estate taxes, where to keep your will, living will, etc.)? (*c*) How is this report helpful in preparing your own will?

7. Make a list of the criteria you will use in deciding who will be the guardian of your minor children if you and your spouse die at the same time.

8. Visit the Prudential Insurance Company of America Web site at http://prudential.com/estateplan. Gather information on various estate planning topics such as an estate planning

worksheet; whether you need an estate plan; when to update your plan; estate taxes, wills, executors, trusts, and so on. Then prepare a report to help you develop your estate plan.

9. Ask your state department of revenue for brochures on state inheritance and gift taxes. What are the exemptions and rates of taxes? How are your property and life insurance treated for the purpose of inheritance tax? Of gift tax?

Internet Connection

ESTATE PLANNING AND CHARITABLE GIVING

Charitable gifts can be an important tool in estate planning. Giving to charity supports a cause and offers benefits such as reduced taxes and increased interest income.

To find ways to plan an estate and help your favorite charities at the same time, use the Internet to find at least three Web sites that suggest general ways to combine estate planning and charitable giving. At the Web sites, look for specific details about planned giving.

Keywords Used	Site Name	Web Site Addresses	Information Offered

1. What basic approaches to estate planning through charitable giving did you find?

_____

_____

_____

_____

2. Which Web sites suggest using donations in estate planning?

_____

_____

_____

_____

3. Choose a charity that accepts donations from people's wills. How does the charity use these gifts?

_____

_____

_____

_____

Case in Point

PLANNING FOR RETIREMENT

Is a bad day fishing better than a good day at the office? Yes, according to a retired dad, Chuck. With his company pension, at least he didn't have to worry about money. In the good old days, if you had a decent job, you'd hang on to it, and then your company's pension combined with Social Security payments would be enough to live comfortably. Chuck's son, Rob, does not have a company pension and is not sure whether Social Security will even exist when he retires. So when it comes to retirement, the sooner you start saving, the better.

Take Maureen, a salesperson for a computer company, and Therese, an accountant for a lighting manufacturer. Both start their jobs at age 25. Maureen starts saving for retirement right away by investing $300 a month at 9 percent until age 65. But Therese does nothing until age 35. At 35 she begins investing the same $300 a month at 9 percent until age 65. What a shocking difference! Maureen has accumulated $1.4 million, while Therese has only $553,000 in her retirement fund. The moral? The sooner you start, the more you'll have for your retirement. Women especially need to start sooner, because they typically enter the workforce later, have lower salaries, and, ultimately, have lower pensions.

Laura Tarbox. owner and president of Tarbox Equity, explains how to determine your retirement needs and how your budget might change when you retire. Tarbox advises that the old rule of thumb that you need 60 to 70 percent of preretire-

ment income is too low an estimate. She cautions that most people will want to spend very close to what they were spending before retiring. There are some expenses that might be lower, however, such as clothing for work, dry cleaning, and commuting expenses. Other expenses, though, such as insurance, travel, and recreation, may increase during retirement.

Questions

1. In the past. many workers chose to stay with their employers until retirement. What was the major reason for employees' loyalty?

2. How did Maureen amass $1.4 million for retirement, while Therese could only accumulate $553,000?

3. Why do women need to start early to save for retirement?

4. What expenses may increase or decrease during retirement?

Retirement Plan Comparison

Financial Planning Activities: Compare benefits and costs for different retirement plans (401K, IRA, Keogh). Analyze advertisements and articles, and contact your employer and financial institutions to obtain the information below.

Suggested Web Sites: www.lifenet.com   www.aarp.org

Your Personal Financial Plan

Type of plan			
Name of financial institution or employer			
Address			
Phone			
Web site			
Type of investments			
Minimum initial deposit			
Minimum additional deposits			
Employer contributions			
Current rate of return			
Service charges/fees			
Safety insured? By whom?			
Amount			
Payroll deduction available			
Tax benefits			
Penalty for early withdrawal: • IRS penalty (10%) • Other penalties			
Other features or restrictions			

What's Next for Your Personal Financial Plan?

- Survey local businesses to determine the types of retirement plans available to employees.
- Talk to representatives of various financial institutions to determine their suggestions for IRA investments.

Name: _____   **Date:** _____

Forecasting Retirement Income

Financial Planning Activities: Determine the amount needed to save each year to have the necessary funds to cover retirement living costs. Estimate the information requested below.

Suggested Web Sites: www.ssa.gov   www.pensionplanners.com

Estimated annual retirement living expenses

Estimated annual living expenses
if you retired today $ _____

Future value for _____ years until
retirement at expected annual
income of _____ % (use future
value of $1, Exhibit A–1 of
Appendix A)   × _____

**Projected annual retirement living expenses
adjusted for inflation** ....   (A) $ _____

Estimated annual income at retirement

Social security income $ _____

Company pension, personal
retirement account income $ _____

Investment and other income $ _____

Total retirement income ....   (B) $ _____

Additional retirement plan contributions (if B is less than A)

Annual shortfall of income after
retirement (A − B) $ _____

Expected annual rate of return on
invested funds after retirement,
percentage expressed as a
decimal $ _____

Needed investment fund after retirement A − B ....   (C) $ _____

Future value factor of a series of deposits for _____ years until
retirement and an expected annual rate of return before
retirement of _____ % (Use Exhibit A–2 in Appendix A)   (D) $ _____

**Annual deposit to achieve needed investment fund
(C divided by D)** .... $ _____

What's Next for Your Personal Financial Plan?

- Survey retired individuals or people close to retirement to obtain information on their main sources of retirement income.
- Make a list that suggests the best investment options for an individual retirement account.

Estate Planning Activities

Financial Planning Activities: Develop a plan for estate planning and related financial activities. Respond to the following questions as a basis for making and implementing an estate plan.

Suggested Web Sites: www.nolo.com   www.webtrust.com

Are your financial records, including recent tax forms, insurance policies, and investment and housing documents, organized and easily accessible?	
Do you have a safe-deposit box? Where is it located? Where is the key?	
Location of life insurance policies. Name and address of insurance company and agent.	
Is your will current? Location of copies of your will. Name and address of your lawyer.	
Name and address of your executor	
Do you have a listing of the current value of assets owned and liabilities outstanding?	
Have any funeral and burial arrangements been made?	
Have you created any trusts? Name and location of financial institution.	
Do you have any current information on gift and estate taxes?	
Have you prepared a letter of last instruction? Where is it located?	

What's Next for Your Personal Financial Plan?

- Talk to several individuals about the actions they have taken related to estate planning.
- Create a list of situations in which a will would need to be revised.

Will Planning Sheet

Financial Planning Activities: Compare costs and features of various types of wills. Obtain information for the various areas listed based on your current and future situation; contact attorneys regarding the cost of these wills.

Suggested Web Sites: www.netplanning.com   www.estateplanninglinks.com

Type of will	Features that would be appropriate for my current or future situation	Cost Attorney, Address, Phone

What's Next for Your Personal Financial Plan?

- Create a list of items that you believe would be desirable to include in a will.
- Obtain the cost of a will from a number of different lawyers.

Name: _____ **Date:** _____

Trust Comparison Sheet

Financial Planning Activities: Identify features of different types of trusts. Research features of various trusts to determine their value to your personal situation.

Suggested Web Sites: www.webtrust.com   www.lifenet.com

Type of trust	Benefits	Possible value for my situation

What's Next for Your Personal Financial Plan?
- Talk to legal and financial planning experts to contrast the cost and benefits of wills and trusts.
- Talk to one or more lawyers to obtain information about the type of trust recommended for your situation.

A Time Value of Money

- "If I deposit $10,000 today, how much will I have for a down payment on a house in five years?"
- "Will $2,000 saved each year give me enough money when I retire?"
- "How much must I save today to have enough for my children's college education?"

As introduced in Chapter 1 and used to measure financial opportunity costs in other chapters, the *time value of money,* more commonly referred to as *interest,* is the cost of money that is borrowed or lent. Interest can be compared to rent, the cost of using an apartment or other item. The time value of money is based on the fact that a dollar received today is worth more than a dollar that will be received one year from today, because the dollar received today can be saved or invested and will be worth more than a dollar a year from today. Similarly, a dollar that will be received one year from today is currently worth less than a dollar today.

The time value of money has two major components: future value and present value. *Future value* computations, which are also referred to as *compounding,* yield the amount to which a current sum will increase based on a certain interest rate and period of time. *Present value,* which is calculated through a process called *discounting,* is the current value of a future sum based on a certain interest rate and period of time.

In future value problems, you are given an amount to save or invest and you calculate the amount that will be available at some future date. With present value problems, you are given the amount that will be available at some future date and you calculate the current value of that amount. Both future value and present value computations are based on basic interest rate calculations.

Interest Rate Basics

Simple interest is the dollar cost of borrowing or earnings from lending money. The interest is based on three elements:

- The dollar amount, called the *principal.*
- The *rate of interest.*
- The amount of *time.*

The formula for computing interest is

$$\text{Interest} = \text{Principal} \times \text{Rate of interest} \times \text{Time}$$

The interest rate is stated as a percentage for a year. For example, you must convert 12 percent to either 0.12 or 12/100 before doing your calculations. The time element must also be converted to a decimal or fraction. For example, three months would be shown as 0.25 or 1/4 of a year. Interest for 2½ years would involve a time period of 2.5.

Example A

Suppose you borrow $1,000 at 5 percent and will repay it in one payment at the end of one year. Using the simple interest calculation, the interest is $50, computed as follows:

$$\$50 = \$1,000 \times 0.05 \times 1 \text{ (year)}$$

Example B

If you deposited $750 in a savings account paying 8 percent, how much interest would you earn in nine months? You would compute this amount as follows:

$$\text{Interest} = \$750 \times 0.08 \times 3/4 \text{ (or 0.75 of a year)}$$
$$= \$45$$

Sample Problem 1

How much interest would you earn if you deposited $300 at 6 percent for 27 months?

(Answers to sample problems are on page 422.)

Sample Problem 2

How much interest would you pay to borrow $670 for eight months at 12 percent?

Future Value of a Single Amount

The future value of an amount consists of the original amount plus compound interest. This calculation involves the following elements:

$$FV = \text{Future value}$$
$$PV = \text{Present value}$$
$$i = \text{Interest rate}$$
$$n = \text{Number of time periods}$$

The formula for the future value of a single amount is

$$FV = PV(1 + i)^n$$

Example C

The future value of $1 at 10 percent after three years is $1.33. This amount is calculated as follows:

$$\$1.33 = \$1.00(1 + 0.10)^3$$

Future value tables are available to help you determine compounded interest amounts (see Exhibit A–1 on page 423). Looking at Exhibit A–1 for 10 percent and three years, you can see that $1 would be worth $1.33 at that time. For other amounts, multiply the table factor by the original amount.

This may be viewed as follows:

Example D

If your savings of $400 earn 12 percent, compounded *monthly,* over a year and a half, use the table factor for 1 percent for 18 time periods. The future value of this amount is $478.40, calculated as follows:

$$\$478.40 + \$400(1.196)$$

Sample Problem 3

What is the future value of $800 at 8 percent after six years?

Sample Problem 4

How much would you have in savings if you kept $200 on deposit for eight years at 8 percent, compounded *semiannually?*

Future Value of a Series of Equal Amounts (an Annuity)

Future value may also be calculated for a situation in which regular additions are made to savings. The following formula is used:

$$FV = \frac{(1 + i)^n - 1}{I}$$

This formula assumes that (1) each deposit is for the same amount, (2) the interest rate is the same for each time period, and (3) the deposits are made at the end of each time period.

Example E

The future value of three $1 deposits made at the end of the next three years, earning 10 percent interest, is $3.31. This is calculated as follows:

$$\$3.31 = \$1 \frac{(1 + 0.10)^3 - 1}{0.10}$$

This may be viewed as follows:

Future value (rounded)	$1		$1		$2.10		FV = $3.31
		Deposit $1 Interest 0		Deposit $1 Interest $0.10		Deposit $1 Interest $0.21	
After year	0		1		2		3

Using Exhibit A–2 on page 424, you can find this same amount for 10 percent for three time periods. To use the table for other amounts, multiply the table factors by the annual deposit.

Example F

If you plan to deposit $40 a year for 10 years, earning 8 percent compounded annually, use the table factor for 8 percent for 10 time periods. The future value of this amount is $579.48, calculated as follows:

$$\$579.48 = \$40(14.487)$$

Sample Problem 5

What is the future value of an annual deposit of $230 earning 6 percent for 15 years?

_____

Sample Problem 6

What amount would you have in a retirement account if you made annual deposits of $375 for 25 years earning 12 percent, compounded annually?

_____

Present Value of a Single Amount

If you want to know how much you need to deposit now to receive a certain amount in the future, use the following formula:

$$PV = \frac{1}{(I + i)^n}$$

Example G

The present value of $1 to be received three years from now based on a 10 percent interest rate is $0.75. This amount is calculated as follows:

$$\$0.75 = \frac{\$1}{(1 + 0.10)^3}$$

This may be viewed as follows:

Present value tables are available to assist you in this process (see Exhibit A–3 on page 425). Notice that $1 at 10 percent for three years has a present value of $0.75. For amounts other than $1, multiply the table factor by the amount involved.

Example H

If you want to have $300 seven years from now and your savings earn 10 percent, compounded _semiannually,_ use the table factor for 5 percent for 14 time periods. In this situation, the present value is $151.50, calculated as follows:

$$\$151.50 = \$300(0.505)$$

Sample Problem 7

What is the present value of $2,200 earning 15 percent for eight years?

Sample Problem 8

To have $6,000 for a child's education in 10 years, what amount should a parent deposit in a savings account that earns 12 percent, compounded *quarterly?*

Present Value of a Series of Equal Amounts (an Annuity)

The final time value of money situation allows you to receive an amount at the end of each time period for a certain number of periods. This amount is calculated as follows:

$$PV = \frac{1 - \dfrac{1}{(1 + i)^n}}{i}$$

Example I

The present value of a $1 withdrawal at the end of the next three years would be $2.49, calculated as follows:

$$\$2.49 = \$1 \left[\frac{1 - \dfrac{1}{(1 + 0.10)^n}}{0.10} \right]$$

This may be viewed as follows:

This same amount appears in Exhibit A–4 on page 426 for 10 percent and three time periods. To use the table for other situations, multiply the table factor by the amount to be withdrawn each year.

Example J

If you wish to withdraw $100 at the end of each year for 10 years from an account that earns 14 percent, compounded annually, what amount must you deposit now? Use the table factor for 14 percent for 10 time periods. In this situation, the present value is $521.60, calculated as follows:

$$\$521.60 = \$100(5.216)$$

Sample Problem 9

What is the present value of a withdrawal of $200 at the end of each year for 14 years with an interest rate of 7 percent?

Sample Problem 10

How much would you have to deposit now to be able to withdraw $650 at the end of each year for 20 years from an account that earns 11 percent?

Using Present Value to Determine Loan Payments

Present value tables (Exhibit A–4) can also be used to determine installment payments for a loan as follows:

$$\frac{\text{Amount borrowed}}{\text{Present value of a series table factor}} = \text{Loan payment}$$

Example K

If you borrow $1,000 with a 6 percent interest rate to be repaid in three equal payments at the end of the next three years, the payments will be $374.11. This is calculated as follows:

$$\frac{\$1,000}{2.673} = \$374.11$$

Sample Problem 11

What would be the annual payment amount for a $20,000, ten-year loan at 7 percent?

Answers To Sample Problems

1. $300 × 0.06 × 2.25 years (27 months) = $40.50.
2. $670 × 0.12 × 2/3 (of a year) = $53.60.
3. $800(1.587) = $1,269.60. (Use Exhibit A–1, 8%, 6 periods.)
4. $200(1.873) = $374.60. (Use Exhibit A–1, 4%, 16 periods.)
5. $230(23.276) = $5,353.48. (Use Exhibit A–2, 6%, 15 periods.)
6. $375(133.33) = $49,998.75. (Use Exhibit A–2, 12%, 25 periods.)
7. $2,200(0.327) = $719.40. (Use Exhibit A–3, 15%, 8 periods.)
8. $6,000(0.307) = $1,842. (Use Exhibit A–3, 3%, 40 periods.)
9. $200(8.745) = $1,749. (Use Exhibit A–4, 7%, 14 periods.)
10. $650(7.963) = $5,175.95. (Use Exhibit A–4, 11%, 20 periods.)
11. $20,000/7.024 = $2,847.38. (Use Exhibit A–4, 7%, 10 periods.)

Exhibit [A–1] Future Value (Compounded Sum) of $1 after a Given Number of Time Periods

Period	1%	2%	3%	4%	5%	6%	7%	8%	9%	10%	11%
1	1.010	1.020	1.030	1.040	1.050	1.060	1.070	1.080	1.090	1.100	1.110
2	1.020	1.040	1.061	1.082	1.103	1.124	1.145	1.166	1.188	1.210	1.232
3	1.030	1.061	1.093	1.125	1.158	1.191	1.225	1.260	1.295	1.331	1.368
4	1.041	1.082	1.126	1.170	1.216	1.262	1.311	1.360	1.412	1.464	1.518
5	1.051	1.104	1.159	1.217	1.276	1.338	1.403	1.469	1.539	1.611	1.685
6	1.062	1.126	1.194	1.265	1.340	1.419	1.501	1.587	1.677	1.772	1.870
7	1.072	1.149	1.230	1.316	1.407	1.504	1.606	1.714	1.828	1.949	2.076
8	1.083	1.172	1.267	1.369	1.477	1.594	1.718	1.851	1.993	2.144	2.305
9	1.094	1.195	1.305	1.423	1.551	1.689	1.838	1.999	2.172	2.358	2.558
10	1.105	1.219	1.344	1.480	1.629	1.791	1.967	2.159	2.367	2.594	2.839
11	1.116	1.243	1.384	1.539	1.710	1.898	2.105	2.332	2.580	2.853	3.152
12	1.127	1.268	1.426	1.601	1.796	2.012	2.252	2.518	2.813	3.138	3.498
13	1.138	1.294	1.469	1.665	1.886	2.133	2.410	2.720	3.066	3.452	3.883
14	1.149	1.319	1.513	1.732	1.980	2.261	2.579	2.937	3.342	3.797	4.310
15	1.161	1.346	1.558	1.801	2.079	2.397	2.759	3.172	3.642	4.177	4.785
16	1.173	1.373	1.605	1.873	2.183	2.540	2.952	3.426	3.970	4.595	5.311
17	1.184	1.400	1.653	1.948	2.292	2.693	3.159	3.700	4.328	5.054	5.895
18	1.196	1.428	1.702	2.026	2.407	2.854	3.380	3.996	4.717	5.560	6.544
19	1.208	1.457	1.754	2.107	2.527	3.026	3.617	4.316	5.142	6.116	7.263
20	1.220	1.486	1.806	2.191	2.653	3.207	3.870	4.661	5.604	6.727	8.062
25	1.282	1.641	2.094	2.666	3.386	4.292	5.427	6.848	8.623	10.835	13.585
30	1.348	1.811	2.427	3.243	4.322	5.743	7.612	10.063	13.268	17.449	22.892
40	1.489	2.208	3.262	4.801	7.040	10.286	14.974	21.725	31.409	45.259	65.001
50	1.645	2.692	4.384	7.107	11.467	18.420	29.457	46.902	74.358	117.390	184.570

Period	12%	13%	14%	15%	16%	17%	18%	19%	20%	25%	30%
1	1.120	1.130	1.140	1.150	1.160	1.170	1.180	1.190	1.200	1.250	1.300
2	1.254	1.277	1.300	1.323	1.346	1.369	1.392	1.416	1.440	1.563	1.690
3	1.405	1.443	1.482	1.521	1.561	1.602	1.643	1.685	1.728	1.953	2.197
4	1.574	1.630	1.689	1.749	1.811	1.874	1.939	2.005	2.074	2.441	2.856
5	1.762	1.842	1.925	2.011	2.100	2.192	2.288	2.386	2.488	3.052	3.713
6	1.974	2.082	2.195	2.313	2.436	2.565	2.700	2.840	2.986	3.815	4.827
7	2.211	2.353	2.502	2.660	2.826	3.001	3.185	3.379	3.583	4.768	6.276
8	2.476	2.658	2.853	3.059	3.278	3.511	3.759	4.021	4.300	5.960	8.157
9	2.773	3.004	3.252	3.518	3.803	4.108	4.435	4.785	5.160	7.451	10.604
10	3.106	3.395	3.707	4.046	4.411	4.807	5.234	5.696	6.192	9.313	13.786
11	3.479	3.836	4.226	4.652	5.117	5.624	6.176	6.777	7.430	11.642	17.922
12	3.896	4.335	4.818	5.350	5.936	6.580	7.288	8.064	8.916	14.552	23.298
13	4.363	4.898	5.492	6.153	6.886	7.699	8.599	9.596	10.699	18.190	30.288
14	4.887	5.535	6.261	7.076	7.988	9.007	10.147	11.420	12.839	22.737	39.374
15	5.474	6.254	7.138	8.137	9.266	10.539	11.974	13.590	15.407	28.422	51.186
16	6.130	7.067	8.137	9.358	10.748	12.330	14.129	16.172	18.488	35.527	66.542
17	6.866	7.986	9.276	10.761	12.468	14.426	16.672	19.244	22.186	44.409	86.504
18	7.690	9.024	10.575	12.375	14.463	16.879	19.673	22.091	26.623	55.511	112.460
19	8.613	10.197	12.056	14.232	16.777	19.748	23.214	27.252	31.948	69.389	146.190
20	9.646	11.523	13.743	16.367	19.461	23.106	27.393	32.429	38.338	86.736	190.050
25	17.000	21.231	26.462	32.919	40.874	50.658	62.669	77.388	95.396	264.700	705.640
30	29.960	39.116	50.950	66.212	85.850	111.070	143.370	184.680	237.380	807.790	2,620.000
40	93.051	132.780	188.880	267.860	378.720	533.870	750.380	1,051.700	1,469.800	7,523.200	36,119.000
50	289.000	450.740	700.230	1,083.700	1,670.700	2,566.200	3,927.400	5,988.900	9,100.400	70,065.000	497,929.000

Exhibit [A–2] Future Value (Compounded Sum) of $1 Paid in at the End of Each Period for a Given Number of Time Periods (an Annuity)

Period	1%	2%	3%	4%	5%	6%	7%	8%	9%	10%	11%
1	1.000	1.000	1.000	1.000	1.000	1.000	1.000	1.000	1.000	1.000	1.000
2	2.010	2.020	2.030	2.040	2.050	2.060	2.070	2.080	2.090	2.100	2.110
3	3.030	3.060	3.091	3.122	3.153	3.184	3.215	3.246	3.278	3.310	3.342
4	4.060	4.122	4.184	4.246	4.310	4.375	4.440	4.506	4.573	4.641	4.710
5	5.101	5.204	5.309	5.416	5.526	5.637	5.751	5.867	5.985	6.105	6.228
6	6.152	6.308	6.468	6.633	6.802	6.975	7.153	7.336	7.523	7.716	7.913
7	7.214	7.434	7.662	7.898	8.142	8.394	8.654	8.923	9.200	9.487	9.783
8	8.286	8.583	8.892	9.214	9.549	9.897	10.260	10.637	11.028	11.436	11.859
9	9.369	9.755	10.159	10.583	11.027	11.491	11.978	12.488	13.021	13.579	14.164
10	10.462	10.950	11.464	12.006	12.578	13.181	13.816	14.487	15.193	15.937	16.722
11	11.567	12.169	12.808	13.486	14.207	14.972	15.784	16.645	17.560	18.531	19.561
12	12.683	13.412	14.192	15.026	15.917	16.870	17.888	18.977	20.141	21.384	22.713
13	13.809	14.680	15.618	16.627	17.713	18.882	20.141	21.495	22.953	24.523	26.212
14	14.947	15.974	17.086	18.292	19.599	21.015	22.550	24.215	26.019	27.975	30.095
15	16.097	17.293	18.599	20.024	21.579	23.276	25.129	27.152	29.361	31.772	34.405
16	17.258	18.639	20.157	21.825	23.657	25.673	27.888	30.324	33.003	35.950	39.190
17	18.430	20.012	21.762	23.698	25.840	28.213	30.840	33.750	36.974	40.545	44.501
18	19.615	21.412	23.414	25.645	28.132	30.906	33.999	37.450	41.301	45.599	50.396
19	20.811	22.841	25.117	27.671	30.539	33.760	37.379	41.446	46.018	51.159	56.939
20	22.019	24.297	26.870	29.778	33.066	36.786	40.995	45.762	51.160	57.275	64.203
25	28.243	32.030	36.459	41.646	47.727	54.865	63.249	73.106	84.701	98.347	114.410
30	34.785	40.588	47.575	56.085	66.439	79.058	94.461	113.280	136.310	164.490	199.020
40	48.886	60.402	75.401	95.026	120.800	154.760	199.640	259.060	337.890	442.590	581.830
50	64.463	84.579	112.800	152.670	209.350	290.340	406.530	573.770	815.080	1,163.900	1,668.800

Period	12%	13%	14%	15%	16%	17%	18%	19%	20%	25%	30%
1	1.000	1.000	1.000	1.000	1.000	1.000	1.000	1.000	1.000	1.000	1.000
2	2.120	2.130	2.140	2.150	2.160	2.170	2.180	2.190	2.200	2.250	2.300
3	3.374	3.407	3.440	3.473	3.506	3.539	3.572	3.606	3.640	3.813	3.990
4	4.779	4.850	4.921	4.993	5.066	5.141	5.215	5.291	5.368	5.766	6.187
5	6.353	6.480	6.610	6.742	6.877	7.014	7.154	7.297	7.442	8.207	9.043
6	8.115	8.323	8.536	8.754	8.977	9.207	9.442	9.683	9.930	11.259	12.756
7	10.089	10.405	10.730	11.067	11.414	11.772	12.142	12.523	12.916	15.073	17.583
8	12.300	12.757	13.233	13.727	14.240	14.773	15.327	15.902	16.499	19.842	23.858
9	14.776	15.416	16.085	16.786	17.519	18.285	19.086	19.923	20.799	25.802	32.015
10	17.549	18.420	19.337	20.304	21.321	22.393	23.521	24.701	25.959	33.253	42.619
11	20.655	21.814	23.045	24.349	25.733	27.200	28.755	30.404	32.150	42.566	56.405
12	24.133	25.650	27.271	29.002	30.850	32.824	34.931	37.180	39.581	54.208	74.327
13	28.029	29.985	32.089	34.352	36.786	39.404	42.219	45.244	48.497	68.760	97.625
14	32.393	34.883	37.581	40.505	43.672	47.103	50.818	54.841	59.196	86.949	127.910
15	37.280	40.417	43.842	47.580	51.660	56.110	60.965	66.261	72.035	109.690	167.290
16	42.753	46.672	50.980	55.717	60.925	66.649	72.939	79.850	87.442	138.110	218.470
17	48.884	53.739	59.118	65.075	71.673	78.979	87.068	96.022	105.930	173.640	285.010
18	55.750	61.725	68.394	75.836	84.141	93.406	103.740	115.270	128.120	218.050	371.520
19	63.440	70.749	78.969	88.212	98.603	110.290	123.410	138.170	154.740	273.560	483.970
20	72.052	80.947	91.025	102.440	115.380	130.030	146.630	165.420	186.690	342.950	630.170
25	133.330	155.620	181.870	212.790	249.210	292.110	342.600	402.040	471.980	1,054.800	2,348.800
30	241.330	293.200	356.790	434.750	530.310	647.440	790.950	966.700	1,181.900	3,227.200	8,730.000
40	767.090	1,013.700	1,342.000	1,779.100	2,360.800	3,134.500	4,163.210	5,529.800	7,343.900	30,089.000	120,393.000
50	2,400.000	3,459.500	4,994.500	7,217.700	10,436.000	15,090.000	21,813.000	31,515.000	45,497.000	80,256.000	165,976.000

Exhibit [A–3]   Present Value of $1 to Be Received at the End of a Given Number of Time Periods

Period	1%	2%	3%	4%	5%	6%	7%	8%	9%	10%	11%	12%
1	0.990	0.980	0.971	0.962	0.952	0.943	0.935	0.926	0.917	0.909	0.901	0.893
2	0.980	0.961	0.943	0.925	0.907	0.890	0.873	0.857	0.842	0.826	0.812	0.797
3	0.971	0.942	0.915	0.889	0.864	0.840	0.816	0.794	0.772	0.751	0.731	0.712
4	0.961	0.924	0.885	0.855	0.823	0.792	0.763	0.735	0.708	0.683	0.659	0.636
5	0.951	0.906	0.863	0.822	0.784	0.747	0.713	0.681	0.650	0.621	0.593	0.567
6	0.942	0.888	0.837	0.790	0.746	0.705	0.666	0.630	0.596	0.564	0.535	0.507
7	0.933	0.871	0.813	0.760	0.711	0.665	0.623	0.583	0.547	0.513	0.482	0.452
8	0.923	0.853	0.789	0.731	0.677	0.627	0.582	0.540	0.502	0.467	0.434	0.404
9	0.914	0.837	0.766	0.703	0.645	0.592	0.544	0.500	0.460	0.424	0.391	0.361
10	0.905	0.820	0.744	0.676	0.614	0.558	0.508	0.463	0.422	0.386	0.352	0.322
11	0.896	0.804	0.722	0.650	0.585	0.527	0.475	0.429	0.388	0.350	0.317	0.287
12	0.887	0.788	0.701	0.625	0.557	0.497	0.444	0.397	0.356	0.319	0.286	0.257
13	0.879	0.773	0.681	0.601	0.530	0.469	0.415	0.368	0.326	0.290	0.258	0.229
14	0.870	0.758	0.661	0.577	0.505	0.442	0.388	0.340	0.299	0.263	0.232	0.205
15	0.861	0.743	0.642	0.555	0.481	0.417	0.362	0.315	0.275	0.239	0.209	0.183
16	0.853	0.728	0.623	0.534	0.458	0.394	0.339	0.292	0.252	0.218	0.188	0.163
17	0.844	0.714	0.605	0.513	0.436	0.371	0.317	0.270	0.231	0.198	0.170	0.146
18	0.836	0.700	0.587	0.494	0.416	0.350	0.296	0.250	0.212	0.180	0.153	0.130
19	0.828	0.686	0.570	0.475	0.396	0.331	0.277	0.232	0.194	0.164	0.138	0.116
20	0.820	0.673	0.554	0.456	0.377	0.312	0.258	0.215	0.178	0.149	0.124	0.104
25	0.780	0.610	0.478	0.375	0.295	0.233	0.184	0.146	0.116	0.092	0.074	0.059
30	0.742	0.552	0.412	0.308	0.231	0.174	0.131	0.099	0.075	0.057	0.044	0.033
40	0.672	0.453	0.307	0.208	0.142	0.097	0.067	0.046	0.032	0.022	0.015	0.011
50	0.608	0.372	0.228	0.141	0.087	0.054	0.034	0.021	0.013	0.009	0.005	0.003

Period	13%	14%	15%	16%	17%	18%	19%	20%	25%	30%	35%	40%	50%
1	0.885	0.877	0.870	0.862	0.855	0.847	0.840	0.833	0.800	0.769	0.741	0.714	0.667
2	0.783	0.769	0.756	0.743	0.731	0.718	0.706	0.694	0.640	0.592	0.549	0.510	0.444
3	0.693	0.675	0.658	0.641	0.624	0.609	0.593	0.579	0.512	0.455	0.406	0.364	0.296
4	0.613	0.592	0.572	0.552	0.534	0.515	0.499	0.482	0.410	0.350	0.301	0.260	0.198
5	0.543	0.519	0.497	0.476	0.456	0.437	0.419	0.402	0.320	0.269	0.223	0.186	0.132
6	0.480	0.456	0.432	0.410	0.390	0.370	0.352	0.335	0.262	0.207	0.165	0.133	0.088
7	0.425	0.400	0.376	0.354	0.333	0.314	0.296	0.279	0.210	0.159	0.122	0.095	0.059
8	0.376	0.351	0.327	0.305	0.285	0.266	0.249	0.233	0.168	0.123	0.091	0.068	0.039
9	0.333	0.300	0.284	0.263	0.243	0.225	0.209	0.194	0.134	0.094	0.067	0.048	0.026
10	0.295	0.270	0.247	0.227	0.208	0.191	0.176	0.162	0.107	0.073	0.050	0.035	0.017
11	0.261	0.237	0.215	0.195	0.178	0.162	0.148	0.135	0.086	0.056	0.037	0.025	0.012
12	0.231	0.208	0.187	0.168	0.152	0.137	0.124	0.112	0.069	0.043	0.027	0.018	0.008
13	0.204	0.182	0.163	0.145	0.130	0.116	0.104	0.093	0.055	0.033	0.020	0.013	0.005
14	0.181	0.160	0.141	0.125	0.111	0.099	0.088	0.078	0.044	0.025	0.015	0.009	0.003
15	0.160	0.140	0.123	0.108	0.095	0.084	0.074	0.065	0.035	0.020	0.011	0.006	0.002
16	0.141	0.123	0.107	0.093	0.081	0.071	0.062	0.054	0.028	0.015	0.008	0.005	0.002
17	0.125	0.108	0.093	0.080	0.069	0.060	0.052	0.045	0.023	0.012	0.006	0.003	0.001
18	0.111	0.095	0.081	0.069	0.059	0.051	0.044	0.038	0.018	0.009	0.005	0.002	0.001
19	0.098	0.083	0.070	0.060	0.051	0.043	0.037	0.031	0.014	0.007	0.003	0.002	0
20	0.087	0.073	0.061	0.051	0.043	0.037	0.031	0.026	0.012	0.005	0.002	0.001	0
25	0.047	0.038	0.030	0.024	0.020	0.016	0.013	0.010	0.004	0.001	0.001	0	0
30	0.026	0.020	0.015	0.012	0.009	0.007	0.005	0.004	0.001	0	0	0	0
40	0.008	0.005	0.004	0.003	0.002	0.001	0.001	0.001	0	0	0	0	0
50	0.002	0.001	0.001	0.001	0	0	0	0	0	0	0	0	0

Exhibit [A-4] Present Value of $1 Received at the End of Each Period for a Given Number of Time Periods (an Annuity)

Period	1%	2%	3%	4%	5%	6%	7%	8%	9%	10%	11%	12%
1	0.990	0.980	0.971	0.962	0.952	0.943	0.935	0.926	0.917	0.909	0.901	0.893
2	1.970	1.942	1.913	1.886	1.859	1.833	1.808	1.783	1.759	1.736	1.713	1.690
3	2.941	2.884	2.829	2.775	2.723	2.673	2.624	2.577	2.531	2.487	2.444	2.402
4	3.902	3.808	3.717	3.630	3.546	3.465	3.387	3.312	3.240	3.170	3.102	3.037
5	4.853	4.713	4.580	4.452	4.329	4.212	4.100	3.993	3.890	3.791	3.696	3.605
6	5.795	5.601	5.417	5.242	5.076	4.917	4.767	4.623	4.486	4.355	4.231	4.111
7	6.728	6.472	6.230	6.002	5.786	5.582	5.389	5.206	5.033	4.868	4.712	4.564
8	7.652	7.325	7.020	6.733	6.463	6.210	5.971	5.747	5.535	5.335	5.146	4.968
9	8.566	8.162	7.786	7.435	7.108	6.802	6.515	6.247	5.995	5.759	5.537	5.328
10	9.471	8.983	8.530	8.111	7.722	7.360	7.024	6.710	6.418	6.145	5.889	5.650
11	10.368	9.787	9.253	8.760	8.306	7.887	7.499	7.139	6.805	6.495	6.207	5.938
12	11.255	10.575	9.954	9.385	8.863	8.384	7.943	7.536	7.161	6.814	6.492	6.194
13	12.134	11.348	10.635	9.986	9.394	8.853	8.358	7.904	7.487	7.103	6.750	6.424
14	13.004	12.106	11.296	10.563	9.899	9.295	8.745	8.244	7.786	7.367	6.982	6.628
15	13.865	12.849	11.939	11.118	10.380	9.712	9.108	8.559	8.061	7.606	7.191	6.811
16	14.718	13.578	12.561	11.652	10.838	10.106	9.447	8.851	8.313	7.824	7.379	6.974
17	15.562	14.292	13.166	12.166	11.274	10.477	9.763	9.122	8.544	8.022	7.549	7.102
18	16.398	14.992	13.754	12.659	11.690	10.828	10.059	9.372	8.756	8.201	7.702	7.250
19	17.226	15.678	14.324	13.134	12.085	11.158	10.336	9.604	8.950	8.365	7.839	7.366
20	18.046	16.351	14.877	13.590	12.462	11.470	10.594	9.818	9.129	8.514	7.963	7.469
25	22.023	19.523	17.413	15.622	14.094	12.783	11.654	10.675	9.823	9.077	8.422	7.843
30	25.808	22.396	19.600	17.292	15.372	13.765	12.409	11.258	10.274	9.427	8.694	8.055
40	32.835	27.355	23.115	19.793	17.159	15.046	13.332	11.925	10.757	9.779	8.951	8.244
50	39.196	31.424	25.730	21.482	18.256	15.762	13.801	12.233	10.962	9.915	9.042	8.304

Period	13%	14%	15%	16%	17%	18%	19%	20%	25%	30%	35%	40%	50%
1	0.885	0.877	0.870	0.862	0.855	0.847	0.840	0.833	0.800	0.769	0.741	0.714	0.667
2	1.668	1.647	1.626	1.605	1.585	1.566	1.547	1.528	1.440	1.361	1.289	1.224	1.111
3	2.361	2.322	2.283	2.246	2.210	2.174	2.140	2.106	1.952	1.816	1.696	1.589	1.407
4	2.974	2.914	2.855	2.798	2.743	2.690	2.639	2.589	2.362	2.166	1.997	1.849	1.605
5	3.517	3.433	3.352	3.274	3.199	3.127	3.058	2.991	2.689	2.436	2.220	2.035	1.737
6	3.998	3.889	3.784	3.685	3.589	3.498	3.410	3.326	2.951	2.643	2.385	2.168	1.824
7	4.423	4.288	4.160	4.039	3.922	3.812	3.706	3.605	3.161	2.802	2.508	2.263	1.883
8	4.799	4.639	4.487	4.344	4.207	4.078	3.954	3.837	3.329	2.925	2.598	2.331	1.922
9	5.132	4.946	4.772	4.607	4.451	4.303	4.163	4.031	3.463	3.019	2.665	2.379	1.948
10	5.426	5.216	5.019	4.833	4.659	4.494	4.339	4.192	3.571	3.092	2.715	2.414	1.965
11	5.687	5.453	5.234	5.029	4.836	4.656	4.486	4.327	3.656	3.147	2.752	2.438	1.977
12	5.918	5.660	5.421	5.197	4.988	4.793	4.611	4.439	3.725	3.190	2.779	2.456	1.985
13	6.122	5.842	5.583	5.342	5.118	4.910	4.715	4.533	3.780	3.223	2.799	2.469	1.990
14	6.302	6.002	5.724	5.468	5.229	5.008	4.802	4.611	3.824	3.249	2.814	2.478	1.993
15	6.462	6.142	5.847	5.575	5.324	5.092	4.876	4.675	3.859	3.268	2.825	2.484	1.995
16	6.604	6.265	5.954	5.668	5.405	5.162	4.938	4.730	3.887	3.283	2.834	2.489	1.997
17	6.729	6.373	6.047	5.749	5.475	5.222	4.988	4.775	3.910	3.295	2.840	2.492	1.998
18	6.840	6.467	6.128	5.818	5.534	5.273	5.033	4.812	3.928	3.304	2.844	2.494	1.999
19	6.938	6.550	6.198	5.877	5.584	5.316	5.070	4.843	3.942	3.311	2.848	2.496	1.999
20	7.025	6.623	6.259	5.929	5.628	5.353	5.101	4.870	3.954	3.316	2.850	2.497	1.999
25	7.330	6.873	6.464	6.097	5.766	5.467	5.195	4.948	3.985	3.329	2.856	2.499	2.000
30	7.496	7.003	6.566	6.177	5.829	5.517	5.235	4.979	3.995	3.332	2.857	2.500	2.000
40	7.634	7.105	6.642	6.233	5.871	5.548	5.258	4.997	3.999	3.333	2.857	2.500	2.000
50	7.675	7.133	6.661	6.246	5.880	5.554	5.262	4.999	4.000	3.333	2.857	2.500	2.000

B Consumer Agencies and Organizations

The following government agencies and private organizations can offer information and assistance on various financial planning and consumer purchasing areas. These groups can serve your needs when you want to

- Research a financial or consumer topic area.
- Obtain information for planning a purchase decision.
- Seek assistance to resolve a consumer problem.

Section 1 provides an overview of federal, state, and local agencies and other organizations you may contact for information related to various financial planning and consumer topic areas. Section 2 covers state consumer protection offices that can assist you in local matters.

Section 1

Most federal agencies may be contacted through the Internet; several Web sites are noted. In addition, consumer information from several federal government agencies may be accessed at www.consumer.gov.

Exhibit [B–1] Federal, State, and Local Agencies and Other Organizations

Topic Area	Federal Agency	State, Local Agency; Other Organizations
Advertising False advertising Product labeling Deceptive sales practices Warranties	Federal Trade Commission 600 Pennsylvania Avenue, NW Washington, DC 20580 1-877-FTC-HELP (www.ftc.gov)	State Consumer Protection Office c/o State Attorney General or Governor's Office National Fraud Information Center Box 65868 Washington, DC 20035 1-800-876-7060 (www.fraud.org)
Air Travel Air safety Airport regulation Airline route	Federal Aviation Administration 800 Independence Avenue, SW Washington, DC 20591 1-800-FAA-SURE (www.faa.gov)	International Airline Passengers Association Box 660074 Dallas, TX 75266 1-800-527-5888 (www.iapa.com)

Exhibit [B–1] Continued

Topic Area	Federal Agency	State, Local Agency; Other Organizations
Appliances/Product Safety Potentially dangerous products Complaints against retailers, manufacturers	Consumer Product Safety Commission Washington, DC 20207 1-800-638-CPSC (www.cpsc.gov)	Council of Better Business Bureaus 4200 Wilson Boulevard Arlington, VA 22203 1-800-955-5100 (www.bbb.org)
Automobiles New cars Used cars Automobile repairs Auto safety	Federal Trade Commission (see above) National Highway Traffic Safety Administration 400 Seventh Street, SW Washington, DC 20590 1-800-424-9393 (www.nhtsa.gov)	AUTOCAP/National Automobile Dealers Association 8400 Westpark Drive McLean, VA 22102 1-800-252-6232 (www.nada.org) Center for Auto Safety 2001 S Street, NW Washington, DC 20009 (202) 328-7700 (www.autosafety.org)
Banking and Financial Institutions Checking accounts Savings accounts Deposit insurance Financial services	Federal Deposit Insurance Corporation 550 17th Street, NW Washington, DC 20429 1-877-275-3342 (www.fdic.gov) Comptroller of the Currency 15th Street and Pennsylvania Avenue, NW Washington, DC 20219 (202) 447-1600 (www.occ.treas.gov) Federal Reserve Board Washington, DC 20551 (202) 452-3693 (www.federalreserve.gov) National Credit Union Administration 1775 Duke Street Alexandria, VA 22314 (703) 518-6300 (www.ncua.gov)	State Banking Authority Credit Union National Association Box 431 Madison, WI 53701 (608) 232-8256 (www.cuna.org) American Bankers Association 1120 Connecticut Avenue, NW Washington, DC 20036 (202) 663-5000 (www.aba.com) U.S. savings bond rates 1-800-US-BONDS
Career Planning Job training Employment information	Coordinator of Consumer Affairs Department of Labor Washington, DC 20210 (202) 219-6060 (www.dol.gov)	State Department of Labor or State Employment Service

Exhibit [B–1]   Continued

Topic Area	Federal Agency	State, Local Agency; Other Organizations
Consumer Credit Credit cards Deceptive credit advertising Truth-in-Lending Act Credit rights of women, minorities	Federal Trade Commission 600 Pennsylvania Avenue, NW Washington, DC 20580 (202) 326-2222 (www.ftc.gov)	Consumer Credit Counseling Service 8701 Georgia Avenue, Suite 507 Silver Spring, MD 20910 1-800-388-2227 (www.nccs.org)
Environment Air, water pollution Toxic substances	Environmental Protection Agency Washington, DC 20024 1-800-438-4318 (indoor air quality) 1-800-426-4791 (drinking water safety) (www.epa.gov)	Clean Water Action Project 317 Pennsylvania Avenue, SE Washington, DC 20003 (202) 547-1196
Food Food grades Food additives Nutritional information	U.S. Department of Agriculture Washington, DC 20250 1-800-424-9121 (www.usda.gov) Food and Drug Administration 5600 Fishers Lane Rockville, MD 20857 1-888-463-6332 (www.fda.gov)	Center for Science in the Public Interest 1875 Connecticut Avenue, NW, Suite 300 Washington, DC 20009 (202) 332-9110 (www.cspinet.org)
Funerals Cost disclosure Deceptive business practices	Federal Trade Commission (see above)	Funeral Service Consumer Arbitration Program Box 486 Elm Grove, WI 53122 1-800-662-7666 (www.funeralservicefoundation.org)
Housing and Real Estate Fair housing practices Mortgages Community development	Department of Housing and Urban Development 451 Seventh Street, SW Washington, DC 20410 1-800-669-9777 (www.hud.gov)	National Association of Realtors 430 North Michigan Avenue Chicago, IL 60611 (www.realtor.com) National Association of Home Builders 15th and M Streets, NW Washington, DC 20005 (www.nahb.com)

Exhibit [B–1]   Continued

Topic Area	Federal Agency	State, Local Agency; Other Organizations
Insurance Policy conditions Premiums Types of coverage Consumer complaints	Federal Trade Commission (see above) National Flood Insurance Program 500 C Street, SW Washington, DC 20472 1-888-CALL-FLOOD	State Insurance Regulator American Council of Life Insurance 1001 Pennsylvania Avenue, NW Washington, DC 20004-2599 1-800-942-4242 Insurance Information Institute 110 William Street New York, NY 10038 1-800-331-9146 (www.iii.org)
Investments Stocks, bonds Mutual funds Commodities Investment brokers	Securities and Exchange Commission 450 Fifth Street, NW Washington, DC 20549 (202) 942-7040 (www.sec.gov) Commodity Futures Trading Commission 1155 21st Street, NW Washington, DC 20581 (202) 418-5080 (www.cftc.gov)	Investment Company Institute 1600 M Street, NW Washington, DC 20036 (202) 293-7700 (www.ici.org) National Association of Securities Dealers 1735 K Street, NW Washington, DC 20006 (202) 728-8000 (www.nasd.com) National Futures Association 200 West Madison Street Chicago, IL 60606 1-800-621-3570 (www.nfa.futures.org) Securities Investor Protection Corp. 805 15th Street, NW, Suite 800 Washington, DC 20003 (202) 371-8300 (www.sipe.org)
Legal Matters Consumer complaints Arbitration	Department of Justice Office of Consumer Litigation Washington, DC 20530 (202) 514-2401	American Arbitration Association 140 West 51st Street New York, NY 10020 (212) 484-4000 (www.adr.org) American Bar Association 321 North Clark Street Chicago, IL 60610 (312) 988-5000 (www.abanet.org)

Exhibit [B-1]   Concluded

Topic Area	Federal Agency	State, Local Agency; Other Organizations
Mail Order Damaged products Deceptive business practices Illegal use of U.S. mail	U.S. Postal Service Washington, DC 20260-2202 1-800-ASK-USPS (www.usps.gov)	Direct Marketing Association 6 East 43rd Street New York, NY 10017 (212) 689-4977 (www.the-dma.org)
Medical Concerns Prescription medications Over-the-counter medications Medical devices Health care	Food and Drug Administration (see above) Public Health Service 200 Independence Avenue, SW Washington, DC 20201 1-800-336-4797 (www.fda.gov)	American Medical Association 535 North Dearborn Chicago, IL 60610 (312) 645-5000 Public Citizen Health Research Group 2000 P Street Washington, DC 20036 (202) 872-0320
Retirement Old-age benefits Pension information Medicare	Social Security Administration 6401 Security Boulevard Baltimore, MD 21235 1-800-772-1213 (www.ssa.gov)	AARP 601 E Street, NW Washington, DC 20049 (202) 434-2277 (www.aarp.org)
Taxes Tax information Audit procedures	Internal Revenue Service 1111 Constitution Avenue, NW Washington, DC 20204 1-800-829-1040 1-800-TAX-FORM (www.irs.gov)	Department of Revenue (in your state capital city) The Tax Foundation One Thomas Circle Washington, DC 20005 (202) 822-9050 (www.taxfoundation.org) National Association of Enrolled Agents 6000 Executive Blvd. Rockville, MD 20852 1-800-424-4339
Telemarketing 900 numbers	Federal Communications Commission 445 12th Street, SW Washington, DC 20554 1-888-225-5322 (www.fcc.gov)	National Consumers League 815 Fifteenth Street, NW Washington, DC 20005 (202) 639-8140 (www.nclnet.org)
Utilities Cable television Utility rates	Federal Communications Commission 1919 M Street, NW Washington, DC 20554 (202) 632-6999 (www.fcc.gov)	State utility commission (in your state capital)

Information on additional government agencies and private organizations available to assist you may be obtained in the *Consumer Action Handbook,* available at no charge from the Consumer Information Center, Pueblo, CO 81009 or online at www.pueblo.gsa.gov.

Section 2

State, county, and local consumer protection offices provide consumers with a variety of services, including publications and information before buying as well as handling complaints. This section provides contact information for state consumer protection agencies. In addition to the primary offices listed here, agencies regulating banking, insurance, securities, and utilities are available in each state. These may be located through a Web search or by going to the *Consumer's Resource Handbook* at www.pueblo.gsa.gov.

Many state consumer protection offices may be accessed through the Web site of the National Association of Attorneys General at www.naag.org or with a Web search for your state consumer protection office using "*(state)* consumer protection agency."

To save time, call the office before sending in a written complaint. Ask if the office handles the type of complaint you have or if complaint forms are provided. Many offices distribute consumer materials specifically geared to state laws and local issues. Call to obtain available educational information on your problem.

State departments of insurance may be accessed online at www.naic.org or www.insurance.about.com/cs/deptsofinsurance.

The Web sites of state tax departments are available at www.taxadmin.org or www.aicpa.org/yellow/yptsgus.htm.

Index